HOLINESS PAST AN[...]

HOLINESS PAST AND PRESENT

Edited by

STEPHEN C. BARTON

T&T CLARK
A Continuum imprint
LONDON • NEW YORK

T&T CLARK LTD

A Continuum imprint

The Tower Building
11 York Road
London, SE1 7NX

370 Lexington Avenue
New York 10017–6503
USA

www.continuumbooks.com

First published 2003

ISBN 0 567 08823 5 (PAPERBACK)
ISBN 0 567 08893 6 (HARDBACK)

British Library Cataloguing-in-Publication Data
A catalogue record for this book is available from the British Library

Typeset by Fakenham Photosetting Ltd, Fakenham, Norfolk NR21 8NN
Printed and bound in Great Britain by Bookcraft, Midsomer Norton

To Ann Loades
Professor of Divinity
respected colleague

Contents

Acknowledgements   x

Contributors   xi

Introduction   xvi
   Stephen C. Barton

Part 1   Holiness in Theory

1   What is Holiness?   3
    John Rogerson

2   Rudolf Otto's *The Idea of the Holy* Revisited   22
    Colin Crowder

3   The Sociology of Holiness: The Power of Being Good   48
    Douglas J. Davies

4   Changing your Holy Ground: An Ecology of Sacred   68
    and Secular in Cities of the Centre and the Periphery
    David Martin

Part 2   Holiness and Scripture

5   Holiness in the Priestly Writings of the   93
    Old Testament
    Philip Jenson

6   'Holy, Holy, Holy': Isaiah's Vision of God   122
    R. W. L. Moberly

7   The Sanctification of Time in the Second   141
    Temple Period: Case Studies in the Septuagint
    and Jubilees
    Robert Hayward

8   Jesus and Holiness: The Challenge of Purity   168
    James D. G. Dunn

9   Dislocating and Relocating Holiness: A New   193
    Testament Study
    Stephen C. Barton

Part 3   Holiness and Christian Tradition

10 Holiness and the Vision of God in the Eastern   217
    Fathers
    Andrew Louth

11 Finding a *via media*: The Moderation of Holiness   239
    in Fourth-century Western Asceticism
    Carol Harrison

12 Benedictine Holiness   260
    Henry Mayr-Harting

13 Holiness in the English Tradition: From Prayer   279
    Book to Puritans
    Gordon Mursell

14 Holiness in the Evangelical Tradition   298
    D. W. Bebbington

15 Holiness in the Roman Catholic Tradition   316
    Sheridan Gilley

16 Mother of God, Mother of Holiness: A Meditation   339
    from Orthodoxy
    Vigen Guroian

Part 4   Holiness and Contemporary Issues

17 Bonhoeffer, Holiness and Ethics   361
    David F. Ford

18 Holiness *in extremis*: Jewish Women's Resistance to   381
    the Profane in Auschwitz
    Melissa Raphael

19 Holiness Ungendered   402
    Susan F. Parsons

20 The Communion of Saints and Other Religions: 421
    On Saintly Wives in Hinduism and Catholicism
    Gavin D'Costa

21 Material Poverty or Poverty of Spirit? Holiness and   441
    the Liberation of the Poor
    Denys Turner

22 Whose Sanctity of Life? Ricoeur, Dworkin and the   460
    Human Embryo
    Robert Song

23 Worship and the Formation of a Holy People   477
    Daniel W. Hardy

Suggestions for Further Reading   499

Index of Modern Authors   507

Acknowledgements

These essays are the happy outcome of a series of research seminars and public lectures on the theme 'Holiness Past and Present' sponsored by the Durham Centre for Theological Research, held at the University of Durham in the academic year 1999–2000. The present series is a successor to two earlier series; the first, *The Family in Theological Perspective*, and the second, entitled *Where Shall Wisdom Be Found?*, have been published already by T&T Clark.

It is a pleasure to record here my thanks to all those who attended the seminars and lectures: postgraduate students, colleagues both in the Department of Theology and the University more generally, and members of the general public. I am especially grateful to those who contributed papers, often travelling considerable distances to do so. For its financial support, I would like to thank the University's Public Lectures Committee.

Stephen C. Barton
Durham
Easter 2002

Contributors

Stephen C. Barton is Reader in New Testament in the Department of Theology, University of Durham and a nonstipendiary priest at St John's Church, Neville's Cross. His special interest is in the use of the Bible in theology and ethics. His most recent books are *Invitation to the Bible* (SPCK, 1997) and *Life Together. Family, Sexuality and Community in the New Testament and Today* (T&T Clark, 2001).

D. W. Bebbington is Professor of History in the Department of History, University of Stirling. A specialist in the history of Evangelicalism and Nonconformity, he is the author of *Evangelicalism in Modern Britain* (Unwin Hyman, 1989; now Routledge), and *Holiness in Nineteenth-Century England* (Paternoster, 2000). He has also co-edited *Evangelicalism: Comparative Studies of Popular Protestantism in North America, the British Isles and Beyond, 1700–1990* (Oxford University Press, 1994).

Colin Crowder is Lecturer in Theology in the Department of Theology, University of Durham, where he teaches philosophy of religion, modern atheism, and religion and film studies. He is the editor of *God and Reality: Essays on Christian Non-Realism* (Mowbray, 1996).

Douglas J. Davies is Professor in the Study of Religion in the Department of Theology, University of Durham. He has major research interests in the relationship between ritual and belief as reflected in the diverse fields of Mormonism, death and cremation, and Anglicanism. Recent books include *Death, Ritual and Belief* (Cassell, 1997), *The Mormon Culture of Salvation* (Ashgate, 2000), and *Private Passions: The Archbishop of Wales's Lent Book for 2000* (Canterbury Press, 2000).

Gavin D'Costa is Reader in Christian Theology at the University of Bristol. He has written four books, most recently, *The Meeting of the Religions and the Trinity* (T & T Clark, 2000) and *Sexing the Trinity* (SCM, 2000). He has edited *Christian Uniqueness Reconsidered* (Orbis, 1990) and *Resurrection Reconsidered* (Oneworld, 1996). He is consultant to the Vatican, the Roman

Catholic Bishops in England and Wales, and to the Church of England's Board of Mission on matters related to other religions.

James D. G. Dunn is Lightfoot Professor of Divinity in the University of Durham, where he teaches New Testament theology and the history of Christian origins. As well as a number of commentaries, his recent books include *The Theology of Paul the Apostle* (T&T Clark and Eerdmans, 1997) and two volumes of collected essays, *The Christ and the Spirit, Volume 1: Christology; Volume 2: Pneumatology* (Eerdmans, 1998).

David F. Ford is Regius Professor of Divinity in the University of Cambridge and a Fellow of Selwyn College. His books include *Self and Salvation. Being Transformed* (Cambridge University Press, 1999); *Theology. A Very Short Introduction* (Oxford University Press, 1999) and *The Shape of Living* (HarperCollins, 2002, 2nd edn.), and he is the editor of *The Modern Theologians* (Blackwell, 1997, 2nd edn.).

Sheridan Gilley is Reader in Theology in the Department of Theology, University of Durham. He specialises in nineteenth- and twentieth-century British and European church history and biography. His publications include *Newman and his Age* (Darton, Longman & Todd, 1990) and he has co-edited *A History of Religion in Britain* (Blackwell, 1994), and *The Irish in Victorian Britain. The Local Dimension* (Four Courts, 1999).

Vigen Guroian is Professor of Theology and Ethics at Loyola College in Baltimore, Maryland, USA. A representative of the Armenian Church, he serves on the Commission on Faith and Order of the World Council of Churches. His most recent publications are *Tending the Heart of Virtue: How Classic Stories Awaken a Child's Moral Imagination* (Oxford University Press, 1998), *Inheriting Paradise: Meditations on Gardening* (Darton, Longman & Todd, 2001), and *Incarnate Love: Essays in Orthodox Ethics* (University of Notre Dame Press, 2002, 2nd edn.).

Daniel W. Hardy taught theology in the University of Birmingham before his appointment in 1986 as Van Mildert Professor of Divinity in the University of Durham and Residentiary Canon of Durham Cathedral. In 1990, he became the first Director of the Center of Theological Inquiry in Princeton, USA. He now lives in Cambridge, England, where he is a member of the Faculty of Divinity. He is the author of *God's Ways with the World* (T&T Clark, 1996).

Carol Harrison is Lecturer in the History and Theology of the Latin West in the Department of Theology, University of Durham. She specialises in the work of St Augustine, and has published *Revelation and Beauty in the Thought of St Augustine* (Oxford University Press, 1992) and *Augustine. Christian Truth and Fractured Humanity* (Oxford University Press, 2000). She is also editor of the Routledge series *The Early Christian Fathers.*

Robert Hayward is Professor of Hebrew in the Department of Theology, University of Durham. He is a specialist in Second Temple and Early Rabbinic Judaism. His recent publications include *Saint Jerome's Hebrew Questions on Genesis* (Clarendon Press, 1995) and *The Jewish Temple. A Non-biblical Sourcebook* (Routledge, 1996).

Philip Jenson is Lecturer in Old Testament and Hebrew at Trinity College, Bristol. He has published *Graded Holiness: A Key to the Priestly Conception of the World* (JSOTSup, 106; JSOT Press, 1992) and several articles on priesthood and priestly theology. His interest in the communication of the significance of the Old Testament to a wider audience is reflected in *Reading Jonah* (Grove Biblical Series 14; Grove Books, 1999).

Andrew Louth is Professor of Patristic and Byzantine Studies in the Department of Theology, University of Durham. Previously, he taught patristics at Oxford, and Byzantine and early medieval history at Goldsmiths College, University of London. His publications include *Denys the Areopagite* (Geoffrey Chapman, 1989) and *Maximus the Confessor* (Routledge, 1996).

David Martin is Emeritus Professor of Sociology in the University of London, London School of Economics, and Honorary Professor in the Department of Religious Studies in the University of Lancaster. Among his recent publications are *Does Christianity Cause War?* (Oxford University Press, 1997) and *Pentecostalism – The World Their Parish* (Blackwell, 2001).

Henry Mayr-Harting is Regius Professor of Ecclesiastical History in the University of Oxford and Lay Residentiary Canon of

Christ Church Cathedral. His recent publications include *Ottonian Book Illuminations: An Historical Study* (Harvey Miller, 2000, 2nd edn.). He is also co-editor, with Richard Harries, of *Christianity: Two Thousand Years* (Oxford University Press, 2001).

R. W. L. Moberly is Reader in Theology in the Department of Theology, University of Durham, where he teaches Old Testament and biblical theology. His publications include *The Old Testament of the Old Testament* (Augsburg/Fortress, 1992) and *The Bible, Theology, and Faith. A Study of Abraham and Jesus* (Cambridge University Press, 2000). He has been an Anglican priest since 1982.

Gordon Mursell is Dean of Birmingham Cathedral. He has published a number of works in the field of Christian spirituality, including *Out of the Deep: Prayer as Protest* (Darton, Longman & Todd, 1989) and, most recently, *English Spirituality* (SPCK, 2001, 2 volumes).

Susan F. Parsons is Director of Pastoral Studies at the Margaret Beaufort Institute of Theology in Cambridge. She is the author of *Feminism and Christian Ethics* (Cambridge University Press, 1996) and *The Ethics of Gender* (Blackwell, 2001), and editor of *Challenging Women's Orthodoxies in the Context of Faith* (Ashgate, 2000). She is also President of the Society of St Catherine of Siena, a charitable trust dedicated to the renewal of Catholic theology in the academy and in the life of the Church.

Melissa Raphael is Senior Lecturer in Theology and Religious Studies at Cheltenham and Gloucester College of Higher Education. She is the author of *Thealogy and Embodiment: The Post-Patriarchal Reconstruction of Female Sacrality* (Sheffield Academic Press, 1996); *Rudolf Otto and the Concept of Holiness* (Clarendon Press, 1997); *Introducing Thealogy: Discourse on the Goddess* (Sheffield Academic Press, 1999); and *The Female Face of God in Auschwitz: A Jewish Feminist Theology of the Holocaust* (Routledge, 2002).

John Rogerson is Emeritus Professor of Biblical Studies, Sheffield University. His latest books are *An Introduction to the Bible* (Penguin, 1999) and *Chronicle of the Old Testament Kings* (Thames & Hudson, 1999). He is also editor of *The Oxford Illustrated History of the Bible* (Oxford University Press, 2001).

Robert Song is Lecturer in Christian Ethics in the Department of Theology, University of Durham. He has written *Christianity and Liberal Society* (Clarendon Press, 1997) and *Human Genetics: Fabricating the Future in a Technological Culture* (Darton, Longman & Todd, 2002).

Denys Turner is Norris-Hulse Professor of Divinity in the University of Cambridge, having taught previously at University College Dublin, the University of Bristol and, as H. G. Wood Professor of Theology, at the University of Birmingham. He is the author of *Marxism and Christianity* (Blackwell, 1983), *Eros and Allegory: Medieval Exegesis of the Song of Songs* (Cistercian Publications, 1995), and *The Darkness of God* (Cambridge University Press, 1995).

Introduction

Stephen C. Barton

One of the convictions lying behind this collection of scholarly essays on holiness is that the language and practices of holiness have atrophied under the impact of modernity and secularisation. Arguably, many people shy away from attention to holiness for fear of the moralising rebuke implied in the tag, 'holier than thou'. But holiness, while it has a properly moral dimension, is much more than that. It has to do, at least in the Judeo-Christian tradition, with the fundamental character of the reality we call God, the One who graces us with His presence and enables us to share His life as gift and grace. This is not a matter of the 'holier than thou'. It is the much more profound matter of discovering, both as individuals and as peoples, that the wellspring of our life and the consummation of creation are hidden in God and share in the glory of God.

In a sermon entitled 'Holy Ground', in which he explores the terrible paradox that places traditionally associated with holiness and the divine presence are places also where human wickedness has manifested itself, Rowan Williams says:

> A human being is holy not because he or she triumphs by will-power over chaos and guilt and leads a flawless life, but because that life shows the victory of God's faithfulness *in the midst* of disorder and imperfection. The Church is holy ... not because it is a gathering of the good and the well-behaved, but because it speaks of the triumph of grace in the coming together of strangers and sinners who, miraculously, trust one another enough to join in common repentance and common praise ... Humanly speaking, holiness is always like this: God's endurance in the middle of our refusal of him, his capacity to meet every refusal with the gift of himself.[1]

---

[1] Rowan Williams, *Open to Judgment. Sermons and Addresses* (London: Darton, Longman and Todd, 1994), 136.

To attend to holiness, therefore, is to attend to a matter that lies at the very heart of what it means to be and become fully human. And in our late-modern (or post-modern) world, with its greater recognition of the local and the particular and of our embodied existence in specific times and places, the way we attend to holiness will be less by way of overarching, universalising theory – although that has its place – and more by way of the study of holy writings and holy people, holy places and holy times.

This helps to explain the structure and content of the present collection. Part 1 consists of essays of a broadly theoretical and methodological kind, including issues of definition (Rogerson), the significance of the contribution of Rudolf Otto (Crowder), and perspectives from the social sciences (Davies, Martin). In Part 2 we turn to biblical and early Jewish writings, with essays on the Priestly Writings of the Pentateuch (Jenson), Isaiah's famous vision of God (Moberly), the Septuagint and Jubilees (Hayward), Jesus (Dunn), and the New Testament as a whole (Barton). Part 3 turns to the Christian tradition for case studies in particular understandings and practices of holiness: in Eastern (Louth) and Western (Harrison) Christianity from the patristic period, in the traditions of Benedictine monasticism (Mayr-Harting), in the English tradition of the Prayer Book and subsequently (Mursell), in the Evangelical (Bebbington) and Roman Catholic (Gilley) traditions, and in Orthodoxy (Guroian). In the final Part, entitled, 'Holiness and Contemporary Issues', attention is given to holiness in practice in recent and current times. Ford writes about Bonhoeffer, and Raphael about Jewish women in Auschwitz; Parsons considers holiness in relation to theories of gender; in an essay of inter-religious scope, D'Costa compares holy lives in Catholicism and Hinduism; Turner offers a liberationist interpretation; Song considers the sanctity of life in relation to our treatment of the human embryo; and Hardy draws out the links between holiness and worship.

The collection is neither rigorously systematic nor exhaustive: the nature of the subject hardly permits of either possibility. Nevertheless, it is likely that the broad coverage and interdisciplinarity of these essays will make them a significant resource for further reflection and investigation into holiness past and present.

PART 1

Holiness in Theory

1

What is Holiness?

John Rogerson

Introduction

There is a very simple and straightforward answer to the question, 'What is holiness?' Holiness is a word in the English language whose meaning depends upon the contexts in which it is used and the interests of those who use it. This may seem to be such an obvious, and even frivolous, answer, that it is hardly worth stating. Yet it is an obvious answer that has been overlooked and ignored in the past hundred years or so, with the result that not only discussions about 'holiness' but about religion in general have been at best confused and, at worst, illogical. Zygmunt Bauman has written recently that,

> More often than not, 'defining religion' amounts to replacing one ineffable by another – to the substitution of the incomprehensible for the unknown ... This is the case with the most popular definitions, which have served mainly to placate the scientific conscience of sociologists eager to declare the embracement of the unembracable: the definitions which 'defined religion' pointing to its relation to the 'sacred', 'transcendental', 'enchanted' or even, in the tamed and thereby vulgarized renditions of Rudolf Otto, the 'tremendous'.[1]

The aim of this paper will be to try to sort out some of the issues that underlie attempts to define or describe 'holiness', 'the

---

[1] Z. Bauman, 'Postmodern Religion?' in P. Heelas (ed.) *Religion, Modernity and Postmodernity* (Oxford: Blackwell 1998), pp. 55–6.

holy', and 'the sacred', to consider some of the questions that these issues raise, and to see how the results affect attempts to describe 'holiness' in the Old Testament.

In an article published recently in the *Zeitschrift für Theologie und Kirche* entitled 'Heilig, heilig, heilig. Zur politischen Theologie der Johannes-Apokalypse', Thomas Söding has argued that the view of the holiness of God in the book of Revelation provides a model for contemporary political theology.[2] His conclusion, that political theology should primarily involve the critique of power, is not my concern here. What is of concern are his remarks about holiness in religions generally and in the Old Testament in particular. Of the former, Söding writes:

> God is holy in his divinity (*in seiner Gottheit*), in his radical difference from what is human and what belongs to the world, in his otherness, in which he conceals each life in himself – as all religions know and as John also sees it. God is the holy one in his majestic aura and his creative potency, in his supernatural splendour and his cosmic presence. Nevertheless to understand holiness in a primal religious way purely simply as transcendence and pure life remains unspecific.[3]

Of the Old Testament he writes:

> God's powerful holiness manifests itself in creating and sustaining, in judging and delivering the world of humankind. According to John, in agreement with the whole Old Testament, God evinces his holiness in his actions, which mediate the historical and cosmic presence of God together with his absolute transcendence. The unity of God's saving activity (*Heilshandelns*) an activity which, this side of all

---

[2] T. Söding, 'Heilig, heilig, heilig. Zur politischen Theologie der Johannes-Apokalypse', *ZThK* 96 (1999), pp. 49–76.

[3] Söding, 'Heilig' p. 55: 'Heilig ist Gott in seiner Gottheit, in seiner radikalen Unterschiedenheit vom Menschlichen und Weltlichen, in seinem Anderssein, in dem er jedes Leben in sich birgt – so wissen es alle Religionen, und so sieht es auch Johannes. Gott ist der Heilige in seiner majestätische Aura und seiner schöpferischen Potenz, in seinem überirdischen Glanz und seiner kosmischen Präsenz. Doch Heiligkeit urreligiös rein als Tranzendenz und pures Leben zu verstehen bliebe unspezifisch.'

mythical cycles, grounds the unity of history in the unity of
space and time, marks the fundamental difference between
the mythological and the biblical-theological understanding
of the holiness of God.[4]

I shall return at the end of this essay to the comments about
what the whole Old Testament says about God's holiness. For
the moment I intend to point out that the claim that 'all
religions' know the holiness of God in his radical difference
and in the way that he conceals each life in his own is
indebted, as are other comments in the article, to the German
translation of Mircea Eliade's *Traité d'Histoire des Religions* as
Söding acknowledges, and that this puts him in a tradition of
speculation about the meaning of holiness that goes back to
Schleiermacher, and which will now be traced and
commented on.

Three Theorists of 'the Holy'

Schleiermacher's *Über die Religion* of 1799 is usually credited
with having established that religion is an autonomous sphere
within human experience that is irreducible, and which can
only be understood according to its own distinctive features.
On page 55 of the 1799 edition he writes of contemplation of
what he calls 'das Universum' and describes it as both the pivot
(*Angel*) of his whole address and the 'the most general and
highest formula (*Formel*) of religion'.[5]

All contemplation is derived from the influence of what is
contemplated upon the one contemplating, from an original

[4] Söding, 'Heilig', p. 56: 'Gottes machtvolle Heiligkeit manifestiert such im
Entstehen und Erhalten, im Richten und im Retten der Menschen-Welt ...
Wie nach dem gesamten Alten Testament erweist Gott auch Johannes zufolge
seine Heiligkeit in seinem Handeln, das immer zugleich mit der absoluten
Transzendenz die geschichtliche und kosmische Präsenz Gottes vermittelt. Die
Einheit des Heilshandelns Gottes, das, diesseits aller mythischen Zyklen, die
Einheit der Geschichte in der Einheit des Raumes und der Zeit begründet,
markiert den substantiellen Unterschied zwischen dem mythologischen und
dem biblisch-theologischen Verständnis der Heiligkeit Gottes.'
[5] F. D. E. Schleiermacher, *Über die Religion. Reden an die Gebildeten unter ihren
Verächtern* (Berlin: de Gruyter, 1999), special edition of the 1799 publication.

and independent action of the former, which is then taken, synthesised and conceptualised by the latter according to his nature.[6]

In further illustration of this point Schleiermacher notes, among other things, that if there were no effluence of light, then the eye would see nothing.[7] Let me emphasise here that I am not concerned with what Schleiermacher might have meant, but what he was understood to have meant by certain later writers. Two points can be made. First, Schleiermacher does not use the terms 'holy' or 'holiness' in his key definition of religion. Secondly, Rudolf Otto's charge in *The Idea of the Holy*, that Schleiermacher's religious category does not primarily refer to an object outside the self, appears to be inaccurate.[8]

There is a direct line from Schleiermacher's 1799 *Reden* to Nathan Söderblom's influential article on 'Holiness' in the *Encyclopaedia of Religion and Ethics* (1913), in that the article begins with a reference to the *Reden* in the opening paragraph. The quotation, 'The idea of God without the conception of the holy is not religion', is followed by an unspecified reference to Schleiermacher's book. Söderblom's main purpose in this opening paragraph is to define religion in relation to something other than God:

Holiness is the great word in religion; it is even more essential than the notion of God. Real religion may exist

---

[6] Schleiermacher, *Religion*, p. 55: 'Alles Anschauen gehet aus von einem Einfluß des Angeschaueten auf den Anschauenden, von einem ursprünglichen und unabhängigen Handeln des ersteren, welches dann von dem letzteren seiner Natur gemäß aufgenommen, zusammengefaßt und begriffen wird.'

[7] Schleiermacher, *Religion*, pp. 55–6.

[8] R. Otto, *The Idea of the Holy. An Inquiry into the Non-Rational Factor in the Idea of the Divine and its Relation to the Rational* (Harmondsworth: Penguin, 1959), p. 24. German original, *Das Heilige. Über das Irrationale in der Idee des Göttlichen und sein Verhältnis zum Rationalen*, 1917. References in this article will be to the 11th edition, Stuttgart/Gotha: Verlag Friedrich Andreas Perthes, 1923. Further material can be found in R. Otto, *Aufsätze das Numinose betreffend* (Stuttgart/Gotha: Verlag Friedrich Andreas Perthes, 1923).

without a definite conception of divinity, but there is no real religion without a distinction between holy and profane.[9]

Söderblom's article is in fact a tour de force of the type that only scholars of his generation could have produced. Dependent upon masses of material gathered by researchers on so-called primitive peoples as well as upon the religions of India, it is both sensitively comprehensive and yet determined to co-ordinate the data into a clear, evolutionary scheme. It centres around the native concepts of *mana* and *taboo* and the analytical concepts of clean/unclean, sacred/profane.

According to Söderblom, holiness begins as the recognition of a mysterious power or entity associated with certain persons, things or events. It is an incohate reaction to what is unknown, startling or terrifying; but as language and social organisation begin to impose order upon it, the holy becomes surrounded by precautions and interdictions which serve to separate it from the ordinary – to protect the ordinary from its danger. The mysterious power begins to be named. Söderblom gives as examples 'the great one', 'the powerful', 'dangerous', 'divine', and incidentally hazards the guess that the original meaning of the Semitic *qds* was 'the extraordinary'.

Once 'the holy' begins to be institutionalised, rites are developed that are designed to acquire and utilise its mysterious power. These include sacrifice. On the other hand, its dangerous qualities, which require taboos, generate rites of cleansing where taboos have been infringed and, morally, penalties such as death for taboo violation. A necessary feature of the mysterious power and the dangers that it poses is its irrationality; here Söderblom mentions well-known Old Testament incidents such as the slaying by God of seventy men of Beth-shemesh who had looked into the Ark of the Covenant after the Philistines returned it, or the striking dead of Uzzah when he touched the Ark to prevent it from falling from the cart being used to take it from Baale-judah (1 Sam. 6.19; 2 Sam.

---

[9] N. Söderblom, 'Holiness (General and Primitive)', *Encyclopaedia of Religion and Ethics* vol. VI (Edinburgh: T&T Clark, 1913), p. 731. A German version of this article is to be found in C. Colpe (ed.), *Die Diskussion um das „Heilige"*, Wege der Forschung CCCV (Darmstadt: Wissenschaftliche Buchgesellschaft, 1977), pp. 76–116.

6.6–7). For Söderblom, the irrational aspect of holiness becomes an important means of linking it with the supernatural; and it must not be forgotten that the sub-title of Otto's *The Idea of the Holy* was *An Inquiry into the Non-Rational Factor* [German *das Irrationale*] *in the Idea of the Divine and its Relation to the Rational.*

However, the irrational aspect of holiness is also a driving force in the evolution of society. The taboo rules of holiness have 'had an inestimable influence on civilisation and the improvement of society. Animal desires were restrained; in the hard school of tabu [*sic*] man was taught self-control.'[10] Further, taboo rules contribute to the human organisation of time and space. An example is the sabbath, where the 'genius of Mosaism' gives a positive character to a taboo day, and time is organised into cycles of seven days.

Another aspect of the irrationality of the holy, its apparently arbitrary, or at least, ambiguous division of things into sacred and profane, also becomes an important factor in the ethical development of the so-called higher religions. Söderblom provides three diagrams in order to illustrate his view of how the notion of holiness has developed:

Diagram A	Holy	Unclean
	Profane	Clean

Diagram A indicates what Söderblom calls 'the old correlation', in which 'holy' and 'unclean' oppose 'profane' and 'clean'. He cites as an example of this Leviticus 10.10: 'You are to distinguish between the holy and the common, and between the unclean and the clean.'

Three factors then modify this scheme, according to Söderblom: the evolution of language; morals, and other practical aims and demands of culture; and the conception of divinity. In the evolution of language, 'profane' or 'common' moves in sense towards 'unclean'. An example is the Hebrew *hillel*, 'to give out for use', which assumes more and more the sense of 'to profane', 'to unhallow' and even to 'to defile'.[11] Söderblom sees a similar evolution in the Greek word *koinos*.

---

[10] Söderblom, 'Holiness', p. 735.
[11] Söderblom, 'Holiness', p. 737.

The moral factor is that as moral sensitivity develops, 'pure' or 'clean' cannot be separated from 'holy'. 'Holy' cannot mean, morally, what is forbidden, but must mean what is commanded. Thus, the ideas of 'holy' and 'clean' are drawn closer together. The third factor, the conception of divinity operating through ritual, transfers the dangerous element of the holy into the unclean. As Söderblom puts it, 'All the dangerous element in religion is included in the unclean, all the valuable element in the clean.' The result of these three factors is what is described in diagram B.

Diagram B	Holy	Clean
	Profane	Unclean

The movement to diagram C is caused by the idea of divinity taking on some of the dangerous aspects of taboo without being associated with 'unclean'. The divinity becomes 'holy' because it is mysterious, powerful, and dangerous. The 'holy' becomes a term for God's essence in relation to himself and not primarily in his relation to humans. Söderblom quotes in this regard Ezekiel 36. 22–3: 'It is not for your sake, O house of Israel, that I am about to act, but for the sake of my holy name ... and I will vindicate the holiness (*v'Qiddashti*) of my great name, which has been profaned (*ham'hullal*) among the nations.' Diagram C represents a stage at which 'holy' is not now identified with 'clean' but with exalted divinity.

Diagram C		Holy	
	Clean		Common
		Unclean	

A final stage in the development of the holy according to Söderblom's scheme occurs when holiness becomes a personal quality of humans as well as of God, in as much as God makes them holy and obliges them thereby to strive for perfection. In ethical religion, holy means 'good' or 'perfect'; yet even so, 'holy' never becomes simply an ethical word. It suggests chiefly divine, supernatural power.

On the face of it, Söderblom's account is a scientific description of the evolution of religion from the standpoint of what he takes to be its most vital component, 'holiness'. It is possible, however, to discern beneath the surface a theistic, if not Christian, apologetic interest. Thus referring specifically to Durkheim's *Les formes élémentaires de la vie religieuse*, Söderblom rejects the view that 'the "sacred" is merely a kind of objectifying and idealising of the community as a power mysteriously superior to the individual'.[12] Later, in discussing the part played by ideas of holiness in moving society towards civilisation, Söderblom asks whether a time will come when humanity can dispense with holiness and be guided by merely rational considerations. He poses the question, 'Has the imperative and absolute form of duty any metaphysical grounds, or is it based on an initial error, by which humanity has been misled, throughout its whole existence?'[13] Although Söderblom gives no answer to the question, there can be little doubt that the future Lutheran Archbishop of Uppsala did not intend his readers to conclude that belief in the supernatural and its moral imperatives was based upon an error which had misled humanity throughout its whole history.

If Söderblom's tour de force was implicitly theistic and Christian, Rudolf Otto's famous account of the same phenomena that Söderblom sought to synthesise was quite explicitly Christian, although this fact emerges only gradually in *The Idea of the Holy*, until it reaches its climax in the concluding sentences, 'We can look beyond the prophet to the one in whom is found the Spirit in all its plenitude, and who at the same time in His person and in His performance is become most completely the object of divination, in whom Holiness is recognized apparent. Such a one is more than Prophet. He is the Son.'[14]

While Otto's two references to Söderblom in *The Idea of the Holy* are complimentary, his whole approach rejects the type of evolutionistic rationalising that characterises Söderblom's

---

[12] Söderblom, 'Holiness', p. 732.

[13] Söderblom, 'Holiness', p. 735.

[14] Otto, *The Holy*, p. 195. German p. 199, 'Über dieser Stufe des Profeten aber läßt sich dann eine noch höhere, dritte denken und erwarten, unableitbar wieder aus der zweiten wie es die zweite aus der ersten war: die desjenigen, der einerseits den Geist in der Fülle hat und der anderseits zugleich selber in Person und Leistung zum Objekte der Divination des erscheinenden Heiligen wird. Ein solcher ist mehr denn Profet – Er ist der Sohn.'

work. In the first place, Otto believes that attempts to account for the holy rationally cannot do justice to what is most significant about it, namely, its non-rationality. It is for this reason that he coins the word 'numinous' in order to describe that non-rational part of the holy that remains when the rational accretions that it has acquired have been stripped away. Secondly, he does not accept that rational, evolutionistic accounts can explain how the diverse phenomena ranging from mana, taboo, ghosts, and demons to monotheistic holiness can be related together, even though these phenomena are not unrelated. He is particularly critical of phrases such as 'gradually evolve' which are used in evolutionistic accounts, without it being shown how ideas evolve.[15] Further, developmental theory 'can never explain how it is that "the numinous" is the object of search and desire and yearning, and that for its own sake and not only for the sake of the aid and backing that men expect from it in the natural sphere'.[16]

How then, does Otto account for the diverse phenomena under consideration? He does so in Kantian-Friesian terms by arguing that 'the holy' is an a priori category.[17] Having said this I must confess that I do not always find it easy to follow Otto's argument, and I am not convinced that it is consistent.[18] In what follows, I attempt to give a coherent account of what I

---

[15] Otto, *The Holy*, p. 58, German p. 53.

[16] Otto, *The Holy*, p. 46. German, pp. 39–40, 'Aus ihn kann sich nie erklären, daß das Numinose gesucht, begehrt, erwünscht wird, erwünscht wird nicht nur um der natürlichen Förderung und Hilfe willen, die man von ihm erwartet, sondern auch um seiner selbst willen, und nicht nur in den Formen des "rationalen" Kultus.'

[17] For Otto's advocacy of Kantian-Friesian philosophy see his *Kantisch-Fries ische Religionsphilosophie und ihre Anwendung auf die Theologie. Zur Einleitung in die Glaubenslehre für Studenten der Theologie* (Tübingen: J.C.B. Mohr, 1909). *The Philosophy of Religion based on Kant and Fries* (London: Williams & Norgate 1931).

[18] G. van der Leeuw, 'Rudolf Otto und die Religionsgeschichte', *ZThK* 19 (1938), p. 75 described the book as 'eine philosophische Fehlgeburt, eine psychologische Verirrung, eine religionsgeschichtliche Einseitigkeit'. But he added 'trotz seiner vielen methodischen und logischen Fehler, trotz seiner Formlosigkeit, hat „Das Heilige" der Generation nach dem Kriege ein neues Verständnis für Religion und religiöse Erscheinungen erschlossen, und das Buch wird diesen Dienst wohl noch vielen Generationen leisten'. Five essays critical of Otto's *Das Heilige* can be found in Colpe, *Die Diskussion um das „Heilige"* (see footnote 9).

think Otto is saying, although I could well be in need of correction.

The a priori category that Otto uses as an illustration of his view is that of causality. It is this category which, observing the temporal sequence of two successive events, posits a causal relation between the two; this is not 'chance external resemblance, but essential correspondence'.[19] In the same way, the impact of 'the numinous' upon reason is schematised by a category, and the result is the apprehension of 'the holy'. This apprehension is, however, affected by what Otto calls 'the law of reciprocal attraction between analogous feelings and emotions'.[20] Not surprisingly, given Otto's Kantian-Friesian interests, the notion of the sublime (where Fries in particular located the essence of the religious), is seen as an analogous feeling likely to be stimulated by the numinous; but also likely to be stimulated are the feelings of awe and dread that lead to belief in ghosts and demons.[21]

How, then, does religion move from 'lower' to 'higher' planes? For Fries it was Kantian critical philosophy that was the ultimate arbiter and purifier of various levels of religious apprehension and its expression. Otto seems to have evoked two different principles. First, as already mentioned, he held that the numinous was such that, however it was apprehended, it became an object sought for its own sake, one that was therefore capable of drawing people to purer notions. Second, and seemingly inconsistently, Otto held that what he called the faculty of divination – his term for the facility by which the numinous was grasped and conceptualised – while being a universal human possibility, was in practice restricted to a few people. As Otto says in a passage in which he criticises Schleiermacher,

> what is a universal potentiality of man as such is by no means
> to be found in *actuality* the universal possession of every

---

[19] Otto, *The Holy*, p. 60, German p. 56, 'nicht äußere zufällige Ähnlichkeit, sondern wesentliche Entsprechung'.

[20] Otto, *The Holy*, p. 140, German p. 142, das 'Gesetz des Sichanziehens sich entsprechender Gefühle'.

[21] See J. F. Fries, *Wissen, Glaube und Ahndung* (Göttingen: Vandenhoeck & Ruprecht, 1905) (edition with identical pagination to the 1805 original edition), pp. 222–33.

single man; very frequently it is only disclosed as a special endowment and equipment of particularly gifted individuals ... Not Man in general (as rationalism holds), but only special 'divinatory' natures possess the faculty of divination in actuality.[22]

Mircea Eliade's *The Sacred and the Profane* begins with a fulsome acknowledgement of the significance of Otto's *The Idea of the Holy*, but proposes a different way of approaching the subject.[23] 'We propose to present the phenomenon of the sacred in all its complexity, and not only in so far as it is *irrational*. What will concern us is not the relation between the rational and the non-rational elements of religion but the *sacred in its entirety*', writes Eliade.[24] Several definitions of the sacred are offered. First, it is an organisational concept, defined in opposition to the profane. Secondly, it is a perceived quality, being 'equivalent to a *power* and, in the last analysis, to *reality*'.[25] Thirdly, it has an existential sense in that '*sacred* and *profane* are two modes of being in the world, two existential situations assumed by man in the course of his history'.[26] Finally, it is an ontological reality which manifests itself in what Eliade calls hierophanies, i.e. 'manifestations of

---

[22] Otto, *The Holy*, pp. 166–7, German, p. 170, ' was allgemein-menschlich ist, wird keineswegs allgemein und von jedem Menschen in actu besessen, sondern kommt sehr häufig nur in Form vorzüglicher Begabung und Ausstattung Einzelner, Begnadeter zu Tage ... Nur divinatorische Naturen haben dieses Vermögen der Divination in actu und nicht der Mensch überhaupt, wie der Rationalismus meint'.

[23] M. Eliade, *The Sacred and the Profane. The Nature of Religion* (New York: Harper & Row, 1961), pp. 8–10. Although the work was written in French in 1956, it first appeared in a German translation in 1957. Reference is made here to the French edition published by Éditions Gallimard, Paris, 1965, under the title *Le sacré et le profane*. Pages 8–10 in English represent pp. 13–14 in the French.

[24] Eliade, *Sacred and Profane*, p. 10, French, p. 14, 'Nous voudrions présenter le phénomène du sacré dans toute sa complexité, et non pas seulement dans ce qu'il comporte d'*irrationnel*. Ce n'est pas le rapport entre les éléments non-rationnel et rationnel de la religion qui nous intéresse, mais le sacré *dans sa totalité*.'

[25] Eliade, *Sacred and Profane*, p. 12, French, p. 16, 'le *sacré* équivaut à la *puissance* et, en définitive, à la *réalité* par excellence'.

[26] Eliade, *Sacred and Profane*, p. 14, French, p. 18, 'deux modalités d'être dans le monde, deux situations existentielles assumées par l'homme au long de son histoire'.

sacred realities'.[27] Hierophanies can be elementary, i.e.
manifestations of the sacred in an object such as a stone or
tree, or supreme, as in the incarnation of God in Jesus Christ.
In each case, people are confronted by a reality which 'does
not belong to our world, in objects that are an integral part of
our natural "profane" world'.[28]

Much of the book is devoted to illustrating this last point
under the headings of sacred space, sacred time and myths, and
the sacredness of nature. Because the examples are drawn from
such a large number of different cultures, religions and times it
is difficult for a non-specialist to judge how far the material is
being interpreted appropriately, but where the Old Testament
is referred to this is often problematic. An example is Jacob's
dream at Bethel (Gen. 28.10–17), where it is assumed that the
biblical account is a true record of an experience by an historical
figure, Jacob. At the same time, some points are made that are
undeniably important. There *are* sacred places and times that
serve to mark off and to define specifically religious areas of life
– Durham Cathedral is one such sacred place. Whether Eliade's
theory best accounts for them is another matter; and I am
inclined to doubt that recent popular and commercial frenzy
about the change in the way we numbered our years from
nineteen-something to two thousand implied a manifestation of
the sacred. However, Eliade's position is clear. In justifying his
deployment of examples from differing cultures and times he
uses the analogy of 'the poetic phenomenon'. If one were trying
to gain a better grasp of the 'poetic phenomenon', it would be
necessary to bring together material from Hindu, Chinese and
Mexican poems as well as from Homer and Dante.[29] The difficulty with this analogy, of course, is that the poetic phenomenon
is a classificatory term only, and does not imply the existence of
a reality beyond the word manifesting itself in the world.

The brief consideration of Eliade has brought us back to the
starting-point, Söding's reference to him in his remarks about

[27] Eliade, *Sacred and Profane*, p. 11, French, p. 15, 'les manifestations des
réalités sacrées'.
[28] Eliade, *Sacred and Profane*, p. 11, French, p. 15, 'la manifestation ... d'une
réalité qui n'appartient pas à notre monde, dans les objets qui font partie
intégrante de notre monde "naturel", "profane"'.
[29] Eliade, *Sacred and Profane*, p. 16, French, p. 19.

the nature of holiness; and the purpose of this historical excursion has been to show some of the assumptions behind influential accounts of 'the holy', so that some fundamental questions can be raised.

In the first place, the three theorists of 'the holy' were all theists and monotheists, which meant that, in their very different ways, they imposed a unity upon their data, implying that one and the same divine reality was ultimately behind all manifestations of 'the holy'. This may, of course, be correct. I certainly do not want to suggest that religious or theological accounts of the many manifestations that are defined as 'holy' are likely to be wrong because they are religious or theological, and that sociological accounts, because they are religiously 'neutral', are more likely to be correct. Personally, I prefer to be agnostic on the matter, and to say that I do not know whether, and if so, how, the data used by Söderblom, Otto and Eliade can be explained in terms of an all-embracing scheme. It would certainly be interesting to see an account of these data from a non-Christian religious perspective; and, of course there is no lack of non-religious accounts of them in psychological or sociological terms.[30]

The problem of imposing unifying forms upon disparate data can also be approached from another angle. Here is Evans-Pritchard criticising Durkheim's definition of religion as beliefs and practices relative to sacred things, that is, things that are set aside from the profane.[31]

> I have made it clear why I think the dichotomy between the 'sacred' and the 'profane' is a false one, and that I have never found it of the slightest value in my field research. Obviously, for dialectical purposes, Durkheim had to make a rigid opposition between the two categories, for if there is to be a 'sacred' there must be a 'profane'; but this is a conceptual, not empirical, antithesis. And are the concepts ours or those

---

[30] See the interesting discussion of Schleiermacher and Otto in W. Pannenberg, *Systematische Theologie Band 1* (Göttingen: Vandenhoeck & Ruprecht, 1988), pp. 151–7.

[31] E. E. Evans-Pritchard, *Theories of Primitive Religion* (Oxford: Oxford University Press, 1965), p. 575; idem, *A History of Anthropological Thought*, London: Faber & Faber, 1981), p. 160.

of the Australian aboriginals? ... In reading the detailed monograph by Dr. and Mrs. Seligman about the Veddas, no such division is suggested as existing among that extremely primitive people. Again, it would be difficult to maintain the existence of such a separation among the Melanesian peoples of whom we have very copious records. I think that Durkheim was here generalizing from his own Semitic background.[32]

Elsewhere, Evans-Pritchard gives an example of what he calls 'situational flexibility'. When the shrines used by the Azande for the cult of ancestors are not in ritual use, they are either ignored or used as convenient props for resting spears against. In other words, this particular piece of sacred space is only sacred when it is being used for ritual purposes; and it is certainly not protected by interdictions.[33]

A third objection that has been mounted to the approach exemplified by Söderblom, Otto and Eliade is that it gives respectability to natural religion at the expense of revealed religion. However, I want to return to a point made by Evans-Pritchard and use it to introduce the final part of this paper.

Holiness and the Old Testament

Evans-Pritchard commented that he had never found Durkheim's distinction between the sacred and the profane to be of the slightest value in his field research. My concern, as an exegete of the Old Testament, is whether the theorising about holiness, some of which has been reviewed, is of any value to Old Testament exegesis; and here, I must admit that I face something of a dilemma. I cannot work as though Durkheim, and before him, Robertson Smith, never drew attention to the sacred/profane distinction. I cannot pretend that Otto never wrote about the feeling of creatureliness and dependence in the face of the 'mysterium tremendum' when I read Isaiah 6.5, where the prophet cries out 'woe is me' when he 'sees' Yahweh and hears the seraphim chant 'holy, holy, holy'. How do I

[32] Evans-Pritchard, *History of Anthropological Thought*, p. 160.
[33] Evans-Pritchard, *Theories of Primitive Religion*, p. 65.

approach the exegesis of Old Testament passages that touch on 'the holy' and 'holiness', especially if I have strong reservations about the work of the theorists on holiness?

What I want to do now is to suggest a different way of approaching the problem, and one that I have not come across in what I have read on the subject of 'the holy' and holiness, although similar ideas are to be found in Pannenberg's account of the dynamics of the tension between unity and plurality in the idea of the divine, as a factor in the development of religions.[34]

The Old Testament contains good deal of material that suggests that some Israelites, at least, could take quite critical stances on the matter of what was holy and sacred. Deuteronomy 12.2–3 commands the Israelites to destroy the sanctuaries, altars and images used by the non-Israelite inhabitants of Canaan to worship other gods. Presumably, these sanctuaries, altars and images were holy places and objects for those whose gods were honoured at and by means of them. For the Hebrew legislators they are abominations that must be destroyed; and presumably there is no fear that such action will bring disaster upon those who carry out the destruction. Indeed, the story of Gideon in Judges 6.25–32 explicitly addresses this issue. Gideon destroys the altar of Baal and cuts down the Asherah pole in Ophrah. When he is threatened with death by the men of the town for doing this, Gideon's father replies to the effect that if Baal really is a god, he will be able to defend his own interests. What these commandments and the Gideon story imply is that one's view of what is and what is not holy will depend upon national and religious loyalty and belief. It is not necessary to believe either that the Israelites really did destroy all pagan shrines and objects in Canaan or that the Gideon story is historically true. The point is that the laws and story must have articulated viewpoints that made sense to the world of the presumed authors, and at least some of the presumed hearers/readers.

The critical attitude to sacred places and objects is not, however, confined to those of non-Israelites in the Old Testament narratives. Hezekiah is said to have destroyed the

---

[34] Pannenberg, *Systematische Theologie, Band 1*, pp. 162–4.

bronze serpent Nehushtan, believed by the people, according
to the biblical text, to have been made by Moses, and to which
the people of Israel burned incense (2 Kgs 18.4). In the terms
of the holiness theorists, this object was presumably possessed
of *mana* which the worshippers hoped to appropriate. It was
the location of a hierophany, to use Eliade's term. For the
reforming king, however, it was a threat to his reforming
programme. He evidently had no fear of the consequences of
destroying such a sacred object. Later in the narrative about
Hezekiah, he is described as stripping the gold from the doors
and doorposts of the Jerusalem temple in order to pay tribute
to Sennacherib (2 Kgs 18.16). This act, presumably of
sacrilege, is nowhere criticised in the biblical narrative, and
Hezekiah is presented as one of the kings of Judah most loyal
to Yahweh.

Passing over the reforms of Josiah, which involved removing
all kinds of objects from the temple, which presumably had
come to be regarded as sacred by someone (see 2 Kgs 23.4–14),
not to mention his destruction of the altars at Bethel and
throughout Samaria (2 Kgs 23.15–20), there is the matter of
the objections that were apparently made to the rebuilding of
the temple in the post-exilic period. These are most forcibly
expressed in Isaiah 66.1:

> Thus says the LORD:
> 'Heaven is my throne
> and the earth is my footstool;
> what is the house which you would build for me,
> and what is the place of my rest?'

The passage goes on to liken those who offer sacrifice to those
who commit all kinds of abomination. Presumably, those who
opposed the rebuilding were not bothered by the thought that
their attitude would rob Jerusalem of its most potent sacred
place.

This relativising view of holiness and its dangers, reminiscent
of Evans-Pritchard's 'situational flexibility', now needs to be
applied to the two narratives mentioned earlier that have long
provided classical support for the holiness theorists, 1 Samuel
6.19 and 2 Samuel 6.6–7. The first passage is set in the narrative
that recounts the return of the Ark of the Covenant from
Bethel after its Philistine sojourn, and is also a classical piece of

textual confusion. The Massoretic Text states that God smote 'seventy men, fifty thousand men', a reading followed by the Authorized and Revised Versions but not accepted by any modern translation including the conservative New International Version, all conveniently ignoring the funda-mental principle of textual criticism that the more difficult reading is to be preferred! The passage from 2 Samuel concerns Uzzah's death when he put out his hand and touched the Ark to stop it from falling from the cart. H. Preserved Smith, commenting on the first passage and the cry of the men of Beth-shemesh 'Who is able to stand before the LORD, this holy God', writes 'The holiness of Yahweh is his apartness from the world. This makes it impossible to approach him except after special ceremonial preparation, and his displeasure is fatal to those who approach him without that preparation (conse-cration).'[35] Addressing the second passage, Arnold Anderson notes the possibility that 'awesome sacrality' was attached to the Ark, and that this belief was the immediate cause of Uzzah's death.[36]

It seems to me that radical questions need to be asked about these stories. Limiting these to the first narrative, it needs to be asked why the men of Beth-shemesh were killed for looking in the Ark when the Philistines who captured it and handled it were not similarly afflicted. It is true that the inhabitants of Ashdod, Gath and Ekron are afflicted with tumours (1 Sam. 5.6–12) when the Ark is brought to their cities, but this seems a lesser, if nonetheless unpleasant, punishment compared with that meted out to the 70 or 50,070 inhabitants of Beth-shemesh.

But the Philistines were arguably not the only non-Israelites

[35] H. P. Smith, *A Critical and Exegetical Commentary on the Books of Samuel* (Edinburgh, 1899), p. 49.

[36] A. A. Anderson, *2 Samuel.* Word Biblical Commentary (Dallas: Word Books, 1989), p. 104. Examples of this type of interpretation abound. P. Kyle McCarter Jr writes: 'The ancient Israelite understood that all sacred things were to be approached with great care and that the manipulation of sacred objects was an activity necessarily insulated by ritual precautions and taboos. The transference of the ark from one place to another, therefore, was not a task to be taken lightly ... Any defect in preparation for or error in the performance of such a rite might provoke a harmful response from a poten-tially beneficial power.' See his *II Samuel,* The Anchor Bible 9 (New York: Doubleday, 1984), p. 170.

to handle the Ark. Although the Ark is not mentioned among the vessels of the Jerusalem temple that were taken by the Babylonian captain Nebuzaradan to Babylon in 587 in 2 Kings 25.13–17, 2 Esdras 10.19–22 laments that 'the ark of our covenant has been plundered'. It is also arguable that the authors of the prose passage in Jeremiah 3.15–18 thought that the Ark was still in Jerusalem during Jeremiah's lifetime.[37] But if the presence of the Ark in Jerusalem in 587 is not insisted on, what is beyond dispute is that 2 Kings 25.13–17 records the removal of sacred vessels from the temple by the Babylonians, without the latter being subjected to any of the afflictions that might be associated with the handling of such potentially dangerous objects.

What this line of argument is leading to is the following proposition: we need to stop reading the Old Testament as though it contained evidence for the evolution of Israel's religion from lower to higher forms over a long period of time. Israel's religion, even in the Second Temple period when the Old Testament assumed its present form, contained popular superstitions, and prophetic and priestly strands which made available to the compilers a rich diversity of material. In putting this into its final form, however, the overriding view of the compilers, so far as the holiness of Yahweh was concerned, was that Yahweh was incomparable, sovereign, beyond the unaided comprehension of humankind, unapproachable yet in the midst of his chosen people. It is in the light of this kind of consideration that narratives such as Genesis 28.10–17 (Jacob's dream at Bethel) or the two incidents in 1 and 2 Samuel 6 should be read, without denying that they may originate in aetiological stories or popular legends. They are object lessons that articulate the view of the writers of the Old Testament of God's incomparability and sovereignty. They are not evidence for 'primitive' views of holiness in terms of *mana* and *taboo*.

This is not to suggest that methods derived from social anthropology cannot illumine those parts of the Old Testament that deal specifically with pollution and defilement, and which

---

[37] See W. McKane, *A Critical and Exegetical Commentary on Jeremiah*, vol. 1 (Edinburgh: T&T Clark, 1986) pp. 72–7 for full discussion of the various possibilities.

define holiness for God's people in terms of ritual purity. It is to suggest that the best place from which to construct an overall framework for approaching the subject of holiness in the Old Testament is a critical reading of Old Testament narratives, rather than generalised theories of 'holiness', however impressive and distinguished they may be.

So, what is holiness? I began by suggesting that it was an English word whose meaning depended on the context in which it was used and the interests of those who used it. While I believe that I have succeeded in establishing something of a case for this, I do not believe that we are left in a Humpty-Dumpty situation. Whatever we think of attempts to account for 'holiness', however understood, in terms of all-embracing theories, these attempts draw our attention to recurrent features of human experience that we ignore at our peril, because they are part of what it means to be human. They share common features: that reality cannot ultimately be totally comprehended in terms of human rationality; that particular times and places can (but not necessarily do or must) assume a significance that points beyond themselves; that experiences of the sublime can induce human feelings of insignificance, uncleanness and danger; that people can feel themselves to be grasped by an unseen reality that becomes something to be after for its own sake and which in this way liberates seekers from self-interest. Further, if the Old Testament is allowed to speak for itself and is not forced into patterns prescribed by phenomenological or anthropological theories (although Old Testament interpretation can learn much from these), it has much to contribute to the question 'what is holiness?' It exhibits a 'situational flexibility' and articulates a critique of holiness as conceived in impersonal terms. This is because it understands holiness as something ultimately grounded in the moral character of the God of Israel, whose chief attributes of unfailing love, mercy and forgiveness mark him off as different from humankind, yet which are intended to transform humanity into what it is unable fully to achieve itself.

2

Rudolf Otto's *The Idea of the Holy* Revisited

Colin Crowder

'A classic', according to Mark Twain, 'is something that everybody wants to have read and nobody wants to read.'[1] This is not, I think, what commentators have in mind when they call Rudolf Otto's *The Idea of the Holy* 'a classic', and there was a time when it seems that everybody wanted to read it. First published in 1917, *Das Heilige* went through 25 editions by 1936, the year before Otto died, and some thirty years later it was still reckoned to be 'probably the most widely read theological work in German of the twentieth century'.[2] An English translation, by John Harvey, was published in 1923, to be followed by translations into Swedish, Spanish, Italian, Japanese, Dutch and French before the decade was out, and abroad the book soon became an even bigger success, commercially speaking, than it had been at home. In the English-speaking world, it popularised the use of 'the holy' as a noun, and introduced a catena of concepts – '*mysterium*', '*tremendum*', '*fascinans*' – which are often recalled long after the original thesis is forgotten (and which might, therefore, continue to influence the ways in which we think about religion, as earlier, and still more exotic imports such as *mana*, *taboo* and *totem* appear to do). It also secured a permanent place in the language for 'numinous', the term Otto derived from *numen*, a Latin word for divinity. While 'numinous' is not unknown in English before the 1920s, given

---

[1] Mark Twain, in his speech 'The Disappearance of Literature', New York, 20th November 1900.

[2] Hans Zahrnt, *The Question of God: Protestant Theology in the Twentieth Century* [1966], tr. R. A. Wilson (London: Collins, 1969), p. 48.

that the naturalisation of *numen* was well under way in the seventeenth century, it is only through *The Idea of the Holy* that it was rescued from obscurity. Many of the illustrative quotations in the new *Oxford English Dictionary* are from the book itself or from works related to it, implicitly and explicitly, and the rest, perhaps, pay tribute to Otto in their own backhanded way, since as Gregory Alles remarks, 'the word ... has become standard English for anything that has a vaguely spiritual or mystical aura'.[3] It is not only the language of scholarship which has been influenced by *The Idea of the Holy*, therefore; yet it *is* the work of a scholar, and its reputation as a classic is bound up with its contribution to various scholarly disciplines, as Melissa Raphael emphasises in the opening lines of her recent study of Otto:

> The twentieth-century history of the concept of holiness is largely unintelligible without reference to that advanced by Rudolf Otto in *The Idea of the Holy*. For nearly eighty years this text has been used as a yardstick against which subsequent studies of holiness have declared and defined their own position. Like other books which have achieved classic status, *The Idea of the Holy* 'exceeds the rules by which any single discipline would claim it', and it has left its mark not only on the history of religions but also on twentieth-century philosophy, psychology and aesthetics of religion, biblical studies, and theology.[4]

Few could dispute its 'classic status', yet somewhere along the line it seems to have become a classic in the Twainian sense, saluted more and more, but studied less and less – although it looks as if even these days might be over. A generation ago, textbooks on theology in the twentieth century often introduced *The Idea of the Holy*, if only to set the scene for the emergence of Karl Barth and 'dialectical theology' after the First World War. By contrast, some recent textbooks scarcely mention it, and those that do are inclined to accept the view

---

[3] Gregory D. Alles, 'Introduction', Rudolf Otto, *Autobiographical and Social Essays*, tr. and ed. Gregory D. Alles (Berlin: Mouton de Gruyter, 1996), p. 3.

[4] Melissa Raphael, *Rudolf Otto and the Concept of Holiness* (Oxford: Oxford University Press, 1997), p. 1, quoting Lynn Poland, 'The Idea of the Holy and the History of the Sublime' (see note 69).

that it is an essay in the phenomenology of religion with limited theological significance in its own right. I suspect that Otto's work has been marginalized in much the same way, and over a similar period, in religious studies, where the theological character of *The Idea of the Holy* is all too apparent. Yet even if the parallel cannot be maintained, I do not think that it is controversial to suggest not only that few people now read the book, but also that few feel that they *ought* to read it; and, if so, there is a sense in which it is no longer the classic that it once was.

What is beyond question, I think, is the claim that the history of the concept of holiness in the twentieth century cannot be comprehended without reference to *The Idea of the Holy*. In this essay, I hope to say something about the book, its place in Otto's work as a whole, and its critical fortunes; but I would also like to raise the issue of whether the book might be of more than purely historical interest after all.

Otto and The Idea of the Holy

The Idea of the Holy occupies a central place in Otto's output, both chronologically and intellectually. As Philip Almond writes, 'this work is the fulcrum of Otto's work on religion; his earlier work points to it, and his later work is in substance a development of it'.[5] In this section, therefore, I approach *The Idea of the Holy* through its author's life and work.

Karl Louis Rudolf Otto (1869–1937) grew up in Peine and Hildesheim, the twelfth of thirteen children born to Wilhelm

---

[5] Philip C. Almond, *Rudolf Otto: An Introduction to His Philosophical Theology* (Chapel Hill, NC: University of North Carolina Press, 1984), p. 8. Almond's introduction to Otto's life and work (pp. 3–25) remains the standard summary in English, and I have drawn on it extensively; I am also indebted to Gregory Alles' translations of Otto's 'autobiographical fragments', in *Autobiographical and Social Essays*. See also Theodore M. Ludwig, 'Otto, Rudolf', in Mircea Eliade (ed.), *The Encyclopedia of Religion* (New York: Macmillan, 1987), vol. 11, pp. 139–41, and, among older works on Otto, Robert F. Davidson, *Rudolf Otto's Interpretation of Religion* (Princeton, NJ: Princeton University Press, 1947), Joachim Wach, 'Rudolf Otto and the Idea of the Holy', in *Types of Religious Experience: Christian and Non-Christian* (Chicago, IL: University of Chicago Press, 1951), pp. 209–27, and Bernard Meland, 'Rudolf Otto', in Dean G. Peerman and Martin Marty (eds.), *A Handbook of Christian Theologians* (Cleveland, OH: World, 1965), pp. 169–91.

Otto, a factory owner, and Katherine Reupke. In 1888, he began his studies in theology at Erlangen, where he hoped to secure the foundations of his strictly orthodox Lutheranism before exposing himself to the ideas of the 'innovators': 'I wanted to study with men of the old school, in order thoroughly to acquire the means for protecting myself against danger.'[6] This is not quite how things worked out, but then at Göttingen (where he studied in 1889 and from 1891 onwards) he did not find the kind of 'naked philosophical rationalism' that he had half anticipated.[7] In both institutions, in fact, a variety of 'mediating' and unambiguously liberal theological voices influenced Otto, and helped him to develop his own voice. At Erlangen, Franz Reinhold von Frank's focus on religious experience – which was central to the theology of the Erlangen School – made a deep impact on Otto's thought, and (even more importantly) it was through Frank that Otto was introduced to the work of Schleiermacher. At Göttingen, his teachers included Theodor Häring, who had succeeded Albrecht Ritschl (perhaps the greatest liberal theologian of the second half of the century), and who, with Herrmann, Harnack, Kaftan and others, played a leading role in the development of Ritschl's legacy. (The debt is acknowledged in the dedication of *The Idea of the Holy* to Häring.) Otto earned his Licentiate of Theology in 1898 with a thesis on Luther and the Holy Spirit, published the same year as *Die Anschauung vom heiligen Geiste bei Luther* – one of the few major works by Otto which, so far as I am aware, has never been translated into English.

In 1899, the year that Otto became a lecturer at Göttingen, he produced a centenary edition of Schleiermacher's *On Religion: Speeches to its Cultured Despisers*, which he followed with an essay on Schleiermacher's 'rediscovery' of religion.[8] At around the same time, he brought out a contribution to 'life of Jesus research', *Leben und Wirken Jesu nach historisch-kritischer*

---

[6] 'My Life' [1891], in Otto, *Autobiographical and Social Essays*, p. 53.

[7] *Autobiographical and Social Essays*, p. 55.

[8] 'How Schleiermacher Rediscovered the *Sensus Numinis*', in *Religious Essays: A Supplement to 'The Idea of the Holy'*, tr. Brian Lunn (London: Oxford University Press, 1931), pp. 68–77.

Auffassung (1901), a work in the Ritschlian tradition which is mentioned, but not discussed, in Schweitzer's book on the 'quest' of the historical Jesus.[9] It was Otto's work on Schleiermacher, however, which pointed forwards to *The Idea of the Holy*, and, more directly, prepared the ground for the philosophical studies that he published in 1904 (when he became an assistant professor at Göttingen) and 1909. Schleiermacher's determination to preserve religion from rationalistic and moralistic reductionism, which, in the *Speeches*, is expressed in terms of the irreducibility of 'feeling' to 'thinking' (metaphysics) and 'acting' (ethics), shaped Otto's programme, but in the details the influence of other late eighteenth- and early nineteenth-century writers was more decisive. His critique of naturalism, *Naturalistische und religiöse Weltansicht*, defended the autonomy of religion in a broadly Kantian way,[10] and the revival at Göttingen of the neo-Kantianism of Jakob Friedrich Fries (1773–1843) opened up philosophical opportunities for Otto that resulted in the publication of *Kantisch-Fries'sche Religionsphilosophie*.[11] Otto withdrew his earlier judgement on the relative merits of Schleiermacher and Fries, now stating that Fries was 'superior in comprehensiveness, thoroughness, and solidity', but his interest in Fries was not primarily historical.[12] Rather, he turned to Friesian philosophy in order to articulate his own convictions, and some Friesian themes – in particular, the emphasis on *Ahndung*, which might be translated as 'intuition', although Fries distinguishes it from 'intuition' in the Kantian sense of the word (*Anschauung*)[13] – occupy an

---

[9] *The Life and Ministry of Jesus* (Chicago: Open Court, 1908). (Albert Schweitzer, *The Quest of the Historical Jesus* [1906], tr. W. Montgomery (London: SCM, 1981), p. 301n.)

[10] Otto, *Naturalism and Religion*, tr. J. Arthur Thomson and Margaret Thomson (London: Williams and Norgate, 1907).

[11] Otto, *The Philosophy of Religion Based on Kant and Fries*, tr. E. B. Dicker (London: Williams & Norgate, 1931).

[12] *The Philosophy of Religion*, p. 15.

[13] David Walford translates *Ahndung* (an archaic form of *Ahnung*) as 'intuitive awareness', suggesting that it designates 'a mode of apprehension which is neither the product of intellection or reasoning, nor capable of conceptual analysis'. ('Translator's Note', in Jakob Friedrich Fries, *Dialogues on Morality and Religion*, ed. D. Z. Phillips, tr. David Walford (Oxford: Blackwell, 1982), pp. xv–xvi.)

important position in *The Idea of the Holy*, although Otto rarely mentioned Fries by name in this and his other later works.

The influence of Luther, Schleiermacher, Kant and Fries on the development of Otto's thought is commonly acknowledged, but commentators almost invariably draw attention to the impact of Otto's travels as well. Back in 1895, he had travelled in Egypt, Palestine and Greece, and certain experiences – including Holy Week in Jerusalem and the Coptic liturgy in Cairo, but also the 'general feeling of the unfathomable depth and mystery of existence and universe' which came over him at the Sphinx in Giza – made a deep impression upon him.[14] In 1911 and 1912, he travelled even more extensively, in North Africa, India, China and Japan, periodically sending letters back for publication in *Die christliche Welt*. These travels enabled Otto to study several religious traditions in their traditional cultural environments, such as Taoism in China, and Buddhism in Burma, Thailand and Japan, with far-reaching consequences for his work. Some years later, Otto established a collection of cultic objects from around the world, and, still more ambitiously, a 'Religious League of Humanity' (*Religiöser Menschheitsbund*), dissolved in 1933. Almond suggests that both ideas were conceived during the journey through India and the Far East, and thinks it likely that Otto began studying Sanskrit at about this time: the first of several translations and studies of texts from India, including three volumes on the *Bhagavad-Gita*,[15] came out as early as 1916. 'From this time on', in fact, 'his work gives as much the impression of a *Religionswissenschaftler* as of a Lutheran theologian or idealist philosopher.'[16]

The Idea of the Holy was completed at Breslau, where Otto had been appointed Professor of Systematic Theology in 1915, but published in 1917, the year that he moved to Marburg, where he succeeded Wilhelm Herrmann, remaining Professor of

[14] The evidence is mostly in unpublished correspondence, cited by Philip Almond, *Rudolf Otto*, pp. 12–15, but Otto mentions the experience at the Sphinx in *The Philosophy of Religion*, p. 137.

[15] *The Original Gita: The Song of the Supreme Exalted One*, tr. J. E. Turner (London: Allen and Unwin, 1939) incorporates translations of all three of these works.

[16] Almond, *Rudolf Otto*, p. 18.

Systematic Theology there until he retired in 1929. Otto's understanding of the book is summarised in its subtitle, 'An Inquiry into the Non-Rational Factor in the Idea of the Divine and its Relation to the Rational', and in his Foreword he presents his credentials as a serious student of 'the *rational* aspect of that supreme Reality we call "God"', referring to his studies in the philosophy of religion. Nevertheless, *The Idea of the Holy* is primarily concerned with 'that which may be called "non-rational" or "supra-rational" in the depths of the divine nature'.[17]

Otto begins by emphasising that for the theist, and for the Christian in particular, God's nature is a *rational* nature: the divine attributes 'constitute clear and definite *concepts*: they can be grasped by the intellect; they can be analysed by thought; they even admit of definition'.[18] But to assume that 'the essence of deity can be given completely and exhaustively in such "rational" attributions' is an error, if an entirely natural one, which leads 'to a wrong and one-sided interpretation of religion':

> For so far are these 'rational' attributes from exhausting the idea of deity, that they in fact imply a non-rational or supra-rational Subject of which they are predicates. They are 'essential' (and not merely 'accidental') attributes of that subject, but they are also, it is important to notice, *synthetic* essential attributes. That is to say, we have to predicate them of a subject which they qualify, but which in its deeper essence is not, nor indeed can be, comprehended in them; which rather requires comprehension of a different kind. Yet, though it eludes the conceptual way of understanding, it must be in some way or other within our grasp, else absolutely nothing could be asserted of it.[19]

This 'bias to rationalization', moreover, is not so much the product of 'Rationalism' as of 'Orthodoxy', which 'found in the construction of dogma and doctrine no way to do justice to

---

[17] Otto, *The Idea of the Holy*, tr. John W. Harvey (London: Oxford University Press, 1923 [all quotations from the 6th, revised impression of 1931]), p. vii.

[18] *Idea*, p. 1.

[19] *Idea*, p. 2.

the non-rational aspect of its subject'; and the failure to recognise the value of the non-rational element in religion 'gave to the idea of God a one-sidedly intellectualistic and rationalistic interpretation'.[20] As he sets his sights on it, Otto asks us to recognise that 'Religion is not exclusively contained and exhaustively comprised in any series of "rational" assertions', and to agree with him that 'it is well worth while to attempt to bring the relation of the different "moments" of religion to one another clearly before the mind, so that its nature may become more manifest.' This is precisely what Otto attempts to do in *The Idea of the Holy*, 'with respect to the quite distinctive category of the holy or sacred'.[21]

He argues that 'holiness', or 'the holy', is a complex category of interpretation and evaluation. It includes a rational element, or 'moment', and as such it is often understood in purely ethical terms, as a way of speaking about the morally good in an absolute form. But it also includes 'a clear overplus of meaning',[22] and for the purposes of the investigation Otto makes use of 'a special term to stand for "the holy" *minus* its moral factor or "moment", and ... minus its "rational" aspect altogether'[23] – this, of course, is *numinous*, which is derived from *numen* in the same way that *ominous* is derived from *omen*. This 'overplus', moreover, is not a secondary development: '"holy", or at least the equivalent words in Latin and Greek, in Semitic and other ancient languages, denoted first and foremost *only* this overplus: if the ethical element was present at all, at any rate it was not original and never constituted the

---

[20] *Idea*, p. 3.

[21] *Idea*, p. 4. The last phrase betrays a gloss on the original, since 'holy' and 'sacred' both translate the single word *heilig*. Otto's translator treats the terms as interchangeable, in this context at least, but he touches on some of the semantic issues in an appendix ('The Expression of the Numinous in English'). The issues are investigated in some detail by Willard G. Oxtoby, 'Holy, Idea of the', in Mircea Eliade (ed.), *The Encyclopedia of Religion* (New York: Macmillan, 1987), vol. 6, pp. 431–8. One might argue, however, that the most misleading aspect of the translation is its title, which turns a book on 'the holy' into a book on 'the *idea* of the holy'; as Eric Sharpe rightly remarks, 'An imperative does not become an idea without losing much of its force.' (Eric Sharpe, *Nathan Söderblom and the Study of Religion* (Chapel Hill, NC: University of North Carolina Press, 1990), p. 211.)

[22] *Idea*, p. 5.

[23] *Idea*, p. 6.

whole meaning of the word'.[24] In time, the meaning of words such as the Hebrew *qadosh*, the Greek *hagios* and the Latin *sacer* broadened to include the rational, moral element, and 'we then use the word "holy" to translate them':

> But this 'holy' then represents the gradual shaping and filling in with ethical meaning, or what we shall call the 'schematization', of what was a unique original feeling-response, which can be in itself ethically neutral and claims consideration in its own right. And when this moment or element first emerges and begins its long development, all those expressions (*qadosh*, ἅγιος, *sacer*, &c.) mean beyond question something quite other than 'the good'.[25]

The isolation of this 'unique original feeling-response' appears to confirm the common supposition that *The Idea of the Holy* represents an analysis of religious experience, but this supposition is misleading in two ways. First, Otto thinks of 'numinous' not only as a quality of experiences, but also as a quality of their object – that is, the transcendent reality which produces them or corresponds to them. Second, he thinks that numinous experience is such that it cannot be broken down into its constituent parts, and so, to this extent, no 'analysis' of the numinous is possible. Both thoughts are present in this passage:

> I shall speak then of a unique 'numinous' category of value and of a definitely 'numinous' state of mind, which is always found wherever the category is applied. This mental state is perfectly *sui generis* and irreducible to any other; and therefore, like every absolutely primary and elementary datum, while it admits of being discussed, it cannot be strictly defined.[26]

As the numinous 'state of mind' is *sui generis*, it can only be approached indirectly, by comparison and contrast with what is more familiar to us – and this is how Otto proceeds in the next few chapters of the book.

---

[24] *Idea*, pp. 5–6.
[25] *Idea*, p. 6.
[26] *Idea*, p. 7.

He gives credit to Schleiermacher for identifying an important element of religious experience in his emphasis on an absolute 'feeling of dependence', but he argues that Schleiermacher misinterprets 'creature-feeling' in failing to see that it is only analogous to (rather than continuous with) our ordinary feelings of dependence, from which it differs not just in degree but in kind as well. Moreover, what he analyses is 'a sort of *self*-consciousness', and, as a result, 'I can only come upon the very fact of God as the result of an inference', that is, by reasoning to some cause to account for the feeling. Even genuine 'creature-feeling' is simply 'a first subjective concomitant and effect of another feeling-element, which casts it like a shadow, but which in itself indubitably has immediate and primary reference to an object outside the self.'[27] The numinous is such that it 'can only be suggested by means of the special way in which it is reflected in the mind in terms of feeling', creating 'this and that determinate affective state', and Otto endeavours, 'by adducing feelings akin to them for the purpose of analogy or contrast, and by the use of metaphor and symbolic expressions, to make the states of mind we are investigating ring out, as it were, of themselves.'[28] It is at this point in the book that Otto begins to characterise the numinous as the *mysterium tremendum et fascinans,* or, rather, introduces the individual elements from which this phrase is constructed. The chapter on the numinous as *mysterium* (in which 'we come upon something inherently "wholly other", whose kind and character are incommensurable with our own')[29] is preceded by an analysis of *tremendum,* which qualifies the substantive in one way (by communicating something of its

---

[27] *Idea,* p. 10. Otto misinterprets Schleiermacher quite seriously, I think, and given Otto's earlier work this might seem puzzling. Some light is shed on the question by Nicholas Lash, in *Easter in Ordinary* (London: SCM, 1988), when he suggests that the conceptual tools used by Schleiermacher 'were such as to enhance the plausibility of the claim, made by a later generation – when the language of "feeling" and "experience" had contracted into empirical description of individual psychological states – that all he was *really* talking about were "subjective", psychic phenomena.' Lash rightly cites as an example Otto's second criticism of Schleiermacher in this passage from *The Idea of the Holy* (p. 130n).

[28] *Idea,* p. 12.

[29] *Idea,* p. 28.

'awefulness', 'overpoweringness' and 'energy'), and is followed
by an analysis of *fascinans*, which qualifies the substantive in
another way (by communicating something of its attrac-
tiveness). The numinous, then, is encountered as the *mysterium
tremendum* and as the *mysterium fascinans*: 'its dual character, as
at once an object of boundless awe and boundless wonder,
quelling and yet entrancing the soul, constitutes the proper
positive content of the "mysterium" as it manifests itself in
conscious feeling'.[30]

All of these themes are set out in six short chapters which,
together, take up less than a quarter of the text. Much of the rest
of the book consists of explorations of the numinous in different
contexts, including the Old and New Testaments and the works
of Luther, but ranging widely over the history of religions.
Willard Oxtoby is not alone, perhaps, in treating three-quarters
of *The Idea of the Holy* as 'a collection of illustrations', and 'a
descriptive inventory of various people's intense experiences of
divine power', but in giving the impression that everything after
the first forty pages is no more than 'optional detail' he goes too
far.[31] It is the later chapters of the book, in fact, which include
some of Otto's most interesting and ambitious speculations,
particularly from a philosophical point of view: i.e. his treatment
of 'the faculty of divination', of the holy as an a priori category,
and of the process of 'schematization' by which the complex
category of the holy emerges from the numinous.

After the publication of *The Idea of the Holy*, Otto continued
to explore the significance of the numinous for various issues in
theology and the history of religions. His essays were first
published as appendices to the book, but as the number of
appendices grew some of them were published separately,
originally in a collection of essays concerning the numinous
(*Aufsätze das Numinose betreffend*, 1923), and later, with new
material, in two further volumes (*Das Gefühl des Überweltlichen*,
1932, and *Sünde und Urschuld*, 1932).[32] In the same period, his
interest in the similarities and differences between religious

---

[30] *Idea*, p. 42.
[31] Oxtoby, 'Holy, Idea of the', pp. 433 and 437.
[32] Some of these essays appeared in translation in the various impressions of
The Idea of the Holy and in *Religious Essays*.

thought in the West and the East led to the publication of his comparative study of Meister Eckhart and Shankara, *West-Östliche Mystik* (1926),[33] followed by a further study of the parallels between Christian and Hindu religious traditions, *Die Gnadenreligion Indiens und das Christentum* (1930),[34] and *Gottheit und Gottheiten der Arier*, a study – so far untranslated – of the religion of our Indo-European ancestors. Some of this work was no doubt influenced by his further travels in the Middle East and India, in 1927–8, and Almond suggests that these may have confirmed Otto's conviction 'that the specific differences between Christianity and Hinduism were a function not of their nonrational core, but of their respective ethical development'.[35] Ethics, and its relation to religion, was central to Otto's work in the final years of his life: he published a series of articles in this area in 1931 and 1932, and, had ill-health not stopped him, he would have given the 1933 Gifford Lectures on the theme of 'Moral Law and the Will of God'. His last work, published posthumously as a book, was an essay on freedom and necessity (*Freiheit und Notwendigkeit*, 1940).[36] But the last work that he saw through the press was a further study of Jesus and primitive Christianity, *Reich Gottes und Menschensohn* (1934),[37] which (quite unlike Otto's earlier book) brings a history of religions perspective to bear on eschatological and Christological issues in the gospel tradition.

The Eclipse of The Idea of the Holy

Given the extraordinary success of *The Idea of the Holy*, both at home and abroad, in the 1920s, 1930s, and beyond, one might

---

[33] Otto, *Mysticism East and West*, tr. Bertha L. Bracey and Richenda C. Payne (New York: Macmillan, 1932).

[34] Otto, *India's Religion of Grace and Christianity Compared and Contrasted*, tr. Frank Hugh Foster (New York: Macmillan, 1930).

[35] Almond, *Rudolf Otto*, p. 24.

[36] It is now available in English, in translations by Gregory Alles, in *Autobiographical and Social Essays*, pp. 274–87, and Thorsten Moritz, in Raphael, *Rudolf Otto and the Concept of Holiness*, pp. 210–21.

[37] Otto, *The Kingdom of God and the Son of Man: A Study in the History of Religion*, tr. Floyd V. Filson and Bertram Lee Wolff (London: Lutterworth Press, 1938).

expect it to feature more prominently in histories of twentieth-century theology and religious studies than it often has. Its place in the history of each discipline might be more secure, perhaps, were it not for the suspicion, common enough in both disciplines, that it ultimately belongs to the other – as I remarked at the outset, there is a tendency in theological circles to treat it as an essay in the phenomenology of religion, whereas in a religious studies context its theological character is likely to be emphasised. Moreover, there is nothing new about this state of affairs, since even in Otto's own lifetime, as Philip Almond rightly remarks, he was too much a historian of religion for the theologians, and too much a theologian for the historians of religion.[38]

Otto's influence on theology was particularly restricted. His description of the divine as *ganz andere*, 'wholly other', impressed Karl Barth, who read *The Idea of the Holy* a few months after he had published the first edition of his commentary on Romans. From the beginning, however, Barth had his reservations, as he explained to Eduard Thurneysen:

> This week I read Otto's *The Idea of the Holy* with considerable delight. The subject has a psychological orientation but points clearly across the border into the beyond with its moments of the 'numinous' which is not to be rationally conceived since it is the 'wholly other', the divine, in God. It opens the way for a basic surmounting of Ritschlianism. Ultimate insights at least begin to appear, though the subject does not quite get moving because of the retention of a theological spectator attitude which is not compatible with the high degree of understanding of the object.[39]

The reservations proved decisive, and in later years Barth rarely mentioned *The Idea of the Holy* except to dismiss it. Lecturing at Göttingen, in 1924 and 1925, he argued that 'the holy' must be

---

[38] Philip Almond, 'Rudolf Otto: Life and Work', *Journal of Religious History* 12 (1983), p. 319. Alles, in his 'Introduction' to *Autobiographical and Social Essays*, pp. 3–25, discusses the perspectives of critics from both disciplines, and I am indebted to his account.

[39] Karl Barth to Eduard Thurneysen, 3rd June 1919, in *Revolutionary Theology in the Making: Barth–Thurneysen Correspondence, 1914–1925*, tr. James D. Smart (London: Epworth Press, 1964), p. 47.

defined in terms of righteousness and mercy, against Otto, or else 'we have the image of a Moloch or Saturn, or at any rate an idol', and not God.[40] Similarly, in the *Church Dogmatics*, he insisted that whatever else Otto's 'the holy' may be, it cannot be understood as the Word of God, 'for it is the numinous, and the numinous is the irrational, and the irrational can no longer be differentiated from an absolutised natural force',[41] and that 'the holy God of Scripture' is not 'the holy', that is, 'that numinous element which, in its aspect of *tremendum*, is in itself and as such the divine'.[42] Back in 1919, Barth had seemed prepared to think of Otto as a sort of 'fellow-traveller', a potential ally in his struggle to overcome the theological legacy of Schleiermacher and Ritschl, but he had soon decided that *The Idea of the Holy* was part of the problem, rather than part of the solution. Given that theology had become 'religionistic', 'anthropocentric' and 'humanistic', what had been required was not 'some kind of further shifting around within the complex of inherited questions', which is what Otto and others had attempted, but 'a change of direction'. 'The ship was threatening to run aground; the moment was at hand to turn the rudder an angle of exactly 180 degrees.'[43]

Barth's dismissal of *The Idea of the Holy* was echoed in the works of other 'neo-orthodox' theologians, although Emil Brunner, who severely criticised it in the 1920s and 1930s, employed some of the themes of 'Rudolf Otto's beautiful book' in the treatment of 'The Holy' in his later *Dogmatics*.[44] Rudolf Bultmann, whose 'existentialist' theology developed the dialectical theology of the early 1920s in a rather different direction,

---

[40] Karl Barth, *The Göttingen Dogmatics: Instruction in the Christian Religion*, ed. Hannelotte Reiffen, tr. Geoffrey W. Bromiley (Grand Rapids, MI: William B. Eerdmans, 1990), I, p. 420.

[41] Karl Barth, *Church Dogmatics* I/1 [1932], eds. G. W. Bromiley and T. F. Torrance, tr. G. W. Bromiley (Edinburgh: T&T Clark, 1975), p. 135.

[42] Karl Barth, *Church Dogmatics* II/1 [1940], eds. G. W. Bromiley and T. F. Torrance, trans. T. H. L. Parker et al. (Edinburgh: T&T Clark, 1957), p. 360.

[43] Karl Barth, *The Humanity of God* [1956], tr. John N. Thomas and Thomas Wieser (Richmond, VA: John Knox Press, 1960), pp. 39, 41.

[44] Emil Brunner, *The Mediator* [1927], tr. Olive Wyon (London: Lutterworth Press, 1934), pp. 68–9; *The Divine Imperative* [1932], tr. Olive Wyon (London: Lutterworth Press, 1937), p. 587; *Dogmatics* vol. I, *The Christian Doctrine of God* [1946], tr. Olive Wyon (London: Lutterworth Press, 1949), pp. 157–74.

saw little or no value in Otto's work. Like Barth, he had made much of the 'wholly other' in some of his earliest writings,[45] but he came to oppose almost everything that Otto – his *bête noire* at Marburg – stood for, and in so doing accelerated the marginalisation of *The Idea of the Holy*.[46] It did, however, influence Paul Tillich. The book had become a 'constitutive element' of his thinking, and so when he moved to Marburg, in 1924–5, he was depressed to see that 'theologians like Schleiermacher, Harnack, Troeltsch, Otto, were contemptuously rejected'.[47] Tillich gave Otto his due in a section on 'God and the idea of the holy' in his *Systematic Theology*,[48] a work he had begun in Marburg some 25 years earlier, but, as Alles comments, he 'systematically retranslated Otto's terms – the numinous, the *mysterium tremendum*, the *fascinosum* – into his own distinctive vocabulary of human concern for the ultimate as both abyss and ground of being'.[49]

By the time that the *Systematic Theology* was published, however, Tillich was teaching in the United States. Back in Germany, the continuing dominance of the movements which had so decisively rejected Otto's work in the 1920s prevented it from exercising any significant influence in theological circles. The influence of *The Idea of the Holy* had been rather more profound (and prolonged) within the study of religion, first in Germany, and subsequently in the English-speaking world; as Tillich had mediated Otto's work to the theologians, so another expatriate, Joachim Wach, mediated it to scholars of religion.[50]

---

[45] Rudolf Bultmann, 'Concerning the Hidden and the Revealed God' [1917], in *Existence and Faith: Shorter Writings of Rudolf Bultmann*, ed. and tr. Schubert Ogden (London: Hodder & Stoughton, 1961), pp. 23–34.

[46] See M. Lattke, 'Rudolf Bultmann on Rudolf Otto', *Harvard Theological Review* 78 (1985), pp. 353–60. (Otto is described as Bultmann's *bête noire* by Mircea Eliade, *No Souvenirs: Journal, 1957–1969*, tr. Fred H. Johnson (New York: Harper & Row, 1977), p. 263.)

[47] Paul Tillich, 'Autobiographical Reflections', in Charles W. Kegley and Robert W. Bretall (eds.), *The Theology of Paul Tillich* (New York: Macmillan, 1952), pp. 6, 14.

[48] Paul Tillich, *Systematic Theology* vol. I (Chicago: University of Chicago Press, 1951), pp. 215–18.

[49] Alles, 'Introduction', *Autobiographical and Social Essays*, pp. 10–11.

[50] Joachim Wach, 'Rudolf Otto and the Idea of the Holy', *The Comparative Study of Religions*, ed. Joseph M. Kitigawa (New York: Columbia University Press, 1958).

Yet from the outset certain features of the book, such as its neo-Kantianism, had been a stumbling-block, and its idiosyncratic, introspective approach to its subject-matter was soon overtaken by new methods informed by phenomenology proper, and by hermeneutics. The 'shift from a concern with experience to a concern with symbolization' was completed by Mircea Eliade, Wach's successor, whose work 'signaled the eclipse of Otto in the English-speaking world'.[51]

Eliade's perspective on *The Idea of the Holy* is an interesting one. His sketch of the book, in the opening pages of *The Sacred and the Profane*, remains useful:

> Its success was certainly due to the author's new and original point of view. Instead of studying the *ideas* of God and religion, Otto undertook to analyze the modalities of *the religious experience*. Gifted with great psychological subtlety, and thoroughly prepared by his twofold training as theologian and historian of religions, he succeeded in determining the content and specific characteristics of religious experience. Passing over the rational and speculative side of religion, he concentrated chiefly on its irrational aspect. For Otto had read Luther and had understood what the 'living God' meant to a believer. It was not the God of the philosophers – of Erasmus, for example; it was not an idea, an abstract notion, a mere moral allegory. It was a terrible *power*, manifested in the divine wrath.
>
> In *Das Heilige* Otto sets himself to discover the characteristics of this frightening and irrational experience. He finds the *feeling of terror* before the sacred, before the awe-inspiring mystery (*mysterium tremendum*), the majesty (*majestas*) that emanates an overwhelming superiority of power; he finds *religious fear* before the fascinating mystery (*mysterium fascinans*) in which perfect fullness of being flowers. Otto characterises all these experiences as numinous (from Latin *numen*, god), for they are induced by the revelation of an aspect of divine power. The numinous presents itself as something 'wholly other' (*ganz andere*), something basically and totally different. It is like nothing human or cosmic;

[51] Alles, 'Introduction', *Autobiographical and Social Essays*, pp. 25, 24.

confronted with it, man senses his profound nothingness, feels that he is only a creature, or, in the words in which Abraham addressed the Lord, is 'but dust and ashes' (Genesis, 18, 27).

The sacred always manifests itself as a reality of a wholly different order from 'natural' realities. It is true that language naively expresses the *tremendum*, or the *majestas*, or the *mysterium fascinans* by terms borrowed from the world of nature or from man's secular mental life. But we know that this analogical terminology is due precisely to human inability to express the *ganz andere*, all that goes beyond man's natural experience, language is reduced to suggesting by terms taken from that experience.[52]

Here and elsewhere, however, Eliade misleads his readers by seriously over-emphasising Otto's focus on the *non-rational*. In so doing, he appears to be providing a justification for his own proposal – 'to present the phenomenon of the sacred in all its complexity, and not only in so far as it is *irrational*'[53] – which it scarcely requires. More significantly, it allows him to 'place' *The Idea of the Holy* in a quite different intellectual and cultural environment than the one in which it had been placed by theologians like Barth and Bultmann. Commenting on the rationalistic character of Wilhelm Schmidt's theory of 'primordial monotheism', Eliade notes that Schmidt was publishing his vast *Ursprung der Gottesidee* as

the Western world witnessed the irruption of quite a number of irrationalistic philosophies and ideologies. Bergson's *élan vital*, Freud's discovery of the unconscious, Lévy-Bruhl's investigations of what he called the prelogical, mystical mentality, R. Otto's *Das Heilige*, as well as the artistic revolutions of dadaism and surrealism, mark some of the important events in the history of modern irrationalism.[54]

---

[52] Mircea Eliade, *The Sacred and the Profane: The Nature of Religion* [1957], tr. Willard R. Trask (New York: Harcourt, Brace & World, 1959), pp. 8–10.

[53] *The Sacred and the Profane*, p. 10.

[54] Mircea Eliade, 'The Quest for the "Origins" of Religion' [1964], *The Quest: History and Meaning in Religion* (Chicago: University of Chicago Press, 1969), p. 46.

In anyone else, a remark of this kind might betray a superficial understanding of *The Idea of the Holy*. The book is concerned not only with the non-rational, but also with 'its relation to the rational', as the subtitle indicates, and Otto makes the strongest possible claims for the rational at the beginning of the first chapter. Otto's contempt for what he describes (in his Foreword to the English translation of the book) as 'the tendency of our time towards an extravagant and fantastic "irrationalism"'[55] is no secret, yet there is something in what Eliade says. Given the propensity of many theologians to 'place' Otto squarely in the nineteenth century, the suggestion that *The Idea of the Holy* is very much a work of its time, in its own way as avant-garde as the works of Bergson and Freud (or even Duchamp and Ernst), is a provocative one. Just as Eliade is reluctant to endorse the view that Otto is a theologian, 'a direct descendant of Schleiermacher', instead of a historian of religions ('it would be better', he suggests, 'to think of him as a philosopher of religion working first-hand with documents of the history of religions and of mysticism'),[56] so he is unwilling to treat him as essentially nineteenth-century in his intellectual outlook.

The Idea of the Holy *Today*

It is one thing, of course, to concede that *The Idea of the Holy* is genuinely interdisciplinary, and more obviously 'at home' in the early decades of the twentieth century than some of its critics have allowed, but it is quite another to conclude that it still speaks to us, within our various disciplines, as the twenty-first century begins. Some recent scholars have drawn attention to the ways in which Otto was 'ahead of his time', especially, but not exclusively, in theology. Philip Almond, for example, notes that 'Otto foreshadowed the modern theological awareness of other religions much more clearly than most of his theological contemporaries',[57] while Gregory Alles sees in 'the desire to

---

[55] Otto, *Idea*, p. vii.
[56] Mircea Eliade, 'The History of Religions in Retrospect: 1912 and After' [1963], *The Quest*, p. 23.
[57] Almond, *Rudolf Otto*, p. 132.

facilitate global religious and moral conversations to promote peace and justice' one of the places where 'Otto's ideas intersect with current sensibilities'.[58] Alles, however, concentrates on the circumstances in which these ideas arose, disclaiming any interest in an 'Otto revival', and Almond is primarily interested in Otto's Friesianism, so both, in effect, root *The Idea of the Holy* in its own time, rather than giving us any reason to expect that it might have something to say to ours.

This is where Melissa Raphael's re-appropriation of *The Idea of the Holy*, in *Rudolf Otto and the Concept of Holiness*, is so striking. Although she argues that Otto's thought 'belongs more to the twentieth century than to the nineteenth',[59] she acknowledges that in some respects *The Idea of the Holy* echoes the assumptions of an earlier era in the study of religion. But she also suggests that, in some other respects, the book prefigures aspects of postmodern thought; and because *The Idea of the Holy* 'represents a confluence of classically modern preoccupations, the romantic criticism of modernity, and elements that anticipate postmodernity, it is not a period piece; indeed, it eludes precise classification within the history of ideas'.[60] Interpreting the book in this way encourages Raphael to assess 'its relevance to contemporary spiritual and theological concerns'.[61] As the 'religious spectrum' of the West becomes increasingly polarised – 'At one end ... fundamentalisms are flourishing, and at the other, syncretism, eclecticism, and other forms of religious tourism are being practised (often for good reasons) under the umbrella of the New Age movement' – Otto's concept of holiness, which 'holds the rational and non-rational elements of religion in creative tension', serves 'a corrective function', and steers a path 'between the extremes of authoritarian rationalism and mystical libertarianism'.[62] In the final chapter of her book, however, Raphael attempts something significantly more ambitious than a sympathetic re-reading of *The Idea of the Holy*, in so far as she co-opts Otto for the purposes of a broadly ecofeminist theological project. This is a bold move, given that

---

[58] Alles, 'Introduction', *Autobiographical and Social Essays*, p. 39.

[59] Raphael, *Rudolf Otto*, p. 3.

[60] *Rudolf Otto*, p. 5.

[61] *Rudolf Otto*, p. 19.

[62] *Rudolf Otto*, pp. 22, 21.

Otto's work is commonly associated with the private, rather than the public and political, and, in particular, that his 'dualism' – in this context, the strong separation of the holy from the natural – has been condemned by many feminist theologians. But Raphael insists that Otto's account of holiness lays the foundation for 'a prophetic theology based on numinous consciousness',[63] and questions the common assumption that emancipatory theology must have a monistic account of holiness:

> Undifferentiated holiness is a genuinely religious ideal, but lacks the transformatory dynamics of models of God and divine–human relations which institute justice as a prerequisite of *shalom*, and, as such, require clear differentiation and demarcation of the holy and what sins by profaning the holy.[64]

In informing a 'prophetic theology', therefore, Otto's account of holiness is still of considerable value.

It remains to be seen whether others will follow Raphael in re-appropriating themes from *The Idea of the Holy* for contemporary purposes in theology and in religious studies. There is no question, I think, of an 'Otto revival', and not only because so much of his work is out of step with the academic fashions of our time. In some ways, the case for returning to *The Idea of the Holy* is not a particularly compelling one. Few scholars believe that the book is exceptionally original; given everything that Otto owes to Schleiermacher and Fries, and shares with contemporaries such as Marett and Söderblom, its distinctiveness lies not so much in its key ideas, perhaps, as in the way it synthesises these ideas into a whole.[65] Fewer still, moreover, think that any of its principal arguments are persuasive; the

---

[63] *Rudolf Otto*, p. 197.

[64] *Rudolf Otto*, p. 186.

[65] Otto acknowledges Nathan Söderblom – whose essay 'Holiness (General and Primitive)', in James Hastings (ed.), *Encyclopaedia of Religion and Ethics*, vol. VI (Edinburgh: T&T Clark, 1913), pp. 731–41, so strikingly anticipates *The Idea of the Holy* – and R. R. Marett in *The Idea of the Holy* (15n, also 20n and 76n), but the extent to which Otto was *influenced* by these and other contemporary writers is unclear. See Almond, *Rudolf Otto*, pp. 58–65, and Raphael, *Rudolf Otto*, pp. 70–3.

problems confronted by Otto's conceptual framework – the law of the association of feelings, schematisation, the holy as an a priori category, and so on – are insurmountable. Even in the less obviously speculative parts of the book he makes assumptions about the experience of the numinous – that it is *universal*, for example, or, with respect to other religious phenomena, that it is *primary* – which are open to all kinds of objections.[66] And yet there seems to be something about *The Idea of the Holy* which, in spite of all its faults, continues to stake a claim on the attention of those who read it.

There is, invariably, a difference between reading someone's work and simply reading about it, but in certain cases – Schleiermacher's, for example, and, I would add, Otto's – the difference between the two can be especially marked. In *The Idea of the Holy*, Otto distinguishes the non-rational and the rational, in the first chapter, and introduces the category of the numinous in the second. But then, at the start of the third chapter, he pauses to issue this striking injunction:

> The reader is invited to direct his mind to a moment of deeply-felt religious experience, as little as possible qualified by other forms of consciousness. Whoever cannot do this, whoever knows no such moments in his experience, is requested to read no further; for it is not easy to discuss questions of religious psychology with one who can recollect the emotions of his adolescence, the discomforts of indigestion, or, say, social feelings, but cannot recall any intrinsically religious feelings.[67]

What is the significance of this passage? It is hard to believe that Otto is encouraging readers to close the book, and the facetiousness of some of the examples of non-religious feelings which he cites might imply that he is trying to reassure his readers, who would hardly identify with such emotional poverty, rather than to alienate them. Most of the chapter is devoted to criticising Schleiermacher, in any case, so it is easy to write off the passage as a casual and oblique dismissal of reductionist interpretations of religious experience, of no

---

[66] See Alles, 'Introduction', *Autobiographical and Social Essays*, pp. 26–38.
[67] Otto, *Idea*, p. 8.

particular significance to the argument of the book. But what happens if it is taken seriously? One critic, Wayne Proudfoot, sees it as essential to the argument, exemplifying the common tendency to smuggle a claim about the cause of religious experience into the identification of the experience *as* religious in the first place. According to Proudfoot, Otto 'has formulated the rules for the identification of the numinous moment in experience in such a way as to prevent the "reduction" of religious experience by its being subsumed under any explanatory or interpretative scheme'.

> The rules have been drawn up so as to preclude any natura-listic explanation of whatever feeling the reader may have attended to in his or her own experience. Such restrictions guarantee ineffability and mystery. If it can be explained, it is not a religious experience. The criterion by which the experience is to be identified precludes certain kinds of explanation. What purports to be a neutral phenomeno-logical description is actually a dogmatic formula designed to evoke or to create a particular sort of experience.[68]

From this perspective, Otto's injunction is the key to the book, in the sense that it is here that its author can be caught in the act of smuggling his conclusions into his premises. But in suggesting that Otto is seeking to *evoke* a specific sort of experience, rather than simply to identify it, Proudfoot inadver-tently signals the possibility of a rather different way of treating Otto's injunction as the key to the book, and one which, unlike his own, brings out what makes the book distinctive. In a remarkable essay on *The Idea of the Holy*, Lynn Poland observes that the book is not only *about* religion, but 'religious writing': 'The numinous must be experienced to be understood, Otto insists; his task is not simply to analyze a religious phenomenon but to produce it in his readers.'[69] Poland, whose interpretation of the book as 'an episode in the history of the sublime' places it in a broader cultural context than that to which it is usually

---

[68] Wayne Proudfoot, *Religious Experience* (Berkeley, CA: University of California Press, 1985), pp. 117–18.

[69] Lynn Poland, '*The Idea of the Holy* and the History of the Sublime', *The Journal of Religion* 72 (1992), p. 175.

assigned,[70] presents a persuasive reading of its rhetoric, revealing the strategies by which Otto attempts to communicate the numinous to his readers. Otto's injunction ('his telling, perhaps teasing, request at the outset of chapter 3'[71]) plays its part in these strategies; *The Idea of the Holy* is, indeed, a book for insiders, but 'its capacity to *produce* insiders' is the key to its continuing power.[72] The more we look, the more apparent it becomes that the book is characterised by something quite other than the 'theological spectator attitude' attributed to it by Barth.

One of the things that *The Idea of the Holy* continues to impress upon its readers, and which accentuates the difference between reading the work and reading about it, is its sheer *seriousness*. It is not only that Otto takes religious experience seriously, from the epistemological point of view, but also that he lays so great an emphasis on experiences of a specific *type*. The first element of the *mysterium tremendum et fascinans* which Otto explores, in the fourth chapter, is the *tremendum*, and the 'element of awefulness' within the *tremendum* is the first to be considered. Otto's interest in 'daemonic dread', 'the uncanny', 'shuddering', and parallel phenomena is striking enough; but the fact that his taxonomy of terror stands where it does in the text, and that it is at this point that he begins to cite vivid examples from the history of religions for the first time, ensures that it makes a particularly strong impression on the reader. His comments on 'the wrath of God', which complete the section, suggest that Otto is well aware that his claims about the persistence of such phenomena even in the most sophisticated forms of religious experience are sure to be resisted:

> 'Wrath' here is the 'ideogram' of a unique emotional moment in religious experience, a moment whose singularly *daunting* and awe-inspiring character must be gravely disturbing to those persons who will recognize nothing in the divine nature but goodness, gentleness, love, and a sort of confidential intimacy, in a word, only those aspects of God which turn towards the world of men.[73]

---

[70] Poland, '*The Idea of the Holy*', pp. 175–6.
[71] Poland, '*The Idea of the Holy*', p. 191.
[72] Poland, '*The Idea of the Holy*', p. 197 (my emphasis).
[73] Otto, *Idea*, p. 19.

Otto's point is that the 'ideogram' of 'wrath', though naïve, is 'most disconcertingly apt and striking', remaining 'an inevitable way of expressing one element in the religious emotion', and in making it he is clearly criticising the theology of a previous age: 'despite the protest of Schleiermacher and Ritschl, Christianity also has something to teach of the "Wrath of God"'.[74] But his recognition that, for some, the point is likely to be 'gravely disturbing' suggests that he foresees that the resistance to his analysis of religious experience might not be exclusively intellectual. Otto tries to co-ordinate the *tremendum* with the *fascinans*, of course, although not all of his critics have given him proper credit for doing so.[75] Nevertheless, I think that there is a sense in which his exploration of the former establishes the *tone* of book, as the consequences of contemplating '"the holy" *minus* its moral factor or "moment"'[76] start to become apparent. One recent study of Otto has sought to account for Otto's distinctive interest in the dark side of the divine, so to speak, in broadly psychoanalytic terms,[77] and even if this approach is not convincing in itself, I think that it would be foolish to deny that, in this particular respect, *The Idea of the Holy* tells us something about its author. It is possible, however, that it can still tell us something about its subject matter that might otherwise be neglected.

Yet Otto insists that there is a limit to what he (or anyone else) can *tell* us. There is much in religion that can be taught, but its 'numinous basis and background' can only be 'induced, incited and aroused': 'If a man does not *feel* what the numinous is, when he reads the sixth chapter of Isaiah, then no "preaching, singing, telling", in Luther's phrase, can avail him.'[78] There is nothing arbitrary about this example, since it is widely recognised that the vision of Isaiah is at the heart of

---

[74] *Idea*, p. 19.

[75] John Oman's influential critique of Otto, in *The Natural and the Supernatural* (1931), is challenged on this point by C. A. Campbell, in *On Selfhood and Godhood* (1957); see John Macquarrie, *Twentieth-Century Religious Thought* (London: SCM Press, 4th edn., 1988), pp. 216–17.

[76] Otto, *Idea*, p. 6.

[77] Donald Capps, *Men, Religion, and Melancholia* (New Haven, CT: Yale University Press, 1997).

[78] Otto, *Idea*, pp. 62, 63.

Otto's thinking on the holy. It is also central to his report of a visit, in May 1911, to a synagogue in Mogador, Morocco, which was originally published in *Die christliche Welt*. It would be quite wrong, as Alles has shown, to propose that it was here that Otto 'discovered' the holy for the first time,[79] but I think that there can be little doubt that the experience made an important contribution to the development of the ideas that appear in *The Idea of the Holy*:

> It is Sabbath, and already in the dark, incredibly filthy vestibule we hear the 'blessings' of the prayers and the scripture readings, those half-sung, half-spoken nasal chants that the synagogue bequeathed to both the church and the mosque. The sound is quite pleasant, and it is soon possible to distinguish certain, regular modulations and cadences, which follow one another like leitmotifs. At first the ear tries to separate and understand the words in vain, and soon one wants to quit trying. Then suddenly the tangle of voices resolves itself and ... a solemn fear overcomes one's limbs. It begins in unison, clear and unmistakable:
>
> > *Qādôš qādôš qādôš ĕlōhîm ădonāy sebāôt*
> > *Māle 'û haŝŝāmayim wehāāres kebôdô!*
>
> > *[Holy, holy, holy LORD God of hosts*
> > *heaven and earth are full of your glory!]*
>
> I have heard the *Sanctus, sanctus, sanctus* of the cardinals in Saint Peter's, the *Swiat, swiat, swiat* in the cathedral in the Kremlin, and the *Hagios, hagios, hagios* of the patriarch in Jerusalem. In whatever language these words are spoken, the most sublime words that human lips have ever uttered, they always seize one in the deepest ground of the soul, arousing and stirring with a mighty shudder the mystery of the other-worldly that sleeps therein. That happens here more than anywhere else, here in this deserted place, where they resound in the language in which Isaiah first heard them and on the lips of the people whose heritage they initially were.[80]

---

[79] Otto, *Autobiographical and Social Essays*, pp. 61–3.
[80] *Autobiographical and Social Essays*, pp. 80–1.

An earlier translation of this passage is quoted by several recent commentators.[81] But Otto's report did not stop there, and the next sentence offers us a sobering reminder that Otto was, in many ways, a child of his age:

> At the same time the tragedy of this people is powerfully impressed upon the soul: they have discarded the highest and most genuine product of their nation and spirit and now sit lamenting by the side of the undecaying mummy of 'their religion', standing guard over its casing and its trappings.[82]

There is nothing quite like this in *The Idea of the Holy*, I believe, but the assumptions that made such an appalling misjudgement possible were buried deep in Otto's thinking, and must be reckoned with in any attempt to re-appropriate the book.

[81] See Peter R. McKenzie, 'Introduction to the Man', in Harold W. Turner, *Rudolf Otto: The Idea of the Holy* (Aberdeen: H. W. Turner, 1974), p. 4; it is quoted by Almond, who, in turn, is quoted by others.

[82] Otto, *Autobiographical and Social Essays*, p. 81.

3

The Sociology of Holiness: The Power of Being Good

Douglas J. Davies

The intention of this essay is to approach the idea of holiness from a sociological perspective, paying particular attention to concepts of reciprocity and moral meaning and to the new forms of identity fostered through processes that transcend 'ordinary' life. By adopting phrases such as 'holiness complex' or 'cluster' to describe the varied foci of identity involved in these processes, I emphasise the complexity of the idea of holiness and seek to avoid the easy trap of assuming it is, essentially, a single phenomenon. This offsets the fact that Otto's *Idea of the Holy* of 1923[1] was overly influential in establishing the idea of the 'holy' as a single category in the minds of many theologians and historians of religion.

Background

Although holiness is a profoundly old-fashioned word, whose postmodern successor would probably be aligned with the currently fashionable concept of the 'sublime', I will not only retain it but also use 'holiness' interchangeably with the 'sacred'. In so doing I am aware that holiness is largely favoured by theologians, while scholars of religion tend to speak of the sacred. Historically, it is worth noting how Robertson Smith's 1889[2] distinction between the holy and the common was eagerly adopted and transformed by Durkheim in his 1912

[1] R. Otto, *The Idea of the Holy* (Oxford: Oxford University Press, 1923).
[2] W. R. Smith, *The Religion of the Semites* (Edinburgh: A&C Black, 1889).

sociological study of primitive religion, published in English in 1915 as *The Elementary Forms of the Religious Life*.[3] This was not long before Barth's *Romans* brought its own theological version of holiness, judgement and identity to bear upon the new century in 1918. It seems as though there was something transcendent in the intellectual air that elicited such a shared perspective. The fact that, at the beginning of the twenty-first century, we should again engage with holiness is not, however, accidental, for the rise of ecologically minded generations is creating a new sense of the pursuit of the sacred. This not only touches the world as a dynamic system with an identity of its own but also reflects the human engagement with nature and cosmos in the search for identity. Numerous other forms of identity, each potentially attracting their own form of 'holiness', are also pursued through sport, leisure, family or other collective activity, all amidst the 'homeless' culture of an increasingly individualist society.[4] This is a timely reminder that the category of 'holiness' may not be the religiously restricted phenomenon that its church-based usage often intimates. So it is that to speak of a 'holiness complex' demands selectivity, not least for contemporary religious activity, in that, for example, even a cursory glance at Gerardus van der Leeuw's[5] foundational study of religion would show that the majority of his 106 sections on the sacred might claim some attention in this connection.

Sociological Classics and Holiness

Here attention will focus on charisma, merit, grace, embodiment, asceticism, ritual purity and impurity, and on sacred space in relation to Mormonism, a breadth of subjects chosen to show the applicability of the social scientific perspective adopted. Theoretically, we move from the two early sociological

---

[3] E. Durkheim, *The Elementary Forms of the Religious Life* (London: George Allen & Unwin, 1915, 2nd edition 1976).

[4] Z. Bauman, *Life in Fragments, Essays in Postmodern Morality* (Oxford: Blackwell, 1995), pp. 46–7.

[5] Gerardus Van der Leeuw, *Religion in Essence and Manifestation* (Boston: Peter Smith [1933] 1967).

sources of Durkheim and Weber to the more recent scholars
Hans Mol[6] and Roy Rappaport,[7] before utilising my own model
of rebounding vitality. Weber stressed the meaning-making
propensity of humanity, not least in the variety of forms
pursued in differing types of salvation. Durkheim, after his
intellectual redirection under the influence of Robertson
Smith, developed his view of the social nature of religion based
on the conviction that social life is primarily moral. He also
emphasised the corporate experience as the context for a sense
of awareness of transcendence. Social anthropologists have
developed the idea of holiness more in the sense of ritual
purity, notably so in the extensive work of Mary Douglas and in
criticism and commentary upon it.[8] Not only would it take this
paper too much into detailed anthropological debate to follow
those arguments, but my concern lies in exploring the relation
between the search for meaning inherent within human
collective behaviour as an intrinsically moral and religious
venture, and the individual realm of moral meaning-making
grounded in the notion of identity. This reflects, for example,
Hans Mol's established description of the process by which
phenomena that confer a sense of identity upon individuals
are, in turn, ascribed with a sacred status.

Holiness Bounding Identity

Rapidly condensing Weber's drive for meaning, Durkheim's
moral society and Mol's generation of identity we arrive at the
formulation that *holiness is the value attributed to a focal source of
identity that furnishes the moral meaning of life for members of a social
group in a process that transcends ordinary levels of experience.* The
phenomena comprising, bounding or conveying that focus
constitute the holiness complex. The source of identity viewed

---

[6] H. Mol, *Identity and the Sacred* (Oxford: Blackwell, 1976).

[7] R. A. Rappaport, *Ritual and Religion in the Making of Humanity* (Cambridge: Cambridge University Press, 1999).

[8] M. Douglas, *Purity and Danger* (London: Routledge & Kegan Paul, 1966). For an extensive consideration of the development and significance of her work see Richard Fardon, *Mary Douglas: An Intellectual Biography* (London and New York: Routledge, 1999), pp. 75–101.

as sacred may take a great variety of forms but is often embodied in some individual, institution or rite. In Buddhism, for example, the figure of the Buddha embodies the principle of enlightenment, while the Sangha symbolises the way of life that makes it possible. The person of the Dalai Lama affords one clear example of the embodiment of identity defining moral ideals.

In Christianity holiness refers primarily to God as the source of salvation, and can be pursued in the direction of ethics, commandments and covenants, and of worship, rituals and devotion. Depending upon context, particular stress may also be laid upon any of the three persons of the Holy Trinity, on some particular church, the Bible or some rite or leader. So it is that we have the Holy Church, Holy Scripture, Holy Eucharist and holy priesthood. Holy baptism is a particularly interesting example since it confers in the most ritually literal fashion a sense of identity upon initiates. The holiness of any particular phenomenon will be stressed when that phenomenon is highlighted as a source of Christian identity. Many a Catholic will, accordingly, speak of the Holy Father, a description utterly alien to most Protestants who are, in their turn, perfectly happy with the idea of the Holy Bible, a text that underwrites their own sense of identity. Similarly the Holy Spirit becomes, sociologically, even more holy in Charismatic movements where the Spirit's manifest presence is foundational for the identity of devotees. In terms of practical ritual, the Holy Eucharist is often seen as a key means of affirming and fostering Christian identity in ordinary life. Other holy foci may be invoked in Christianity as and when necessary, as with particular saints, or particular holy sites. In each case we find the holy status invoked as and when it is related to the generation of meaning, morality or identity.

The sociology of holiness is thus grounded in the sociology of meaning generation, especially in moral meaning underlying human identity. This brief description of identity formation highlights the process involved rather than its substance and, while it may be problematic in theological terms to equate the Buddha with Guru Nanak, Christ, or Mohammed, the sociological issues are clear in that the growth of religious groups is associated with the growth of focal points of holiness. As a group grows numerically it increasingly draws an expanding

sense of its own identity from its founder, reformer or key institution. As the strength of identity of the group grows so does
the holiness of the focal source of moral meaning. At the same
time, a group is likely to define itself in terms of what it is not,
with notions of error and boundary markers increasing in
importance. It will assert its difference from other groups and,
as often as not, its leader will assume increasing significance,
one defined in terms of a special divine status. In this sense one
might argue for the holiness of Jesus of Nazareth as something
that grows and is increasingly affirmed as the Christian group
draws away from Jewish and other groups. In strictly sociological terms this means that the deity of Christ increases as the
distinctive identity of the Church increases. This approach
would suggest that it is unlikely that Jesus would be accorded a
very high status in terms of holiness in a group of Jews who still
retained a shared Jewish identity, or, as in the case of Islam,
where his status is high as a prophet of God but not as a
defining source of identity. This kind of argument has, of
course, been developed in Maurice Casey's studies of early
Christianity.[9] Here, then, is the barest basis for one sociological
approach to holiness.

Cases and Consequences

A recent, and major, anthropological contribution to the idea
of holiness comes in Roy Rappaport's posthumously published
Ritual and Religion in the Making of Humanity (1999), an
extensive analysis of the holy in which anthropological and
theological ideas jostle for attention. He is convinced that the
holy is 'rooted in the organic depths of human being' due to
the very structure and organisation of the brain, of human
language and the way in which the brain is affected by ritual
activity (p. 230). He takes holiness to be 'a property of religious
discourse', related to that 'quality of unquestionableness'
associated with the religious language used in ritual (p. 281). It
is in liturgy that doubt is transcended and there is created a

---

[9] M. Casey, *From Jewish Prophet to Gentile God* (Cambridge: James Clarke &
Co., 1991).

'closed loop of authority and legitimacy', a loop that leads him to speak of the cybernetics of the holy (p. 430). For Rappaport, then, the holy is a quality of a certain type of information system, one that is, in a sense, relatively informationless. By this he means, for example, that devotees gain little new propositional information in liturgy. Old words are repeated and, unlike in lectures or seminars, new words and concepts are not introduced as a matter of course. Rather, the meaning of a ritual lies in the traditional certainty derived from it rather than from novel information. Accordingly, the sense of the holy comes in and through ritual, giving an impression of oneness and unity, and conveying an awareness of the unquestioned certainty of the way things are. I would extend Rappaport's idea of a 'closed loop of authority and legitimacy' in yet another way to stress the mutual interrelation of the individual's gaining a sense of identity from the source of holiness and that individual's ascription of holiness to that source of identity. This is necessary since Rappaport did not utilise Mol's work.

Charisma and Holiness

This intimacy of relation between authority and identity is valuable for the sociology of holiness because the notions of charisma, prophet, charismatic leader and followers all cohere within the holiness complex. Sociologically speaking it is not difficult to relate the notions of charisma and holiness and to extend them by including Durkheim's discussion of the transcendence attained in ritual. The theoretical similarity between Weber's charisma and Durkheim's transcendence is not new,[10] but to pursue the dynamics of that similarity in relation to holiness is worthy of development. Here I can but note how religious devotees perceive in certain leaders that attractive quality of religious power designated as charisma. It is often qualified by an idea that the leader, prophet or guru has been divinely appointed, inspired or charged with a soterio-logical mission in which they are caught up and from which a new sense of identity grows. Such holiness marks a particular

---

[10] M. Weber, *The Sociology of Religion*, tr. E. Fischoff, Introduction by Talcott Parsons, (Boston: Beacon Press, 1965) pp. xxiv–xxxv.

kind of relationship – a soteriological relationship. With respect
to its prime focus in the leader, prophet or guru, holiness
concerns the embodiment of soteriological power: holiness is
active and manifest. As far as the devotee is concerned holiness
is also evocative, eliciting a response and an acknowledgement
of the power present in the charismatic figure.

Embodiment and Holiness

A crucial feature of the holiness complex is that it is particular
bodies that manifest supernatural power. It is precisely when
religious values and ideals come to be embodied within a
distinct charismatic figure that holiness emerges as a kind of
demonstration that truth is not some abstraction to be enter-
tained philosophically, but is a dynamic power to be
encountered relationally. But to stress the nature of charismatic
leaders and groups does not mean that we can ignore that sense
of holiness that may befall an individual in solitude.
Malinowski[11] long ago pressed this point as against Durkheim's
strong emphasis upon the group effect. Here human imagination and creativity come into play as the sense of the oneness,
and perhaps also the strangeness of things combine with a
moral drive and become embodied within an individual. It is
the very awareness of the emergence of a sense of self as one in
whom these factors, as it were, materialise and are realised, that
furnishes that awe and wonder documented so firmly by
William James. It probably also lies at the heart of mystical
experience.

Ritual and Holiness

To talk of the embodiment of values is to move into a discussion
of ritual as the formal manipulation of symbols of prized
identity and of transcendence. I raise this issue of transcendence to emphasise this quality of otherness – this sense that all
is not grasped, or that individuals or groups are aware of the

---

[11] B. Malinowski, *Magic, Science and Religion and Other Essays* (New York,
Doubleday [1948] 1974), pp. 58–9.

need to reach beyond themselves. This was perfectly apparent to Otto when he spoke of the 'overplus of meaning' associated with the numinous. I will develop this within my own model of 'rebounding vitality'. Meanwhile I highlight holiness in action rather than as any abstract category of the philosopher of religion: the holiness complex embraces experiences of place, person or time. Rappaport highlights this in terms of what he calls the 'ultimate sacred postulates' of a religion and the way in which they come to be deemed incontrovertible through ritual. This view resembles the long-established cultural definition of religion given by Clifford Geertz with its 'aura of factuality' deemed to surround systems of ritual symbols.[12] Our beliefs seem so real to us, with faith grounded in absolutes and ultimates, echoing Tillich's existential theology of 'ultimate concern' – one that Rappaport cites with approval.

Rebounding Vitality and Holiness

Against this background I pursue holiness in terms of what I have developed elsewhere as the notion of rebounding vitality,[13] an idea elaborated from the dual source of Maurice Bloch's idea of rebounding conquest[14] and Stanley Tambiah's notion of ethical vitality.[15] This model interprets a variety of religious ritual and I have, for example, used it in discussing the diverse topics of death ritual[16] and what we might call the conversion of Peter in the Acts of the Apostles.[17]

While Maurice Bloch does not concern himself with holiness as such, his thesis in *Prey into Hunter* provides a synonymous idea

[12] C. Geertz, 'Religion as a Cultural System', in M. Banton, ed., *Anthropological Approaches to the Study of Religion* (London: Tavistock, 1966).

[13] D. J. Davies, 'Rebounding vitality: Resurrection and Spirit in Luke-Acts', in M. D. Carroll, R. D. J. A. Clines and P. R. Davies (eds.) *The Bible in Human Society* (Sheffield: Sheffield Academic Press, 1995), pp. 205–44.

[14] M. Bloch, *Prey into Hunter* (Cambridge: Cambridge University Press, 1992).

[15] S. J. Tambiah, 'The Ideology of Merit and the Social Correlates of Buddhism in a Thai Village', in E. R. Leach (ed.) *Dialectic in Practical Religion* (Cambridge: Cambridge University Press, 1968), pp. 41–121.

[16] D. J. Davies, *Death, Ritual and Belief* (London: Cassell, 1997).

[17] See footnote 13.

in the transcendent order encountered by devotees during ritual, especially rites of initiation. Bloch's thesis is that the natural process of birth, maturation and death is found wanting by most traditional societies. Accordingly they establish a ritual world that symbolically destroys the ordinary form of natural life and replaces it with a higher order scheme of things. This often involves the sense of destruction of a given nature and its replacement with a supernatural quality of life. The old nature is destroyed and a new nature conferred through ritual, a conquest of nature occurs in the rebounding process in which new energy or power is brought to neophytes after initiation. This is made possible through ritual contact with the supernatural realm of gods, ancestors or spirits that provides the dynamism to symbolically destroy ordinary human nature and effect its transformation into a higher order of being or spirituality. In this scheme of things holiness is the quality of the transcendent order – the realm of deities, spirits and ancestors – which gives the power to conquer pre-existing human nature and to transform it into the new level of dynamic spirituality. Bloch develops Van Gennep's earlier and widely accepted theory of rites of passage, adding to it the understanding that 'initiates never again fully leave the sacred but ... achieve a combination of the sacred and the profane which is of a very special hierarchical kind'.[18] In Bloch's terms it is the ritual of rebounding conquest that frames this destruction of the old and creation of the new in rituals of initiation. Although he does not stress the language of identity and identity formation, his argument deals with the same kind of issues already raised earlier in this chapter.

I have developed this approach through what I call the model of rebounding vitality derived, in part, from the notion of ethical vitality originally introduced by Stanley Tambiah to account for the moral power generated through a life obeying moral rules in village Buddhism. He showed how merit is generated by those who adhere to religious rules for specific periods of time, arguing in particular that 'it is the sacrifice of this human energy', especially youthful vitality and sexual energy, 'that produces ethical vitality which can counter karma

---

[18] Bloch, *Prey into Hunter*, p. 15.

and suffering'.[19] In other words he identifies a power that can be used to soteriological advantage, whether ultimately in the next life or proximately in this one.

Merit and Holiness: The Power of Being Good

The merit generated through ethical vitality can be viewed as a kind of commodity, a soteriological commodity, exchangeable for aspects of well-being and salvation. This brings us to the second part of this essay and its subtitle, 'The power of being good': for merit can also be used to transform identity and, in that sense merit-making is a feature of the holiness complex. But this central point is paradoxical, for while being good generates benefit, it also raises problems for experiences of transcendence. I cannot pursue this issue very fully here but some attention must be drawn to these two aspects of the paradox. The first concerns the kind of reciprocity underlying a great deal of human social life, and the second involves a mode of transcending it.

Ordinary Reciprocity and its Transcendence

Marcel Mauss first drew theoretical attention to the normality of reciprocity in his gift theory of 1925.[20] There he described the social demands and expectations of life through which relationships are constructed, affirmed or weakened. Such reciprocity extends into the cultural realm of ethics and underlies that sense of pay for work done, of rewards for services rendered, and of responsible community participation as demonstrated some thirty years ago by Fürer-Haimendorf for South Eastern Asian societies.[21] In essence this form of reciprocity yields rewards for services rendered. Merit is accorded to those who keep the rules, laws or commandments. Merit can then become a powerful religious commodity

---

[19] Tambiah, 'The Ideology of Merit', p. 105.
[20] M. Mauss, *The Gift* (London: Cohen and West, 1954).
[21] C. von Fürer-Haimendorf, *Morals and Merit* (London: Weidenfeld & Nicholson, 1967).

precisely because it is a potent moral-social commodity. In Christianity it comes to be focused in Christ, most especially in Protestant thought which regards it as dangerous to talk in terms of other sorts of merit, whether that of the Church, saints or any other figure. The Reformation focused on this topic in the form of indulgences and the associated idea that merit was transferable from the moral treasury of the Church to the moral poverty of individual members, all under the agency of the Church. It was not that reformation theology disagreed with the power and significance of merit or of merit-transfer, it simply disagreed with its prime location and mode of transfer. Issues of merit, demerit and the consequences for well-being continue to be important to this day, as evidenced in popular ideas of ultimate heavenly rewards and proximate illness and misfortune.

Recently Maurice Godelier has reassessed notions of reciprocity in his volume *The Enigma of The Gift*, a third of which is devoted to the idea of the sacred as 'a certain type of relationship that humans entertain with the origin of things'.[22] The precise nature of that relationship is that 'real humans disappear and in their stead appear duplicates of themselves, imaginary humans'. This brings Godelier to the heart of his affirmation, that 'the sacred can appear only if something of human beings disappears'. He sees human beings as engaged in a process of denaturing themselves as they engender gods. Real human abilities are reduced as the gods are given superhuman powers.

Godelier's enigma helps emphasise the second general aspect of reciprocity that I have deemed paradoxical: one that is well-expressed in Otto's 'overplus of meaning'. It is not that Godelier's thesis can be harmonised with Otto but that it highlights an area of discontinuity between the outcome of pious endeavour and the perception of sheer generosity in divine benevolence towards humanity. In traditional Christian terms this concerns the conflict between the grammar of discourse of grace and works. The simple answer to this problem is to argue that works and wages belong to a different logical type than do faith and grace. Both faith and grace then

---

[22] M. Godelier, *The Enigma of the Gift* (Cambridge: Polity Press, 1999), p. 171.

operate upon a different axiom than do work and wages. But there is, I think, more to it even than that, for there is also a shift in identity involved in these contexts in which religious endeavour is overcome and replaced by faith and grace in the Christian scheme of sacrifice. In Pauline terms it is not simply that the law is replaced by gospel, the flesh by the spirit, but that a new person emerges. It is precisely because of the process of identity transformation through transcendence that discourse on human achievement cannot co-exist with that of grace. This view reinforces Godelier's stance in that such moments often create new images of both the divine and the human. By extension I think we can also argue that they possess profound consequences for theology, as in the case of Christology where the rise of the Christian community, along with periods of theological creativity, yield new images of humanity and divinity. Much of the theology of the Reformation, echoing as it does aspects of biblical and Patristic spirituality, has to do with this very theological paradigm shift – one that has been repeated in the rise of numerous new religious movements inside and beyond Christianity.

Super-plausibility and Holiness

To deal with such paradigm shifts in spirituality is to encounter an aspect of the drive for meaning, and for moral meaning, that is deeply human and of real significance to the notion of holiness. Let me approach this question through the sociology of knowledge and in terms of what I will call super-plausibility, a phrase reminiscent of Otto's 'overplus of meaning'. The essential argument is that ordinary life leads to the construction of schemes of plausibility. The very nature of language and the customary rules of existence generate a world of meaning in which people become relatively secure. Sociologists of knowledge often speak of the plausibility structures of such life, inherent as they are in contexts of family, work, leisure, politics, religion, economics and the very cultural history of a people. But, contexts emerge in which these solidities are brought into question, may be destroyed and may have to be replaced. Such changes can occur at national or personal levels and may simply involve the replacement of one normality by another.

But there are other changes that involve significant discontinuity. At the personal level these include certain forms of
religious conversion or insight-generation – a feature of which
is that the newly discovered level of interpreting the world is of
a different type than what it replaces. It is this higher-order
scheme that comprises what I call super-plausibility and, in the
religious world, super-plausibility is associated with holiness.
Holiness is an attribute of that kind of super-plausibility that
confers an enhanced moral meaning to existence and actively
transforms the pre-existing scheme of knowledge and
experience. It is associated with the emergence of a very
powerful sense of identity both in individuals and groups, one
that, in appropriate contexts, affords an adaptive advantage
over other, less secure identities and may be expressed in many
different ways.

This is reflected textually when, for example, Job's
experience contrasts the hearing of the ear with the seeing of
the eye: 'I had heard of thee by the hearing of the ear but now
my eye sees thee' (Job 42.5). So too in the Bhagavad Gita, when
the divine form is manifested to Arjuna, his hair stands on end
and, filled with dread, he bows to the earth: 'things that were
not revealed before I see, my heart is thrilled yet trembles
fearfully'.[23] In some Sikh scriptures, too, there is a new level of
insight:

> When by the grace of the Guru I was granted understanding,
> I saw that there is One God. And I saw that there is no other
> beside Him. Saith Nanak: 'These eyes of mine were blind,
> But when I met the True Guru, they were graced with divine
> Light.'[24]

This higher-order knowledge is often deemed to derive from
a supernatural source; it comes by revelation, expressing the
fact that holiness can often be analysed in terms of an active or
passive mode. In the contexts just mentioned it comes upon a
person who is the passive recipient of active revelation. When
considered in terms of sacred places and rites the sacred can be

[23] Bhagavad Gita 11.45.
[24] Radhakrishnan, *The Sacred Writings of the Sikhs* (London: Allen & Unwin,
1960), p. 130.

viewed as a more passive focus to be approached with due reverence and care.

Active Holiness

The active processes of identity transformation take on additional significance when allied with the notion of truth, with ultimate sources of life and with missionary work and evangelism. This sense of super-plausibility associated with an increased sense of identity can be seen in the Charismatic Movement and, to a degree, in earlier Holiness Movements. For these it is not sufficient simply to be a water-baptized Christian, nor indeed a Spirit-baptized Christian, but higher modes of spiritual influence are involved as with a second-blessing of the Spirit, or a move into perfect love, or the influence of another wave of Charismatic gift-reception. There is a certain escalation of notions of truth, identity and spiritual experience in these traditions and it is associated with the fragmentary tendency in Protestant religiosity.

Asceticism

One recent sociological analysis of such fragmentary groups raised an interesting point as far as holiness is concerned, when Moscovici argued that asceticism could be interpreted as 'the degree of purity attained in the accomplishment of religious duties'[25] assumed by Protestant denominations and sects as they competed for status and religious priority in such an arena. He reckons that one reason why asceticism became the modus operandi of Protestant groups was precisely because Protestantism did not succeed in achieving a single universal form with a directing hierarchy. Since groups will usually compete amongst themselves for members there must be some basis of and for competition, and asceticism is one potential path. This is not, of course, to suggest that asceticism might not serve similar processes in other major Christian traditions.

[25] S. Moscovici, *The Invention of Society*, tr. W. D. Halls (Cambridge: Polity Press, 1993), p. 161.

Complex Societies and Holiness

In increasingly complex societies the precise nature of the moral community will always need to be defined, indeed it often is so defined whether indicatively and formally, or practically through the establishment and maintenance of boundaries. One way of discussing fundamentalist and sectarian groups, for example, is to see them as generating distinctive forms of holiness. Unlike the Holiness Movements of the nineteenth and early twentieth centuries, whose Protestant roots fed the desire for behavioural control, and whose holiness lay in pure thoughts, controlled speech and the avoidance of alcohol, we might define contemporary Holiness Movements – though they are never so approached in the sociological literature – as pursuing contact with power in nature, in self and in their ecological relationship. It is not too difficult to see conceptual relationships between the old Christian Holiness Movements, grounded in the covenant of grace, and the new secular holiness movements focused on the ecological covenant. Attitudes of respect towards and concern for the earth, as well as for human life itself, involve attitudes of the sacred. Similarly, reverence for life, albeit an older motif, is also utilised afresh in many a New Age context. The venerable historian of religion, Mircea Eliade, a scholar much preoccupied with the manifestation of religious power in sacred phenomena, regularly argued that 'the sacred is an element in the structure of consciousness and not a moment in the history of consciousness'.[26] This I would echo for the notion of holiness, for holiness is one aspect of the human drive for meaning, particularly the drive for moral meaning, that pertains to the very structure and organisation of social groups, even though it may take one form in the classic Holiness Movements and another in New Age movements. In both there is a sense of power, and this cannot be ignored even though it is an extremely difficult topic to describe with care.

It is well known that evangelical Holiness Movements espoused a sense of power coming with particular forms of

---

[26] M. Eliade, *No Souvenirs: Journal, 1957–1969* (New York: Harper & Row, 1977), p. 313.

committed living in a spirituality of discipleship to which David Bebbington has drawn attention.[27] But, in some New Age movements too there is also something of a sense of power. This emerges within people as they see themselves living according to the principles that underlie life itself, as in the idea of ecology as an expression of a form of secular covenant between human beings and the nature of the world itself. It is interesting, for example, even to see interpretations of New Age religious experience being couched in the conceptual categories of Rudolf Otto's idea of the holy.[28] The point I emphasise is the relationship between human endeavour and the sense of being related to the source of human existence, a relation that involves a strong moral valuation and subsequent sense of identity.

Ritual Purity and Ritual Impurity

One aspect of the relationships fostering holiness is that of ritual purity, a term denoting the quality of such relations. It describes the status of an individual in relation to certain others and to tasks that may or may not be performed. In this sense ritual purity is in no way a mysterious term but involves issues of bureaucratic legality bounding the sacred. Someone either is or is not ritually pure and, as such, may or may not engage in some form of activity. The 'practice of purity', as Michael Carrithers describes it for contemporary Jainism, is one form of maintaining Jain identity and, in particular, of ensuring the appropriate status of a family and its daughters such that they will be eligible for marriage within the wider Jain world.[29] In this case purity is closely linked both to sexual abstinence and the necessity of virgin brides on the one hand, and to the

[27] D. W. Bebbington, *Evangelicalism in Modern Britain: A History from the 1730s to the 1980s* (London and New York: Routledge, 1989), p. 151ff.

[28] W. J. Hanegraaf, 'Reflections on New Age and the Secularisation of Nature', in J. Pearson, R. H. Roberts and G. Samuel (eds.), *Nature Religion Today* (Edinburgh: Edinburgh University Press, 1998), p. 31.

[29] M. Carrithers, 'The foundations of community among southern Digambar Jains: An essay on rhetoric and experience', in M. Carrithers and C. Humphries (eds.), *The Assembly of Listeners: Jains in Society* (Cambridge: Cambridge University Press, 1991), p. 279.

practice of fasting, especially by mothers as the moral guardians of family and hence of community life, on the other. Here ritual purity is an idea intimately associated with the notion of embodiment. It is the very nature of the human body that engenders questions on ritual purity. Bodily emissions, especially of blood or semen, are regularly deemed to render an individual ritually impure for some tasks. Amongst the most explicit in the contemporary world is that of India and its caste system, where both the social status of caste and sub-caste groups and the behaviour of individual members are related to ritual purity.

Peter's Dream

Much better known to Christian theology is the ritual purity of Judaism which can, for example, be explored in the telling biblical example of Peter's 'conversion'.[30] His metamorphosing insight lay in the fact that God 'had taught him' not to call anyone unclean or common. Here 'holiness' takes the form of 'people counted in' on the basis of their attitude of belief in Jesus. Belief replaces ethnicity, yet it remains integral to identity. This inevitably makes Christ the focus of a new identity and also makes him holy. This is a potentially interesting idea, viz. the holiness of Christ, sociologically speaking, is the result of his being the defining focus and boundary of the identity of the Christian community. It seems as though holiness is an attribute of identity – defining elements, whether focal, boundary or ritual.

Mormonism and Holiness

Another brief example of the holiness complex lies in Mormonism's development of its own sense of identity. I have fully discussed this issue elsewhere[31] but, briefly, holiness is an important word in Latter-day Saint culture, as one might

---

[30] Davies, 'Rebounding vitality'.
[31] D. J. Davies, *The Mormon Culture of Salvation* (Aldershot: Ashgate, 2000), pp. 30–3.

anticipate in a group emerging in Protestant and revivalist America of the 1820s and 1830s. It reflected that Judaeo-Christian strand of thought stressing the morality of a community rather than the perfectionist stream of Methodism's perfect love. Within Mormon spirituality the very word 'holiness' came to serve as a root metaphor – whether applying to God: 'I am God, Man of Holiness is my name',[32] to Adam, 'Man of Holiness' in the Joseph Smith translation of Genesis 6.60, or to God's chosen 'city of holiness'.[33] Mormonism certainly did not follow that strand of American theology overseen by Charles Hodge of Princeton who has been described by Thomas E. Jenkins as using the 'concept of holiness to create a neo-classical character for God' in such a way that 'holiness could not be personified'.[34]

Mormons saw holiness as a call to a moral life within a divinely ordered community, and holiness marked one's identity as a Latter-day Saint in a community of Saints. Holiness was intimately associated with obedience to divine revelations and church leaders and its prime symbol was the temple. More than the prophet and more than the Book of Mormon, temples symbolised the heart of the divine restoration of truth and of that true ritual that alone would give access to ultimate salvation. When the first temple was built at Kirtland, the dedicatory prayer – a significant phenomenon in Mormonism – petitioned God that the Saints might 'feel thy power, and feel constrained to acknowledge that thou hast sanctified it, and that it is thy house, a place of thy holiness' (*Doctrine and Covenants*, 109.13). Subsequent temples have the words 'Holiness to the Lord' placed on their walls and, for example, in the Salt Lake City Temple these words are even found on the doorknobs.

Entry to Mormon temples is restricted to Saints living what is often called a morally pure life that is in accord with Christian principles and in support of Church teaching and leaders. This is assured through an interview with a Mormon bishop prior to

[32] Moses 7.35.
[33] Moses 7.9.
[34] T. E. Jenkins, *The Character of God* (New York: Oxford University Press, 1997), p. 51.

receiving a certificate granting access to the temple and its
saving ritual. This has the effect of highlighting the style of life
consonant with Mormon identity. It is a lifestyle and an identity
radically related to aspects of embodiment. Within the temple
the clothing of the world is abandoned, washings and anointing
lead to establishing covenants with God and promises to live a
moral life. The special temple garment is then given, in the rite
called the Endowment, and is, thereafter, always worn under-
neath ordinary clothing. In this way the body comes to
resemble the temple: both must be holiness to the Lord. The
undergarment symbolises self-control and identity as a temple
Mormon. Here we possess an extremely sharp example of the
relationship between holiness, identity and embodiment, all as
part of a transformation of human nature into a divine nature
through contact with supernatural power.

Conclusion

This chapter has rooted the idea of holiness largely within a
sociological consideration of human existence concerned with
the development of human identity amidst a social world of
moral meaning. While it has focused on several established
concepts involved in the study of religion, including charisma,
embodiment, merit, grace, conversion and ritual, it has also
introduced new forms of analysis and interpretation of these
both through the notions of rebounding vitality and super-
plausibility. This underpins the proffered definition of holiness
as 'the value attributed to a focal source of identity that
furnishes the moral meaning of life for members of a social
group in a process that transcends ordinary levels of
experience'. By viewing holiness sociologically, as an attribute
of sources of religious identity, we have gone some way to
emphasise the dynamism experienced by individuals and
groups when the ordinariness of life is transformed by a higher-
order power. It is precisely this realm of dynamic experience
that raises ideas of transcendence and encounter with what are
deemed to be supernatural powers. Although it is not easy to
achieve, in terms of relating social scientific and theological
methods, these social scientific considerations could be
developed quite extensively in relation to wider theological

considerations to provide, for example, complementary forms of interpretation within areas of Systematics, Missiology and Pastoral Theology.

The future of holiness is directly related to the extent to which individual identity is achieved through specifically religious ends. In a society of fragmented ideological groups and individuals the firmest types of holiness are likely to accompany more sectarian and 'cult-like' activities where ideological and moral certainties provide an anchor for identity. But just how the notion of 'religion' should be defined may, increasingly, prove a difficult task. It is likely, for example, that with the growth of ecological concerns some may find their identity coming to sharper focus through an explicitly 'healthy and natural' lifestyle. What was once couched in terms of ritual purity may now adopt a more scientific foundation with, for example, food free of genetic modification and organically produced coming to constitute a 'pure' form. When combined with bodily training, what might be called New Age 'food-laws' will furnish a holiness code of embodied existence that will also confer a firm sense of purposeful identity set within a wider universe for which one feels a sense of moral responsibility. Food and bodies stand as natural symbols open to a wide variety of interpretation and use, showing that while 'holiness' can be an attribute of a variety of moral stances it is never far removed from the establishment of a purposeful identity. When an individual, then, gains an added sense of self from living in accord with a proffered ideal, whether the Holiness Code of Leviticus or the ethics of holistic food and medicine, the power of being good should never be ignored. This has not been the place to explore just how theological analyses might engage with social scientific considerations of holiness in relation to the development of identity. Enough has been said, however, to alert theological readers to the sociological fact that there is a power in being good, one that both individuals and societies demand if they are to flourish communally.

4

Changing your Holy Ground: An Ecology of Sacred and Secular in Cities of the Centre and the Periphery

David Martin

Sacred Hearts in Evolution

This essay, or book in embryo, attempts to fuse several frameworks, the first of which concerns the relation between the specifically Christian 'sacred', transcending location and outside the city, and its incorporation into the generic 'sacred' of established power within the cities of space and time, with the result that images of universal fraternity come to be juxtaposed with images of hierarchy and political potency. The second framework involves a comparative sociology in time and space of changing kinds of holy ground; in time, from sacred monarchy and holy city to (say) art gallery and concert hall; in space, from American separation of powers to Latin/European conflict of powers and the ethno-religiosity most clearly exemplified in ex-communist Europe.

The third framework deploys notions of centre and periphery, or fields of cultural and political magnetism as they encounter resistant identities: for example, London–Dublin, Paris–Strasbourg, Rome–Milan. Some of these identities are also zones of transition, such as Strasbourg, lying at a religio-linguistic frontier, and Timişoara likewise, at a multiple frontier between West and East. Another and profound expression of relations between sacred centres and peripheries relates to what are called here 'cities of perpetual recollection', above all Rome (ancient and Christian), Athens (classical and Byzantine) and Jerusalem (the universal symbol and multiple temporal reality). Such cities have their intertwined genealogies in places like Paris and London, and in this essay there is a focus on these genealogies in the affiliated cities of London and Boston.

It is worth noticing that each of the examples chosen in the course of the comparisons in cultural space and time selects a different theme: in Helsinki it is the sacred in mutation through different styles; in Rome the successive exemplars of a mythic national history; in Budapest the theme of imposition and expulsion, including the sacred space of minorities. The whole argument is pervaded by the concept of sacred geography, which is the literal and symbolic build up of sacred potency with greater proximity to the centre.

Sacred geography, as dealt with here, mainly concerns whose insignia dominate the high places to proclaim the governing group, idea of presence, whether at the centre or the redoubts of the periphery. Clearly the emplacements of the sacred change form, focus and location over time, and some are effaced or forgotten as the ceremonies of antique power fall into disuse or the memories of wars fade away.[1] At the same time neglected sites can acquire fresh meanings and attract new pilgrims.[2] More and more 'secular' spaces open up, which come loosely to be called 'temples' of entertainment or commerce, and popular idols emerge whose deaths require the perpetual tribute of visitation, as at Strawberry Fields, New York, or Gracelands, Memphis.[3] What I am trying to do in focusing on such themes in the context of the city is to harness the work of people like Mumford and Girouard to the purposes of a comparative sociology of religion, in this case as represented in the socio-historical categories of my *A General Theory of Secularisation*.[4]

[1] Jon Davies and Isabel Wollaston (eds.), *The Sociology of Sacred Texts* (Sheffield: Sheffield Academic Press, 1993).

[2] Grace Davie, *Religion in Modern Europe. A Memory Mutates* (Oxford: Oxford University Press, 2000), chapter 9.

[3] Erika Doss, *Elvis Culture, Fans, Faith and Image* (Kansas City: University of Kansas Press, 1999). One of the first temples of commerce was the Galleria Vittorio Emmanuele II in Milan, built to symbolise the new moral authority of the Italian nation.

[4] David Martin, *A General Theory of Secularisation* (Oxford: Blackwell, 1978); Mark Girouard, *Cities and People* (New Haven: Yale University Press, 1985); Lewis Mumford, *The City in History* (New York: Harcourt, Brace, 1961). Cf. also

Those categories are based on historical filters, governed by degrees and kinds of pluralism and monopoly, which radically alter the flow of secularisation and inflect the shifting foci of the sacred. Here they are reduced to three broad kinds: the northern Protestant universe, the southern Catholic (or Latin) universe, and the ethno-religiosity characterising Eastern Europe. For simplicity's sake, I mostly omit the special kind of territorial pluralism found in countries like Switzerland, Holland and Germany, cut into segments by the historic frontiers of the Reformation.

Taking the northern Protestant universe first, it is broken down into degrees of pluralism, which yield a continuum from the unfettered religious competition of the USA, with its historic separation of church and state, to the virtual monopoly and historic fusion of church and state in Scandinavia, with Britain and its immediate sister societies lying somewhere in between. This continuum can be read architecturally in the contrasting arrangements of Washington, London and Helsinki. In Washington the 'sacred field' is dominated by classical temples and the Capitol, with the national cathedrals held at a distance. In London the weak nexus of church and state is represented by the sacred cluster at Westminster, while in St Paul's – another 'Capitol' – the Enlightenment and religion are not separated but rather conjoined. In Helsinki the church, the university and the administration dominate the central square – Enlightenment and faith in active co-operation, except that monuments elsewhere testify to a mirror monopoly represented by Social Democracy.

Contrasted with this northern universe is a much larger universe in southern Europe and South America, comprising Latin Catholic societies. From Spain to Mexico and Uruguay, this vast cultural expanse is prone to revolutionary upheavals in

---

Peter Hall, *Cities in Civilization* (London: Weidenfeld & Nicolson, 1998); Alexandra Richie, *Faust's Metropolis. A History of Berlin* (New York: Carroll & Graf, 1998); Eve Blau and Monika Platzer (eds.), *Shaping the Great City. Modern Architecture in Central Europe 1890–1937* (New York and London: Prestel, 1999); Aidan Southall, *The City in Time and Space* (Cambridge: Cambridge University Press, 1998); Roy Porter, *London. A Social History* (London: Hamish Hamilton, 1994). One should also consult the numerous books of David Starkey with respect to the sacred and rituals of proximity, as they admix the political and the religious.

which church power and, by extension, religion itself becomes a central issue. This pattern was inaugurated in France and then widely exported elsewhere. Paris, therefore, provides a paradigm case of a city where religious and secular emplacements (which can also be seen as rival forms of sacrality) face each other in contestation, claiming rival genealogies. The Sacré Coeur was erected on Montmartre expressly as a warning to the faithless city below. President Mitterand had to be mourned both in Notre Dame and the Place de la Bastille.[5] Of course, the capital cities of Latin America have their own spatial realisations of this conflict, coding the balance of advantage in the struggle. In Mexico City the National Memorial and the shrines of Our Lady of Guadelupe are both massive, whereas in Guatemala City a miniature version of the Eiffel Tower suggests a partial victory for the anti-clerical radicals.

The remaining category is Eastern Europe, where ethno-religiosity has emerged as the characteristic form in response to German, Austrian, Ottoman, Tsarist and Soviet domination. With nation and church partially fused, ecclesiastical buildings symbolise resurgent nationhood as, for example, the recently completed St Saba cathedral in Belgrade, Serbia, or the Alexander Nevsky cathedral in Sofia, built in the 1880s in gratitude for recent liberation at Russian hands. The manner in which Budapest was annotated by the insignia of Russian Communist power bred a national reaction in which religion played a complex part. That association was weakest in countries where religion itself was part of the history of foreign domination, as had been the case in the Czech Republic. Yet even in the heart of Moscow, at the centre of the empire, the reaction after 1990 meant that the Cathedral of our Saviour, razed by Stalin, rose again, a symbol of the fusion of Russian nationality and Orthodoxy.

Peripheries

So far the focus has been on the centre, but the topic of ethno-religiosity also introduces the countervailing power of the

---

[5] Davie, *Religion in Modern Europe*, pp. 78–9.

periphery. Whereas concentrated religious and political power, relating human to divine kingship (as well as checking human arrogance by divine judgement) come together at the centre, there are also alternative foci in defensible niches ranged along the margin. The heartland in Madrid, Prussia or the Île de France, seeks expansion, but then encounters recalcitrant otherness, perhaps in island or highland. Paris meets heretical Languedoc – a confrontation which can be translated as northern power meeting southern power, because each criterion of otherness has a tendency to mesh with other criteria allied in self-defence. Then at a later stage, when secular power has captured the centre, it seeks to expand its own particular language and control, and at that point a coalition of local language, religion, culture and mythic history will often come together to defend the heretical enclaves: the Cévennes and Alsace, Britanny, the Massif Central and Languedoc. Perhaps that is part of the meaning of relatively remote shrines in Rocamadour or Lourdes, or even Lisieux. Whereas the sacred places were once close in at Rheims or Chartres, representing an older map of power, now they are mostly at a distance, defensible redoubts of religion.

Peripheries may manifest themselves in micro-nationalism or else in nations which eventually gain independence. Recently Slovakia, Slovenia, Croatia, Serbia, Bosnia, Montenegro and Macedonia were subsumed in wider entities, but are now, to this or that extent, autonomous. The best-known instances are Poland and Ireland: these are the North-East and North-West areas of a national Catholicism respectively under the alien rule of Russia – an Orthodox or atheist power – and of Britain – a Protestant or religiously indifferent power. Scandinavia may look culturally unified, but in Norway one finds an historic contrast between secular Oslo and pietist Bergen, which has had long-term political and linguistic correlates; and in Finland there are national enclaves in Lappland in the far north and in the south-east (Russian) and the south-west (Swedish). Thus in Bergen one 'reads' the shrines of past pietist leaders like Hauge, while in Oslo the murals in the Civic Hall create a shrine of modern Social Democracy.[6]

---

[6] Stein Rokkan and H. Valen, 'Regional Contrasts in Norwegian Politics', in

Spain provides particularly clear examples of centre and periphery, maybe because, like France, it occupies a rough and geographically bounded square, with micro-nationalisms in corners and mountain niches such as the Basque Country, Aragon, Catalonia and Galicia. The site of Madrid for the capital city was chosen by a centralising monarchy precisely because it was at the centre, and the main alternative centre is probably Barcelona, capital of an autonomous Catalonia where most people speak Catalan. Barcelona contains much evidence of resistance, to French and to Spanish alike, as well as an arch set up to mark the triumphal arrival of Philip V in 1714 intent on reincorporation. El Pilar in Zaragoza is a great pilgrimage centre of another region with aspirations, and Santiago is likewise the heart of the North-West periphery in Galicia. Montserrat, just outside Barcelona, not only plays a major role in Catalonian autonomist sentiment but has inscribed around its inner cloister its own geopolitical vision of a Mediterranean north and south restored to Catholic hegemony. As a matter of interest, Barcelona is as much a periphery of Paris as of Madrid, and it is to Paris that the tracks from the Central Station make their way. Here in Barcelona runs a double border, and there is a different atmosphere, to the rest of Spain, almost Milanese in its industrial spirit.

Certain kinds of peripheries have a special importance as zones of transition, coding the rival pressures exercised by major linguistic, ethnic and religious blocs, and also containing mixed populations. The Protestant periphery in eastern Hungary crosses the contemporary frontier into a mixed area of western Romania, which is mainly lowland, with cities like

---

Erik Allardt and Y. Littumen (eds.), *Cleavages, Ideologies and Party Systems* (Helsinki: Westermark Society, 1964). For cognate regional contrasts in Spain cf. Daniele Conversi, *The Basques, Catalans and Spain* (London: Hurst, 1977). A parallel approach can be found in Hugh Kearney, *The British Isles. A History of Four Nations* (Cambridge: Cambridge University Press, 1989). There may be material of interest in my own discussion of the two rival Irish 'peripheries' of the British Isles in chapter 3 of Liah Greenfield and Michel Martin (eds.), *Center. Ideas and Institutions* (Chicago and London: Chicago University Press, 1988). The whole volume works through the problematic of centre and periphery, an acknowledgement of its origins in the seminal work of Edward Shils. The discussion of Germany by Thomas Nipperdey has a particular value for the present essay.

Timişoara displaying markers of rival identities in juxtaposition. Here West meets East, Catholicism meets Orthodoxy, and the Hapsburgs the Ottomans. The comparable area in western Europe is semi-Protestant Alsace, poised between French and German culture, and looking back over a millennium to the ancient Middle Kingdom of Lotharingia. Strasbourg is today an international city housing the European Parliament, and it seems that cities close to junctions, like Brussels, Geneva and Helsinki, often take on this kind of role.

Holland, Switzerland and Germany have been omitted, but in different ways they have a federal character which ameliorates the stark contrasts of the centre and periphery, though these have been tense enough in the past. The recent debate about keeping Catholic *gemütlichkeit* Bonn as capital of Germany rather than transferring it to a post-Protestant Berlin in Prussia gave evidence of such residual tensions, though it seems pretty clear that Berlin is, in fact, being constructed as the capital of the whole of northern Europe. After all, it belongs to the 'Mittel Europa' where ideas of a heartland originally came from.

The USA is another federal society which solved the problem of the centre by creating a new city (as did Australia by creating Canberra), and this allowed Washington to be built explicitly to code American constitutional arrangements. In federal societies one often has groups of cities representing a core area: Geneva, Bern, Zürich; or Boston, Philadelphia, New York and Washington. The nearest approach to a periphery in the USA is the South (and South-West), with its ring of cities: Austin, Dallas, Houston, Nashville, Memphis, Atlanta. To take only one example from this list, Dallas certainly measures itself militantly against the cities of the North-East. The Baptists are closest in to the centre and then the Methodists, and then Our Lady of Guadelupe, the Catholic cathedral of the rapidly expanding Hispanic community. At the dead centre is Thanksgiving Square, where nothing happens and the building there escapes all local identifications by resembling the Mosque of Samarra in Iraq.

There is only one North American periphery of the European kind, in Québec, and the French Catholics show how well they understand sacred geography in their careful colonisation of one of the key prominences of Montreal. The remaining European echoes are all at the margins: the Catholic cathedral squares of Santa Fé and New Orleans. There are also minor echoes of the British established forms, as at Williamsburg, Virginia, for example, but above all in the Caribbean. (Indeed, it was a town in Jamaica which suggested this whole concept to me, with its three concentric circles: Anglican church with police station, a High Street with the Methodist and Baptist churches, and an outer ring of Pentecostal chapels.)

Chosen Cities and Selected Themes

The framework having been set out it can now be used to focus more directly on the varied and evolving forms of sacred and secular space, taking selected cities in turn: Helsinki (north), Rome (south), Bucharest and Budapest (ethno-religion in Eastern and Central Europe) and London and Boston (with their differing degrees of pluralism). Helsinki exemplifies religious monopoly in the Scandinavian mode, but reinforced by a subordination to Sweden and Russia which helped fuse together nation, language and religion. In the case of Rome, the emphasis lies on the tension between Catholic religious monopoly and the late emergence of liberal nationalism (as well as the emergence of a radical politics). In Bucharest and Budapest you encounter an Orthodox and a Catholic dominance respectively, overprinted by secularist oppression, with a mixed zone in between. London and Boston can be viewed as an evolutionary sequence. Although the Anglican establishment in England imploded during the mid-seventeenth-century Republic, the net result in 1660 was a restoration of Church and King with some opportunity for a further expansion of pluralism later – whereas in Boston the Puritan establishment collapsed, first into several quasi-establishments and then into unrestricted pluralism.

Since the following analyses are mere indications which select varied themes for emphasis, I have to preface them with a thematic index. In Helsinki I select the idea of the sacred in mutation through different kinds of space, and especially through different styles, while in Italy the focus is on the successive markers and exemplars of a mythic national history, part of which is now mere inscription out of mind, if not out of sight.[7] In Budapest and Bucharest the main theme selected has to do with imposition, followed by expulsion, and the sub-theme concerns the space of minorities. Among the variety of themes evoked by London and Boston, there is the fragmen-tation and literal dislocation of Protestant continuity and commemoration alongside a mutation in the idea of the city itself, which can still be realised in a common central space, but increasingly confines particular religious genealogies to private space. The other themes touched on include the special clue provided to the nature of national or regional tradition by the placing of the 'unknown warrior' and by the style and wording of war memorials; then there is the contrast between sequences where nation and national church predate enlightenment, as in England, and the kind of problematic sequence found in Italy, where the church comes first and is at odds with an emergent enlightenment as well as with liberal nationalism and political radicalism.

Helsinki

First, then, we turn to Helsinki, a city relatively easy to read because the independent history of Finland is quite recent. Moreover, the building of Helsinki has been more intentional than accidental, and can easily be divided into periods.

The first period precedes the founding of the modern city and comprises the eighteenth-century fortresses built by the Swedish overlords on the island of Suomenlinna, which in their way exemplify the same kind of religio-political nucleus found in the Peter and Paul cathedral fortress in St Petersburg. The second period represents Finland's incorporation as a Grand Duchy of Russia and is the explicit realisation of an enlightened

---

[7] Adrian Hastings, *The Construction of Nationhood. Ethnicity, Religion and Nationalism* (Cambridge: Cambridge University Press, 1997); Liah Greenfield, *Nationalism: Five Roads to Modernity* (Cambridge, MT: Harvard University Press, 1992); Linda Colley, *Britons: Forging the Nation 1707–1837* (New Haven: Yale University Press, 1992). I very much agree with Adrian Hastings' emphasis on the early origins of nationalism, on the religious and especially the biblical element, and on England as the proto-nation.

autocratic idea, executed in neo-classical 'empire' style, echoing St Petersburg, with cathedral, university, government and police taking up all four sides of the central square. To the east, on a commanding bluff, stands the Orthodox cathedral, built about half a century later, in Byzantine style. To the south is the Alexander Esplanade, with other civic or national buildings, fronting the harbour, also in empire style. This is the externally imposed centre now fully appropriated by Finland.

One of the paradoxes of the spaces created by enlightened autocracy is the opportunity they offer in later periods to mass movements for mobilisation. In Helsinki the main square is filled from time to time with thousands of people – manifestly now a democratic nation in communion with itself and listening to 'Finlandia'. But one thinks also of the crowds assembled before the Hofburg in Vienna or massed in Berlin and Rome to render adulation to dictators. There are also the crowds which attacked the Winter Palace, and the very different crowds which brought down the East German regime after their nightly vigils in Leipzig outside the Nicolaikirche. Uses alter spaces.

The third period in Helsinki, covering an inner ring and especially the Central Station square, represents an emergent national self consciousness, and is mainly built in a Finnish version of *Jungendstil* (or art nouveau), sometimes with evocation of the landscape and animals associated with the national epic. The main buildings of Helsinki at the turn of the century are the new kind of secular temple, represented by the Atheneum (National Gallery), with its art dedicated to the Finnish artistic revival, the National Theatre and the Central Station. Art nouveau is frequently regarded as the style of a bourgeois materialism which, for the first time, allots a very minor role to ecclesiastical architecture (Gaudi in Barcelona excepted), though the widespread symbolist influences of the same time have a clear spiritual aspect, as is illustrated in Simberg's work (1915) for Tampere cathedral in central Finland.[8] Secular and sacred trends exist in counterpoint.

[8] Rosemary Hill, 'Gorgeous and a Wee Bit Vulgar', *The Times Literary Supplement*, 5th May 2000, pp. 18–19. Simberg has a major exhibition of his work at the National Gallery in Helsinki and should be placed in apposition to the recent exhibition (2000) of German symbolist art at the Civic Gallery, Birmingham.

In the twentieth century after 1917 Finland endured a brutal civil war of whites and reds, which helps account for the difficulties of memorialisation. But thereafter democracy was fully established, with a democratic and modernist architecture to accompany it, including the circular 'rock church' let into the soil and rock of a Helsinki square and a required stop for tours (which seem also to be pilgrimages). Perhaps the most frequented building of contemporary Helsinki is Stockmann's, at the far end of the Alexander Esplanade: a temple of commerce in the ubiquitous succession of the gallerias that originated in Milan and Naples.

Rome

Part of the analytic conundrum set by Italy arises from the range of conceivable centres from Venice to Palermo, along the elongated peninsula, and part from the way the only possible centre, in Rome, simultaneously houses ancient Rome, the national capital, and the headquarters of Catholicism. The rivalry of ancient Rome with Catholic Rome was temporarily solved by supercession, as in churches like Santa Maria Sopra Minerva, but the much more recent rivalry of nation and Church has been symbolised by the way St Peter's is faced off by the Victor Emmanuel monument (containing the unknown warrior), though compromise is also signalled by the Via della Conciliazione connecting the two. Conflict in Italy has been endemic since the ecclesiastical and the civic subdivided many centuries ago, as they did in Florence in the two main piazzas of the Duomo and the Signoria. The Church clashed with many of the city states, then inaugurated a Counter-Reformation, which inhibited the opening up begun by the Renaissance, and then tried in turn to repress enlightenment, liberal nationalism and socialism. Somehow the resultant anti-clericalism co-exists with Catholicism, though the careful placing in Rome of the monuments to Garibaldi and to Bruno (burnt in 1600 for heresy) symbolises the depth of hostile sentiment.[9] In Ferrara a

---

[9] Eamon Duffy, *Saints and Sinners. A History of the Popes* (London and New Haven: Yale University Press, 1997), p. 237.

plaque to resistance heroes manages also to excoriate 'the Pharisees in Rome'.

The periphery of Italy is in fact the industrial power house of Milan (the 'Middle City'), but, like Barcelona, Milan faces away from the national centre toward the heartlands of Europe. Yet whatever the North-South divide, the whole country, Rome included, recapitulates a semi-mythic national history. Every city and town honours in its squares, monuments and streets, the great names of the renaissance including Savonarola, then Tasso and Ariosto, and then the giants of the Risorgimento, Mazzini, Cavour and Garibaldi, as well as the composers of opera, Verdi, Donizetti and Bellini. After that the memorials are to those dead in the struggle for independence (and to the dates of its key events), to the dead in the world wars, to the resistance, to the ubiquitous dissident Marxist Gramsci, and latterly to holocaust victims.

This national genealogy can be assimilated to a much wider European genealogy memorialised in almost any major city. It begins with a culture hero (Romulus and Remus), a patron saint (Stephen, Wenceslaus), a warrior (El Cid, Alfred, Olaf), an exemplary poet who brought the language to maturity (Dante, Eminescu), a reformer (Michael Agricola, Luther, Savonarola), a hero of exploration (Columbus, Cartier, Magellan, and King Henry), and a hero of knowledge (Galileo, Marconi, Pasteur). Thereafter come the founders of liberal nationalism and memorials to the victims of the wars. But this sequence immediately suggests a question, signalled earlier, about what sectors of the past are reduced to mere masonry or aide-memoires. In Bologna, for example, once in the Papal States (and once renowned as a red and anti-clerical city) there are many inscriptions and arches to papal power and munificence. Europe as a whole may have a sacred-secular genealogy comprising an 'army of martyrs', but some of the ranks are blanks. What, moreover, of the protecting powers of the city – Stephen overlooking Budapest, Santa Maria della Salute guarding Venice from plague, the figure of Christ at Corcovado overlooking Rio, our Lady overseeing Santiago de Chile? Exactly what meaning do they retain?

Ethno-religion in Central/Eastern Europe

In turning to East-Central and Eastern Europe the focus is not so much on the tension between religion and nation as in Italy or France, as on their fusion, and on the patterns of domination and release from domination which welded nation and faith together.

In the imperial heartland of Europe, of course, in between the rival poles of Berlin and Vienna, one has the urban forms of enlightened autocracy, with their huge palaces and clear subordination of the Church, whether Catholic or Protestant. Berlin, for example, is defined not by its spires but by its state buildings and museums. But these imperial territories give way at points east to other territories where the Catholic religion (in the case of Austria, for example) has been discredited by association with conquest, expulsion and repression, notably in what is now the Czech Republic but also to some extent in Hungary, and these are countries where national myth has some connections with Protestantism. Protestant Eastern Hungary was long outside the Hapsburg empire and remained centred in Debrecen, with its 'Great Reformed Church' and statue of Kossuth in the central square, as well as its famous educational institutions. Indeed, in Budapest itself Kossuth – of Lutheran background – has a statue and a square near a Lutheran church containing a commemorative museum. The Hungarian reaction to the Hapsburgs is also symbolised by the dismantling of the Austrian fortifications once overlooking the city. At the same time almost all the emplacements along the hill of Buda (as on Castle Hill, Prague) represent Catholic and monarchical power. Apart from the (rebuilt) Gothic church of St Matthias, the key statues are St Stephen and the figure of a woman, now relieved of her attendant Russian soldier.

Budapest, then, is a complicated case; equally part of a Dual Monarchy with Austria and site of a liberal nationalism. But its crucial modern history is of Soviet domination, after an invasion defined by the victors as defeat rather than liberation, which was followed by the decapitation of the Church. The slow process of religious and national recovery beginning in the 1970s meant that in the 1990s all the insignia of Communist rule (arches and sculptures) were expelled to a park on the edge of the city. Today almost all the rival sign languages, whether political or religious, are compromised one way or another, as is indicated by the rivalrous ambiguity over national holidays. For an unambiguous statement of a national Catholic identity, where once the ceremonies of Church, state and military were enacted before the Second World War, one has to go to the vast shrine at Ezstergom high above the Danube, about 30 miles north-west of Budapest. This is Canterbury and Windsor combined and the cathedral is modelled on St Peter's.

The other theme introduced by Budapest, apart from domination and expulsion, is the role and space of the minority, especially the Germans and Jews who together made up nearly half the population. The sacred buildings of minorities – Calvinist, Lutheran and Jewish – are virtually all in the lower city, and most resplendent of these is the newly restored synagogue, originally put up in Moorish style to avoid any misidentification with Christianity. Also in Pest are the main emplacements of the liberal revolution, notably the National Assembly, built along the Danube in fantastic neo-Gothic and with a clear reminiscence of the Houses of Parliament built along the Thames.

Bucharest represents the same pattern of superimposition and expulsion as Budapest, except that the Communist dictatorship of the Ceauşescus tried to harness an autonomous nationalism to its cause and also rope in a persecuted Church. The megalomaniac plans of Nicolae and Elena Ceauşescu swept aside a great deal of old Bucharest to create a triumphal way much longer than its Parisian model, with a palace at the end which was nearly as large as the Pentagon and surrounded by a Bernini-like piazza. As Napoleon explicitly aimed to outdo ancient Rome, so Nicolae Ceauşescu aimed to outdo Napoleon. The earlier nexus of patriarchal cathedral and national assembly building, standing for the fusion of church and nation against earlier Ottoman rule, was rendered diminutive. Now, however, 'Babylon the Great has fallen' and the palace is an empty, unusable shell.

In between Orthodox Bucharest and semi-secular Budapest are the marchlands at the junction of East and West, Byzantium and Rome, Ottomans and Hapsburgs. In these areas, either side of the present Hungarian-Romanian border, there exists a pluralism made up of ethno-religions, Protestant and Catholic

Hungarians (working together), Romanians, a few remaining Germans and hardly any remaining Jews.

In Timişoara the contemporary sacred finds its most poignant realisation in crosses at either end of the main square in front of the opera house and the Orthodox cathedral. Here people gather to remember every Ascension Day. In December 1989 a minor affray between police and members of the Hungarian Protestant church tucked away in a side-street, spilled over into vast demonstrations in the main square in which hundreds were shot down on government orders. There is an interesting contrast here between the earlier commemorations of liberal nationalist revolutions: those were secular in form, but these in Timişoara, as in so many other cases in Eastern Europe (such as the crosses in Gdansk (Poland)), are Christian. Here one notes an instructive reversal of roles. In the Campo del Fiori, Rome, there is a secular memorial to Bruno who suffered at the hands of the Church, and in Eastern Europe there are religious markers remembering those who suffered under secular ideology.

A Tale of Affiliated Cities: London and Boston

London is a city whose religio-political revolutions in 1642–60 and 1688–9 paved the way for the more 'enlightened' revolutions of Boston and Philadelphia. London is also a city where the early fusion of Church and nation (accelerating in the years 1547–53) precluded the kind of struggle between Church and change found in Italy, allowing enlightenment to seep quietly into Church, state and elite culture, all more or less interconnected.[10] If one adds to that the security afforded by the English Channel and a slow, sequential development taking place in conjunction with what was possibly the first instance of emergent national self-consciousness, then it is not surprising that the vast growth of London was more accidental than intentional. Though the confrontation of monarch and parliament left behind what is now a minor devotion to Charles, king and

[10] Cf. Vicenzo Ferrone, *The Intellectual Roots of the Italian Enlightenment* (New Jersey: Humanities Press, 1995) and Diarmaid MacCulloch, *Tudor Church Militant* (London: Allen Lane, 1999).

martyr, as well as a Cromwellian sentiment, the sense of Protestant nationhood, forged especially against France, has acted as a persistent source of unity. The paring back of autocratic and centralising power and the centrality of commerce has inhibited Baroque extravagance in favour of moderate Palladianism, and prevented any realisation of the various plans to create triumphal ways in the grand manner from the Palace to St Paul's or Regent's Park.[11] Liberal nationalism and imperial pride have created monuments like Nelson's in Trafalgar Square, but London never acquired the profile of statues to national heroes found in countries where national independence was contested. So just as there is no pantheon of revolutionary icons like Voltaire, so the squares are not dedicated to people like Cavour or Masaryk, or the dates of sanguinary uprisings.

Obviously the established Church colonises the twin heartlands of administration in Westminster and commerce in 'the City', and as a repository of the nation the Church records its history and imperial expansion, above all in the royal mausoleum of the Abbey. However, the inscribed tablets of that imperial history are rarely read, though they tell an extraordinary tale, and its vaults are rarely opened up for inspection. Nowadays that may even be true of the monuments to national heroes like Nelson and Wellington in the crypt of St Paul's. A Victorian sense of expansiveness was replaced in the early twentieth century by national mourning, and the sacred was re-sited for the rest of the century at the cenotaph (or 'empty tomb'), which is only cryptically Christian, and at the grave of the Unknown Warrior in Westminster Abbey. The space between No. 10 and Big Ben is still the space where processions come and go, and where crowds congregate for crisis or celebration, but when the Dome was built for the millennium nothing much could be found to fill the faith zone except eclectic wisdoms.

Just beyond the central area there begins an eighteenth- and early nineteenth-century London of squares where light-filled

[11] Martin Daunton, 'The Unhealthy Heart of Empire', *The Times Literary Supplement*, 17th Dec. 1999, p. 32; Jonathan Schneer, *London 1900. The Imperial Metropolis* (New Haven: Yale University Press, 1999).

churches were built for persuasion rather than for mystery and
gesture. They served to provide civic space with a rational
punctuation. This is the alternative trajectory to the kind of
enlightened autocracy rejected with the expulsion of the
Stuarts, and it links London not only with Hanoverian Dublin
and Edinburgh 'New Town', but with the civic and commercial
virtue of republican Philadelphia. St-Martin's-in-the-Fields,
Christchurch, Philadelphia and the King's Chapel, Boston are
cut out of the same template, which is the defining ecclesiastical style not only of New England but the USA itself. What
distinguishes enlightened London from coeval cities in the
USA is the absence of any venue to display the Bill of Rights or
other sacred document. By the same token, the Royal Courts
of Justice in the Strand (dating from 1882), in spite of their
Solomonic symbolism, are not shrines for interpreting the
written principles of the Constitution like the Supreme Court.

There are two main religious genealogies set against
Anglican establishment; first, the nonconforming traditions of
Puritan dissent and Evangelical revival, both replicated in
America, and then the (largely) ethno-religion of Catholicism,
also of course taken by migrants to the USA, though somewhat
later. The spatial realisations of nonconformity are fragmented
like its history, though one can locate a direct confrontation
with the nexus of established power in the Methodist Central
Hall, built opposite the Abbey in the early 1900s in deliberately
distinctive Baroque. But whether nonconformity is represented
by the rational interiors of later dissent, or by the populist
auditories of evangelical preaching, it still fails to create a chain
of continuous memory in particular sacred locations. Perhaps
the closest approximation is Bunhill Fields Burial Ground,
where those who know where they stand walk in circum-
spection, as they would walk also in Copps Burial Ground
overlooking the Old North Church in Boston, or in the
graveyard of the King's Chapel. That is a paradox, because
discontinuity may well have something to do with the Protestant
dismissal of the dead and refusal to recite a spiritual genealogy
– which in turn prompts a query about the evanescence of
words as compared with gesture, embodiment and holy place.
Is the ideational and the notional something cast on the air so
that even the commemoration of the Smithfield martyrs and
Tyndale in London, or of Cranmer, Ridley and Latimer in

Oxford, or of Calvin in Geneva and Luther in Erfurt, no longer evokes memory? Maybe the martyrs of the Reformation have become relegated to a sacred now defunct, even though Tyndale still stands on the Embankment. Or is it that what was once shared national myth is now too particular and specific to be allowed the status and visibility of accepted icons in the neutral public realm? (Except, of course, in Ulster, which is precisely why contention turns on which flags should fly on public buildings.)

How then is Catholicism different? Catholicism is the other alternative tradition in Britain, part of a triangle of power, and linked, of course, to ethnic memory and survival. But it establishes continuity in place, so that in Westminster Cathedral at the other end of Victoria Street from the Abbey the recusant tradition is carefully tended. The sacred here is not a matter of monuments to be examined but of prayers to be said. And the architecture signals difference by its evocation of Siena and St Irene in Constantinople, as does Brompton Oratory nearby by its reference to Il Gesù in Rome.

In Boston (and Cambridge) the sacred is the city itself, as in a picture by Vermeer or Canaletto, and it comes in successive incarnations: 'the city set on the hill' of the New Testament and the Puritans, the heavenly city of the eighteenth-century philosophers, and the world of civilised seriousness. It is fitting that Cambridge, England, as the Puritan, renaissance and right-thinking university, should be progenitor to another such genealogy in Cambridge, Massachusetts. The heartland between Boston Common and the North End is occupied by the sacred, represented as a civic idea of the *res publica*, and the monuments belong to the advance of that idea from the Pilgrims and Mary Dyer, executed in 1660 as a Quaker, to the revolutionaries, and on again to the abolitionists and the dead of the Civil War, including the black battalion raised to fight in it. The public statues, as you might expect, are to founders, peacemakers, scholars, ministers, reformers and exemplars. There are few rites needed to sustain the sacred city, unless you count the recitation of the semi-mythic history of successive liberations which has its tourist realisation in 'The Freedom Trail' and its black equivalent. Each minority has its own sector: the Italians in North End, the Jews in Brookline, the Armenians in Watertown, and so on, and there is a holocaust memorial (and Irish recollections) close to the oldest part of the city in the region of government centre.

The Common is, of course, common ground, and the churches around it belong to the old Protestant establishments – Episcopalian, Congregational and Unitarian – representing a qualified pluralism. If there is a concentration of holy ground it probably lies in the tract between Park Street Congregational, where the campaign to abolish slavery was begun, and the Capitol, golden capped on Beacon Hill, resembling the Dome of the Rock, with the (Swedenborgian) Church of the New Jerusalem next door. On Beacon Hill itself there is (appropriately enough) no temple of any kind (except a meeting house), but just the quiet air of seriousness.

There are two major realisations of that seriousness to be explored, omitting (as I have throughout this essay) the search for a sacred nature and for rural innocence found locally in Thoreau. One realisation is found in the art galleries of Boston and Cambridge, where the common iconostasis of the Church is infinitely fragmented for the purposes of private contemplation, and in the symphony hall, where transcendental sounds create a high mass without a creed for the musically educated. There is a transition here of some importance, which might provide a facing panel to be placed against the architectural transitions noted in Helsinki. It is a shift from a concentration on the great choral works of the Christian tradition, which inspired the early founding of the Boston Handel and Haydn Society at Park Street Congregational, to absolute music without verbal symbol or historical narrative.[12] This can be labelled music of the highest class. What it marks is an extension of the space for contemplation from church to concert hall, but not one where the latter displaces the former. The universe simply expands with the proliferation of temples – and stadia and gallerias.

The second realisation of seriousness is in the founding of universities, such as the creation of Boston University by the

---

[12] Michael Broyles, *Music of the Highest Class. Elitism and Populism in Antebellum Boston* (New Haven and London: Yale University Press, 1992). This offers an interesting linkage of music, class, morality and the sacred. Cf. Albert Blackwell, *The Sacred in Music* (Cambridge: Lutterworth Press, 1999).

Methodists in 1839. After the Puritan university establishment of Harvard (and Princeton and Yale) comes an evangelical sequence at Boston (and at Emory and Duke).

There is another transition here, which involves the kind of extrusion from public space suggested in relation to the effacement of Tyndale. No one tradition may occupy public space except to exemplify a shared humane principle. So the memorial to Martin Luther King stands outside his old Divinity School of Boston University, but the Methodist tradition itself is confined to the private space of Marsh Chapel just behind it. Here, in the sacred centre of the university, the stained glass tells a particular narrative from Epworth in Lincolnshire, Aldersgate Street London and Wesley's Oxford, to Boston and the USA. It is also *inside* the myriad churches that you discover not only all the other particular genealogies, from Brazilian Pentecostals to the local Christian Science establishment, but the secret communion of church and state as flag and altar recombine. The Americans have simply removed the sacred altar from public space, as they have in Washington, to restore their intimacy in private.

Cities of Perpetual Recollection

Behind every city of Christian (and Jewish) civilisation lie the cities of perpetual recollection, Rome, Athens and Jerusalem, each positioned at 'the centre' of the earth in the Mediterranean, except that Jerusalem is also incorporated in another map of sacred geography which transfers the centre to Arabia. Thus, the different geopolitical magnets bearing on the sacred in Jerusalem ensure segmentation, so the Dome of the Rock is superimposed on the site of the Temple under the oversight of the Church of the Ascension.

The three cities of Rome, Athens and Jerusalem traditionally represent law, wisdom and faith, and almost every city will contain some recollection of them.[13] In Bologna the church of

---

[13] Sheridan Gilley, 'What has Athens to do with Jerusalem?' in Stephen Barton (ed.), *Where Shall Wisdom Be Found?* (Edinburgh: T&T Clark, 1999), chapter 11; and Jaroslav Pelikan, *What has Athens to do with Jerusalem?* (Ann Arbor: University of Michigan Press, 1997). Pelikan emphasises symbolic

Santo Stefano actually houses an ancient complex originally known as Sancta Jerusalem. Venice grandiloquently called itself 'The Jerusalem of the West' – the universal city. In Boston, for example, it is Athens that is recalled in Cambridge, Rome that is precisely replicated at MIT in the form of the Pantheon, and the idea of Jerusalem that is realised in 'The city set upon a hill'. There are also, maybe, secondary and tertiary layers among cities of perpetual recollection, such as Florence and Venice, and London and Paris. Boston clearly recalls London and Paris, above all in Commonwealth Avenue where it sets in line its own genealogy from Leif Erikson to the abolitionists. These secondary and tertiary cities make their own references back: London in its recollection of Jerusalem through the circular Temple and the Jerusalem Chamber, and Paris in its repeated recall of Rome.[14] Then Rome itself remembers Jerusalem as, for example, in Santa Croce in Gerusalemme. These references back to sacred genealogies are, like the resurrection appearances, claims to authority as well as glances and recognitions. They point to foundations, as well as original building blocks transferred to new edifices. Thus the Pope visits Jerusalem and Galilee, and wishes to make his way back to the Abrahamic source in Ur of the Chaldees to say that this beginning is still present in this our end.

There is a paradox running through these claims and recognitions because they relate to the tension between the sanctity of power and the power of sanctity. The primary Christian symbol set on top of St Peter's and St Paul's simultaneously to identify, claim and acknowledge, has to do with a Galilean periphery that sought to appeal to the centre in Jerusalem and was forcibly ejected. That means that the sacred can stand against power as well as for it, so that the hall of meat-hooks in Berlin where Bonhoeffer and his companions were strung up is

---

transfers, commandeering the classical world and Jerusalem for the purposes of Western iconography, politics and sanctuaries, e.g. in Florence, Bologna and Rome. Cf. 'Babylon or Jerusalem?' chapter 17 of Girouard, *Cities and People*.

[14] Robert Berger, *A Royal Passion. Louis XIV as Patron of Architecture* (Cambridge: Cambridge University Press, 1994). One might also note the Victorian recall of Rome in the Albert Hall, London, and the recall of Venice in Manchester.

also sacred, part of the genealogy of Golgotha. So, too, the crosses in no-man's land just to the west side of the Berlin Wall.

One ends on that note because the word 'sacred' has throughout been let fall where it will, according to context, which reinforces its association with power. Given the ubiquity of power that is inevitable, indeed a near tautology, which is at least as evident in the works of enlightened empire at Sans Souci or the Winter Palace as in the works of Christian empire at Ravenna and Monreale. In the overwhelming mosaics of Ravenna and Monreale, Jerusalem is juxtaposed to the insignia of power at the heart of the holy. This is, in part, the sacralisation of the geopolitical. Yet the core of Christianity is evidently a reversal of that, so that the juxtaposition within the city of supreme judge with the judiciary, and of the Majesty on high with human kingship, dissolves into a different judgement made by a powerless king outside the city wall. The point is that the centripetal suction of power constantly pulls such potent reversals into its own ambit, so that Christianity remains defined in all its high places by a double entendre: a temple converted into a human body (or bread) shared out for all, and a body that has been turned back once again from bead into a stone.

Notes for a Theological Commentary

Given that this essay has sketched a projected book, these notes offer a different level of commentary.

If we suppose that there are general realisations of 'the sacred' demarcated from profanity, ritually and spatially, then the Christian realisation is infused with a very specific content. That is because of the distinctive kinds of transcendence arising in what Jaspers called the Axial Age, some centuries either side of Christ.[15] Christianity witnessed to a realm beyond mundaneity, yet sought to transform it. The high tension with the real that resulted necessarily generated two basic social forms: radical rejection of power through the cross and the

---

[15] As discussed in Samuel Eisenstadt, *Fundamentalism, Sectarianism and Revolution* (Cambridge: Cambridge University Press, 1999).

expectation of the peaceable kingdom, and radical adjustment to power in which the signs of rejection were juxtaposed to the insignia of hierarchy and domination. In the former case Jerusalem became the sign of the universal city, without location or demarcation, home of peace and justice, while in the latter, Jerusalem was made captive to the imperial and territorial idea embodied in Terra Sancta and allied to Rome and Athens – though formally distinguished from them in the crucial idea of the Two Cities.

Because Christianity has to make its way in 'the world' (and the peaceable kingdom stays *in potentia*), the sacred in the temporal cities of 'Christian' civilisations carried a double entendre: it is simultaneously a demarcated colony of the perfect and a replication of the insignia of power – as at Ravenna and Monreale.[16] If we set on one side the scientistic notion of Christianity as falsified propositions rather than signs of a transforming divinity, then the question becomes: do we believe those signs have been spilled out historically, and done their works, as Gauchet maintains, for example, in Nation or City 'set on a hill' or University, each seen as transmuted Church?[17] If not, then Christian worship maintains the boundary between the real and perfect viewed as the incarnate colony of heaven, and does so under two signs: the broken sign of frustration as the site of God's redemptive Word, and the unutterable sign of the plenitude of Being, in both of which we commune and participate. For that to cease, therefore, is an emptying out of creative tension, a loss of the sense of redemption's cost, and the slimming down of the potential for transfiguration. Humanity has been returned to Nature and its immanent sanctities.[18]

---

[16] Cf. Eve Borsook, *Messages in Mosaic. The Royal Programmes of Norman Sicily 1130–1187* (Woodbridge: The Boydell Press, 1990) and Alick McLean, chapters 4 and 5 in Rolf Toman (ed.), *Romanesque* (Koln: Könemann, 1997). These books discuss the carefully asserted links and genealogies between Ravenna, Aachen, Monreale – and Jerusalem. McLean further discusses the monastery as heavenly Jerualem.

[17] Marcel Gauchet, *The Disenchantment of the World* (Princeton: Princeton University Press, 1997).

[18] I wish to express my thanks for the time and space offered to me at the Bellagio Centre, Lake Como.

PART 2

Holiness and Scripture

5

Holiness in the Priestly Writings of the Old Testament

Philip Jenson

Holiness is a key idea both in scholarship and the life of the church. Theologians seek to explore the character of the holy God, ethicists reflect on the holy life, and historians of religion investigate the experience of the holy. The Bible is a major source for this reflection, and from a statistical point of view the priestly writings that extend from Exodus 25 to Numbers include the majority of occurrences of the holiness root (*qdš*).[1] Although some theological traditions (particularly in the Protestant mould) have marginalised these texts, they comprise the majority of the laws revealed at Sinai. They describe the nature of the holy Tabernacle, the holy priesthood, the various kinds of impurity that are incompatible with holiness, and the holy life that is required of the holy people. The events and laws associated with Sinai not only comprise the heart of the Pentateuch, but Christians and Jews have traditionally read them as the authoritative grounding for all subsequent developments in language and theology. Thus the importance of a study of holiness in the priestly writings can hardly be overestimated.

Yet such a study is not easy. The priestly writings are a crystallisation of several sources or traditions and represent the endpoint of a long development. Further, these different priestly strands do not all speak with the same voice. Add to this the way in which the various forms of the holiness root are used

---

[1] See the statistics in H.-P. Müller, '*qdš*', *Theological Lexicon of the Old Testament, Vol. 3* (Peabody, MS: Hendrickson 1997), pp. 1103–18.

in a complex and many-sided way. All too often interpreters have approached these texts with a specific idea of holiness, and then interpreted the texts selectively in the light of that idea. Yet careful surveys of the linguistic details also have their limitations, for holiness is far more than a matter of language. The topic calls for an engagement with the larger theological and interpretive issues.

I shall begin this paper with some linguistic issues concerning translation and definition. I shall then go on to consider three authors who have discussed the disputed issue of how holiness is related to ethics. The markedly different approaches raise wider issues of theology (or ideology) and method, the subject for the third and final section. By the end I hope to have shown that the priestly writings provide a distinctive and significant perspective on holiness that remains of abiding value.

Holiness and Language

The Translation of 'Holiness'

In his paper in this collection (see Chapter 1) John Rogerson emphasised that holiness is a word, an English word whose meaning reflects the interests of those who use it. But for a student of the Hebrew Bible, the starting point is on the words that lie behind the English translations 'holy' or 'holiness', the various forms of the Hebrew root *qdš*. Various other English words are used to translate different forms of this root. In addition to the adjective 'holy', we have 'sacred' (and 'sacral'). As for verbs, the basic form can be translated 'become holy', but causative forms are usually translated 'consecrate' and 'sanctify' (in addition there is the obsolete 'hallow'). Nouns have played a particularly significant role in the wider discussion. The translation of Otto's classic work has popularised 'the holy', while Eliade refers constantly to 'the sacred'. A holy place may also be called a 'sanctuary', although the reader of the English Bible cannot be sure whether this translates *qōḏeš* or *miqdāš*.

An example from Exodus illustrates the challenge of translation and its influence on how a reader might understand the meaning of the word. The New Revised Standard Version

(NRSV) translates *qōḏeš* as holy in most cases, but why does it insist on 'sacred vestments' (Exod. 28.2, 4; 29.29),[2] sacred offerings (Exod. 28.38; Lev. 22.2) and sacred poles (literally *)ašērôt*; Exod. 34.13)? In one baffling case the identical phrase in the same verse is translated both 'sacred anointing oil' and 'holy anointing oil' (Exod. 30.25).[3] The growth of the use of 'sacred' in modern translations is striking, when one considers that the word was not used at all in the Authorised Version (AV) and only once in the Revised Standard Version (RSV; Exod. 30.25).[4]

The shift appears to be due to the popularity of 'the sacred' as a key analytical category for Eliade and other historians of religion. 'The sacred' was an important unifying concept in the study of very different belief systems. However, the attempt to discover what was in common for a wide range of exotic religions has contributed to 'sacred' becoming an outsider's term.[5] The practical effect is to distance the reader from the 'sacred' objects described in these texts. To call garments 'holy' makes a more direct claim for their divine character than to call them 'sacred'. Perhaps this is an example of Protestant suspicion of the ritual, but it probably reflects a more general trend since it is also found frequently in Jewish (New Jewish Publication Society) and Catholic (New Jerusalem Bible) translations. Another factor may be a desire to vary the language of translation. The freer Revised English Bible (REB) has more occurrences of 'sacred' than the more literal NRSV. Yet the effect is to increase variety at the expense of unity. It is less evident how the priestly writings attempt to subsume under the category of holiness all kinds of objects, people and times.

A different kind of problem is illustrated when we turn to the verb, in particular the piel of *qdš* that usually describes the activity of making something holy. In Leviticus 16.19 the verb is

[2] But sometimes 'holy vestments' (Exod. 31.10; Lev. 16.4)! For some general comments see C.-B. Costecalde, 'Sacré', *Dictionnaire de la Bible, Supplément* X/59 (1985), cc. 1353–6 [1346–93].

[3] [A]nd you shall make of these a sacred anointing oil blended as by the perfumer; it shall be a holy anointing oil' (Exod. 30.25). REB and NAB have 'sacred anointing oil' consistently; NJB has 'holy anointing oil'.

[4] 'Sacred' is used 107 times in the NRSV; 156 times in the NJPS (plus 'sacral' 14 times); 161 times in the NJB; 131 times in the NIV; 206 times in the REB.

[5] W. G. Oxtoby, 'Holy, Idea of the', *Encyclopedia of Religion* 6 (1987), pp. 434–5 [431–8].

used of what the priest does to the altar of burnt offering. How shall we translate it? Normally 'consecrate' is a good equivalent (so New International Version, NJPS), even though the 'holy' connection is not evident. Certainly it evokes a formal and ritual solemnity that is fitting for Leviticus 16. Yet in English 'consecrate' (and the Good News Bible 'make holy') usually implies an initial and non-repeatable consecration, whereas here the ritual happens every year. NJB suggests 'set apart', but the emphasis on separation is an inadequate rendering (see below). The majority of versions go back to the old word 'hallow' (AV, RV, RSV, NRSV, REB), acknowledging the repetitive character of the ritual (cf. the use of the word in the Lord's Prayer), but also preserving the link to 'holy'. The main drawback is the use of rather antiquated language that again reinforces the distance between reader and text.

The Meaning of *qdš*

If the subtleties of the various English translations of *qdš* are a challenging topic, then all the more so is the clarification of the original Hebrew root. Consider the following desiderata for a comprehensive study.

1. There are several words formed from the *qdš* root, including various forms of the verb, nouns (*qōdeš* and *miqdāš*),[6] and the adjective (*qādôš*). Both the common elements and the distinctive aspects of the meanings of these words should be traced. For example, it has been argued that the adjective *qādôš* is used in a distinctive way (see below).

2. But meaning is a matter not so much of isolated words, but how words are used with others in sentences and discourses. The semantic field of holiness at its broadest includes not only synonyms, such as *ṭāhēr* (clean or pure) and *ḥērem* (dedicated or devoted), but also antonyms such as *ḥōl* (common or profane) and *ṭāmē* (unclean or impure or polluted). In addition, there are syntagmatic relations.

---

[6] In addition there is the noun *qādēš* (and *qᵉdēšâ*) referring to a 'temple prostitute'. However, this does not occur in the priestly writings.

Some objects, people and times may be described as holy, but not others.

3. In addition, the various priestly writings reflect a variety of cultural and historical contexts. In historical-critical study of the priestly writings, this is most evident in the distinction between the Priestly source (P) and the Holiness Code (H, mainly Lev. 17—26).[7] These sources make use of the holiness vocabulary in characteristic and distinctive ways, yet there is also much common ground.

4. Nor can the larger debate about the meaning of holiness be ignored. Studies of Israel's neighbours will be relevant, as well as anthropological studies of traditional societies in which purity laws remain very significant. To these should be added the influential writings of philosophers of religion. The different perspectives that emerge provide many potential points of illumination, but also raise the possibility that ideas of holiness are inappropriately applied to these specific texts.

5. Finally, the meaning of holiness is not merely an interesting academic linguistic and cultural question. The biblical writings use the language to make claims about the reality of God and His relation to the world. Yahweh, not any other god, is the source of holiness. There are matters of truth and faith at stake.

All these complex factors might need to be borne in mind in the quest for the meaning of holiness in the priestly texts. Who is sufficient for all these things!

Definitions of Holiness

Fortunately there is another point of entry. Rather than work upwards from a detailed linguistic analysis, another approach is to survey some of the broad-brush definitions of holiness and explore their adequacy and usefulness. It is striking how diverse

---

[7] It is generally agreed that other texts belong to the same tradition as the Holiness Code (e.g., Lev. 11.43–45), but opinions differ as to the details. Knohl's work is particularly influential. See his summary in I. Knohl, *The Sanctuary of Silence: The Priestly Torah and the Holiness School* (Minneapolis: Fortress, 1995), pp. 104–6.

these definitions turn out to be, and the following is one
attempt to analyse and evaluate the main proposals. Of course,
it is likely that any particular discussion will refer to more than
one approach, for texts may be found to support all of them.

Separation

Separation has often been regarded as the key idea in holiness.
Leviticus 10.10 reads, 'You are to distinguish (*lᵉhab̲dîl*) between
the holy and the common, and between the unclean and the
clean.' Eichrodt can represent this approach:

> In so far as their meaning can be determined etymologically,
> the cognate stems in the various languages indicate the holy
> as *that which is marked off, separated, withdrawn from ordinary
> use.*[8]

Separation is certainly necessary in order to attain and maintain
a new status of holiness. One form of the verb (the piel of *qdš*)
usually indicates the event when a person or an object is made
holy. The climax of the description of the making of the
Tabernacle is its consecration (Exod. 40.9–11), and in order to
minister in it Aaron and his sons must also be consecrated
(Exod. 40.13; Lev. 8.30). The ritual is a good example of a rite
of passage, in which those undergoing it are separated from
their previous status in order to take on a new status. This separation
must be maintained. Holiness is incompatible with
impurity, and so walls and barriers protect the holy parts of the
Tabernacle from encroachment upon it. Similarly the priests
must ensure they are not contaminated by impurity when they
approach the Tabernacle to minister in it.

However, the etymological derivation of *qdš* from a root
meaning 'cut' or 'separate' is highly speculative, and the
approach to its meaning through etymology has now largely
been abandoned. What matters above all is how texts use words.
And while essential, it is not clear that separation is the primary
content of holiness. In particular, holiness is a positive attribute

---

[8] W. Eichrodt, *Theology of the Old Testament, Vol. 1* (London: SCM, 1961), p.
270.

or status, not a negative one. This seems no different in principle from the necessity for a just judge to shun the taking of bribes (Deut. 16.19), but justice is a positive vision not merely separation from unjust practices. Snaith emphasises that it is as much separated *for* as separated *from*.[9] The process of discernment that Leviticus 10.10 refers to is in matters of doubt and emphasises only the boundaries between the various terms, not their primary content.[10]

Power

Eichrodt goes on to find a second nuance to holiness, that of power:

> The concept of holiness as it emerges from this system of ideas, therefore, is that of a *marvellous power*, removed from common life, impersonal and bound up with particular objects.[11]

A similar definition by Müller makes it clear that he and Eichrodt are drawing on a complex prior understanding of the nature of religion in general, when he writes:

> The proto-Sem[itic] root apparently already describes the status or character of holiness; it indicates, then, a conception of numinous quality sui generis ... For a dynamistic-magical religiosity, *qdš* is primarily associated with the concept of might ... The 'holy' in the sense of that imbued with mana includes, first, objects ... some processes establish power matrices and are consequently taboo.[12]

Even allowing for the compressed nature of a lexical entry, the meaning of these sentences is obscure. Taboo and mana are particularly unfortunate terms. It is doubtful that these

---

[9] N. H. Snaith, *The Distinctive Ideas of the Old Testament* (London: Epworth Press, 1944), p. 30.

[10] See particularly the critique of this idea by Costecalde, 'Sacré', cc. 1356–61.

[11] Eichrodt, *Theology*, pp. 270, 271. Compare E. Jacob, *Theology of the Old Testament* (London: Hodder and Stoughton, 1958), p. 87: 'The essential aspect of holiness is that of power'.

[12] Müller, '*qdš*', pp. 1107–8.

concepts, derived from Melanesia, analysed by Victorians, adapted by historians of religion, and borrowed by biblical scholars, can shed much light on holiness in the Bible.[13] The influence of Otto is also evident in the way that the dynamic, numinous quality of the holy is emphasised.

Now it is certainly true that the interaction of the unholy with holiness can have dramatic and powerful consequences. When Nadab and Abihu offer strange fire before Yahweh, fire comes out from the presence of the Lord and consumes them. Moses quotes Yahweh: 'Through those who are near me I will show myself holy [the niphal of *qdš*]' (Lev. 10.3). But is this, like separation, a secondary consequence rather than a primary quality of holiness? The divine fire here is the result of an inter-action between two incompatible things, the unauthorised use of 'strange fire' and the holy. Nothing would have happened, no power would have been manifest, if Nadab and Abihu had not acted foolishly. In the priestly texts an encounter with the 'numinous' is by no means normative or even normal for holiness.[14] The extraordinary coming of God at the conclusion of the consecration of the Tabernacle (Exod. 40.34–5) and following the ordination of Aaron and his sons as priests (Lev. 9.23–4) are unique and unrepeatable events. Furthermore, they are described in terms of the glory of Yahweh, not his holiness.

Just as separation may be the focus of a form of the verb, this dynamic power may be the special nuance of the adjective. Jan Wilson has suggested that:

> there is a dynamism associated with those objects called *qādôš* that is missing from those called simply *qōdeš*. While *qōdeš* simply denotes a state of belonging to the realm of the divine, those things which are *qādôš* all possess the ability to move things (or people) into, or at least, towards, the realm of the divine.[15]

---

[13] For a cautious and wide-ranging study of taboo see F. Steiner, *Taboo* (Harmondsworth: Penguin, 1967).

[14] 'Relationship, not manifestation, is the primary implication of *qodesh*'; Steiner, *Taboo*, p. 85.

[15] E. J. Wilson, *'Holiness' and 'Purity' in Mesopotamia* (AOAT; Neukirchen-Vluyn: Neukirchener Verlag, 1994), p. 88.

Thus God is *qādôš*, as is the sacrificial court (Exod. 29.31) and the water used to test the woman suspected of adultery (Num. 5.17). Yet here again there may be a linguistic explanation of this 'dynamism'. When objects and people are described with an adjective, it is because the interest is on their manifesting such behaviour in certain contexts. Is it any different from observing that a just king tends to act dynamically in moving situations into a state of justice?

The idea of power also seems to lie behind Milgrom's exposition of holiness. He adopts an evolutionary theory of the development of religion that begins with animism: 'Natural objects ... are invested with supernal force.' He goes on to argue that the biblical understanding of holiness demonstrates a sharp distinctiveness. 'Holiness is not innate. The source of holiness is assigned to God alone ... The Bible exorcises the demonic from nature; it makes all supernatural force co-extensive with God.'[16] However, there is relatively little evidence for the demonic as a significant influence on the development of priestly ideas.

At one significant point Müller raises what I consider to be a crucial question:

> [T]he experience of the holy as the 'wholly other' presup-poses, for the most part, a point of departure in an understanding of the profane that has been suggested only by the absence of the numinous in modern concepts of normalcy.[17]

Ironically, Müller's understanding of normalcy may derive from a modern philosophical framework. Peter Brown gives a pertinent warning: 'It is a reflex of historians of distant periods to assume that what they themselves do not possess, the men of the past had in superabundance.'[18] I suspect that in Israel, as in most cultures, the normal interaction that a person had with

---

[16] J. Milgrom, 'The Changing Concept of Holiness in the Pentateuchal Codes with Emphasis on Leviticus 19', in J. F. A. Sawyer (ed.), *Reading Leviticus: A Conversation with Mary Douglas* (Sheffield: Sheffield Academic Press, 1996), pp. 65–6 [65–75].

[17] Müller, '*qdš*', p. 1104.

[18] P. R. L. Brown, *Society and the Holy in Late Antiquity* (Berkeley: University of California Press, 1982), pp. 229–30.

God and the holy was in ways that can only be described as routine and unexciting. Power, like separation, is indeed associated with holiness, but only at a secondary level.

Wholly Other

The dominant influence on many discussions of holiness is Otto, particularly when there is reference to 'the numinous' and the 'Wholly Other'. For example B. W. Anderson combines several perspectives in the following definition, but the main one is clearly that of Otto:

> holiness belongs essentially to the divine, whether experienced in Israel, Canaan, or elsewhere. It is the Wholly Other, which exceeds everything worldly: all human conceptuality, all moral categories, all metaphors. It is the power that belongs to 'the very essence of deity.' It may be more fundamental in the Godhead than the personal traits that are emphasized in biblical tradition.[19]

Otto made a sharp distinction between the supra-rational element of the divine nature, and those attributes that can be rationally understood through analogy with human characteristics.[20] It is indeed the case that in the Bible only God is the source of holiness. He alone can consecrate the priests and the Tabernacle, and the sacrificial rituals He has ordained are the source of the most holy parts of the sacrifice (Lev. 2.3, 10). There is no clear secular use of the 'holy' root.

Yet an emphasis on otherness can reflect unnecessary doubts about the ability of language and human analogies to refer to God. The modern character of these doubts is indicated by the way that dissatisfaction with the limits of human language did not seem to be a great problem for the biblical writers. Instead they assumed that God would be described adequately, though

---

[19] B. W. Anderson, *Contours of Old Testament Theology* (Minneapolis: Fortress Press, 1999), pp. 46–7. See similarly J. Joosten, *People and Land in the Holiness Code: An Exegetical Study of the Ideational Framework of the Law in Leviticus 17–26* (Supplements to Vetus Testamentum, v. 67; Leiden; New York: E.J. Brill, 1996), p. 123.

[20] R. Otto, *The Idea of the Holy* (Harmondsworth: Penguin, 1959 [1923]).

not exhaustively, in language that was also used of worldly things and people. However much the supra-rational character of religious language is asserted, it remains human language. Nor does putting key ideas into Latin help. Whether it be *mysterium tremendum* or *numen praesens*, these can only be understood on the basis of common or uncommon human experience of a sensible world. C. S. Lewis put it well:

> Nature never taught me that there exists a God of glory and of infinite majesty. I had to learn that in other ways. But nature gave the word *glory* a meaning for me. I still do not know where else I could have found one. I do not see how the 'fear' of God could have ever meant to me anything but the lowest prudential efforts to be safe, if I had never seen certain ominous ravines and unapproachable crags.[21]

This is not to say that holiness does not refer to something that is distinctively divine – only that even this distinctiveness has to be expressed through ordinary human language, people and objects, though perhaps extraordinarily ordered. God may be called holy, but unless there were other things that are also called holy, we would not be able to understand anything about what it meant. Metaphor, symbol and analogy allow us to understand the lesser known (the holy God) in terms of the materially constructed (the holy Tabernacle). The importance of religion as a basis for God-talk was underestimated by Otto, who inherited the Lutheran emphasis on inner experience.[22]

'Wholly Other', paradoxically, illustrates this very point. The experience of God as 'other' is dependent on the experiencing of human others. Likewise, 'wholly' cannot imply an absolute difference (concerning which we could only be silent). Rather it is a rhetorical expression of incomparability. It does describe a different class of being, but by means of an exceptional extension of what is known about human beings. Metaphor, not mysticism, is the way forward.

---

[21] C. S. Lewis, *The Four Loves* (London: Fontana, 1963 [1960]), p. 229.
[22] M. Raphael, *Rudolf Otto and the Concept of Holiness* (Oxford: Clarendon Press, 1997), pp. 19, 160–5.

Character

A traditional understanding of holiness is that it is the distinctive characteristic of divinity. Thus Olyan writes: 'God's quintessential characteristic is holiness, and it imbues all aspects of his being and presence'.[23] David Wright gives a similar definition: '[Holiness] is defined on the one hand as that which is consistent with God and his character, and on the other as that which is threatened by impurity.'[24]

The emphasis on God's character helpfully corrects approaches to holiness that suggest it is an impersonal force or power. The distinction between the personal God and the holy God that Anderson makes in the quotation above is an unnecessary one if the biblical orientation is taken as primary. God's holiness is never abstract, but always expressed through his relatedness, and particularly to his people. This is expressed in the personal pronouns of descriptions such as 'my sanctuary' (Lev. 19.30), 'my holy name' (Lev. 20.2), and 'my holy Sabbaths' (Lev. 26.2). Although these come in the Holiness Code (Lev. 17.26), they simply make explicit what is implied by the narrative setting of the entire priestly instruction at Sinai.

For character is indicated above all by how a person acts in a story. The language of holiness is introduced at key points in the biblical story, on those occasions when God acts in particularly significant ways.[25] Holiness has to be understood in relation to the actions and purposes of the holy God. A key element to the plot of the biblical story is that God wishes to form a people who become holy as he is (Exod. 19.6; Lev. 19.2).[26] Thus in Genesis 2.1–3 the holy Sabbath is related to the rest of God, and Israel's system of festivals and rituals is a

---

[23] S. M. Olyan, *Rites and Rank: Hierarchy in Biblical Representations of Cult* (Princeton, NJ: Princeton University Press, 2000), p. 17.

[24] D. P. Wright, 'Clean and Unclean (OT)', *Anchor Bible Dictionary* VI (1992) pp. 729–41, 237. Compare also J. Milgrom, *Leviticus 1–16: A New Translation with Introduction and Commentary* (AB; New York: Doubleday, 1991), p. 730: 'Holiness is the extension of his [God's] nature; it is the agency of his will.'

[25] Cf. G. A. Lindbeck, *The Nature of Doctrine: Religion and Theology in a Postliberal Age* (London: SPCK, 1984), p. 121.

[26] See now the exposition of J. Bailey-Wells, *God's Holy People: A Theme in Biblical Theology* (JSOTSup 305; Sheffield: Sheffield Academic Press, 2000).

celebration and establishment of this sabbatical pattern.[27] The manifestation of holiness in Exodus 3.5 is closely related to God's call to Moses and his purposes in making for himself a holy people (Exod. 19.5–6). From the point of view of the canon and the story it tells, the extensive vocabulary of holiness in the priestly writings comes firmly in the context of the covenant with God at Sinai, who instructs his people in matters relating to his holiness.

Yet if 'separateness' is too narrow a category, then character may be so broad that it calls out for further specification. Even if holiness is the distinctive character of divinity, it can still be related to other aspects of God's character, as well as to the earthly realm. Further, a character can often be defined by the discerning exposition of external features associated with that character, such as the character of their home or what they avoid. The abundant use of the holiness root in the priestly writings to apply to objects suggest that there is more to be said. The absolute opposition between holiness and impurity is a further potential clarification of the character of holiness.

Realm or Sphere

It is time to come to the definition I find most helpful. It is based on perhaps the most basic experience we have, that of space. It is interesting to note how even a conceptual theologian such as Tillich begins his discussion with a three-dimensional affirmation:

> The sphere of the gods is the sphere of holiness. A sacred realm is established wherever the divine is manifest. Whatever is brought into the divine sphere is consecrated. The divine is the holy.[28]

Holiness in this approach is anything that belongs to God's realm or sphere of existence, over against other places that do not have the same direct relation to it:

---

[27] P. P. Jenson, *Graded Holiness: A Key to the Priestly Conception of the World* (JSOTSup 106; Sheffield: JSOT Press, 1992), pp. 192–7.

[28] P. Tillich, *Systematic Theology, Vol. 1* (London: SCM, 1978), p. 215.

holiness (and its opposite, the profane) represents the divine relation to the ordered world, and the clean (with its opposite, the unclean) embraces the normal state of human existence in the earthly realm. The holy–profane pair represents (positively and negatively) the divine sphere, and this may be distinguished from the human sphere (which is marked by the opposition between clean and unclean). The presence of a holy God and a holy sanctuary in the midst of Israel ensures that these two points of view overlap in a complex way.[29]

The noun *qōḏeš* often means simply the holy place, the Tabernacle. Objects and people that are consecrated exist in the bounded space of the tabernacle. Priests need to be holy if they are to minister in the sanctuary, but it is recognised that they may become impure outside their sphere of ministry. The furniture in the tabernacle emphasises that it is regarded as a house for God, the bounded space where he dwells or appears. The realm of God in heaven is mirrored or manifest on earth in the Tabernacle. 'In accordance with all that I show you concerning the pattern of the tabernacle and of all its furniture, so you shall make it' (Exod. 25.9).

Space is such a fundamental aspect of human existence and comprehension that this allows a concrete basis for reflection that can be developed in more abstract directions. Its basis in material reality avoids the approach to holiness that focuses on an individual's experience of the numinous. Starting from here it is possible to accommodate many of the other definitions of holiness that have been considered.

Thus the realm of God is not to be identified with this world, a world where impurity and sin are to be found, and so the holy has to be kept separate. But the distinction is not absolute. The tabernacle partakes of the holy quality of God's dwelling. There is a complex overlap between the realms that allows a careful communication of that holiness, but at the same time preserves God's realm from defilement. Because those who live in God's

---

[29] Jenson, *Graded Holiness*, p. 48. For similar expressions see J. A. Naudé, '*qdš*', *New International Dictionary of Old Testament Theology and Exegesis* 4 (1997), p. 879 [877–87] and R. D. Nelson, *Raising Up a Faithful Priest: Community and Priesthood in Biblical Theology* (Louisville: Westminster John Knox, 1993), p. 26.

realm must behave accordingly, so Israel is called to reflect God's character through obedience to his commandments (Lev. 11.44–45; 19.2). This general holiness is an emphasis of the Holiness Code, and stands alongside a narrower, restricted understanding. Because the holy refers to God's realm, it includes another idea that is often associated with holiness – ownership or belonging.

But what about those texts that speak of the sanctification of time, particularly the Sabbath? Even here space can be a fruitful means for reflecting on the character of holy time. The Sabbath is the day when God's realm expands to embrace the people and the land in a special way. Heschel explores this analogy:

> Judaism teaches us to be attached to *holiness in time*, to be attached to sacred events, to learn how to consecrate sanctuaries that emerge from the magnificent stream of a year. The Sabbaths are our great cathedrals; and our Holy of Holies is a shrine that neither the Romans nor the Germans were able to burn ... Jewish ritual may be characterized as the art of significant forms in time, as *architecture of time*.[30]

However, there is one other concept that, though not equated with holiness, is closely associated with it and needs to be discussed: the presence of God.

Presence

'And have them make me a sanctuary (*miqdāš*), so that I may dwell among them' (Exod. 25.8). The Lord states 'I appear in the cloud upon the mercy seat' (Lev. 16.2). God's presence in the midst of Israel is the goal of the construction of the Tabernacle, and it is in the holy of holies at the centre of the camp that he promises to appear. Yet there is a distinction between the concepts. Holiness is a necessary but not an exhaustive precondition for God's presence to be manifest. It might be possible for a place to be holy, but God not to be fully present. From an ancient Near Eastern perspective, it was

---

[30] A. J. Heschel, *The Sabbath: Its Meaning for Modern Man* (New York: Farrar, Straus & Giroux, 1951), p. 8.

possible for the gods to be absent without compromising the holiness of a temple. The special appearances of Yahweh in the Tabernacle argue for something similar to be the case for the priestly perception of holiness.

A particular issue is the graded character of holiness and presence. The priestly writings made various distinctions between the holy of holies, the holy place, and other impure places that are at the farthest remove from holiness. This has suggested to me and to others that holiness is not an either/or concept, but one that admits of gradations. However, although Jan Wilson adopted the 'realm' definition of holiness, he has argued that it 'would seem to be absolute and not admit gradations.'[31] Instead he suggests that the grading is due to a differentiated quality of presence:

> whereas virtually everything within the tabernacle compound qualified as *qōdeš* because it belonged to the realm of the divine, the concept of gradation became operative when nearness to YHWH was considered.[32]

The priestly writings have only partly adapted *qōdeš* so that they have taken on some of this graded character. So we find *qōdeš qādāšîm* used occasionally of the innermost room of the Tabernacle, but elsewhere it is simply referred to as *qōdeš*, the holy place (e.g. 'the sanctuary inside the curtain', Lev. 16.2). In an intriguing revisionist interpretation, Wilson suggests that Otto may be describing not holiness, but 'deity itself, and the phenomena associated with the presence of deity'.[33] His book should have been called 'The Presence', not 'The Holy'!

His reasoning is attractive, but not entirely persuasive. As is well known, there is a tension between the more stable, static ideas of God's permanent dwelling, and the texts that speak of him coming and making himself present in an active and dynamic way. These are often assigned to different sources. The classic discussion by von Rad, sharply distinguishes the 'two completely different "theologies"' associated with the Tent (the theology of manifestation) and the Ark (the theology of

---

[31] Wilson, '*Holiness*', p. 89.
[32] '*Holiness*', p. 90.
[33] '*Holiness*', p. 56.

presence).[34] Yet this is too easy a resolution of a fundamental theological paradox. There is a tension between the regular, assured presence of God in the sanctuary, and an awareness of his sovereign freedom to appear at certain times, or even to abandon his sanctuary. Brueggemann has expressed it well:

> How Yahweh, the God of Israel, is present constitutes a major concern to both ancient Israel and the early church. There is no clear or single resolution of the question, but only a variety of explorations of it. Israel's struggle can be articulated in concerns which are in tension but which must be held together. The central polarity concerns the freedom of Yahweh and his accessibility. It was of primary importance to have regular, reliable access to the Holy One around which the community gathers and focuses. It is the responsibility of cult to regularize such access ... At the same time, Yahweh had shown himself to be free and sovereign, captured in no cultic theory or practice, but abroad in the land according to his inscrutable purposes.[35]

It is the context that determines the quality of holiness and presence. Frequently it is sufficient to speak in simple terms of holy/profane, present/hidden, but the complex phenomenon of the cult requires a more nuanced approach to holiness that may helpfully be analysed as graded. Although the vocabulary of graded holiness may be partial and inconsistent (but not absent or illogical), the elaborate construction of the Tabernacle (and other temples) points to a variegated manifestation of God's holiness. There is never unmediated or direct access either to God's presence or his holiness. The material character of the Tabernacle gives it a stability that corresponds to the promise of assured presence (cf. 'before the Lord'). But neither presence nor the sanctuary's holiness is fully assured, although the implications of this are not fully worked out in the priestly writings. The danger of defilement qualifies the

---

[34] G. von Rad, *Old Testament Theology, Vol. 1* (London: SCM, 1962), p. 237.

[35] W. Brueggemann, 'Presence of God, Cultic', *Supplement to Interpreter's Dictionary of the Bible*, ed. K. Crim (Nashville, 1976), p. 680 [680–3]. The accessibility of the holy is interpreted somewhat negatively by H. Ringgren, '*qdš*', *Theologische Wörterbuch zum Alten Testament* 6 (1989), c. 1192 [1179–1204] in terms of control.

assurance of its holiness (Lev. 15.31) just as surely as sin and disobedience will ensure that the people will be expelled from God's presence (Lev. 26.33).

If we ask which of the two concepts is the more fundamental, then it must be the presence of God, if only because of its well-attested and diverse vocabulary.[36] Holiness is a precondition for his presence on earth. The focus in the priestly writings is on the construction, maintenance and proper use of the holy realm that is the special focus of God's presence. But perhaps because the assurance or manifestation of his presence is a matter more for God than priestly legislators, less is said about it. Only at unique or rare events – the first consecration of the Tabernacle (Lev. 9) or the Day of Atonement (Lev. 16) – is there a special manifestation of God's presence.

Holiness and Ethics

A number of later traditions regarded holiness as having a very prominent ethical content. How far is this true of the priestly writings, or was their concern strictly to do with ritual matters? After all, the qualification for being a holy priest was not a high degree of moral integrity, but birth into a priestly family and conformity to the purity rules. In this section I shall look at three important discussions of this topic, by Israel Knohl, Walter Brueggemann and Mary Douglas.

Israel Knohl

Most of the previous discussion has assumed that the priestly writings can be discussed as if they presented a unified perspective. But can the assorted texts from Exodus 25 onwards be treated as a reasonably unified whole? Elliger and Milgrom have distinguished several different layers within P.[37] Most

---

[36] Unlike holiness, presence comprises a large and complex semantic field with no central term. It may be indicated by verbs (to draw near, *qrb*; to appear, niphal of *r'h*; to dwell, *škn*), nouns (presence or face, *pānîm*; glory, *kābôd*), adjectives (near, *qārôb*), and prepositions (before, *lipnê*; in the midst, *b⁽tôk*).

[37] See the detailed analyses in K. Elliger, *Leviticus* (HAT; Tübingen: Mohr-Siebeck, 1966); Milgrom, *Leviticus 1–16*.

important of all is the identification of a distinctly different
point of view found in Lev. 17–26 and a number of other texts:
the Holiness Code (H). As its name suggests, holiness plays a
prominent role in this source.

Scholars have generally regarded H as a distinct source that
the priestly writing (P) has integrated. Recently Israel Knohl
has mounted a powerful challenge to the consensus.[38] He
argues that the Holiness School (HS – his term for the Holiness
Code) is later than the Priestly Torah (PT) and was intended as
a theological and ethical corrective. As is well known, holiness
in the Holiness Code is extended to all the people and given a
prominent ethical dimension, 'You shall be holy, for I the
LORD your God am holy' (Lev. 19.2). The content of Leviticus
19 combines ritual and ethical instruction, including 'you shall
love your neighbour as yourself' (v. 18). The Priestly Torah, on
the other hand, restricts holiness to priests. Aaron and his sons
undertake a unique consecration that is restricted to the
Aaronic family (Lev. 8–9). Numbers 16–17 describes a protest
against this restricted holiness that leads to a decisive divine
ruling in favour of Aaron.

Knohl sets up a sharp contrast between these two sources or
schools or circles. The 'concept of holiness in Priestly Torah has
a ritual character devoid of any moral content'. Service of the
holy by the priests relates to procedures rather than morals:
'The sacred enclosure is a kind of minefield, in which the cultic
ordinances served to mark a narrow path where the slightest
deviation may be fatal.' The reason for this is because the social-
moral order is established at creation. The revelation of the holy
at Sinai is quite distinct from this and the ritual-cultic sphere is
the only object of interest for the priests.[39] There are opaque
barriers between the realm of the holy and ordinary everyday
life. It is not that the Priestly Torah has no ethics. Rather, it is a
common human possession and nothing to do with the cult.

The Holiness School represents a reaction to this and an
attempt to integrate holiness with morality as well as the cult. It

---

[38] Knohl, *Sanctuary*. See also Milgrom, 'The Changing Concept of Holiness'
and D. P. Wright, 'Holiness in Leviticus and Beyond: Differing Perspectives',
Interpretation 53 (1999), pp. 351–64.
[39] Knohl, *Sanctuary*, pp. 137–48.

teaches that the people are to echo the holiness of the temple and the priests in their daily lives, by keeping both the moral commandments and the ritual ones (such as the wearing of tassels). The priests retain a special degree of holiness, but the Levites and the people also have degrees of holiness, and these must be maintained and increased. The separation to God is not just a once for all event (so the Priestly Torah), but dependent on the fulfilling of all the commandments.

Knohl presents his case with a wealth of detail, and his main proposals about the relative dating of the sources is persuasive. Yet there are certain problems with his overall approach that affect his view of how ethics and holiness relate. From a source-critical point of view, it is possible that his key distinctions should not be made so absolutely. The interspersing of Holiness Code texts through the Priestly Torah suggests that the early editors saw substantial continuity.[40] There are a few texts that tell against his strong arguments from the ethical silence of the priestly writings (e.g. Lev. 16.21).[41] How far is the contrast between the general, ethical holiness of the Holiness School and the particular, cult-oriented holiness of the Priestly Torah a matter of context rather than conflict? An alternative view is suggested by Robert DiVito: 'Societies actually differ from each other not in the values they share in common, absolutely speaking, but in the ranking of these values and in the degree of their explicitness about them.'[42]

A similar approach is suggested by interpretations that work with the final form of the canonical text, rather than sources in isolation. The priestly writings (including the Holiness Code) come in the middle of the reasonably coherent, overarching story that begins in Genesis and continues on past Sinai. Exodus sets the Priestly Torah's exclusive definition of priestly holiness within a general exposition of Israel's special status and a paradigmatic statement of its general holiness: 'you shall be for me a priestly kingdom and a holy nation' (Exod. 19.6).

---

[40] Cf. Olyan, *Rites and Rank*, p. 122.

[41] Milgrom, *Leviticus 1–16*, pp. 19–26. Knohl responds in *Sanctuary*, pp. 225–30.

[42] R. A. DiVito, 'Old Testament Anthropology and the Construction of Personal Identity', *Catholic Biblical Quarterly* 61 (1999), pp. 217–38 [p. 238]. He alludes to the work of the anthropologist Kluckhohn.

From a canonical point of view priestly holiness is an exceptional outworking of this general holiness. From a source-critical point of view, the traditional late dating of P makes it unlikely that there is an absolute contradiction between the general and the restricted ideas of holiness.

Walter Brueggemann

The recent writing of Walter Brueggemann explores the tension between the cultic and the ethical in a very different way. In 1989 he wrote the following in his introduction to Gammie's *Holiness in Israel*:

> The priestly tradition focused on separateness and cleanness bespeaks the ultimacy, mystery, and unapproachability of God. In Israel, however, a sense of wonder in the face of majesty is never undifferentiatedly religious. The prophetic tradition concerns justice and social caring as the substance of God's holiness. There is no way to harmonize or finally adjudicate between these two tendencies in the God of Israel. Prerational majesty and critical social passion belong to God; both are there in a fruitful tension. The stress on cleanness prevents God's holiness from being reduced to moral requirement. Conversely, the urgency of justice precludes holiness from being generic, disinterested religion.[43]

Brueggemann assigns to the prophets the interests and concerns Knohl finds in the Holiness School. His strong contrast between the traditions is reminiscent of Knohl's opposition between the Priestly Torah and the Holiness School, and similar objections apply. But it is very possible that the biblical writers themselves were aware of the value of the fruitful tension that Brueggemann sets out. Later editors did not seem to have an uneasy conscience in recording and acknowledging both traditions.

A priori it would be surprising if priests did not have some ethical awareness, just as it is unlikely that the prophets did not

---

[43] W. Brueggemann, 'Editor's Foreward', to J. G. Gammie, *Holiness in Israel* (Minneapolis: Fortress, 1989), p. xi.

see some good in the cult, even if it needed to be reformed and refined. It is generally recognised now that the prophetic critique of the cult was contextual and limited. The paradigmatic example of this confluence is Ezekiel, who found ways to combine his prophetic and priestly callings in a way that was not a pale or uneasy harmonisation. The language of holiness and justice may remain distinct, but there is no clash between them, and Ezekiel upholds God's character as both holy (Ezek. 43.7) and just (Ezek. 18).

Brueggemann discusses the same tension in his recent theology but resolves it in a very different way. He traces two trajectories in Moses' interpretation of the command of Yahweh (i.e., in the writings that follow the making of the covenant). The first is that of social justice, centred on the book of Deuteronomy. The second is the trajectory of purity, focused on the priestly writings and designed to counter the threat of disorder. However, once again, a wedge is driven between the cultic and the ethical. In the purity trajectory the 'threats of disorder are not primarily understood to be moral. Rather, the power of disorder is palpable, material, physical, and can be managed only by careful and powerful attention'.[44]

There follows an intriguing redescription:

> The focus of this tradition of holiness, which we may find rooted in the first three commands of the Decalogue, is that those zones of life that are inhabited by Yahweh in an intense way must be kept pure and uncontaminated.[45]

This raises a number of issues that are not really explored: the meaning of purity, the relation between purity and holiness, and the unity of the Decalogue. The issues are sharply posed by a specific consideration of homosexuality, which is condemned in two texts in the Holiness Code (Lev. 18.22; 20.13):

> the enormous hostility to homosexual persons (and to proposals of justice for them) does not concern issues of

---

[44] W. Brueggemann, *Theology of the Old Testament: Testimony, Dispute, Advocacy* (Minneapolis: Fortress, 1997), p. 191.

[45] Brueggemann, *Theology*, p. 192.

justice and injustice, but rather concerns the more elemental issues of purity – cleanness and uncleanness.[46]

His conclusion is telling:

> My own judgement is that, following Fernando Belo in Christian extrapolations from the Old Testament, the justice trajectory has decisively and irreversibly defeated the purity trajectory. Thus the purity trajectory of the text may help us understand pastorally the anxiety produced by perceived and experienced disorder, but it provides no warrant for exclusionary ethical decisions in the face of the gospel.[47]

Homosexuality is a notoriously complex issue, but simply from a methodological point of view this contrast seems overstated. The zeal of the Holiness Code for social justice is evident, while Deuteronomy has significant things to say about the cult in a positive way (e.g., Deut. 15.19). The New Testament may reinterpret but does not fully abandon the purity trajectory. Brueggemann is in danger of reducing the purity/holiness trajectory to subjective feeling (shades of Otto!). In previous pages he has noted some of the advantages and weaknesses of both trajectories, but here an absolute and one-sided decision appears to have been made without any qualification. In his preface to Gammie the two are understood to be complementary and kept in creative tension. Here they have become contradictory and exclusive. This seems inconsistent with his earlier emphasis on the canon as supplying crucial complementary perspective for biblical theology.[48]

Mary Douglas

Brueggemann cites Mary Douglas in his exposition of purity and impurity, but it is striking that his approach does not engage in depth with her interests in the social and theological

---

[46] Brueggemann, *Theology*, p. 195.
[47] Brueggemann, *Theology*, p. 196.
[48] E.g., W. Brueggemann, *The Creative Word: Canon as a Model for Biblical Education* (Philadelphia: Fortress, 1982).

functions of the purity laws. Her attitude is also very different. As an anthropologist her breadth of reading and interests and openness to other cultures have allowed her to approach the priestly texts with sympathy and insight. Aware of the danger of reductionism, she has explored the complex interplay between the body, society and the cosmos with patience and imagination. However, these larger interests mean that she sometimes pays insufficient attention to the precise use of language.

For example, in her earlier work she starts with the idea of holiness as separation, but then goes on to refer to a complex cluster of concepts including wholeness, completeness and perfection.

> Granted that its root means separateness, the next idea that emerges is of the Holy as wholeness and completeness ... To be holy is to be whole, to be one; holiness is unity, integrity, perfection of the individual and the kind ... If the proposed interpretation of the forbidden animals is correct, the dietary laws would have been like songs which at every turn inspired meditation on the oneness, purity and completeness of God.[49]

The strength of the approach is its attempt to provide a comprehensive understanding of holiness as part of a system that also includes impurity. Yet it is difficult to relate these rather abstract nouns to the specific ways the priestly writings speak of holiness. Although sacrificial animals and priests had to be unblemished to minister at the altar (Lev. 21.16–23; 22.17–25), this is not the same as being impure.[50] And while impurity is often caused by the breaking of bodily boundaries,[51] this is not always true. Further, holiness cannot simply be understood as the opposite of impurity, although the two are absolutely incompatible.

Her latest book, *Leviticus as Literature*, tackles the problem from another point of view. The starting point is that Leviticus represents a very different way of thinking than we are familiar

---

[49] M. Douglas, *Purity and Danger* (London: Routledge & Kegal Paul, 1966), p. 51.

[50] Milgrom, *Leviticus 1–16*, p. 721.

[51] M. Douglas, *Purity and Danger*, pp. 51, 54, 57.

with, the kind of causal and personal speech that is very evident in Deuteronomy:

> Leviticus is analogical thinking, highly classified, intellectually subtle, theologically all-encompassing. Deuteronomy is rational thinking, emotional, politically sophisticated, theologically superficial.[52]

One abiding puzzle in the priestly writings is the nature of contagion, the ability of both holy and impure objects to transmit their holiness or impurity to others. Rather than developing the implicit medical analogy of contagion, Douglas appeals to societies with a strong discourse of honour:

> The nearest usage in European language for the idea of contagion is in the discourse of honour, especially with reference to the virtue of women or the honour of a knight ... defilement as a violation of holiness is a particularly apt expression for an attack on the honour of God perceived as a feudal lord. The word for holy has the sense of 'consecrated', 'pledged', 'betrothed', as 'sacrosanct' in modern English, something forbidden for others, not to be encroached upon, diluted, or attacked.[53]

The analogy is illuminating, though directed more to understanding the nature of impurity than holiness. But her emphasis on the analogical character of priestly thinking may shed light on how holiness and ethics are related. With persuasive thoroughness she shows that the priestly writings developed a comprehensive set of analogies embracing the whole of life, and she suggests that this also includes the moral realm. The holy sanctuary (like Mount Sinai) is divided into three parts (most holy place, holy place, outer court), as is the holy sacrificial body (entrails, midriff, head and feet) and the holy people (high priest, priests, people). These in turn are related to the system of purity and impurity. These cannot be fully separated from the rules of right behaviour built into creation and given special force by the making of the covenant

---

[52] M. Douglas, *Leviticus as Literature* (Oxford/New York: Oxford University Press, 1999), p. 174. For her critique of Knohl see pp. 128–31.

[53] Douglas, *Leviticus*, pp. 146–7.

with Israel. Both ritual and moral commandments require conformity to the will of God, and obedience to the one reinforces and expresses the other. 'The idea of goodness in Leviticus is encompassed in the idea of right ordering. Being moral would mean being in alignment with the universe, working with the laws of creation.'[54] The explicit moral dimension of the Holiness Code (and parallel later developments) would then be drawing out implications of the priestly view that are implicit.

Although the exegetical basis for her remarks is relatively thin, this is a common problem in the discussion. All approaches to the priestly writings struggle with the preponderance of detail over explanation. But in my opinion her insights are well worth exploring, and the general approach promises more than many of the alternatives.

Holiness and Ideology

We have moved a long way from linguistics. The discussion of the meaning of holiness has become entwined with significant judgements about method in biblical criticism and biblical theology. These in turn are dependent upon basic commitments relating to the character of the Bible and the God of whom it speaks. Theological reflection today is increasingly being carried out in an awareness of the growing challenge of ideological criticism, that is, criticism carried out from the outside of the tradition, and often from points of view that are set over against the text. It is often associated with the hermeneutic of suspicion, particularly in relation to the interests of the authors.

In a relatively mild form this is seen in the discussion of holiness and ethics. Brueggemann clearly favours Deuteronomy over the priestly trajectory, but attempts to see positive value in the priestly tradition. Knohl's preference for the perspective of the Holiness School over the Priestly Torah is equally clear. Douglas's approach is a startling reversal of the traditional negative evaluation of the priestly perspective.

---

[54] Douglas, *Leviticus*, p. 44.

Ideological criticism would explore how these critical and theological judgements relate to the faith of these scholars, who represent the liberal Protestant, non-orthodox Jewish and Roman Catholic traditions respectively.

However, more hostile attitudes are evident in the history of interpretation of these texts, and I expect them to increase in future years.[55] The priestly writings have largely avoided this fate so far, I suspect, because of their complexity. To expend the necessary effort it helps to be pious and committed! For example, the language of ideological criticism was anticipated in a remarkable way by Samuel Terrien. Despite his sterling efforts to explore the cultic expression of God's presence, he wrote in 1982:

> The realm of the sacred, even if its conscious intention is to reach the masses through festive ceremonies, is in fact the privileged ground of an esoteric club, a restricted oligarchy of vested interests.[56]

Here we have the characteristic revisionist method of the hermeneutics of suspicion. The 'in fact' in the quotation indicates that the conscious and determinate intentions of the author lose out in favour of the subconscious. A strong ideological framework for interpretation is suggested by the way in which these unintended motives are stated in anachronistic terms. The language of privilege and interests betrays the roots of such criticism in the Marxist materialist and economic criticism of class. This has now become the external Archimedian point from which the priestly writings may be weighed and found wanting.

Such criticism is in continuity with the long-standing Protestant bias against the priestly perspective. We may go back to Wellhausen's patronising comment on holiness:

---

[55] But see R. A. Kugler, 'Holiness, Purity, the Body and Society: The Evidence for Theological Conflict in Leviticus', *Journal for the Study of the Old Testament* 76 (1997), pp. 3–27; F. Landy, 'Leviticus, Deconstruction and the Body', *Journal of Hebrew Scriptures* 11 (1999) [http://www.arts.ualberta.ca/JHS/].

[56] S. Terrien, 'The Numinous, the Sacred and the Holy in Scripture', *Biblical Theology Bulletin* 12 (1982), p. 101 [99–108].

[T]he ideal of holiness governs the whole of life by means of a net of ceremonies and observances which separate the Jew from the natural man. 'Holy' means almost the same as 'exclusive.' Originally the term was equivalent to divine, but now it is used chiefly in the sense of religious, priestly, as if the divine were to be known from the worldly, the natural, by outward marks.[57]

The hostility of these remarks is not evident in the writings of Otto, Eliade and others, but their writings may well illustrate a similar external standpoint, derived not so much from the Bible as from a particular theory of religions. From a prior understanding of the nature of the holy the specific and unique aspects of the priestly concept of holiness are reinterpreted in terms congenial to their larger project. For example, the constant reference to the holiness of specific people and material objects is marginalised in favour of those texts that can be interpreted in terms of an experience of the holy.[58] Perhaps because of their firmer grasp on the particular Jewishness of the priestly texts, this universalising tendency is less evident in Jewish scholarship.

It is probably clear by now that my sympathies lie with those who seek to read the Bible as canonical scripture. As such there will be a reluctance to write off any of the voices of Scripture, however foreign they appear to be. In fact, that willingness to struggle with hard texts that come from a very different culture can lead to insights into the character both of the Bible and the present day. The emphasis of the priestly writings on the close relationship between holiness and the material and human realities of the cult goes counter to most of the assumptions of modernism and postmodernism. Yet it is perhaps this very aspect that has the potential to recover an awareness of the holy God that has almost disappeared in many churches.[59]

---

[57] J. Wellhausen, *Prolegomena to the History of Israel* (Edinburgh, 1885), p. 499.
[58] Note the handful of texts discussed by Otto, *Holy*, pp. 87–97.
[59] See the comments by the Orthodox theologian A. Walker, *Telling the Story: Gospel, Mission and Culture* (London: SPCK, 1996).

Conclusion

To sum up and hint at wider implications:

1. The idea of holiness in the priestly writings is subtle, diverse, and richly developed. I have suggested that a fruitful starting-point for understanding and exploring the concept of holiness in the priestly writings (and perhaps elsewhere) is to relate it to the idea of God's realm or place.

2. Holiness is not primarily a moral term, but neither is it inherently amoral. The chief concern in the priestly legislation is that holiness be kept apart from the impure. However, it is also clear that the holy God will not tolerate sin and injustice among his holy people, an emphasis found particularly in the Holiness Code. Different parts of the priestly tradition show stronger and weaker developments of the moral dimension, but the affirmation of both moral and cultic aspects of holiness in the final form of the canonical text warns us against a sharp separation of these aspects.

3. Discussion of the meaning of holiness in the priestly writings often requires a consideration of the wider philosophical debate about the nature of religion. Ideological criticism has alerted us to the way in which both sympathetic and unsympathetic treatments reflect theological commitments that are, in turn, related to views on the nature of truth and method.[60] For those prepared to take these texts seriously, I would contend that they comprise an invaluable challenge and resource for the church today as it seeks to worship the holy God and live as his holy people.

---

[60] Cf. K. Vanhoozer, *Is there a Meaning in this Text? The Bible, the Reader and the Morality of Literary Knowledge* (Leicester: Apollos, 1998).

6

'Holy, Holy, Holy': Isaiah's Vision of God

R. W. L. Moberly

Isaiah's vision of God in the Jerusalem temple is one of the most famous and enduringly influential passages within the Old Testament. Not least, the incorporation of the seraphic cry, the *trisagion*, within Jewish and Christian worship has ensured that Isaiah's vision of the worship of God has been in some way appropriated by believers generally in every generation. In this paper I would like to consider again certain aspects of what might be the import of this famous text.

Some clarificatory remarks about scope and method should be made. First, I cannot here consider the extensive history of the reception of Isaiah 6. Nonetheless I work from within the general context of Jewish and Christian reception, in that I presuppose that the biblical text is not just the interesting account of an ancient religious experience conceived in the categories of Jerusalemite temple ideology, but is also an enduring and critical constituent within Jewish and Christian conceptions of the one true God. Secondly, I wish to offer a close reading of certain parts of Isaiah's vision, and will need to cross-refer to other Isaianic and Old Testament texts in order to elucidate the meaning of key terms and concepts. In doing this I wish to prescind from difficult compositional and dating questions both within the book of Isaiah itself and in the relationship of the book of Isaiah to other Old Testament texts. The achieved portrait of Isaiah is our concern.[1] Thirdly, I do

---

[1] The question of how an awareness of the likely complex tradition-history and composition of the text may affect an interpretation of the achieved

not wish to discuss all the intriguing issues that the text raises, whether, for example, the text-critical problems,[2] or the significance of the first-person form of the narration.[3] I will rather offer an outline of the narrative as a whole with attention paid only to selected detail. Fourthly, there is no space to discuss how the immediately following chapters of Isaiah, or the book as a whole, envisage the outworking of what Isaiah is commissioned to do. Fifthly, I have little to add to the debate as to why Isaiah's vision is chapter 6 rather than chapter 1 of the book bearing his name, when chapter 1 would seem the more logical position to place it, not least by analogy with Jeremiah and Ezekiel (and, with a slight difference, Moses in Exodus). What matters for our purposes is that the vision entails a commission (which is undoubted), not whether it constitutes Isaiah's call to be a prophet (which it may or may not).

However, if one wishes to take seriously the present form of the book, certain contextual points may briefly be made. Chapter 1, an apparent summary of much of Isaiah's message, at the outset depicts YHWH as the Holy One of Israel (*qᵉdoš yisra'el*, 1.4), and concludes with the divine purification of a corrupt city so as to restore justice and righteousness (1.21–7, *mišpat*, *sᵉdaqa* are the obvious key words) – with also a warning

---

portrait cannot be predicted in advance and is likely to vary from passage to passage and verse to verse. I take it for granted, however, that an interpretation which is aware of such complexity will not be identical to one which is unaware.

[2] Some of the relevant literature is listed in Hans Wildberger, *Isaiah 1–12* (Minneapolis: Fortress, 1991), p. 246f.

[3] This has usually been construed in terms of the quest for the historical Isaiah, for which first-person reference has seemed particularly promising. However, the form in which the quest has usually been expressed, Budde's hypothesis of an Isaiah Memoir, is no longer tenable (see H. G. M. Williamson, *Variations on a Theme: King, Messiah and Servant in the Book of Isaiah* (Carlisle: Paternoster, 1998), ch. 3; Brevard S. Childs, *Isaiah* (Louisville: Westminster/John Knox, 2001), pp. 42–4), and we should probably rethink the possible significance of the first-person form. Stuart Weeks offers the suggestive proposal that 'prophets, in the early prophetic literature, are presented in the first person when required to describe situations in which they act or speak as individuals in their own right' as distinct from when they act as a divine spokesman or agent ('Whose Words? Qoheleth, Hosea and Attribution in Biblical Literature', in Peter J. Harland and Robert Hayward, eds., *New Heaven & New Earth: Prophecy & the Millennium: Essays in Honour of Anthony Gelston* (Leiden: Brill, 1999), pp. 151–70, esp. p. 165ff, quote p. 169).

of fire that will not be quenched (*kbh* with negative) for those
who are unresponsive (*poše'im*, 1.28–31; *pš'* being a key term,
introduced in 1.2), a note with which the whole book ends
(66.24, *poše'im*, *kbh* with negative). Chapters 2 to 4, mostly
oracles addressed to a corrupt Judah and Jerusalem, are framed
by pictures of Jerusalem as it is meant to be, in the latter case
(4.2–6, esp. 3–4) with people who can be designated holy
(*qadoš*) explicitly as a result of divine purification through blasts
of burning justice (*b'ruah mišpat ub'ruah ba'er*). Thus a process
of purification, in which the imagery of burning features prominently,[4] and which is directed to the ends of justice,
righteousness and holiness is a fundamental concern of these
early chapters. Chapter 5 initially indicts Israel as a whole in
the song of the vineyard, which climaxes in the absence of the
appropriate fruit from the vineyard, that is justice and righteousness (*mišpat*, *s'daqa*, 5.1–7). The continuing indictment
utilises once more the key word-pair of justice and righteousness, this time as a quasi-definitional explication of the
holiness of YHWH (5.16). The subsequent oracles of
judgement speak of divine anger but not of purification, and
conclude in two fearsome images – first of a lion roaring and
irresistibly consuming its prey (5.29), and secondly the roaring
of a stormy sea where a sailor can see no security but only
enveloping darkness (5.30). Against this forbidding backdrop
Isaiah's vision in chapter 6 is now set.

Verses 1–5

Isaiah's vision is of YHWH as king – though with characteristic
Hebrew reserve the account makes no attempt to depict YHWH
in himself, for YHWH is primarily depicted by what is seen and
said around him. Whether or not the opening reference to king
Uzziah means that the divine kingship is being situated in
relation (presumably of contrast) to human kingship,[5] is

---

[4] Significant also is the account of YHWH's judgement on the arrogance of
Assyria, where the imagery of sickness alternates with that of fire, and where
YHWH does not simply send fire but becomes fire (Isa. 10.17).

[5] Although one would be unwise to over-interpret a straightforward chronological marker, formulated in terms of regnal year, if that is what the opening

unclear. What is clear is the royal nature of the divine vision. This derives on the one hand, of course, from Isaiah's own words explicitly depicting YHWH as king (*melek*, v.5). On the other hand, however, there is also the intrinsic symbolism of the vision: throne, train,[6] palace,[7] attendants (however the seraphim are to be envisaged) who stand and wait on one who sits (a traditional posture of authority), the proclamation of the whole earth as YHWH's 'glory' (*kabod*, 'glory' being that which accompanies and designates a king, 8.7aβ), and fundamentally the very nature of the exalted position in which YHWH is depicted. Likewise the hardening of a people's hearts and the laying waste of their land which is envisaged later in the chapter is the kind of act which invites depiction as an act of sovereign power (comparable to YHWH's overthrow of the king of Egypt in Exodus). Thus in one way or other the symbolism, assumptions and language of the narrative consistently envisage the kingly nature of YHWH.

---

four words are, the question, of course, is whether that is all these words are meant to be. In favour of a purely chronological function is the exactly parallel formulation of the death of Ahaz (Isa. 14.28), which introduces an oracle against Philistia, which relates not in any way to Ahaz but rather to a perceived deliverance from Assyrian domination (14.29–31, esp. in relation to 14.24–27). In favour of a possible greater significance could be the wording *hammelek `uzziyyahu*, instead of `*uzziyyahu melek yehuda* (by analogy with Isa. 1.1), which could anticipate and contrast with the depiction of YHWH as *hammelek* (6.5); for a suggestive account in these terms, see Martin Buber, *The Prophetic Faith* (Harper: New York, 1949), p. 126f. Although I incline to favour the former in terms of likely authorial intention, I would not wish to rule out the possibility that the text in its present form may have resonances that are both potentially significant and originally unintended.

A characteristic reflection (different from the above, yet not unrelated) on wider resonances is offered by von Rad, who comments on the religio-historical uniqueness within Old and New Testaments of the dating of particular revelations in terms of particular historical events, such that 'Words such as "in the year that King Uzziah or King Ahaz died" ... set the tone for the Christian "suffered under Pontius Pilate"' (*Old Testament Theology* II (London: SCM, 1965,1975), p. 363; similarly, Childs, *Isaiah*, p. 54.

[6] The precise nature of the *šulim* is disputed, but it remains most likely that it depicts the hem or train of a long royal robe.

[7] The Hebrew *hekal* can mean both a royal palace and also the central chamber of a temple. If, as seems likely, the vision is of YHWH's palace, that is not an alternative to the temple, for the latter symbolically represents the former. The point would be that Isaiah's vision sees God in that majestic context which the temple serves to replicate.

Within this context the divine attendants speak. What might one expect to hear them say? Given the symbolism of the moment, one would surely expect to hear the words *yhwh malak*, 'YHWH rules/is king', as in one of the divine kingship psalms.[8] For this would further underline the royal majesty of the God whom Isaiah sees. The fact that these are not the words Isaiah hears suggests that the kingship of YHWH is not so much proclaimed in the words of the seraphim as it is interpreted. Given that YHWH is king, as the symbolism of the vision makes clear, what does his kingship mean, what does it entail? It is this that the seraphim proclaim: God's kingship entails his holiness.

The first part of the seraphic cry, the threefold proclamation of YHWH's holiness, is remarkable for its emphasis. The standard Hebrew idiom for emphasis is simple repetition,[9] so had the cry been solely 'holy, holy', i.e., 'utterly holy', that would have sufficed to emphasise the holiness of YHWH.[10] The threefold repetition, therefore, is grammatically puzzling.[11] Although this could be taken as a 'super-superlative' of unlimited emphasis[12] – 'YHWH is utterly, utterly holy' – it should probably be envisaged as a single 'holy' followed by an intensifying 'holy, holy'/'utterly holy' (a construal suggested also by the Massoretic notation).[13] Either way, the consensus of

---

[8] Pss. 93, 95–99. Apart from the specific wording *yhwh malak*, the kingship of YHWH is presented in a variety of ways in these psalms.

[9] For example: with adjectives, *ra`ra`*, 'quite worthless' (Prov. 20.14), *`amoq `amoq*, 'extremely deep' (Eccles. 7.24); with nouns, *be'rot be'rot*, 'full of pits' (Gen. 14.10), *šalom šalom*, 'perfect peace' (Isa. 26.3).

[10] Surprisingly, the Qumran text of Isaiah has *qadoš* only twice. Perhaps this is conforming the text to standard Hebrew idiom. There is little reason to suppose that the Qumran reading is more original than that of MT, and the MT is certainly the best received reading.

[11] One might argue that the text envisages two or more seraphim, each calling out a single 'holy', and that this undermines the case for an idiom of superlative emphasis. If, however, the text wished to specify different speakers it would likely repeat the speech introduction, *w''amar* (cf. Amos 6.10); and, even if the hypothesis were granted, the present text, as written text, could have a syntax and meaning different from that of the envisaged underlying oral speech.

[12] The closest parallel is Ezekiel 21.32 [English 27], where the threefold *`awwa* indicates total and complete ruin. The threefold repetitions in Jeremiah 7.4 and 22.29 seem to have a rhetorical function other than that of emphasis.

[13] I am grateful to Stuart Weeks for directing attention in discussion to the 1 plus 2 structure.

translators both ancient and modern to keep the threefold wording means that the rhetorical form of the seraphic cry (to be replicated by worshippers) is retained to some extent at the expense of its idiomatic sense. Such an emphatic formulation is tantamount to a definition of the nature of YHWH, and as such its sense is well captured by the later formulation within the book of Isaiah that 'his name is holy' (*qadoš š^emo*, Isa. 57.15).

These two Isaiah texts (6.3; 57.15) thus invite classification alongside the canonically primary passages about the name, and nature, of YHWH in Exodus 3.14, 34.6–7; though the context of the latter – on the lips of YHWH, to Moses alone, at Sinai – gives the latter a foundational role which Isaiah cannot replicate. It is noteworthy, however, that the first significant usage of 'holiness' within Israel's story (excluding the consecration of the sabbath at creation, Gen. 2.3, which is prior to the particular story of Israel) is when Moses first approaches God at the burning bush (Exod. 3.5) and first learns that God's name is YHWH. When God is not revealed as YHWH, as in the patriarchal context (Exod. 6.2–3), holiness is not an issue. The corollary of this is that when God is known as YHWH, holiness is intrinsic to his name and nature.[14] So Isaiah is making explicit what is implicit in Exodus.

What it means that YHWH is 'holy' has already been specified in the previous chapter of Isaiah, where divine holiness is closely linked with moral integrity (not that the two are co-extensive, but that the latter supremely exemplifies the former): 'But YHWH of hosts is exalted in justice, and the holy God shows himself holy in righteousness.'[15] The significance of this for understanding the seraphic cry will become evident as the narrative proceeds.

Isaiah's response to what he sees and hears is a cry of anguish.[16] For he now sees himself as being at one with the

---

[14] I have argued this more fully in my *The Old Testament of the Old Testament: Patriarchal Narratives and Mosaic Yahwism* (Minneapolis: AugsburgFortress, 1992), ch. 1.

[15] See my 'Whose Justice? Which Righteousness? The Interpretation of Isaiah 5.16', *Vetus Testamentum* 51 (2001), pp. 55–68.

[16] Brown-Driver-Briggs 17 characterises the interjection '*oy* as 'an impassioned expression of grief and despair'.
It is unclear whether *ki nidmeti* represents an extension of the cry of anguish

people of Israel as 'unclean' (*tame'*), a condition far removed – perhaps as far removed as it possibly could be – from that of holiness.[17] Specifically, it is Isaiah's lips, just as the lips of the people, that are unclean. Why this reference to the lips? First, it resonates in context with the hearing of the words of the seraphim. With their lips they can proclaim the holiness of YHWH; whereas the prophet and the people appear to be in some way failing to make, or even to be disqualified from, such proclamation, because their lips, being unclean, are incompatible with the content of what is proclaimed. This does not necessarily rule out the possibility that the words of the *trisagion* could already have been in use in the temple liturgy; though it must surely at least make one think twice about the common assumption that the words of the seraphim are words that a Jerusalemite would hear anyway in the temple (R. E. Clements, for example, simply asserts as apparently self-evident that the words of the seraphim in v. 3 'must derive from a choral antiphon actually sung in the Jerusalem temple').[18] For one natural reading of the text is that Isaiah responds thus to the call of the seraphim precisely for the reason that that which the people of Israel should say, i.e., the *trisagion*, they do not say.

A second reason for referring to lips could be the assumption that lips should express the content of heart and mind – a characteristic Old Testament understanding, given classic

---

('for I am lost'), or whether it expresses a reason for the anguish ('for I was silent'), or something else. See the standard commentaries for discussion. Most suggested renderings are compatible with the tenor of this present interpretation.

[17] See Philip Jenson, *Graded Holiness: A Key to the Priestly Conception of the World* (JSOTSup 106; Sheffield: JSOT Press, 1992), ch. 2 for a survey of the terminology. It is debatable whether *tame'* is the ultimate antithesis to *qadoš*, but such an understanding would fit well in Isaiah 6.

[18] R. E. Clements, *Isaiah 1–39* (NCB; Grand Rapids: Eerdmans, 1980), p. 74. Cf. Wildberger's assertion that 'without a doubt, the Trisagion was part of the liturgy in the Jerusalem cult' (*Isaiah 1–12*, p. 265); Wildberger does not argue the point, but sees it as an uncontroversial part of the wider pattern for which he argues (cf. *Isaiah 1–12*, pp. 24f., 261f.) of the Jerusalem cult adopting and adapting religious understandings such as holiness and kingship from the Canaanite cult of El. In fact there is no unambiguous evidence for the use of the *trisagion* even in the Second Temple, never mind the First Temple (see Robert Hayward, 'The Chant of the Seraphim and the Worship of the Second Temple', *Proceedings of the Irish Biblical Association* 20 (1997), pp. 62–80).

expression by Jesus in his dictum that 'out of the abundance of the heart the mouth speaks'.[19] This could underline the concern that Isaiah and Israel do not acknowledge God at all with the words they should use because the reality of their hearts and minds is quite otherwise. But it is also compatible with Israel already using the words of the *trisagion* and the prophet now perceiving a gulf that has opened up between what he and the people say and what in reality they are – the problems of at least ignorance, and more likely inconsistency, insincerity, hypocrisy. This latter is the problem given memorable expression in Isaiah 29.13 where the prophet announces God's astonishing overthrow of a people who 'draw near with their mouth and honour me with their lips while their heart is far from me'. But whether or not Israel's use of the *trisagion* is presupposed, the important and indisputable point is that the disposition and way of life of the prophet and Israel, in whichever way it is reflected in what they say, is fundamentally incompatible with the holiness of YHWH as proclaimed by the seraphim. It is this incompatibility which is immediately addressed as the narrative proceeds.

Verses 6–8

A seraph approaches the prophet with a glowing, i.e., red-hot, coal taken from an altar, presumably the incense altar (Exod. 30.27), which stands within the main chamber of the sanctuary, rather than the altar of the whole burnt offering in the forecourt.[20] The obvious symbolic potential of incense (as in the ritual for the purification of the tabernacle, Lev. 16.12–13) is beside the point in this context (apart from the fact that it is probably the incense smoke which is part of the awesomely charged context of Isaiah's hearing the cry of the seraphim,

---

[19] Matthew 12.34b, in the context of 12.33–7, and Luke 6.45b, in the context of 6.43–5. In this dictum in these contexts Jesus is not denying the problem of deception and hypocrisy, which is clearly recognised elsewhere. In each context the saying functions as a challenge to integrity on the part of disciples, so as to prevent hypocrisy arising. But when deception or hypocrisy is present, the same principle is used to affirm that the reality of the person will become evident through that person's words and deeds (Matt. 7.15–20).

[20] Cf. Wildberger, *Isaiah 1–12*, p. 269.

v. 4), where it is the coal rather than the incense to which attention is drawn. The purpose of the glowing coal is to purify – perhaps as metal is purified (Num. 31.22f.), a common image in the Old Testament for the transformation of human life into what it is meant to be[21] – a purification clearly consonant with that already depicted in the opening chapters of the prophetic book.[22] When the coal touches Isaiah's lips, his sin is thereby dealt with, thus confirming the purifying power of the glowing coal (and also illustrating the earlier contention that the lips, in their ability to speak and represent the heart and mind, stand for the whole person in a morally accountable perspective).

The imagery of this purification is stark. A burning coal is so hot and searing that it is normally untouchable, a point implicit in the seraph picking up and carrying the coal with tongs.[23] Yet such a coal is applied directly to the prophet's lips. One might well expect the text to speak next of a shriek of agony (perhaps again with the *'oy* of v. 5 or a comparable ejaculation) and something such as the smell of burning flesh. Yet the text says nothing about scorching and pain – the 'feelings' or the 'experience' of Isaiah – but focuses instead on the purifying, transformative significance of the encounter.

The act of purification is followed by Isaiah's hearing God himself speak for the first time, a hearing which in its specific content may only be possible after the preceding purification. What he hears is expressed as an open question, yet in context

---

[21] There is a fuller discussion of the imagery and its significance in my *The Bible, Theology and Faith: A Study of Abraham and Jesus* (Cambridge Studies in Christian Doctrine; Cambridge: Cambridge University Press, 2000), pp. 99–100, 105.

[22] Curiously, Motyer denies this with a categorical assertion that 'In the Old Testament fire is not a cleansing agent but is symbolic of the wrath of God' (*The Prophecy of Isaiah* (Leicester: IVP, 1993), p. 77 [cf. p. 66 on Isa. 4.4]). His discussion of symbolism seems insufficiently attuned to the Isaianic context.

[23] It is very unlikely that *b'yado rispa* means explicitly 'in its hand was a glowing coal', for the idiom really means 'carrying a glowing coal', the precise means of that carrying being specified in the clause about the tongs which follows. To suppose that the seraph first took the coal with tongs and then transferred the coal to its 'hand' (a part of the body which we don't even know a seraph possessed) before applying it to Isaiah's lips would be comparable to supposing that the depiction of a bird's foot as having a *kap* (Gen. 8.9) envisaged birds possessing the same smooth patch of skin that characterises a human hand palm or foot sole.

is directed specifically to him (unless Isaiah is thought to be present in the 'divine council' in such a way that others there might also be able to respond, by analogy with the picture in 1 Kings 22.19–22). Instead of being rendered incapable of speech by the glowing coal, Isaiah's lips are not mutilated but rather are enabled to speak two words of pure responsiveness to God, words which may in effect be an equivalent to the *trisagion* in their appropriateness in God's presence.

First, Isaiah says *hin^eni*, conventionally rendered 'here am I' but perhaps better captured by 'I am ready'. As Jon Levenson says with regard to Abraham's identical response to God's momentous summonses in Genesis 22.1, 11 (and also to Isaac, Gen. 22.7): 'In none of these verses is there an inquiry about the Patriarch's location. What is at stake, instead, is his readiness to act upon a command from God (vv. 1,11) and to face the human consequences (v. 7).'[24]

Secondly, Isaiah says *š^elaheni*, 'send me'. Being 'sent' by God is one of the most fundamental terms and concepts of Hebrew prophecy.[25] It depicts the prophet as responsive and accountable to God, with a purpose which is not his own but God's – the prophet lives and speaks both *from* God and *for* God. As such, his life becomes bound up with God in a way that is not so for most others, with the consequence that his life takes a different course from that of Israel generally.[26] This word on Isaiah's lips thus expresses the unreserved reorientation of his life in relation to God – some of the cost of which will be made clear in the awesome content of the commissioning which directly follows.

---

[24] Jon D. Levenson, *The Death and Resurrection of the Beloved Son: The Transformation of Child Sacrifice in Judaism and Christianity* (New Haven and London: Yale University Press, 1993), p. 126f. Levenson commends E. A. Speiser's one word translation of *hinneni* as 'Ready'.

[25] This is, of course, a prime reason for seeing the passage as depicting Isaiah receiving his prophetic vocation and not just a specific commissioning.

[26] Numerous passages in the book of Isaiah express a sharp distinction between the way of the prophet and the way of the people, e.g., Isa. 8.11–13, 17–18; 22.1–4, 12–14. Similar distinctions can be found in many other prophetic books.

Verses 9–13

The key to understanding the commissioning is, I suggest, implicitly contained in v. 5. There the prophet's anguished cry was related to the fact that he was a man of unclean lips 'in the midst of a people of unclean lips'. The purification in vv. 6–8 has solved the problem posed by Isaiah's own unclean lips, and he now speaks words of appropriate responsiveness to God. But what about the people of unclean lips? It is they to whom the focus now shifts in vv. 9ff. That is to say, I suggest that the structure of the text is that the seraph with the glowing coal relates to Isaiah, as Isaiah with his message relates to the people. Isaiah's purification by the coal is parallel to, and is the means towards, the people's purification by the prophetic message – with the goal for each that there should be response to God commensurate with the *trisagion* of the seraphim. This structural point coincides with a basic axiom of prophecy,[27] that one of the prime tasks of the prophet is to bring about genuine turning to God (*šub*) on the part of those to whom they speak.

It is in the light of these two points that we must try to understand the amazing message that Isaiah is given to speak in v. 9b: 'Hear constantly, but understand nothing; see unceasingly, but perceive nothing', and YHWH's astonishing depiction to Isaiah of his task in v. 10 as stupefying, dulling and blinding the people lest a more positive response enable the people to turn to God (*šub* – that prime purpose of prophecy)[28] and be healed

---

[27] Whether, as a matter of history, Hebrew prophecy was always understood thus is a matter of legitimate debate. However, when the canonical prophets are read in canonical context, it becomes natural to take the explicit articulations of the repentance-seeking purpose of prophecy in Jeremiah and Ezekiel (and the post-exilic summary of Zech. 1.4–6) as heuristically regulative for their predecessors also, as long as the distinctive voices within, and varying genres of, prophetic literature are fully respected.

[28] There is a difficult semantic problem as to whether *wašab* should be construed as a use of *šub* in its own right, i.e., 'and repent', or whether it is used modally as an idiom of repetition (as indubitably in 6.13aβ), i.e., 'and again be healed'. See Georg Sauer, 'Die Umkehrforderung in der Verkundigung Jesajas', in H.-J. Stoebe, J. J. Stamm and E. Jenni, eds., *Wort – Gebot – Glaube: F/S W. Eichrodt* (Zürich: Zwingli, 1970), pp. 277–95, esp. 279–84. As far as I can see, however, there is a consensus (rightly or wrongly; few scholars really argue the point) that the Massoretic vocalisation, *wašab*, makes 'repent' the more likely construal, whereas a modal vocalisation would be *wešab*; the real issue,

(language that resonates with the book's opening image of battered and broken Israel, a condition understood to be the consequence of sin, 1.4, 5–6). That this is a hard and unsparing message and understanding of the prophetic task is clear both from Isaiah's response of 'How long, Lord?' (v. 11a), and from God's unambiguous answer that it will go on until the land is utterly desolate, with those to whom Isaiah is sent removed from it (vv. 11b–13).

Among the many things that could be said, and have been said,[29] about this passage I offer solely four observations. First, it is surely right to see a high level of a certain kind of irony in the passage. If there is good reason to suppose that God's purpose in sending Isaiah is to purify the people, that is to bring them to turn to God (*šub*), then the statement that God wants Isaiah so to act as to prevent this cannot be a genuine negation of the characteristic prophetic task but, rather, an ironic reconstrual of what that task will involve. This is so not least because hardening people's hearts is not as such something that the prophet himself, rather than God, could do; and the specific words that YHWH tells Isaiah to speak are nowhere spoken by him, and the form which Isaiah's message does take could not be predicted on the basis of 6.9–10. *Of course* God's purpose is that the people should turn back to him. But the act of turning is problematic, beyond normal comprehension.

Secondly, the underlying concern is that of searing purification, that which for a nation might be equivalent to Isaiah's red-hot coal. The text is unsparing in its depiction of the devastation and desolation of the land – yet the implicit purpose is to

---

therefore, is whether or not the Masoretic pointing represents the original sense, and what is its status if it represents a reconstrual of the text. Thus hermeneutical issues about the level on which one reads the text affect decisions as to what constitutes the text to be read. Given our concern to understand the received portrait of the prophet, it seems natural to follow the Massoretic construal, which is unambiguous also in the Targum, and which is already present in the LXX (which was not ignorant of the modal use of *šub*, for it renders *šub* in v. 13 by *palin*), as long as this is not done with disregard for the semantic problem.

[29] Material relating to the early history of interpretation is conveniently set out in Craig A. Evans, *To See and Not Perceive: Isaiah 6.9–10 in Early Jewish and Christian Interpretation* (JSOTSup 64; Sheffield: JSOT Press, 1989).

transform those who are afflicted thus, for the presupposition is that YHWH smites his people in order to bring them to turn (*šub*) to him (Isa. 9.12, [English 13]; cf. the refrain in Amos 4.6–11). This is not the only way in which YHWH relates to his people as a whole, as not least the latter part of the book of Isaiah makes clear, but its presupposition is nonetheless deeply rooted in many parts of the Old Testament.

Thirdly, the process of purifying goes on far beyond what anyone would expect. The desolation of vv. 11–12 might surely be considered sufficient to achieve its purpose; but it is not. This is the point of v. 13. The interpretation of this verse is fraught with difficulties, yet at the risk of oversimplifying, I wish to offer a reading of the received text on the grounds that as it stands it does make sense. The prime point is in v. 13a, 'And if there is still a tenth in it [the land], it will again be for burning'. The use of *ba'er*, 'burning', recalls the imagery of the red-hot coal, and resonates with the imagery of purification through fire elsewhere in Isaiah 1–5.[30] The assumption appears to be that such burning is intrinsic to the holy nature of YHWH, whose prime symbol at Sinai is fire, and so burning continues constantly, primarily to purify and restore but also to consume those who do not respond but persist in their sin (cf. 1.28–31; 66.24).

This general idea of renewed burning for a remaining tenth is then given an illustration – it is like a great tree (an oak or terebinth) where something remains standing even when it is felled (v. 13bα). The general point of the illustration would appear to be that the people of Israel is initially like a great tree.

---

[30] Wildberger (*Isaiah 1–12*, pp. 142, 251) argues that *b'r* (Pi.) in Isa. 6.13 means 'graze until bare', on the basis of similar usage and meaning in Isa. 3.14; 5.5. Even if this be granted (though it is arguable) as a possible hypothesis for the meaning of *b'r* (Pi.) in some contexts, it remains doubtfully applicable to Isa. 6.13. Moreover when Isa. 6.13 is read in its literary and canonical context within the present shape of Isa. 1–12, where astringent purification is a recurrent concern, Wildberger's proposed meaning must surely be excluded. The root *b'r* occurs seven times in Isa. 1–12, thrice in the Qal where its meaning is clearly 'burn' (1.31; 9.17; 10.17) and four times in the Pi'el (3.14; 4.4; 5.5; 6.13) where, even if this is a different root *b'r* whose meaning is not 'burn' (which is debatable), it should mean something like 'devastate', for the envisaged scenarios are of violent devastation – of a kind readily associated with the total destructiveness of fire.

When it is felled, one might think that was the end of what was inflicted upon it. But it is not, for when a tree is felled something still remains standing. The specific point of the analogy is that what remains standing of the tree corresponds to the tenth which survives the initial devastation of the land. The further burning of the tenth corresponds to what people can do with the standing remains of a tree, that is, burn with fire what was not initially felled.

It is intriguing that the verse then concludes with a note (v. 13bβ) that picks up and interprets the 'what remains standing' (*massebet*). The note interprets the *massebet* as belonging to the land ('its') and as being 'a holy seed' (*zera' qodeš*), a term which could naturally refer to Israel (as analogous to 'holy people/nation', *goy qadoš*, Exod. 19.6, *'am qadoš*, Deut. 7.6), and certainly has this signification in its only other use, in Ezra 9.2. Two assumptions are usually made about this note. One is that it expresses a note of hope, an interpretation at least as old as the Targum,[31] and ubiquitous among modern commentators. The other is that it is a later addition to the text, probably from the post-exilic period.[32] Whatever may be the case about the date of the note, the assumption I wish to query is that the note is a hopeful one, at least as that is usually understood. The usual assumption appears to be that what remains standing is that which stands when YHWH's action against Israel is finished, a stump of tree out of which new growth can take place (cf. the similar imagery in Isa. 11.1); thus it depicts a purified Israel having renewed life. Yet, as already indicated, the stump is not that which is spared further burning but that which receives it.

The wording of the note relates clearly to its Isaianic context. The use of 'a holy seed' recalls the seraphim's acclamation of God's majesty as 'holy'. Israel is 'a holy seed' because Israel is understood as the offspring of YHWH (Isa. 1.2, *banim*),[33] and so

[31] See, e.g., Bruce D. Chilton, *The Isaiah Targum* (Aramaic Bible 11; Edinburgh: T&T Clark, 1987), p. 14f.

[32] See, e.g., H. G. M. Williamson, *The Book Called Isaiah: Deutero-Isaiah's Role in Composition and Redaction* (Oxford: Clarendon Press, 1994), p. 35, for a succinct statement of a widely held position.

[33] This imagery is commonly used of Israel elsewhere in the Old Testament; cf. Exod. 4.22f. ('son'), Deut. 14.1 ('sons'). A highly suggestive penetration of the significance of the imagery is Jon D. Levenson, *Death and Resurrection*.

in some way partakes of the nature of the divine parent, in this instance in terms of holiness. The problem, however, is that Israel fails to realise in its life that which it intrinsically is through its generative divine vocation – it fails to live in a holy way, as its God is holy (cf. Lev. 19.2). Israel has become unclean (Isa. 6.5), and so needs God's purifying fire to engender holiness. The note is not therefore hopeful in the sense that it already envisages Israel as made holy by God's purifying acts (vv. 11–13bα) and so able to grow again from a stump into a tree. Rather, because YHWH is holy, and because Israel is intrinsically holy, but fails in practice to be holy, the text pictures purification as in effect also intrinsic to the relationship between YHWH and Israel, and as such a poten-tially unceasing process. In its own way, however, it is hopeful, for it presupposes YHWH transforming Israel into that which it is meant to be (as metal that is purified becomes the strongest and most serviceable), and Isaiah's own words after the red-hot coal and the divine invitation demonstrate the reality of positive response to YHWH.[34]

Fourthly, two partial parallels from elsewhere in the Old Testament may illuminate something of the dynamics of Isaiah 6.9–13. First, there is Joshua's challenge to Israel in Joshua 24.19–20. After Joshua's strong initial challenge to Israel to serve YHWH as he, Joshua, does and will do (24.1–15, esp. 14–15), Israel respond positively in unreserved terms, 'Far be it from us to turn away from YHWH ... we too will serve YHWH' (24.16–18). That might appear to be all that is necessary to conclude matters. But it is not. Joshua rejects the people's words (24.19–20). The words sound plausible and genuine, and may even be well-intentioned, but Joshua sees them as superficial in relation to what is actually involved in faithfulness to YHWH. Israel 'cannot' (*lo' tuk^elu*) serve YHWH, first because he is a holy God (*^elohim q^edošim hu'*), secondly because he is a

---

[34] One obvious question concerns how my proposed interpretation relates to the 'remnant' (*š'r*) elsewhere in Isaiah. I would suggest that my reading is compatible with whatever shape Isaiah's understanding of 'remnant' is thought to take. For if v. 13bβ does not picture a 'remnant' in quite the way that is usually supposed, the way the text neither envisages nor rules out a 'remnant' remains congruous with that hope for the future which 'remnant' may express.

jealous God (again, the language of Sinai, esp. Exod. 34.14) and thirdly because he will not forgive Israel's sins – if the people of Israel are unfaithful to YHWH then he will destroy them. Israel then affirm their loyalty to YHWH nonetheless (v. 21). Joshua then reminds them of the binding nature of their commitment, for those witnesses who will be able to testify and hold them to their commitment are they themselves (v. 22a). When the people accept this (v. 22b), Joshua finally challenges the people actually to remove foreign deities and to adhere to YHWH alone (v. 23). Only when the people again respond affirmatively (v. 24) does Joshua make the covenant. The narrator subsequently notes that Israel's serving YHWH was of significant duration (v. 31).

Three features of this are particularly significant for our discussion. First, the recognition of the complexity of true turning to YHWH, not least because (in modern terms) the subconscious or only partially conscious complexities of the human personality may be at odds with its conscious intentions. Secondly, the appeal to YHWH's holiness as a reason for rejecting a turning to YHWH which is judged to be superficial. Thirdly, the rhetorical freedom with which basic axioms (Israel's ability to serve YHWH, YHWH's mercy towards sinful Israel)[35] may be denied, not so as really to deny them but so as to generate a deeper awareness of the seriousness of the issues at stake and a correspondingly more genuine responsiveness to God. There are, I suggest, parallels to all these in Isaiah 6.9ff.

The other Old Testament parallel is Zechariah 13.7–9. This is a mysterious and difficult passage in many ways, with unresolved questions both as to its literary context,[36] and in relation to its historical context of origin, an issue bound up with the identity of the shepherd who is to be struck down. For our purposes what matters is the actual depiction of the text. First, a sword striking down the shepherd is seen as preliminary

---

[35] These are axioms within the book of Deuteronomy (e.g. 30.11–14; 9.4–10.22), whose language and assumptions are in significant ways adopted within Joshua 24.

[36] How should one understand Zech. 13.7–9 in its present context in relation to 13.2–6; 14.1ff.? How does it relate to the obviously associated passage in 11.17? How should one evaluate the frequently proposed textual relocation of 13.7–9 to immediate proximity to 11.17?

to God's action against the sheep/little ones, i.e., against a people as a whole apart from their leader. The action is clearly of hostile import, from the fact that two-thirds of those in the land will perish – where presumably the depredations of a victorious invading army (who wield the sword which strikes the shepherd) are the outworking of God's hand turned against the sheep. This is a picture of great devastation and destruction. Yet things do not end here. On the contrary, the text may imply that it is only now that the purifying action of God really begins to take effect. For the third which survives is now to be subjected to refining, just as silver and gold are refined, a process which takes place 'in the fire' (*ba'eš*).[37] This may well imply that what happens to the surviving third is even more severe than what happened to the two-thirds. As such it could seem to envisage annihilation. Yet the text is clear that it is not annihilation but purification that is the purpose of it all, with the end result of a restored relationship of covenantal mutuality between YHWH and his people.

The significance of Zechariah 13.7–9 for Isaiah 6.9ff. is twofold. On the one hand, there is a picture of divine action in relation to people which initially sounds solely destructive, but which is clearly understood as beneficial because purifying. On the other hand, it is a process which continues, even intensifies, at just the point where one might suppose that the initial purpose had already been accomplished. As such it seems to presuppose the kind of problematic dynamics of human turning to God which characterises also Isaiah 6.

Conclusion

As we have seen, holiness is a basic concern of Isaiah 6. The seraphim proclaim YHWH's holiness at the beginning, Israel is characterised as YHWH's holy offspring at the end, and the content in between depicts a searing purifying process to transform those of unclean lips into those who embody that

[37] The symbolic resonances of 'fire' are many. In addition to its symbolising affliction (cf. Zech. 3.2; Isa. 43.2), it also symbolises the presence of YHWH (Exod. 3.2; 19.18), and in a context such as this it may well be that both symbolisms are implicit.

holiness which is intrinsically theirs as the people of YHWH. This process achieves its goal with Isaiah himself. How and in what way Isaiah's words will achieve the further goal for the people is not specified, although the rest of the book regularly returns to this issue in one way or another. It is noteworthy that the particular moral aspect of holiness which is characteristic of Isaiah, that is the realisation of holiness in the practice of justice and righteousness (5.16), is not as such central, for the emphasis rather is on the purifying process necessary to make justice and righteousness truly characteristic of the life of Israel. But the combination of purifying process with resultant justice is itself a characteristic Isaianic linkage.

The implied understanding of Israel as God's people holds two features in tension. On the one hand, if a human community is to be refined, the basic assumption is hopeful. Israel's life is a mixture of pure and impure, in which it is possible for the dross to be burnt away and that which remains to become truly itself and of most value. On the other hand, there is nothing facile about the hope, for it is dullness, not readiness, of response which features prominently in the text, apart from Isaiah himself. If holiness is to be achieved, so that the people of YHWH become like their God, it will be through a process demanding and problematic beyond normal imagining.

However, it is the majesty of YHWH which is the prime image in the text, and his holiness is a corollary of that majesty. What this surely means, among other things, is that the sovereignty of God is intrinsically directed towards the transformation of his people so that they display his own characteristics; and it means that the power and purpose to bring about that transformation is as limitless as the divine sovereignty, even if the means adopted may often appear ineffective or even counter-productive.

To conclude. The text of Isaiah 6 is hardly 'Bright the vision that delighted / Once the sight of Judah's seer', for its imagery is fearful and unsparing and its tenor rather 'I tell you naught for your comfort.' Yet the majesty of God is revealed and his holiness proclaimed so that his people may become what they have already been called to be. If the imagery makes no concessions, it also thereby encourages readers to suppose that here they encounter no pretext or pretence, but rather truth about

God and themselves. Those who today seek truth, and who are open to recognising in the Hebrew Scriptures an enduring critical witness to the nature of God and of humanity, could well ask themselves whether that which the text envisages may yet remain true even when the Jerusalem temple and its symbols have passed away. Within a Christian context, T. S. Eliot gives incomparable expression to what I have argued to be the central concern of Isaiah 6, in part IV of *Little Gidding*:

> The dove descending breaks the air
> With flame of incandescent terror
> Of which the tongues declare
> The one discharge from sin and error.
> The only hope, or else despair
>   Lies in the choice of pyre or pyre —
>   To be redeemed from fire by fire.
>
> Who then devised the torment? Love.
> Love is the unfamiliar Name
> Behind the hands that wove
> The intolerable shirt of flame
> Which human power cannot remove.
>   We only live, only suspire,
>   Consumed by either fire or fire.[38]

[38] I am grateful to the Durham Old Testament postgraduate seminar, and also to Prof. Chris Seitz, for many suggestions and comments upon a draft of this paper, which have led to its improvement.

7

The Sanctification of Time in the Second Temple Period: Case Studies in the Septuagint and Jubilees

Robert Hayward

Introduction

It is a striking fact that the first occasion on which the Hebrew Bible speaks of something being holy or sanctified, using the common Hebrew root *qdš*, is with reference to the sacred time of the Sabbath day. The passage in question is the famous verse Genesis 2.3, which tells how, after completing the works of the six days of creation and resting on the seventh day, God blessed that same seventh day and sanctified it, because he had rested from all his work. As far as the Hebrew Bible is concerned, therefore, the sanctification of time takes precedence over the sanctification of space (e.g., the Temple), of objects (e.g., the altar, Temple furniture and holy vessels), and of persons (e.g., priests or Levites).[1] If we read the Hebrew Bible as a straightforward narrative, this precedence of the sanctification of time is quite literally perceived in historic time; for it is only many generations after the days of creation that we next find the Bible using

---

[1] On holiness in the Hebrew Bible, see particularly J. Milgrom, *Leviticus 1–16. A New Translation with Introduction and Commentary*, Anchor Bible 3 (New York: Doubleday, 1991), pp. 729–34. Milgrom will offer an extended discussion of the notion in the second part of this same commentary (forthcoming). He also discusses the term 'sanctification' in Excursus 27 of *The JPS Torah Commentary. Numbers* (Philadelphia/New York: Jewish Publication Society, 5750/1991), pp. 384–6.

the root *qdš* in any form, and that with regard to the 'holy
ground' where Moses stood gazing in awe at the burning bush
(Exod. 3.5).[2] Indeed, we have to read further into Exodus before
we encounter another sanctified time, that of the Pesah (12.16);
and only with Exodus 19.6 do we encounter the command that
persons, namely the house of Jacob, the sons of Israel, are to be
'a kingdom of priests and a holy nation' (Exod. 19.3, 6). This
'time gap', as it were, between the command to sanctify the
Sabbath given at the beginning of history, and the designation of
Pesah as a holy season in the time of the Exodus, presented
ancient exegetes with pressing questions. Had time been
sanctified in the period between Adam and Moses, and, if it had
been, who had sanctified it, in what ways, and by what authority?

The Bible, however, feels it necessary to express the priority
of sanctified time in more sophisticated ways as well. Exodus
31.12–17 sets out detailed commandments for the observance
of the Sabbath in a compact and carefully constructed section
of text which stands as the seventh and final set of instructions
concerning the sanctified place of Israel's worship, the
Tabernacle. The six preceding sets of instructions all relate to
the Tabernacle: its altar of incense (Exod. 30.1–10); the half-
shekel Temple levy (30.11–16); the laver (30.17–21); the
anointing oil (30.22–33); the incense (30.34–8); and those
responsible for building the shrine (31.1–11). As Nahum Sarna
points out, when Exodus once again takes up the story of the
construction of the Tabernacle, it begins with a reiteration of
the law of Sabbath (Exod. 35.1–3). We can do no better than to
rehearse his own appreciation of this literary structure, which,
he says,

> is intended to make an emphatic statement about the
> hierarchy of values that informs the Torah: the Tabernacle
> enshrines the concept of holiness of space; the Sabbath
> embodies the concept of the holiness of time. The latter
> takes precedence over the former, and the work of the
> Tabernacle must yield each week to the Sabbath rest.[3]

[2] The root *qdš* appears as a place-name Qadesh at Gen. 14.7; cf. Gen. 16.14;
20.1, where we find Qadesh-Barnea, but these verses seem devoid of religious
overtones or significance.

[3] See N. Sarna, *The JPS Torah Commentary. Exodus* (Philadelphia/New York:
Jewish Publication Society, 5751/1991), p. 201.

It would be difficult to exaggerate the enormous support which the Bible's emphasis on the pre-eminence of sanctified time must have given to Jews in the Diaspora. Throughout the period of the Second Temple, millions of Jews, indeed the majority of the Jewish people, lived outside the boundaries of the Holy Land, and had only limited access to the sanctified ground of the Temple in Jerusalem. For these Jews in particular, sacred time, and the process of the sanctification of time, saw in truth a 'God send'. Through careful observance of the Sabbath and the festivals, they could still participate in the sanctification of time, even though they might be unable to bring the requisite sacrifices or to carry out the ceremonies whose performance was restricted to the Temple and its courts.[4]

There was yet another important respect in which the sanctification of time, as set forth in the biblical record, was to prove a powerful influence on both Diaspora Jews and on those resident in the Land of Israel. The sacred times which the Bible orders for observation are all of them concerned with the ordered progress of the year through its seasons, as week succeeds week with its regularly occurring Sabbath; as month succeeds month with its regularly observed new moon day (see Num. 28.11–15); as season succeeds season as God promised in his covenant with Noah (Gen. 8.22; cf. Jer. 5.24); and as the three great Festivals speak of spring, summer and autumn. All biblical sacred time speaks of the *order* in creation; the three great festivals also bring to Israel's attention the fruits of that created order which give sustenance to human beings. Thus Pesah-Mazzoth occurs at the time of the barley harvest, the first sheaf of barley being offered to the Lord on the day following Pesah (see Lev. 23.4–14; cf. Exod. 23.15); Shavu'oth or

---

[4] On the importance of Sabbath and Festivals among faithful Jews of the Diaspora, see E. Schürer, *The History of the Jewish People in the Age of Jesus Christ*, vol. III.1, rev. and ed. G. Vermes, F. Millar and M. Goodman (Edinburgh: T&T Clark, 1986), pp. 140–5, and literature there cited. A valuable collection of literary, papyrological and inscriptional evidence regarding observance of Sabbath and festivals in the Diaspora from Second Temple times and later is now available in M. H. Williams, *The Jews among the Greeks and Romans: A Diasporan Sourcebook* (London: Duckworth, 1988): see index under 'fasts, feasts and festivals' and 'Sabbath, Sabbatical Year'.

Pentecost, fifty days after the offering of the `omer (barley sheaf), coincides with the wheat harvest, and wheaten loaves are offered (Lev. 23.17; cf. Num. 28.26–31); Sukkoth falls at the time of the vintage and the harvest of autumn fruits (Lev. 23.33–6). The sacred times of the Jewish calendar thus have a universal significance, demonstrating God's ordered design of the world and his continuing involvement in it, and his ceaseless goodness in providing human beings with food. Proper observance of these sacred times, in whatever place a Jew might happen to be, constitutes the due response of the creature to the creator of all things. Philo of Alexandria, that greatest of Jewish Diaspora philosophers, was never to tire of pointing this out; and it was he more than anyone else in Second Temple times who insisted that the Jewish people, by duly observing their sacred times, rendered back to the creator the gratitude which was due to him from the whole human race. In this sense, Philo was wont to argue, the Jews are the priestly race of humanity, keeping sacred time and giving thanks to God on behalf of the race of men.[5]

The links which the Bible establishes between sacred time and the created order, however, do not exhaust what it has to say about the meaning of sacred time as such. For the sanctification of time, or at least the sanctification of some particular times, is inextricably bound up with the history of Israel as a people. Thus Pesah and the seven days of Mazzoth year by year represent Israel's going forth from slavery in Egypt, the affliction they endured before that Exodus, their preservation from the last plague against Egypt, and the great miracle at the Red Sea which brought about their redemption (Exod. 12.21–8, 34, 39–42). At Sukkoth, Jews are to live in temporary huts or booths, so that they may know how God made Israel dwell in booths when he brought them out of Egypt (Lev. 23.42–3).

Although Shavu`oth is not named in Exodus 19.1, we read that in the third month, which is the month of that festival, the

---

[5] See Philo, *De Sac* 63; *De Mig. Abr.* 91–2; *Quis Rerum* 226; *De Spec. Leg.* I. 97; II. 162–170; cf. *De Vita Mosis* II. 133–5; and discussion in J. Laporte, *Eucharistia in Philo*, Studies in the Bible and Early Christianity 3 (Toronto: Edwin Mellen, 1983).

Israelites assembled at Sinai to receive the Torah: later generations of Jews, represented by the Chronicler (2 Chron. 15.10),
were to associate this third month with a renewal of a covenant,
of which more must be said below. Even the Sabbath itself
might be linked to the particular history of Israel, according to
Exodus 31.12–17, in that it is a perpetual sign between God *and
Israel* that in six days God made heaven and earth, the historical
aspects of that sign being markedly to the fore (Exod.
31.16–17).

This tendency of the Bible to relate the sanctification of time
to events or periods in Israel's history, however, remains for the
biblical writers precisely that – a tendency. Many of the sacred
times are not at all said to carry with them the recollection of
some historical happening. Thus the new moon days, the
eighth-day celebration following Sukkoth known as Shemini
`Atzeret, New Year's Day itself (Rosh Ha-Shanah) and
the holiest of all days, Yom Kippur, are not associated by the
biblical writers with historical events in the life of the Jewish
people. Despite what was noted about Shavu`oth in the
preceding paragraph, it is not at all certain that the festival was
linked with the giving of the Torah in biblical times, even
though the Chronicler's note is suggestive, and commentators
suggest that that author had Pentecost in mind as the time
when King Asa ordered a renewal of the covenant.[6]
Nevertheless, this recorded tendency of the biblical writers to
bring the sanctification of some particular times into association with episodes in Israel's history was not lost on later
interpreters; and one of the characteristic developments in the
Second Temple Period of Jewish understanding of sacred time
consists precisely in the extension of this biblical tendency to
relate holy time to history.

What has been said so far makes up a necessary introduction
to the substance of this paper, which will consider in detail two
literary productions of the Second Temple Period and their
distinctive religious attitudes to the sanctification of time. The

---

[6] *Possibly* the Chronicler implies that the renewal of a covenant in King Asa's
reign (2 Chron. 15.10) took place on the Feast of Shavu`oth; but it is not clear
which particular covenant is being renewed, and the Giving of the Law may
not be in mind at all: see S. Japhet, *I and II Chronicles. A Commentary* (London:
SCM, 1993), pp. 724–5.

second of these writings, the *Book of Jubilees*, received its final redaction in the Land of Israel around the middle of the second century BCE, and represents a major rewriting of Genesis and Exodus 1—20. No serious student of this book doubts that it has quite definite views on time and its sanctification, which its author takes some pains to make clear.[7] The first document to be considered, the Septuagint Pentateuch, is the work of Diaspora Jews, probably resident in Alexandria, translating the Hebrew Torah of Moses into Greek.[8] Although the Septuagint is still best known, and most often used, in inter-textual criticism of the Hebrew Bible, it should not be forgotten that what the Egyptian-Jewish translators of the third century BCE effected was, in the words of John W. Wevers, 'the earliest exegetical source that we have for understanding the Pentateuch'. Consequently, he continues, the Septuagint should be 'the first document to which one turns when trying to understand the Torah'.[9] In this paper, then, our main concern will not be text-critical, evaluating LXX readings in the light of the Hebrew MT and Qumran biblical texts, and vice-versa; rather, the evidence of the LXX in its own right will make up our object of study. To put matters more simply: we shall attempt to put ourselves in the place of Greek-speaking Jews who knew little or no Hebrew as they read their Septuagint, and ask what they may have made of the Greek text that confronted them. We shall find that the translation itself had created a dynamic with regard to sacred time which some, at least, felt compelled to develop along quite individual lines.

---

[7] For discussion of the date and composition of Jubilees, see G. W. E. Nickelsburg, *Jewish Literature between the Bible and the Mishnah* (London: SCM, 1981), pp. 78–9; J. VanderKam, 'The Putative Author of the Book of Jubilees', *Journal of Semitic Studies* 26 (1981), pp. 202–17.

[8] For the dates and provenance of the Greek translations of the Pentateuchal books and the Prophets, see E. Tov, *Textual Criticism of the Hebrew Bible* (Assen: Van Gorcum, 1992), pp. 136–7; E. Schürer, *The History of the Jewish People*, vol. III.1, pp. 474–93; and especially M. Harl, G. Dorival and O. Munnich, *La Bible Grecque des Septante. Du Judaïsme hellénistique au Christianisme ancien* (Paris: Cerf, 1988), pp. 83–111.

[9] See John W. Wevers, *Notes on the Greek Text of Genesis*, Septuagint and Cognate Studies 35 (Atlanta: Scholars Press, 1993), pp. xiv–xv.

The Septuagint and the Hellenisation of Time

While the Greek-speaking world which nourished Egyptian Jewry was in many respects *sui generis*, the overwhelming importance over it of imported Greek traditions, institutions and religion cannot be denied. Once the dynasty of the Ptolemies had been established, the Greek language and Greek customs had naturally come to dominate native Egyptian culture; and the Jews, particularly those settled in Alexandria, were inevitably going to be conscious of the power of Hellenism and of the Greek-speaking court with its complex system of royal administrators.[10] The Greek conquerors, too, naturally felt bound to transplant into their newly acquired territory of Egypt fundamental Greek institutions such as the gymnasium and its ephebate, and the ever-popular dramatic entertainments of tragic and comic plays. Presiding over all these things were the Greek gods, at whose regularly recurring festivals, and in whose honour, were celebrated games and athletic contests, often enhanced by the performances of tragic plays celebrating the heroes of Greek epic and the glorious past of the Hellenes. Indeed, it seems that the Ptolemies and the administrators of Alexandria were especially keen to encourage drama in its various forms.[11] Although little remains to the present day in the way of Greek-Egyptian dramatic literature (with one notable exception, as we shall see presently), the names of dramatists are known, and it appears that their work was highly regarded in antiquity – the group known as the Alexandrian Pleiad being famed particularly for its tragedies.[12]

---

[10] The standard work on the history, culture and society of Alexandria in the Greek period is P. M. Fraser's *Ptolemaic Alexandria*, 3 vols. (Oxford: Clarendon Press, 1972). He discusses the literature associated with that city, which will particularly concern this essay, in vol. 1, pp. 495–716. For a succinct, but scholarly account of Ptolemaic Alexandria and the Jews, see Martin Hengel, *Judaism and Hellenism*, 2 vols. (London: SCM, 1974), particularly vol. 1, pp. 35–57, 65–70, and his comments on LXX in vol. 1, pp. 100–2.

[11] See the evidence collected and discussed by Fraser, *Ptolemaic Alexandria*, vol. 1, pp. 618–22; vol. 2, pp. 870–9.

[12] This literary Pleiad included at least eight names in its number, even though the constellation known as the Pleiades has only seven stars. Most of the writers in this group wrote tragedies, but very little of their work survives, and information about them is scanty. They seem to have flourished in the early to mid-third century BCE. For the little known about them, see Fraser, *Ptolemaic Alexandria*, vol. 1, pp. 619–20, and vol. 2, pp. 871–4.

Given all this, it is of some interest to record that the translators of the LXX Pentateuch were not averse to making
occasional, but telling, use of technical terms which were used
in classical and later Greek formally to refer to the constituent
elements of tragic and comic plays; and these the translators
used with particular reference to certain Jewish festival days,
that is, with reference to sanctified time. The first of these terms
to be considered here is the word *exodion*, which was used to
speak of the concluding section of a tragic play immediately
preceding the departure of the players from the stage. The
word signifies a 'finale', the part of the play in which the
dramatic action is brought to a fitting and satisfactory
conclusion. Such is its general and common meaning. Other
senses attested in the lexicon are 'gateway' and 'outgoing'; but
the connection of the word with the drama is primary and
assured.[13] Strikingly, it is this word which the translators of LXX
chose to render the Hebrew technical expression `atzereth` on
the three occasions it appears in the Pentateuch, at Leviticus
23.36, Numbers 29.35 and Deuteronomy 16.8. The Hebrew
word itself has been the subject of considerable discussion; in
the light of this, most students understand it to signify 'solemn
religious assembly'.[14] The biblical Hebrew verb *ātzar*, however,
has the sense of 'retain, shut up', suggesting the meaning
'conclude', thus it is hardly surprising that, in Rabbinic
Hebrew, `atzereth` comes to mean specifically a 'concluding
festival', and it is most probable that the LXX translators of the
Pentateuch had in mind this sense of the word when they translated it as *exodion*.[15]

---

[13] For the dictionary definition, see H. G. Liddell and R. Scott, *A
Greek–English Lexicon*, revised and augmented by H. Stuart Jones and R.
McKenzie (Oxford: Clarendon Press, 1996), p. 596, with entry in Supplement,
p. 121 emending entry on use of the word by LXX, such that it is given as
'outgoing, terminating day of feast'. The meaning 'gateway' is found in Pap.
Oxy. 243. 16. While it might be suggested that LXX, by using *exodion* to render
`atzereth`, have managed to invest the Greek with some new significance, it
remains most likely that readers of that version who knew Greek but not
Hebrew would, in the first instance of seeing it, associate the word with
dramatic performances.

[14] See J. Milgrom, *The JPS Torah Commentary. Numbers*, p. 249.

[15] See *b. Hag* 18a. In early Rabbinic parlance generally, however, the term
was often applied without further specification to Shavu'oth: e.g., *m. RH* 1.2;

To a reader of the Pentateuch whose first and main language was Greek, however, *exodion* could hardly fail to be redolent of the drama. In the case of its use in Deuteronomy 16.8, the LXX speak of the concluding seventh day of the Mazzoth festival as an *exodion* – this day forming the conclusion of the Passover celebrations of God's redemption of the people from Egypt. There is nothing strange in considering the Pesah, its attendant ceremonies, and the great events which it recalls, as a drama. It might even be said to invite such a description, since the events accompanying Israel's deliverance from the pursuing army of Pharaoh were celebrated in a grand poem, lofty in theme, elevated in style. The Hebrew Bible calls this 'Song at the Sea' simply *haššîrāh*, 'The Song' (Exod. 15.1); and the LXX took the opportunity to declare that Miriam and her companions joined in it *meta tumpanōn kai chorōn*, literally 'with drums and choruses'. There can be no word more likely to be associated with the drama, in the mind of anyone imbued with the culture of the Greeks, than 'chorus'. Without the chorus and its stately dance accompanying the verse-form appropriate to the theme of a particular play, there could be no drama: the chorus, in many respects, makes up the 'meat' of the play, commenting throughout on the actions and dispositions of the main characters. Now LXX of the Pentateuch use the word twice only: Exodus 15.20, to describe the poetry and accompanying dance of those singing 'The Song', and during the episode of the calf (Exod. 32.19), when a ghastly parody of the celebrations at the Red Sea was undertaken in the name of something falsely supposed to have 'brought Israel up out of Egypt' (Exod. 32.4). We may leave aside this later episode, even though it confirms in a backhanded kind of way the translators' notion of chorus as particularly appropriate to a commemoration of the Exodus. It is 'The Song' itself which should claim attention, since almost in the manner of a Greek choral ode it describes the actions, emotions and consequences of those involved in the experience at the Red Sea. The Bible furthermore indicates that Moses and the Israelites sang the poem, and were 'answered' by Miriam in another song (Exod.

Meg. 3.5; *Sheb.* 1.1; 2.1; *Bikk.* 1.3, 6, 10, a usage already attested to by Josephus, *Antiquities* III.252; *Targum Neofiti* Exod. 34.22; Deut. 16.10.

15.22): in this way we are to envisage, perhaps, a double chorus, of the sort familiar also from Greek tragic plays.[16] Those so inclined might be able to discern here strophe and antistrophe, as now one, now another group of singers moved to and fro in solemn choreography.

At this point it should be noted that the Hebrew Bible speaks, on a number of occasions, of 'doing' or 'performing' the Pesah, using the common verb `asāh (e.g., Exod. 12.47, 48; Deut. 16.1). LXX invariably translated this verb with the equally common Greek *poiein*. Unlike its Hebrew counterpart, however, the Greek can have the sense of 'perform, put on a dramatic production'. The verb is used of celebrating Mazzoth at LXX Exodus 23.15, where it lacks any equivalent in the corresponding Hebrew text. Taken on its own, this information may not mean much; but it should not be forgotten that the LXX translators will have been aware of the musical performances explicitly tied to Pesah by the Chronicler (2 Chron. 29.25–30; 35.15), and emphasised at 2 Chronicles 30.21, where we read that the priests and Levites praised the Lord day by day throughout the time of Pesah and the seven days of Mazzoth, singing with mighty instruments to the Lord.[17] This choral aspect of the festival, which, strikingly, is not subject of any explicit command in the Pentateuch, heightens its dramatic character, and there is little doubt that such musical performances of which the Chronicler was a witness were continued into the days of the LXX translators and beyond, since Jubilees 49.6 takes for granted, without any discussion, a musical dimension to the festival.[18]

---

[16] LXX use the word *choros* also at Ps. 149.3 and 150.4 in the setting of the worship of God. Later on, Philo was to make much of the chorus at the Exodus and the song which was sung by two groups, one of men, the other of women: see his description of the 'fiftieth day festival' celebrated by the Egyptian Therapeute, *De Vita Cont.* 83–8, and cf. *De Vita Mos.* I. 180; II. 256–7.

[17] On the supposed textual difficulty in 2 Chron. 30.21, see Japhet, *I and II Chronicles*, p. 954, who (rightly in our view) defends the reading of the Masoretic text 'with powerful instruments' as making good sense and not requiring emendation. For the use of psalms and music at Pesah in the time of the Chronicler, see further J. B. Segal, *The Hebrew Passover* (Oxford: Oxford University Press, 1963), pp. 227–30.

[18] 'And all Israel was eating the flesh of the paschal lamb, and drinking the wine, and was lauding and blessing, and giving thanks to the Lord God of their

Yet another aspect of Pesah which might be held to heighten the dramatic nature of the festival is the character of the meal which is an integral part of it. Already the Bible itself envisaged children asking to know what the rite might signify (Exod. 12.26), and it was from this biblical question and its answer that there developed, in the course of time, a domestic drama involving dialogue between the head of the household and other participants in the service. This is not the place to discuss the origins and development of the Passover Haggadah or the Seder meal; but it should be noted that some element of question and answer, or of ritualised dialogue, was implicit from the beginning in the biblical injunctions for the festival.[19] These also include the famous and specific command to a father to 'declare' to his son that Pesah is being celebrated and mazzoth eaten because of what the Lord did for him in Egypt (Exod. 13.8). In the Diaspora particularly, where Pesah would be observed without the Temple service and the sacrificed lamb, a development and expansion of a ritual dialogue between the head of household and his fellow diners was almost inevitable.[20] Underlying all the biblical commandments about Pesah is the conviction that this festival, *par excellence,* encapsulates fundamental national experiences which every Jew is under an obligation to appropriate and to make his own. Rabban Gamaliel's famous comment on Exod. 13.8 in *m. Pes.* 10.5 (itself spoken at the Seder meal) – that in every generation a man must consider himself as if he had gone forth from Egypt – represents a faithful distillation of what the Bible has to say of

---

fathers ...': translated by R. H. Charles, *The Book of Jubilees* (London: Black, 1902), p. 254.

[19] On the history and development of the Passover Haggadah and Seder, see A. Z. Idelsohn, *Jewish Liturgy and its Development* (New York: Schocken, 1960), pp. 173–87; J. Tabory, 'The Passover Eve Ceremony – An Historical Outline', *Immanuel* 12 (1981), pp. 32–43; Baruch M. Bokser, *The Origins of the Seder: The Passover Rite and Early Rabbinic Judaism* (Berkeley: University of California Press, 1984).

[20] See also Exod. 12.26, where children are envisaged as asking: 'What mean ye by this service?' and the formal answer set out in the following verse. Whereas MS of Exod 12.26 reads literally 'What is this service to you?', LXX significantly make the children ask only 'What is this service?' *tout court.* The latter demands a formal explanation of the rite itself, rather than a meditation on it.

the festival's meaning when it comes to Jewish identity: the law of Numbers 9.13, that a man who fails to observe Pesah brings upon himself the penalty of *kārēth* ('then that soul shall be cut off from its people'), makes the same point in a negative fashion. The observation of this festival, and the business of being a Jew, are inseparable, both in biblical and Rabbinic law.

Given all this, it is not difficult to understand how Pesah in particular might be regarded as the celebration of a national epic. That it was so regarded in some educated Jewish circles of the Egyptian Diaspora is incontestable, because the story of Pesah and the deliverance of the Jews from Egypt was turned into a Greek tragedy, substantial fragments of which survive. The author of this play was one Ezekiel, often referred to as 'the Jewish tragedian': although little is known of his life, it seems probable that he lived and wrote in Alexandria sometime in the second century BCE.[21] The evidence of the LXX, which has been surveyed briefly here, is far too fragmentary to provide the basis of an argument that the translators of that version themselves thought of the biblical events, and the festival of Pesah, as a tragic drama. But the language which they had used at key points might be construed by readers as an invitation to look upon things in such a way. Perhaps Ezekiel the Tragedian did that very thing. In any event, his work offers a vivid demonstration of how some Diaspora Jews, at least, had come to understand the sanctified time of the Passover and Unleavened Bread in terms quite different from anything set forth explicitly by the Hebrew Bible itself. In Ezekiel's Hellenistic drama, the very events celebrated at length in the Pesah ceremonies and the following seven days of Mazzoth are made into the subject of a play, in much the same way as grand events in the past of the Greeks and other nations had already begun to provide topics for tragic dramas in Ptolemaic Alexandria.

From the classical period of Greek tragedy, the *Persae* of Aeschylus is perhaps the only play to leave the realms of myth

---

[21] See H. Jacobson, *The* Exagoge *of Ezekiel* (Cambridge: Cambridge University Press, 1983), pp. 1–16; R. G. Robertson, 'Ezekiel the Tragedian', in J. H. Charlesworth, ed., *The Old Testament Pseudepigrapha*, vol. 2 (London: Darton, Longman & Todd, 1985), pp. 803–7.

to celebrate an historical happening.[22] It is certainly the best-known play of this kind. But the plays of the Alexandrian Pleiad, that group of dramatists spoken of earlier, very often dealt with historical events and epic happenings;[23] and on any showing, the story of the Jews' oppression in Egypt and their subsequent deliverance is an epic theme. As to the time when this play might have been performed, we need only remind ourselves that, in the Greek-speaking culture which nurtured Ezekiel, the production of plays was invariably associated with the festival of some deity or another.

Evidence that Jews in the Egyptian Diaspora were able to consider their national history recorded in the Pentateuch as a kind of drama is not confined to the work of Ezekiel. It is evident that some Gentile dignitaries were sympathetic to such Jewish efforts, and encouraged them. Thus we read in the *Epistle of Aristeas,* a work of uncertain date (but most likely written sometime in the second century BCE),[24] that when King Ptolemy read the Greek Pentateuch for the first time, he exclaimed:

> How is it that after such great works were (originally) completed, none of the historians or poets took it upon himself to refer to them? (*Arist.* 312)

He receives the reply that the laws are holy, and come from God; and that those who attempted to represent them in some other way inevitably came to a bad end. In particular, a tragic

---

[22] Convincing evidence for Ezekiel's familiarity with the plays of Aeschylus, with the *Persae* and *Supplices* in particular, and with other classical and Hellenistic plays of an historical-epic character, is considered in detail by Jacobson, *The* Exagoge, pp. 23–8.

[23] Thus the poet Lycophron wrote a play about historical events which took place in the city of Cassandrea, which was built in the year 310 BCE: see Fraser, *Ptolemaic Alexandria*, vol. 1, p. 619.

[24] The author of *Aristeas* is generally said by students of the work to have been an Egyptian Jew, probably resident in Alexandria; the dating of his work, however, is beset with problems, although some time in the second century BCE seems possible for its production. For provenance, authorship and date, see the comprehensive discussion in Schürer, *History of the Jewish People*, vol. III. 1, pp. 677–87, and literature there cited; A. Pelletier, *Lettre d'Aristée à Philocrate*, Sources Chrétiennes 89 (Paris: Cerf, 1962), pp. 56ff.; R. J. H. Shutt, 'Letter of Aristeas' in J. H. Charlesworth, ed., *Old Testament Pseudepigrapha*, vol. 2, pp. 7–11.

poet named Theodectus declared that, when he had attempted to include a biblical passage in a play that he was writing, he was smitten with cataract of the eyes and became blind, and recovered only after sustained prayer to God (*Arist.* 314–316).

At the very least, these words suggest that the use of biblical themes for dramatic purposes was not confined to the work of Ezekiel the Tragedian;[25] we may perhaps sense, informing the words attributed to King Ptolemy, a hint that dramatic presentation of biblical events might serve to promote Jewish interests in a cultural environment that was far from hostile towards that people and its laws. As an apologetic device, there can be little doubt that public recognition among Greeks that Jews had a history and a set of traditions worthy of proclamation in festival drama would be enormously effective.[26] And as we have seen, some of the language of the LXX relating to festivals, especially to the Pesah and Mazzoth, lent itself to this development in a natural and unforced manner.

One further episode in Israel's history as presented by the LXX requires particular attention. This is the famous encounter between Jacob and a mysterious, supernatural being at the ford of Jabboq, which resulted in the change of his name to Israel.[27] It will not be necessary here to labour the fundamental importance of names and their significance for ancient Jewry; nor need we elaborate on the specific weight which might be accorded to the name of an ancestor of a whole

[25] Jacobson, *The* Exagoge, pp. 17–20, considers in some detail the kind of audience for which Ezekiel might have written, and deals with some religious objections which ancient (and modern) Jews might present to a play of this kind.

[26] While the Greek upper classes in Egypt seem to have paid little attention to Jewish literature in the third century BCE, by the second century their estimation of the Jews and their writings had changed for the better, especially since Ptolemy VI Philometor (180–145 BCE) held the Jewish people in high regard: see Fraser, *Ptolemaic Alexandria*, vol. 1, pp. 714–15.

[27] Gen. 32.22–32; 35.9–15. See N. Sarna, *The JPS Torah Commentary. Genesis* (New York: Jewish Publication Society, 5749/1989), pp. 226–7; Excursus 24 and 25, pp. 403–5; G. Wenham, *Word Biblical Commentary 2 Genesis 16–50* (Dallas: Word Books, 1994), pp. 292–8, and literature cited there, pp. 292–3. For the development of the biblical narrative and its later interpretations, see W. T. Miller, *Mysterious Encounters at Mamre and Jabbok*, Brown Judaic Studies 50 (Chico: Scholars Press, 1984).

national group.[28] What does concern us, however, is the manner in which Jacob received this name, as the outcome of a struggle of some kind. The Bible states *wayyē 'ābēq 'ĭš 'immô 'ad 'lôt haššahar* (Gen. 32.25), which should be taken to mean that 'a man intertwined, entangled himself with him until the dawn rose'.[29] The verb *ābaq* is used only here and in the following verse in the whole Pentateuch; and its meaning is not absolutely certain. There is a noun *ābāq* meaning 'dust' (cf. Exod. 9.9; Deut. 28.24; Isa. 5.24; 29.5), which allowed Aquila, according to some manuscript witnesses, to explain the verb here as a reference to fighting men rolling in the dust by translating *ekonieto*. He has presumably linked the Hebrew verb with the better known noun meaning 'dust', which LXX themselves had rendered as *koniortos*, 'dust', on every occasion this noun is used in the Hebrew Bible. LXX, however, have translated Genesis 32.25 with the words *kai epalaien anthrōpos met 'autou heōs prōi*, 'and a man wrestled with him until early morning'. Their choice of the common verb *palaiein* is in need of explanation.

A pagan reading LXX's account of Jacob's exchange with the mysterious 'man' might easily imagine the two as engaged in a wrestling bout of a kind commonplace in his own society. Not only was wrestling an essential part of the educational curriculum offered to young men in the gymnasium; it also featured prominently in the regularly recurring athletic contests so beloved of the Greek cities. These were generally held in honour of some god or hero, and sometimes commemorated a mythical event; but they always brought great honour to the victor, who might be crowned with a laurel wreath or granted some other mark of esteem. Wrestling in athletic contests had sacral associations which could not be divorced from the cult of the god in whose honour the games were

---

[28] Cf. B. Weber, 'Nomen est Omen: Einige Erwagungen zu Gen 32.23–33 und seinem Kontext', *Biblische Notizen* 61 (1992), pp. 76–83.

[29] Such is Rashi's understanding of the root, which he associates with its Aramaic cognate on the basis of *b. Sanh.* 63b and *Men.* 42a: see M. Rosenbaum and A. M. Silbermann, *Pentateuch with Targum Onkelos, Haphtaroth and Rashi's Commentary*, 5 vols. (New York: Hebrew Publishing Company, n.d.), vol. 1, p. 159; cf. L. Koehler and W. Baumgartner, *The Hebrew and Aramaic Lexicon of the Old Testament*, rev. W. Baumgartner and J. J. Stamm (Leiden: Brill, 1994), vol. 1, p. 9.

celebrated, and the victor was thus inevitably associated with the god as his special votary or favourite. Wrestling occupied a central place in such games; and there is little doubt that LXX wished to represent Jacob as an accomplished wrestler, since they make him the subject of verbs which were used as technical terms in the sport (e.g., Gen. 27.36, *epterniken ... deuteron*).[30] They find no difficulty, therefore, in presenting the ancestor of all Jews as one skilled in the arts and sciences which Greeks looked upon as fundamental to their own civilisation; and their choice of words in describing the episode of how Jacob became Israel lay at hand for others to use, if one may so express it, in more dramatic ways. Indeed, this whole section may be summarised by saying that the LXX translators, in choosing the words they did to speak of Jacob-Israel and the festivals of Pesah and Mazzoth, opened up for future generations the possibility of presenting the early history of Israel as a great epic almost in the Greek style; the sanctified time of Pesah and Mazzoth and their ceremonies constituting a kind of dramatic representation of these set forth for public display in honour of the God of Israel.

Jubilees and the Retrieval of Time

While the translations of the LXX imply a particular relationship between the sanctified time of the festivals and wider Jewish history which appears to have been taken up and developed by later Greek-speaking Jews, the *Book of Jubilees*, in some respects, represents a vigorous reaction against that reaching out of Jews to a wider cultural world so far described in this essay. The qualification 'in some respects' is important here because, in spite of many differences, the LXX translators and Jubilees turn out, on closer inspection, to share certain common concerns. At first blush, however, it cannot be denied

---

[30] On Jewish knowledge of technical terms used by Greek athletes and competitors in the games, see H. A. Harris, *Greek Athletics and the Jews* (Cardiff: University of Wales Press, 1976); and on the specific use by LXX of terms associated with wrestling in respect of Jacob, see M. Harl, *La Bible d'Alexandrie. 1 La Genèse* (Paris: Cerf, 1994), pp. 218–19, 243.

that Jubilees seems to breathe an atmosphere quite different from LXX, Ezekiel, and the world of Alexandrian Jewry.

This is not surprising. The book was written, in part, as a protest and polemic against the agenda of those Jews and others in the Land of Israel who, from the reign of Onias III onwards, were seeking to change ancestral customs – even, perhaps, to the extent of attempting to substitute in Jerusalem a Greek constitution or a set of Greek laws for the Torah of Moses.[31] As such, it represents a powerful demand that Jews remain faithful to the commandments of the Torah, and particularly that they observe meticulously the laws regarding the sanctification of time. Its specific order that Jews adhere to a solar calendar is perhaps its best-known characteristic; for the purposes of this essay, it should be remembered that this solar calendar is no human invention, but the calendar of heaven itself, recorded on the 'heavenly tablets' (see especially Jub. 6.29–38). Failure to observe it properly is fraught with terrible consequences for Jews, who would consequently 'forget the feasts of the covenant and walk according to the feasts of the Gentiles, and show themselves equally misguided and ignorant' (Jub. 6.35).[32]

Perhaps to reinforce this basic tenet, the author further develops a tendency already noted among later biblical writers like the Chronicler, by linking every conceivable festival to an historical event: for Jubilees, these events turn out to have occurred in the lives of the Patriarchs.[33] Festivals which play a relatively minor role, or no role at all in the Bible, Jubilees

---

[31] On this particular point, see the important essay by Getzel M. Cohen, 'The Antiochenes in Jerusalem', in J. C. Reeves and J. Kampen, eds., *Pursuing the Text. Studies in honour of Ben Zion Wacholder on the Occasion of his Seventieth Birthday*, JSOTSup 184 (Sheffield: Sheffield Academic Press, 1994), pp. 243–59. On the provenance and date of Jubilees, see above, note 7. The work is sometimes defined as 'rewritten Bible': see G. W. E. Nickelsburg, 'The Bible Rewritten and Expanded' in M. E. Stone, ed., *Jewish Writings of the Second Temple Period*, CRINT section 2 (Assen: Van Gorcum, 1984), pp. 97–106; J. C. Endres, *Biblical Interpretation in the Book of Jubilees*, CBQMS 18 (Washington: Catholic Biblical Association of America, 1987).

[32] For a convenient introduction to and explication of this calendar and its major ramifications, see now J. VanderKam, *Calendars in the Dead Sea Scrolls. Measuring Time* (London: Routledge, 1998), pp. 27–33.

[33] For the wider implications of this, see G. A. Anderson, 'The Status of the Torah Before Sinai', *Dead Sea Discoveries* 1 (1994), pp. 1–29.

brings to the fore and dignifies by association with some noble ancestor. Thus Shavu'oth or Pentecost, the least emphasised of the three major biblical festivals, is elevated by Jubilees to supreme importance as the feast of the covenant, commemorating God's covenants with Noah (6.20–21), Abraham (14.20; 15.1–10) and Moses (6.11), as well as other covenants recorded in the book (e.g., 22.1; 29.1–7). Yom Kippur, the holiest of all days, is associated with Jacob, who on that day was confronted by his sons with Joseph's robe stained with goat's blood, and mourned his death (34.10–14). Rosh Ha-Shanah is a day when Jacob built an altar to God (31.3); Passover occurs when Abraham offered up his son Isaac (17.15 ff.); Tabernacles was celebrated by both Abraham (16.20–31) and Jacob (32.4–15); and the new moon days of the first, fourth, seventh and tenth months (with the exception of the seventh not otherwise singled out by the Bible for special attention), are to be observed as marking events befalling Noah and his ark (6.23–8). Towering over all these, however, is the Sabbath.[34] The author begins and ends his book with reference to it: a large section at the start of his work (2.17–33) corresponds to laws of the Sabbath which conclude Jubilees (50.6–13), and both sections are unstinting in their praise of this great day. It is 'a day of festival and a holy day: and a day of the holy kingdom for all Israel' (50.9), and the Creator of all things 'blessed this day which he had created for a blessing and sanctification and a glory above all days' (2.32).

Jubilees goes to some lengths, then, to show how the regular sanctification of time begins, not in the days of Moses, but, as far as the present world order is concerned, in the days of Noah. The universe we inhabit is founded on God's covenant with Noah made at Shavu'oth, which the author of Jubilees openly declares to be the earthly celebration of a festival celebrated in heaven from the days of creation (6.18). On the

---

[34] One of the major organising principles of Jubilees, through which its author gives a coherent account of the rationale of Festivals and Sabbaths, is the covenant: although over thirty years old, the sustained discussion of this subject by Annie Jaubert is still fundamental. See her *La Notion d'Alliance dans le Judaïsme aux abords de l'ère chrétienne* (Paris: Seuil, 1963), pp. 89–115, and cf. M. Testuz, *Les Idées religieuses du Livre des Jubilés* (Paris: Librairie Minard, 1960), pp. 140–64; for the importance of Sabbath, see Charles, *Jubilees*, pp. 17–21.

proper sanctification of this day the well-being of the whole universe depends: it is associated with a man from whom, in the last resort, the whole human race is descended. Nonetheless, the sanctification of this day is ordered to the children of Israel alone (6.22), and the other festival days come to be sanctified only with the passage of time. Thus the feast later known as Pesah and the following Mazzoth is not celebrated until Abraham's time (17.15—18.19), nor is Sukkoth (16.13–21); and Jacob is the first to mark Rosh Ha-Shanah by building an altar (31.3). The Sabbath cannot properly be celebrated on earth until certain conditions are met, as we shall see presently; for the moment, however, it is enough to observe how adroitly Jubilees has combined and developed the biblical notions that sanctified time marks the regular passage of the seasons and their gifts, and marks events in the life of the chosen people. This was so from the beginning of the present world order and, given that all time is to be measured by a calendar divinely sanctioned and observed in heaven itself, there is the underlying sense that all time is in some sense sacred for Israel, so long as this rightful calendar is followed.

It might be objected that Jubilees has more to say about sacred time as linked to events in Patriarchal history than to sacred time's importance in the general cosmic order itself. It is certainly true that this book wishes to root the sanctification of time in the very beginnings of the Jewish people, ascribing such sanctification to their pious ancestors; but this characteristic of the book is conditioned by two key considerations yet to be touched upon, namely the angels and the Sabbath. Regarding the former, Jubilees is clear that there are many different classes of angels (92.2–3), but that the two highest orders, the angels of the Presence and the angels of Sanctification, are entrusted with a heavenly service of God which is (or ideally should be) exactly parallel to Israel's earthly service (15.27–8; 31.14). Israel's service of God, therefore, is a reproduction on earth of a heavenly reality; and in no case is this more strongly marked than the Sabbath.[35]

---

[35] For a discussion of this, with bibliography, see C. T. R. Hayward, 'Heaven and Earth in Parallel: The Key role of Angels in ancient Judaism', in D. Brown and A. Loades, eds., *Christ: The Sacramental Word* (London: SPCK, 1996),

First, it should be observed that, of all celestial beings, only the angels of the Presence and the angels of Sanctification are ordered by God to keep Sabbath (2.17–18); correspondingly, Israel alone among the nations is permitted to keep Sabbath on earth (2.19–20, 31). Secondly, just as God declares this Sabbath to be blessed and holy, so he correspondingly declares that Jacob is blessed and holy (2.23–4, 28, 31–2). Third, the first Sabbath is declared after God has completed twenty-two works of creation (2.15); and Jacob correspondingly arises after twenty-two heads of humanity counting from Adam onwards (2.23). As R. H. Charles justly remarked of all this at the turn of the century, 'not till Jacob's time could the Sabbath be rightly observed on earth'.[36] The full significance of Charles's observation will be apparent when we consider what Jubilees has made of Jacob-Israel and his sanctification of the various festival days recorded in the Jubilees schema. By way of elucidation, we need to recall the simple fact that 'Israel' is to consist of twelve tribes descended from the twelve sons of Jacob whose name is changed to Israel. According to Exodus 19.4, 6, God ordered Moses to command 'the house of Jacob' and 'the sons of Israel' to be a 'kingdom of priests and a holy nation'. In the whole Pentateuch it is only in Exodus 19.4 that we find the phrases 'the house of Jacob' and 'the sons of Israel' in the same verse; in any event, the expression 'the house of Jacob' is very rarely used in the books of Moses.[37] The author of Jubilees took this biblical information very seriously when it came to defining Israel as the kingdom of priests and a holy nation.

As a consequence of his reading of Exodus 19.4, that writer was convinced that it was impossible to speak of Israel until 'the house of Jacob' was complete: in other words, only when the birth of Benjamin, Jacob's youngest son, is assured and imminent, will Jubilees countenance the change of Jacob's name to Israel, and envisage the emergence in history of the 'kingdom of priests and holy nation'.

---

pp. 57–74; C. T. R. Hayward, *The Jewish Temple. A Non-biblical Sourcebook* (London: Routledge, 1996), pp. 85–107.

[36] See Charles, *Jubilees*, p. 18.

[37] The only other occurrence of the expression in the Pentateuch is at Gen. 46.27, where it refers to the sum total of Jacob's descendants who went to Egypt.

The author of Jubilees, then, had to wait until he could relate the biblical story of Jacob's second visit to Bethel, recorded in Genesis 35.1–15, before he could say anything about Jacob's change of name to Israel. Only at this point in the biblical narrative is Benjamin's birth recorded (Gen. 35.16–21), a detail which is seized upon and emphasised in his retelling of the story (Jub. 32.3). It is, of course, the case that the Bible records Jacob's change of name during that second visit to Bethel (Gen. 35.10); and this, likewise, becomes a focal point in the version of events given by Jubilees. But it does so in a highly distinctive way. The Bible twice tells how Jacob's name was changed to Israel, and the first account (Gen. 32.25–31) is the longer and better known of the two stories, describing Jacob's struggle with a supernatural being and his consequent designation as Israel. This earlier account of things Jubilees entirely suppressed; and it is not difficult to see why. The author is profoundly hostile to the Jewish adoption of Greek customs, and the biblical story of Jacob's struggle could lead, as we have seen that it did lead in the LXX version, to a portrayal of the Patriarch as a wrestler, an athlete whose prowess might not easily be distinguished from that of a victor in the Greek games. Furthermore, the chosen race of kings and priests descending from Jacob will be keeping Sabbath in union with the angels of the Presence and the angels of Sanctification: nothing could be more unsuitable, unthinkable indeed, than a suggestion that their ancestor Jacob had fought with a supernatural being, perhaps so that he could obtain the name Israel by showing his athletic superiority.

The author of Jubilees evidently felt called upon to rework the text of Genesis in such a way that Jacob's reception of the new name Israel was associated, not with a supernatural struggle, but with the sanctification of time – and that in a quite explicit manner. Jubilees 32, which represents a lengthy and complex reworking of Genesis 35's account of Jacob's second visit to Bethel, describes in detail how Jacob celebrated the feast of Sukkoth, a matter of which the Bible itself is utterly ignorant. During that festival, Jacob appointed Levi as priest. Earlier, Judah had been blessed as ancestor of kings: he is to provide the royal tribe. Benjamin's birth is imminent. The stage is thus set by Jubilees for the completion of 'the house of Jacob'. This house now has a priesthood formally constituted in the person

Holiness and Scripture

of Levi, and a royal house provided in the family of Judah. All that remains is the solemn designation of this 'house of Jacob' as 'Israel'.[38]

That momentous event, according to Jubilees, took place on the day following the seventh day of the feast of Sukkoth, on that 'extra' eighth day known more commonly as *Shemini `Atzeret.* Jubilees 32.27–9 absolutely insists that this day is 'written on the heavenly tablets' and is included 'among the feast days according to the number of the days of the year'. The Jewish tradition in general, however, makes little of this 'eighth day of solemn assembly'; indeed, most Talmudic discussion of the day is concerned with its status vis-à-vis Sukkoth, and has little to say about its origins or subsequent liturgical place in Jewish life.[39]

For Jubilees, however, it takes on tremendous significance, for the simple reason that it falls on the twenty-second day of the seventh month. The number 22 links it with the 22 works of creation preceding Sabbath, and with the 22 heads of humanity from Adam to Jacob, both of which represent points at which God's plans for the universe are brought to completion. By insisting on the sanctity of the twenty-second day of the seventh month at this point in Jacob's life, and by ensuring that this day will be observed by his descendants for evermore, the author of Jubilees is telling his readers that yet another completion and ·

---

[38] For discussion of the weighty matters necessarily only touched upon in this paragraph, see R. A. Kugler, *From Patriarch to Priest: The Levi-Priestly Tradition from* Aramaic Levi *to* Testament of Levi (Atlanta: Scholars Press, 1996); J. C. Endres, *Biblical Interpretation*, pp. 139–50, 205; J. Kugel, 'Levi's Elevation to the Priesthood in Second Temple Writings', *Harvard Theological Review* 86 (1993), pp. 1–48; J. C. VanderKam, 'Isaac's Blessing of Levi and his Descendants in *Jubilees* 31', in D. W. Parry and E. Ulrich, eds., *The Provo International Conference on the Dead Sea Scrolls* (Leiden: Brill, 1999), pp. 497–519; J. C. Vander-Kam '*Jubilees*' Exegetical Creation of Levi the Priest', *Revue de Qumran* 17 (1996), pp. 359–73.

[39] See *b. Sukk.* 47a. The fact that the keeping of *Shemini `Atzereth* is ordered by Lev. 23.36, while the day is apparently ignored by Deut. 16.15, may have suggested to some that it had a secondary status: hence the insistence of Jubilees that it is like the other Feasts in rank and status. For the Synagogue service see L. N. Dembitz, article 'Shemini `Azeret', in *The Jewish Encyclopedia*, vol. XI (New York: Funk & Wagnalls Co., 1905), p. 270; and on the biblical background, see J. Milgrom, 'The Eighth Day, Meaning and Paradigm', in *Leviticus 1–16*, pp. 592–5.

fulfilment of God's plan has been reached in time: Jacob becomes Israel, and Sabbath can be observed on earth. From now on, the seventh day of the week, which follows the completion of the 22 works of creation, can be properly observed as Sabbath on earth after Jacob's name becomes Israel, on the twenty-second day of the seventh month. It would be difficult to imagine a more direct way for the author of this remarkable book to indicate to his readership that the identity of Israel is inseparable from the Jewish process of sanctifying time.

There is a coda to this aspect of Jubilees. The 'eighth day' of solemn assembly constitutes the very last day of the cycle of festivals ordered by the Bible. That is to say, it is the last festival day in the year, chronologically speaking, and is called `atzareth by the Pentateuchal legislation in Leviticus 23.38 and Numbers 29.35. We saw earlier that LXX translated this term as *exodion*, thereby allowing the reader to envisage this day as something corresponding to the grand finale of a tragic play or epic drama. There can be little doubt, from the evidence set out in the preceding paragraphs, that the author of Jubilees likewise understood the first ever earthly celebration of *Shemini `Atzeret*, by Jacob renamed Israel, as the triumphant conclusion of a momentous story, telling how 'Israel' came to be a people made up of the twelve sons of Jacob, formally constituted as 'a kingdom, priests and a holy nation'. Since Jacob is universally acknowledged by students of Jubilees as the central character of the book, this supreme moment of his story represents a grand finale all of its own.

Final Observations and Conclusion

The Bible is unambiguously clear in its demands that the Jewish people should observe Sabbath and certain other set days as holy. In this essay, we have surveyed two major Jewish literary productions of the Second Temple Period, namely LXX and the *Book of Jubilees*, enquiring into their particular under-standings of what the sanctification of time might signify for Jews who read these works. The writings come from different geographical areas, and from different centuries. The LXX Pentateuch originated in a Greek milieu relatively friendly

towards Jews; Jubilees, by contrast, displays a readily compre-
hensible and justifiably mordant attitude to the Greek world.
LXX quite happily use words associated with Greek drama,
athletic contests and cultural activities in speaking of Jewish
festivals and of Jacob who becomes Israel. Jubilees carefully
avoids any hint that Jewish sacred time might bear comparison
with Greek festivals, and passes over in silence any biblical
suggestion that Jacob-Israel might have something in common
with a Greek athletic hero.

Jubilees is concerned also to answer the question, implied
by the Bible, how time was sanctified in the days from Adam
to Moses; and from the few scraps of information about altars,
sacrifice and prayer in the book of Genesis builds up a
comprehensive picture of Jacob-Israel's ancestors as pious Jews
who observed such sacred time as had been revealed to them.
Angels play a central role in instructing these ancestors in
what time should be consecrated, and the proper manner of
their observance: Israel's status is that of earthly representa-
tives of heavenly order, a privilege restricted to the chosen
people. While Jubilees leaves no room for doubt that Israel's
identity is tied up with the sanctification of time, and goes to
great lengths to demonstrate the primary importance of such
sanctification as indicated by the Bible, LXX display a subtlety,
indeed a complexity, which draws the reader by degrees into
serious consideration of the place that Jews occupy in the
predominantly Greek world of Ptolemaic Egypt. By opening
up the possibility of a dramatic interpretation of two major
Jewish festivals (Pesah-Mazzoth and Sukkoth), the translators,
at least in principle, allow for a rapprochement between Greek
high culture and Jewish tradition. The apologetic possibilities
in this process as far as Jews are concerned are obvious, and
need no rehearsal here: the tragedian Ezekiel's working out of
LXX's hints so as to produce a full-scale Greek play on the
Exodus could only strengthen any already existing sense of
Jewish-Greek alliance against native Egyptian hostility and
animus towards both parties. LXX by allusion, and Ezekiel in
fact, look outwards to Greek culture, art and social life, and
in their own distinctive ways offer to their readers or hearers
a sense of who Jews are seen to be as they celebrate their
major festivals. LXX in particular come close to portraying
Jacob-Israel as a typical Greek athlete-hero, whose victory in

the wrestling bout marks him out as the honoured votary of his God.[40]

The circumstances prevailing in the land of Israel when Jubilees received its final redaction ensured that the author-compiler of that book would insist that Israel's sanctification of time was *sui generis* on earth, replicating an authentic heavenly reality. Even so, it is possible to discern in Jubilees an epic-dramatic quality in its presentation of the life of Jacob-Israel, whose life story is carefully brought to its climax in the celebration of *Shemini `Atzeret*, the final day of the annual festival cycle, and the inauguration on earth of Sabbath observance. For Jubilees, this last is always the high point of the sanctification of time, since the Sabbath is the great day in heaven. Whatever the details surrounding the first celebrations of the festivals in history, all sacred time – Sabbath, Shavo'oth, Pesah, Sukkoth and the rest – remains essentially a heavenly reality determined by divine decree. Hence flows the author's certainty that celebration of these days according to a false calendar will result in universal disruption. In particular, ignorance of the correct calendar will ensure that Jews 'forget the feasts of the covenant and walk according to the feasts of the Gentiles' (6.35). At first sight, this looks strange: surely a mere slip in the calendar in itself is unlikely to lead Jews to 'walk according to the feasts of the Gentiles'? A moment's reflection on what has been said in this essay about LXX and Ezekiel, however, may provide a clue to what the author of Jubilees had in mind.

Among the Greeks, including those of Alexandria, it was the cult of Dionysus which was most famously associated with the production of tragic and comic plays. The greatest of all the festivals in honour of this god was in the Athenian city Dionysia, copied by Greeks throughout their diaspora, and celebrated at the end of March.

Now Pesah may fall towards the end of this same month; and this observation may have influenced Egyptian Jews like Ezekiel

---

[40] For the measure of accommodation of Judaism to the Greek world of Egypt and Alexandria, especially with regard to the story of the Exodus, see the Introduction to A. le Boullec and P. Sandevoir, *La Bible d'Alexandrie. 2 L'Exode* (Paris: Cerf, 1989), pp. 25–70.

in their writing of plays with biblical themes. What could be more fitting than a public recitation of the epic story of the Jews at the time when the Greeks were celebrating their greatest festival of drama? Indeed, an already existing general association between Pesah and the Greek Dionysia, in the minds of some Jews at least, might account for the action of the extreme 'Hellenisers' during the great crisis initiated by Antiochus Epiphanes in the land of Israel. Second Maccabees 6.6 tells how the decrees of that monarch meant that one could not keep Sabbath, nor observe the feasts of the fathers, 'nor so much as confess himself a Jew', a combination of complaints which in some measure confirms our observations about the links between sanctification of time and Jewish identity in the period we are discussing. Rather, says 2 Maccabees 6.7, when the feast of the Dionysia came round, Jews were compelled to process in honour of Dionysius wearing ivy wreaths, perhaps, may one suggest, because there was already in the minds of those Jews who favoured Greek culture a sense that the Pesah and Dionysia were in some sense related?[41]

If, for our *exodion* so to speak, we turn to the later history of the Jews, there can be little doubt that the author of Jubilees showed the more profound sense of what the sanctification of time might mean for Jews and Jewish identity. Despite his peculiar halakhic rulings, which at times differ significantly from the authoritative teaching of the Rabbis, he and the Sages are at one in insisting that God is the one who has ordered that time be sanctified, and that the Jewish observances of the proper times, days, seasons and festivals is the outcome of obedience to divine commandments. In this, he is at one with the great prayers of the Synagogue service which, though formalised long after his days, nonetheless breathe the same spirit:

---

[41] See further J. Knabenbauer, *Commentarius in duos Libros Machabaeorum* (Paris: Lethielleux, 1907), pp. 342–3; F.-M. Abel, *Les Livres des Maccabées* (Paris: Gabalda, 1949), pp. 362–3. Dionysius, in fact, was held to be the ancestor of the Ptolemies: see Schürer, *The History of the Jewish People*, rev. and ed. G. Vermes, F. Millar and M. Black, vol. II (Edinburgh: T&T Clark, 1979), p. 35, citing Justin, *Epitome* xv. 4.2–3; and his cult was widely known in the land of Israel, ibid., pp. 35–7, 43, 51.

O Lord our God, bestow on us the blessing of *thy* appointed times for life and peace ... even as thou hast been pleased to promise that thou wouldst bless us ... Sanctify us by thy commandments, and grant our portion in thy Law ... and let us inherit, O Lord our God, with joy and gladness thy holy Sabbath and appointed times ... Blessed art Thou, O Lord, who hallowest the Sabbath and Israel and the seasons.[42]

[42] See Service for Festivals, S. Singer, *The Authorised Daily Prayerbook of the United Hebrew Congregations of the British Commonwealth of Nations* (London: Eyre and Spottiswoode, 5722/1962), p. 312.

8

Jesus and Holiness: The Challenge of Purity

James D. G. Dunn

Jesus and Holiness

As a student, my first reflections on biblical holiness were very much influenced by Norman Snaith's *The Distinctive Ideas of the Old Testament*,[1] and Rudolf Otto's *The Idea of the Holy*.[2] Snaith noted that the roots of the concept of 'holiness' are close to the related concepts of mana and taboo. For Otto, 'holiness' speaks first of all of the manifest presence of the divine, the numinous which evokes a sense of fearful, shuddering awe, *mysterium tremendum et fascinans*. In the Old Testament we think obviously of the typical theophany, illustrated particularly by Exodus 19.16–24 and Isaiah 6. In the account of the frightening manifestation at Sinai we read that 'the Lord descended upon it in fire; and the smoke of it went up like the smoke of a kiln, and the whole mountain quaked greatly' (Exod. 19.18); and the people are repeatedly warned not to infringe the border of the mountain 'lest the Lord break out against them' and they die (19.12–13, 21–2, 24). And in Isaiah's account of his vision of the Lord's holiness, we read that 'The foundations of the thresholds shook at the voice of him who called, and the house was filled with smoke' (Isa. 6.4). People and things and places set apart to God were seen to share in this holiness, whose

---

[1] N. Snaith, *The Distinctive Ideas of the Old Testament* (London: Epworth, 1944), ch. 2.

[2] R. Otto, *The Idea of the Holy* (London: Oxford University, 1923).

dangerous, destructive power is forever illustrated by the cautionary tales of Nadab and Abihu in Leviticus 10.1–3 (destroyed by the fire which came forth from the holy God, when they tried to offer 'unholy fire before the Lord'), of Achan in Joshua 7 (stoned because he took 'some of the devoted things' and provoked the Lord's anger), and of Uzzah in 2 Samuel 6.6–8 (struck dead when the Lord 'broke forth upon Uzzah' when he put his hand on the ark of the covenant'). In the New Testament there are overtones of the same understanding in such passages as Acts 5 (the fate of Ananias and Sapphira, provoking great fear in the church and all who heard of it) and 1 Corinthians 11.29–30 (failure to discern the body of Christ resulting in illness and death). I mention this at the start partly because I still want to maintain that wherever the concept of 'holiness' appears in the biblical material, underlying it is the sense of the mysterious otherness and aweful power of the divine, of God, and that the holiness of people, places and things is essentially derivative from that primary source of holiness, 'holy' as related to the divine, to God. I mention this also partly to make the further point that the presence of 'holiness' in the biblical tradition should not be limited to places where the *qadosh/ hagios* word group appears.[3]

This recognition of the fundamental character of 'holiness' in the biblical tradition seems to be borne out, at least to some extent, when we turn to examine the theme or perception of holiness in relation to Jesus and his ministry. Five 'holiness' sayings are attributed to Jesus, two at least with a good claim to be recognised as dominical sayings, not least because the theme is so lacking in prominence in the tradition; that is to say, it is unlikely that these sayings derive from a later desire to promote the theme. The Lord's Prayer petitions that God's name may be 'sanctified' (*hagiasthetô* – Matt. 6.9/Luke 11.2), an echo of the sense that holiness is first and foremost God's holiness. In Mark 8.38/Luke 9.26 Jesus speaks of 'the holy angels' (Matt. 16.27 lacks the adjective) – again the sense of 'holy' as pertaining to the divine/heaven. Matthew 24.15 speaks of the Temple as 'the holy place', though the Markan parallel (13.14) lacks the

---

[3] For example, they do not appear in 2 Sam. 6.6–8; in Acts 5 only in reference to 'the Holy Spirit' (5.3); and not at all in 1 Corinthians 11.

reference – again the sense of 'holy' as set apart to God, as applicable to the place where God's name, God's *shekinah* dwells.[4] Similarly Matthew 23.17 and 19 (again without Synoptic parallel): it is 'the Temple which makes holy (*hagiasas*) the gold (of the Temple)', 'the altar which makes holy (*hagiazon*) the gift (on the altar)'. Otherwise we have only Matthew 7.6 ('Do not give the holy/that which is holy [*to hagion*] to the dogs', again without Synoptic parallel) – where again the sense is of the reverence due to that which has been dedicated to the sphere of God's presence and service. We could also add at least one of the references to 'the holy spirit' in the Jesus tradition, since Jesus' warning about blasphemy against the Holy Spirit never having forgiveness (Mark 3.29) certainly evokes the same sense of the aweful fearfulness of 'the holy'. Probably worth mentioning in the same connection is the Baptist's prediction that the Coming One would 'baptise in holy spirit and fire', which presumably owes at least something of its threatening tone in the Q version (Matt. 3.11/Luke 3.16; Mark 1.8 omits 'and fire') to the presence of the word 'holy', bearing in mind not least the background of the Baptist's imagery in Isaiah 4.4 and 30.27–8.[5]

We might also ask whether Jesus' presence evoked any sense of 'the holy' in those he met, bearing in mind that we are not looking simply for occurrences of the concept itself. Here we could refer to Mark 1.24/Luke 4.34 – the cry of the demoniac in the Capernaum synagogue, 'I know who you are, the holy one of God (*ho hagios tou theou*)'. Since 'holy one of God' is hardly a Christological title which we find in the earliest churches, it is more likely that we have here the remembrance of a demoniac's response when confronted with the charismatic power of one already recognised as a holy man.[6]

---

[4] For the holiness of the temple, its furniture, offerings and priests in the Old Testament see, e.g., D. P. Wright, 'Holiness (OT)', *Anchor Bible Dictionary* 3, pp. 239–43.

[5] See further my 'John the Baptist's Use of Scripture', in C. A. Evans and W. R. Stegner, eds., *The Gospels and the Scriptures of Israel* (JSNTS 104; Sheffield: JSOT Press, 1994), pp. 42–54.

[6] Cf. particularly G. Vermes, *Jesus the Jew* (London: Collins, 1973), who most effectively drew attention to the parallels between Jesus and holy men/charismatic rabbis like Honi the Circle-drawer and Hanina ben Dosa. 'There is no

Instances where individuals are reported as falling before Jesus in reverence could be cited in the same connection,[7] though how far along the spectrum, respect–reverence–awe, we actually are in these cases is by no means clear. The impact of Jesus is also attested by references to hearers being 'amazed' at his teaching,[8] though the emphasis in these cases is usually on Jesus' unexpected authority. The best example of this category is probably Mark 10.32: 'They were on the road, going up to Jerusalem, and Jesus was walking ahead of them; and they were filled with awe (*ethambounto*), while those who followed behind were afraid (*ephobounto*)'.[9] Other instances could be cited for discussion – the response of the disciples to Jesus' stilling of the storm (Mark 4.41), Herod's attitude to the Baptist and response to the reports about Jesus (Mark 6.14–16, 20), the transfiguration (Mark 9.2–8 pars.), or the centurion's exclamation at the cross (Mark 15.39) – but considerable discussion would be required, and quite probably little more would be added to what we have so far gleaned.

The results of this attempt to develop the theme of Jesus and holiness, as attested in the Jesus tradition and earliest memories of his ministry, have been significant but modest. As already noted, the motif of 'holiness' is not prominent in these traditions, with many of the explicit references in the Evangelists' narratives quite conventional in character ('the holy Spirit', 'the holy city'). The things Jesus is remembered as saying on the theme do reflect something of the fundamental sense of the aweful holiness of God; and we may well have in the Jesus tradition various memories of the impact Jesus made as evoking some sense of the holy. But these memories do not amount to a sustained reflection on the theme of holiness.

However, a narrow focus on the theme of 'holiness' is by no means the whole story. It does not require a detailed familiarity

---

reason to contest the possibility, and even the probability, that already during his life Jesus was spoken of and addressed by admiring believers (sic) as *son of God* (p. 209).

[7] *Proskuneô* – Matt. 8.2; 9.18; 15.25; 20.20; Mark 5.6; 15.19(!).

[8] Mark 1.22, 27/Luke 4.32, 36; Mark 6.2 pars.; Mark 10.26/Matt. 19.25; Mark 11.18; Matt. 7.28–9; 22.33.

[9] See also my earlier discussion in *Jesus and the Spirit* (London: SCM, 1975), ch. 4 (here, pp. 76–7).

with the biblical tradition to recognise that the themes of holiness and of purity are closely related.[10] What precisely the relation between holiness and purity is would require more discussion than is appropriate here. Perhaps it will suffice to say that the purity/impurity distinction is most simply understood as the human response made necessary by the fascinating but threatening character of divine holiness; the awareness of holiness brings consciousness of impurity, as classically in the vision of Isaiah ('Woe is me ... for I am a man of unclean lips' – 6.5). It is also certainly significant that of the two pairs, holy/profane and pure/impure, the two dynamic partners are 'holiness' and 'impurity', with 'profane' and 'pure' as more neutral concepts. It is the negative, inhibiting effect of impurity, as preventing access to or relation with the holy, which sets impurity as the effective antithesis to the positive, outgoing power of the divine holiness. If, then, we are to grapple adequately with the theme of Jesus and holiness we must enquire also about his attitude to purity and impurity. But in order to do that we must first ask about the importance of purity and impurity in the Judaism of Jesus' time within which he was brought up.

Purity in Second Temple Judaism

Recent study has done much to clarify the importance of purity concerns in Judaism at the time of Jesus. We can best approach the subject by looking briefly, first at what E. P. Sanders has called 'Common Judaism',[11] and then at the two groups or factions within Second Temple Judaism, the Pharisees and Essenes, which most emphasised purity as a concern not to be limited simply to the Temple. The contribution of Marcus Borg deserves particular note, since among recent scholars he has made most play on the theme of holiness and purity as social factors of first importance within the Judaism of Jesus' time.

---

[10] See, e.g., P. P. Jenson, *Graded Holiness: A Key to the Priestly Conception of the World* (JSOTS 106; Sheffield, JSOT Press, 1992) especially chs. 2 and 3; D. P. Wright, 'Holiness (OT)' and 'Unclean and Clean (OT)', *ABD* 3.237–49 and 6.729–41.

[11] E. P. Sanders, *Judaism Practice and Belief 63BCE–66CE* (London: SCM, 1992).

Finally, we need to look more closely at the relation between impurity and sin as perceived within the factionalism of late Second Temple Judaism. In this way we may hope to clarify the context within which and in relation to which Jesus spoke and acted on the issue of purity and impurity.

Purity in Common Judaism

We can be fairly confident, to put it no more strongly, that the bulk of Jews in the land of Israel at the time of Jesus observed the central rules of purity. By these I mean, first of all, following Sanders,[12] the laws on clean and unclean food and on not eating blood. If Emperor Caligula was aware that Jews did not eat pork (as Philo reports),[13] then we can be sure that the laws of 'kashrut' and 'kosher' food were widely practised in Diaspora communities; and if in them, how much more in the land of Israel itself. In the same connection, we may recall the words attributed to Peter in Acts 10.14: 'I have never eaten anything common/profane and unclean' (*pan koinon kai akatharton*).[14] If so for Peter, one of Jesus' closest disciples, an unlettered man (according to Acts 4.13), then it is a fair guess that observance of the law of clean and unclean was equally important for most Jews of the time.

Second, corpse impurity, impurity from discharges from the sexual organs and impurity of skin disease. It is important to note that such impurity was contagious: contact with a corpse or with menstrual blood or genital discharges rendered the person impure. Sanders' observation that impurity was not sin is also important: impurity was an unavoidable consequence of daily life; the impure did not need forgiveness but cleansing. The only problem with impurity is that it made participation in

---

[12] Sanders, *Judaism*, pp. 214–30.

[13] In his *Legatio* 361, Philo reports Caligula as interrupting his hearing of the Alexandrian Jews' delegations with the abrupt question, 'Why do you refuse to eat pork?'

[14] In ordinary Greek *koinos* means simply 'common, ordinary'. The sense 'profane, defiled, unclean' derives from the use of *koinos* as equivalent to the biblical *tame'* (e.g., Lev. 11.4–8; Deut. 14.7–10) or *chol* (Lev. 10.10; Ezek. 22.26; 44.23); hence the use of *koinos* in 1 Macc. 1.47, 62 ('unclean food'), Mark 7.2, 5 ('defiled hands') and Acts 10.14 and 11.8.

the Temple services impossible; impurity prevented access to the holy.[15] We can be confident that such purity concerns were widespread within common Judaism; the archaeological evidence of many *mikwaot* (immersion pools), not only in Sadducean priestly households, but also in houses of (other) aristocrats, and public pools adjacent to Temple and synagogue is hard to dispute.[16] And although the logic of purity is that it was only necessary in order to attend the Temple, there is evidence that purity rituals were practised more widely by those who could hardly attend the Temple regularly, and even in the Diaspora.[17] Once again we may deduce that if such concerns were so strong in the Diaspora, how much stronger must they have been among ordinary (religious) Jews in the holy land itself.

Purity among the Pharisees

There continues to be a substantial consensus that the Pharisees were basically a purity sect, whatever wider influence or political power they may or may not have exercised prior to or at the time of Jesus.[18] This is certainly the implication of the name by which they are known. The name 'Pharisees' (*perushim*) is generally derived from the root *parash*, 'to separate'; 'Pharisees' were 'separatists'. The obvious implication is that they were so called because they tried to separate themselves within or even from the rest of Israel, again with the clear implication that the motivation for such separation was purity driven. That is, they sought to separate themselves as much as possible from the impurities which characterised daily living for most of their compatriots.

The logic behind this attitude has been spelled out in recent years most clearly by Jacob Neusner. The Pharisees

---

[15] Sanders makes the point repeatedly in his *Jesus and Judaism* (London: SCM, 1985), pp. 182–92.

[16] Sanders, *Judaism*, p. 223.

[17] On the evidence for Diaspora observance of purity rules see E. P. Saunders, *Jewish Law from Jesus to the Mishnah: Five Studies* (London: SCM, 1990), pp. 258–71.

[18] See, e.g., those cited in my *The Partings of the Ways between Christianity and Judaism* (London: SCM, 1991), pp. 289–90, nn. 13, 19.

were concerned to keep the purity laws, which governed
access to the Temple and participation in the Temple cult,
outside the Temple; they wished to extend Temple holiness
throughout the land; they wanted the whole land to be, as it
were, the Temple – holy place and holy land in an unbroken
continuum. The biblical warrant would no doubt have been
Exodus 19.5–6: 'You shall be a kingdom of priests and a holy
nation.' This seems to have meant that the Pharisees, although
most of them not priests themselves, attempted to live like
priests, observing outside the Temple the purity laws which,
strictly speaking, were only necessary for service within the
Temple. In particular, Neusner sees this concern for purity
focused especially in the meal table: even everyday food
should be eaten in a state of purity, as if one was a priest
serving in the Temple.[19]

Purity at Qumran

No one doubts that purity was a central concern of the Qumran
community. Although purity was necessary only for participation in the Temple cult, the new covenanters evidently
regarded the Temple and its priesthood as defiled, and
therefore set up their own community to serve as an alternative
Temple community in place of the Temple.[20] In its defining
document, *The Rule of the Community*, Qumran saw itself as 'the
community of holiness' (1QS 9.2), 'a council of holiness' (1QS
5.2; 8.21), 'the holy congregation' (1QS 5.20; 1Qsa 1.9, 12), 'a
holy house for Israel', 'separated (*yibbadelu*) from the
habitation of ungodly men', 'to atone for the land' (1QS 8.5–6,

---

[19] This is a position Neusner has maintained since his earliest major study
on the subject, *The Rabbinic Traditions about the Pharisees before AD 70* (Leiden:
Brill, 1971), vol. 3, p. 288. Sanders objects to Neusner on these points, but
concedes a good deal of key ground while disputing its significance,
and concentrates his discussion on the question of the Pharisees' political and
social significance (*Judaism*, chs. 18–19). He also ignores the significance of
the name 'Pharisees' itself.

[20] See further B. Gartner, *The Temple and the Community in Qumran and the
New Testament* (SNTSMS 1; Cambridge: Cambridge University Press, 1965),
chs. 2–3; G. Klinzing, *Die Umdeutung des Kultus in der Qumrangemeinde und im
NT* (Göttingen: Vandenhoeck, 1971), vol. 2.

13).[21] In the recently published 4QMMT the explanation is given that 'we separated ourselves (*prshnu*) from the multitude of the people', and the editor reconstructs the following phrase, understandably, as 'and from all their impurity' (C7).[22] The verb ('separated') in this case is the same as the root (*prsh*) from which the *perushim*, Pharisees, gained their name ('Separatists'). And the implied rationale, as Qimron recognises, is the same: they separated themselves from their fellow Jews in order to maintain their own purity/holiness. As an instructive footnote, it is relevant to note that the same motivation is implicit in the Antioch incident in Galatians 2.11–14 where at the coming of the 'certain men from James', Peter 'separated himself' (*aphôrizen* – the equivalent Greek verb) from table fellowship with the Gentile believers, and 'the rest of the Jews [Jewish believers]' followed suit (2.12–13); the Jewish believers were evidently anxious to avoid the Gentile impurity which would put in some peril their standing within Israel. If such concerns were so prominent among the Jewish disciples of Jesus, how much more at Qumran.

It is not surprising, then, that we find such an emphasis on purificatory washings and on the rules governing the purity of the community meal in the sectarian documents of Qumran. For example, 'the purity of the many' is a phrase which occurs regularly in the procedures for admitting new member and for community discipline (1QS 6.16–17, 24–25; 7.2–3, 15–16, 19).[23] And in the conveniently named 'Annex to the Community Rule' it is made clear what the ideal for the community was – a community in effect of priests, with no man defiled by the impurities of a man permitted to enter the assembly (1Qsa 2.3–4). No one who would be disqualified to serve as a priest by reason of physical defilement or blemish (Lev. 21.17–21) should be allowed to take his place among the congregation, for the holy angels were there, present among the congregation (1Qsa 2.5–10).

---

[21] See also M. Newton, *The Concept of Purity at Qumran and in the Letters of Paul* (SNTSMS 53; Cambridge: Cambridge University Press, 1985), pp. 39–40.

[22] E. Qimron and J. Strugnell, *Miqsat Ma'ase Ha-Torah* (DJD 10.5; Oxford: Clarendon Press, 1994).

[23] Newton, *Concept of Purity*, pp. 10–26.

Purity and Politics

Borg has coined the phrase 'the politics of holiness'.[24] By that he means first to remind us that 'politics' is the name we give to the task of organising community. In what re-emerged after the exile as a small Temple state, the ethos and organisation of political, economic and social life was bound to be largely determined by relationship to the Temple, the focus of holiness. Under the political domination of Syria, and subsequently of Rome, the politics of holiness required resistance, and increasingly, separation. 'To be holy meant to be separate from everything that would defile holiness. The Jewish social world and its conventional wisdom became increasingly structured around the polarities of holiness as separation.'[25]

Borg's concern is timely. It would be a serious mistake to think of concerns for holiness in Second Temple Judaism as remote from the messiness and nastiness of political life. The Temple was the focus of political and economic power in the little state of Judea; its religious significance as 'the holy place' was thoroughly mixed up with its political and economic power. The policy (politics) of separation already noted for both Pharisees and Qumranites was as much an act of resistance to domination by impure foreigners as it was an attempt to be Israel in the midst of a Temple state where lack of concern about impurity was regarded as still far too rife.

Impurity and Sin

Borg's reminder that the significance of holiness/impurity extends well beyond the immediate realm of the Temple cult, is also a reminder that the distinction between impurity and sin can be too strongly pressed as well. Sanders may be justified in pointing out that, strictly speaking, impurity is not sin. But when maintaining holiness and separating from impurity in

[24] M. Borg, *Conflict, Holiness and Politics in the Teaching of Jesus* (New York: Edwin Mellen, 1984); also *Jesus: A New Vision* (San Francisco: Harper & Row, 1987).
[25] Borg, *Jesus*, pp. 86–7.

order to be Israel become the reason why one Jew separates from another, then more than a statement about impurity which can be removed by immersion at the end of a day or a week is clearly in view. There is also conflict implied, resistance to and condemnation of the other from whom one finds it necessary to separate oneself. And in such polemic the language of sin quickly appears.

In fact, impurity and sin were not categories held clearly apart in Israel's concern for holiness, as the Holiness Code of Leviticus 17–26 itself attests (e.g. 19.8; 20.17; 22.9). Isaiah's reaction to the vision of Yahweh's holiness is a confession of impurity ('I am a man of unclean lips'), which results in his *sin* being forgiven ('This has touched your mouth; your guilt is taken away, and your sin forgiven'). And in the factionalism which characterised Second Temple Judaism from the second century BCE onwards, it was common to denounce as breach of the law (sin) activities carried out by another faction in what the writer's faction regarded as a state of impurity, or to use the language of impurity in condemning what the writer's faction regarded as failure to keep the law.[26] Thus, for example, 1 Enoch 5.4 denounces fellow Jews: 'You have not persevered, nor observed the law of the Lord. But you have transgressed, and have spoken proud and hard words with your unclean lips (*en stomati akatharsias humôn*)'. In the Psalms of Solomon (a document often linked to the Pharisees) the self-styled 'righteous' attack their opponents as 'sinners', probably the Hasmonean Sadducees; their sin is particular that they defiled the sanctuary (1.8; 2.3; 8.12–13, 22) and committed all kinds of uncleanness (*pases akatharsias* – 8.12); 'there was no sin (*hamartia*) they left undone in which they did not surpass the gentiles' (8.13). The same attitude is clearly evident in the Essene/Qumran denunciation of their religious and political opponents as the wicked, the men of the lot of Belial, who have departed from the paths of righteousness, transgressed the covenant and suchlike (e.g. CD 1.13–21; 8.3–19; 1QS 2.4–5; 1QH 10(2).8–19; 1QpHab 2.1–4; 5.3–8).

---

[26] On the factionalism of Second Temple Judaism see my 'Pharisees, Sinners, and Jesus', *Jesus, Paul and the Law: Studies in Mark and Galatians* (London: SPCK, 1990), pp. 61–88 [71–7]; also *Partings*, pp. 102–7.

In consequence, it is necessary to qualify Sanders' observation that impurity as such is not sin. That is certainly true when we are simply talking about 'common Judaism'. But the last two hundred years of Second Temple Judaism evidently witnessed an intensification of holiness concerns within several at least of the factions of the period. In the intra-Jewish polemic which resulted, impurity was seen as an occasion for sin, precisely because in the eyes of several factions, (all) other Jews were ignoring the disqualifying effect of the purity/impurity legislation as interpreted within that faction's halakhah. 'Sinner' was a polemical condemnation by one faction of the adherents of another.[27] And lest the talk of 'sin' and 'sinner' be regarded as mere rhetoric, we should simply remind ourselves that in Jewish scripture and tradition, the designation 'sinner' was a damning indictment: the 'sinner' was excluded from the covenant and debarred from participation in the world to come.[28]

The sort of halakhic dispute in view is nicely illustrated once again by 4QMMT, which itemises the halakhic rulings ('works of the law'), including issues of purity, on which the sect differed from others in Israel. This in fact is a mild statement of the case, seeking a positive response, and not using the language of 'sin' and 'sinner'. But even so, these relatively minor disagreements were considered of sufficient importance as to require the writer's community to 'separate' from the rest of Israel (C7). And the evangelistic invitation made at the end, that if the recipients of the letter come to the same conclusion (that the letter's halakhic rulings are correct), 'it shall be reckoned to you for righteousness' (C30–31). The point, though more softly and less stridently made, is the same: failure to observe such purity concerns, as interpreted by each faction in the land of Israel, was reckoned by that faction to imperil final acquittal and salvation by God. In factional polemic, impurity is never 'minor';[29] impurity and sin go hand in hand.

---

[27] The failure to appreciate this factional use of the term 'sinner' was my main criticism of Sanders' *Jesus and Judaism* (see n. 26 above).

[28] See further my 'Jesus and Factionalism in Early Judaism', in J. H. Charlesworth and L. J. Johns, eds., *Hillel and Jesus: Comparisons of Two Major Religious Leaders* (Minneapolis: Fortress, 1997), pp. 156–75 [164–70].

[29] In order to minimise the significance of Pharisaic purity concerns,

Given, then, the importance of purity concerns within Second Temple Judaism, both at the level of common Judaism and in Judaism's factions, what can we say about Jesus' own attitude on such matters?

Jesus and Impurity

The most obvious way to proceed is to enquire whether there is any indication in the Jesus tradition that Jesus referred to or reacted in relation to the purity concerns within Second Temple Judaism, as outlined above. It will be most convenient to look at the three areas, Common Judaism, Pharisees and Qumran, in reverse order.

Jesus and Qumran

We cannot make any assumptions about how well known the Qumran community was in the rest of the land of Israel. So we cannot assume that Jesus would have known of it in any detail. And there are no explicit references whatsoever to Qumran in the Jesus tradition. But there is one lively and entirely relevant possibility which we should note.

This is the Qumran practice, already noted, of debarring from participation in the community any who were lame or blind or crippled (1Qsa 2.3–10; the same formula and attitude is present also in 1QM 7.4–6; 4QDamascus Document[b], fr.17, col.1.6–9; 11QTemple 45.12–14). As also noted above, the influence of Leviticus 21.17–21 is clear: those who were debarred by Levitical law from the priesthood by reason of their physical defect were also debarred from the Qumran community. The sectarian logic is the same as in regard to impurity: defect and impurity were equally disenabling conditions; the holiness of the community, marked by the presence of the holy angels (1Qsa 2.8–9; 1QM 7.6; 4QD[b], fr.17, col.1.9), required the exclusion of all such defects.

Sanders speaks of 'minor gestures towards extra purity' (*Jewish Law*, pp. 232–5), entirely missing the importance such 'minor gestures' can assume within inter-factional polemic.

The point of interest here is that in one of his table-fellowship scenes, Luke has Jesus referring twice to the importance of inviting to the festal table 'the maimed, the lame and the blind' (Luke 14.13, 21). The repeated mention of just these categories of physical defect, debarred from priesthood and so also from the table of the Qumran community, strongly suggests that the tradition had the Qumran practice very much in mind. Jesus was remembered, in the tradition used by Luke at any rate, as one who deliberately set his face against the purity concerns of Qumran, by indicating that those whom Qumran debarred from the holy community should be precisely the sort of people that sympathisers with Jesus' priorities should invite to their own tables.[30] Here we can see in Jesus' ministry (or arising directly out of it) a strong protest and challenge against a prominent concept of holiness within the Judaism of his day, and a corresponding call to a re-ordering of priorities.

Jesus and Pharisees

That Jesus was also remembered as reacting against the purity concerns of many Pharisees is indicated by the episode narrated in Mark 7.1–13/Matthew 15.1–9. The episode relates how 'the Pharisees and some of the scribes who had come down from Jerusalem' criticised some of Jesus' disciples for eating food with 'common/defiled hands (*koinais chersin*)' (Mark 7.2, 5). In the story, Jesus responds by arguing in effect that such rulings are merely human tradition which actually missed or obscured the point of God's commandment, and he illustrates the point by referring to the 'corban' ruling, which allowed a son to escape his obligation to support his parents by dedicating the income in question to the Temple (Mark 7.9–13/Matt. 15.3–9).[31]

In his influential *Jesus and Judaism* Sanders was very suspicious of the historical value of the Markan account, since we have no

---

[30] For fuller detail see my 'Jesus, Table-Fellowship, and Qumran', in J. H. Charlesworth, ed., *Jesus and the Dead Sea Scrolls* (New York: Doubleday, 1992), pp. 254–72.

[31] See further my *Partings*, p. 100.

other evidence that Pharisees practised handwashing in the
period before 70CE; at best a small number of *haberim* would have
practised it in relation to their own table-fellowship, but would
hardly expect it of others; in effect, the halakhoth which build
up into the Mishnah tractate *Yadaim* most likely came from the
period 70–200.[32] Two considerations tell against this line of
argument. For one thing, hands were the part of the body most
susceptible to impurity by reason of what they might touch – as
the *Letter of Aristeas* explains in reference to 'the custom of all
Jews' in washing their hands during prayer: 'for all activity takes
place by means of the hands' (*Aristeas* 304–306).[33] The logic
which led Diaspora Jews to the practice of handwashing as
'evidence that they have done no evil' (306) is not likely to have
been unmatched by Pharisaic concern to ensure that they ate
their food in purity.[34] And for another, Mark 7 is clearly drawing
on earlier tradition: the criticism about 'common' hands has to
be explained as referring to 'unwashed hands' (7.2), and the
whole practice within Judaism has to be explained by the added
note in 7.3–4, which clearly disrupts the earlier form of the story
(hence the awkward resumption in 7.5). Since, by common
consent, the composition of Mark's Gospel itself is to be dated
about 70, it follows that the tradition on which Mark drew here
must have pre-dated 70 by some years. That is, Mark 7.2, 5 is itself
evidence for a Pharisaic practice of handwashing before eating
food prior to 70CE. The point of Sanders' argument therefore
seems to be lost: it is one thing to conclude 'that there was no
substantial conflict between Jesus and the Pharisees',[35] because
there is no evidence of such Pharisaic concerns before 70CE; but
if the encounter between Jesus and some Pharisees reported in
Mark 7.1–5 reflects pre-70 conditions, then there is no reason
why the encounter could not have involved Jesus himself.[36]

---

[32] Sanders, *Jesus and Judaism*, pp. 185–7, 264–6; see also *Judaism*, pp. 429 and
537 n. 39.

[33] Cf. Mark's attribution of the practice of handwashing before meals to 'all
Jews' (Mark 7.3).

[34] The relation of the Pharisees to *haberim* is unclear; but at the very least the
overlap between the two was considerable, as Sanders acknowledges (*Jesus and
Judaism*, p. 187).

[35] Sanders, *Jesus and Judaism*, p. 265.

[36] In his second Jesus book, *The Historical Figure of Jesus* (London: Penguin,

Here then is substantive evidence that Jesus probably objected to the purity concerns of the Pharisees as they were pressed upon his disciples. His own concern seems to have been that in focusing on such a ritual matter, which could be observed merely by engaging in a formal act, they were building human tradition on divine commandment and thus obscuring the commandment of God. Both versions of the story (Mark and Matthew) cite Isaiah 29.13, thus emphasising the contrast between the merely outward or superficial act and worship from the heart: 'this people honours me with their lips, but their heart is far from me; in vain do they worship me, teaching as instructions the precepts of human beings'.[37] Jesus is thus remembered as looking for response from the heart, and regarding insistence on such a halakhah as handwashing before eating food as likely to obscure the more important concern.

The picture of Jesus drawn by this account correlates well with the immediately subsequent (Mark) or integrated (Matthew) account of Jesus' questioning of the corban ruling. The ruling, presumably then current, that oaths made by responsible people were inviolable (Num. 30.2–15), was undermining the fifth commandment ('Honour your father and your mother'), which Jesus regarded as having the higher priority (Mark 7.9–13/Matt. 15.3–6).

Similarly with the two episodes where Jesus is remembered as challenging Pharisaic halakhah regarding the sabbath. In the one case, the disciples plucking ears of corn on the sabbath (Mark 2.23–28 pars.), Jesus' response makes it clear that he saw the satisfaction of hunger as a higher priority than the elaboration of the fourth commandment, such as we have attested already in Jubilees 2.17–33 and 50.8–12 and in the Essene Damascus Document (CD 10–11). Indeed, according to the tradition as remembered (or elaborated) by Mark, Jesus' defence of his disciples indicates the way that humans, for whom the sabbath was given, should observe the sabbath (Mark

---

1993) Sanders is more restrained on the subject (p. 219), though he still ignores the factional use of 'sinners' (p. 227), that is, the fact that many Jews were designated as 'sinners/wicked' by this or that faction because they sat loose to what the faction regarded as important.

[37] Note the interesting echo of this Jesus tradition in Col. 2.22, in the LXX form of Isa. 29.13 rather than its MT form.

2.27). Observance of the sabbath is not in question; but the reckoning of the sabbath as given for human benefit, rather than the sabbath as requiring human service, amounts to a significant change of perspective.

Similarly with the second sabbath incident recalled by all three Synoptics – the healing of the man with the withered hand (Mark 3.1–5 pars.). Here, more explicitly, Jesus presses beyond questions of halakhic debate to a fundamental principle: the doing of good must always have priority over the doing of evil; the saving of life must always have priority over killing; and that principle applies to the sabbath (Mark 3.4/Luke 6.9).[38] In short, in both cases Jesus is remembered as pressing to a more fundamental principle, as relativising the well-intentioned halakhoth of the Pharisees in the light of that principle, and as protesting against any traditions which prevented or obscured that priority. This attitude is clearly consistent with what we have seen in regard to Jesus' protest and prioritising in the case of purity matters.

We noted above the degree to which the factionalism of Second Temple Judaism seems to have intensified purity concerns; also the fact that accusations of impurity and of disobedience to the law (sin) were part and parcel of the inter-factional polemic of the period. This observation is relevant here too, since Jesus is also remembered as, in effect, rebuking such polemic and its categorisation of those who disregarded or opposed a faction's rulings on such matters as 'sinners'. In Mark 2.15–17 pars. all three Synoptics narrate, as the sequel to the call of Matthew, Jesus dining with 'many tax collectors and sinners'; all three recall the Pharisees criticising Jesus because he was eating with tax collectors and sinners; and all three give Jesus' response, 'Those who are well/strong have no need of a doctor, but those who are ill; I did not come to call righteous but sinners.'

It would appear likely from this that many Pharisees used the same righteous/sinner contrast which is so characteristic

---

[38] Significantly, Matt. 12 transforms the episode back into one of halakhic dispute by replacing Mark 3.4 with an allusion to a dispute presumably between Pharisees and Essenes, in which Pharisees allowed an owner to rescue his sheep from a pit on the sabbath (Matt. 12.11/Luke 14.5), whereas Essenes disallowed it (CD 11.13–14 = 4QD, fr.3, col. 1.8–9 = 4QD^e, fr.10, col. 5.18).

of the Psalms of Solomon in particular, and, no doubt, with the same theological rationale: those who disregarded or opposed what the Pharisees ruled as essential to the proper keeping of the law were failing to keep the law – were 'sinners'. The case for this conclusion is strengthened by the Q recollection that Jesus was widely criticised for his levity and festive habits, as 'a glutton and a drunkard, a friend of tax collectors and sinners' (Matt. 11.19/Luke 7.34). Luke elaborates the point by going on to narrate the case of a woman 'who was a sinner' who anointed Jesus' feet at table and was accepted by Jesus despite his Pharisaic host's protest (Luke 7.36–39); by subsequently observing that the parables of the lost were told by Jesus in response to the Pharisee's criticism that 'This man receives sinners and eats with them' (15.2); and by going on to include the contrast between the Pharisee and tax collector praying in the Temple, the latter of whom was justified because he confessed himself a 'sinner' (18.10–14), and the account of Jesus going to dine with the tax collector Zacchaeus, despite the crowd's murmuring that Zacchaeus was a 'sinner' (19.7). The consistency of the testimony, that here indeed was a point of confrontation between Jesus and many Pharisees, together with its consistency with the language of inter-factional polemic, thus calls for a revision of Sanders' earlier attempts to minimise the grounds for dispute between Jesus and the Pharisees.[39] On the contrary, it would appear that many Pharisees regarded Jesus with his disciples and sympathisers as one more faction within Judaism which, like other factions, had to be confronted and rebutted if their own credibility (among themselves as well as with the people) was to be sustained. Once again, Sanders ignored the intensification of such concerns occasioned by the factionalism of the period.

In which case, it becomes relevant once again to note that Jesus protested against such boundary drawing within Judaism and in effect called for a reordering of priorities. In the saying Mark 2.17, he does not dispute the claims of 'the righteous' to be righteous; on the contrary, the parallelism of the saying implies that the righteous, since they are strong/well, have no

[39] Above, n. 35.

need of a doctor.[40] Jesus' criticism is rather to be understood as directed against the self-styled 'righteous' for dismissing others as 'sinners'; he protests against the faction which maintains its own integrity by denying that other Jews (unobservant in its view) have a share in the benefits of God's covenant. Nor should we ignore that the protests on both sides focus on table-fellowship: Jesus was criticised for eating with sinners; and he evidently of deliberate choice made a point of doing so. But the rules governing table-fellowship are essentially purity rules. So once again, the protest is in terms of what Jesus evidently judged to be wrong priorities: the concern to avoid impurity was preventing the engagement with others which Jesus saw as fundamental to his mission, and, indeed, as central to the kingdom of God, if the parable of the wedding feast (Matt. 22.1–10/Luke 14.15–24; cf. Matt. 8.11–12/Luke 13.28–29) is to be given due weight.

To sum up, the very purity concerns which constituted Pharisees as a faction, the 'Separatists', seem to have raised issues on which many of them clashed with Jesus. For his part Jesus protested against these Pharisees for giving too much weight to what they (the Pharisees) counted as impurity and as therefore to be avoided. In contrast, Jesus regarded several rulings that resulted from such concerns as 'human tradition', which obscured more basic principles of the law, as indeed of human well-being and community. And he wholly disregarded the factional judgmentalism which dismissed those non-observant of Pharisaic halakhah as 'sinners'. On Jesus' view, God was more concerned for such 'sinners' than for the 'righteous'.

Jesus and Common Judaism

Jesus is also remembered as reacting against not only the inten-sified purity concerns of Pharisees and (probably) the Qumran community, but also in relation to the purity concerns of

---

[40] Cf. the tribute which the father pays to the elder brother in the parable of the Prodigal Son: 'Son, you are always with me, and all that is mine is yours' (Luke 15.31).

common Judaism. This is the clear impression given by the sequence of stories told by the Synoptic Evangelists, with Mark in particular bringing this feature to the fore. Jesus is recalled as touching a man with a contagious skin disease (*lepros*) and declaring him cleansed there and then (*katharistheti*) (Mark 1.41 pars.), thus flying in the face of the clear laws on how such uncleanness must be dealt with by the priest (Lev. 13—14).[41] He justifies his disciples' plucking of the corn on the sabbath by citing as precedent David's breach of the holiness of the tabernacle sanctuary (Mark 2.26 pars.). In Mark 5.1–20 the resonances of common purity concerns are almost deafening: Jesus encounters a man 'with an unclean spirit', who lived among the tombs (thus incurring corpse impurity); he sends the unclean spirits into pigs (unclean animals); and all this happens in Gentile territory (outside the holy land). And in Mark 5.24–34 Jesus is touched by a woman with a continuing haemorrhage, that is, in a constant state of blood impurity; the description of her condition in 5.25 echoes Leviticus 15.25 – a woman having 'a flow of blood' (*hrusei haimatos*) – though Leviticus 15.25 envisages a condition persisting only over 'many days', whereas the Synoptic tradition indicates a condition lasting 'twelve years' (Mark 5.25 pars.). Jesus was evidently clearly remembered as one who sat loose to many of the purity restrictions which regulated social behaviour and communication.

More difficult to gain a clear perspective on is the key episode on true cleanness which follows the handwashing dispute in both Mark 7 (7.14–23) and Matthew 15 (15.10–20). The problem is partly that the Markan version poses the antithesis in very sharp terms: 'There is nothing from outside a person entering into him which is able to defile (*koinôsai*) him' (7.15); 'Everything which from outside enters into a person is not able to defile (*koinôsai*) him, because it does not enter into his heart but into his belly and into the drain ... it is what comes out of the person, that defiles (*koinoi*) the person'

---

[41] The fact of holiness confronted by a defilement which prevented social intercourse may help explain the strength of language used by Mark in the episode: 'deeply moved', possibly 'angered' (1.41); 'sternly charged him', almost 'snorted at him' (1.43).

(7.18–20). And partly that Mark (or already the tradition which he received) adds the explanatory note: 'cleansing (*katharizôn*) all foods' (7.19), universally understood as Mark's interpretative conclusion that by this saying Jesus had nullified or rescinded the laws of clean and unclean foods. Yet, how it could be that Jesus had so spoken and been so understood when, as already noted, Acts 10.14 presents a Peter who had never hitherto 'eaten anything common (*koinon*) or unclean', remains a serious question to the many scholars who take this passage as the yardstick of Jesus' radicalism.[42] For myself, I am persuaded that the softer Matthean version is probably closer to what Jesus actually said: 'It is not what goes into the mouth which defiles (*koinoi*) a person, but what comes out of the mouth' (Matt. 15.11); 'Do you not understand that everything which goes into the mouth passes into the belly and is expelled into the drain? It is what comes out from the mouth, from the heart, that is what defiles (*koinoi*) the person' (15.17–18).[43] If this is the case then we cannot say with any confidence that Jesus called for a total disregard for the laws of clean and unclean. But he did indicate, in typically prophetic fashion, that moral impurity should be regarded as more serious than ritual impurity, and in effect called for higher priority to be given to the moral purity of a person rather than to a person's ritual purity. The teaching is consistent with Jesus' exposition of the commandments against murder and adultery: the root causes of unjustified anger and despising of the other, of lustful looks and aspirations are just as serious (Matt. 5.21–2, 27–8). In the context of Mark 7 and Matthew 15, then, purity of heart is reckoned as so much more important than the ritual washing of hands as to render the latter inconsequential.

We should also note the parable of the Good Samaritan in Luke 10.29–37. The choice of a Samaritan as the story's hero would have been striking enough. Given the antagonism between Jews and Samaritans, and not least over the Samaritan Temple at Gerizim, it is highly probably that Josephus'

---

[42] Here Sanders does have a fair point (*Jesus and Judaism*, pp. 266–7).

[43] See further my 'Jesus and Ritual Purity: A Study of the Tradition-History of Mark 7.15', *Jesus, Paul and the Law: Studies in Mark and Galatians* (London: SPCK, 1990), pp. 37–60.

description of them as 'apostates from the Jewish nation' (*Ant.* 11.340) would have been widely shared; Samaritans were 'sinners' indeed! But the fact that the two chosen as foils to the good Samaritan were both functionaries of the Temple, the priest and the Levite, is almost as significant. In a purity-conscious culture, where the Temple was the focus of natural purity, the implication would be clear to most of Jesus' hearers. The priest and Levite kept as far away from the man fallen among thieves as possible (they 'passed by on the other side'); why else than because they were afraid of contracting blood or corpse impurity? The fact that the parable says that the priest was 'going down' the road, that is away from Jerusalem (as by implication also the Levite), simply underscores the point: purity concerns were of such importance to them, that even though they had (presumably) already completed their spell of Temple service in Jerusalem (where their purity really mattered), they still sought to avoid any possibility of contracting impurity. In which case, the criticism of an over-emphasised purity concern is all the sharper; Jesus' priority was people more than purity.

We need not add any more evidence on the point. Had space permitted, it would certainly be interesting to probe more deeply into the Temple incident which Jesus himself provoked (Mark 11.11–19 pars.).[44] Purity issues must have been involved in at least some measure, since Temple and purity were symbiotically related, though despite the popular title for the incident, 'the cleansing of the Temple', the only real hint of purity concerns as such lies in any echo of Malachi 3.1–3 and Psalms of Solomon 17.30 which may be implied.[45]

More immediately to the point are the emphases which Borg in particular has drawn out from much the same evidence. One is, as already noted, the social and political dimensions of such purity concerns, and therefore of Jesus' reaction to them. We should not permit Jesus' protest and re-prioritisation to be limited in their reference to the sphere of individual or

---

[44] Sanders brought the Temple incident to central focus in Life of Jesus research (*Jesus and Judaism*, ch. 1), but the purity aspect has not been central in the resulting debate.

[45] See, e.g., the brief discussion in my *Partings*, pp. 47–9.

personal piety. A counter-concern for unclean individuals and 'sinners' to be accepted within society and at meal tables meant a redrawing of norms and practice in social etiquette and behaviour. The questioning of the importance of the multiplying halakhoth relating to sabbath observance, the downgrading of the distinction between clean and unclean foods, the ignoring of the internal boundaries within Galilean and Judean society and the challenging of hostile national sentiment to the Samaritans, all had significant ramifications for the ways in which the national life of Judea and Galilee were ordered politically and socially. And if indeed Jesus did call in question priestly prerogative, in pronouncing lepers clean and sins forgiven, or indeed the power the high priestly families exercised through the Temple, then it is no wonder that he was handed over by them to the secular power to be dispatched with usual Roman brutality. Jesus' protest and re-prioritisation, not least in the matters of purity, had in the end touched a raw nerve at least once too often in the politics which governed Jewish society.

The other point made by Borg also deserves some emphasis. It is that the Jesus tradition recalls Jesus as countering the disenabling effects of uncleanness with, as we might say, the positive, transforming power of holiness.[46] Jesus was well-known as a successful exorcist, for expelling 'unclean spirits' as a holy man acting by the power, the (holy) Spirit, of God (Mark 1.23–7; 3.11; etc.; Matt. 12.28/Luke 11.20). He touched the leprous man, and instead of being rendered unclean, it was the leprous man who was made clean (Mark 1.41–2). In the same way, he was touched by the woman with the haemorrhage, and instead of being defiled by her blood impurity, 'power went forth from him' and healed her (5.27–30). Sharing in table-fellowship with him rendered factional polemic between Jews irrelevant: 'sinners' were to be sought out, not expelled; welcomed not denounced. He pronounced sins forgiven, as though he were the priest officiating at the individual's sin offering in the Temple (Mark 2.5 pars.; Luke 7.48). His coming to the Temple possibly echoed the coming of the messenger of the covenant in Malachi 3.1–3, who was to be 'like a refiner's fire ... (to)

---

[46] Borg, *Conflict, Holiness and Politics*, pp. 134–6.

purify the sons of Levi and refine them like gold and silver'. The weight of evidence is somewhat mixed, but the impression of a person with tremendous presence emerges with growing force. The fact that this impression is of a piece with our initial reflections on Jesus and holiness should not surprise us.

Conclusion

I framed this paper around the issue of purity because I had it in mind to discuss the relation of inward purity to outward, formal or ritual purity. None of the material or participants in the various debates we have reviewed would have any doubt that there is a distinction between the two kinds of purity. And all would no doubt agree that inward purity is the more important: circumcision of the heart and not just of the flesh (Deut. 10.16; Jer. 4.4). The interesting question is how the two are related – whether it is possible to have the one (inner purity) without the other (outward purity). The debate on the question ranges from those who see the two as one (*ex opere operato*), through those who see the two as inner and outer aspects of the same single reality, through those who see the one as symbolic of the other (the weight to be given to the term 'symbol' as itself part of the debate, from 'reality-effecting symbol' to 'mere symbol'), to those who would be willing to or even wish to dispense with the outward altogether as of any religious/spiritual significance. Do our findings on the subject of Jesus and holiness have anything to say to this debate?

If the above review is at all on target, then we can surely say that Jesus would not have placed himself at either end of the range of debate. By ignoring purity and food laws to the extent that he did, he certainly indicated that he did not regard them as indispensable. But neither did he dispense with the Sabbath or attendance at Temple or synagogue, and while he evidently did not continue the Baptist's practice of baptising would-be followers, the memory of his last supper with his inner group is clear. We should also note that Jesus worked within the rules and conventions of the day in recognising a link between uncleanness and sin, and in requiring the leprous man to show himself to the priest and to offer for his cleansing what Moses commanded (Mark 1.44).

Holiness and Scripture

What Jesus did seem to object to was the application of purity rules simply to exclude from community, without anything more being done for the person(s) thus reckoned unclean. And what made him even more angry was the factional use of purity rules to dispute right of access to the holy to others who did not share the faction's interpretation of the purity laws. In such circumstances, purity of heart rendered such factional disputes irrelevant; the humble confession of sin to God by the sinner was what assured the sinner's acceptance by God, not the Pharisee's testimony of halakhoth observed (Luke 18.10–14). Holiness was more important for Jesus as a power which cleanses uncleanness and dissolves impurity than as a status (of person or place) constantly threatened by the 'common' and profane.

9

Dislocating and Relocating Holiness:
A New Testament Study
Stephen C. Barton

Introduction

Holiness is a subject which has become marginalised in the
moral and theological discourse of the late-modern West. The
reasons for this are numerous and complex. One is a by-
product of Enlightenment epistemology and has to do with the
neutering of theology as a discipline of prayer and holy living in
favour of the scientific study of phenomena known as 'natural
religion' and 'the sacred'.[1] A second is the invention of the
secular with its hostility to the particularity and rootedness of
the traditions, practices, communities, times and places which
make formation in holiness possible. Yet a third reason is
related to the curiously 'gnostic', individualistic model of the
self in late modernity, with the associated tendency to seek
escape from history and the givenness of the body, bodily relatedness and bodily discipline. A fourth is a consequence of our
consumerist mentality and 'do-it-yourself' cultural ethos, the
result of which is that the passing (and often highly syncretistic)
fashions of 'spirituality' are in the ascendant and the schooling
by faith communities over time in the contemplation of God
and the life of virtue is neglected.[2]

---

[1] See on this Nicholas Lash, *The Beginning and the End of 'Religion'*
(Cambridge: Cambridge University Press, 1996).
[2] Cf. Linda Woodhead, 'Sophia or Gnosis? Christianity and New Age
Spirituality', in S. C. Barton, ed., *Where Shall Wisdom Be Found?* (Edinburgh:

But this brief sketch may be one-sided. Or, to put it another way, if holiness has been marginalised for the kinds of reasons I have given, we may be in a position now to see with greater clarity what we have lost. It may even be the case that there are developments in late (or post-) modernity which are cause for hope. Among these, I would include the following. In terms of the history of moral thought, there is the advocacy of a return to virtue ethics in the tradition of Aristotle and Aquinas, an advocacy in which Alasdair MacIntyre, amongst others, has played a major role.[3] In developments in the understanding of the self, there is a growing disenchantment both with Cartesian individualism and with that part of the legacy of the Enlightenment which requires that method take precedence over understanding and knowing take precedence over being.[4] At the same time, there has been a rediscovery of 'the body', including its permeability, genderedness, inter-dependence and inter-relatedness in history and society. This has allowed a shift from the spiritualised self as product of the will to the embodied self as given and shaped in relationship with others.[5] Finally, and by no means unconnected with this, it could be said that postmodernity marks a renewed recognition of the local and the particular, of the embededness of every person in a history and a tradition, a time and a place. As Edith Wyschogrod has shown in *Saints and Postmodernism*, holy places, holy times, holy writings and holy people are able to serve once more as contours on the map of what it means to be truly human.[6]

If this last point is valid, then a way is opened for a recovery of the study and pursuit of holiness in church and academy as

---

T&T Clark, 1999), pp. 263–77. Relevant also is *Concilium* 1999/4 on *Faith in a Society of Instant Gratification* (London: SCM, 1999).

[3] See Alasdair MacIntyre, *After Virtue. A Study in Moral Theory* (London: Duckworth, 1981); also the special issue of *Studies in Christian Ethics*, 12/1 (1999) on Virtue Ethics.

[4] See for example the essay by Stanley Hauerwas, 'The Sanctified Body: Why Perfection Does Not Require a "Self"', in his recent collection, *Sanctify Them in the Truth* (Edinburgh: T&T Clark, 1998), pp. 77–91.

[5] See for example, Sarah Coakley, ed., *Religion and the Body* (Cambridge: Cambridge University Press, 1997).

[6] Edith Wyschogrod, *Saints and Postmodernism. Revisioning Moral Philosophy* (Chicago: University of Chicago Press, 1990).

a vital dimension of human life under God. Naturally, a crucial part in such a pursuit will have to be given to the contemplation of those sources which holy people have found to be sacramental and sanctifying. Supreme among those sources for Christians are the Scriptures of the church along with the millennia-old traditions of remembrance and interpretative enactment by means of which, through the inspiration of the Holy Spirit, the Scriptures continue to speak as oracles of God. Which brings me, in this essay, to the New Testament.

My aim in what follows is not to give a comprehensive or systematic account of holiness in the New Testament. That has been done well by others, and time and space do not allow a study along those lines here.[7] What I propose to do instead is to make a series of observations about holiness in early Christian testimony, drawing upon a wide range of what strike me as relevant New Testament texts. In so doing, my primary intention is not that of historical reconstruction, although what I say presupposes the necessity for interpretation of understanding the texts in their originating and subsequent historical contexts. Rather, what I propose is to attend to the meaning of the text in ways that I hope will be fruitful for a late-modern reappropriation of the concept and practice of holiness.

Holiness and the Presence of God

The first point I would like to make is that the idea of holiness in the New Testament, as in the Old Testament, is related to an understanding of *who God is and where God is to be found,* a sense of both the incomparability of God in his transcendent otherness and yet also of the accessibility of God arising out of his covenantal love and mercy. A key scriptural text is Exodus

---

[7] See for example, David Peterson, *Possessed by God. A New Testament Theology of Sanctification and Holiness* (Leicester: Apollos, 1995). For a comprehensive survey of the Old Testament, see J. G. Gammie, *Holiness in Israel* (Minneapolis: Fortress, 1989). Very useful also are the articles 'Holiness (OT)' and 'Holiness (NT)' by, respectively, David P. Wright and Robert Hodgson Jr. in the *Anchor Bible Dictionary*, Vol. 3. It is surprising that the special issue of *Interpretation*, 53/4 (1999), on 'Holiness and Purity', has no essay on the New Testament. I hope that the present essay will help to fill the gap.

19—20, in particular Exodus 19.4–6, the words of the Lord to Moses out of the mountain:

> You have seen what I did to the Egyptians, and how I bore you on eagles' wings and brought you to myself. Now, therefore, if you will obey my voice and keep my covenant, you shall be my own possession among all peoples; for all the earth is mine, and you shall be to me *a kingdom of priests and a holy nation.*

Note the two main metaphors. Israel is lifted up out of slavery and called and graced by God to be a 'kingdom of priests' and a 'holy nation'. Here we have the two main ingredients of holiness: worship and obedience. And these two ingredients are displayed in these two successive chapters of Exodus. Chapter 19, with its heavy symbolism of theophany, temple and cult,[8] displays the incomparable holiness and transcendence of God which calls forth worship and brings Israel into being as a kingdom of priests. Chapter 20 sets forth how life as a kingdom of priests is to be sustained: by becoming a holy nation in conformity to the 'ten words' that God speaks directly to the people. The narrative logic is clear. The experience of the holy otherness of God is an invitation to become a priestly kingdom who celebrate God's holiness in worship. But the liturgical or cultic community has to be also the moral community which celebrates God's holiness in lives devoted to doing God's holy will.

We need not doubt that this scriptural understanding of holiness was fundamental for both early Judaism and Christianity, even if in different ways. In early Judaism in its various manifestations, the holiness of God was understood as that which distinguished every critical sphere of life: the people, the land, the temple and the torah.[9] These spheres of life were holy because God was present in and through them. They were set apart for God in various significant ways – through circumcision and purification, the ritual ordering of

---

[8] Cf. R. W. L. Moberly, *The Old Testament of the Old Testament* (Minneapolis: Fortress, 1992), pp. 102–3.

[9] See further, J. D. G. Dunn on what he calls the 'four pillars' of Second Temple Judaism, in *The Partings of the Ways* (London: SCM, 1991), pp. 18–36.

space, time and people, the offering of worship and sacrifice, and the practice of obedience.[10] As the gift of God in creation and election, they mediated God's presence.

In early Christianity, the claim is made that God is to be found somewhere new, though not in an unanticipated place. God is present in the person of the Son of God, himself the One in whom dwells the Holy Spirit of God (cf. John 1.1–18, 29–34, etc.). This claim represents a dislocation and relocation of holiness. It represents also an extension and intensification of holiness. No single way of putting the matter is able to capture the nature of the change. But there can be no doubt that the reinterpretation of holiness and its corollaries represented by the claim that 'God was *in Christ*' (2 Cor. 5.19) signifies a development of momentous proportions. The people, the land, the Temple and the torah could be understood no longer as sufficient testimony to God's presence in holiness, even if, in various significant ways and while they lasted, they remained vital as partial testimony, at least.[11]

Now, however, God is to be sought and found elsewhere. Entirely indicative of this is the fact that when the Exodus 19 text is employed in 1 Peter, its referent is no longer the elect nation of Israel. Rather, it refers to the Church, now predominantly Gentile:

> But you are a chosen race, a royal priesthood, a holy nation, God's own people, that you may declare the wonderful deeds of him who called you out of darkness into his marvellous light. Once you were no people but now you are God's people; once you had not received mercy but now you have received mercy (1 Pet. 2.9–10; cf. also Rev. 1.6).[12]

[10] See further Robert Hayward's essay in this volume. Useful also are the sources collected in G. W. E. Nickelsburg and M. E. Stone, eds., *Faith and Piety in Early Judaism* (Philadelphia: Fortress, 1983).

[11] Nicely nuanced on this whole question is William Horbury's essay, 'Land, Sanctuary and Worship', in J. Barclay and J. Sweet, eds., *Early Christian Thought in its Jewish Context* (Cambridge: Cambridge University Press, 1996), pp. 207–24.

[12] See further Jo Bailey Wells, *God's Holy People. A Theme in Biblical Theology* (Sheffield: Sheffield Academic Press, 2000).

Holiness, Kingdom and Spirit

If my first point was about who God is and where God is to be found, my second and related point is about *the Kingdom of God and the Spirit of God*. The idea and practice of holiness in the New Testament are deeply indebted to the belief that the life, death and resurrection of Jesus of Nazareth marks the coming of God in power and the inauguration of the new age of the eschatological Spirit.[13] Jesus made the holiness/Kingdom connection himself: 'Our Father who art in heaven, *hallowed [hagiasthētō] be thy name. Thy kingdom come.* Thy will be done, on earth as it is in heaven' (Matt. 6.9–10). The sanctifying of God's name is brought about by the breaking in of God's rule, proclaimed and enacted by Jesus, God's Son, and bringing healing and restoration to God's people.

The impact of this 'Kingdom' eschatology is that holiness looks different now – or, perhaps we should say, holiness of a different kind comes to the fore.[14] Thus, for example, the reason why the Jesus of the Synoptic Gospels is not preoccupied with matters of ritual purity after the fashion of the priests, Pharisees and Qumran sectaries is not that he was 'anti-cult' (cf. Matt. 23.16–22), but that his horizon was dominated by a greater reality: the coming of God as King in mercy and justice. The reason why he was critical of the temple in Jerusalem was not because he believed that God was present there no longer, but because he saw it as inadequately fulfilling its holy vocation to be 'a house of prayer for all the nations' (Mark 11.17).[15] The reason why he wept over the holy city was not because he had no sense of a holy people and a holy place, but because he saw it as impervious to the summons to repentance and renewal brought by himself and the prophets before him (Luke 13.31–35). Yet again, the reason why he ate with 'tax collectors and sinners' and gained a reputation as a 'glutton and a

[13] Cf. G. J. Thomas, 'A Holy God Among A Holy People In A Holy Place: The Enduring Eschatological Hope', in K. Brower and M. Elliott, eds., *The Reader Must Understand* (Leicester: IVP, 1997), pp. 53–69.

[14] On what follows, see now, Scot McKnight, *A New Vision for Israel. The Teachings of Jesus in National Context* (Grand Rapids: Eerdmans, 1999).

[15] Cf. Morna D. Hooker, 'Traditions about the Temple in the Sayings of Jesus', *Bulletin of the John Rylands Library*, 70 (1988), pp. 7–19.

drunkard' is not because he was a notorious libertine who disregarded torah, but because he believed that torah, as an instrument of grace, had to be interpreted in the light of the gracious in-breaking of God as 'good news to the poor' (Luke 4.18; cf. 15.1–32).[16]

This eschatological reinterpretation of holiness is not limited to the Synoptic Gospels either. In the Fourth Gospel, Jesus' resurrection from the dead inspires a process of *anamnesis* whereby his riddling words about the destruction and rebuilding of the temple are interpreted with reference to a different temple where God is to be found, 'the temple [*naos*] of his [i.e. Christ's] body' (John 2.21). In the same Gospel, it is because the eschatological 'hour' both 'is coming and now is' (John 4.21, 23), that the true worship of God is restricted no longer to a holy mountain, whether in Samaria or Jerusalem. It takes place, instead, 'in spirit and truth' (John 4.23). Such worship is open, furthermore, to a new people: to anyone who believes in and becomes united to Jesus. In so far as this new people is represented by the disciples, it is an eschatological people purified by the death of God's Son (John 13.1–11), sanctified by the prayer of the Son to the Father (John 17.17–19), and blessed by the Son with the Holy Spirit (John 20.22).

The Acts and the Epistles display this same eschatological thrust. In particular, in the light of the coming of the end-time Spirit, holiness as ritual purity is displaced and relativised by holiness as charismatic endowment. In the words of Peter to the Gentile centurion Cornelius,

> You yourselves know how unlawful it is for a Jew to associate with or to visit [*kollasthai ē proserchesthai*] any one of another nation; but God has shown me that I should not call any man common or unclean [*koinon ē akatharton*] ... While Peter was still saying this, the Holy Spirit fell on all who heard the word (Acts 10.28, 44).[17]

---

[16] See further, Stephen C. Barton, 'Parables on God's Love and Forgiveness (Luke 15:1–32)', in R. N. Longenecker, ed., *The Challenge of Jesus' Parables* (Grand Rapids: Eerdmans, 2000), pp. 199–216.

[17] See J. D. G. Dunn, *The Acts of the Apostles* (Valley Forge, PA: TPI, 1996), pp. 131–46.

The Levitical conception of holiness as separation[18] is reinter-preted eschatologically and pneumatologically here so that the integrity of a new people of God can be affirmed and celebrated.

Holiness and the Self

This brings me to a third point. The idea and practice of holiness in the New Testament is related to a *re-valuation of the self* – above all, in relation to God, but also, as a direct corollary, in relation to others. This is expressed in a multitude of ways. In the gospels, for example, there are the powerful and subversive metaphors of childlikeness and rebirth. Access to God's holy presence involves turning to God in repentance and becoming 'like a child' (Matt. 18.3; cf. 5.3–11) – in Johannine terms, being 'born again/from above' through baptism and the Spirit (John 3.3–6). These are metaphors of reordering grace on God's side and humble dependence on the part of humankind. In this light, holiness is a gift, to be received in humility by faith. It is not a capacity but a charism, not a matter of the human will to power but of God's will to bless.

In addition to metaphors, there are narratives also. Think of the momentous exorcism story of Mark 5. The casting out of the 'legion' of unclean spirits (vv. 2, 13) into the (unclean) swine who plunge into the sea and are drowned expresses something of the sanctifying presence of God in Jesus bringing a new sense of self, not only to the demonised man (v. 15, 18–20), but also – if only they would receive it (vv. 16–17) – to a nation possessed by the demons of subjection to imperial Rome (Mark 5.1–20). The story of the Good Samaritan is pertinent also (Luke 10.25–37). Here, true holiness is shown to be a matter not so much of separation from corpse impurity – the (no doubt legitimate) motivation of the priest and Levite in 'passing by on the other side' (vv. 31–2) – as of acting with compassion towards the poor. That it is a Samaritan who

---

[18] On which see Philip P. Jenson, *Graded Holiness. A Key to the Priestly Conception of the World* (Sheffield: JSOT Press, 1992), and also his essay in this volume.

models this holiness is an intimation of the significant change in the understanding of the sanctified self which the teaching of the Lukan Jesus represents.

Other New Testament texts portray the self in relation to God differently, according to genre. Of great significance is the common designation 'saints' (*hagioi*), a biblical term with eschatological connotations designating those set apart by God to be the people of God and witness to the holiness of God. Typical is the opening of Paul's Letter to the Romans, where holiness terminology is pervasive (Rom 1.1–7). Paul himself, as apostle, is 'called [and] set apart' (*klētos [kai] aphōrismenos*); the gospel he preaches is a message foretold 'in the holy scriptures' (*en graphais hagiais*); the One to whom he testifies was 'designated [*oristhentos*] Son of God ... according to the Spirit of holiness [*kata pneuma hagiōsunēs*]'; and the believers he is addressing are 'God's beloved [*agapētois theou*] in Rome, who are called to be saints [*klētois hagiois*]'. The First Letter to the Corinthians begins similarly: 'To the church of God which is at Corinth, to those sanctified in Christ Jesus [*hēgiasmenois en Christō Iēsou*], called to be saints [*klētois hagiois*] ...' (1 Cor. 1.2). What we have here is a fundamentally scriptural, covenantal understanding of the self. What is novel is the extension of this self-understanding to a *corpus mixtum*, to a fellowship made up of people – Jews and Gentiles – whom traditional notions of the sanctified person kept apart.

Complementing the terminology of election and sanctification is the language of cult and temple applied both to Christian believers individually and corporately. In 1 Corinthians, for example, Paul says to the fornicators, 'Do you not know that your body is a temple of the Holy Spirit within you [*naos tou en humin hagiou pneumatos*], which you have from God?' (1 Cor. 6.19). But earlier in the same letter, the temple metaphor is applied in identical terms to the warring factions in the church as a whole: 'Do you [plural] not know that you are God's temple and that God's Spirit dwells in you? If anyone destroys God's temple, God will destroy him. For God's temple is holy, and that temple you are' (1 Cor. 3.16–17; cf. also 2 Cor. 6.14—7.1). As at Qumran, the language of holiness, temple and cult traditionally associated with the Temple in Jerusalem is applied to a group of people. Its reappropriation in this way

testifies to the continued potency of such language for both
self- and community-definition in relation to God.[19]

Holiness, Tradition and Corporate Memory

One reason for its potency – and this is my fourth point – is that
the idea and practice of holiness were *rooted deeply in a shared
tradition and corporate memory*. The first Christians had a
profound holiness tradition ready-to-hand and embodied in
the Judaism which gave them birth.[20] They did not start *de novo*,
with a clean slate. A good example is the ethical instruction in
1 Thessalonians 4.1–12, itself having significant points of
contact with the teaching in 1 Peter 1.13—2.3, 11–12.[21] Here
we have paraenesis which follows a recognisable pattern. It
combines foundational statements about the holiness of God
and God's call to sanctification with concrete instruction in
matters to do with sexual, business and social life, all reinforced
by motivational statements to do with the judgement of God
and concerns about outsiders. The principal features are
evident in the central section:

> For this is the will of God, your sanctification [*ho hagiasmos
> humōn*]: that you abstain from unchastity [*apo tēs porneias*];
> that each one of you know how to take a wife for himself in
> holiness and honour [*en hagiasmō kai timei*], not in the
> passion of lust like heathen who do not know God; that no
> man transgress or wrong his brother in this matter [or, as an
> alternative translation, 'defraud his brother in business'],
> because the Lord is an avenger in all these things as we

[19] Cf. Brian S. Rosner, 'Temple and Holiness in 1 Corinthians 5', *Tyndale
Bulletin*, 42 (1991), pp. 137–45.
[20] Cf. Brian S. Rosner, *Paul, Scripture and Ethics* (Leiden: E. J. Brill, 1994);
and more generally, Wayne A. Meeks, *The Origins of Christian Morality* (New
Haven: Yale University Press, 1993).
[21] I am following here Robert Hodgson's excellent study, 'Holiness
Tradition and Social Description: Intertestamental Judaism and Early
Christianity', in Stanley M. Burgess, ed., *Reaching Beyond: Chapters in the History
of Perfectionism* (Peabody: Hendrickson, 1986), pp. 65–91. Cf. also, J. A. D.
Weima, ' "How You Must Walk To Please God": Holiness and Discipleship in
1 Thessalonians', in R. N. Longenecker (ed.), *Patterns of Discipleship in the New
Testament* (Grand Rapids: Eerdmans, 1996), pp. 98–119.

solemnly forewarned you. For God has not called us for uncleanness, but in holiness [*epi akatharsia all' en hagiasmō*]. Therefore whoever disregards this disregards not man but God, who gives his Holy Spirit [*to pneuma autou to hagion*] to you (1 Thess. 4.3–8).

This material relates only loosely to its present context in 1 Thessalonians[22] and, by virtue also of points of contact with the tradition in 1 Peter, may well be pre-Pauline tradition. In fact, Robert Hodgson has argued convincingly that its roots lie in the Holiness Code of Leviticus 17–26 and the mediation of that code in the ethical exposition of various forms of inter-testamental Judaism – namely, the Septuagint, Pseudo-Phocylides, and the Damascus Document. He also shows that the development and adoption of this holiness tradition is characteristic of the kind of society or group 'determined to construct its own self-identity and status, and concerned to establish and maintain boundaries between itself and outsiders'.[23] Just as this tradition allowed the various 'Judaisms' to negotiate their respective relations both internally and with outsiders (i.e., other Jews, proselytes and pagans), so too it allowed the persecuted Christian community in Thessalonica (cf. 1 Thess. 2.14) to define and order its common life with a view both to the increase of love within the brotherhood (4.9–10) and to proper behaviour towards outsiders (4.12).

Other examples of the rootedness of early Christian holiness in Scripture, tradition and contemporary Jewish practice could be given. One such, not unrelated to the 1 Thessalonians text just discussed, is the influential role of the traditions behind the second century Noachide Commandments in the shaping of early Jewish-Christian halakah on relations with Gentile converts, recently explored by Markus Bockmuehl.[24] He shows how significant in Judaism were the halakhic concerns under-lying the Noachide Commandments for the formation of a Jewish ethics for Gentiles. According to Bockmuehl, the Commandments, as formalised by the rabbis, constituted a kind

---

[22] Robert Hodgson, 'Holiness Tradition', p. 70.
[23] 'Holiness Tradition', p. 82.
[24] Markus Bockmuehl, 'The Noachide Commandments and New Testament Ethics', *Revue biblique* 102 (1995), pp. 72–101.

of natural law or constitution of universal application by virtue of its association with the primeval period of human history before the covenants with Abraham and Moses (cf. Gen. 1—11, esp. 9.4–6). He also shows how this tradition of 'public ethics' in Judaism decisively shaped the form and content of early Christian halakah in the context of the apostolic mission to the Gentiles.

This makes intelligible the ruling – with its (to our ears!) strange collocation of moral and ritual commands – agreed at the Apostolic Council, reported in Acts 15. In the words of James, the leader of the Jerusalem Church: 'Therefore my judgment is that we should not trouble those of the Gentiles who turn to God, but should write to them to abstain from the pollutions of idols [*tōn eidōlōn*] and from unchastity [*tēs porneias*] and from what is strangled [*tou pniktou*] and from blood [*tou haimatos*]' (15.19–20; cf. v. 29). In other words, Gentile converts do not have to become proselytes, and therefore do not come under the laws governing proselytes, such as circumcision and sabbath observance. Rather, what we have here is the momentous acceptance that Gentiles are saved *as Gentiles.* But how then are they to live? This is a question which the gospel message about the crucified Messiah and the coming of the Spirit did not answer in any straightforward way. The main ingredients of an answer, however, lay close at hand. The Gentiles are to live according to this well-known tradition (associated with God's pre-Mosaic covenant with Noah) governing the behaviour of resident aliens in Israel (cf. Lev. 18–20; Ezek. 33.23–6; Wis. Sol. 14.12–31; Jub. 7). That is to say, they are to avoid idolatry, sexual immorality, and the consumption of animal blood (extending, no doubt, to the shedding of blood as well).[25] It is by no means coincidental that Paul's instructions to the Gentile Christians in Corinth have essentially the same content. The Corinthians are to 'flee sexual immorality [*pheugete tēn porneian*]' and they are to 'flee idolatry [*pheugete apo tēs eidōlolatrias*]' (1 Cor. 6.18; 10.14).

---

[25] Markus Bockmuehl, 'The Noachide Commandments', pp. 93–5.

Holiness and the Crucified Christ

But if early Christian holiness is rooted deeply in tradition and the communal bearers of that tradition, namely Israel and the Jews – if, to put it another way, early Christian holiness is shaped by the remembrance and enactment of the story of Israel both in contemporary Judaism and in its own common life – there is also an element of profound and disturbing discontinuity and dislocation. I refer to the disturbing implications of *the death of the Messiah* for holiness as traditionally conceived.

The apostle Paul saw this clearly. Identification with Christ in his death becomes the very essence of his apostolic self-understanding and turns his vision of a 'blameless' (*amemptos*) life upside-down: 'circumcised on the eighth day, of the people of Israel, of the tribe of Benjamin, a Hebrew born of Hebrews; as to the law a Pharisee, as to zeal a persecutor of the church, as to righteousness under the law blameless. But whatever gain I had, I counted as loss for the sake of Christ . . .' (Phil. 3.5–11). The marks of holiness, of being set apart for God, are listed systematically only to be put aside, shockingly, as 'loss' (*zēmia*) and 'refuse' (*skubala*). The message of the cross, as he says to the Corinthians, is a *skandalon* to Jews and *mōria* to Gentiles. Now, wisdom, righteousness, sanctification [*hagiasmos*] and redemption are to be found somewhere quite new and unexpected: 'in Christ Jesus' crucified and risen. Therefore, says Paul, 'Let him who boasts, boast of the Lord' (1 Cor. 1.30–1).[26] Commenting on such texts, Paul Minear puts it this way:

> For execution by crucifixion to become the criterion of holiness, and of God's holiness at that, became the supreme scandal . . . It is easy enough to accept, in theory, the idea of God as the sole source and criterion of holiness; but it is anything but easy when such holiness is defined by the awful dereliction on Golgotha.'[27]

---

[26] Noteworthy, in this scriptural citation in 1 Corinthians, is the fact that 'the Lord' is reinterpreted Christologically to refer to Christ. This represents an 'extension' of monotheism in a Christological direction, itself indicative of the development of the idea of holiness in a Christological direction taking place in early Christianity.

[27] Paul S. Minear, 'The Holy and the Sacred', *Theology Today* 47 (1990–91),

The Epistle to the Hebrews may be read, at least in part, as an attempt to address precisely this issue.[28] It does so by a reinterpretation of cultic holiness in the light of the death of Christ as the sacrifice to end all sacrifice (cf. Heb. 7.23–8; 9.11–12; 10.5–18). For the author of Hebrews, the holiness of God revealed in the death of the Son of God is a holiness offered, ironically and paradoxically, through the profanity and defilement of a corpse. Now, that which sanctifies is precisely the dead corpse outside the camp:

> For the bodies of those animals whose blood is brought into the sanctuary by the high priest as a sacrifice for sin are burned outside the camp. So Jesus also suffered outside the gate in order to sanctify the people [*hina hagiasei . . . ton laon*] through his own blood. Therefore let us go forth to him outside the camp and bear the abuse he endured (Heb. 13.11–13).

Holiness as separation – of life and death, male and female, priest and lay, Jew and Gentile, purity and impurity – is displaced by *holiness as solidarity*: the solidarity of Jesus the great high priest in sharing human nature as flesh and blood and, above all, in accepting the defilement of death (cf. Heb. 2.14–15, 17). Timothy Radcliffe puts the matter well:

> [W]hat underpins this new theology of solidarity is a more fundamental innovation, which is a transformation of God's relationship to suffering and death. God had been perceived as the source of all life and holiness precisely in his separation from death ... But in Christ God's creative act happened in a grasping of the ultimate impurity and its transformation so that 'through death he might destroy him who has the power of death'.[29]

---

pp. 5–12 [p. 8]. I should say, that while Minear's essay makes many worthwhile observations, in my opinion it polarises in a quite tendentious way the distinction (such as it is) between 'the holy' and 'the sacred'.

[28] See on this Timothy Radcliffe's profound essay, 'Christ in Hebrews: Cultic Irony', in G. Turner and J. Sullivan, eds., *Explorations in Catholic Theology* (Dublin: Lindisfarne Books, 1999), pp. 1–16.

[29] Radcliffe, 'Christ in Hebrews', pp. 9–10.

Furthermore, because temple order was held to reflect the divine ordering of creation and sacrifice was understood as the way to heal and sustain the cosmos,[30] what Hebrews says about Christ as sustainer of creation by his word (1.2–3), and great high priest in his death, implies a significant development in understanding both of creation itself and God in relation to creation. God's holy otherness is not just that of transcendence, of distance from creation, sin and death. Remarkably, it is seen now even more in terms of immanence, of closeness to creation, of making atonement for sin once and for all, of embracing death in order, by death's defeat, to bring life. This closeness is communicative. Christ's high priesthood makes possible the priesthood of people of all kinds and conditions, who now 'have confidence to enter the sanctuary by the blood of Jesus . . . through the curtain, that is, through his flesh' (Heb. 10.19–20). Christ's being made perfect (*teleios*) through suffering makes possible the perfecting (*teleioō*) of all who are being sanctified (2.10–11; 10.14; 12.2). Christ's entry through death and resurrection into the 'rest' (*katapausis*) of eschatological sabbath allows him to lead all who hope in him, not least the weak and suffering, into that 'rest' also (3.7—4.13).[31] Christ as the mediator of a new covenant has given access to the realm of true worship and true holiness, in hope of which the author's addressees are to live lives of peace and love: 'But you have come to Mount Zion and to the city of the living God, the heavenly Jerusalem, and to innumerable angels in festal gathering, and to the assembly of the first-born who are enrolled in heaven, and to a judge who is God of all, and to the spirits of just men made perfect . . .' (12.22–4).

It would be a curious misreading of Hebrews to claim that its underlying logic is 'anti-cult' and that its understanding of holiness is non-sacerdotal. To the contrary, the language and practice of temple cult and priestly holiness constitute the

---

[30] 'Christ in Hebrews', pp. 3–8; cf. also, C. T. R. Hayward, 'Sirach and Wisdom's Dwelling Place', in S. C. Barton, ed., *Where Shall Wisdom Be Found?*, pp. 31–46.

[31] For more on the motif of 'rest' see C. K. Barrett, 'The Eschatology of the Epistle to the Hebrews', in W. D. Davies and D. Daube, eds., *The Background of the New Testament and its Eschatology* (Cambridge: Cambridge University Press, 1956), pp. 363–93 [pp. 366–73].

author's symbolic world through and through. If that world is a 'shadow' (*skia*: 8.5; 10.1) of an even greater reality taking place in heaven and revealed by Christ's suffering and death, it serves a crucial role nevertheless.[32] But that is not the author's concern. What he wants to show – as a basis for the encouragement of those who have 'drooping hands and weak knees' (12.12)[33] – is how much the dispensation of the new covenant sealed by Christ's blood transcends all that has gone before, including the conception and practice of holiness.

Holiness and the Unity of Humankind

My last point is a kind of 'sociological' (or ecclesiological) corollary of all that I have said about holiness up to now. It is that the New Testament witnesses to a profound sense that the holiness of God revealed through the Spirit in the life, death and resurrection of the Son of God makes possible, both in principle and in representative practice, *the unity of humankind.* With respect to Hebrews, the reinterpretation of holiness in terms of a holiness of solidarity in God's relations with creation makes possible a new solidarity within the created order itself. The locus of this new solidarity is the Church.[34] It is the solidarity which binds together all who follow the example of those who from the creation of the world have lived 'by faith',

[32] Note, however, Markus Bockmuehl's observation in his essay, 'The Church in Hebrews', in M. Bockmuehl and M.B. Thompson, eds, *A Vision for the Church* (Edinburgh: T&T Clark, 1997), p. 145: 'The author's vision, then, is almost exclusively of a Church of the Word ... One could argue that his theology is somewhat arid in this respect, given his failure to develop the complementary themes of Christ's presence through the Spirit or in the sacraments. And yet we are probably well advised not to extrapolate overmuch from the silences conditioned by the writer's central aim. In extolling the superiority of Christ's once-for-all redemption over the Old Covenant's sacrificial ritual it is after all hardly surprising that he should concentrate on the sufficiency of the *word* of Christ's achievement rather than, say, on a re-enacted liturgical drama.'

[33] On the pastoral concerns of Hebrews, see William L. Lane, 'Standing Before the Moral Claim of God: Discipleship in Hebrews', in R. N. Longenecker, ed., *Patterns of Discipleship in the New Testament*, pp. 203–24.

[34] See further, Nils Dahl's profound study, 'Christ, Creation and the Church', in W. D. Davies and D. Daube, eds., *The Background of the New Testament and its Eschatology*, pp. 422–43.

all who in hope join the pilgrimage to heaven following in the way Jesus by his death has opened up (Heb. 11.1—12.2).

To make the point clear, we need to underscore what was said above about creation. In the priestly conception, as Mary Douglas has helped us to see,[35] the transcendent holiness of God is expressed on earth by an ordered series of separations marked out by clear boundaries (cf. Gen. 1.1—2.4; Lev. 19—26, esp. 20.22–6). Typically, these boundaries are expressed in binary oppositions understood as given in creation and revelation. These oppositions are what mark out the Jews as God's holy people, Israel as the holy land, the Temple as the place where God dwells, and so on.

But the death and resurrection of Christ, as the event which inaugurates the coming near of God in salvation and judgement, comes to be seen as a new act of creation, indeed, the bringing into being of a new creation (*kainē ktisis*) remade 'in Christ' (cf. 2 Cor. 5.17). This new creation is an unmaking and remaking of the old. The extent of this unmaking is almost unimaginable. In fact, its perception and recognition required a transformation of the imagination of the kind which only the language and thought-forms of apocalypse could bring about. As an unmaking of the old, the new creation means that the old oppositions are reinterpreted, transcended, in some cases left behind altogether. In consequence, what was separated previously could now come together in a new unity – a unity, it should be said, not of sameness, but of *diversity in oneness*. The revelation of Christ as God's gift of redemption and sanctification to the world made possible, in principle at least, the unity of humankind.

That this was recognised very early on is clear in the justly famous pre-Pauline 'baptismal reunification formula'[36] which

---

[35] Among her many contributions in this area, see especially *Purity and Danger* (London: Routledge & Kegan Paul, 1966). For an appropriation by a New Testament scholar, see Bruce J. Malina, *The New Testament World* (London: SCM, 1983), pp. 122–52. For a recent symposium on her work, see J. F. A. Sawyer, ed., *Reading Leviticus. A Conversation with Mary Douglas* (Sheffield: Sheffield Academic Press, 1996).

[36] I have borrowed the phrase from Wayne A. Meeks' excellent study, 'The Image of the Androgyne: Some Uses of a Symbol in Earliest Christianity', *History of Religions* 13 (1974), pp. 165–208.

Paul quotes in Gal 3.27–8: 'For in Christ Jesus you are all sons of God [*Pantes gar huioi theou este ... en Christō Iēsou*], through faith. There is neither Jew nor Greek, there is neither slave nor free, there is no male and female; for you are all one in Christ Jesus [*pantes gar humeis heis este en Christō Iēsou*].' Here, baptism is a rite of new creation which is at the same time a return to Eden (cf. 1 Cor. 15.22, 45). In the new creation, 'all' are sons of God, 'all' are united as 'one' in Christ (cf. also 1 Cor. 12.13; Col. 3.11).

The unity of the new creation in Christ is also celebrated in the Epistle to the Ephesians (2.11–22)[37] in a passage worth quoting at length:

> But now in Christ Jesus you [Gentiles] who once were far off have been brought near in the blood of Christ. For he is our peace, who has made us both one [*ta amphotera hen*], and has broken down the dividing wall of hostility, by abolishing in his flesh the law of commandments and ordinances, that he might create in himself one new man in place of the two [*tous duo ktisei hen*], so making peace, and might reconcile us both to God in one body [*tous amphoterous en heni sōmati*] through the cross, thereby bringing the hostility to an end ... for through him we both have access in one Spirit [*en heni pneumati*] to the Father. So then you are no longer strangers and sojourners, but you are fellow citizens with the saints and members of the household of God ... Christ himself being the cornerstone, in whom the whole structure is joined together and grows into a holy temple [*naon hagion*] in the Lord; in whom you are also built into it for a dwelling place of God in the Spirit.

The language and conceptuality of *oneness* is quite emphatic: one new person, in one body, in one Spirit and belonging to one household. Furthermore, this oneness is interpreted explicitly in terms of holiness: Jews and Gentiles together form part of one 'holy temple' where God himself is present as Spirit.

But the motif of the unity of humankind resulting from God's redeeming and sanctifying work in Christ is found

---

[37] For a full bibliography and discussion, see Andrew T. Lincoln, *Ephesians* (WBC 42, Dallas: Word Books, 1990).

elsewhere, particularly in the Fourth Gospel. More than the other gospels, John places heavy emphasis on the oneness of the Father and the Son and the oneness of believers.[38] Taken as a whole, the Gospel represents a claim that the one true God has made his presence uniquely known in the person of the Son with whom he is one, belief in whom brings a new oneness into being, an eschatological unity of people drawn from every nation. Two passages are most striking. In chapter 10, Jesus reveals himself, polemically, as 'the *good* shepherd' who knows his sheep by name and whose death on their behalf will bring into 'one flock [*mia poimnē*]' under 'one shepherd [*heis poimēn*]' sheep from different folds. Furthermore, in so laying down his life in obedience to the Father's will, Jesus the Good Shepherd can affirm at the end of the discourse: 'I and the Father are one [*hen*]' (10.30). Why this emphasis on oneness? Because unity is a mark of the sanctifying presence of the one true God with his people. As a corollary, that sheep from different flocks (i.e., Jews and Gentiles) can be spoken of as 'one', in unity under 'one shepherd', is profound testimony to the truth of the revelation which has brought them together.

The other passage is John 17, the prayer of Jesus prior to his ascent to the Father via death on the cross:

> Holy Father, keep them in thy name, which thou hast given me, that they may be one, even as we are one [*hina ōsin hen kathōs hēmeis*] ... [F]or their sake I consecrate [*hagiazō*] myself, that they also may be consecrated [*hēgiasmenoi*] in truth. I do not pray for these only, but also for those who believe in me through their word, that they may all be one [*hina pantes hen ōsin*]; even as thou, Father art in me, and I in thee, that they also may be in us, so that the world may believe that thou hast sent me (17.11–22).

Once again, the oneness of believers (including those of the second and subsequent generations) is a sign of the Father's sanctifying presence. It is made possible by the 'consecration'

---

[38] I am indebted here to C. T. R. Hayward, 'The Lord is One: Some Reflections on Unity in Saint John's Gospel', an unpublished paper presented at the New Testament Postgraduate Seminar of the Department of Theology, University of Durham, on 3 March 1997.

of the Son to the Father in death, which in turn unites believers in the Son with the Father also. And in the ongoing court-like contest of testimony for and against the truth of the revelation of the Father in the Son, this unity has a probative aspect: 'I in them and thou in me, that they may become perfectly one [*hina ōsin teteleiōmenoi eis hen*], *so that the world may know* that thou hast sent me' (17.23).

Conclusion

Nicholas Lash has made the point that Christian doctrine should function as 'a set of protocols against idolatry'.[39] It strikes me that what we discover about holiness in the New Testament may serve the battle against idolatry also, not least in that period of Western cultural history we call late (or post-) modernity. According to Lash:

> The metanarratives which postmodernists like Lyotard rightly find incredible are those that speak of everywhere from nowhere in particular. But, between such dead, destructive, universals, on the one hand and, on the other, the night battle of innumerable merely private, tribal tales and pastimes (each of which, someone will say, is 'true for me'), there remains the sacramental possibility: the possibility of sense, and life, and peace, and friendship, instantiated and offered and received. But ... only from some particular place, in some particular configuration, shaped by particular experience and memory, can such comprehensive possibility be glimpsed, and born. Incarnation is particular; Bethlehem's world-birth took place then, and there. Without such reference, such rootedness, all large talk, all grand designs, are not merely abstract but destructive, hegemonic, riding roughshod over other stories, other places, other people.[40]

The ideas and practices of holiness displayed in the New Testament are far from being abstract, and need not be

---

[39] Lash, *The Beginning and the End of 'Religion'*, p. 194.
[40] *The Beginning and the End of 'Religion'*, p. 197.

'hegemonic'. As we have seen, holiness in early Christianity is shaped by the revelation of the presence of God in the history of Israel dislocated and relocated, developed and reinterpreted, under the inspiration of the Spirit in the light of the death and resurrection of Christ. The transforming effect of that revelation is particular and embodied. It is individual and social. It arises out of a tradition and gives rise to the development of tradition. It is a matter, not just of beliefs, but of practices and disciplines. It finds its focal point in the worship and witness of communities of faith.

Thus, a good case can be made for the claim that, in its own time and place, the doctrine of holiness in early Christianity constituted a 'protocol against idolatry'. Even more, however, we might wish to affirm a positive side – what Lash calls 'the sacramental possibility': that holiness in early Christianity is the discovery of the forgiveness of sins, of peace in place of hostility, above all, of life out of death made possible through the life out of death of God's own Son. And because, in the faith of Christians, that life out of death is an eschatological reality, it is a reality, a holy mystery, still true today.[41]

[41] For their critical help with an earlier version of this essay, I am grateful to John Barclay, Stanley Hauerwas, Melissa Raphael and Francis Watson, and to the members of seminar groups in the Durham Department of Theology and the Cambridge Faculty of Divinity.

PART 3

Holiness and Christian Tradition

10

Holiness and the Vision of God in the Eastern Fathers

Andrew Louth

Seeing the Unseeable God

In the epistle to the Hebrews, the author commends the pursuit of 'holiness, without which no one shall see the Lord' (Heb. 12.14). The conviction that the vision of God is only accessible to the holy is one that is very widespread: it is by no means a distinctively Christian sentiment – most religions associate very closely access to the sacred with holiness, though there may well be different ideas about what constitutes holiness: it may be ritual purity, it may be the holiness, in the sense of being set apart, that belongs to a priestly caste by birth or consecration. In the Christian tradition, however, such holiness entails moral purity, and generally any notion of ritual purity includes, though may not be exhausted by, moral purity, though this is not peculiar to Christianity, either. This conviction, that the vision of God requires holiness, is also repeated in one of the beatitudes: 'Blessed are the pure in heart, for they shall see God' (Matt. 5.8). Often, especially in the psalms, purity of heart is presented as the esssential quality required in those who turn to God. In that great prayer of repentance and contrition, Psalm 50 (or 51), the psalmist prays, 'Create a pure heart in me, O Lord' (Ps. 50.10), and in Psalm 23 (or 24), one who wishes to ascend the mount of the Lord and stand in his holy place is required, among other things, to be 'pure in heart' (Ps. 23.4). (Learned Hebraists among you who have immediate recall of the original Hebrew text may protest that the words for purity in these verses are not the same, but I am following the LXX, as

217

did the Fathers to whom I shall eventually come, and the LXX
has *katharos* in both psalms.)

So the verse from Hebrews with which I began, and the
Beatitude, are drawing on a long biblical tradition in making
holiness, or purity of heart, a prerequisite for any authentic
encounter with God. Both of these verses, however, speak of
this encounter with God in terms of vision, of seeing God. This,
too, has a long tradition in the biblical writings, but it is
complex. The last verse of the Johannine prologue encapsulates something of the complexity of the biblical tradition of the
vision of God: 'No one has ever seen God; the only-begotten
God [or Son], who is in the bosom of the Father, he has
declared [or better: explained] him' (John 1.18). What is
meant by this 'explanation' has already been asserted a few
verses earlier: 'And the Word became flesh and dwelt among
us, and we beheld his glory, the glory as of the only-begotten
from the Father, full of grace and truth' (1.14). The vision of
God is impossible – no one has ever seen God – and yet the one
who both is in the bosom of the Father and became flesh has
manifested his glory, a glory coming from the Father, and thus
'explained' him. The vision of God is impossible, and yet
possible, indeed actual. A similar paradox is to be found in the
Old Testament: the vision of God is impossible, indeed rather
worse than that – to see God means death, for humans cannot
bear the reality of God, as Semele discovered when she asked to
see Zeus as he was in all his divine splendour – and yet in the
Bible we mostly learn about this through exceptions to it,
through examples of those who have seen God and lived. Jacob,
for instance, after struggling all night long with 'a man', and
only being defeated by a mysterious touch to his thigh, is given
the name Israel, and realizes that he has been struggling with
God. As he grasps this, he exclaims, 'I have seen God face to
face and my life has been preserved' (Gen. 32.30). Hebrew
scholars tell us that the name Israel means 'one who strives with
God', but the Greek Fathers, following Philo, almost invariably
took it to mean 'one who sees God'. Similarly, Manoah,
Samson's father, reacts to his encounter with God by saying to
his wife, 'We shall surely die, for we have seen God' (Judg.
13.22). But he doesn't: as his wife wisely points out, God would
hardly have accepted their sacrifice and revealed the fate of
their son, if he had meant to destroy them.

This paradox of the vision of God – as something that human beings cannot bear, and yet something that is only revealed by exceptions to this rule – is developed at greater length in the case of Moses. We are told in Exodus that 'the Lord used to speak to Moses face to face, as a man speaks to his friend' (Exod. 33.11). And yet in that very chapter of Exodus, we are told of Moses' request to God to be allowed to see his glory. To which request he gets the reply, 'I will make all my goodness pass before you, and will proclaim before you my name "The Lord"; and I will be gracious to whom I will be gracious, and will show my mercy on whom I will show mercy. But', the Lord continues, 'you cannot see my face, for man cannot see my face and live.' God, however, offers Moses what seems to be a compromise: 'Behold, there is a place by me where you shall stand upon the rock; and while my glory passes by I will put you in a cleft of the rock, and I will cover you with my hand until I have passed by; then I will take away my hand, and you shall see my back [as the Revised Standard Version coyly translates it: the LXX says 'behind']; but my face shall not be seen' (Exod. 33.18–23). With Moses the paradox becomes even starker: God is said to speak with him as with a friend, and yet to see God 'face-to-face' is denied to Moses: all he is allowed is a glimpse of God's behind.

The Fathers and the Vision of God

I have dwelt on the idea of the vision of God in the Bible – there are other obvious places I could have mentioned, notably Isaiah's vision of God in the Temple in Isaiah 6, and Ezekiel's vision of God in the first chapter of his book of prophecy – and I have done this, because I think we need to familiarise ourselves with all this, before we look at what the Fathers had to say on holiness and the vision of God, because almost all they have to say took the form of reflection on the biblical paradox of the vision of God: the terms in which they themselves pondered on the vision of God were determined by their reflection on these passages. In particular, perhaps, the story of Moses: the pattern set by Philo, with his account of Moses as a kind of archetype of human encounter with God, was followed by the Fathers, not least the Greek Fathers, with whom I shall principally be dealing. Starting with Clement of Alexandria, we find this way of seeing the pattern of Christian discipleship, our following of Christ, reflected in the account of the life of Moses developed by Origen, the Cappadocian Fathers, then later still by the writer who called himself Dionysios the Areopagite, and then by Maximos the Confessor, and beyond. Even when it is not explicit (and it often is), we often find that reflection on the life of Moses is implicit in what the Fathers have to say about the vision of God.

The paradox of God's revelation to Moses is often dwelt on: God seems to reveal himself to Moses, and yet at the same time to deny that revelation. Often the focus of this reflection is not the revelation to Moses in the cleft of the rock that we have just looked at, but God's first revelation to Moses in the Burning Bush. You will recall that in this encounter, God tells Moses that he has chosen him to save the people of Israel from their captivity in Egypt. In order to give him authority among the Israelites – and also to reassure himself – Moses asks for God's name. The Fathers frequently pick up the puzzle of God's reply: *ehyeh asher ehyeh*. They note what might seem to us the evasiveness of 'I am that I am' or 'I will be what I will be', offered in English translations, but express this in ontological terms, for the LXX translates this 'I am the one who is'. What might that mean? God as the one who is, as opposed to those who are not, like us, for instance? It was a common enough conceit among second- and third-century Platonists that God alone truly is, that compared with Him our participation in being is frail and uncertain. And if that is true – that God alone truly is – how can we, who more nearly are not, ever come to know Him? What sort of a revelation is it, if God reveals himself as beyond anything that we are ever likely to grasp? As a young Slovene thinker has put it, 'To think of oneself as non-existent is the crucifixion of thought.'[1] Very quickly such thoughts become commonplace among Christian thinkers: thoughts that express the fundamental unknowability of God. How are we to respond to a God whose mystery is utterly unfathomable? For

---

[1] Gorazd Kocijančič, 'He Who is and Being: On the Postmodern Relevance of Eastern Christian Apophaticism', in Robert F. Taft SJ ed., *The Christian East. Orientalia Christiana Analecta* 251 (Rome: 1996), pp. 631–49, [p. 641].

the Christian Fathers the answer lies in the person of Jesus. Clement of Alexandria gives a Christian interpretation of Moses' being allowed to see the behind of God along these lines: what Moses (or the Christian) is being told by this story is that we cannot gaze on the face of God, but what we can do is follow along behind. God's reply to Moses tells the Christian who reads it that what he must do is follow Christ, become his disciple. This following Christ is the human way of seeing God, at least in this life: and such human following of one who, sharing the divine life, embraced human life as Jesus of Nazareth, means that we come close to God, that we are, in some way, assimilated to the divine life. And Clement, who among the Fathers is the fondest of pointing to the convergence of Platonism and Christianity, argues in this way that following Christ and assimilation to God amount to the same thing.

Seeing God – Becoming God

Assimilation to God – in Greek, *homoiôsis Theô(i)*, a direct quotation from Plato's dialogue the *Theætetus* – is one of the earliest ways in which the Greek Christian understanding of the goal of the human life as deification, becoming God, finds expression. Finding the right word for this took some time, but from the end of the fourth century, mainly following the usage of Gregory Nazianzen, one of the so-called Cappadocian Fathers (the one the Greek tradition came to call 'the Theologian'), the term *theôsis* became established. Neither term nor concept became as established in Western theology as in the East (though many Western theologians, both Catholic and Protestant, have exaggerated Latin unfamiliarity with this term), but we need to grasp something of its significance in Eastern theology if we are to make much progress. My stressing its Platonic provenance may lead you to think of it as an alien intrusion into Christianity, but though Platonism provided convenient terminology, *what* was being expressed by such terminology was, I think, authentically Christian. Let us turn back to the Scriptures. Another text on the vision of God I might have cited earlier is from the first Epistle of John: 'Beloved, now we are children of God, and it is not yet clear what we shall be. We know that when he appears we shall be like him, for we shall see him as he is' (1 John 3.2). Seeing God as he is is a transforming vision, in which we are assimilated to God.

There seem to me to be two points we need to grasp here. The first has to do with a difference between the prevailing notions of our culture and that of the Fathers. It was a commonplace to many philosophers of antiquity and late antiquity that 'like is known by like'. Most of the Fathers were acquainted with theories of knowledge, according to which, in order to know anything, the organ of knowledge had in some way to be conformed to the object of knowledge. Such theories of knowledge were only a corollary of a more deep-rooted conviction that we are deeply affected – ultimately, perhaps, determined – by the object of our concerns: who we are is determined by what we are concerned about. And who we *really* are is determined by what is our deepest concern. We can, for instance, become deeply concerned about money and its acquisition: this will affect the way we look at things; we will be interested in what things are worth, meaning what they can be sold for. Everything will be judged in terms of realisable value; even people will be valued either as opportunities for raising money, or, if they are 'possessed' – as wife or husband or child – as evidence of our resources. This is the point of the myth of King Midas: everything he touched turned to gold – i.e., the substance of money – even his daughter. In a more modern idiom, he knew the price of everything, but the value of nothing. Such an approach to knowledge starts from the opposite end of the spectrum to what we would probably do today: modern theories of knowledge are about gathering information; the philosopher of antiquity – whether pagan or Christian – was more concerned with the pursuit of wisdom. But in the case of God, the question of how we come to know him is even more radical, for God cannot be someone about whom we simply have information. Seeing God is not just catching sight of him – those, like me, who once sat at the feet of Professor Donald MacKinnon in Cambridge are never likely to forget a sentence from C. C. J. Webb that he constantly recalled: 'We could not allow the name of God to a being on whose privacy an Actæon could intrude, or whose secrets a Prometheus

could snatch from him without his assent.'[2] Nor could seeing
God be a matter of surveying him with approval or interest.
To see God is to encounter him and be transformed in the
process. Both of these considerations lie behind John's
assertion that 'we shall be like him, for we shall see him as he
is', and perhaps, still more, the Fathers' universal
endorsement of this.

The way the Fathers expressed this idea that knowledge of
God is deification takes some such form as this. Our ultimate
human concern is God: it is only with God that we encounter
what is beyond the finite and the transient, or rather the One
who is beyond, beyond anything we can imagine. This takes
expression in the doctrine that human beings were created, as
Genesis tells us, 'in the image of God'. We are created with an
affinity for God, found in our being created in His image. That
image is fulfilled, so far as that is possible for finite creatures, by
being brought to full likeness in the vision of God, a vision that
transforms us into God. Deified human beings become
completely, perfectly human: their nature expresses fully what
we are meant to be. Human beings whose concern falls short of
God are denying themselves their full humanity.

Knowing the Uncreated God in Darkness

The fourth century was the century that saw the conversion of
the Emperor Constantine and the beginning of the transformation of the Roman State into a Christian Empire. The same
century saw a change in Christian doctrine – or perhaps better,
a radical realisation of the implications of Christian doctrine
for our understanding of how things are, of what we might call
metaphysics or ontology. For the Council of Nicæa, called by
the Emperor Constantine in 325, declared that Our Lord Jesus
Christ is one in being, *homoousios*, with God the Father, and by
the end of the century it was a settled conviction of Orthodox
Christianity that Father, Son and Holy Spirit were one God,
sharing a single being or nature, which was radically different

---

[2] C. C. J. Webb, *Problems in the Relations of God and Man* (London: James
Nisbet, 1911), pp. 25–6.

from the universe that had been brought into being out of nothing, *ex nihilo*, by God. God's being is uncreated; in contrast, everything in the universe – human beings and everything on the earth, the earth itself, the sun and moon and the stars, and also any other beings such as angels or demons – for them, to be means to be created. The implication of this metaphysical gulf between the uncreated being of God and the created being of all else was quickly grasped, notably by the Cappadocian Fathers, St Basil the Great, his friend St Gregory of Nazianzus, and his younger brother St Gregory of Nyssa. Its principal implication was that it undermined the fundamental ontological divide of Platonic metaphysics between the spiritual world and the material world: both the spiritual world and the material world were now seen to be created. The natural affinity between God and spiritual beings, including humans (or at least their souls), posited by Platonism was abolished: the most spiritual archangel was no closer to God than a stone, for both were created *ex nihilo* by God. The human defining character-istic of being in the image of God no longer meant some natural spiritual affinity (as earlier Christian theologians had tended to suppose), but a special grace, though an enduring one, whereby human beings had been elected from the realm of creatures to the possibility of direct communion with God.

What all this meant for our understanding of human knowledge of God was worked out most clearly by Gregory of Nyssa, especially in one of his last works, the *Life of Moses*. Gregory sees significance in an aspect of the story of Moses that had not been made much of before: what he sees as a progression from light to darkness in his deepening encounter with God. A progression *from* light *to* darkness, not darkness to light. At the Burning Bush, God manifested himself as light, a light that drove away the errors of Moses' earlier ignorance: here there is a movement from darkness to light. But thereafter Moses' engagement with God takes him into deeper and deeper darkness. He receives the law by ascending Mount Sinai, and as he ascends he disappears into the cloud; after he has received the law, he draws near 'to the thick darkness where God was' (Exod. 20.21). Light–cloud–thick darkness: as Moses gets closer to God, he finds himself in ever-more-impenetrable darkness. Gregory himself explains this progression in these terms:

What is now the meaning of Moses' entry into the darkness and of the vision of God that he enjoyed in it? The present text would seem to be somewhat contradictory to the divine apparition he had seen before [at the Burning Bush] ... But we should not think that this contradicts the entire sequence of spiritual lessons which we have been considering. For the sacred text is here teaching us that spiritual knowledge first occurs as an illumination in those who experience it ... But as the soul makes progress, ... so much the more does it seem that the divine nature is invisible ... The true vision and the true knowledge of what we seek consists precisely in not seeing, in an awareness that our goal transcends all knowledge and is everywhere cut off from us by the darkness of incomprehension.[3]

The vision of God is not quite what one might imagine: it is a continual reaching out after God in a darkness of unknowing. Gregory unfolds what this means in various ways: the finite creature's reaching out after God is never ending, for God is always beyond; the creature's desire for God is never satisfied, but in a way is satisfied by not being satisfied; seeing God, Gregory says elsewhere, 'means following Him wherever He might lead'[4] – that is how Gregory interprets the passage in which Moses is denied the vision of God's face but allowed to see his behind. We find here, in an elaborated form, the paradox we noticed earlier in the scriptural teaching about the vision of God as impossible and yet granted.

This emphasis on the ineffability of God becomes a fundamental theme of Greek theology from the end of the fourth century onwards: as well as the Cappadocian Fathers, we find it eloquently expressed in St John Chrysostom.[5] In all of them it follows from the fundamental gulf now seen to exist between the uncreated God and what he has created *ex nihilo*. But it is

---

[3] Gregory of Nyssa, *Life of Moses* II. 162–3 (ed. Jean Daniélou SJ, *Sources Chrétiennes 1ter*, Paris: Le Cerf, 1968, p. 211). Translation from *From Glory to Glory*, texts from Gregory of Nyssa's mystical writings, selected and with an Introduction by Jean Daniélou SJ, translated and edited by Herbert Musurillo SJ (London: John Murray, 1962), p. 118.

[4] Gregory of Nyssa, *Life of Moses*, II. 252 (ed. Daniélou, p. 280).

[5] See especially, John Chrysostom's homilies on the incomprehensibility of God (ed. A.-M. Malingrey, *Sources Chrétiennes 28bis*, Paris: Le Cerf, 1970).

not a doctrine of agnosticism: it is not that we know nothing
about God, but that nothing that we know about him measures
up to the reality that God is. We know that God is, for sure, and
a great deal has been revealed about God's activity in creation
and about his continual attempts to draw fallen humanity back
to communion with him, notably in the Incarnation, when God
himself assumed human form to redeem us. But none of this
knowledge gives us more than a glimpse of the transcendent
reality of God. We do not know God's essence. St Basil summed
this up in a letter to a friend: 'we say that from his activities (or
energies) we know our God, but his essence itself we do not
undertake to approach; for his activities descend to us, but his
essence itself remains unapproachable'.[6]

Apophatic and Cataphatic Theology

This balance between a fundamental stress on God's ineffability, combined with grateful acknowledgment of what God has
made known of himself, above all in the Incarnation, became
characteristic of Greek theology. The writer who took the name
Dionysios the Areopagite borrowed from Neoplatonic terminology to express this distinction, and spoke of apophatic and
cataphatic theology: theology of denial and theology of affirmation. We affirm everything that Scripture asserts of God, but
at the same time we deny it, because God ineffably transcends
any concept or image that we have of him. Dionysios finds a
symbol of the coincidence of both apophatic and cataphatic
theology in the 'dazzling darkness' of God's revelation: a
radiance that is overpowering, that conceals, as it reveals.[7]

There is however a deeper significance in the relationship of
apophatic and cataphatic theology, and this draws us back to
our theme of holiness and the vision of God. Cataphatic

---

[6] Basil, *ep.* 234 (*The Letters*, ed. R. J. Deferrari, Loeb Classical Library
(London: Heinemann), vol. III, p. 372).

[7] For the image of 'dazzling darkness' (Henry Vaughan's inspired rendering
of *hyperphotos gnophos* in the last verse of his poem 'The Night'), see Dionysios
the Areopagite, *Mystical Theology*, 1.1 (ed. A. M. Ritter, *Corpus Dionysiacum* II,
Patristische Texte und Studien 36, Berlin and New York: Walter de Gruyter,
1991, p. 142, lines 1–2).

theology – what is declared in revelation, and what we discern of God's activity from the created order – affirms something about God; apophatic theology declares that all this falls short of God, and so appears to undermine the theology of affirmation. In reality, though, it undergirds it. For two reasons: first, without the denial of apophatic theology, the affirmations about God in concepts and images would become idolatrous, we might imagine that we had actually grasped the reality of God, and then we would really be lost; but secondly apophatic theology is based on the conviction born of our engagement with God that God is beyond anything we can conceive: it is not an abstract denial, but a checking of our faculty of knowing by our awareness that the God we know is beyond what we imagine. Modern Orthodox theology expresses this by saying that through God's activities towards us we know something about him, but we know this as flowing from a personal reality that cannot be captured by anything that we say about him: it is the mystery of personal communion with God, in however fleeting a form, that makes us deny the ultimacy of anything we say about God. As the great Romanian theologian, Fr Stăniloae, put it: 'the mystery of the personal reality of God is experienced, properly speaking, through the renunciation of all the words that point to the attributes and activities of God directed towards us'.[8] This same way of seeing the apophatic as grounded in the reality of person-to-person experience of God is affirmed by Vladimir Lossky:

[A]pophaticism, so far from being a limitation, enables us to transcend all concepts, every sphere of philosophical speculation. It is a tendency towards an ever-greater plenitude, in which knowledge is transformed into ignorance, the theology of concepts into contemplation, dogmas into experience of ineffable mysteries. It is, moreover, an existential theology involving man's entire being, which sets him upon the way of union, which obliges him to be

---

[8] Dumitru Stăniloae, *Teologia Dogmatică Ortodoxă* (București: Editura Institutului Biblicşi de Misiune al Bisericii Ortodoxe Române, 1996[2]), I, p. 107. Translation (modified) from Dumitru Stăniloae, *The Experience of God*, trans. and ed. Ioan Ioniță and Robert Barringer (Brookline, MA: Holy Cross Orthodox Press, 1994), p. 142.

changed, to transform his nature that he may attain to the true *gnosis* which is contemplation of the Holy Trinity. Now, this 'change of heart', this *metanoia*, means repentance. The apophatic way of Eastern theology is the repentance of the human person before the face of the living God.[9]

Apophatic theology, then, is that dimension of theology that prevents us from turning aside from the face-to-face encounter with God that lies at the heart of any genuine knowledge of God, at the heart of the vision of God. The development we have traced so far in patristic reflection on the vision of God finds its focus in Byzantine theology in pondering a biblical event that we have so far not mentioned: the Transfiguration of Christ on a mountain, traditionally identified as Mount Tabor.

The Transfiguration of Christ in Uncreated Light

In his Transfiguration, we seem to have the vision of God enacted in the life and person of Christ for those apostles – the inner three, Peter, James and John – who were privileged to behold it. The significance of the events that accompanied the Transfiguration – the dazzling light, the presence of Moses and Elijah, Peter's bewilderment and his suggestion that they put up three booths, the descent of the Cloud and the voice, the terror of the disciples and their final vision of Jesus alone – all these are teazed out in patristic exegesis. It is a theophany: the divine nature of Jesus is manifest to the disciples. But to manifest Jesus' divine nature is to manifest him as one of the Trinity, something symbolised by the descent of the Cloud, the Shekinah of the divine presence, representing the Holy Spirit, and the voice of the Father declaring Jesus his beloved Son. The radiance in which Jesus is transfigured renders his human nature transparent to the divine nature, and the presence of Moses and Elijah, recalling the principal parts of the Hebrew Scriptures, the Law and the Prophets, often provokes comment about how, in the light of Christ, the meaning of the Scriptures becomes transparent. But this

---

[9] Vladimir Lossky, *The Mystical Theology of the Eastern Church* (London: James Clarke, 1957), p. 238.

radiance produces terror among the disciples; they fall on their faces: the revelation is overwhelming, more than humankind can bear. All the themes we have encountered so far about the paradox of the vision of God come into focus in such a reading of the Transfiguration.

From the very beginning the Fathers were fascinated by this mystery: Irenæus' famous assertion – *Gloria enim Dei vivens homo, vita autem hominis visio Dei,* 'the glory of God is a live human being, and a truly human life is the vision of God'[10] – that striking assertion occurs in a chapter in which, without explicitly mentioning the Transfiguration, Irenæus draws together all the themes brought into focus in that mystery. But in patristic reference to the Transfiguration, it soon becomes apparent that the Fathers are not talking about an event confined to the life of Jesus; they are talking about an experience known and experienced in the life of the Church. So we read in the late fourth-century Macarian Homilies, 'as the body of the Lord was glorified, when He went up into the mountain and was transfigured into the divine glory and into the infinite light, so are the bodies of the saints glorified and shine like lightning' (XV.38).[11] You will recall that in the accounts of the Transfiguration, particular attention is directed to the face of Christ: it was altered, St Luke says (Luke 9.29); it shone like the sun, according to St Matthew (Matt. 17.2). So too in the transfiguration of the saints: it is said of St Antony, the great ascetic of the Egyptian Desert, that if someone who did not know him visited him when he was in the company of other monks, they would immediately know who he was 'as if drawn by his eyes'. This was because of the 'great and indescribable charm' of his face, an outward sign of his 'settled character and the purity of his soul'.[12]

In the Byzantine period, all this seems to come together. St Maximos the Confessor, in the seventh century, reflected frequently on the Transfiguration. He uses Dionysios' language of apophatic and cataphatic theology to interpret the mystery.

---

[10] Irenæus, *Adversus Hæreses* IV.20.7, ed. W. W. Harvey (Cambridge: Typis Academicis, 1857), vol. II, p. 219.

[11] Makarios, *Hom.* 15. 38. ed. H. Dörries, E. Klostermann and M. Kroeger, Patristische Texte und Studien 4 (Berlin: Walter de Gruyter, 1964), p. 149.

[12] Athanasius, *Vita Antonii* 67, tr. R. T. Meyer, Ancient Christian Writers 10 (London: Longmans, Green & Co., 1950), p. 77.

The light irradiating his body and his clothes, so that the human aspect of Christ becomes transparent to the divine nature, speaks to Maximos of the transparence and limpidity of Scripture and creation to those whose understanding has been purified and attuned to Christ, to those able to receive the light of Christ: the phrase from the psalm, 'in your light shall we see light' (Ps. 35 [36].9), is never far away in patristic interpretation of the Transfiguration. That is the cataphatic side, as Maximos puts it, the affirmative side of the Transfiguration. But the face, the face altered and shining like the sun: that draws us into a mystery beyond anything we can understand, into the mystery of the person of Christ, the divine Person who assumed our human nature. The face of Christ – face and person are the same word in Greek: *prosôpon* – speaks of the 'characteristic hiddenness of his [divine] being'.[13] This is the face-to-face encounter with Christ, it is that to which all the radiance draws us, but it is an unfathomable mystery: we simply gaze and are struck with awe at the ineffable personal encounter that lies behind all that is revealed in the radiance flowing from his body and his clothes. What we have here in Maximos is a kind of fusing together of the mysticism of darkness we have found in Gregory of Nyssa, and a mysticism of light, which the Transfiguration more naturally symbolises. The light of the Godhead irradiates the created humanity of Christ and draws us into a state where the whole of the cosmos is revealed as irradiated by the light of the Godhead, but the light itself, because it is the light of the uncreated Godhead, because it is itself uncreated, cannot be grasped by our human faculties: it is dazzling, a 'dazzling darkness', as the Welsh poet Henry Vaughan put it, a light that, drawing us into itself, draws us into the unfathomable mystery of the reality of God.

Such an emphasis on the Transfiguration might be thought to overshadow the more profound mysteries of the Cross and Resurrection. I do not think that is so: the Transfiguration

---

[13] Maximos, *Quæstiones et Dubia* 191, line 48, ed. J. H. Declerck, Corpus Christianorum Series Græca 10 (Turnhout: Brepols, 1982), p. 134. The Transfiguration is also interpreted by Maximos in his *Capita theologica et œconomica* 13–18 (Patrologia Græca [= PG] 90. 1129C–1133B), and in *Ambiguum* 10. 17, 31 (PG 91. 1125D–1128D, 1160B–1169B).

speaks of a transfiguration within us, and the cross is the measure of the transformation needed if we are to be open to the light of Mount Tabor and of the Garden of the Resurrection: Maximos' apophatic interpretation of the Transfiguration makes it emblematic of what Lossky has called, in the phrase already quoted, 'the repentance of the human person before the face of the living God'. There is, very likely, a contrast in the understanding of these mysteries between the West, which has tended to emphasise the Cross, and the East, which looks beyond the suffering of the Cross to the victory manifest in the Resurrection and prefigured in the Transfiguration; but I do not want to be polemical here. It is nevertheless the case that Byzantine theology came more and more to lay emphasis on the Transfiguration as archetypal of the human encounter with God.

A thousand years ago, at the turn of the last millennium, a remarkable monk, St Symeon the New Theologian ('new' in contrast with the other 'theologians' of the Greek tradition, St John the Evangelist and St Gregory of Nazianzus) introduced a fresh note into Byzantine theology by speaking of his own experiences of the uncreated light of the Godhead: hitherto the Byzantine tradition had been remarkably shy of autobiography. Throughout his writings he describes these experiences, and sees them revealing the reality of what it is to be Christian: a response to God's presence to humanity in the Incarnate Christ, a presence extended to us now through Gospel and Sacrament, and made our own in felt experience, most typically experience of the uncreated light of the Godhead. His first experience was a kind of conversion experience, to which, as he says, he was only haltingly faithful. He was praying, he says, in his usual place, and suddenly 'he saw nothing but light all around him, and did not know whether he was standing on the ground ... Instead he was wholly in the presence of immaterial light, and seemed to himself to have turned into light.'[14] What is said in the Gospels of the transfigured Christ is true of Symeon: he is irradiated by light; he has become light. Transfigured, Christ is manifest as he truly is, and we can only know this if we too are

[14] Symeon the New Theologian, *Catechesis* 22.93–4, 97–8, ed. Basile Krivochéine, *Sources Chrétiennes* 104 (Paris: Le Cerf, 1964), p. 372.

irradiated by the same light. In passing, some of you may find the words I have just quoted familiar: if so, it is probably because they are the motto that stands at the beginning of the score of John Tavener's *Ikon of Light*, the text of which is drawn from one of St Symeon's prayers beseeching the transforming presence of the Holy Spirit. That experience was transient, and Symeon tells us he was not faithful to it: he turned his back on it and pursued for some years the career of a courtier. His later visions are rather different. They are less dramatic, but leave him with a deep longing for God, a longing that leads him to become a monk, to embrace a life of obedience to his spiritual father, of simplicity and prayer. Gradually, the experience of light becomes not an overwhelming exception, but quieter and more normal: such experiences came to accompany the times when he received holy communion, for instance. He speaks of this progress in these terms:

> Like a star that rises, You manifest yourself from afar, You grow slowly. Not that You change in so doing, but You open the mind of Your servant that he may see. You manifest yourself like the sun, little by little, and gradually the darkness flees and disappears. I believe it is You who come, You who are present everywhere. When You encompass me altogether, Saviour, as in the past, when you surround me completely, I am freed from my troubles, freed from the darkness, from temptations, from the passions, from all thoughts. I am filled with joy and an indescribable happiness (*Hymn* 51.35–46).[15]

Symeon's influence was eventually to be considerable. Even if he was controversial in his lifetime, as the shadows of the declining Byzantine Empire lengthened, the monks of Byzantium, especially on the Holy Mountain of Athos, came to treasure such experiences of the divine uncreated light. But again it became controversial. At the beginning of the fourteenth century, a Greek monk from the West, from Calabria, called Varlaam, rejected such experiences of the divine light as hallucinations, on the grounds that God was

---

[15] Symeon the New Theologian, *Hymn* 51.35–46, ed. J. Koder, *Sources Chrétiennes* 196 (Paris: Le Cerf, 1973), pp. 186–8.

utterly unknowable: there could be no experience of God, we could only know about God by inference, from creation and from revelation. We cannot now go into the controversy that ensued, called the 'Hesychast' controversy, from the ideal of *hêsychia*, or stillness, that lay at the heart of the contemplative life of the monks maligned by Varlaam, or the 'Palamite' controversy, after St Gregory Palamas, himself a former monk of Athos, later archbishop of Thessaloniki, who defended the monks against Varlaam.[16] To oversimplify, Varlaam seems to have grasped one aspect of the biblical paradox with which we began – the emphasis on God's transcendence or unknowability – but neglected the other side – the reality of God's self-communication. Much of the argument turned on the interpretation of the Transfiguration, for, the monks argued, if Varlaam is right, what was the light in which Christ was transfigured on Tabor? It was, Varlaam asserted, some kind of created light, a symbol of the glory of God. For the monks, however, the light of Tabor was the uncreated light of the Godhead; it was the same light that they hoped to see in their own life of prayer. If we look back at the biblical ideas with which we began, we can, I think, see that the monks were right, for there is no contrast in the Bible between the face-to-face vision of God and experience of his glory: when Moses is denied the face-to-face vision of God, it is God's glory that passes by while he is hidden in the cleft of the rock; the glory of the Father that is declared by the Word, according to John's prologue, is not a compensation, a kind of *pis aller*, for a face-to-face vision of God that we are denied because of God's transcendence. To encounter God's glory is to encounter God Himself, not some sort of symbol of the divine presence, which is less than God, not in fact God at all. St Gregory Palamas, drawing on ideas in the earlier Greek Fathers, affirmed this by making a distinction within God between his essence and his energies. God in Himself, in his essence, is utterly unknowable,

---

[16] The most important of Gregory Palamas' defences of the hesychast monks is his *Triads in defence of the holy hesychasts*, edited by Jean Meyendorff (Louvain: Spicilegium Sacrum Lovaniense, Études et Documents 30–1, 1973). A briefer defence is found in his *150 Chapters*, edited by Robert E. Sinkewicz (Toronto: Pontifical Institute of Medieval Studies, Studies and Texts 83, 1988).

none of our concepts or images measures up to the reality of what God is; but at the same time God makes himself known to us in his energies – his activities in creation or redemption, activities manifesting his attributes of goodness, mercy, judgment and love – but the one we encounter in these energies is not some created representative, or symbol, of God: it is God Himself. One of these uncreated energies of God is his uncreated light, his glory, which irradiated the human reality of Christ at the Transfiguration, and which some monks rightly claimed to see when, in their prayer, they attained a state of simplicity and purity of heart.

Uncreated versus Created Light

That is no more than a sketch of what the Greek and Byzantine Fathers understood by holiness and the vision of God. It is very inadequate and introductory; there is much more that could be said about the Hesychast doctrine of beholding the uncreated light of the Godhead: there is the role of the body, for instance, barely touched on, the way in which the response in ascetic struggle to Christ's call restores a psychosomatic unity to human beings that has been broken and distorted by the Fall. But what we have seen is an understanding of the vision of God in which the light of God's glory transfigures the one able to behold it, so that that 'holiness without which no one shall see God' is seen to be a simplicity before God, and transparence to his radiance, the result of an unremitting life of love and self-denial, so that someone holy in this sense is one in whom the glory of God's love is palpable.

But you might say that this is all very well, but it is very remote from the lives we live at the beginning of the twenty-first century. I would like to end this paper by addressing some remarks to that charge. First, I want to draw attention to something historical. The last two centuries have seen extraordinary changes in the kind of society we know, at least in the West: changes that have extended extraordinary freedoms, not just political, to the individual, and led to dramatic transformations in our relationship with nature and the environment, so that we are less and less at the mercy of the unpredictability of our environment, indeed more and more the environment itself seems to be at our mercy. The progress of science, and especially its technological applications, together with an explosion in the production and processing of information, has produced a global awareness (again, only on the part of a highly powerful minority), unlike anything known before. But parallel with that, and scarcely noticed, during those two centuries, there has been a striking rediscovery and revival of the hesychast way of prayer that we have just looked at. In 1782 a large volume called the *Philokalia* was published in Venice, an anthology of hesychast spirituality. The last two centuries have seen the quiet but inexorable growth of its influence: it has been translated into many languages, the English translation now nearly complete,[17] and the last few decades (in the now fragmented Soviet bloc, the last decade) have seen an enormous increase in monasticism, inspired by hesychast spirituality, not to mention its influence on styles of lay spirituality, even outside the Orthodox Church. I do not think that that parallelism is a matter of chance, it is rather a matter of divine providence. Hesychast spirituality has experienced a revival because it has something to say to our heavily technologised society, in which the world we encounter increasingly bears the marks of human shaping, almost to the exclusion of the hand of the Creator.

That was my historical point; my other two points are concerned with the relevance of aspects of the hesychast doctrine of the uncreated light. First, that doctrine speaks of a vision of God face-to-face in the uncreated light. Whatever is meant by a vision of the uncreated light it does not mean some sort of harsh, overwhelming, impersonal radiance: the kind of harsh, unforgiving radiance of the searchlight or the naked light bulb that has been found so often this century on closely guarded frontiers and in interrogation cells. The doctrine of the uncreated light is about the reality, the experienced reality, of the 'light of the knowledge of the glory of God, in the face of Christ' (2 Cor. 4.6). The face of God, as the Transfiguration

---

[17] *The Philokalia. The Complete Text,* compiled by St Nikodimos of the Holy Mountain and St Makarios of Corinth, translated from the Greek and edited by G. E. H. Palmer, Philip Sherrard and Kallistos Ware, 4 vols. (out of 5) published so far (London and Boston: Faber & Faber, 1979–1995).

reveals, is a human face, a particular face: it is not an overwhelming, boundless infinity, in which everything is swallowed up, but a particular face, the face of Jesus, looking at us in judgement, certainly, but in love and grace, mercy and forgiveness. A particular face: it could be different, it is not universal, nor is it perfect, with the smooth perfection and symmetry of a film star. In the East, the icon of Christ, of the face of Christ, is recognisable: as a photograph bears a known and loved likeness. It is recognisable, because it is not perfect: it is in fact lop-sided. The earliest icon of the face of Christ we have, the Christ of Mount Sinai, as it is called, an early sixth-century icon, has established itself as the model, to the exclusion of all else. And it is a curiously lop-sided face, it is particular, unique even. The Jewish philosopher, Emmanuel Levinas, has spoken about the ultimacy of the face, its resistance to what is true universally and everywhere, and also the fragility of the face, that bears the meaning of person, but can so easily be erased – or liquidated, to use a twentieth-century Soviet coinage.[18] As I understand it, the doctrine of the uncreated light of the Godhead affirms this sense of the ultimacy of the face: the uncreated light, which is God himself, is the light of the countenance, not the light of a searchlight; it is the light of the radiance of love, and elicits love, and radiance, from those who spare it time and attention. There is a poem of Rilke's, in which a defeated Russian Tsar retreats to his private chapel, and there prays before an icon of the Mother of God: he looks at her, her veil, her hands,

> but the countenance is like a door
> opening on to the warm twilight,
> in which smiles from her gracious lips
> seem to stray with their light, and disappear.[19]

The face speaks of a uniqueness that only the Creator can make, and of love and compassion that is eroded, even as that sense of uniqueness is lost sight of.

[18] See especially Emmanuel Levinas, *Totalité et Infini. Essai sur l'extériorité* Phaenomenologica 8 (The Hague, Boston and London: Martinus Nijhoff, 1961, 1971), in particular the third part, 'Le Visage et l'extériorité', pp. 161–225.

[19] Rainer Maria Rilke, 'Die Zaren', in *Das Buch der Bilder* cited from *Werke*, Band I, 1 (Frankfurt am Main: Insel Verlag, 1966 [1984 reprint]), p. 191. My translation.

But, and this is my second point, the uncreated light is an *uncreated* light: it is beyond the reach of human making. Much of the burden of Heidegger's philosophy was about the trivialisation of human life brought about by concentration on the seemingly limitless possibilities opened up by human technological ingenuity: we are led to concentrate on what things are for, how we can use them, in ever more diverse ways, and find ourselves 'forgetful of being', as Heidegger rather gnomically put it – forgetful of the realm anterior to the realm of things, and also to the realm of personal relationships that make up the societies in which we find ourselves so much at home. When he came to reflect on what art can be, must be, in such a society as ours, he made a distinction between the 'world', in which we find ourselves so easily at home, a network of meaning conferred and interpreted that does not reach beyond itself, and what he called the 'earth', 'Erde', something altogether more primordial and uncontrollable. It is the role of the true artist to tap in some way this realm of 'Erde' so that it emerges and makes itself felt in the true 'work of art'.[20] This sense of a world over which we have so much control, such increasing control, so that what we control manifests such a complexity and self-sufficiency that we no longer need look beyond it, seems to me the greatest danger of the society in which we live. The hesychast witness to the uncreated, and our need for engagement with the uncreated reality of God, seems to me needed more than ever in such a society.

I want to close on a more personal note. There is one thing that has struck me ever since it came to my consciousness: especially as when I was born it was not there, and yet ever since my ninth month it has always been there, and will remain. The feast of the Transfiguration of Our Lord in both the Western and the Eastern Churches falls on 6 August. The first 6 August of my life saw another light, dwarfing any created light ever seen before. For, as you will all have guessed, that 6 August fell in 1945, the day when the first atomic bomb exploded above Hiroshima. So the feast of the Uncreated Light has been ever

---

[20] See Martin Heidegger, 'Der Ursprung des Kunstwerkes', which exists in various forms. I have used that published in *Holzwege* (Frankfurt am Main: Vittorio Klostermann, 1950, 1963), pp. 7–68.

since then the anniversary of the most destructive created light ever known. It is as if we have a choice: our created light or God's Uncreated Light; destruction or life; faces melting in the blast of nuclear explosion or faces affirmed by the light of uncreated love. There, I think, is the relevance of the quest for the Uncreated Light of the Godhead that lies at the heart of the understanding of holiness and the vision of God in the Eastern Fathers.

11

Finding a *via media*: The Moderation of Holiness in Fourth-century Western Asceticism

Carol Harrison

Moderation and compromise are probably not words that occur very often in relation to holiness. They are not, I must admit, very common in most Patristic literature either. The reflections of the fathers seem to veer like dodgem cars between dangerous extremes, and sometimes clash head-on with a huge bump. It is the bumps, the clashes, the exhilarating collisions, which I would like to examine in this paper – the confrontations and debates which lead to a plea for careful driving.

When we turn to examine the ways in which the early Christians understood and defined themselves in relation to the world, to their society and culture, the idea of holiness predominates. They understood themselves to be leading the highest, most excellent, true and perfect life, in holding to their faith in Christ and in following his teaching. They were a holy people, set apart by God, for God. They had turned their backs on the gods of paganism and, in so doing, on a society and culture determined, in almost every aspect, by their worship. The emergence of Christianity from this world, the ambiguous, faltering process of Christianisation, is also, necessarily, the history of the emergence of a distinctively Christian idea of holiness – of what exactly it is that sets the Christian apart, of what is distinctive about Christian faith and life. This happened in innumerable ways, in many different contexts. In this paper, I would like to concentrate on one of them: the practice of asceticism, of setting oneself apart, of attempting to achieve holiness, by voluntary self-denial.

Holiness Defined by Persecution

It was straightforward for the early Christians to understand the need for self-denial, to the point of self-sacrifice, when the Church, because of its refusal to worship the gods who protected the well-being of the Empire, was persecuted by the Roman state as a hostile, anarchic, anti-social and unpatriotic threat. Christians were forced, as it were, to become holy, to practise asceticism; they were unremittingly set apart and pushed into self-denial so long as they held to their faith. They were forced to extremes – either faithfulness, death and salvation or apostasy, life and damnation. At this precipitous edge it was easy to understand the essentials of the faith, the nature of Christian holiness, the need for asceticism. The essence of the faith was, in a way, imposed upon them by the Romans, who were fulfilling prophecy and enabling Christians to literally follow Christ to death. This experience was, unsurprisingly, to determine the nature of Christian life and self-understanding, even when the persecutions ceased.

But I am not going to go on, as you might fear, and suggest that asceticism, in the form of Christian monasticism and the desert fathers and mothers, flourished in the fourth century simply as a reaction to the end of the persecutions; that it was an attempt to revive the martyr spirit, to retain the identity of the early church, to perpetuate and maintain Christian holiness in a hostile and ambiguous world of inward and outward temptation and worldliness. This traditional line must be re-evaluated in the light of the extraordinary flowering of scholarship on forms of asceticism in the Patristic era.

The Ascetic Ideal and its Inspiration

It is quite clear, as New Testament scholars have known all along, that other forms of asceticism, in addition to the most extreme and definitive one of martyrdom, were present within Christian life from the very beginning, and are not at all dissimilar to the forms which are often identified as part of the so-called fourth-century revolution. A desire to set oneself apart, to attain holiness by self-denial, was an intrinsic feature of Christian life from the very beginning, quite apart from that imposed by the Romans. One of the most common, and certainly one of the most prominent forms this took in the patristic era was the practice of celibacy or virginity. The ideal of the virgin life was, for most of the fathers, the acme of the Christian life, its greatest grace, its highest calling, its definitive model and supreme achievement. It coloured everything they had to say.

Why was this? I do not intend to answer this question in any great depth but it must be raised, and possible responses aired, before we move on to examine the debates and controversies its practice aroused, and before we can appreciate the elements of compromise and moderation which they introduced into the early Christian ideal of holiness.

Why virginity? Virginity was not a new ideal. It was present in some forms of Judaism (particularly in the Dead Sea Scroll community); in pagan culture, particularly as part of the highly respected philosophical ideal of single-minded devotion to the search for truth; in heterodox communities such as the Gnostics and Manichees, the Encratites, Marcionites and Montanists, where it frequently had dualistic, eschatological overtones; in traditional Roman respect for the vestal virgins and the *univira* (the once-married woman).

Perhaps most importantly, the fathers believed that they found it in Scripture. Adam and Eve, the archetypal and perfect human beings, were held by almost all of them to be either virginal or sexless. There was no sexual intercourse, no child-birth in paradise. Both are the result of, and necessitated by, the Fall; they are at once a consolation and a punishment for humanity's loss of perfection. A return to paradise, to what humanity was created and intended by God to be, therefore demanded virginity. This was confirmed by the fact that both Mary and Jesus were held by the fathers to be virgin, and by numerous passages in the New Testament which were read in an ascetic sense, as advocating virginity. It was not difficult to adduce passages from the gospels, such as Matthew 19.12 concerning those 'who have made themselves eunuchs for the sake of the kingdom of heaven', or Mark 12.25 concerning the woman who had had seven husbands, where Jesus observes, 'For when they rise from the dead, they neither marry nor are given in marriage, but are like angels in heaven.' Paul, of course, provided even more ammunition for the ascetic arsenal, especially in 1 Corinthians 7, for example verse 29: 'Let those who have wives live as though they have none.' The gospels were also replete with passages that did little to recommend family life as an ideal but which, interpreted in the right way, bolstered the ascetic agenda: what else was one to make of passages suggesting that hatred of one's own family was the precondition for discipleship (Luke 14.26), or of Jesus' rejection of his blood relations in favour of those who do the work of God (Mark 3.31–5)?

Virginity then, was part of the context of early Christianity and its Scriptures could be read as endorsing it. But this does not really answer the question as to *why* the early Christians adopted it as the defining feature of Christian holiness. The problem is that the works of the fathers are replete with exhortations to, defences of, encomiums upon, virginity, but suggest very little as to *why* it is so important, except by inference and context. It is as if they already have the agenda, and it reads virginity, so that every debate which arises, each problem that must be dealt with, is answered according to this agenda. What we find ourselves reading in patristic literature, more often than not, is propaganda: propaganda for the ascetic, virgin life. The texts will be misunderstood if we read them otherwise and this is no doubt why so much of recent scholarship has concentrated on the rhetorical function of ascetic literature and exegesis – for that is precisely what it is – rhetoric with the aim of teaching, persuading and motivating the reader to adopt the ascetic, virginal life.

Nor, of course will it do to say that the fathers were simply prompted by Scripture. There is so much there (especially in the Old Testament) to militate against the ascetic agenda, and as Elizabeth Clark has brilliantly demonstrated in her most recent book, what is really going on is simply exegesis with a set pattern, so that texts are tailored to fit the particular author's understanding of the Christian life of asceticism and virginity. The extraordinary lengths to which some authors went to make awkward garments fit becomes a laughable changing-room drama. As Clark puts it, 'Procreating Israelites could be exegetically displaced by renunciatory Christians.'[1]

---

[1] E. A. Clark, *Reading Renunciation: Asceticism and Scripture in Early Christianity* (Princeton: Princeton University Press, 1999), p. 203.

The question then still remains, why virginity? We can only speculate and it seems to me that there are no hard and fast answers. The speculation of scholars has ranged over a wide field: perhaps Christians were seeking not only to emulate, but to supersede the ascetic ideal of pagan philosophy which still evidently carried enormous weight in cultured circles; perhaps the revival of the ancient philosophical ideal of singleness, unity, wholeness and harmony in late second-century Neopythagoreanism and third-century Neoplatonism meant that it still exerted a magnetic influence; perhaps Christian interpretation of virginity was intended as a corrective or counterweight to heterodox views; perhaps it was theologically motivated and the story of Adam and Eve did indeed provide a powerful paradigm for pre-lapsarian human life which should be followed; perhaps the adoption of such a high moral code, which could command universal respect and praise, was regarded as essential for Christians who were subject to criticism from all quarters, even when persecution had ended; perhaps the results of the ascetic life to some extent justified the means and furthered its propagation, for example, it endowed its proponents with authority (maybe in contradistinction to church authority or clerical hierarchy) and its female practitioners with the opportunity to undo the curse of Eve, to obtain freedom from the social, sexual constraints which would otherwise condemn them to a life of marriage, childbearing, servitude and subjection. Perhaps, finally, there is some truth after all in the theories which see its phenomenal increase in popularity after the Constantinian revolution as a mark of the church's desire to retain its original identity as a martyr church, at odds with a hostile world, a pilgrim church alienated from its true homeland, a church with a sharp cutting edge of moral resolution and firmness rather than one made up of woolly opportunists and nominal converts, a holy church of spiritual rigour removed from comfortable compromise with the secular still, all-too-pagan, authorities. There is probably some truth in all of these suggestions but I do not think that any one of them provides a complete answer.

I would like to pursue one suggestion which I have not elaborated on so far but which I think might bear running with for a while, especially since it has some relevance to the specifically Western debates we will be considering later. When we ask what is being set apart and what the individual celibate Christian is denying him or herself in espousing virginity as definitive of true Christian life and holiness, we are forced to acknowledge the rather awkward fact that the vast majority of married humanity and the everyday, ordinary life of most of the Empire's population, is what is being renounced and effectively written off as inadequate, or at least, as not meeting the highest calling of the Christian life. This raises a host of questions: is the Christian ideal of holiness really so morally demanding, so exclusive, as to marginalise and exclude all but a very small, elite minority? Was married life, sexual activity and the bringing up of children so morally reprehensible as to fall so far short of the Christian calling? Were all Christians expected to follow the rarified high moral ground of the virgins or was there space for the gentle slopes of decency within the Church? What implications did this have for a Christian theology of marriage and sexuality? Was the traditional model of human society really so far removed from what God had intended? Was social convention and expectation indeed so radically misguided that it had to be so violently opposed and overturned? The fact that these questions were real ones, which were asked, debated or defended by the fathers, suggests that at the heart of the ascetic ideal was a desire, whether conscious or not, to separate oneself from traditional society, from the common and accepted pattern of marriage and children which had hitherto been regarded as a duty in order to foster, protect and continue that society. It was certainly this issue which seems to have been at the forefront of Western debates.

Augustine's *Confessions* are one of the most revealing accounts of what conversion to Christianity meant in the fourth century. Books 1–8 not only detail the doubts and uncertainties of an intellectual whose mind must be satisfied before he can accept the faith, they also portray with astonishing and acute psychological introspection the battle of the will to overcome temptation and illicit desires in order to single-mindedly and single-heartedly accept Christianity. The mark of his will's conversion was, for Augustine, his willingness to abandon his one-time mistress and to wholeheartedly embrace celibacy. He did not, at this point, wish to become a monk, or to pursue any other religious vocation, he merely wished to be baptised and to become a lay Christian, single-mindedly devoted to God. He would have heard the virtues of celibacy extolled in the highest terms by Ambrose, the Bishop of Milan, who eventually baptised him in 387. It was his friend Ponticianus' account of the conversion of two civil servants to a life of celibacy after reading the great Eastern classic of the ascetic life, the *Life of Antony*, that was one of the final weights in the balance which precipitated his conversion. The final one was, of course, the ascetic admonition of St Paul in Romans 13.14 to 'make no provision for the flesh, to gratify its desires'. All the influences which we mentioned above were probably at play in Augustine's mind. His *Confessions* and his conversion are strong evidence for the prevalence of the ascetic ideal and the powerful pull which it could exert upon an individual Christian convert, away from traditional social structures towards a radically new and revolutionary way of life.

Western Asceticism

In order to discuss, and attempt to resolve, some of the questions which we have seen this new, alternative way of life posed, we perhaps need to examine in a little more detail the specific nature of Western asceticism. As in the East, there is evidence for the practice and exaltation of asceticism, usually in the form of virginity, from a very early date. This most often seems to have taken the form of female virginity, either in the household or some sort of community. The West was no doubt influenced by Eastern models, partly through the travels of Westerners such as Cassian, Rufinus and Jerome in the East, and by the visits of Easterners such as Athanasius to the West. Some of the key texts of Eastern asceticism, including the *Life of Antony*, were translated into Latin early on. They, together with the work of Western writers, led Westerners to attempt to follow the Eastern pattern and to create an ascetic life for themselves in accordance with the desert ideals. Despite attempts by some to live the anchoritic ideal, the form of Western asceticism was generally communal, either in the household or, later, the monastery. The practices of the former were diverse, ranging from a virgin daughter or son within the household, the spiritual cohabitation of a man and a woman, to a small community of virgins or lay 'servants of God'. Monastic houses arose, not least, perhaps, because some of asceticism's most prominent exponents, including Augustine at Hippo and Martin at Tours, were either aristocrats or cultured intellectuals, or both, and hence prime candidates for the role of bishop, or a priestly ministry, who then had to attempt to reconcile this way of life with the ascetic ideal. The evolution of the monk-bishop and of the clerical community as a sort of monastery and seminary in one meant, also, that Western asceticism tended to be city based, unlike the Eastern desert model, and more involved with the various aspects of the wider society. Moreover, as the *Lives* of Ambrose, Martin and Augustine attest, the monk-bishop increasingly assumed, in popular perception, the authority traditionally attributed to the Eastern 'holy man'.[2]

It is individuals who stand out in the West as proponents of the ascetic ideal; cultured, well-educated and before their ascetic renunciation, well-placed and well-off. They form a sort of 'Western community', overcoming geographical distance by exchange of letters and ideas. This applies not just to the men who became bishops and founders or members of monastic communities, but also to women. The role of rich, aristocratic, educated and therefore influential women, or *conversi*, as they became known, is an especially interesting aspect of asceticism in the West. Often the wives, widows, daughters or sisters of senators, they founded or joined communities, sometimes leaving their children in order to do so, and disposed of their wealth to further the ascetic cause, acting very much as patrons or benefactors. They studied Scripture, learnt biblical languages and read the fathers. Jerome's small community with Paula and her daughter Eustochium in Bethlehem, Melania and Rufinus in Jerusalem, Marcella[3] and Asella[4] in Rome, are perhaps the most famous examples.

---

[2] See P. Rousseau, 'The Spiritual Authority of the Monk-Bishop: Eastern Elements in some Western Hagiography in the Fourth and Fifth Centuries', *Journal of Theological Studies* 22 (1971), pp. 380–419.

[3] Jerome, *Letter* 127.5.

[4] Jerome, *Letter* 24.4.

Reactions to Ascetic Practice

The reactions that asceticism inspired and the questions that initiated a clearer definition of holiness in the West might now be raised in this context. The fact that so many of the well-known proponents of asceticism in the West, both men and women, had previously belonged to the aristocracy, or were cultured intellectuals, holding, or at least educated for, high office, could not but cause a reaction. They belonged to an elite, to those who formed, cultivated and ensured the continuance of Roman identity and culture. That they should so dramatically turn their backs on it by giving up their privileged lives, their professions and vast wealth, their duties and responsibilites, represented a revolutionary move. Their much-valued moderation and temperance gone, they appeared, according to their more extreme critics, in dirty habits, smelly, unwashed, unshaven, with long beards and wasted, pale faces;[5] they were in every sense unrecognisable. They were met with shocked and hurt incomprehension[6] from their families and friends and by derision and mockery from their pagan peers. As Jerome puts it, they 'appeared strange, ignominious and debasing' to outsiders.[7] They were compared by pagans to swine or elephants;[8] a miserable, morbid species who shunned the light in favour of barren inhospitable places, they mortified, tortured and tormented themselves, abandoning all contact with the human society they so hated.[9]

They could not be ignored. On being widowed, Jerome's good friend, the well-known and respected senator Pammachius, donned a habit and continued to mix with his colleagues in the senate.[10] The two noble Aquitainians,

---

[5] See Dom Gougard, 'Les Critiques Formulées Contre les Premiers Moines D'Occident', *Revue Mabillon* 24 (1934), pp. 145–163 [160]; J. Fontaine, 'L'Aristocratie Occidentale devant le Monachisme', *Revista di Storia e Letteratura Religiosa* 15, (1979), pp. 28–53 [p. 36 n. 24], for references to these characteristics.

[6] E.g., Ambrose's letter to Sabinus concerning Paulinus of Nola's conversion (Ambrose, *Letter* 58.5).

[7] Jerome, *Letter* 127.5.

[8] Libanius, *Oration* 30.8.

[9] Rutilius Namatianus, *On His Return* 1.5.515–26.

[10] Jerome, *Letter* 66.4.6.

Paulinus of Nola and Sulpicius Severus, both abandoned high office to pursue asceticism through the monastic life. Honoratus, the great landowner, relinquished all his possessions and retreated to the barren and arid island of Lerins. Augustine, the up-and-coming rhetor, with such a promising career ahead of him, retreated to the semi-monastic communities of Cassiciacum and Thagaste before establishing a monastic house for clergy at Hippo. Martin, the soldier, became a monk, and was eventually consecrated Bishop of Tours. The increasing number of monk-bishops were also subject to criticism since there were those who doubted whether the monastic vocation was compatible with the office of bishop.[11]

This aristocratic, intellectual espousal of asceticism was not, as we have already noted, confined to men. High-ranking, notable women of the most influential families were also abandoning the well-nigh inevitable roles of wife and mother in order to espouse the ascetic life. In many ways their actions had wider repercussions than those of men in relation to traditional social structures.[12] The family had long been the crux of Roman society, a microcosm of social peace and order, a building block for the wider state. The fact that such prominent women defied social expectation and convention by choosing to remain unmarried turned things on their head. The much valued *concordia,* or harmony of the household, from which order and peace in the state derived, was vitiated by such a severe blow to the authority which the head of the household, the paterfamilias, had hitherto held. By renouncing marriage and children these women were seen as failing in their duty, abrogating their responsibility to continue and ensure the family's future. Even when they did marry, there is evidence of the power of the ascetic ideal in the fact that Christian women married later, had fewer children and tended not to remarry if

[11] See C. Stancliffe, *Saint Martin and His Hagiographer: History and Miracle in Sulpicius Severus* (Oxford: Oxford University Press, 1983), pp. 292–5; pp. 299–300 in relation to Martin of Tours; Gougard, 'Les Critiques' p. 162 in relation to Honoratus of Arles.

[12] I am very much indebted in the following paragraph to the article of H. Drijvers, 'Virginity and Asceticism in Late Western Elites' in *Sexual Asymmetry* eds., J. Blok and J. C. Gieben (Amsterdam: 1987), pp. 241–73.

widowed.[13] The future of the aristocratic family was also jeopardised by the redeployment of its financial resources by these women in favour of the church, often to the detriment of legal heirs and even their own children.[14]

A good deal of Western ascetic literature seems to be directed towards this phenomenon, either to encourage, instruct and admonish the women, as in Jerome's letters, to present an apology to defend and explain their actions to those (especially their families) who were being deprived of their status, wealth and future, or to criticise those avaricious, worldly priests or monks who sought to profit from them by obsequious ingratiation, flattery, seduction or deception.[15]

Evidence derived from the lives of aristocratic, high ranking, educated individuals, is, of course, extremely partial. They were a privileged elite, a very small minority of the wider population. There were no doubt many other, less prominent or influential ascetics pursuing the virgin life in a much less dramatic way. The vast, silent majority of the population, were no doubt married, bringing up children and getting on with the everyday occupations they had always pursued in a conventional and traditional way. This does not mean that the evidence is not important. The individuals we have mentioned were undeniably influential in defining and shaping the identity and self-understanding of the church precisely because they did hold important social or ecclesiastical positions. They had influence, authority, a voice (even though that of the women is almost always mediated to us through a male author) and they inspired a large body of literature. As we have seen, their words and actions met with incomprehension, misrepresentation, resistance and criticism, not least because, by embracing virginity, they were breaking with tradition, overturning social convention and custom, threatening, it seemed, the very foundations of human society.

[13] Drijvers, 'Virginity', p. 257.
[14] Jerome, *Letter* 108.15; 31 on Paula.
[15] See Stancliffe, *Saint Martin*, pp. 269–70.

Ascetic Debates in Fourth-century Rome

It was in the theologically traditional and socially conservative city of Rome that some of their most extreme critics,[16] as well as some of their most extreme practitioners and defenders, emerged. It is to Rome in the fourth century that I would now like to turn, in order to present the debates of this century in microcosm.

It was, of course, to Rome that Jerome retired, between AD 382–5, after his unsatisfactory attempt to lead the anchoritic life in the desert of Chalcis. It was he, more than any other individual, who acted as spiritual advisor, mentor, teacher and acolyte to the aristocratic women inspired by the likes of Athanasius to embrace the ascetic, virgin life. It was he, among all the fathers, who expounded the most extreme ascetic ideal as the prerequisite for authentic Christian faith. He was insistent that Adam and Eve were virgins before the Fall and that this was and should be mankind's natural state;[17] sexual desire by contrast, was no more than a 'natural tendency to evil'.[18] He had no time, it seems, for any compromise whatsoever, most especially for marriage, or heaven forefend, remarriage. The only use he could imagine for the former was the creation of a new generation of Christian ascetics,[19] the latter was no better than the brothel. God's command to 'increase and multiply' in Genesis, along with the numerous passages of the Old Testament which might be read as endorsing marriage and children, were subjected to thorough-going ascetic exegesis and read strictly according to its agenda.[20] Rather, Jerome stressed that Christ was a virgin, Mary a virgin, the apostles, either virgin or continent after marriage, just as bishops, priests and deacons should be.[21]

---

[16] See D. G. Hunter, '*On the sin of Adam and Eve*: A little-known Defence of Marriage and Childbearing by Ambrosiaster', *Harvard Theological Review* 82.3 (1989), pp. 283–99.

[17] Jerome, *Letter* 22.19.

[18] Jerome, *Letter* 22.24.

[19] Jerome, *Letter* 22.20; 66.3.

[20] For good examples of this see Clark, *Reading Renunciation*. Among the ascetic strategies adopted she mentions inter-textual exegesis, difference in times and figurative exegesis.

[21] Jerome, *To Pammachius* 21.

It was quite clear to him that since the number of the saints was now complete, there was no need for reproduction.[22] In a society where *pietas* or loyalty to one's family, was one of the highest virtues, it was Jerome who advised the widow Floria, 'Honour your father, but only if he does not separate you from your true Father';[23] the virgin Paula, who had abandoned her two youngest children, that 'too great affection [for her children] is lack of affection for God';[24] and used the account of James and John leaving their father to follow Christ to enourage ascetics to leave behind their families.[25] It was he who was blamed by an outraged populace when Paula's convalescent daughter Blesilla died, apparently worn down to death by the harsh ascetic observances of fasting and nightly vigils he had recommended.[26] When her mother fainted at her daughter's funeral the people grumbled, 'How long must we refrain from driving these detestable monks out of Rome? Why do we not stone them or hurl them into the Tiber?'[27]

Jerome's teaching was expressed in strict hierarchical terms: merit and future reward followed the degree of ascetic achievement attained in this life. The virginal state was the highest, followed by widowhood and then marriage; it was gold to their silver or hay,[28] and, as in the parable of the talents, would receive a hundredfold reward, whereas the widow could only expect to receive sixty-fold and the married thirty-fold.[29] In fact, Jerome thought he was being generous. It was, of course, unfair of God to give the same reward for different merits,[30] but others he knows of do not include the married in their hierarchy of merit and reward at all. Nevertheless, Jerome's version of the Christian life struck many as shockingly elitist, negative about the body and sexuality, derogatory of marriage

---

[22] Jerome, *Against Helvidius* 20–21.
[23] Jerome, *Letter* 54.3.
[24] Jerome, *Letter* 39.6.
[25] Jerome, *Letter* 38.5.
[26] Jerome, *Letter* 39.6.
[27] Jerome, *Letter* 39.6.2 quoted by Stancliffe, *Saint Martin*, p. 276; Gougard, 'Les Critiques', p. 135.
[28] Jerome, *To Pammachius* 2.
[29] Jerome, *Against Jovinian* 2.33.
[30] Jerome, *Against Jovinian* 2.23 .

and family relationships, and, above all, exclusive. As might be expected, he was not without his critics.

But Jerome, though he was (and is) usually taken as a convenient Aunt Sally among Christians, was not alone. As he himself points out, appealing to Tertullian, Cyprian and Ambrose, he is merely voicing Western consensus on these matters: 'Read them,' he retorts, 'and in their company accuse me or free me.'[31] He might equally have appealed to the majority of Greek fathers.

There is no doubt that Jerome's language lacks moderation but the fact that he became so embroiled in ascetic debates and hostile criticism is perhaps due to the presence of an heretical sect who were prominent in Rome, who had just been legally condemned and who appeared, unfortunately, to resemble his thought, and that of other extreme ascetics, very closely. These were the Manichees: dualists, determinists, a type of fourth-century Gnostic who reviled creation, the body, matter and the reproduction of matter, as the work of an evil, hostile, alien demiurge and whose elite – the elect – practiced severe ascet-icism in fasting and celibacy, in order to distance themselves from evil matter and liberate the divine spark or light trapped within them.

It had become commonplace to label any manifestation of extreme asceticism as Manichean and thereby to suggest that it was unacceptably severe and probably heretical.[32] Christian ascetics were understandably acutely sensitive to the charge since, although they could refute the charge of dualism, their ascetic practice seemed to endorse such beliefs. It seems that a good deal of the hostile reaction to asceticism was in fact directed against the Manichees, first of all, and then, by inference, to those Christians who seemed so vehemently to defend such practices. Were they not Manichees too?

It is clear that from the 380s onwards there was definite unease and disquiet in some quarters at the extreme ascetic practices of certain Christians at Rome. This uneasiness found expression in works which both defended Christian marriage

---

[31] Jerome, *To Pammachius* 17.
[32] E.g. Jerome, *Letter* 22.13.3, in reference to Roman women; Rufinus, *Apology* 25.42–43, in reference to Jerome.

and sexuality, and urged moderation in ascetic practice. Against the Gnostics, authors such as Ambrosiaster, Helvidius, Jovinian, Viligantius and Augustine echoed the earlier defence of Christian marriage and sexuality which had already been articulated with such eloquent moderation by the likes of Clement of Alexandria in the third century. In their own ways they each attempted to walk the difficult tightrope across the chasm which had opened up between ascetic extremism, which verged on heresy, on the one hand, and the moral complacency and compromise made possible by a Christian empire on the other.

Towards a via media

What was this *via media*?[33] Writing in the early 380s, the Roman priest who has become known to us as Ambrosiaster, composed a treatise entitled *On the sin of Adam and Eve*.[34] In it he mounts a carefully argued case for procreation by appealing to the 'innate power' for procreation which human beings share with all living things, and which was called forth in the command to the first couple to 'increase and multiply'. This divine injunction was obviously one of the most sensitive texts in early ascetic debates and enjoyed as many different interpretations as there were shades of opinion and ascetic, or non-ascetic inclination. Ambrosiaster, as one might expect, takes it literally, and in a startling and gloriously subversive way, breaks with all previous literal interpretations by quietly assuming that it must refer to Adam and Eve *before* the Fall. Thus he initiates a revolution in Patristic thought by supposing that Adam and Eve would have married and had children by sexual intercourse in paradise itself. Nor, he assures his reader, is the time for procreation over, as some suggest. So long as creation continues it is part of a larger whole and must also continue – to reject it is to lean towards Manicheism, to impugn the value of creation and the clear testimony of Scripture (where he cites verses to

---

[33] The following section owes a great deal to the work of David Hunter, whose articles on Western asceticism have highlighted many important and interesting aspects and have very much set the agenda for future work.

[34] See Hunter, 'A little known Defence'.

illustrate the congruence between Christ's teaching and that of the Old Testament, in opposition to the discontinuities which extremists were fond of highlighting). Furthermore, he held that sexual relations are wholly unaffected by the Fall. What has changed is what Genesis tells us changed: death, the pain of childbirth and the toil of working the soil. Ambrosiaster's one concession to the ascetic agenda in this treatise is an argument for the celibacy of the clergy, not on the grounds that marriage and sexual relations are in any way illicit – what he has in mind in general is a post-marital celibacy after having children – but because the priest must be purer because he acts in the place of Christ and ministers holy things.

As David Hunter, who has brought this important, but hitherto little-known treatise to scholars' attention, suggests, Ambrosiaster was probably writing with Jerome in mind, not least his *Letter* 22, which I have had occasion to refer to already, and his treatise *Against Helvidius*. We know little about Helvidius apart from what Jerome reveals: that he undermined Mary's perpetual virginity by asserting that she had children after Jesus was born. The merit of Mary's virginity was also questioned towards the end of the 380s by the Roman monk Jovinian who seems to have taken the same position as Ambrosiaster towards Roman asceticism and, no doubt influenced by him, launched a rather more vociferous and popular attack upon those Christian ascetics such as Jerome, Ambrose and Pope Siricius whose extremism seemed to him to be no better than, and as open to condemnation as, Manicheism.[35]

Hunter has convincingly argued that Jovinian's first opponents were, in fact, the Manichees at Rome, but that Catholic ascetics, by attacking him, and thus implicitly defending the Manichees, tarred themselves with the Manichean brush.[36] Against the Manichees' docetic Christology, Jovinian rejected the doctrine of Mary's perpetual virginity, even after giving birth to Christ;[37] against their emphasis on the superiority of virginity and the hierarchy of

[35] Jerome, *Against Jovinian* I.5.

[36] D. G. Hunter, 'Resistance to the Virginal Ideal in Late-Fourth-Century Rome: The Case of Jovinian', *Theological Studies* 48 (1987), pp. 45–64.

[37] Ambrose, *Letter* 42.

merit it accrues, he questioned the value of fasting and stressed the power of baptism in making all people equally holy whatever their ascetic practice.[38] He also argued that there were no otherworldly rewards graded according to ascetic practice but one reward for all – virgin, widowed or married – who keep their baptismal vows,[39] and that baptism places the Christian beyond temptation.[40] Against the Manichees' rejection of the Old Testament and their criticism of the ethics of the Patriarchs, in particular, Jovinian interpreted Genesis 1–3 literally, and cited passages from both Testaments, including the Song of Songs, to endorse the goodness of Christian marriage.[41]

Although Jovinian was condemned by the Synod of Milan in 393, and exiled by Honorius in 398, his teaching remained popular[42] and his ideas could not be ignored by the church. His position was clear cut: anyone who denigrated marriage by making it inferior to virginity was condemning marriage, and was therefore a Manichee and a condemned heretic. There was with Jovinian, as with Jerome, no middle way. The extremely hostile reception which Jerome's treatise against Jovinian received in Rome, with its exaltation of the superiority of virginity and its denigration of the married life, is evidence of the Roman Christians' real sense of the dangers of extreme asceticism and of the need for a reaction against it. The Aquitainian priest Vigilantius' condemnation of various aspects of the ascetic life towards the end of the fourth century, such as enforced clerical celibacy, the monastic life and alms sent to the Jerusalem poor, is further evidence of currents of resistance to the ascetic ideal.[43] But was Jovianian's equally extreme rejection of any form of ascetic practice and his assertion of the unassailability and equality of all baptised Christians, in merit and reward, really the answer? Could the value of virginity be retained without lapsing into heretical

---

[38] Jerome, *Against Jovinian* 1.3.
[39] Jerome, *Against Jovinian* 1.3.
[40] Jerome, *Dialogue Against the Pelagians* I.16.
[41] Jerome, *Against Jovinian* I.5.
[42] Hunter, 'Resistance', p. 48 n.14 cites Siricius *Letter* 2.2.3; Jerome, *Against Jovinian* 2.36; Augustine, *On the Merits and Forgiveness of Sins* 3.13.
[43] See Jerome's *Against Vigilantius*.

Manicheism?[44] Could the goodness of marriage be upheld without rejecting ascetic practices altogether?

It is rare in history to have two such extreme positions so clearly and sharply polarised by two individuals. For whatever reason, the church had long exalted virginity. Yet it had also fought a long battle against the threat of Gnosticism and that radical dualism which, in its thorough-going asceticism, led to the rejection of creation, the human body and sexuality and the Scriptures of the Old Testament. The church was made up of a large majority of married couples with families.

In the work of Ambrosiaster we have already seen a reaction to the specific dilemma posed in Rome in the fourth century. It fell to Augustine, a new convert from Manicheism, in Rome at the time Jovinian was making his ideas known, to take up Ambrosiaster's insights and secure a workable *via media* for the church.

Augustine's Moderation of Holiness

In what remains of this paper I can only briefly point the way forward. We have seen that it was Manicheism that lay at the heart of the ascetic debates and divisions in Rome. Augustine, who had spent nine years as a Manichean hearer, who had lived with a concubine and had a child, who was converted to a Christian life which for him demanded celibacy to be genuine and who went on to live the rest of his life as a monk, was uniquely placed to appreciate what was at issue.

In innumerable treatises we find Augustine forced onto the precarious tightrope walk of ascetic debate. In his early works, where he is eager to dissociate himself from the Manichees, he stresses the goodness of creation which is the work of the divine Creator (*On the Nature of the Good*); he enters the battlefield of scriptural exegesis against Faustus and uses all the strategies at his disposal to reclaim the Old Testament as a work reflecting Christian morality that endorses marriage and sexual

---

[44] The fact that it was legally and officially defined as a heresy, and had been implicated in the reasons for Priscillian's condemnation, would only add weight to Jovinian's teaching.

intercourse (*Against Faustus*); he moves, gradually, towards a literal interpretation of Genesis and interprets 'increase and multiply', like Ambrosiaster, to mean that Adam and Eve were intended to procreate by sexual intercourse in paradise.[45] The natural human state, before the Fall, was therefore a gloriously social one: the first human beings were intended to marry, to procreate, to found a society and share a common life. How revolutionary this was it is difficult to overestimate.

In two works written at the turn of the fourth century Augustine specifically addresses the debate between Jerome and Jovinian. In *On the Good of Marriage* he takes the line that virginity is better but marriage is most certainly a good. Indeed he describes three 'goods' of marriage: children (*proles*), fidelity (*fides*) and the sacrament (*sacramentum*). The most revealing section is the one on fidelity, where Augustine effectively baptises the Roman ideal of married life as one of harmony and concord – *concordia* – by describing it as a religious concord – *concordia religiosa*. Referring to Acts 4.32 – a text which, significantly will also be determinative of his description of the common monastic life – he suggests that the union of man and wife in marriage, with one heart and one mind towards God, signifies the unity of the heavenly city. Marriage, in this treatise, is considered and defined not so much as a sexual relationship but as a social bond of friendship, fellowship and mutual affection.[46] Nor is the sexual relationship a result of the Fall. Rather, Augustine places it as part of the 'friendly fellowship of marriage' which might legitimately be motivated, not by a desire for procreation but simply by the duty which spouses owe to one another.[47]

Having reinstated marriage in the Christian life, against the Manichees and extremists such as Jerome, Augustine goes to equal pains to reinstate the value of asceticism against Manichean misinterpretation of it and the outright rejection of it by extremists such as Jovinian. To an extent, he does this in the same ways as he re-established marriage, by radically re-thinking

---

[45] Augustine, *Literal Commentary on Genesis* 9.3.6.

[46] Augustine, *On the Good of Marriage*, e.g. 1.1.

[47] *The Good of Marriage* 4.4. I owe this insight to D. G. Hunter 'Augustinian Pessimism? A New Look At Augustine's Teaching on Sex, Marriage and Celibacy', *Augustinian Studies* 25 (1994), pp. 153–77.

and re-defining it. In *On Holy Virginity* he is quite clear that
virginity is superior to marriage, but he is careful to guard
against any hint of superiority in the virgin ascetic. Virginity, he
makes clear, is a gift of grace. It is given to those who can receive
it and is not in any way merited. Further, the virgin cannot claim
superiority of virtue to a married person because virtue is hidden
within the soul, and some virtues, like humility, obedience and
readiness for martyrdom, are greater than virginity and might
well be present in the married person and absent in the virgin
ascetic.[48] In fact this treatise is not so much on the practice of the
ascetic life, as a warning against the sin of pride and an exhor-
tation to humility. Virginity is superior because it allows virgins
to single-mindedly and single-heartedly devote themselves to
God; it lends itself more readily to a community united in heart
and soul, selflessly seeking the common good; it comes closer to
the heavenly society of the saints. At least it does in theory and
ascetics strive to realise it in practice, but as we shall see, they are
just as unlikely to realise it as the married majority.

As the fifth century progressed Augustine's ideas in these two
treatises on marriage and virginity were subjected to fresh
reflection and elucidation when he was forced to counter the
thought of Pelagius – a Jerome and a Jovinian rolled into one.
Like Jerome, Pelagius was an extreme ascetic, with a following
of noble Roman aristocrats eager to excel in the virgin life; like
Jovinian he rejected any double standard and thought that all
Christians were equal, that there were no distinctions of merit.
Pelagius, however, thought that equality rested on the call to
ascetic perfection, based on baptismal initiation, a perfection
which, he maintained was realisable by all.[49]

The *via media* which Augustine had developed between
Jerome and Jovinian was reconfirmed in his long dispute with
Pelagius. Against the Pelagian charge (made by Julian of
Eclanum) that he remained a Manichee in teaching a doctrine
of original sin, Augustine reiterated his stress on the goodness
of conception, birth and marriage and even conceded
that libido might have operated (albeit in a different way from
that in which we now experience it) in paradise. Against the

---

[48] Augustine, *On Holy Virginity* 44.45–6.
[49] See, e.g. Pelagius' *Epistle to Demetrias*.

Pelagian claim that all were called to perfection and all were capable of attaining it Augustine argued that no one could attain it in this life – neither the married person nor the virgin ascetic or monk. All were subject to original sin, and life inside the cloister, or behind the veil, was just as ambiguous, just as subject to temptation and sin, as life outside and beyond it. What mattered was not physical virginity but single-minded, whole-hearted devotion to God; not personal achievement, but dependence upon grace; not self-referential pride, but humble service of the common good; not the solitary life, but the common life – a community with one heart and mind towards God. Original sin proved to be the final leveller, the middle way between asceticism and ordinary life. In Augustine's thought it reconfirmed human solidarity, not only in sin, but in dependence upon grace, and its need for charity, humility, faith and mutual inter-dependence.

Conclusion

A pagan critic seems to have seen to the heart of the ascetic debate and the way in which it divided the Christian church. Celsus not only accused Christians of trying to destroy family life by encouraging children to convert against their parent's wishes, but also of threatening the stability of the Empire if they all withdrew from society and did not care for the accepted, normal life.[50]

Augustine seems to have achieved a middle way, not only between Christian disputes concerning the nature of asceticism, but between Christianity and its secular context. There was to be no setting apart, no separation from anything: holiness was unattainable and would only be realised in the final separation of the last judgement in the life to come. In this life, ascetic and married, Christian and pagan, belonged to a world dominated by the solidarity of sin, the ambiguities of grace and the common life of humility, faith and charity. It was within this ambiguous, fragile context that holiness was to be sought and, in some cases, through grace, partially attained.

---

[50] Origen, *Against Celsus* 3.55; 8.48 – cited by Drijvers, 'Virginity', p. 253.

12

Benedictine Holiness

Henry Mayr-Harting

Introduction

Although I went to two Benedictine schools, it was only at the
second, Douai, that Benedictine spirituality or holiness (I use
the two words interchangeably) came to mean anything to me.
On one of my earliest days at Douai, in the autumn of 1949,
some of us new boys were detailed to pick potatoes on the
monastery's land. There was a good deal of silly talk and
horseplay. Nobody had told us that the short, dumpy, snubby-
nosed man wearing green corduroy trousers, quietly and
uncensoriously picking potatoes alongside us, was the abbot.
Abbot Sylvester Mooney was one of the few authentic saints
whom I have encountered in my life. But it was only later when
one had face-to-face talks with him, when one learned how he
daily walked up and down the church meditating for half an
hour before morning office began at five, and when one
realised that he never cut monks down but always gave them a
helping hand, that one came to know gradually of his sanctity.
There was nothing dramatic or pushed-under-one's-nose about
it. On every great festival of the church he came down to the
school to give a brief address to the senior boys. Highly intel-
ligent and widely read as he was, he never tried to impress but
conveyed his good wishes in a simple, slightly shy, and often
moving way, and then looked demure while *ad multos annos* was
sung for his benefit. He was re-elected abbot every eight years
by the community, from the age of 43 for 40 years, and at the
age of 83 he would certainly have been re-elected had he not
then been adamant on standing down. Very unusually for an

ex-abbot, the monks insisted that he should continue to live at Douai, where, as he became ill in high old age, he was tenderly cared for by them, and he died aged 102. When I came to know him, he was in his sixties.

There are three phrases by which I would sum up Benedictine holiness: completely undemonstrative, deeply conventual, and lacking any system of expertise. When I was an Oxford undergraduate in the 1950s the Catholic Chaplain was Monsignor Valentine Elwes, known to everyone as Father Val. Regrettably, he only really recognised the existence of public schools, but he used to make an interesting contrast between the Sunday mass-going habits of those who had gone to Jesuit and to Benedictine schools. The Jesuits, if they went to mass at all, would turn up, on time, to the eight o'clock mass. The Benedictines, all of whom went to mass, would show up only at the 11.15, and many of them late.

With these remarks by way of introduction, I shall divide my paper into two parts, one on the *Rule of St Benedict* itself, and one on Augustine Baker's *Holy Wisdom*.

The Rule of St Benedict

The *Rule of St Benedict*, an incisive masterpiece, was written as a guide to the monastic life around the year 550. Benedict of Nursia was a Central Italian of not very good family, who lived his life amidst the turmoil and warfare caused by the barbarian incursions into the Roman Empire. Apart from his *Rule*, practically all we know about Benedict comes from the *Dialogues* of Pope Gregory the Great, a work about the Holy Men of Central Italy written in the 590s. The evidences of impoverishment in sixth-century Italy are written all over Gregory's book, and Benedict's *Rule* shows that he envisaged a community that was far from rich, unlike so many Benedictine monasteries later. The *Rule of St Benedict* shows, however, that all this was turned from economic and social calamity, into the seizure of a spiritual opportunity.

Benedictine scholars used to think that the *Rule* had been written as a blue-print for the whole of Western monasticism. But that opinion has not stood close scrutiny. Only in the time of the Emperor Charlemagne and his successors in the ninth century, more than two hundred years after it was written, did it become *the* authoritative prescription for monasteries, to the exclusion of all else.

To what did it owe its success? Partly to its inherent wisdom. Partly to the admiration of the influential early English Christians, especially Bede. Partly to its not being too precise in its detailed stipulations (a feature of which we shall see that Augustine Baker availed himself), but containing much in the way of general spiritual precept. And partly to its brilliant rhetoric.

To the last I was personally exposed from an early age, for I went to a prep school run by Benedictine monks. Each day after lunch, one of the boys read a passage of the *Rule* in front of the monks and the whole school. 'Wine is no drink for monks', we would read with a satirical glance at the community unless we were paralysed with giggles, 'but since nowadays monks cannot be persuaded of this, let us at least agree to drink temperately and not to saturation, for wine maketh even the wise to fall away.' The monks paid no small attention to Benedict's injunctions not to spare the rod against 'the shameless and callous, the proud and the disobedient'. Every Friday one term, at the regular inspection by the headmaster of our form room, I was found to be the only boy with an untidy desk. Every week he and I would walk over to his study after the inspection, talking amicably as we went, so that he could cane me. For in the issue of caning boys, the 1940s were closer to the 550s than to the 1990s! That headmaster was Father David Parry, who has since become world famous – as an expert in mystical prayer.

It is important to establish from the outset the atmosphere of the *Rule*. On a casual glance it may seem rather forbidding. Benedict's monks were to be men of *gravitas*, serious in manner and of few words; as to laughter, that was practically forbidden. One could have too much, even of edifying conversations, for in much speaking sin was inescapable. To speak befits the master; to be silent and to listen becomes the disciple. The monk should not be wordy in prayer. Prayer should be brief and pure, unless – and here comes one of Benedict's masterly riders – unless perhaps it be prolonged by an inspiration of divine grace. As for idle talk which provoked laughter, he condemned it with a perpetual ban (an *aeterna clausura*). The trouble with laughter was that it broke the fragile spell of listening, concentration and meditation. Benedict might allow himself the occasional chuckle – monks who are late for the night office, he says, should stand *inside* the oratory where they could be seen by everyone. If they were to remain outside, 'there will perhaps be someone of the type who will go back to bed and sleep'. But laughter, never!

Pope Gregory the Great, when he wrote his *Dialogues*, was equally witty, and equally opposed to laughter. There was a holy man called Isaac from near Spoleto. He was a model of humility, of prayerfulness, of voluntary poverty, of charity, of prophetic insight, and of the performance of miracles to relieve the poverty of others. His one trait that seemed reprehensible, said Gregory with genuine disapproval, was that at times he gave way to extreme laughter. Why, it was hard to tell. Perhaps, opined the pope, because so holy a person needed at least one drawback to remind him of his fallibility.

The evil of much talk and uncontrolled laughter has to be understood alongside one of Benedict's main aims – to establish a culture of listening. The opening words of the *Rule* are: 'hearken, my son, to the precepts of the master [i.e., the author of the *Rule*] and incline the ear of thy heart'. Not just one's ear, but one's heart and inclination. It wasn't all one-way listening by the disciple to the master or the abbot. On important business, the abbot was to call together the whole community for counsel. 'Now the reason,' says Benedict, 'why we have said that all should be called to council, is that God often reveals what is better to the younger.' How contrary to this was the spirit of Master Thompson of Trinity College, Cambridge, who once notoriously said, 'none of us is infallible, not even the youngest!' Again, Benedict speaks about the reception in the monastery of pilgrim monks. 'If such a monk should reasonably, modestly and charitably censure or remark upon any defect, let the abbot *consider* the matter prudently, lest perchance the Lord will have sent him for this very end.'

Benedict's idea of mutual listening was part of his total concept of a monastic community, which may best be described as trying, on this earth, to work towards the fellow citizenship of the heavenly kingdom. It was not a new idea, for instance, to say that the social distinctions of the world should not be reflected in a community of monks who had, in a sense, contracted out of the world. But in the dislocations and insecurities of Central Italian society caused by the wars between the Byzantines and the Goths in the 530s and 540s, when we know that people were only too inclined to stand on their social dignity, Benedict set about the elimination of every social distinction with a ruthlessness never before witnessed in monasteries.

No monk was to protect or exercise any sort of patronage over another, least of all if they were blood relations. Everyone, except the sick, should eat the same food and should wear well-fitting and serviceable but cheap clothes. Nobody was to avoid the menial tasks of working in the kitchen. If a present were sent to anyone, the abbot should see it first. 'If the abbot allow it to be received,' Benedict continues, 'it shall be his to decide to whom it is to be given; and let not the brother to whom it was [first] sent be vexed thereat, lest occasion be given to the devil.' Prep school boys of the 1940s, who depended on pots of marmite and jars of jam sent from home to palliate the repulsive bread of those times, were naturally outraged at having to read this out, and at the idea that their precious parcels might be directed to someone else, very likely an enemy! They had not yet read the anthropologists who would have told them what gift-giving and gift-receiving could be, as a form of social climbing.

Benedict insisted that rich and poor should equally be accepted as monks if they were suitable, and the same went for the reception of guests. Indeed, he says, 'it is most especially in the reception of poor guests and of pilgrims that attentive care is to be shown, because in them is Christ the more received. Dread is enough of itself to secure honour for the rich.' When I was an undergraduate, travelling along the pilgrimage routes to Santiago de Compostella to study Romanesque art and architecture, I came one evening to the monastery of Santo Domingo de Silos in Spain, looking scruffy enough with my rucksack, and in a rather unbathed state. When supper time arrived at nine o'clock, I was asked to wait outside the refectory door while all the monks went in. Then the abbot came up, a tall man with the typical dark good looks of a Mediterranean ecclesiastic, high forehead and aquiline nose, like a churchman who could have stepped out of a Ravenna mosaic, and washed my hands, the jug of water and bowl being carried by a junior monk. I shall never forget the kindly smile, totally devoid of patronisation, that he gave me as he followed this prescription of the *Rule of St Benedict*.

The most powerful of all Benedict's devices for breaking up social distinctions in the monastic community was his principle of seniority. It was simple compared with anything that had gone before. It was entirely based on time of entering the monastery. This was a clear criterion in itself which left all considerations of former wealth, age and social class irrelevant. All monks were to go to communion, intone the psalms, and stand in choir, in this order. With a rhetorical flourish, typical of Benedict, he adds, 'let him who came to the monastery at the second hour of the day, whatever be his age or dignity, know that he is junior to him who came at the first hour'. It may be surprising to some that I treat this as a brilliant novelty, since it is the very order of seniority which obtains amongst the fellows of colleges, and so we take it for granted. But that is because it is under the influence of Benedict that our colleges have come to use this as one means to achieve classlessness. I know of only one exception to this rule of seniority in any collegiate institution of either Oxford or Cambridge. If the person who came to Christ Church at the second hour of the day were a canon, he would not be junior to him who arrived at the first hour, unless perchance he had been pipped at the post by another canon!

Benedict is at his most impressive in the way he envisages authority to work in the community. Christian monasticism was originally a mainly Eastern phenomenon, which was domiciled in the West during the fifth and sixth centuries. That domiciling, for whatever reasons, involved a considerable heightening of abbatial authority. Benedict was no exception; the abbot stands four-square in the centre of the *Rule*. But his authority was far from unrestrained. I am not speaking of constitutional restraints. People in the sixth century were not constitutionalists, and Benedict's *constitutional* restraints on the abbot were nugatory. I am speaking of restraint by Benedict's assumption of *shared* moral and spiritual objectives; by the erection of a *yardstick* external to his will against which the abbot's actions could be measured; and by the development of a notion of *stewardship* which made the abbot accountable to God for his flock. It may be naïve to think of these as restraints at all, but I believe it to be unhistorical to think of constitutional checks as the only form of restraint. One of the greatest rulers of the medieval West, the Emperor Charlemagne, based much of his rule on the assumption of shared moral objectives. And, of secular rulers, he was the first great propagator of the *Rule of St Benedict*.

The nineteenth-century historian, Lord Acton, argued that the greatest contribution of the Christian church to liberty had been the holding up of an external yardstick of morality against rulers' actions, which might often be ignored, but never went away. It is fashionable nowadays to mention Acton only to deride him, but I cannot see much cause for derision in that argument. As to Benedict's idea of authority as a stewardship, it passed directly into a work by the greatest of Benedict's admirers, Pope Gregory the Great, a work which would shape the notion of authority altogether for centuries to come – his *Pastoral Care*. How original Benedict was, I do not care to discuss, for he had that kind of originality which made every point, wherever it came from, his own. But I do say that Benedict was one of the actual fountain sources of the idea that authority, not just monastic authority but *all* authority, should be limited, an idea which has been a powerful yeast in the history of Europe.

Early in the *Rule*, Benedict discusses what kind of a man the abbot should be. The abbot is understood to act in the monastery in the place of Christ. His commands and teaching should be infused into the minds of his disciples like the leaven of divine justice. In other words obedience is not due *because* the abbot says or commands, but because through his words, Christ is able to act as a leaven in the monks' minds. 'Let the abbot constantly remember,' Benedict continues, 'that at God's awe-inspiring judgment, both matters will be under scrutiny: *his teaching* and the disciple's obedience.' At once we are in a world of authority and obedience as reciprocal responses, both dependent on service of Christ, rather than vertical dictation. Such ought to be the exercise of all authority over adults in the Christian Church. Obedience is the first grade of humility, because it involves the voluntary submission of the will to Christ. Moreover, the brethren should not only obey their abbot, but also live in mutual obedience to each other, 'knowing that by this way of obedience, they will reach God'. Benedict makes it clear that he speaks not of obedience in all things without reasonable question, but of an inclination for Christ's sake to obey.

The abbot must realise that he has taken on a difficult task as a leader of souls; it is a stewardship, which requires infinite discretion and adaptability to individual dispositions. One he must humour, another rebuke, another persuade, according to each one's disposition and understanding, in such a way, 'that he may not only suffer no *loss* in the sheep committed to him, but may even rejoice in the *increase* of a good flock'. How every tutor will know what all this means, considering the damage that can be done by rebuking an undergraduate who needs encouragement, or indeed occasionally by encouraging an undergraduate who needs a rebuke!

You may like a story of a twentieth-century abbot, Cuthbert Butler, of Downside, who treated junior monks with perfect humour. A certain junior frequently omitted to ring the prescribed bells for prayers and offices, according to the *Rule*, when he was 'antiphoner'. Abbot Butler often supplied the omissions himself. One day he left in the junior's room a note to this effect: 'Shall be away today. Please get another to ring the Angelus, E.C.B.'

When Benedict speaks of the appointment of the abbot, he returns to the theme of what an abbot should be like. He should set himself to be loved, rather than feared. He must realise that he has to help, more than to rule; to hate vices but love the brethren; to distrust his own weakness; and to be prudent in correction, lest while he is over-anxious to scour the rust, the vessel crack:

> Let him remember that he has undertaken the care of sickly souls, not a violent rule of the healthy. And let him *fear* the prophet's threat, through which God is saying: 'What you saw was fat, you took; and what was weak, you threw aside.'

Here Benedict has passed beyond justifying an abbot's authority to his subjects, telling him rather what he must say to *himself* in the depths of his own conscience.

When we read such language, it is no wonder that an idea developed of the Benedictine abbot as a mother, as well as a father. Such was St Anselm in a later age, sitting beside the bed of an old and sick monk, Herewald, who was unable to take solid food, feeding him with the juice of grapes crushed in his own hand.

Wholly remarkable is Benedict's discussion of how an abbot should treat his prior. Benedict was rather ambivalent about priors. On the one hand, they were needed; on the other hand, they could give rise to conflict. If the latter occurred, and the prior came to hold the *Rule* in contempt, he was to be corrected up to four times verbally. Should he not amend, he should be deposed from his office; and if even after that he would not be quiet and obedient in the community, he should be expelled from the monastery.

But then Benedict adds one more, miraculous, sentence, which lights up his whole view of authority in the community with one flash:

> Yet let the abbot bear in mind that he must give God an account of all his judgments, lest perchance his mind be inflamed by the fire of envy and jealousy.

The *Rule of St Benedict* is studded with quotations from and allusions to the Bible, always used with superb appositeness. But there is more than rhetoric in that use; there is vision. Given that scholarly editions of the *Rule* have been available for decades, there is a feature of it to which (speaking personally) I should have tumbled much sooner than I did. Amidst so profoundly biblical a piece of writing, the vision of authority and community is most of all a Pauline vision.

Now, after talking with an authority on Paul about this, I am not looking to read too consistent a view of either authority or community into Paul's letters; nor to suggest that compared with the rest of Scripture, Benedict's allusions to St Paul are numerically overwhelming. I speak of what *Benedict* took from St Paul, and I do say it was pivotal.

Here, apropos of the abbot standing in the person of Christ, is St Paul writing to the Corinthians: 'To whom ye forgive anything, I forgive also; for if I forgave anything, for your sakes I forgave it in the person of Christ.' Benedict's Prologue says, in a tissue of Pauline allusions:

> Let us never let go his [i.e. the Master's or *Rule's*] instructions, but rather hold fast to his teaching in the monastery until death; and let us share patiently in Christ's sufferings, so that we may also merit to have a share in his kingdom.

Benedict's monks are to the abbot as sons to a father; for as the Apostle says, 'you have received the spirit of adoption of sons, whereby we cry abba! Father!'

As a teacher, says Benedict, let the abbot always follow the example of the Apostle, who says, 'reprove, entreat, rebuke'. Paul says this in the Second Epistle to Timothy, which no scholar now (unlike Benedict) thinks was written by Paul himself, but most scholars would agree is Pauline in spirit. In any case, Paul says something in the Letter to Philemon, which nobody has questioned as his work: 'I might be bold in Christ,' says Paul, 'to *command* thee, but for love's sake, I rather *beseech* thee, being now such an one as Paul the aged, and now also a *prisoner* of Jesus Christ' (vv. 8–9).

When Benedict speaks of seniority in the monastery regardless of previous social class, he says, again in Pauline language, 'whether slave or freeman, in Christ we are all one'. When he discusses the concern with which the abbot should treat an erring brother, by sending some of the wiser brethren, 'as it were secretly to console the vacillating brother, lest he be swallowed up with overmuch sorrow', he is resorting to Corinthians. And he does not pass over the issue of kitchen service without an allusion to Galatians: 'serve one another in love'. The idea of the stewardship of authority is not absent from 1 Timothy, Chapter 3. I could go on with this, if you wanted me to nail every last detail. But I hope that what I have said is enough to start us on the *via Paulina Benedicti*, the Pauline road of Benedict.

It is almost, therefore, as if Benedict, in his masterpiece, were saying to us: 'This is my ideal of a community of monks, and of the exercise of authority within that community. But there is little peculiarly monastic about it, though if a community of monks may suggest to the rest of the church how to live, so much the better.' Hence, when we experience the extraordinary grace and power of Benedict's vision, it is the grace and power of a vision that had already been put before the *earliest* Christians, and that has been there for all Christians to see ever since.

Augustine Baker's Holy Wisdom

Now to move on eleven centuries to the seventeenth century and Augustine Baker's *Holy Wisdom*, published posthumously in 1657 as an amalgam of Baker's spiritual treatises. Born in Abergavenny in 1575, David Baker studied at Oxford and was converted to Catholicism in 1603. He took the Benedictine habit and the name in religion of Augustine, in 1605 at Santa Giustina, Padua. From 1619 his contemplative life intensified and he spent long hours in prayer. In 1624 he became the spiritual director of a nunnery in Cambrai, and it was in this position that he composed most of his spiritual writings. He died in 1641. For over two centuries after it was published, *Holy Wisdom* was not much read. But through the interest of Abbot Norbert Sweeney it underwent a revival which has made it a potent influence in the English Benedictine Congregation ever since. Above all it was advanced by the notable scholar and leader of men, Abbot Cuthbert Butler of Downside, to whom I have referred already. The eighteen-year-old Butler read it for his Lenten book as a novice in 1877. This is what he wrote about it subsequently, as quoted by David Knowles in his celebrated memoir of Abbot Butler:

> Before Christmas of the noviciate *Sancta Sophia* was put into our hands; it formed the staple of our spiritual reading for the rest of the noviciate; our Novice Master exhorted us to study it in private and analyse it ... It became in the fullest sense our text book of the spiritual life ... From the first I felt a strong attraction for *Sancta Sophia* – its logical order, its philosophical sweep of the spiritual life, its lofty ideal, its piety in tone, its eloquence in language, all combined to influence my fervour and enthusiasm. It came to us also recommended by the highest authority ... Under these circumstances it is not surprising that I do not wish to make any absurd claim to high spirituality; I mean that we took Fr. Baker's theory as the orthodox theory of Benedictine life, and tried to walk along the earlier stages of his system, hoping that, as he says, when we came to 'almost a declining age' we might be found worthy to enter on some of the higher paths ... Substantially I have ever been faithful to my first love, and to this day [1891] I regard my early

acquaintance with and admiration for *Sancta Sophia* as one of
the chief graces of my life. It gave me a definite theory of the
spiritual and monastic lives, and a high ideal to aim at ...
From *Sancta Sophia* I got a firm grip of the great and fundamental principle that the Benedictine Order is
contemplative ... After my profession I began to read some
of the books most recommended by Fr. Baker; thus I read all
of St Theresa's works I could lay my hands upon; and soon I
turned to Cassian and the *Lives of the Fathers of the Desert*.

Thereafter, Butler recommended it to all his monks, and read
it regularly to his novices, including the great monastic
historian, David Knowles himself, during the summer holidays.

Two things strike me about *Holy Wisdom*: how far it all looks
from the brass tacks of the *Rule of St Benedict*, and its notable
aversion to spiritual directors and the use of images in prayer.

Baker was very aware that some regarded the practice of
contemplation, the attending to inner divine inspirations, and
the aspiration, through contemplation, to perfect union with
God, as prejudicial to the due authority of superiors, and their
external calls to obedience and regularity – by regularity
meaning of course the monastic offices. I hesitate to quote him
directly, because the average length of his sentences is some
twelve lines of print. But, with that trenchancy which rarely fails
Holy Men who know that God is on their side – and I doubt that
more trenchant twelve-liners have often been written in English
– he feels obliged to tackle head on those who, 'either out of
ignorance, passion or interest', have espoused this anti-
contemplative view. Never did Baker play fast and loose with
the primary duty of obedience laid down in the *Rule*. He even
said that if superiors ordered their monks or nuns to cut down
on the time of contemplation, they must in the last analysis be
obeyed, whatever the cost to their subjects' souls, and even
greater cost to their own.

It is vital to understand in what way to take Baker in all this.
The *Rule of St Benedict* has 73 chapters, and I was speaking about
the first 72 in the first half of my paper. Chapter 73 takes off
into the spiritual stratosphere. The *Rule*, it says, is a first step.
For monastic perfection one must move on to the teachings of
the Old and New Testament, to the Catholic Fathers, to Cassian
and the spiritual fathers, to Basil:

Whoever, therefore, thou art that hastenest to thy heavenly country, fulfil first of all by the help of Christ this little Rule for beginners. And then at length, under God's protection, shalt thou attain those aforesaid loftier heights of wisdom and virtue.

'Those loftier heights of wisdom and virtue'; *that* is what *Holy Wisdom* is about. It is a guide to following the last chapter of the *Rule*; and Baker not only frequently cites the texts which it mentions, especially Cassian, but was also widely read in the medieval and sixteenth-century mystical writings which would serve this end.

Even when writing of Benedict's earlier chapters, he puts on them what one might call a Chapter 73 spin. He acknowledges, for instance, that in Chapter 20 of the *Rule*, Benedict says, 'our prayer ought to be short and pure, unless it chance to be prolonged by the inspiration of divine grace'. Yes, says Baker, but under the inspiration of divine grace, which is the whole object and substance of contemplation, Benedict allows the liberty that prayer may be prolonged. So smitten did Baker become with the priority of the contemplative life over every other, that he latterly put it above the vital work of the English Mission, though no coward himself. Of course, if a monk were ordered to England by his superiors he must go. But he should not angle to put himself into the way of being sent, for the English Mission would inhibit his contemplative life with inevitable damage to his soul.

Here I think Benedict would have been with Baker. It is true that Gregory, in the *Dialogues*, represents Benedict engaging in some missionary activity in the vicinity of Monte Cassino. But Gregory himself believed that the contemplative life should bear fruit in the active, missionary life. For him the contemplative life was no abiding habitation as it was for Benedict. Most Benedictines in later ages approximated more to Gregory than to Benedict, or to Augustine Baker. They were Chapter-1-to-72-men rather than Chapter-73-men. I persevere with Baker not because he was typical, but because there was something quintessentially Benedictine about his contemplative *persona*.

Hence we come to the second point that strikes me about *Holy Wisdom*; its aversion to spiritual directors and the use of images in prayer. The trouble with directors was that they would impose system and external observances to the smothering of divine inspiration in the soul. Moreover, he wrote, 'it is too general a humour in directors nowadays to make themselves seem necessary unto their disciples, whom they endeavour to keep in a continual dependence, to the great prejudice of their progress in spirit, besides many other inconveniences not needful to be mentioned particularly'. And then he breaks into a series of uncharacteristically brief sentences as he particularises these inconveniences, most of all that God works according to our natural complexions of soul which directors rarely understand, and that directors induce scrupulosities and excessive soul-baring in their charges.

As to the use of images in prayer, Baker uses 'images' invariably as a pejorative. The opposite words, always used in a favourable sense, are 'abstraction' or 'affection'. Images might be useful in maintaining a right intention in external works of charity, but their use, he opined, seldom was efficacious in raising or fixing the affections on God. True contemplative souls, who are much superior to those in the active life, are so by reason of their more profound, pure and *imageless* recollections. Divine inspiration is given free rein when the soul is untroubled by the exercise of the imagination, senses or passions. The triumph of the spiritual life is achieved with what Baker calls the attainment of the 'divine inaction', which I believe knowledgeable writers on spirituality call the *via negativa*!

What are images? Baker supposes that one knows, and never explains or gives examples. One gasps to realise that he must mean principally images of Jesus, the kind of thing the *Imitation of Christ* means when it says (II, 7) 'be resolved to study Christ in all his actions to penetrate into his designs, and to do, suffer and live as he did'. Baker nowhere mentions the *Imitation of Christ*, and the *Imitation* is not *full* of images but, as one sees from this passage, Thomas à Kempis's whole system implies them. Moreover, Baker disliked system as much as he disliked directors and images. What I think shows clearly that he must have meant, for a large part, images of Jesus, was that he advises against a contemplative's playing an unnecessary part in external affairs because these excite the passions, cause bad images in the mind, and necessitate the conjuring up of good images at prayer in order to dispel the bad ones. And these good images, believe it or not, are a *drag* on the contemplative soul – for no other reason than that they are images at all.

If it sounds as if I am on the verge of scoffing at *Holy Wisdom*, it is because, no mystic myself, I do not believe that this could ever be my way personally. Besides, some of it seems to fall dangerously close to the area of G. K. Chesterton's epigrammatic warning, 'when Jones follows the inner light, Jones follows Jones'. But it is certainly no laughing matter. From what some of the monks said when I was at a Benedictine school, they gave the impression of being Bakerites; and from their lives they also gave the impression, to quote Knowles, of 'a deep spirituality drawing its strength from a hidden source'. That is to say, one can only speak with respect of where the Baker non-method can lead.

I have to say, however, that Baker appears to have put himself at odds, over this matter of images, with a large part, though certainly not all, of the medieval Benedictine tradition. Consider, for instance, the English Cistercians of the twelfth century. First of all, Ralph Haget, abbot of Fountains in the 1190s, was on Baker's side, so to speak. Hugh of Kirkstall records an incident in his life that might have come out of the early Wesleyans.

One Sunday when the community were at Lauds, the psalm *Confitemini Domino* was being sung, when the man of God was carefully attending to the meaning of that psalm the hand of the Lord was upon him and he saw a great and glorious sight, the Trinity itself in three persons. I asked him under what form or appearance that revelation was made. He answered – and here comes the imagelessness of the inspiration – 'Nothing was there of form or figure, and yet I saw in a blissful vision the Persons in Unity. I saw and knew the unbegotten Father, the only-begotten Son, and the Holy Spirit proceeding from both. The vision lasted while two whole verses of the psalm were being completed. From that moment no misfortune, no sadness has ever come to me which could not be mitigated by the remembrance of that vision ... And such a confidence and hope was poured into my soul by this showing, that I could never after doubt of my salvation.'

This contrasts markedly, however, with the treatise on prayer which Ailred of Rievaulx wrote for his sister who was a recluse, which is *based* on images and use of the imagination. It is all about how his sister should put herself into the shoes of those around Christ, and imagine what it was like. Here is a passage from it on the Woman taken in Adultery:

> Let the woman taken in adultery occur to your *imagination*, and how Jesus asked her what she had done. *Remember* how he wrote in the ground, and said, 'let him among you who is without sin cast the first stone'. When he had frightened everyone with this saying and expelled them from the Temple, *imagine* how he raised his eyes to her and offered her forgiveness in a gentle and sweet voice. *Think* how he sighed, and with tears in his eyes, said, 'Has no one condemned you? Neither will I.'

Moreover there was not in the Middle Ages so sharp a distinction between the observance of the monastic offices and the contemplative life of Benedictine monks as is implied in Baker's approach. When one considers the christological illustrations of so many psalters, such as the Stuttgart Psalter (c. 830) or the St Alban's Psalter (c. 1130), it is clear that as monks recited the psalms, they were encouraged at appropriate verses to recollect, however fleetingly, images of the life of Christ.

Baker was reaching back for his inspiration to late medieval writers such as Walter Hilton and the anonymous author of the *Cloud of Unknowing*, and further back to a kind of spiritual expertise represented *par excellence* in Cassian. What was he reaching back past? I have already mentioned Thomas à Kempis, and Baker can have been no friend to the *devotio moderna*. There will be others who can better set Baker into his right place in the sixteenth/seventeenth-century spiritual map than I can. But a dominating landmark in his spiritual scenery must have been the *Spiritual Exercises* of St Ignatius of Loyola (1526). Everything that Baker abhorred is writ large in this work.

The spiritual director is a *sine qua non* of the *Exercises*, making sure that the exercitant spends a full hour on each of the five stated contemplations a day, and curbing him from rash promises in the flush of his fervour. The scrupulous examination of conscience, reviewing year-by-year the sins of the exercitant's life, is their foundation. System, the precise system of a sort of military campaign, dominates the *Exercises*. Above all, images called to mind in prayer are their staple diet. The meditation on hell begins, 'here it will be to see in imagination the length, breadth, and depth of hell'. And then follow five points involving each sense: 'to see in the imagination the vast fires, to hear the wailing and howling, to smell the sulphur and corruption, to taste the bitterness of tears, to touch the flames which envelop and burn souls'. This may not be much to modern taste, but there is also in the *Spiritual Exercises* a systematic deployment of the life of Christ to evoke images, often very movingly, as in this simple point on the Last Supper and the persons at it: 'listen to their conversation and likewise seek to draw fruit from it'. It is no wonder that with all this, on top of Ignatius's conversion experience, his new order was called the Society of Jesus.

Baker never mentions Ignatius or the *Spiritual Exercises* by name, whether from holy charity, or because it was far more blistering not to, is unclear. But there cannot be a doubt that he had the work in the front of his mind. He was in fact the beginning of a phenomenon that was still very present when I was boy and youth – the defining of Benedictine spirituality by defining it as against what was Jesuitical. What was more natural to a Benedictine who had grown up in the Wales and England of Elizabeth I, where Jesuit and Catholic were almost synonymous?

Some of you may think that I have been asked to talk of holiness but have talked of spirituality, a related subject, you will say, but not the same thing. Yet I think that I have been relevant. In other contexts holiness may be the result of all kinds of human rituals and projections; rituals of asceticism, consecration or canonisation, projections onto space or place, person or object. But I see no way of defining Benedictine holiness except in terms of the spirituality from which it grows.

When Eigil of Fulda wrote the life of his monastery's saintly founder, Sturm, in the ninth century, stressing not Sturm's miraculous powers nor his prayer, but his capacity to achieve concord amongst the brethren, he wrote from the ideal viewpoint of a conventual spirituality expressed through the mutually listening community. It was as if he were a Chapter-1-to-72-man. But when David Knowles wrote his *Monastic Order* and *Religious Orders in England,* he wrote more as a rather hard Chapter-73 judge. A typical instance is his five pages in *Religious*

Orders, volume 2, about Thomas de la Mare, Abbot of St Albans. For all that he was a great peer of the realm, who would ride in state to the Lords in Parliament, this abbot was energetic in his monastic duties, punctilious in his observance, and the soul of kindness to his monks, consoling them when they were ill and performing the most menial tasks for them. He was truly loved rather than feared. Yet Knowles, in a phrase noted earlier, doubted 'whether he gave also an impression of a deeper spirituality drawing its strength from a hidden source'. He followed this up by adding, 'we may perhaps be allowed to feel that the ultimate touch of holiness was wanting, and that de la Mare was neither a Wulfstan nor an Anselm'. Here, as elsewhere, an important secret of Knowles as monastic historian is revealed. He wrote as one who, when a Benedictine novice, had imbibed Augustine Baker's *Holy Wisdom* under his abbot, Cuthbert Butler.

Bibliographical Note

The standard edition of the *Rule of St Benedict* is *La Règle de Saint Benoît,* eds. Adalbert de Vogüé and Jean Neufville, 6 vols. *Sources Chrétiennes* nos. 181–86 (Paris: Editions de Cerf, 1978–1980 [1971–1972]). This, and the excellent *The Rule of Saint Benedict, in Latin and English,* ed. and tr. Justin McCann (London, 1952) identify most of the scriptural citations. The *Dialogues of Pope Gregory the Great* are edited as *Dialogorum Libri IV de Miraculis Patrum Italicorum,* ed. Adalbert de Vogüé, *Sources Chrétiennes* nos. 251, 260, 265 (Paris: Editions de Cerf, 1978–1980). Translation: *Saint Gregory the Great: Dialogues,* tr. Odo J. Zimmerman, *Fathers of the Church,* vol. 39 (New York: Catholic University of America, 1959). For Gregory's *Regula Pastoralis,* eds. F. Rommel, C. Morel and B. Judic, *Sources Chrétiennes* nos. 381–82 (Paris, 1992). For Augustine Baker's *Holy Wisdom,* I have used the edition of Norbert Sweeney (London, 1876). For Ignatius of Loyola, Louis J. Puhl *The Spiritual Exercises of St Ignatius* (Chicago: Loyola University Press, 1951). An important article for Augustine Baker's reading and his manuscripts is Jan T. Rhodes, 'Dom Augustine Baker's reading lists', *Downside Review,* 111, 384 (July 1993), pp. 157–73; and also Geoffrey Scott, 'The Image of Augustine Baker', forthcoming in *Augustine Baker: A*

Quatcentenary Celebration Conference, May 2000. David Knowles's memoir of Abbot Cuthbert Baker is reprinted in his book *The Historian and Character* (Cambridge: Cambridge University Press, 1963), pp. 264–342. The passage about Ralph Haget is cited from David Knowles, *The Monastic Order in England* (Cambridge: Cambridge University Press, 1940), pp. 357–8; that on Thomas de la Mare from the same author's, *The Religious Orders in England*, vol. 2 (Cambridge: Cambridge University Press, 1955), p. 47. The passage from Ailred of Rievaux's *De Institutione Inclusarum* is my own translation of *Aelredi Rievallensis Opera Omnia*, eds., A. Hoste and C. H. Talbot, *Corpus Christianorum, continuatio medievalis* I (Turnholt, 1971), p. 665. One should also note Bernard Green, *The English Benedictine Congregation: A Short History* (London: Catholic Truth Society, 1980), pp. 19–22, on Augustine Baker, and the items by Justin McCann and Hugh Connolly in his bibliography, at p. 98.

I have been helped in the writing of this paper by one Benedictine monk, Jeremias Schroeder (now Archabbot of St Ottilien), and one Jesuit priest, John Moffatt.

13

Holiness in the English Tradition: From Prayer Book to Puritans

Gordon Mursell

This is an extract from one of the sermons of the sixteenth-century English bishop Hugh Latimer:

I read once a story of a holy man (some say it was St Anthony), which had been a long season in the wilderness, neither eating nor drinking any thing but bread and water: at the length he thought himself so holy that there should be nobody like unto him. Therefore he desired of God to know who should be his fellow in heaven. God made him answer, and commanded him to go to Alexandria; there he should find a cobbler which should be his fellow in heaven. Now he went thither and sought him out, and fell in acquaintance with him, and tarried with him three or four days to see his conversation. In the morning his wife and he prayed together, then they went to their business, he in his shop, and she about her housewifery. At dinner time they had bread and cheese, wherewith they were well content, and took it thankfully. Their children were well taught to fear God, and to say their *Paternoster*, and the Creed, and the Ten Commandments; and so he spent his time in doing his duty truly. I warrant you, he did not so many false stitches as cobblers do now-a-days. St Anthony perceiving that, came to knowledge of himself, and laid away all price and presumption. By this ensample you may learn, that honest conversation and godly living is much regarded before God, insomuch that this poor cobbler, doing his duty diligently, was made St Anthony's fellow. So it appeareth that we be not destituted of religious houses: those which apply their business uprightly and hear God's word, they shall be St

279

Anthony's fellows; that is to say, they shall be numbered amongst the children of God.[1]

Latimer's version differs significantly from the original, which appears in the *Lives of the Desert Fathers*. In that version, St Antony duly visits the cobbler in Alexandria, but gets a different answer: the original cobbler tells the saint that he gave a third of his income to the Church, another third to the poor, and kept the rest for himself. This didn't strike St Antony as particularly impressive, since he himself had given away everything he owned. So he pressed the cobbler to reveal where his true holiness lay. 'The humble tradesman, who venerated Antony, then told him his soul's secret: "I do not do anything special. Only, as I work I look at all the passers-by and say, 'So that they may be saved, I, only I, will perish.'"'[2]

The differences are intriguing. The original cobbler exemplifies the ascetic, self- and world-denying holiness of early monastic Christianity. But Latimer's cobbler exemplifies a quite different kind of holiness. He is married, with children (St Antony would never have approved of *that*). He has a trade, and he is good at it: no cheating the customers with false stitches. His wife runs the house. And their children have been taught how to pray, what to believe and what to do as devout Christians. The old monastic view of holiness as separation *from* the world has been supplanted by the new Reformation view of the godly life *in* the world. In short, the cobbler has been transformed from a monk into a Protestant.

Holiness and the Reformation

This is not simply a different view of what holiness consists of. Martin Luther did not deny the genuine holiness of some Catholic ascetics; indeed he had a particularly high esteem for St Bernard of Clairvaux ('a man so godly, so holy, and so chaste, that he is to be commended and preferred above them

[1] Hugh Latimer, 'Sermon 5 on the Lord's Prayer', in *Sermons*, ed. G. E. Corrie (Parker Society; Cambridge: Cambridge University Press, 1844), pp. 392–3.

[2] English text in O. Clément, *The Roots of Christian Mysticism*, Theodore Berkeley (London: New City, 1993), p. 302

all'[3]). But the reason he approved of St Bernard was not because of the latter's holiness: rather it was because of his faith: 'he took hold of that one thing which was necessary, and so was saved'.[4] For Luther, holiness (whatever form it takes) is not enough to earn salvation: it can only be a response to something God has done in justifying you. Latimer's cobbler had heard God's word, and been justified: his godly way of life, his *holiness*, was a sign of his having been saved.

This is not to imply that holiness in sixteenth-century England had lost its original meaning of separation, being set apart for the service of God. But it does imply that, as the Protestant Reformation became established, the different (and for a long time mutually antagonistic) versions of Christianity that were in existence were obliged to decide for themselves exactly what it meant to be holy. Where medieval monasticism had tended towards the assumption that holiness meant the separation of the spiritual from the physical, and thus the physical cutting-off of the holy person or place from their surroundings, sixteenth-century Christians found that assumption questionable. Calvin, for example, who (like Luther) believed holiness to be a sign of having been saved, rather than a means of earning salvation, believed that holiness consisted, not in separation from the world, but in separation from evil.

> When mention is made of our union with God, let us remember that holiness must be the bond; not that by the merit of holiness we come into communion with him (we ought rather first to cleave to him, in order that, pervaded with his holiness, we may follow whither he calls), but because it greatly concerns his glory not to have any fellowship with wickedness and impurity.[5]

In what follows, we shall look at how holiness was understood in the first two centuries of the English Reformation, and at

[3] Martin Luther, *Commentary on Galations* 4.30, 1575 English translation, ed. P: S. Watson (London: James Clarke, 1953), p. 439.

[4] Luther, *Commentary*, p. 439.

[5] John Calvin, *Institutes of the Christian Religion*, translated by Henry Beveridge (London: James Clarke & Co., 1957), 3:6:2.

how Christians of different theological traditions who were obliged to co-exist with one another sought to give expression to a vision of 'the holy' which would heighten the distinctiveness (and, they hoped, the superiority) of their particular tradition. For some, such as Roman Catholics or Baptists, this might involve a clear sense of separation, if not from the world, then from the spiritual values and practices of the society in which they lived (though, in a society in which tolerance was far from being established as a virtue, such a sense of separateness had to be practised with an emphasis on interiority rather than on some form of publicly differentiated lifestyle). For others, and in England supremely for members of the new established Church, a different dilemma arose. If holiness could no longer be equated with withdrawal from the world in the manner of the old monks and nuns, then of what did it comprise? Strenuous and celibate asceticism was unlikely to appeal to the increasingly literate and confident laity who formed the backbone of the new Church's membership. But if holiness were to be reduced to some form of gentrified piety, the Church ran the risk of having little that was distinctive to offer to those who sought to draw closer to God.

Holiness and the Church of England

We may best approach the Church of England's understanding of holiness by thinking about buildings. By the reign of Elizabeth I, English churches had undergone a fundamental facelift: images and altars had been replaced by pews, royal coats of arms and boards containing improving and didactic texts. The church building was no longer to be regarded as holy because the sacrament was reserved in it, or celibate priests ministered in it, but because the godly worshipped in it: Calvin explicitly warned against assuming the prayer was somehow more holy simply because it was practised in a church building.[6] And the emphasis has shifted from the *rite* to the *word*. The anonymous author of the official homilies published for use in English churches declared that the church building is to be a

---

[6] Calvin, *Institutes* 3:20:30.

place of reverence, of hearing rather than speaking.[7] It was the willingness of worshippers to 'hear, and receive thy most holy Word', as the Prayer Book put it, that determined whether either they or their parish church were holy or not. Holiness was rooted in human conformity to the word of God, a word that was no longer only (or even primarily) a word of *power* so much as of *instruction*, and a word that was (at least in its spoken form) accessible to all, no longer the exclusive preserve of Latinate clergy and scholars.

This is not, however, to say that the Prayer Book, even in its Protestant 1552 format, represents Calvinism swallowed whole. It included, originally as part of the order of worship for Ash Wednesday, a Commination service, in which particular sins (mostly drawn from Deuteronomy 27) were denounced and God's anger against sinners declared.[8] The service was drawn from the practice of the early Church; and in effect it replaced old medieval rituals (among them the rite of excommunication) in which power is conceived through rituals or images: here it is conveyed through words.[9] The ferocious tone of the service underlines a different theological approach from that of Latimer. Here the language explicitly evokes Jesus' parable of the Last Judgment in Matthew 25: we risk eternal punishment if we do not return to Christ and abandon our 'ungodliness'. It is true that the Articles of Religion unequivocally affirm the Lutheran doctrine of justification by faith alone.[10] Yet holiness of life is not simply a response to what God has done for us in Christ, though it is certainly that. Rather it is the fruit of our co-operation with God. We are at once saved and sinners; God looks upon us and sees both.[11]

[7] 'Of the Right Use of the Church or Temple of God', in *Certain Homilies Appointed to be Read in Churches in the Time of the Late Queen Elizabeth* (Oxford: Oxford University Press, 1840), p. 152. See also 'An Homily for Repairing and Keeping Clean, and Comely Adorning of Churches', in ibid, p. 243.

[8] In later editions of the Prayer Book, the Commination service stood on its own.

[9] See C. J. Sommerville, *The Secularization of Early Modern England: From Religious Culture to Religious Faith* (New York and Oxford: Oxford University Press, 1992), pp. 50 and 141.

[10] See *Articles of Religion* XI

[11] See *Articles of Religion* XVI for an insistence upon the possibility of Christians continuing to sin after baptism.

The Prayer Book rarely speaks of holiness explicitly. But there is a profound sense in which the entire Book is concerned with it. Where holiness in the Protestant tradition is a process of separation from the world into a gathered church, holiness in the tradition of the Church of England is better seen as a process (beginning not with conversion but with baptism) whereby all of our selves are brought into unity with the redeeming Christ, in a church virtually coterminous with society around it. Hence the sonorous words of the prayer of oblation:

> And here we offer and present unto thee, O Lord, ourselves, our souls and bodies, to be a reasonable, holy, and lively sacrifice unto thee.

Hence too the eucharistic theology of Richard Hooker, who maintained that 'the real presence of Christ's most blessed body and blood is not ... to be sought for in the sacrament, but in the worthy receiver of the sacrament',[12] for Christ's presence is personal, and it is a personal union with him to which we should aspire.

The conviction of Church of England theologians that holiness consisted in our personal and corporate conformity to the will of God and the likeness of Christ means that it becomes inseparable from justification. John Donne, though deeply influenced by Calvinist theology, nonetheless declared in one of his sermons:

> It is not only the selling all we have, that must buy that pearl, which represents the kingdome of Heaven; The giving of all that we have to the poor, at our death, will not do it; the pearl must be sought, and found before, in an even, and constant course of Sanctification; we must be thrifty all our lives, or we shall be too poor for that purchase.[13]

'An even and constant course of Sanctification': the holy life becomes an integral dimension of the process of

---

[12] Richard Hooker, *Of the Laws of Ecclesiastical Polity* 5:67:6, in *The Works of ... Mr Richard Hooker,* ed. John Keble, 2nd edn. (Oxford: 1841), p. 352.

[13] John Donne, 'Sermon 1' in *The Sermons of John Donne,* eds. G. R. Potter and E. M. Simpson (Berkeley: California University Press), vol. 1, p. 156.

salvation. And George Herbert argued that holiness of life meant not the pursuit of private piety, or intellectual study, but love of neighbour: 'there is no greater sign of holinesse, then [*sic*] the producing and rejoycing in another's good'.[14] And,

> The Countrey Parson's Library is a holy life; for besides the blessing that that brings upon it, there being a promise, that if the Kingdome of God be first sought, all other things shall be added, even it selfe is a Sermon.[15]

Jeremy Taylor and Thomas Traherne

The Church of England writer who explored the nature of holiness in most depth during the seventeenth century was Jeremy Taylor (1613–67), sometime royalist chaplain and later Bishop of Down and Connor in Ireland. Like John Donne, Taylor saw holiness as a lifelong process of growth in conformity to the will of God: 'our holiness must persevere to the end. But … it must also be growing all the way',[16] and the person who is 'grown in grace' is the one who 'hath made religion habitual to his spirit'.[17]

In his two great treatises on *Holy Living* and *Holy Dying*, Taylor suggests three basic principles for holy living. The first is to take care of our time. He offers a range of ways in which we can exercise 'care of our time'.[18] We should avoid idleness, 'the greatest prodigality in the world',[19] (though he acknowledges

---

[14] George Herbert, *The Country Parson* 6, in *The Works of George Herbert*, ed. F. E. Hutchinson (Oxford: Clarendon Press, 1941), p. 234. Calvinists, and Herbert too, believed holiness to be itself a gift from God, not in any way to the credit of those who manifested it; and one sign of it was precisely this rejoicing in another's good.

[15] Herbert, *The Country Parson* 33, in *The Works*, p. 278.

[16] Jeremy Taylor, *Unum Necessarium* 1:44, in *The Whole Works of the Right Rev Jeremy Taylor DD*, ed. R. Heber, rev. by C. P. Eden (London: Brown, Green & Longmans, 1856), vol. 7, p. 39.

[17] Jeremy Taylor, *A Course of Sermons* 2:14, in *The Whole Works*, vol. 4, p. 503.

[18] Jeremy Taylor, *Holy Living*, ed. P. G. Stanwood (Oxford: Clarendon Press, 1989), pp. 19–27.

[19] Taylor, *Holy Living*, p. 21. He suggests that we should 'sometimes be curious to see the preparation which the sun makes, when he is coming forth from his chambers of the East' (p. 21).

that due relaxation is vital[20]). He encourages us to intersperse
our busy work with ejaculatory prayers, and warns against
useless busyness ('there are some people, who are busie, but it
is as Domitian was, in catching flyes'[21]). Above all we must seek
to 'redeem the time', ending each day by examining carefully
but without fussiness all that we have done.[22]

But holy living involves much more than good use of time.
We must aspire to purity of intention,[23] doing all for the glory
of God. Taylor has no shortage of vivid illustrations to make his
point: 'if a man visits his sick friend, and watches at his pillow
for charitys sake, and because of his old affection we approve it:
but if he does it in hope of legacy, he is a Vulture, and onely
watches for the carkasse'.[24] Instead Taylor offers a shrewd way
of discerning whether or not we have yet made this purity of
intention our own:

> He that does his recreation, or his merchandise cheerfully,
> promptly, readily and busily, and the works of religion slowly,
> flatly, and without appetite, and the spirit moves like *Pharaohs*
> chariots when the wheels were off, it is a signe, that his heart
> is not right with God, but it cleaves too much to the world.[25]

The third basic principle for holy living is 'the practise [*sic*]
of the presence of God':[26]

> God is wholly in every place, included in no place, not bound
> with cords (except those of love) ... we may imagine God to

[20] *Holy Living*, pp. 24–5.

[21] *Holy Living*, p. 23; cf. p. 24: 'As much as may be, cut off all *impertinent and
uselesse imployments* of your life, unnecessary and phantastick visits, long
waitings upon great personages, where neither duty nor necessity, nor charity
obliges us, all vain meetings, all laborious trifles, and whatsoever spends much
time to no real, civil, religious, or charitable purpose.'

[22] *Holy Living*, p. 26.

[23] *Holy Living*, pp. 27–34.

[24] *Holy Living*, p. 28.

[25] *Holy Living*, p. 32.

[26] *Holy Living*, pp. 35–42. For the eucharistic implications of this in Taylor's
work, see H. McAdoo, *The Eucharistic Theology of Jeremy Taylor Today* (Norwich:
Canterbury Press, 1988). Taylor insists on the real presence of Christ in the
Eucharist, and that the body of Christ present there is the same body as
suffered at Calvary, albeit present in a different manner (Jeremy Taylor, *The
Real Presence* 1:11, *The Whole Works*, vol. 6, p. 19).

be as the Aire and the Sea, and we all included in his circle, wrapt up in the lap of his infinite nature, or as infants in the wombs of their pregnant Mothers: and we can no more be removed from the presence of God, than from our own being.[27]

But this is not just a matter of *discerning* God's presence: it is a matter of *reverencing* it:

> God is in every creature: be cruel towards none, neither, abuse any by intemperance. Remember that the creatures and every member of thy own body is one of the lesser cabinets and receptacles of God. They are such which God hath blessed with his presence, hallowed by his touch, and separated from unholy use by making them to belong to his dwelling.[28]

This active awareness of the presence of God also informs the writing of Taylor's near contemporary Thomas Traherne (1636–74), poet and theologian, whose understanding of holiness is deeply influenced by Platonism. For Traherne the whole created order speaks eloquently of the presence and beauty of its Creator, and nothing more so than the human creatures who bear their Creator's image. And to be created in that image is to be created with a divine longing for what God alone can satisfy. This is how Traherne put it:

> To be Holy is so Zealously to Desire, so vastly to Esteem, and so Earnestly to Endeavour it [the end for which we were created] that we would not for millions of Gold and Silver, Decline, nor fail, nor Mistake in a Tittle. For then we Pleas God when we are most like Him. We are like Him when our Minds are in Frame. Our Minds are in Frame when our Thoughts are like his.[29]

Here we come close to union with God; but it is an intellectual union, a union of minds and thoughts, in a typically Platonising formula. Some of the 'Latitude-men' (broadly,

[27] *Holy Living*, p. 35.

[28] *Holy Living*, p. 40.

[29] Thomas Traherne, *Centuries* 1:13, in *Poems, Centuries and Three Thanksgivings*, ed. A. Ridler (Oxford: Oxford University Press, 1966), p. 171.

theologians associated with the University of Cambridge who were criticised for their relative lack of interest in the specifics of Christian doctrine) followed Traherne in using the language of deification to denote the ultimate goal of the Christian's union with God. Thus John Smith (?1616–52) declared that

> It is most God-like and best suits with the Spirit of Religion, for a Christian to live wholy [*sic*] to God, to live the life of God, having his own life hid with Christ in God; and thus in a sober sense he becomes Deified.[30]

Holiness in the Puritan and Quaker Traditions

We have come a long way from the world-view of Calvin and Latimer; and it is time to return to them. In the Reformed tradition, holiness involved separation from immorality and any kind of wickedness in response to God's free gift of salvation. We should be holy, because God is holy.[31] But we could not become like God, for the Reformers constantly stressed the absolute distinction between God and all human creatures. Latimer put it like this:

> 'Wilt thou call him "Father", which is so holy a God, and thou art so wicked and miserable a sinner?' This the devil will say, and trouble our minds, to stop and let us from our prayer ... Our sins let us, and withdraw us from our prayer; but our Saviour maketh them nothing; when we believe in him, it is like as if we had no sins. For he changeth with us: he taketh our sins and wickedness from us, and giveth unto us his holiness, righteousness, justice, fulfilling of the law, and so, consequently, everlasting life.[32]

It is important simply to note how Latimer stresses the absolute gulf between God's holiness and human wickedness in order to lay all his emphasis on God's utterly free and undeservable act of mercy in changing us: God looks on us, and sees Christ in

---

[30] John Smith, *Select Discourses* 9, in *The Cambridge Platonists*, ed. C. A. Patrides (London: Edward Arnold, 1969), p. 167.

[31] See Calvin, *Institutes* 3:6:2.

[32] Latimer, 'Sermon 1 on the Lord's Prayer' (1552), in *Sermons*, pp. 329–30.

our place, and imputes Christ's holiness to us. We are holy, if we believe in Christ's saving death on our behalf.

It is this kind of approach which characterises the thought of John Bunyan. For him, as for Calvin and Latimer, holiness, or sanctification, is not the *cause* of our salvation, but the *fruit* of it.[33] And to be holy does not mean living *like* Christ, in the sense of seeking some personal and ontological union with him: rather it means responding through faith to what Christ has already done for us.[34] It is true that sometimes Bunyan uses language which sounds close to that of Hooker, or the Latitude-men: thus in *A Defence of the Doctrine of Justification*, he says that

> Christ came not to restore, or to give us possession of that which was once our own holiness [i.e., the holiness of Adam or of the old Law], but to make us partakers of that which is in him.[35]

But Bunyan would have been horrified at any comparison between his thought and that of the Latitude-men (whom he memorably excoriated in *The Pilgrim's Progress* in the person of Mr Facing-Bothways). Holiness for Bunyan is always God's holiness imputed to us, not our own intrinsic capacity to be holy.[36] And the crucial reason why this matters is because true holiness confers freedom, that enduring inner freedom which is wholly God's gift, and which derives from committing one's soul unconditionally into God's hands.[37] For Bunyan, the

---

[33] See John Bunyan, *The Pharisee and the Publicane*, ed. O. C. Watkins, in *The Miscellaneous Works of John Bunyan* vol. 10 (Oxford: Clarendon Press, 1988), p. 186. For Calvin, 'justification is based on what Christ has done for us: sanctification is based on what he does within us', L. J. Richard, *The Spirituality of John Calvin* (1974), p. 106.

[34] See John Bunyan, *A Defence of the Doctrine of Justification*, ed. T. L. Underwood, in *Miscellaneous Works*, vol. 4 (Oxford: Clarendon Press, 1989), pp. 7–130, esp. p. 330; see also I. Rivers, *Reason, Grace, and Sentiment: A Study of the Language of Religion and Ethics in England, 1660–1780* (Cambridge Studies in Eighteenth-Century English Literature and Thought, 8), vol. 1 (Cambridge: Cambridge University Press, 1991), p. 142.

[35] Bunyan, *A Defence*, *Miscellaneous Works*, vol. 4, p. 297.

[36] See e.g. John Bunyan, *Ebal and Gerizzim* in *Miscellaneous Works*, ed. R. Sharrock, vol. 6 (Oxford, Clarendon Press, 1980), p. 111.

[37] 'Holiness and liberty are joyned together, yea our call to liberty, is a call to holiness', John Bunyan, *Seasonable Counsel*, in *Miscellaneous Works*, vol. 10, pp. 32–3.

trouble with the Latitude-men's view of holiness was that it was
'no other than what is common to all the men on earth',
whereas for him true holiness had to comprise three things: the
Holy Spirit, faith in Christ, and 'a new heart, and a new spirit'.[38]
In *The Pilgrim's Progress*, Faithful speaks of

> A life of holiness; heart-holiness, family-holiness (if he hath a
> Family) and ... Conversation-holiness in the world: which in
> the general teacheth him, inwardly to abhor his sin, and
> himself for that in secret, to suppress it in his Family, and to
> promote holiness in the World; not by talk only ... but by a
> practical subjection in Faith, and Love, to the power of the
> word.[39]

The prominent role Bunyan gives to the Holy Spirit is not
dissimilar from that given to it by the Quakers, though their
understanding of holiness differs from his. For George Fox,
holiness required a direct experience with God such as the
great figures of the Bible had had. But this is no pious elitism.
On the contrary: Fox believed that 'every man was enlightened
by the divine light of Christ' – though only those who believed
in it emerged from the condemnation into the light of life.[40] It
is a distinctive dimension of Quaker spirituality that even the
wicked possess the Holy Spirit.[41] Fox says that 'the least babe
might see him'.[42]

But there is another point too. Fox frequently describes the
Friends' experience of the power and blessing of God, or
the Holy Spirit: it is noteworthy that this is often a corporate
experience, as at Pentecost, rather than an individual one. In
his preface to Fox's *Journal*, William Penn speaks of the two
stages of justification: both 'justification from the guilt of the
sins that are past, as if they had never been committed, through
the love and mercy of God in Christ Jesus' and 'the creature's
being made inwardly just through the cleansing and sanctifying

---

[38] Bunyan, *A Defence*, in *Miscellaneous Works*, vol. 4, pp. 286 and 288.

[39] John Bunyan, *The Pilgrim's Progress* Part I, ed. J. B. Wharey, 2nd rev. edn.
R. Sharrock (Oxford: Clarendon Press, 1960), p. 83.

[40] George Fox, *Journal*, ed. N. Penney, 8th edn (London: Society of Friends,
1902), vol. 1, p. 34.

[41] See Fox, *Journal*, vol. 2, pp. 34–5.

[42] *Journal*, vol. 2, p. 35.

power and Spirit of Christ revealed in the soul which is commonly called sanctification'.[43] And, as he goes on to make clear, this interior sanctification leads directly to (and is inseparable from) love of neighbour, even of one's enemy, and a practical concern to do good.

The Congregational theologian John Owen also attached great importance to the work of the Holy Spirit in relation to holiness. For him, as for most Puritans, justification is a once-for-all event; but sanctification, the means by which we are made holy, is 'continually to be renewed and gone over again, because of the remainder of sin in us and the imperfection of our grace'.[44] And the Holy Spirit assists in that process by preserving that vital 'principle of spiritual life and holiness communicated unto us in our regeneration';[45] by exciting us to good actions, both morally and 'really and internally'; by granting us experiences of the truth; and by increasing the presence of grace within us.[46] This is crucial, for 'grace gives beauty'; and 'the spiritual beauty and comeliness of the soul consists in its conformity unto God'.[47] For Owen, holiness is as much for the good of others as for ourselves: 'holiness makes a man a good man, useful to all; and others eat of the fruits of the Spirit that he brings forth continually'.[48] And this holiness is accessible to everyone 'much of the glory of heaven may dwell in a simple cottage, and poor persons, even under rags, may be very like unto God'.[49] Above all, though, for Owen, Christ's holiness is profoundly *attractive* to the believer, alluring us and drawing us towards him; and it works in us in three ways: by *contemplation* (by which we are changed into his likeness); by *admiration* ('that beauty of God which attracts the love of a believing soul, and fills it with a holy admiration of him'), and by granting us *delight* in obedience to Christ.[50]

---

[43] See Penn's Introduction to Fox's *Journal*, vol. 1, p. xxix.

[44] John Owen, *Pneumatologia* 3:5, in *The Works of John Owen DD*, ed. W. H. Goold (London and Edinburgh,: Johnstone and Hunter 1850–5, repr. 1965–8), vol. 3, p. 325.

[45] Owen, *Pneumatologia* 4:3, in *Works* vol. 3, p. 409.

[46] *Pneumatologia* 4:2, in *Works* vol. 3, pp. 389–91.

[47] *Pneumatologia* 4:4, in *Works* vol. 3, p. 429.

[48] Owen, *Of Communion*, in *Works* vol. 2, p. 186.

[49] Owen, *Pneumatologia* 5:1, in *Works* vol. 3, p. 583.

[50] *Pneumatologia* 5:1, in *Works* vol. 3, p. 586.

For Richard Baxter, holiness was, in effect, synonymous with godliness, and found its supreme expression in the life of the Christian family: we return here to Latimer's cobbler. Both holiness and godliness denote a total Christian life, in which family piety, worship, moral uprightness and good relations with others are inseparably bound together: hence it is not only important for the individual, but brings peace and harmony to an entire nation:

> Godliness takes away the ball of the world's contention, that sets men every where together by the ears ... If all the ambitious climbers and state-troublers were truly godly, they would quietly seek for higher honours. If all the covetous noblemen, soldiers, landlords, and rich men were truly godly they would never set both city and country into combustions, and poor oppressed families into complaints, for the love of money. If thieves turned godly you might travel safely, and spare your locks and keep you purses ... What is there for societies to strive about, when the bone of contention is taken away, and godliness hath cast down the idol of the world, that did disturb them?[51]

For Baxter, holiness not only brought security and happiness; it also brought honour,[52] the only honour that endures because it consists in recognising our true dignity as those who are created and renewed in the image of God himself.[53] Last but not least, godliness makes us happy, here and now:[54] our holy desires for others' good, albeit unfulfilled, bring us happiness.[55] Hence, for Baxter:

> Holy families are the seminaries of Christ's church on earth, and it is very much that lieth upon them to keep up the interest of religion in the world ... Oh, that God would stir up the hearts of people thus to make their families as little

---

[51] Richard Baxter, *A Saint or a Brute* 2:4, in *The Practical Works of the Rev Richard Baxter*, ed. W. Orme (London: James Duncan, 1830), vol. 10, p. 186; see also p. 184.

[52] Baxter, *A Saint or a Brute* 2:9, in *Works* vol. 10, pp. 258–91.

[53] *A Saint or a Brute* 2:9, in *Works* vol. 10, p. 270.

[54] *A Saint or a Brute* 2:10, in *Works* vol. 10, pp. 295–400.

[55] *A Saint or a Brute* 2:10, in *Works* vol. 10, p. 305.

churches, that it might not be in the power of rulers or pastors that are bad to extinguish religion, or banish godliness from any land![56]

Union with Christ: Puritan Mysticism

Bunyan's reference to participation in Christ's holiness, Owen's stress on being transformed through contemplation into the likeness of Christ, and the Quaker (and Richard Baxter's) emphasis on the social implications of holiness, suggest some interesting correspondences between Anglican and Dissenting approaches to this subject. And it prompts a further question: is holiness, in the Puritan vision, primarily a matter of obedience to Christ, or does it imply some measure of intimacy, even union, with Christ? Puritan writers certainly conceived of an intimate and personal union between the individual Christian and Christ, though a union that never dissolved each other's identity. Thus John Owen argues for a union between the Christian and Christ that is similar to that of the union of diverse natures *within* Christ: 'There may be a manifold union, mystical and moral, of divers, of many persons, but a personal union there cannot be of any thing but of distinct natures.'[57] We always remain distinct persons in our relationship with God.[58] Richard Baxter, speaking of our communion with Christ in heaven, puts it thus:

> What can you desire yet more? Except you will, as some do, abuse Christ's expression of oneness to conceive of such a union, as shall deify us; which were a sin one step beyond the

---

[56] Richard Baxter, *The Poor Man's Family Book*, in *Works* vol. 19, pp. 484–5 and 503; cf. Richard Baxter, *A Christian Directory* 2:3, in *Works* vol. 4, pp. 66–90; William Perkins, *A Warning Against the Idolatry of the Last Times*, in *The Works of William Perkins*, Courtenay Library of Reformation Classics 3 (Appleford: Sutton Courtenay, 1970), vol. 1, pp. 714–16; G. Wakefield, *Puritan Devotion* (London: Epworth, 1957), p. 55. For family piety among Puritans in general, see C. Hill, *Society and Puritanism in Pre-Revolutionary England* (New York: Schocken, 1964), pp. 443–81, and Diane K. Tripp, 'Daily Prayer in the Reformed Tradition: An Initial Survey', in *Studia Liturgica*, 21 (1991), pp. 190–2 and 206–10.

[57] Owen, *Pneumatologia* 8:4, in *Works* vol. 4, pp. 384–5.

[58] *Pneumatologia* 8:4, in *Works* vol. 4, p. 385.

aspiring arrogancy of Adam; and, I think beyond that of the devils. A real conjunction, improperly called union, we may expect; and a true union of affections. A moral union, improperly still called union, and a true relative union, such as is between the members of the same politic body and the head: yea, such as is between the husband and the wife, who are called one flesh. And a real communion, and communication of real favours, flowing from that relative union. If there be any more, it is acknowledged unconceivable, and consequently unexpressible, and so not to be spoken of. [59]

Baxter's use of marital imagery is characteristic of Puritan writings just as of Catholic ones. John Owen, commenting on the Song of Songs (which was, of course, the favourite mystical text for Catholic theologians of the spiritual life), comes very close to identifying the spouse in the Song with the individual Christian, not simply (as is commonplace) with the Church as a whole:

Christ gives himself to the soul, with all his excellencies, righteousness, preciousness, graces, and eminencies, to be its Saviour, head, and husband, for ever ... in carrying on this union, Christ freely bestoweth himself upon the soul ... And this is the soul's entrance into conjugal communion with Jesus Christ as to personal grace – the constant preferring him above all pretenders to its affections, counting all loss and dung in comparison of him. [60]

How does this union come about? John Owen has no doubt about that: it is the fruit of Christ's death, in which we participate by faith. This participation is no mere intellectual assent: it is a sharing in Christ's dying and rising, for 'there is almost nothing that Christ hath done ... but we are said (in scripture) to do it with him'. [61] By this participation we die to sin as Christ did, though this is hard spiritual work. Owen notes that

Sin is never more alive than when it is thus dying. But there is a dying of it as to the root, the principle of it – the daily

[59] Baxter, *The Saint's Everlasting Rest* 1:4, in *Works* vol. 22, p. 54.
[60] Owen, *Of Communion* 2:3, in *Works* vol. 2, pp. 56–8.
[61] *Of Communion* 2:6, in *Works* vol. 2, p. 155.

decaying of the strength, power, and life of it; and this is to be had alone in Christ.[62]

The reason we seek this union with Christ through his death is because Christ draws us, attracts us by his intrinsic beauty, transforming us into his own likeness and making us his marriage partner.[63] So Richard Sibbes (d. 1635), one of the most remarkable Puritan writers on the spiritual life, says that

> you may know by this altering, changing, transforming power, whether he be in you or not. He alters and changes us to his own likenesse; that as he is set down in the Gospel in his life, conversation, and disposition; so (if we have entertained him, and he be in us) we should have the same disposition, the same mind, and the same will with him.[64]

We become Christlike as we respond to Christ's call; and then (as Owen puts it), for the Christian 'every day whilst we live is his wedding-day'; and every day Christ shares his secrets with us.

Some Puritans went further still. John Everard maintained that Christ must be born in us as he was in Mary: we must become the Virgin, feeling the child beginning to be conceived in us.[65] For Everard, Christ is in us already, by virtue of our creation;[66] but his coming-to-birth in us must be the beginning of a conscious, and costly process, whereby he grows up to full humanity within us.[67] This process has six stages, beginning with condemnation of self,[68] continuing with conformity to Christ as head, and concluding with *deiformity*:

---

[62] *Of Communion* 2:3, in *Works* vol. 2, p. 100.

[63] For this idea among Puritans, see J. C. Brauer, 'Puritan Mysticism and the Development of Liberalism', in *Church History* 19 (1950), pp. 151–70, esp. p. 152; J. C. Brauer, 'Francis Rous, Puritan Mystic 1579–1659: An Introduction to the Study of the Mystical Element in Puritanism', unpublished dissertation, Chicago University, 1948; and B. J. Gibbons, *Gender in Mystical and Occult Thought: Behmenism and its Development in England* (Cambridge: Cambridge University Press, 1996), pp. 66–8.

[64] Richard Sibbes, *The Saints Cordialls* (London: Henry Cripps, 1658), p. 364.

[65] John Everard, *The Gospel-Treasury Opened: or, The Holiest of all unvailing . . .* (collection of sermons); 2nd edn. (London: R. Harford, 1659), p. 54.

[66] Everard, *The Gospel-Treasury*, p. 57.

[67] *The Gospel-Treasury*, p. 63.

[68] *The Gospel-Treasury*, pp. 221–30.

When indeed we are no longer men but gods; mistake me not, that is, when we act no longer ourselves, but God acts in us; that if we do anything, yet we see and feel, and confess it is God that doth it, that if we speak, it is Christ that speaks; if we think, it is Christ that thinks.[69]

This is still not ontological union: rather it is Christ living in us, making us Christlike. An even more mystical form of Puritan holiness is to be found in the writings of Jane Lead (1624–1704), an enthusiastic disciple of the German mystical writer Jakob Boehme and leader for many years of the Philadelphian Society, established in London to promote Boehme's ideas. In *The Enochian Walks with God* she uses the imagery of ascent, popular among mystical writers:

If once you can clear and get off here, from these low clogging and heavy sandy ways, then you may enter into these high and pleasant walks with God, which, when you are once come into, you will meet with those various sweets and delights, that will engage you to keep to them.[70]

For Lead holiness was unambiguously about separation, a point to which she frequently returns. Hence getting clear of 'these low clogging and heavy sandy ways' involves renouncing, as far as possible, all earthly concerns and vexations, and cleansing the mind of all that is transitory through 'the spring of the Holy-Ghost'.[71] But this is no solitary journey: she follows Boehme in maintaining that seven angels (or 'qualifying spirits') keep us company: 'holy, passive-patience', humility, a lively hope, 'a super-celestial wisdom', the spirit of faith, the 'live-coal of Flaming Love', and 'impregnable strength and power'.[72] And its ultimate goal is deification:

When the Soul shall be brought forth as a well-tuned Instrument, new strung and qualified, in the deified man, where the holy Spirit moves every Property.[73]

---

[69] *The Gospel-Treasury*, pp. 132–3.
[70] Jane Lead, *The Enochian Walks with God* (London, 1694; repr. Glasgow: John Thomson, 1891), p. 6.
[71] Lead, *The Enochian Walks with God*, p. 23
[72] *The Enochian Walks with God*, pp. 35–7.
[73] Jane Lead, *The Revelation of Revelations* (London, 1683), p. 4.

Conclusion

The fact that Protestant mystics like Jane Lead can use the same language of deification that is normally associated with Catholic and (perhaps supremely) with Orthodox writers does not mean they meant the same thing by it. But it underlines the immense richness and sophistication of seventeenth-century Puritan and Nonconformist spirituality. The English seventeenth century was one of the most socially disruptive and politically turbulent in the entire history of the nation; yet it witnessed the development of spiritual traditions of remarkable power and depth. And that in turn suggests two conclusions: first, the enormous impact of the Reformation in stimulating new and important ways of living the Christian gospel; secondly, the enduring capacity of the biblical and patristic notion of holiness to inspire all those who sought to appropriate it for their own age. Had he lived longer, Latimer would surely have suggested some other models of holiness for the astonished St Antony to contemplate. But he was burnt at the stake for his religious views; and that may serve to remind us of one less appealing truth: the worrying potential of holiness and savagery to co-exist.

And yet paradoxically, that may serve to underline the significance, for those living at the start of the twenty-first century, of the fact that, for all the figures and traditions explored here, the search for holiness involved the whole person in an attempt to appropriate the life and gospel of Christ and to live these to the full in such a way as to draw others to do the same. For them, holiness was not some specialist option for the few, but the full Christian life as it was always intended to be lived. Nothing less, in their view, was good news for the world.

14

Holiness in the Evangelical Tradition

D. W. Bebbington

Evangelicalism is the prevailing form of Protestantism in the modern world. In English-speaking lands, the tradition encompasses members of most denominations except the Unitarians and other bodies disavowing historic orthodoxy. In the Church of England, Evangelicalism has been the third option alongside High and Broad Churchmanship. While including the Evangelical party in the Church of England, however, the tradition takes in the whole popular movement that ranges from the traditionalist Free Church of Scotland to innovative Pentecostalism. Although there is a world-wide movement possessing similar characteristics, this paper concentrates on its British expression. It arose virtually simultaneously in the 1730s in Wales, England, Scotland and the British colonies in America. It created the new phenomenon of Methodism, but it also reinvigorated the established churches and the Old Dissent. It increased its impact at all social levels up to the middle of the nineteenth century, when it reached the peak of its influence. It remoulded the language of the other Christian traditions, so that Victorian High and Broad Churchmen spoke very like Evangelicals. By the early twentieth century, however, the movement had fallen on evil days: its numbers decreased, it tended to split into theologically opposed camps and it became socially marginalised. There has been a resurgence in the later twentieth century within the churches, though hardly within society at large. Its current trajectory suggests that it is likely to play a more salient role in the twenty-first century than in the twentieth.

Evangelical Holiness Characterised

Evangelical versions of holiness were rooted in the distinctive features of the movement. First was its insistence on conversion as the start of the Christian life. Conversion could be instant or gradual, but in either case it was essential. For the Evangelical, the world was divided into two groups, believers and unbelievers, and the line of separation was a decisive turning from darkness to light. A measure of sanctity was a presumptive indication that the change had taken place. Thus Hannah More, an Evangelical bluestocking at the end of the eighteenth century, wrote that, 'Holiness of life is the only true evidence of a saving faith.'[1] Without the emergence of holiness, the process of sanctification, it could be judged that a sinner was still unconverted. Theologically the event of conversion was described as justification, the putting right of the sinner by God. There was no doubt about the relationship of justification and sanctification. 'Sanctification is a fruit of justification', John Clayton, a London Congregational minister, declared in 1813. 'It never exists without justification.'[2] The insistence that sanctification came second was a corollary of justification by faith. Holiness entailed good works; but good works could not earn salvation; a right relationship with God was his gift to those who put their trust in Christ. Therefore holiness must follow, not precede, justification. It was a fundamental belief of Evangelicals that holiness was only for the converted.

A second characteristic was a stress on the doctrine of the atonement. It was not the teaching or example of Christ that brought salvation to the soul. Rather it was the work of Christ in dying on the cross that conveyed the forgiveness of sins. Charles Simeon, the leader of the Evangelicals in the Church of England at the start of the nineteenth century, published a sermon entitled 'Christ Crucified, or Evangelical Religion Described'. In it he urged that by appeal to the cross 'holiness in all its branches must be enforced and a sense of Christ's love

---

[1] J. M. Gordon, *Evangelical Spirituality. From the Wesleys to John Stott* (London: SPCK, 1991), p. 107.

[2] J. H. Pratt, ed., *The Thought of the Evangelical Leaders* (Edinburgh: Banner of Truth Trust, 1978), p. 520.

in dying for us ... inculcated as the main spring of all our obedience'.[3] The quest for sanctity was to be an expression of gratitude for the atonement. There was a sense in which the cross eclipsed the life of discipleship altogether. A person could never achieve assurance of salvation through obedience to the Almighty. That experience could come only through the death of the Saviour. 'Sanctification', according to William Goode, a leading Evangelical clergyman, in 1804, 'is not the ground of our comfort. The work of Christ is the only ground of comfort.'[4] The pursuit of holiness should never lead believers to place their confidence elsewhere than in the cross. The atonement was to be the foundation of all spiritual experience.

The Bible, thirdly, was the guide to the nature of holiness. Evangelicals were Bible people. Scripture was the kernel of their private devotional reading as well as, through preaching, the central element in public worship. In his book on *God's Way of Holiness* (1874), the Scottish Presbyterian Horatius Bonar recommended that 'the whole soul be fed by the study of the whole Bible'.[5] The absorption of Scripture teaching was equated with the cultivation of godliness. The Bible thus provided more than a specification of what the Christian life entailed: it also imparted the power to fulfil the divine requirements. C. H. Spurgeon, Baptist minister in London and the greatest of Victorian preachers, put the principle in a nutshell: 'It is the Word of God which sanctifies the soul.'[6] The Bible was the chief instrument in the living of a holy life.

The result of holiness, finally was vigorous activity. The Evangelical ideal of sanctity was much closer to that of Martha than to that of Mary in the gospel story: it was less concerned with contemplation than with busyness. 'Activity for God', according to the American Methodist holiness preacher James Caughey, 'is a consequence of a *healthy* soul, as green to a healthy leaf'.[7] The logic was impeccable: once converted to

---

[3] Gordon, *Evangelical Spirituality*, p. 97.

[4] Pratt, ed., *Thought of the Evangelical Leaders*, p. 314.

[5] Gordon, *Evangelical Spirituality*, p. 140.

[6] C. H. Spurgeon, *Twelve Sermons on Sanctification* (London: Passmore & Alabaster, n.d.), p. 94.

[7] J. Caughey, *Earnest Christianity Illustrated* (London: Partridge & Co., 1857), p. 103.

God, any individual should try to bring the same momentous experience to others. Mission was therefore the lifeblood of the Evangelical movement. At home John Wesley was celebrated for spending his life in constant travel to preach the gospel through the British Isles. Abroad Evangelicalism gave rise to the modern missionary movement. But activism, as the work of the missionaries themselves reveals, was not confined to pioneering evangelism. From the start, missionaries were preoccupied with the temporal welfare of the lands they entered, as William Carey's campaign against widow burning in India illustrates. As time went on, an increasing proportion concentrated on education, medicine and industrial development. Equivalent charitable effort was the central aim of many of the great domestic Evangelical agencies such as the Ragged School Society. Rank-and-file members were caught up in the flurry of doing. Sophia Nixon, for example, a Wesleyan convert in 1835, confided to her diary her eagerness to be holy; her obituarist recounts that she lived 'in the healthy and bracing breeze of incessant employment and activity'.[8] Evangelicals believed that devotional exercises must always issue in concrete deeds.

These, then, were the most salient features of the holy life in the Evangelical tradition. It would be quite wrong, however, to portray so diverse a movement as having a single understanding of anything, let alone so protean a concept as holiness. On the contrary, Evangelicals differed sharply among themselves over questions surrounding sanctification. So the main task here is to survey the various strands in Evangelicalism for their contrasting views in the field. Four chief sub-traditions are readily identifiable: the Reformed, the Wesleyan, the Keswick and the charismatic. Each will be explored in turn. The aim will be not only to bring out the most striking elements in their perceptions of sanctity, but also to diagnose their cultural affinities. That exercise goes a long way towards explaining why there have been different understandings of holiness.

---

[8] L. Wilson, 'Female Spirituality amongst Nonconformists, 1825–1875', unpublished Cheltenham and Gloucester College of Higher Education Ph.D., 1997, p. 70.

Reformed (or Calvinist) Holiness

The first sub-tradition was the Reformed or Calvinist strand. In the eighteenth century, nearly all Anglican Evangelicals other than Wesley's followers adopted Reformed teaching, but they tended to play it down because Calvinism seemed tainted with memories of the Puritan revolution. Simeon eventually publicly repudiated Calvinism altogether. Most Evangelical Anglicans thereafter sat loose to distinctively Reformed views, but their theology continued to be moulded more by it than by any other source and a few including the redoubtable J. C. Ryle, first Bishop of Liverpool from 1880, remained self-conscious Calvinists. Evangelical Dissenters, both Congregationalists and Baptists, were tied to their Calvinist moorings for longer, but gradually cast them off during the later nineteenth century. Presbyterians in Scotland and Calvinistic Methodists in Wales were confessionally Reformed, and so retained more of their doctrinal legacy than English Nonconformists, but followed broadly the same path. By the first half of the twentieth century Calvinism was at a low ebb. In its second half, however, the distinguished Welsh minister of Westminster Chapel, Martyn Lloyd-Jones, propagated a revival of Reformed teaching, especially through his sponsorship of the Banner of Truth Trust that republished Calvinist classics. What was the understanding of holiness in these circles?

Calvinist Evangelicals were constantly aware of two traps into which the unwary might stumble. One was the legalist snare: the notion, condemned in the New Testament by the apostle Paul, that human beings could obtain acceptance by the Almighty through fulfilling the demands of God's law. This was what Josiah Pratt condemned in 1804 as 'a self-righteous spirit': people might suppose that they could become holy by their own effort, independent of divine grace. The early Evangelicals saw this opinion propagated in the eighteenth century by many latitudinarian churchmen. The other threat was what Pratt called 'an Antinomian spirit': the assertion that believers were exempt from obeying the law of God and so need not exert themselves to obtain holiness. A handful of hyper-Calvinists took this ground, at least in theory. The best known were Robert Hawker, a Plymouth clergyman around the turn of the nineteenth century, and William Huntington, a former coalheaver who became an Independent preacher in London and delighted to place 'S.S.', denoting 'Sinner Saved', after his name. These men taught imputed sanctification, that is the idea that a person is wholly sanctified from conversion onwards and contended that the need for holiness of life should not be mentioned in preaching. Mainstream Evangelicals such as Simeon were horrified at this view, which seemed calculated to foster immoral behaviour. They insisted that, just as holiness was unattainable without divine help, so it must be sought through human endeavour. The achievement of sanctity was a result of synergy, divine and human.

It was furthermore, a gradual process. Over time, progress was to be expected in the Christian life. 'A man,' remarked Ryle, 'may climb from one step to another in holiness.'[9] Slowly old motives were transformed and new habits consolidated. There could nevertheless be a falling back into sinful ways – what Evangelicals called backsliding – but the remedy was to break with sin and return to the paths of righteousness. The whole business necessarily took time. 'The new heart of a saint of God', according to a Presbyterian minister at the turn of the twentieth century, Alexander Whyte, 'was never attained at a bound.'[10] Steady progress was the best that could be expected.

Spiritual development did not mean that a believer escaped from the blandishments of sin. There was always, even after a long pilgrimage, an enemy within, what John Newton, the eighteenth-century Anglican clergyman and hymnwriter, called 'the inseparable remnants of a fallen nature'.[11] The flesh, in Pauline terms always contended with the spirit. The hostility between the two aspects of human nature remained down to the grave. Not until death and the entrance on glory was the tension relieved. Hence there was a need for constant vigilance, dedication and effort. The Christian life was an arena of perpetual conflict. Calvinists readily employed military imagery in their exposition of spirituality. 'A holy violence,' declared Ryle, 'a conflict, a warfare, a fight, a soldier's life, a wrestling,

[9] J. C. Ryle, *Holiness*, 3rd edn. (London: William Hunt & Co., 1887), p. 29.
[10] Gordon, *Evangelical Spirituality*, p. 246.
[11] B. Hindmarsh, *John Newton and the English Evangelical Tradition* (Oxford: Clarendon Press, 1996), p. 256.

are spoken of as characteristic of the true Christian.'[12] Ryle was drawing on the long Christian tradition that depicted the quest for sanctity as a *pugna spiritualis*, a spiritual battle. The Calvinist approach was not far removed from that of the bulk of Christendom, Eastern as well as Western.

The Reformed understanding of holiness, in fact, had deep roots in the epoch before the rise of Evangelicalism. Its classic texts were not from the revival period at all, but from the previous century. John Goode, a Dissenting minister at an Evangelical discussion group in 1809, naturally appealed to the definition of sanctification in the catechism of the Westminster Assembly. Ryle in the late nineteenth century included among his authorities on the subject Richard Sibbes, Thomas Manton, John Owen and Thomas Brooks – all Puritan divines.[13] These were still the authors being republished by the Banner of Truth Trust at the end of the twentieth century. There was, therefore, a strong sense of continuity with the past about the Calvinist advocates of holiness.

Nevertheless one element of the Puritan attitude was firmly repudiated. Seventeenth-century Calvinist authors had encouraged their readers to doubt their salvation. Only if they were aroused to be seekers, it was assumed, would they be likely to find. Hence authentic spirituality in the seventeenth century entailed intense introspection to discover whether there were any green shoots of a harvest of grace in the field of the soul. Evangelical Calvinists of the eighteenth century onwards however, would have nothing of that. Except in the most conservative circles of English Strict Baptists and Scottish Free Churchmen, they held that assurance of salvation, though by no means certain for believers, was at least to be coveted. Only if they possessed an assured hope would they turn from spiritual hypochondriacs into dedicated participants in mission: 'assurance is to be desired', according to Ryle, 'because it tends to make a Christian an active working Christian'.[14] The confident knowledge of God, which was the

---

[12] Ryle, *Holiness*, p. xxvi.

[13] Pratt, ed., *The Thought of the Evangelical Leaders*, p. 464; Ryle, *Holiness*, pp. xxix, 48n, 460–71.

[14] Ryle, *Holiness*, p. 163.

essence of assurance, formed an Evangelical species of the Enlightenment's characteristic preoccupation with epistemology. Calvinism had been sufficiently adapted to the times to take up a much stronger estimate of the knowability of the Almighty. The conception of the holy life current among Evangelical Calvinists was powerfully moulded by long-standing Christian tradition, especially in its Protestant variant, but adapted to the intellectual environment created by the Enlightenment.

Wesleyan Holiness

The second strand for consideration is that associated with John Wesley. The Wesleyan teaching contrasted with the Reformed position by asserting that before death a state of perfect holiness is attainable on earth. This was one of the distinctive views that brought eighteenth-century Methodists into conflict with Calvinist contemporaries. It was part of the Wesleyan theological package labelled Arminianism, after the seventeenth-century continental opponent of Reformed doctrine, Jacobus Arminius. The central conviction setting Arminians apart from Calvinists, was the belief that all might be saved: not, of course, that all would be saved but that all had the power to respond to the gospel. Yet Wesleyan holiness teaching should not be seen as a corollary of Arminianism. For one thing Arminius himself had not upheld it; for another the General Baptists, who, like Wesley, were Arminians, did not embrace his view of sanctification. All branches of Methodism, however, officially maintained the Wesleyan position during the nineteenth century. Although in practice the holiness tradition within Methodism gradually decayed, it enjoyed a resurgence in the 1870s. This so-called 'holiness revival' was much weaker in Britain than in the United States but it did give rise to a number of small holiness bodies including, in its early days, the Salvation Army. By the twentieth century, however Wesleyan teaching had become marginal, being sustained in the later part of the century only by the Church of the Nazarene and a small number of Methodists. The Wesleyan tradition has largely fallen by the wayside.

The outstanding primary source is John Wesley's *Plain Account of Christian Perfection* (1766–89). In it Wesley teaches the

possibility of entire sanctification, what he prefers to call
'perfect love'. This was held to be a state in which the believer
commits no sin. It is not just that sinful acts have ceased; it is
also that there is no longer any stimulus to sin. The condition
was described in questions and answers summarising the
proceedings of the first Methodist Conference in 1744:

Q. What is it to be *sanctified?*
A. To be renewed in the image of God, in *righteousness and
   true holiness.*
Q. What is implied in being a *perfect Christian?*
A. The loving God with all our heart, and mind, and soul
   (Deut. 6:5).
Q. Does this imply that *all inward sin* is taken away?
A. Undoubtedly: or how can we be said to be *saved from all
   our uncleanness?* (Ezek. 36:29)[15]

The doctrine spread in the much more palatable form of the
hymns of John Wesley's brother, Charles:

> Answer that gracious end in me
> For which thy precious life was given:
> Redeem from *all iniquity,*
>   Restore and make me meet for heaven.
> Unless thou purge my *every stain,*
>   thy suffering and my faith is vain.[16]

Here was a direct challenge to Reformed teaching. Far from the
Christian life being a perennial struggle between the implanted
spirit and the sinful flesh, it was possible to break free from sin
altogether. This was strong meat, and it turned the stomachs of
Calvinists.

The Wesleyan conception focused on what its opponents
often called 'the second blessing'. After conversion, on this
view, there was a fresh crisis in which the believer entered on a
state of perfect blessedness. It was received instantaneously.
Before that point, Wesley found, converts often struggled for
years in the search for sanctity. Most, including Wesley himself,

---

[15] F. Whaling, ed., *John and Charles Wesley. Selected Prayers, Hymns, Journal
Notes, Sermons, Letters and Treatises* (London: SPCK, 1981), p. 319.
[16] Whaling, ed., *John and Charles Wesley*, p. 317.

never professed to have discovered the blessed state at all. Those who did entered on it by faith alone. Sanctification, like justification, was given to faith, not achieved as a result of works. The Calvinist supposition that there must be sustained effort in the struggle against sin was rejected. On the contrary, there could be a serene reliance on Christ as the guarantor of Christian perfection. Peace, according to its advocates, had superseded the state of war in the soul. Nevertheless, Wesley and his followers readily admitted that perfect love could be lost. The condition of sanctity could be attained and forfeited repeatedly as a person lapsed into deliberate wrong. Errors that were not deliberate, however, were not classified as sins at all. They were merely 'infirmities'. For that reason Wesley denied that there was such a thing as 'any *absolute perfection* on earth'.[17] It was a concession that made the experience seem attainable. Wesley was nevertheless portraying a state of sanctity far higher than that envisaged by his Calvinist opponents.

Although Wesley always remained the leading authority in the Methodist holiness tradition, there were significant modifications in its content over time. In the middle years of the nineteenth century there was a process of American democratisation. Visiting preachers from the United States, James Caughey and Phoebe Palmer, proclaimed a version of Wesleyan holiness for the masses. Wanting to maximise the numbers enjoying the experience, they tried to make the way of securing the blessing easier. There was no need to wait, as earlier Methodists had supposed, until a believer wrestled through to full salvation. Instead it was possible to believe for entire sanctification on the spot. By contrast with Wesley, they claimed that no feeling of confirmation – 'the witness of the Spirit' – was necessarily to be expected. Faith would always be honoured by God. Consequently numbers professing entire sanctification increased under their preaching; but the experience was normally less deeply rooted. At the same time, and on into the twentieth century, another factor came into operation. Exponents of the Wesleyan tradition smoothed away its sharp edges. William Arthur, a Wesleyan connexional official, for example, published *The Tongue of Fire* (1856) to urge entire

---

[17] Whaling, ed., *John and Charles Wesley*, p. 307.

sanctification, but wrapped up his subject in such oblique genteel language as to tone down the distinctiveness of the experience. He was catering for a Methodist public that was upwardly socially mobile. Professions of perfection seemed out of place in Victorian suburbia. Growing respectability dictated that talk about instantaneous holiness should be either modified or abandoned. Consequently the tradition fell into decay.

The decreasing popularity of holiness on Wesleyan lines was also partly the result of the fading of the intellectual context in which it had originally been created. It was the product of the Enlightenment of the eighteenth century. John Wesley has increasingly been recognised in recent years as an Enlightenment thinker. Although he retained a streak of superstition and credulity, he was a persistent assertor of the claims of reason in religion. Doctrine, he argued, should be accepted only if it was reasonable. The New Testament, in the first Epistle of John, taught that 'he that is born of God sins not'. It was a rational inference, Wesley insisted, that freedom from sin was possible. In keeping with the spirit of the age, Wesley was committed to empirical method. He therefore investigated the cases of Methodists claiming entire sanctification, and in many instances concluded that their claims were valid. He, like his era, was an optimist about human potential. Why should not human beings be capable of rising to sublime heights of sanctity? The result was an understanding of holiness cast in an Enlightenment mould. It is true that some late Victorian Methodists injected the Romantic style of thinking into Wesleyan teaching and so caught the wind of later cultural trends. There was however a more thorough Romantic revamping of holiness available in the alternative Keswick tradition which gained far more influence than its Wesleyan counterpart. As the legacy of the Enlightenment in the exaltation of reason, empiricism and optimism weakened in society, so Wesley's ideal of holiness ceased to exert a powerful appeal

The Keswick Holiness Tradition

The Keswick movement that has just been mentioned forms the third strand of Evangelical holiness teaching. Its central contention, like Wesley's, was that sanctification is possible by faith. Unlike Wesley, however, it maintained that the sinful nature is never extinguished during life on earth. Keswick teaching was so called because it was the message of the annual convention held from 1875 in the Lake Disrict town. The immediate source of the novel theory was an American couple, Robert and Hannah Pearsall Smith, who toured Britain in the early 1870s propagating what was often called 'the higher life'. Conferences in Oxford in 1874 and Brighton in 1875 laid the foundations for Keswick. The whole movement was nearly wrecked through an indiscretion by Robert Pearsall Smith at Brighton: he offered spiritual guidance to a young woman privately in a hotel room and had to be hurriedly shipped back to America. Once the annual convention had been launched, however, it went from strength to strength. Its journal *The Life of Faith* gained a mass circulation. Keswick sanctification doctrine became the norm in conservative Evangelical circles during the first half of the twentieth century fading only in the 1950s and 1960s. For nearly a century it enjoyed considerable support.

Sanctification, on the Keswick understanding, was originally received in a moment. This belief shows the debt of Keswick, through the Pearsall Smiths and others, to the Wesleyan tradition before it. Every annual convention came to the point where a speaker would call on his hearers to receive entire consecration. Ryle, from his unreconstructed Reformed perspective, protested against 'the theory of a sudden, mysterious transition of a believer into a state of blessedness ... at one mighty bound'.[18] Faith, according to Keswick, was the only initial condition of receiving. Faith, furthermore, had to be exercised permanently. Only if a person continued to trust would sin continue to be defeated. There had to be what was often termed a 'moment-by-moment' form of dependence on God. By this means sin was not eradicated, as contemporaries in the Wesleyan succession claimed, but repressed. 'The flesh', in the words of Evan Hopkins, the movement's leading theological exponent down to the First World War, 'is ... effectively counteracted by ... the Holy Ghost within us, so that we

---

[18] Ryle, *Holiness*, p. xxiv.

can walk in the paths of continuous deliverance from it'.[19] Hence there was no persisting struggle between spirit and flesh, as traditional Calvinists believed, but rather an experience of 'victory', a common Keswick slogan. The whole convention position can best be understood as an attempt to remodel Wesley's teaching so as to make it palatable to those possessing a Reformed inheritance. Consecration was available in an instant through faith, as Wesley had contended; but there was no question of the elimination of sin from the human life. Keswickers were always hot in denial of the charge that they were 'perfectionists'.

Like the Wesleyan approach Keswick teaching underwent change over time. In its early days it remained particularly malleable. It was the achievement of Evan Hopkins and Handley Moule, Bishop of Durham from 1901 to 1920, to formulate it in acceptable theological terms. Moule's commentary on the book of Romans was an important text. In the 1879 edition, written before the time of his spiritual consecration, Moule expounds chapter 7 as an account of the apostle Paul's experience as a mature believer of internal conflict between the flesh and the spirit – the standard Reformed view. In a revision published in 1894, after he gave his allegiance to Keswick, however, he reinterprets the passage as an account of the tensions in the life of someone yet to reach the moment of personal sanctification.[20] Only in chapter 8, on this view, does the apostle describe the life of victory. Here was a scholarly apologia intelligible to the theologically literate.

Subsequently, however, others put a different spin on the Keswick message. In the inter-war years, Graham Scroggie, a Scottish Baptist minister, provided more careful biblical exegesis than had been customary on the convention platform. He also presented the difference between the unconsecrated and the consecrated believer as that between those who take Christ as Saviour only and those who accept him as Lord as well.[21] The Lordship of Christ involved no complexities about

[19] E. Hopkins, *Hidden yet Possessed* (London: Marshall Brothers, 1894), p. 63.

[20] Gordon, *Evangelical Spirituality*, pp. 210–11.

[21] I. M. Randall, *Evangelical Experiences. A Study in the Spirituality of English Evangelicalism, 1918–1939* (Carlisle: Paternoster, 1999), pp. 26–8.

interior pneumatological repression: it was an altogether simpler message. At the same period another group whose members were attracted to Keswick spirituality, but who found its conservative theology and undenominational ethos repellent, established an alternative convention at Cromer on the Norfolk coast. The addresses at Cromer tended to pantheism but still called for the utmost spiritual dedication. The message of Keswick was adapted in different ways so as to have a wider appeal.

The people most drawn in during the earlier years of the movement had been the educated, the prosperous and the young. Keswick was closely associated with the rise of the Inter-Varsity Fellowship of Christian Unions that consisted of undergraduates with precisely such characteristics. These students were young people possessing sufficient wealth to be able to attend conventions and a reading habit that allowed them to absorb Keswick literature. They were part of the sector of society most likely to be influenced by the gradually spreading Romantic cultural mood of the later nineteenth century. Keswick's appeal was grounded in its penetration by the spirit of the age. Its epicentre, symbolically, was in the Lake District, the home of Wordsworth and Coleridge. Those poets were in vogue among convention-goers, who descanted in the manner of Wordsworth on the 'chastening and purifying effect' of 'nature's panorama'.[22] The serene side of the Romantic ethos, Wordsworth's beloved tranquillity, was also reflected in the atmosphere of the movement, dwelling on the peace and rest enjoyed by the consecrated soul. There were also Romantic affinities in Keswick's doctrinal approach. On the one hand, its adherents tended to be less precise in dogmatic formulation than other Evangelicals, so mirroring the intellectual influence of Coleridge on Anglican Broad Churchmanship. On the other, they were almost unanimous in embracing the premillennial advent hope, the doctrine of the imminent Second Coming of Christ, which was closely related to Romantic thought. The heavy debt of the Oxford Movement and the succeeding style of High Churchmanship to the Romantic temper of the age is generally acknowledged. Keswick should

<hr/>

[22] *Christian*, 25 July 1895, p. 14.

be seen as an Evangelical parallel to that High Church idiom. Both enjoyed growing appeal in the period of the dissemination of Romantic cultural norms to a wider public, the later nineteenth and early twentieth centuries, and both faded afterwards. Keswick's brand of holiness should be diagnosed as an adaptation of the Evangelical tradition to a Romantic cultural setting.

Charismatic Renewal

The final strand of Evangelical holiness teaching is that associated with charismatic renewal. Its exuberant style of worship has transformed much of the Evangelical world, and its influence has extended far beyond those boundaries into, for example, the Roman Catholic Church. Yet, as Roman Catholic participants have declared, the movement has drawn them into embracing customary Evangelical priorities such as detailed Bible study. Renewal sprang originally from the Pentecostal sector of Evangelicalism, its most distinctive feature in the early days being speaking in tongues. Nevertheless, the charismatic movement was not simply an extension of classic Pentecostalism. Leaders of the Pentecostal movement looked on the outgrowth of renewal in the historic churches with reserve and sometimes with dismay. They were aware that charismatic spokesmen failed to accept standard Pentecostal doctrine, and uneasily conscious of a tangible difference in ethos. There is more of a similarity, in fact, between charismatic renewal and the inter-war Oxford Group movement led by Frank Buchman. Both cast aside inherited ways in order to minimise the cultural distance between adherents of the movements and their secular contemporaries. Both, for instance eagerly used the slang of their times in preference to the accepted language of Zion. The great upsurge of the charismatic movement came in the 1960s, was simultaneous with the rise of youth culture and had close affinities with it. It took two forms: renewal in the historic denominations, fostered until 1980 by the Fountain Trust; and the creation of fresh bodies, usually called house churches until they started buying disused cinemas to accommodate their throngs of worshippers, and now normally called 'New Churches'. On the eve of the twenty-first century charismatic renewal is a vigorously growing sector of British Christianity.

The charismatic conception of holiness is in some ways elusive, because the term itself has not been favoured since it savours of off-putting religious language. Even the words 'sin' and 'salvation' have been much rarer in charismatic-influenced worship songs than in traditional hymnody. An approved phrase, however, was 'spirituality in depth'.[23] What were its salient features? In the first place the movement laid great stress on the physical, a point illustrated, for example, by the characteristic raising of the hands in worship. Hence spiritual wholeness and physical health were often linked. There have been many expressions of the ministry of healing. Most typical, however, was concern for the welfare of the place where the physical and the spiritual most obviously intersect – the human consciousness. 'Inner healing' was in vogue. Psychological healing was so generally practised in the earlier days of renewal, according to Michael Harper, the organiser of the Fountain Trust, that it actually diverted the movement from trying to reach the unconverted.[24] Holiness meant a well-adjusted mind, complete with unpolluted depths.

Salvation was also often reinterpreted, in charismatic circles, in terms of relationships. Progress in salvation, what traditionally would have been called sanctification, was understood as advance in relationship with God and with fellow Christians. The principle of community was baptised into use. Christian communities, sometimes semi-monastic though rarely celibate, sprang up in many parts of the country. House churches insisted on close bonds between individual believers, often entailing the subordination of those judged to be less advanced in the faith. 'Everywhere,' according to a leader of the Isca Christian Fellowship, 'everything is based on relationships.'[25] Holiness was embodied in right relationships.

Perhaps the supreme feature of charismatic spirituality, however, was what can appropriately be termed holy worldliness. By contrast with received Evangelical Nonconformist

[23] *Anglicans for Renewal* 24 (1985), p. 26.
[24] E. England, *The Spirit of Renewal* (Eastbourne: Kingsway, 1982), p. 159.
[25] R. Forster, *Ten New Churches* (n.p.: M.A.R.C. Europe, 1986), p. 125.

inhibitions, Gerald Coates, one of the most prominent New Church leaders, considered it a virtue to declare that one drank alcohol.[26] Coates's teaching was evaluated by a Calvinist to be formally antinomian.[27] There must be no pretence; one should follow one's real feelings; the public self should mirror the inner self. There should be authenticity. A former Durham vicar and future Archbishop of Canterbury, George Carey, declared in 1985 that through renewal he discovered liberty. 'It shattered,' he explained, 'my evangelical rigidity.'[28] The charismatic movement undermined previous assumptions about how the Christian ought to behave. There was to be no retreat from the world for the sake of sanctity.

Like the Keswick movement of the late nineteenth century, charismatic renewal in the late twentieth century disproportionately attracted the educated, the prosperous, and the young. Is adherents were overwhelmingly graduates rather than the masses. This was the section of British society most affected by fresh cultural currents. From the 1960s the rising tide was what has come to be labelled Postmodernism, although its lineage can be traced back to the Modernist avant-garde of the early twentieth century. The prominent features of charismatic spirituality are discernibly Postmodernist in style. Inner healing was predicated on the depth psychology stemming from Freud and Jung that steadily came into its own as the twentieth century advanced. The exaltation of relationships typified in the Bloomsbury Group, became normal in the advanced circles of the late twentieth century. And holy worldliness entailed an erosion of boundaries that is perhaps the most striking feature of Postmodernist discourse. Insofar as there existed a concept of holiness in the renewal movement, it was strongly tinctured by the rising cultural mood of its time. Postmodernism shaped charismatic versions of spirituality.

---

[26] A. Walker, *Restoring the Kingdom* (London: Hodder & Stoughton, 1985), p. 89.

[27] A. Munden, 'Encountering the House Church Movement: "A Different Kind of Christianity"', *Anvil* 1 (1984), p. 211.

[28] *Anglicans for Renewal* 21 (1985), p. 8.

Conclusion: Holiness in Context

These four strands show that the scrutiny of holiness has to take into account the social context of ideas. It must be, in a strong sense, a study in the relationship of gospel and culture. The Evangelical tradition has given rise to an approach to the holy life that is recognisably distinctive, displaying the characteristic marks of conversion, cross, Bible and activism. These elements have endured from the early eighteenth century down to the present day. Yet the tradition has been repeatedly transformed by its environment. The inherited Calvinist doctrine of gradualism by works was challenged in the eighteenth century by Wesleyan teaching about a crisis of sanctification by faith. Wesley's new version of holiness reflected his immersion in the thought of the Enlightenment. In the late nineteenth century Keswick offered a fresh presentation of sanctification by faith in terms more acceptable to Calvinists by adopting Romantic categories of thought. A century later charismatic renewal built on Postmodernist premises as it formulated its understanding of the Christian life. The resurgence of Reformed teaching in the late twentieth century means that in coming years the Evangelical world is likely to be increasingly polarised between the Calvinist and the charismatic views. The Wesleyan and Keswick interpretations have become negligible as the cultural forces with which they were associated have faded away. What survive are the stance with the longest pedigree, which tends to attract those of a reading and conservative inclination, and that with the greatest contemporary resonance, which draws on a much larger constituency. Sanctity has been understood in different ways in accordance with the changing assumptions of the age. Without doubt, therefore, holiness in the Evangelical tradition has been shaped by its cultural setting.

15

Holiness in the Roman Catholic Tradition

Sheridan Gilley

The history of sanctity in the modern Roman Catholic Church draws on two thousand years of history over the whole of the ancient classical world and medieval Europe and most of the earth since Christianity became a global religion through the Portuguese and Spanish missions of the sixteenth century. Of course, the cult of saints, of prayer to the dead who are alive in God's presence, also flourishes in the Orthodox and Oriental Churches, and in religions external to Christianity.[1] Hagiography 'was the most widely-used and long-lived genre of Late Antiquity and the Middle Ages',[2] and its modern literature is also vast. Even the modern secular world has its radical movements from the time of the French Revolution that have produced pantheons of saints and martyrs, borrowing from the imagery of Christianity,[3] and much in the subject which looks

---

[1] On the cult of saints in Islam, see Marc Gaborieau, 'The Cult of Saints Among the Muslims of Nepal and Northern India', in Stephen Wilson, ed., *Saints and their Cults: Studies in Religious Sociology, Folklore and History* (Cambridge: Cambridge University Press, 1985), pp. 291–308; Chase Robinson, 'Prophecy and Holy Men in Early Islam', and Josef W. Meri, 'The Etiquette of Devotion in the Islamic Cult of Saints', both in James Howard-Johnston and Paul Antony Hayward, *The Cult of Saints in Late Antiquity and the Middle Ages: Essays on the Contribution of Peter Brown* (London: Oxford University Press, 1999), pp. 241–62, 263–86.

[2] Mary-Ann Stouck, *Medieval Saints: A Reader* (Peterborough, Ontario: Broadview Press, 1999), p. xvii.

[3] See Albert Soboul, 'Religious Feeling and Popular Cults during the French Revolution: "Patriot Saints" and Martyrs for Liberty', in Stephen Wilson, ed. *Saints and their Cults*, pp. 217–32.

Roman Catholic to Protestants is shared with other religions and traditions.

Nor is the theme of sanctity without contemporary interest. Theologians like Hans Urs von Balthasar, the nearest that modern Roman Catholicism has to an official Doctor of the Church, continue to reflect upon the theme,[4] which has also become the material for the investigation of such recent preoccupations as gender relations.[5] With so vast a subject, even in Roman Catholic terms, it is difficult to begin, but here are three stories about modern Roman Catholic saints.

The first is that of the youngest of the five surviving children of a devout Norman watchmaker and jeweller, Marie-Francoise-Thérèse Martin, born in 1873. At the age of 14 she went with her father on pilgrimage to Rome and, in an audience with Pope Leo XIII, seized his knees and demanded that she be allowed to enter at once the local Carmel in Lisieux, where two of her sisters were nuns already. She had to be carried off by attendants. She became a Carmelite at 15, was professed as Sister Thérèse of the Child Jesus and of the Holy Face, and died unknown to the world in 1897 aged 24, promising to spend eternity doing good on earth. One of her sisters put together three letters she had written and published it as the *History of a Soul* (1898). It became a runaway best-seller, with an attendant cult of its author as 'the Little Flower'. By 1918, the Carmel in Lisieux was receiving 1800 letters a day, asking for prayers in her name and reporting miracles and spiritual favours. Her teaching of a 'little way' of loving and suffering in small things had reached millions. In 1923, she was beatified by Pope Pius XI, who canonised her in the Holy Year of 1925, an action which he called the 'star' of his pontificate. She had longed to be a soldier, a missionary and a philosopher: in 1927 she was declared, with Francis Xavier, the principal patroness of missions; in 1944, a secondary patroness of France, with her

[4] See Lawrence S. Cunningham, 'Current Theology: Saints and Martyrs: Some Contemporary Considerations', *Theological Studies*, 60 (1999), pp. 530–1, with many contemporary references.

[5] E.g., John Kitchen, *Saints' Lives and the Rhetoric of Gender: Male and Female in Merovingian Hagiography* (New York and Oxford: Oxford University Press, 1998).

own favourite saint, the warrior St Joan of Arc; and in 1997 a Doctor of the Church.

The second example: in 1954, a barque was rowed across the Venetian lagoon through a multitude of waiting boats and ships. It contained the incorrupt body of Giuseppe Melchiorre Sarto, the son of a municipal messenger who had worked all his life for three shillings a day in the north Italian village of Riese. The corpse had been engaged upon a triumphant grand tour of Italy, in a black and gilded hearse. Sarto had been a popular priest-catechist in an obscure provincial town, a seminary professor and Bishop of Mantua, and then Cardinal Patriarch of Venice. In 1903, the Austrian Emperor vetoed the election to the papacy of the aristocratic Cardinal Rampolla, and Sarto was elected Pope under the name of Pius X. Pius was an administrative genius, who gave the Curia its most fundamental reform since the sixteenth century. He had an irresistible charm to his Italian flock, and devoted his Saturday afternoons to explaining the faith in catechetical lectures to crowds of several thousand in the courtyard of Pope Damasus. He also performed abundant miracles, even through a nun's sock. He was said, though here the evidence is contradictory, to have died of grief because of the outbreak of the First World War. He was beatified in 1951 and canonised in 1954.

The third example is that of Maria Goretti, born in Ancona in 1890, the daughter of a peasant farmer who had died when she was ten. Maria was a cheerful, devout and otherwise unremarkable girl, who at the age of 12, was stabbed resisting an attempt to rape her by a young man called Alexander Serenelli. She died the following day forgiving her murderer. Her killer was sentenced to life imprisonment, repented in 1910, after a dream in which Maria offered him flowers, and was released from gaol in 1929. He trudged back to Maria's village where her mother cooked him a simple meal. Maria was canonised in the Holy Year of 1950. She is a patron saint, we should now say, of the victims of paedophilia, and in her the Roman Church 'also honours innumerable others who, in similar circumstances, prefer death to dishonour'.[6]

---

[6] David Hugh Farmer, *The Oxford Dictionary of Saints* (London: Oxford University Press, 1987), p. 188.

What, then, can be learned from these stories?

First, all three are untypical in the speed of their canonisation. Twentieth-century canonisations until quite recently have been of people who died long ago, like the fifteenth-century St Joan of Arc, canonised in 1920, or the Forty Martyrs of England and Wales, who died between 1575 and 1680, and were canonised in 1970. In the modern era, Thérèse of Lisieux holds the record of 27 years between her death and canonisation.

But my stories say a good deal about the modern Catholic Church. It is obviously significant that the list includes a Frenchwoman and two Italians, from the Mediterranean heartland of the Church. Of all the saints in the Western tradition, the most fertile of imitation and the nearest to an *alter Christus* has been the Italian St Francis, with the widest of cults after the Blessed Virgin. Most modern Roman Catholic canonised saints have been Italian, French or Spanish. It is also significant that two of the saints in the list are women. Although only about 20 per cent of saints papally canonised by Rome have been women, scholars have detected an internal feminisation of Catholic piety in the nineteenth century, when many men lapsed from religious practice while most women remained faithful.[7] Again, it is notable that one of the women is a nun; it helps to have a great religious order like the Carmelites to push and fund a cause for canonisation, and the Carmelites felt no little pride in adding a little Thérèsa to their already great Theresa, St Teresa of Avila, who was also (in 1970) declared a Doctor of the Church. There are other St Theresas, the latest another Carmelite, the former Jewish convert executed by the Nazis, Edith Stein, St Teresa Benedicta of the Cross. Only about 20 per cent of the saints canonised by Rome have been lay people, rather than priests or religious. Again, as in the three examples, the bias of canonisation is to holy virginity, the smallest category of saints, feminists might note, being happily married women. Maria Goretti renewed

[7] See Olwen Hufton, 'The Reconstruction of the Church, 1796–1801', in Gwynne Lewis and Colin Lucas, eds., *Beyond the Terror: Essays in French Regional History, 1794–1815* (Cambridge: Cambridge University Press, 1983), pp. 21–52.

older Catholic memories of the early Christian women martyrs of the Roman canon like Felicity, Perpetua and Agnes, but in the contemporary world reflected a modern purity movement within Italian Catholicism very like that half a century before among non-Catholic feminists in England. It is Popes who canonise, and it might be thought that they have an interest in canonising Popes, but St Pius X is the first pope to have been canonised since the sixteenth-century St Pius V, and there have been only three canonised popes since the thirteenth century, the earliest of these being the very uncharacteristic former hermit Pope Celestine V, who resigned the papacy, a sin for which Dante put him in hell. Canonised cardinals are almost as rare.

Saints are acknowledged by canonisation, which in its primitive form meant putting his or her name in the list or canon of the saints on the altar for commemoration. The most necessary element of such canonisation is still present in all three modern examples: the evidence of democracy, *vox populi, vox dei*, that the saint has a popular following – that there are people who think that he or she is a saint. Saints' cults must consist in part in communal and collective remembrance. The initial questions to witnesses in canonisations is not 'is X a saint?', but 'do people think he is?' In this respect, the popular impulse of the earliest canonisations remains in the present system.

There are about 10,000 venerated saints in the *Acta Sanctorum*,[8] which has been scientifically compiled by the Jesuit Bollandists from the seventeenth century,[9] and is still going strong, although the Inquisition closed it down once for twenty years for denying that Elijah had founded the Carmelite order.[10] But this number excludes many of the thousands of saints, perhaps especially those of Celtic Christianity, who have never had more than local recognition. There are, moreover,

---

[8] Johannes Bollandus and Godefridus Henschenius, *et al.*, original series, *Acta Sanctorum*, 58 vols. (Antwerp, Brussels, Tongerloo and Paris, 1643–1867).

[9] Hippolyte Delehaye, *The Work of the Bollandists through Three Centuries, 1615–1915* (Princeton: Princeton University Press, 1922); Dom David Knowles, 'The Bollandists', in *Great Historical Enterprises: Problems in Monastic History* (London: Thomas Nelson & Sons Ltd, 1963), pp. 1–32.

[10] Wilson, *Saints and their Cults*, p. 31.

about 500 saints in this body of 10,000 who have been canonised by the Popes, and it is only in the present century that papal canonisations by Rome have become frequent. The inflation in numbers for this century runs thus: four canonisations by Pius X in a pontificate of eleven years, three by Benedict XV in eight years, thirty-two by Pius XI in seventeen years, thirty-two by Pius XII in twenty-one years, ten by John XXIII in four years,[11] well over a hundred by Paul VI in fifteen years and about three hundred by John Paul II in twenty-two years – more than all his predecessors put together. Some of John Paul's list are mass canonisations: as of no fewer than 117 Vietnamese martyrs in 1988, as earnestly requested by the Vietnamese bishops, to the fury of the Communist government of Hanoi. Indeed the twentieth century has been more fertile of martyrs than any time since the pagan persecutions.

The abundance of recent canonisations has also to do with the desire to make the saint more typical of the universal Church, as declared in Pope John Paul's own missionary travels, which often feature local canonisations. The promotion of young lay candidates has the same motivation, as of Marcel Callo, a 23-year-old Frenchman who died while a volunteer missionary in a Nazi prisoner-of-war camp in Germany, and later attracted a posthumous cult among German prisoners of war.[12] The inflation in saint-making is also the result of recent changes in the procedure of canonisation itself, as shall be shown. In short, this is an interesting contemporary topic, which is of more than merely historical, academic or theological interest.

In all this, there is a subtle and complicated relationship between popular piety and ecclesiastical authority, as the cult of the saints blows where it wills with the Spirit, and serves other interests than those of the Church. Devotion to the saints often has a wider clientele than among those who regularly go to Mass, and peasant and even working-class devotion often places

---

[11] See Pierre Delooz, *Sociologie et Canonisations* (The Hague: Martinus Nijhoff, 1969), pp. 463–5.

[12] Kenneth L. Woodward, *Making Saints: How the Catholic Church Determines Who becomes a Saint, Who Doesn't, and Why* (New York: Simon & Schuster, 1990), pp. 147–9.

a higher value on the saints than on the sacraments.[13] The hostility of Mass-centred Irish Catholics in America to the saint-centred devotions of immigrant Italians, and the rivalries of different Madonnas among these Italians, show the kind of tension which saints' cults can create within Roman Catholicism itself.[14]

The main official division of the saints in the modern missal and breviary derives from the early centuries of Christianity. In the beginning were the martyrs, of whom Stephen was the first, and whose passion narratives told of witness through suffering endured like Christ's through the power of God. Then, proceeding from Apostles came the confessors, some, like the Desert Fathers, distinguished by the white martyrdom of asceticism, and, where appropriate, distinguished as bishop, priest and deacon, monk, virgin and widow. Another category, that of doctor, was to be applied to learned theologians, while Kings, Queens and Emperors kept their royal titles in glory. Edith Stein and Maximilian Kolbe, both executed by the Nazis, have a privileged position as both martyrs *and* confessors, after controversies over whether they could be classified as martyrs for the faith or as victims of Nazi politics. At least from the time of the martyrdom of Polycarp, c. AD 150, the feast days of saints have been their death days; not their birthdays, when they were born in sin, but their death days, their heavenly *dies natalis*, when they were reborn in glory.

The origin of saints' cults has been a matter of confessional controversy – Protestant scholars tending to argue that they were inspired by the example of pagan gods or heroes. In some cases that seems to be partly true, as the early Christians exploited both the resemblances as well as differences between Christian and pagan usage.[15] SS Cosmas and Damian may have taken over some

[13] See Stephen Wilson, 'Cults of Saints in the Churches of Central Paris'; and Pierre Sanchis, 'The Portuguese *romarias*', both in Wilson, *Saints and their Cults*, pp. 233–60, 261–89.

[14] See Silvano M. Tomasi and Edward C. Stibili, eds., *Italian-Americans and Religion: An Annotated Bibliography* (New York: Centre for Migration Studies, 1978).

[15] William Horbury, 'The Cult of Christ and the Cult of the Saints', *New Testament Studies* 44 (1998), pp. 444–69.

functions from Aesculapius and Castor and Pollux,[16] but the martyrs who were the first saints to be venerated had died opposing paganism.[17] William Horbury has sought to show that the cult of the saints in Christianity also derived directly from honouring angels and the holy dead (patriarchs, prophets and martyrs) in Judaism, and that there is significant evidence for this in the New Testament, as in the immediate presence of the patriarchs Abraham, Isaac and Jacob and the prophets Moses and Elijah.[18] Horbury also argues for a Jewish origin of the cult of tombs and relics, which dates in Christianity from the second century at least, as the martyrdom of Polycarp testifies. The bones of the martyrs were venerated as relics and were incorporated into altars, which thereby also become tombs: a practice required by the Seventh General Council of Nicaea in 787 and still persisting today.[19] Saints are said to be 'raised to the altars' on their canonisation, and their shrines and relics work miracles. The spread of relics led to the spread of cults. The principle emerged, beginning with St Jerome, that they were owed a veneration or *dulia*, inferior to the *hyperdulia* offered to the Virgin, the saint of saints, and cult of cults, and the worship or adoration or *latria* offered to Christ and God.[20] The cultus of saints swept up the following: the founding missionary bishops of the ancient churches, like St Denis in France and St Augustine in England; non-humans, the angels – a prayer to St Michael the archangel used to conclude every Latin Low Mass; pre-Christian members of the Old Covenant like St John the Baptist; and partly or wholly imaginary figures from ancient folklore like St Catherine of Alexandria and St Christopher, or from the Christian Apocrypha, like the internationally popular St Anne, Our Lord's grandmother, who first appears in the *Protoevangelium of James*.

Purely imaginary or 'constructed'[21] saints are a subject in themselves, and not all are of ancient invention. The popular cult of St Philomena resulted from the misreading of an

[16] Wilson, *Saints and their Cults*, p. 2; but for the contrary view, see Hippolyte Delehaye, *The Legends of the Saints*, tr. Donald Attwater (London: Geoffrey Chapman, 1962), p. 141.
[17] Wilson, *Saints and their Cults*, pp. 2–3.
[18] Horbury, 'The Cult of Christ', pp. 444–69.
[19] Wilson, *Saints and their Cults*, p. 5.
[20] *Saints and their Cults*, p. 4.
[21] Delooz, *Sociologie et Canonisations*, p. 195.

inscription found in the Roman catacombs in 1802. The translation of the nearby body was accompanied by miracles, and
three subsequent visionaries saw Philomena in glory, one of
them the modern French patron saint of parish priests, the
nineteenth-century St Jean-Baptiste Vianney. After enquiry,
Rome abolished the cult of St Philomena in 1961.[22] A large
number of venerable figures for whom there was no clear
historical evidence were removed from the calendar by Pope
Paul VI in 1970, though, as in the case of St Christopher, their
cults have continued, sometimes on an international scale.

Saints are, by definition, holy, but there is a problematic
relationship between sainthood and sanctity, quite apart from
the consideration that martyrdom may cover unholiness of life.
Like St Dismas, the good thief who died on the cross beside
Christ, a saint may simply have died well. A single sentence,
'Lord, remember me when you come into your kingdom', was
enough for paradise; it spoke and speaks for all humanity. But
some early saints seem to have been bad men on the right side,
especially when they are in that dubiously canonisable category,
the theologian. The irascible and disputatious St Jerome
deserved his halo, lion and cardinal's hat of tradition as a
scholar, rather than a saint. St Cyril of Alexandria was a great
champion of orthodoxy against Nestorianism, but there is
a view of Cyril as a theological thug. He was certainly not a
conventionally 'nice' or pleasant person, and I would not
believe Cyril to be a saint did Holy Church not bid me do so.

At first, canonisations were episcopal, the act of canonisation
itself consisting in a recitation of the candidate's life and
miracles before the bishop. The diocesan origins of any process
of canonisation survived into the modern era in a division into
two parts – an Ordinary or Episcopal process belonging to the
bishop, and an Apostolic process reserved to Rome. There were
(and are) local lists of saints, embodying the identities of
monasteries, villages, towns and nations, and for trades, guilds
and professions. Their roles became too numerous to

---

[22] Caroline Ford, 'Female Martyrdom and the Politics of Sainthood in
Nineteenth-Century France: The Cult of Sainte Philomène', in Frank Tallett
and Nicholas Atkin, eds., *Catholicism in Britain and France since 1789* (London:
The Hambledon Press, 1996), pp. 115–34.

enumerate, though usefully summarised by Stephen Wilson as 'universal assistance, patronage, and political functions',[23] involving the cure of diseases, the protection of places and institutions from famine and conquest, the expression of communality, and the glorification of an order or royal dynasty or (as in the case of St Thomas à Becket) of opposition to one. Late medieval devotion to the fourteen Holy Helpers, the Vierzehnheiligen, offered protection in every area of life. Among the outrée is the Portuguese princess St Wilgefortis or St Uncumber, a lady who was given a miraculous moustache and beard to deliver herself from an unwanted suitor. She relieved or disencumbered other women of unwanted husbands for a peck of oats, and was deservedly popular in late medieval England.[24]

There was, therefore, a pluriformity of functions performed by saints' cults in late antiquity and the Middle Ages. For Peter Brown, the cult of the holy man was, on balance, a form of spiritual and social liberation, through the humanisation of an older natural religion, a source of 'that freedom of action from which the miracle of justice, mercy, and a sense of solidarity with their fellow humans might spring'.[25] In a recent response to his work, Philip Rousseau emphasises the role of holy men as mediators and teachers, distinguishing between 'the episcopal programme of homily and sacrament and the ascetic programme of wisdom, dialogue, and moral effort'.[26] Claudia Rapp stresses the key activities of the Eastern saints of late antiquity as those of intercession and ascetic example.[27] For Paul Hayward, with the outlook of a rather instrumentalist sociologist, and as an admirer of Gibbon, saints' cults were 'fraudulent to some degree' and 'self-serving', 'the fantasy of an elite threatened by violence and

[23] Wilson, *Saints and their Cults*, p. 16.

[24] Farmer, *Oxford Dictionary of Saints*, pp. 437–8.

[25] Peter Brown, *The Cult of the Saints: Its Rise and Function in Latin Christianity* (London: SCM Press, 1981), pp. 126–7; see also Howard-Johnston and Hayward, *The Cult of Saints*, p. 4.

[26] Philip Rousseau, 'Ascetics as mediators and as teachers', in Howard-Johnston and Hayward, eds., *The Cult of Saints*, p. 59.

[27] Claudia Rapp, ' "For next to God, you are my salvation": Reflections on the Rise of the Holy Man in Late Antiquity', in Howard-Johnston and Hayward, *The Cult of Saints*, pp. 63–82.

competition',[28] and arose from relic-shrines which were exploited by local aristocratic interests and then by kings and bishops. Richard Price suggests the continuities of hagiographic models as the stories of one generation of saints influence another.[29] More negatively, in Freudian mode, Michael Carroll has derived Marian and saints' cults in Italy from the anxieties produced by a dangerous environment,[30] and in Ireland, from a subconscious resentment of the imposition of Tridentine disciplines from the sixteenth century.[31] Such complexities of interpretation do not admit of easy resolution by evidence, reflecting the complexities of human psychology itself.

Such complexities are reflected in the way that cults rise and fall, as can be seen in the distinctly modern popularity of St Joseph. Moreover, the functions of particular saints have changed over the centuries, as appears from art. For the later Middle Ages, St Anthony of Padua, bearing the Christ Child, expressed tenderness for children; or with a piglet, care for animals. But in the painting by Sebastian del Piombo, he is a sage; for Tiepolo, a healer; in another work, in Admiral's uniform, he drives the Moors from Oran;[32] though 'on the rosters of at least two Portuguese regiments'[33] in popular culture, he now finds lost objects.

The seven champions of Christendom are an oddly assorted lot: St Denis of France was an amalgam of the perfectly historical third-century Bishop of Paris with St Paul's disciple Dionysius the Areopagite (Acts 17.34) and the fifth-century

---

[28] Paul Hayward, 'Demystifying the role of sanctity in Western Christendom,' in Howard-Johnston and Hayward, *The Cult of Saints*, pp. 141, 131.

[29] Richard Price, 'The Holy Man and Christianization from the Apocryphal Apostles to St Stephen of Perm', in Howard-Johnston and Hayward, *The Cult of Saints*, pp. 215–40.

[30] Michael P. Carroll, *Madonnas that Maim: Popular Catholicism in Italy since the Fifteenth Century* (Baltimore and London: The Johns Hopkins Press, 1992), p. 145.

[31] Michael P. Carroll, *Irish Pilgrimage: Holy Wells and Popular Catholic Devotion* (Baltimore and London: The Johns Hopkins Press, 1999), p. 167ff.

[32] Pierre Delooz, 'Towards a Sociological Study of Canonised Sainthood in the Catholic Church', in Wilson, *Saints and their Cults*, p. 195.

[33] *Saints and their Cults*, p. 37.

'Pseudo-Areopagite' and authority on Christian mysticism who was given the Areopagite's name – the whole fused by the royal monastery of St Denis near Paris into the special protector of the insecure French monarchy.[34] St Iago – St James the Great – became the Moorslayer; St George, God bless him, killed mostly Frenchmen. These complexities refute the idea that saints, though holy, have historically always been simply exemplars of holiness; they have been far more protean. Saints have been like modern academics, appointed for their research but then expected to teach, administer and give pastoral care. Sometimes, as in their triumphs of asceticism, the sanctity of the saints is more for edification than imitation. Some insignia of sanctity are both moving and repulsive, like the tradition, again begun by St Francis and copied by many hospital saints, of reverencing the sick to the extent of licking their sores. Some of the fasting prodigies of the past might be regarded as anorexic, though as in the case of St Rose of Lima, they went with beautiful characters. Like St Thérèse, saints are in heaven to do good on earth. But the luxuriance of saints' cults does raise the issue of the need for the regulation by authority of such a multiform world of popular devotion, and for a body of saints who are for everyone.

All saints and cults must be local in origin. The idea in the West of such a universal list for Christendom and its calendar, of collective remembrance for everyman, depended on the growth of papal power.[35] The first authenticated papal validation of a saint was Pope John XV's canonisation of a German, Bishop Ulrich of Augsburg in 993. In 1170 Pope Alexander III, who had reprimanded a Swedish bishop for allowing the veneration of a monk killed in a brawl, tried to reserve the power to canonise to the Holy See. In 1234, Gregory IX's decretals made this binding on the universal Church, and established the principle that a candidate for canonisation must exhibit both virtues and miracles. Thus the classic formula

---

[34] Gabrielle M. Spiegel, 'The Cult of St Denis and Capetian Kingship', in Wilson, *Saints and their Cults*, pp. 141–68.

[35] See 'Canonisation of Saints (History and Procedure)', *New Catholic Encyclopedia*, 14 vols (Catholic University of America: McGraw-Hill Book Co., 1967) (henceforth cited as *NCE*), vol. 3, pp. 55–61.

emerged that the saint must have practised in heroic or extraordinary degree the three Christian virtues of faith, hope and charity, together with the four cardinal virtues, defined in Aristotle's *Nichomachean Ethics*, of justice, prudence, fortitude and temperance. This framework was first clearly applied to the canonisation of St Bonaventure in 1482.

It was in the fourteenth century, however, during the exile of the popes at Avignon, that a proper canonical procedure emerged in which the petitioners for a canonisation, represented by a Procurator, contested the sanctity of the candidate in a public trial, in which an official Promoter of Justice or of the Faith – the famous Devil's Advocate – contested their witnesses and evidence. New local saints who had not undergone this procedure were described as *beati*, in an attempt to reserve supreme honours to those who had been papally approved, though beatification was taken into the papal system as the last stage before canonisation itself. Beatification permitted and permits the veneration of the saint in particular places and institutions; canonisation extends that cultus to the universal Church, though given that there are far more saints than vacant days in a year, many have never been included in the ordinary universal calendar, their cult belonging to particular dioceses, countries or religious orders.

The advent of the attempt at papal control of canonisation meant a new emphasis on members of religious orders who were either radically committed to holy poverty and chastity, like St Francis, or were spectacularly learned, like St Thomas Aquinas, and were of an otherworldly interior piety. The women canonised were chiefly mystics like St Bridget of Sweden and St Catherine of Siena. This close association between sainthood and prayer, between holiness and inner devotion and mystical attainment, has continued down to the present, and come to form a major part of the idea of heroic sanctity, creating a problem for those for whom holiness is more obviously practical and external. A saint is what he or she *is* rather than what he or she *does*.

In reaffirming the cult of the saints at the Council of Trent, the Church thought it necessary to purge some cults which had attracted Protestant ridicule. In the thoroughgoing reforms of the Vatican administration which created the modern Roman congregations, Sixtus V placed the procedure of canonisation under the auspices of the Congregation of Rites in 1588, with a Cardinal and other ecclesiastical dignitaries, and the Congregation evolved a set of rules and precedents which were formalised by Urban VIII in 1642. The saint had to be judged to have exercised the virtues in an exceptional or heroic degree, that is, with a perfection surpassing the ordinary. Urban also made a clear distinction between the recognition of individuals 'formally' canonised by Rome and those whose cult could be 'equipollently' recognised as being older than a century, on the basis of historical enquiry, and so of equivalent status and power. Some famous national saints – St Wenceslas, duke (not king) of Bohemia, St Stephen, king of Hungary, and St Margaret, Queen of Scotland – and a number of monastic founders like St Bruno the Carthusian and St Norbert the Premonstratensian, received equipollent canonisation after centuries of cultic veneration. This distinction was administratively formalised in 1930 in Pope Pius XI's Historic Section for the Oldest Causes, and such canonisations, on the basis of a long-established cult, still continue: a famous example came with the Pope's visit to Prague, that least Catholic of nominally Catholic cities, in the midst of the Velvet Revolution in 1989, to canonise the medieval Agnes of Bohemia, an occasion attended by the hero of the Prague Spring, Alexander Dubček and by the largest Catholic crowd since the Communists assumed power, in fulfilment of the prophecy that her canonisation would bring the nation its freedom.

It was, however, Voltaire's favourite pope, the genial and brilliant eighteenth-century canonist Prospero Lambertini, Benedict XIV, famous for chatting to ordinary Romans outside their public taverns, and with a long experience as a Devil's Advocate, who codified the whole subject in his five-volume work, *De servorum dei beatificatione et beatorum canonizatione, Concerning the beatification of the Servants of God and the canonisation of the Blessed* of 1734–38, only part of which has been translated into English, and that was in the middle of the nineteenth century.[36] In its developed form the process is a

---

[36] The translation is the work of the Fathers of the London Oratory, as part of their celebrated mid-Victorian series *The Saints and Servants of God*, on which see Sheridan Gilley, 'Supernaturalized Culture: Catholic Attitudes and Latin

characteristic product of the bureaucratic care and caution of the Roman legal mind, the more careful and cautious because theologians have generally regarded canonisation as an expression of the pope's infallible prerogative in questions of faith and morals. This claim is only said to cover the period of the modern procedure, from 1588, when rigorous testing began. Here in the matter of Roman saint-making, there is a striking example of the interaction of the worshipping or Priestly, and authoritative or Regal, Offices of the Church, according to Newman's classic formulation.[37]

The Church claims, however, to have the power to discern saints by identifying their virtues,[38] the theological virtues of faith, hope and charity, conceived as a consequence of infused grace, and the four cardinal or moral virtues of justice, prudence, fortitude and temperance. The latter, though pagan in origin, had been interpreted by Saints Ambrose and Augustine in a Christian sense, and Aquinas and the scholastics further enriched them by extension: thus justice covers religion, piety, gratitude, liberality and affability; fortitude embraces magnanimity, patience and constancy; temperance includes abstinence, sobriety, humility, meekness, modesty and chastity. They are naturally acquired by the habitual exercise of the will to a given end, and perfected in the theological virtues, through the infusion of divine grace, creating a fixed disposition in the soul to do what is right, an idea rather weakly corresponding to the English word 'habit'.

Heroic charity goes far beyond what is customary or ordinary, and it is by it that we are 'made partakers of the divine nature', according to 2 Peter, though falling short of God Himself ('the perfect participation and similitude of God and Christ, is

---

Lands', in Derek Baker, ed., *The Materials, Sources and Methods of Ecclesiastical History: Studies in Church History*, vol. 11. (Oxford: Blackwell, 1975), pp. 309–23. The translation is entitled *Heroic Virtue: A Portion of the Treatise of Benedict XI, on the Beatification and Canonization of the Servants of God*, 3 vols (London, Dublin and Derby: Thomas Richarson and Son, 1850–2), and begins with the twenty-first chapter of the third book. It is referred to below as Benedict XIV.

[37] John Henry Newman, 'Preface' to *The Via Media of the Anglican Church*, 2 vols (London: Basil Pickering, 1877), vol. I, pp. xiff.

[38] The principal older work on the subject, by Canon Macken, strives to emphasise the 'scientific' character of the process, but is extremely confusing. Thomas F. Macken, *The Canonisation of Saints* (Dublin: M. H. Gill & Son, 1910).

altogether impossible').[39] Of the three theological virtues, the greatest of course is charity, and the heroic virtue of the saint arises from an intensity of charity, which makes possible the performance of the other virtues, theological and cardinal, to an heroic degree. Prudence has been thought to have a similar superintending role to charity over the cardinal virtues. Charity always accompanies the seven gifts of the Holy Spirit, according to Isaiah 11.2, 3, of 'wisdom, understanding, counsel, fortitude, knowledge, godliness, the fear of the Lord', as supernatural habits infused by grace which are superior to the cardinal virtues, though inferior to the theological ones.[40] Springing from the same source, the heroic virtue of the saint in one area will be mirrored in another, so that charity and courage would be expected from the one man, though 'it is not necessary that all of them [the virtues] should have been in the heroic degree, for S. Jerome thinks that never happened'.[41] In this respect, heroic virtue is a state, embracing all the virtues, which does not exclude venial sin, if it is properly repented and overcome. Moreover, heroic virtue 'does not remove the passions, but restrains and conquers them' by the intellect and will under grace,[42] and practice makes perfect so that the virtuous state should be attended by the 'ease, readiness, and delight'[43] in virtue which are a mark of its heroism.[44]

Moreover as Benedict XIV stressed, sanctity or heroic virtue 'properly consists in simple conformity to the Divine Will, 'according to the condition of the servant of God, or beatified person, and according to the circumstances in which he was placed during his life.'[45] Although Benedict showed a special interest in the special terms of deciding the sanctity of royal persons,[46] his criteria implied a sanctity for everyone. A soldier, a sailor and a candlestick maker would each be expected to exercise heroic virtue in a manner appropriate to their worldly

---

[39] Benedict XIV, vol. 1, p. 20.
[40] Benedict XIV, pp. 44–6.
[41] Benedict XIV, p. 41.
[42] Benedict XIV, p. 58.
[43] Benedict XIV, p. 44.
[44] Benedict XIV, p. 32.
[45] Benedict XIV, p. 72.
[46] Benedict XIV, vol 2, pp. 277ff.

calling, as a good soldier, sailor or candlestick maker, as showing virtue in an heroic degree in the affairs of everyday life. What is fortitude or obedience in a soldier might be different in a butcher or baker, though Benedict in his treatise gave special consideration to the virtues required of popes and cardinals in their calling, which may be why so few have been canonised.

This emphasis upon the virtues is in some tension with the contemplative dimension of sanctity, the conception of the saint as a tyro of prayer, a mystic, who has achieved in exceptional degree a knowledge of God, even though this knowledge is also, like heroic virtue, a gift of grace and a fruit of charity. A particular problem concerns the charismata of the Spirit, deriving from 1 Corinthians 12, as Benedict discusses them in his work: the word of wisdom and of knowledge, of healing and miracles, of prophecy, of discernment of spirits, of transport, ecstasy and rapture, visions and apparitions and revelations, with their dimension in what Herbert Thurston calls the physical phenomena of mysticism,[47] especially as they have been common in saints dedicated to the contemplative life.

There is here a great cultural gulf, as Euan Cameron has recently pointed out, between Protestant and Catholic Europe about the miraculous dimension of these charismata; Protestants generally confining the miraculous to Scripture,[48] or as it might be put more crudely, reserving their belief in miracles for Sundays. In Catholic Europe the problem has been a different one: of getting miracles in perspective and distinguishing true miracles from false ones. Benedict XIV was concerned to put them severely in their place in his treatise *De Beatificatione*, insisting that they were not proof of sanctity, being possible to sinners, and that where apparently miraculous acts have occurred, it must be shown that they have neither a natural nor a diabolical explanation. Even where miraculous, Benedict insists that charismata are generally graces *gratis datae*, graces 'chiefly given for the profit of

---

[47] Herbert Thurston, *The Physical Phenomena of Mysticism*, ed. J. H. Crehan (London: Burns & Oates, 1952).

[48] Euan Cameron, 'For Reasoned Faith or Embattled Creed? Religion for the People in Early Modern Europe', *Transactions of the Royal Historical Society*, (1998), p. 187.

others',[49] as for the extension of the Church or the sanctification of the faithful rather than for the sanctification of the individual who receives them, and therefore not necessarily proofs of sanctity.

Part of Benedict's treatise is an analysis of the personality to whom charismata occur. Even a genuine mystic may be under a natural or diabolical influence rather than a divine one, the subject either of possession or just bad digestion or a vivid imagination. But nor are these things to be dismissed a priori, for all things are possible to God. Rather, they are to be judged by their fruits in the virtuous life. These include visions, which may be intellectual or corporeal, as in St Bridget of Sweden's revelations of hell, or more recently, the angelic appearances to Hans Urs von Balthasar's inspiration, Adrienne von Speyr; locutions, like the voices that spoke to Joan of Arc; the reading of hearts, the penetration into the secret thoughts of others; hierognosis, or the ability to discern other holy persons or objects; the flames of love, sensations of the body which can blister the skin, or in the case of St Philip Neri, resulted in an actual enlargement of the heart; the stigmata, which first occurred to St Francis, the appearance of Christ's wounds on the body; tears of blood or a bloody sweat, like Our Lord's in Gethsemane; the mystic's sensation that Christ's heart has replaced his own; compenetration, or passing through other bodies; bilocation and agility, or the passing of the body from one place to another; levitation; inedia, or abstention from food for long periods, especially by living on the Blessed Sacrament; transfigurations, aureoles and illuminations round the saint's body, possibly suggested by Our Lord's transfiguration; the proverbial 'odour of sanctity', sweet odours from the saint, whether living or dead; and bodily prodigies, the absence of rigor mortis, with posthumous suppleness of the body, and incorruption.[50]

The last, incorruption, has been common among saints, and evoked inspections of the tomb. There seems to be no historical doubt about the incorruption of the body of St Cuthbert for a thousand years. Such matters constitute a puzzle to the secular

---

[49] Cameron, 'For Reasoned Faith', p. 88.
[50] See J. Aumann, 'Mystical Phenomena', *NCE*, vol. 10, pp. 171–4.

historian, as to what is so well attested by evidence. There is a tradition, beginning with St Catherine of Siena, a highly public figure in her own lifetime, for the mystic who was married to Christ to develop a wedding ring of flesh. Were those who saw Catherine's ring all liars? Numerous highly respectable witnesses, including a Spanish peer and his wife, testified to the levitations of the seventeenth-century St Joseph of Copertino, while a guard of Protestant doctors was unable to prevent Anne Catherine Emmerich's survival for a decade upon the Blessed Sacrament. There is excellent medical evidence that Padre Pio's hands and feet bled for years until he died, and then healed without scars a few months before his death. Yet however the Church regards them, a reputation for wonders is often important for the origins and popularity of a cult, even if the lack of such wonders in the life of a saint is no obstacle to ultimate success in canonisation. If, as Benedict XIV insists, sanctity (heroic virtue) properly consists in simple conformity to the Divine Will expressed in an exact and constant fulfilment of the duties of one's proper state, then no lifetime prodigies are required.

The actual process of canonisation itself was incorporated into the new Code of Canon Law in 1918. It was changed by Pope Paul VI, who in his Apostolic Letter of 19 March 1969 turned the double ordinary, or diocesan and apostolic process, into a single one, and in his Apostolic Constitution of 8 March of the same year, created the Sacred Congregation for the Cause of Saints, as distinct from the Congregation of Rites responsible for the liturgy. Pope John Paul II, in the Apostolic Constitution _Divinus perfectionis Magister_ of 25 January 1983, and by the subsequent norms of the meeting of the Sacred Congregation for the Causes of Saints of 7 February, further simplified and recodified centuries of Roman practice, combining a complexity of procedure with a certain simplicity of principle.[51] It is easy to exaggerate the character of the changes as the victory of the historians over the Roman advocate lawyers deputed in adversarial manner to contest the

---

[51] What follows is heavily dependent upon the English translation of the Latin text (_Acta Apostolicae Sedis_, 9 April 1983, Part 1, no. 4), very kindly provided by Mr Gerard Tracey of the Birmingham Oratory.

evidence of sanctity,[52] as the process has always been essentially investigative in the manner of continental law. First, the Actor or persons or petitioners supporting the candidature of the saint can collect the evidence of his reputation for sanctity and wonders, his *fama signorum* for miracles, though in a manner which does not involve paying him the unauthorised cult, say, of organised pilgrimage to his tomb, or depicting him with a halo, prohibited by Urban VIII's bull of 1634. Such activity could kill a cause, so there was a carefully defined check upon the devotion required for it to succeed. The Actor, by a letter of appointment or *mandatum procurationis*, appoints a representative called a 'Postulator' for the official process of enquiry itself, and it is the Postulator who has the duty of conducting the investigations into the cause and reporting his findings to the bishop. The Actor begins the process by presenting a written petition (a *supplex libellus*) to the Bishop of the diocese chiefly concerned with the candidate's life, together with 'any existing biography of any import', a list of his publications and of witnesses to his virtues and martyrdom, and of witnesses to the contrary. The bishop is to publicise the petition to his own diocese and, if thought necessary, through other dioceses, and decides after discussion of any objections with the postulator as to whether to go further. If the matter is taken further, the bishop has the candidate's published writings investigated by two competent theological censors to be assured that they contain nothing against faith and morals, with a similar subsequent enquiry by historical experts into any unpublished letters and diaries. The cause of Jean-Jacques Olier, the founder of the seminary of Saint-Sulpice, was blocked for writing a dangerously speculative work upon the Virgin Mary, until it was discovered to be by someone else.[53] Newman's cause is only halved by the irrelevance of his writings before his conversion to Catholicism. Everything here is also to be delivered over to the Promoter of Justice, whose task is to ensure correct procedures and to frame the questions for the interrogation of witnesses. After the Sacred Congregation in Rome has considered and passed a *brevis notitia* from the Bishop

---

[52] See Woodward, *Making Saints*, pp. 90–5.
[53] Woodward, *Making Saints*, p. 80.

(enquiring if Rome might have any objections), the Bishop or his delegate then authorises the examination of the Postulator's witnesses. A careful transcript of all the testimony (from family, acquaintances, etc.) is taken down by a notary and inspected by the Promotor of Justice for any new witnesses or documents. The whole transcript is hand-copied, carefully sealed and sent to the Sacred Congregation for the Cause of Saints, with supporting documents, the candidate's publications, a declaration of *super non cultu*, according to the bull of Urban VIII, and a letter from the Bishop or his delegate testifying to the trustworthiness and legitimacy of the whole. There is a separate enquiry on miracles.

All is passed for consideration to the College of Realtors in Rome, one of whom is assigned by a *Congressus Ordinarius* (ordinary meeting) of the Congregation to the cause. It is his task, with an assistant, to prepare the *Positio* on the virtues or martyrdom of the candidate. The *Positio* can be considered by historical Consultors who are experts in the area, and theological Consultors for an opinion of the merit of the cause, together with the judgement of the Promotor of the Faith for the cause (the Devil's Advocate), and responses to any of the Promotor's criticisms from the Realtor. All this goes for further consideration by a *Congressus Peculiaris* of the Cardinals and Bishops of the Congregation. The Realtor also has to prepare a *Positio* on alleged miracles, which also goes before a meeting of the Congregation. Until recently two miracles were required for the beatification of a non-martyr, and even this is a long way from canonisation, which may only follow after many years.

It is a mild irony that the ceremony of canonisation proceeds with a petition to the pope to number the blessed among the saints *instanter, instantius, instantissime.* The ceremony in St Peter's includes a procession with the saint's banner, the singing of the Veni Creator for the guidance of the Spirit, the Te Deum, in rejoicing, and the Litany of the Saints, a tremendous invocation and roll-call of the Holy Dead from the Apostles down, and including the newly-proclaimed member of the elect, concluding in a Pontifical Mass. Churches can be dedicated anywhere to the saint, his name can be invoked in prayer, there can be an annual feast in his honour, and he can be depicted with a halo, as in glory.

There is, then, underlying the cult of saints, the theme of a deified humanity, yet it is a universal calling, if we are all to be in glory. Holiness, sanctification, lies within the reach of all, the point stressed by St Thérèse in her *History of a Soul*. Saints simply do that which God intends us to do, in that state of life to which he calls us, and woe betide us if we don't. That makes holiness ordinary, yet it is extraordinary, for the virtues of the saint are heroic, and how can we by imitation be heroes? This viewpoint is put by C. S. Lewis, who complained that he had grown up in a

'low church' *milieu* ... too cosily at ease in Sion. My grand-father ... used to say that he 'looked forward to having some very interesting conversations with St. Paul when he got to heaven'. Two clerical gentlemen talking at ease in a club! It never seemed to cross his mind that an encounter with St. Paul might be rather an overwhelming experience even for an Evangelical clergyman of good family. But when Dante saw the great apostles in heaven they affected him like *mountains*. There's lots to be said against devotions to saints; but at least they keep on reminding us that we are very small people compared with them. How much smaller before their Master?'[54]

The paradox of holiness is that the saints are there to show us what we could be, even if we can't be. They are ordinary because they are of us, and extraordinary because they are beyond us: as Gladstone wrote of his dead friend Cardinal Manning, even after the worst had been said, he could 'only look at him as a man looks at the stars'.[55] The saints are those of whom the world was not worthy. Through the writing of this essay I have been haunted by the concluding lines of Shaw's play *St Joan*: 'O God that madest this beautiful earth, when will it be ready to receive Thy saints? How long, O Lord, how long?' Yet in spite of Shaw, Joan triumphed at

---

[54] C. S. Lewis, *Letters to Malcolm: Chiefly on Prayer* (London: Geoffrey Bles, 1964), p. 23.

[55] W. E. Gladstone to E. S. Purcell, 14 January 1896, in D. C. Lathbury, ed., *Correspondence on Church and Religion of William Ewart Gladstone*, 2 vols (London: John Murray, 1910), vol 2, p. 341.

the last, and a Christian must hold that 'the only tragedy in life is not to be a saint',[56] to be other than as God would have us be.

---

[56] Raïssa Maritain, *Les Grandes Amitiés* (Paris: Desclée de Brouwer, 1949), pp. 117ff.; cited by Michael J. Kerlin, 'Anti-Modernism and the Elective Affinity between Politics and Philosophy', in Darrell Jodock, ed., *Catholicism contending with Modernity: Roman Catholic Modernism and Anti-Modernism in Historical Context* (Cambridge: Cambridge University Press, 2000), p. 313.

16

Mother of God, Mother of Holiness: A Meditation from Orthodoxy

Vigen Guroian

Echoing Verdi's 'La donne e mobile', G. K. Chesterton remarks at the start of his fantasy tale *The Napoleon of Notting Hill*: 'Men are men, but Man is a woman.' Chesterton explains that he is taking note of the 'changeful, mystical, [and] fickle' character of the human race as a whole. No doubt the prejudice in this remark would raise more than a few eyebrows among today's readers. I, however, am investing this expression with a different meaning. I have in mind a particular woman – the Holy Virgin, Mary, and Mother of God. For if the Church is right about human existence, Mary's sanctified life is a model of holiness and perfection for all persons, men and women alike, and fickleness could never be attributed to her character.

By naming Mary the Second Eve and Handmaid of the Lord, the ancient tradition affirms that the mother of Jesus exercised her freedom and made her choice to bear the Son of God with complete sobriety. Whereas Eve asked no questions of the Serpent and was foolishly deceived through her passions by that tempter, Mary scrupulously interrogated the angelic visitor. Only when she felt assured that no deception lay in his proposal and that this was truly the will of God, did Mary consent to conceive and give birth to the Second Adam who opens the closed gates of Paradise (Luke 1.31). Only then did Mary pronounce: 'Behold the handmaid of the Lord; be it unto me according to thy word' (Luke 1.38, King James Version).

No less important, from that moment on, states St Luke, Mary kept all the things she heard and saw about the mystery of redemption, pondering them in her heart (Luke 2.19). In these

ways, we may say that Mary *is* the woman who teaches us that
Man, by which we mean mature humanity (Eph. 4.13), *is* a
woman.

Mary, the Heart of the Church's Holiness

When, in the Epistle to the Ephesians, St Paul speaks of mature
(or perfect) manhood, he is reflecting upon the sanctification
by which persons enter into the holiness of God. 'Put off your
old nature which belongs to the former manner of life and is
corrupt through deceitful lusts, and be renewed in the spirit of
your minds, and put on the new nature, created after the
likeness of God in true righteousness and holiness' (Eph.
4.22–4, Revised Standard Version).

Eastern Christian writers describe Mary as the bridge from
Old Testament righteousness to its fulfilment and completion
in the holiness of the New Covenant. This conviction moved
the ninth-century Byzantine church father, John of Damascus,
to declare: 'The name of the Mother of God contains all the
history of the divine economy in this world.'[1] In other words,
Mary is the heart of the church's holiness.

Mary's holiness and relationship to the church is profoundly
expressed in Eastern Christian iconography. Naturally, she
appears in festal icons that are specifically about her life, such
as the Birth of the Mother of God, the Annunciation, and the
Dormition (or Assumption) of the Mother of God.
Disagreement over whether or not Mary should appear in
Pentecost icons of the Descent of the Holy Spirit, however, is
especially interesting for our purpose. It raises important
questions about the special character of Mary's holiness – about
the above claim, namely, that she is the heart of the church's
holiness.

In most Byzantine or Russian icons of the Descent of the
Holy Spirit, Mary is not included among the twelve apostles and
evangelists seated in a semi-circle.[2] In other instances, however,

---

[1] *Exposition on the Orthodox Faith*, 3:12, as quoted by Vladimir Lossky, *The
Image and Likeness of God* (Crestwood, NY: St Vladimir's Seminary Press, 1974),
p. 202.

[2] 'Tradition says that, to fulfil the prophecy of Joel (Joel 2.28–9), the Holy

notably in Armenian gospel illuminations and some Russian and Byzantine iconography, Mary is not only present, but in some cases conspicuously at the centre of the circle, an unchallenged focal point of the scene. In his excellent study of *The Resurrection and the Icon*, Michael Quinot, however, objects to this practice. He maintains that it 'relegates the apostles to a secondary position ... [and] makes the icon of Pentecost an icon of the Mother of God'.[3] Yet Quinot approves of the dominant position of Mary in icons of the Ascension. Here, he asserts, Mary is appropriately represented as the Mother of the Church.[4]

Yet why cannot Quinot's justification for Mary's presence in the Ascension icons also legitimately serve for icons of the Descent of the Holy Spirit in which she is included among the gathered apostles and evangelists? The Armenian illuminated miniatures in which Mary is present and at the centre of the Pentecost scene seem to me to emphasise two important theological matters about Mary and the Church. First, they remind us that, like Mary at the Annunciation, the Church is visited by the Spirit and thus enabled to give birth to faith and holiness. Second, they emphasise that Mary is herself the preeminent embodiment of the Church's holiness, greater even than John the Baptist or any of the apostles.

Christ's speech to the Apostle John from the Cross supports this interpretation: 'Then saith he to the disciple, "Behold thy mother"' (John 19.27, KJV). The Eastern tradition has interpreted this to mean that Mary is also the Mother of the Church, the mother of all who are members of the mystical Body of Christ. The twentieth-century Russian Orthodox theologian Sergius Bulgakov maintains: 'The churchliness of the Church

---

Spirit descended not only on the twelve chosen Apostles, but also upon all who were with them "with one accord in one place" (Acts 2.1) ... that is, on the whole Church. That is why [in] the icon there are represented Apostles not belonging to the twelve – Apostle Paul (sitting with Apostle Peter at the head of the circle of Apostles), and among the seventy, Luke the Evangelist ... and Mark the Evangelist.' Quoted from Leonid Ouspensky and Vladimir Lossky, *The Meaning of Icons* (Crestwood, NY: St Vladimir's Seminary Press, 1983), p. 208.

[3] Michael Quinot, *The Resurrection and the Icon* (Crestwood, NY: St Vladimir's Seminary Press, 1997), p. 190

[4] Quinot, *Resurrection and Icon*, p. 183.

and power of entering into it are centred in the Mother of God and those who have this power [which is of the Spirit] come particularly close to her.'[5] Bulgakov's words call to mind the traditional icon of the Dormition of the Mother of God in which she in her casket is in the middle encircled by apostles and disciples. The Dormition icon is based not at all upon biblical testimony but rather the early tradition that at her death the apostles came together one last time in Jerusalem to honor the Mother of the Lord. Like the Pentecost icons in which Mary is present, the Dormition icon emphasizes that she is the heart of the Church's holiness. She is presented, even in death, as the first among those honoured in the communion of saints. The Byzantine sticheron hymn for Great Vespers proclaims that Mary herself *is* 'the Holy Place of God'.

In sum, Mary is the Mother of God and also the mother of the new humanity, the Church. Paul Evdokimov writes: 'The *synergy* of the holiness of Israel and of the Spirit culminates in the Virgin', and so it is by 'the Holy Spirit *and* the Virgin's *fiat* that every believer is born again.'[6] Eve is the old, sinful humanity's fleshly mother by whom death spread to the whole of the race: Mary is the new humanity's spiritual mother from whom the only begotten Son of God took flesh purely, without corruptibility, and raised the race to eternal life. The *fiat* of the Virgin, in Evdokimov's turn of phrase, makes it possible for persons to become her children and to be adopted as brothers or sisters of her resurrected Son. Our relationship to Jesus is never simply one-on-one, because he has a mother whom he has given to us as our mother, as he did to John. For this reason, a Christian's holiness is not solely his or her possession. Holiness is born and realised in relationship to Christ and our Mother Mary. Holiness consists in keeping and remembering what God has done for us in Christ by his mother. Holiness is in the manner of the service Christians render to others, as Mary did by declaring herself the handmaid of the Lord.

---

[5] Sergius Bulgakov, *A Bulgakov Anthology*, eds., James Pain and Nicolas Zernov (Philadelphia, The Westminster Press, 1976, originally published in London: SPCK, 1976), p. 96. Excerpted from Sergius Bulgakov, *The Burning Bush*.

[6] Paul Evdokimov, *Woman and the Salvation of the World* (Crestwood, NY: St Vladimir's Seminary Press, 1994), p. 194.

Holiness is not individual, it is ecclesial, entirely related and connected to the other great marks of the Church: namely, unity, catholicity and apostolicity.

While it is, of course, true that Jesus is every Christian's supreme model of holiness, Mary, nevertheless, is the first disciple and Christian. She, in her holiness, marks the path every Christian should follow. Jesus addressed the multitude on the mountain with the Beatitudes and then summed them up by saying 'You, therefore, be perfect, as your heavenly Father is perfect' (Matt. 5.48, RSV). The words are Christ's. But it is no less a truth of the Christian faith that Mary gave birth to these words by willingly giving her flesh to the One who uttered them. Indeed, his birth depended upon her free consent and obedience to the Father. 'The incarnation was not only the work of the Father and His Virtue and His Spirit,' writes the fourteenth-century Byzantine theologian Nicholas Cabasilas, 'it was also the work and will of the Virgin. Without the consent of the All Pure One and the cooperation of her faith, this design would have been unrealizable.'[7] Last, Mary is filled with grace because she fulfils all of the 'Amens', all the 'thy-will-be-done-s' of the history of the people of God.

'The Holy Spirit shall come upon you' (Luke 1.35, KJV)

The Holy Spirit descended twice upon Mary. The first was at the Annunciation, the second at Pentecost. The first was functional, for by it Mary conceived. It concerned her alone. She did not share it with others, except through the gift of her Son. Vladimir Lossky explains that 'this objective function of her divine maternity becomes the subjective way of her sanctification'. In time, Lossky continues, Mary realised 'in her consciousness, and in all her personal life, the meaning of the fact of her having carried in her womb and having nourished at her breast the Son of God'.[8]

In his Hymns on the Nativity, St Ephrem the Syrian reflects a tradition commonly accepted already in the fourth century that

---

[7] Quoted by Lossky, *Image and Likeness*, p. 202.
[8] Lossky, *Image and Likeness*, pp. 206–7.

the Divine Word has had four births. He was begotten of the Father before all ages, born of a woman, baptised in the River Jordan, and resurrected on the third day. In a profound paradox, Mary herself, by having borne Jesus, experienced a second, spiritual birth, like unto baptism. For by having carried the Word in her womb and given birth to him Mary was herself sanctified. Thus in Hymn 16, Mary proclaims: 'Son of the Most High, Who came and dwelt in me, / [in] another birth, he bore me also / [in] a second birth. I put on the glory of Him / Who put on the body, the garment of His mother.'[9]

In light of these things, we may argue confidently that Mary brought a special holiness with her to the upper room at Pentecost, where again the Holy Spirit visited her. Vladimir Lossky observes:

> What degree of holiness able to be realized here below could possibly correspond to the unique relationship of the Mother of God to her Son, the Head of the Church, who dwells in the heavens? Only the total holiness of the Church, the compliment of the glorious humanity of Christ, containing the plenitude of deifying grace communicated ceaselessly to the Church since Pentecost by the Holy Spirit.[10]

No doubt the second descent of the Holy Spirit upon Mary at Pentecost affected her personally. But on this occasion she was in the company of others and the ancient tradition conjectures that she was given the full understanding that she was not only the Mother of her Lord but of each person onto whom the Spirit descends. This is the reason why the church affirms the special place of Mary as Queen of the Kingdom of Heaven. In this regard, however, it needs to be said that even with this estimate of Mary's place in the scheme of redemption, Orthodox Christianity has not embraced a doctrine of the Immaculate Conception. It seems more consistent with the gospel story that Mary, like the rest of humanity, was born into the sin of the first Eve. Otherwise, the importance of her humanity is diminished. She becomes merely a predestined

---

[9] Ephrem the Syrian, *Ephrem the Syrian, Hymns* in the Classics of Western Spirituality (Ramsey, NJ: Paulist Press, 1989), p. 150. Hymns of Nativity, 16: 11.
[10] Lossky, *Image and Likeness*, p. 207.

instrument of grace and the exemplary character of her achievements of humility and purity and freely pronounced willingness to be of service to God fades. But it is also appropriate, even necessary, to say that by her birth-giving and motherly relationship to Jesus through the Holy Spirit, Mary overcame our sinful condition and became, by virtue of her special holiness, the mother of our salvation.

'Behold the handmaid of the Lord; be it unto me according to thy word' (Luke 1.38, KJV)

As early as the second century, Irenaeus, bishop of Lyons, raised the two important themes of the New or Second Eve and the Virgin's *fiat*, and identified their importance for the Christian understanding of holiness. He writes:

> And just as it was through a virgin who disobeyed that man was stricken and fell and died, so too it was through the Virgin, who obeyed the word of God, that man resuscitated by life received life. For the Lord came to seek back the lost sheep, and it was lost; and therefore He did not become some other formation, but he likewise, of her that was descended from Adam, preserved the likeness of formation; for Adam had necessarily to be restored in Christ, that mortality be absorbed in immortality, and Eve in Mary, that a virgin, become the advocate of a virgin, should undo and destroy virginal disobedience by virginal obedience.[11]

Now traditional Christianity interprets this obedience as a proof of Mary's freedom, not her servitude – a judgement that contradicts contemporary feminist criticism that Mary's obedience is a sign of weakness. I could draw from Byzantine, Armenian or Syrian liturgies to show how the traditional argument unfolds. However, permit me at the start to cite a less familiar source of the early church. The fifth-century Syriac writer Jacob of Serug, in his series of homiletic poems on the Mother of God takes up these themes of Mary's freedom and

---

[11] St Ireneaus, *Proof of the Apostolic Preaching*, Chapter 33, in the Ancient Christian Writers, No. 16 (Mahwah, NJ: Paulist Press, 1952), p. 69.

obedience in a compelling way. In the homily entitled 'Concerning the Blessed Virgin Mother of God, Mary', Jacob writes of God's respect for the human freedom of Mary.

> The holy Father wanted to make a mother for his Son,
>   but He did not allow that she be his mother because of his choice.

> Maiden, full of beauty hidden in her and around her,
>   and pure of heart that she might see the mysteries which had come to pass in her.

> This is beauty, when one is beautiful of one's own accord;
>   glorious graces of perfection are in his will.

> However great be the beauty of something from God,
>   it is not acclaimed if freedom is not present . . .

> Even God loves beauty which is from the will:
>   He praises a good will, whenever this has pleased Him.

> Now this virgin whom, behold, we speak of her story
>   by means of her good will, she was pleasing and was chosen.[12]

There will be those who object even to this way of putting the matter. Mary's circumstance alone, they may say, puts her in a subservient position. God and Mary are not equals and God does the proposing, not she. Genuine freedom entails equal position and autonomy, which Mary lacks personally, socially and religiously. This modern view, or some variant of it, affects much contemporary Christian theology in a variety of expressions on dogmatic and moral issues. The subject calls for more attention. But suffice to say here that traditional Christian teaching is of another mind.

The dogma of the Annunciation is not the revelation of a solitary and autocratic God; nor is the Annunciation a story of human subservience to such a God. Mary is called to an act of kenosis or self-emptying, suffering love, imitative of her own Son's, even before he himself has revealed it to the world. For

---

[12] Jacob of Serug, *On the Mother of God*, Homily I (Crestwood, NY: St Vladimir's Seminary Press, 1998), p. 25.

by conceiving the holy child, she risks humiliation and social ostracism. But whatever the Father asks of the mother, he asks also of his Son, who 'emptied Himself ... taking the form of a bondservant, and coming in the likeness of men' (Phil. 2.5–11, New King James). This passage from Paul's Letter to the Philippians is a reading for the feast of the Birth of the Mother of God. St Paul argues that the kenosis of the Son of God lights the way towards a religious affirmation of human freedom and holiness. The true end of human freedom is voluntary self-limitation in loving service to others and to God. God holds to this law of love when he condescends to become one of us. Mary is the first human being to obey this command wholly and consummately.

So we may say that Mary's actions at the Annunciation foreshadow and complement the act of divine self-limitation lifted up and praised by St Paul in his great hymn of the Letter to the Philippians. As Alexander Schmemann has said, the Annunciation is about 'the dependence of the Incarnation itself, of the Divine plan itself, on the free and personal choice of Mary, on her free acceptance of the Divine challenge'. And hence – and this is such an important and powerful insight:

> the divine plan and 'nature' are revealed as focused in a free person ...
> Salvation is no longer the operation of rescuing an ontologically inferior and passive being; it is revealed as truly a *synergia*, a cooperation between God and man. In Mary obedience and humility are shown to be rooted not in any 'deficiency' of nature, aware of its own 'limitations,' but as the very expression of man's royal freedom, of his capacity freely to encounter Truth itself and freely receive it. In the faith and experience of the Church, Mary truly is the very icon of 'anthropological maximalism,' its *epiphany*.[13]

'Mary ... is the very icon of "anthropological maximalism," ' says Schmemann. What is the meaning and content of this 'anthropological maximalism'? First, it is not, as so much modern and postmodern opinion holds, a matter of power.

---

[13] Alexander Schmemann, *The Virgin Mary*, Sermons, vol. 3 (Crestwood, NY: St Vladimir's Seminary Press, 1995), p. 53

Mary is not 'empowered'. Perhaps this term has a proper use when used to say that persons have human rights and that, therefore, the marginalised, impoverished and the persecuted need to be 'empowered'. Mary's magnificat, however, is not liberationist in this thoroughly modern sense. Rather, it is *doxological* in a profound, ancient sense. In praising God we give ourselves over entirely to God and in turn he delivers us from sin and death. In the same manner, by giving ourselves over to God, we praise God as his holy people. Mary sings this praise in her magnificat and announces the beginning of the great reversal.

> He that is mighty has done to me great things; and holy is his name. And his mercy is on them that fear him from generation to generation. He hath shewed strength with his arm, he hath scattered the proud in the imagination of their hearts. He hath put the mighty from their seats, and exalted them of low degree. He hath filled the hungry with good things and the rich he hath sent empty away (Luke 1.49–53, KJV).

Mary, says a Byzantine hymn of the Annunciation, *is* 'the Living City of Christ the King'.[14]

Second, this 'anthropological maximalism' does not mean 'self-fulfilment'. The meaning of Mary's holiness and perfection is not about the empty self filling itself with experiences or possessions that will enable the self to realise its own 'potential' and gain happiness. This, in fact, is the character and behaviour of the First Adam and the First Eve. And we know where that got the first couple. Blessedness, in biblical terms, is the self's abandonment of all such desire for self-gratification in order to be filled with God's grace. To be maximally human means, in this sense, precisely what the church has said about Mary, that she is filled with grace. As Evdokimov says, 'The human vessel proves itself worthy of the Uncontainable who takes His substance from this vessel.'[15] Mary is the first to prove herself worthy. As St Cyril of Alexandria says:

---

[14] Mother Mary and Kallistos Ware, tr., *The Festal Menaion* (London: Faber & Faber, 1977), p. 438.

[15] Evdokimov, *Woman and Salvation*, p. 194.

'Mary, the ever-Virgin, [is] the holy temple (namely) of God', the sanctuary.[16] Henceforth, she and every person upon whom the Holy Spirit descends is prepared to grow 'to mature manhood, to the measure of the stature of the fullness of God' (Eph. 4.13, RSV).

'Then said Mary unto the angel, "How shall this be, seeing I know not a man?"' (Luke 1.34, KJV)

Often I hear from my college undergraduates and in church parishes a description of the Christian faith as 'blind faith', as if the height of Christian faith is to believe without knowing. This is an odd expression and an unfortunate cliché. It exposes a deep misunderstanding about the Christian life. Christian humility certainly requires that those who call themselves by the name of Christian should not boast of their faith. Nonetheless, faith as we find it in Mary requires the believer to seek out God, to know God's purposes. In a real sense, holiness is seeking to be filled with the knowledge of God in order to exercise one's own will in conformity with God's purpose.

Orthodox liturgies and hymns of the Annunciation emphasise this relationship of faith, knowledge of God and holiness. Mary's encounter with the archangel Gabriel is dramatically cast in the form of a dialogue so that any notion that Christian faith, or holiness, is dependent upon an unquestioning attitude is dismissed. Mary listens to what Gabriel has to say – that she has been chosen by God to give birth to the great One whose Kingdom is without end. Then she challenges him with questions. Let me quote at length from this cycle of dialogues spread throughout a number of Byzantine services for the Annunciation. They do not appear in the immediacy of one another as my juxtaposition of these passages may suggest.

> Mary said to the Angel: 'Strange is thy speech and strange thine appearance, strange thy sayings and thy disclosures. I am a Maid who knows not wedlock, lead me not astray.'

---

[16] Quoted by Evdokimov, *Woman and Salvation*, p. 196.

'Thou dost appear unto me in the form of a man,' said the undefiled Maid to the chief of the heavenly hosts: 'how then dost thou speak to me of things that pass man's power? For thou hast said that God shall be with me, and shall take up His dwelling in my womb; how, tell me, shall I become the spacious habitation and the holy place of Him that rides upon the cherubim? Do not beguile me with deceit.'

'O Angel, help me to understand the meaning of thy words. How shall what thou sayest come to pass? Tell me clearly, how shall I conceive, who am a virgin maid? And how shall I become the Mother of my Maker?' [said the Theotokos].

'O Virgin thou dost seek to know from me the manner of thy conceiving, but this is beyond all interpretation. The Holy Spirit shall overshadow thee in His creative power and shall make this to come to pass' [answered the Angel].

My mother Eve, accepting the suggestion of the serpent, was banished from the divine delight: therefore I fear thy strange salutation, for I take heed lest I slip' [answered the Theotokos].

'I am sent as the envoy of God to disclose to thee the divine will. Why art thou, O Undefiled, afraid of me, who rather am afraid of thee? Why, O Lady, dost thou stand in awe of me, who stand in reverent awe of thee?' [said the Angel].

'I cannot understand the meaning of thy words. For there have often been miracles, wonders worked by the might of God, symbols and figures contained in the Law. But never has a virgin borne child without knowing a man' [answered the Theotokos].

'Divine joy is given to thee, O Mother of God. All creation cries unto thee: "Hail, O bride of God". For thou alone, O pure Virgin, wast ordained to be the Mother of the Son of God' [said the Angel].

'May the condemnation of Eve be brought to naught through me; and through me may her debt be repaid this

day. Through me the ancient due be rendered up in full'
[answered the Theotokos].[17]

There is the story in a nutshell, as the saying goes. And it is
an interesting account that requires some commentary. Jacob
of Serug enters the conversation again, because although he
cannot be commenting directly on these passages (they enter
Byzantine liturgy much later), he, like his predecessor Ephrem
the Syrian, is certainly someone who inspired the content and
form of liturgical developments.

Most important is how Jacob contrasts the character and
behaviour of Eve and Mary. 'Eve had not questioned the
serpent when he led her astray', Jacob observes. She remained
silent and fell to the guile of the serpent and his treachery.
Mary, however, 'heard truth from the faithful one, / nevertheless in this way she had sought out an explanation'. Eve was
told she might become a goddess by eating from a tree but did
not even ask how that was possible. Whereas, 'the Watcher told
... [Mary] that she would conceive the Son of God, / but she
did not accept it until she was well informed'.[18] Vladimir Lossky
lends insight here when he observes that 'scriptural evidence
teaches us that the glory of the Mother of God does not reside
merely in her corporeal maternity, in the fact that she carried
and fed the Incarnate Word'.[19] Rather, Mary's holiness has
everything to do with her character. Nor is her virtue merely
the product of grace that is simply infused in her in the same
manner as she is impregnated. Her integrity and freedom
remain. Her virtue is the sum of her intentions and acts. And as
we have seen, Orthodox liturgy goes to great lengths to say that
this is so. A synergy is at work because it is equally true that, as
Jacob says, 'God purified one virgin, and made her his
Mother'.[20] Jacob continues:

She was pleasing as much as it is given nature to be beautiful
...

---

[17] Mother Mary and Kallistos Ware, tr., *Festal Menaion*, pp. 437, 440, 449,
450, 452, 453.
[18] Jacob of Serug, *On the Mother of God*, Homily 1, p. 32.
[19] Lossky, *Image and Likeness*, pp. 197–8.
[20] Jacob of Serug, *On the Mother of God*, Homily 1, p. 35.

Hitherto she strove with human virtue,
  but that God should shine forth from her, was not of her
  own doing.

As far as the just ones drew near to God,
  the most fair one drew near by virtue of her soul.

But that the Lord shone from her bodily,
  His grace it is, may He be praised because of so much
  mercy![21]

Mary's supreme act of acceptance to give birth to the Son of
God, permits God also to translate her – and all believers
ultimately – to that condition 'where Eve and Adam were
placed, before they sinned'.[22] The nature of Mary's faith must
be considered, together with the nature of her intentions and
the disposition of her will. Her holiness is defined by the purity
of her motives, by her discernment, and the knowledge of God
that she sought, gained and kept in memory for the sake of
the whole church. 'For if Mary had not sublime impulses, / she
would not have arrived to speak before the Watcher.'[23] The
wisdom that Eve sought for the wrong motives, Mary gained
through her purity of heart. Jacob concludes:

Blessed Mary, who by her questions to Gabriel,
  taught the world this mystery which was concealed.

For if she had not asked him how it would be,
  we would not have learned the explanation of the matter of
  the Son.

The beauty of the matter which appeared openly is because
  of her,
  she was the reason that it was explained to us by the angel.

By that question, the wise one [Mary] became the mouth of
  the Church;
  she learned that interpretation for all Creation.[24]

---

[21] *On the Mother of God*, Homily 1, p. 26.
[22] *On the Mother of God*, Homily 1, p. 36.
[23] *On the Mother of God*, Homily 1, p. 38.
[24] *On the Mother of God*, Homily 1, p. 38.

'Yea, a sword shall pierce through thy own soul also' (Luke 2.35, KJV)

Simeon, of course, speaks these words to Mary, upon blessing Jesus at the Temple in Jerusalem. 'Behold, this child is set for the fall and rising again of many in Israel; and a sign which shall be spoken against. Yea, a sword shall pierce through thy soul also that the thoughts of many hearts may be revealed.' From the beginning the Church has interpreted this speech as prophecy of the great grief and suffering that Mary herself would endure as she watched her Son's crucifixion, death and burial. This must certainly be counted as central to the story of her holiness and how that holiness redounds to the entire church. Mary is the great intercessor because she has come nearer to the suffering of her Son than any mortal and was first witness to his resurrection. Mary's holiness is tied to this suffering and joy, which she has taken with her to heaven in order to plead for the relief of suffering among her children, and for the forgiveness of their sins. A Byzantine hymn for Ascension reminds us of this:

> O Lord, having fulfilled the mystery that was hidden from before the ages and from all generations, as Thou art good, Thou didst come with thy disciples to the Mount of Olives, having together with Thyself her that gave birth to Thee, the Creator and Fashioner of all things; for it was meet that she who, as Thy Mother, suffered at the Passion more than all, should also enjoy the surpassing joy of the glorification of Thy flesh.[25]

The tradition is not sentimental about this. The redemptive character of Mary's suffering at the foot of the Cross as she watched the life of her son ebb away and her great grief afterwards at the deposition of his body is the struggle of fallen humanity against the temptations of rebellion and despair. The patristic writers portray a complex reception of Simeon's prophecy and, by extension, a complicated response of the Mother of God to her son's Passion. Mary leads us on a *journey*

---

[25] *The Pentecostarion* (Boston, MA: Holy Transfiguration Monastery, 1990), p. 327. Entreaty at Great Vespers.

to perfection. She herself is not instantly holy. She too, like the full company of disciples, must pass through the scandal of the Cross and be purified by the fire of the Spirit. The sword foretold by Simeon is emblematic of the doubt and fear that rushed through the disciples at Jesus' capture, trial and crucifixion. In his seventeenth homily on St Luke, Origen comments: 'What ought we to think? That while the apostles were scandalized the Mother of the Lord was immune from scandal? If she had not experienced scandal during the Lord's passion, Jesus did not die for her sins.'[26]

This is strong speech. But it saves the veneration of Mary from shallow sentimentalism and ensures that believers leap not too quickly to the triumph of Resurrection Sunday. Moreover, it secures a sober recognition of Mary's humanity, that, although she takes the name of the Mother of God, she is not removed from our human condition. The great sixth-century Byzantine hymnist, St Romanos the Melodist, takes up this theme in his homiletic poem for the Feast of the Meeting of the Lord. He places these words in the mouth of Simeon:

> So much is the mystery contradicted that in your own mind doubt will arise.
> For when you see your Son nailed to the Cross, O All-Unblemished,
> Remembering the words which the angel spoke and the divine conception
> And the ineffable wonders, at once you will doubt.
> The misgivings caused will be like a sword for you
> But after this he will send your heart swift healing
> and so his disciples unassailable peace,
> > *the only Lover of mankind.*[27]

Here is the realism in the Church's memory of Mary's suffering; and it is indispensable to the Easter faith.

As I have said already, the Byzantine liturgies for all of the major Feasts of the Virgin Mary, include a reading of

---

[26] Quoted in Luigi Gambero, *Mary and the Fathers of the Church: The Blessed Virgin in Patristic Thought* (San Francisco: Ignatius Press, 1999), pp. 77–8.

[27] St Romanos, *On the Life of Christ: Kontakia* (San Francisco: HarperCollins, 1995), p. 32.

Philippians 2.2–11 in order to emphasise Mary's participation in the kenosis of her Son, especially his death on the Cross. In some icons of the Annunciation, Gabriel holds a cross to signify the same. And in virtually all icons of the Virgin holding the child this connection of Mary with the suffering of the Cross is conveyed. Paul Evdokimov comments on the famous icon of Our Lady of Vladimir that strongly expresses this understanding of Mary's suffering:

> Mary's face is elongated, her nose long and pointed, her mouth thin and narrow, her eyes big and dark under arched eyelashes. The eyebrows are slightly raised with folds between them. The fixed stare of the eyes looks off into eternity and gives the face an expression of a dense and gripping affliction. The corners of the mouth reinforce this sadness. The shadows of the eyelashes make the pupils appear darker, and the eyes seem to be plunged into an unfathomable depth, inaccessible to the look of the spectator ...
>
> Christ presses his face affectionately against his mother's and is completely absorbed in the movement of tenderness and consolation. His attention, attuned to Mary's state of mind, is very visible in the focused movement of his eyes and makes us think of another icon, the Burial of Christ: 'Do not cry for me, O Mother ...'[28]

Postscript

In June 1997, I was one of forty scholars and churchmen who attended a three-day meeting in Paris to begin planning commemorative events for the celebration of the 1700th Anniversary of Christian Armenia in 2001. His Holiness Karekin I, Catholicos of All Armenians (of blessed memory) was present and on the Sunday of our departure there was a Pontifical Mass.

I arrived at the church a few minutes before the start of the Divine Liturgy and was ushered in as a guest to the first row of pews. As I was taking my seat, I turned to see a young woman in a wheelchair being pushed down the middle aisle towards

---

[28] Paul Evdokimov, *The Art of the Icon: A Theology of Beauty* (Redondo Beach, CA: Oakwood Publications, 1990), pp. 256–6.

where I was seated. Her husband and her young son of perhaps ten years accompanied her. The mother held a small child to her bosom on her lap, and as I looked upon them I saw that both of the woman's legs had been amputated. I struggled not to stare, but I could not help myself. Deliberately, I turned my head and looked up to the high altar. My perspective had changed but, shockingly, not the subject. It was as if I was staring into a looking glass. Armenian churches do not have a Byzantine iconostasis, so that the view is unobstructed to the seven-storied altar. Above and at centre there is always an icon of the enthroned Theotokos with child.

Suddenly a commotion arose. Someone hurriedly pushed the wheelchair to the side of the aisle to make way for the pontifical procession. As Catholicos Karekin I neared the woman I saw him make a gesture towards her as if he wanted to stop. This was not possible and so His Holiness went forward and seated himself in the bishop's throne immediately in front of us. I glanced toward the mother and her child and saw the pained disappointment in her eyes. Some time passed, until the Catholicos rose from his seat, came to the centre, and turned to give the sign of peace. But he did not retreat. Instead, he stepped down towards the woman and her child, laid his right hand upon them and spoke a blessing. The woman's face shone with a light from within.

I do not know for certain how this young mother had become crippled. I suspect that she lost her legs in the earthquake of December 1988 that took upwards of 50,000 lives in Armenia and maimed tens of thousands more. Nor do I know what kind of a life this mother had lived before she was crippled. I do not know whether she was a virtuous woman. Nevertheless, she left me with a priceless gift. For as I received communion that morning, I was conscious in a way I had not ever been before of the presence of the Mother of God. I was thankful in a way I had not been before of Mary's compliance with the invitation of the Holy Spirit to carry the divine Word in her womb and to give him her flesh to wear as our Saviour. And I was newly conscious of her affliction and her protection and of her profound connection with her son's sacrifice, the Eucharist, and its promise of holiness.

Instinctively, I turned towards the mother and child in their wheelchair throne. But they were gone. They had left the church, the blessing having been received. The way that God speaks to us and invites us into his life are as varied as the stars in the heavens. He may call us with the voice of an angel, through a vision, or in the fleshly presence of one of his children. On this particular day, God spoke to me through my crippled sister, my mother, who sat no more than five feet from me under the icon of her own womanly flesh and motherly love. I had at last embraced the Mother of our Lord as my mother and fount of holiness.

O Mother-of-God, tabernacle of the light of the unbounded sun of life, thou didst become the dayspring of the sun of righteousness and didst shed forth light on those who sit in darkness; wherefore we all praise thee always.

O thou undefiled temple and burning-bush who art not consumed, thou didst bear in thee the fire of the Godhead that is not burnt, wherewith the flame of the passions of our nature was burnt and consumed, wherefore we all praise thee always.

O thou living ark of the tables of the testament of the new covenant, through thee was cast up the way to the land of the promise, the Word that was fashioned in thee by the Spirit; wherefore we all praise thee always.[29]

[29] The Armenian Midday Hymn for the Feast of the Annunciation. Tiran Nersoyan, *The Divine Liturgy of the Armenian Apostolic Orthodox Church,* 5th edition (London: Saint Sarkis Church, 1984), pp. 146–7.

PART 4

Holiness and Contemporary Issues

PART V

Holiness and Contemporary Issues

17

Bonhoeffer, Holiness and Ethics

David F. Ford

The aim of this paper is to explore the contribution of Dietrich Bonhoeffer (1906–1945) to the theme of holiness.[1]

In this country Bonhoeffer leapt to prominence in John Robinson's *Honest to God* in 1963,[2] which was largely focused on a few passages of Bonhoeffer's last writings gathered in his *Letters and Papers from Prison*, and which closely associated Bonhoeffer with Rudolf Bultmann and Paul Tillich. This concentration on the prison correspondence, together with a tendency to see it in some discontinuity with earlier works, and also to link Bonhoeffer too closely with dissimilar contemporaries, had a long innings. But the definitive basis for putting it firmly in the past is now in place with the completion of the 17 volumes of *Dietrich Bonhoeffer Werke*,[3] (henceforth DAW) which are being translated into English.

A new stage of appreciation of Bonhoeffer can now begin, and in my opinion he might well be one of the twentieth-century Christian theologians whom it is most fruitful for the twenty-first century to study. I will not try to substantiate that in any detailed or comparative way, but simply summarise my own conclusions about his significance and potential, before going

---

[1] In writing this paper I have benefitted greatly from correspondence with Dr Stephen Plant, from the years of supervising Dr Ann Nickson's dissertation on Bonhoeffer, and from intensive conversation with Rachel Muers and Paul Janz, each of whom energetically rose to the challenge of this topic and have contributed to the result in ways to which footnotes cannot do justice.

[2] J. A. T. Robinson, *Honest to God* (London: SCM Press, 1963).

[3] *Dietrich Bonhoeffer Werke* (Munich: Christian Kaiser Verlag, 1986–1999).

on to try to illustrate them in relation to the theme of holiness, as exemplified mainly in his work, the *Ethics*.[4]

Bonhoeffer's Significance

In approaching this I am continuing what was begun in a recent book, *Self and Salvation: Being Transformed*.[5] There, Bonhoeffer is discussed alongside Thérèse of Lisieux in relation to Edith Wyschogrod's category of 'saintly singularity'[6] which she developed expressly to enrich what she regards as the impoverished field of philosophical ethics. Bonhoeffer's significance is manifold – his deep Christian and theologically aware involvement in academic, church, cultural and political life; his daring reappropriation of his Lutheranism, incorporating strong Catholic and other characteristics; his 'view from below … from the perspective of the outcast, the suspects, the maltreated, the powerless, the oppressed, the reviled – in short, from the perspective of those who suffer';[7] his reinterpretation of key historical periods; the integrity of his theological thought united with a life ending in martyrdom; and the fresh understanding of holiness that emerges from all this.

On holiness, his letter from prison on 21 July 1944 is a classic summary statement illustrated by a vivid anecdote. He appreciates Christianity's

> profound this-worldliness, characterized by discipline and the constant knowledge of death and resurrection. I think Luther lived a this-worldly life in this sense.
>
> I remember a conversation I had in America thirteen years ago with a young French pastor. We were asking ourselves quite simply what we wanted to do with our lives. He said he

---

[4] Dietrich Bonhoeffer, *Ethics* (London: SCM Press, 1955); *Dietrich Bonhoeffer Werke* Band 6 *Ethik* Herausg. Ilse Tödt, Heinz Eduard Tödt, Ernst Feil, Clifford Green (Munich: Christian Kaiser Verlag, 1992) [hereafter DBW 6].

[5] David F. Ford, *Self and Salvation: Being Transformed* (Cambridge: Cambridge University Press, 1999).

[6] Edith Wyschogrod, *Saints and Postmodernism* (Chicago and London: Chicago University Press, 1990).

[7] Dietrich Bonhoeffer, *Letters and Papers from Prison* (London: SCM Press, 1971), p. 17.

would like to become a saint (and I think it's quite likely that he did become one). At that time I was very impressed, but I disagreed with him, and said, in effect, that I should like to learn to have faith. For a long time I didn't realize the depth of the contrast. I thought I could acquire faith by trying to live a holy life, or something like it ...

I discovered later, and I'm still discovering right up to this moment, that it is only by living completely in the world that one learns to have faith. One must completely abandon any attempt to make something of oneself, whether it be a saint, or a converted sinner, or a churchman (a so-called priestly type), a righteous man or an unrighteous one, a sick man or a healthy one. By this-worldliness I mean living unreservedly in life's duties, problems, successes and failures, experiences and perplexities. In so doing we throw ourselves completely into the arms of God, taking seriously, not our own sufferings, but those of God in the world – watching with Christ in Gethsemane.[8]

This triple simultaneity of throwing oneself completely into the arms of God, living completely in the world, and completely abandoning any attempt to make a saint of oneself is at the heart of Bonhoeffer's conception of holiness and points to his distinctive contribution to our theme. It pervades the *Letters and Papers from Prison*, and it is in line with his earlier writings. But it receives its most thorough theological treatment in his *Ethics*, and that will be my main focus in what follows.

Holiness Prior to the Ethics

One could write many papers on holiness in Bonhoeffer prior to his *Ethics*. Just confining oneself to his books, the theme recurs in many forms. It is there in the very title of his dissertation *Sanctorum Communio*,[9] and the interweaving of both sociality and the reality of Jesus Christ with holiness is maintained throughout his theology. His Habilitationsschrift,

---

[8] Bonhoeffer, *Letters*, pp. 369f.
[9] Dietrich Bonhoeffer, *Sanctorum Communio. A Theological Study of the Sociology of the Church*, Dietrich Bonhoeffer Works, vol. 1 (Minneapolis: Fortress Press, 1998); German DBW 1.

Act and Being,[10] is perhaps the least appreciated and discussed of his works. A strong case can be made[11] for it offering the epistemology and ontology which underlie his later work, and this means that it is relevant to the *Ethics* as well. I will briefly take this up later in discussing the relationship of epistemology to ethics and holiness. And at the end of *Act and Being* there is a discussion of 'being in Christ', culminating in a section on 'The Definition of Being in Christ by Means of the Future: The Child',[12] which is tantalising in suggesting a conception of holiness that includes a theology of childhood and intergenerational responsibility.[13] His University of Berlin lectures in 1932–3, *Creation and Fall*,[14] developed basic thoughts about humanity which remained central to his later thought, and the same is true about his understanding of Jesus Christ as it appears in his other Berlin lectures, *Christology*.[15]

The books arising out of Bonhoeffer's years heading the seminary for the Confessing Church at Finkenwalde are his fullest treatment of holiness and related themes. In a full study *The Cost of Discipleship*[16] would perhaps be the main work to bring into dialogue with the *Ethics*, and its importance lies not just in its well-known exposition of the Sermon on the Mount but also in its final section on the Church which includes a treatment of holiness under the heading of 'The Saints'.[17] *Life Together*[18] was written in a concentrated period in 1938 after the

---

[10] Dietrich Bonhoeffer, *Act and Being. Transcendental Philosophy and Ontology in Systematic Theology,* Dietrich Bonhoeffer Works, vol. 2 (Minneapolis: Fortress Press, 1996); German DBW 2.

[11] Cf. Paul D. Janz, *Redeeming Modernity. Rationality, Justification, and Penultimacy in the Theology of Dietrich Bonhoeffer.* Unpublished Ph.D. Dissertation, University of Cambridge, 2000.

[12] Bonhoeffer, *Act and Being,* pp. 157ff.

[13] I am grateful to Rachel Muers for her thoughts on this.

[14] Dietrich Bonhoeffer, *Creation and Fall: A Theological Exposition of Genesis 1–3,* Dietrich Bonhoeffer Works, vol. 3 (Minneapolis: Fortress Press, 1997); German DBW 3.

[15] Dietrich Bonhoeffer, *Christology* (London: Collins, 1978); German DBW 12.

[16] Dietrich Bonhoeffer, *The Cost of Discipleship* (London: SCM, 1959); German DBW 4.

[17] Bonhoeffer, *Cost of Discipleship,* pp. 245ff.

[18] Dietrich Bonhoeffer, *Life Together* and *Prayerbook of the Bible* Dietrich Bonhoeffer Works, vol. 5 (Minneapolis, Fortress Press, 1996); German DBW 5.

Gestapo had dissolved the seminary, and describes the shaping of daily Christian living before God in community – a concentrated, practical evocation of everyday holiness.

Bonhoeffer saw the *Ethics* as the culmination of his theological work, but before turning to it I want to draw attention to one very early excursion into ethics when he was in Barcelona in 1928–9, his 'Basic questions for Christian ethics'.[19] Here he foreshadows many later ideas, and in particular makes clear the inseparability of Christian ethics from a radical holiness pervading the whole of life. The theological reason for this is the basic biblical one that God is holy, and Christian ethics are part of living before the face of God, obeying God's call and will.[20]

Holiness in the Ethics

The contents and ordering of the ethical writings of Bonhoeffer between 1940 and his arrest in 1943 continue to cause disputes among scholars. The best recent account of the issues is given by Clifford Green in the additional chapter included in the revised edition of his book *Bonhoeffer. A Theology of Sociality*.[21] He describes what he terms 'the most complex textual issues in the Bonhoeffer corpus',[22] and they are by no means irrelevant to the interpretation of the work. As we shall see, it is especially important for the theme of holiness that DBW 6 places the section called 'Christ, Reality and the Good. Christ, Church and World' first.

But before exploring the significance of where Bonhoeffer began it is worth reflecting a little on terminology. This volume of essays takes holiness as its topic. Bonhoeffer uses the word

[19] '*Grundfragen einer christlichen Ethik*' DBW 10, S.323–45.

[20] E.g., '*Der Sinn der gesamten ethischen Gebote Jesu is vielmehr der, dem Menschen zu sagen: Du stehst vor dem Angesicht gottes, gottes Gnade waltet über dir, du stehst aber zum Andern in der Welt, musst handeln und wirken, so sei bei deinem Handeln eingedenk, dass du unter Gottes Augen handelst, dass er seinen Willen hat, den er getan haben will.*' DBW 10, S.329.

[21] Clifford J. Green, *Bonhoeffer. A Theology of Sociality*, rev. edn (Grand Rapids and Cambridge, UK: Eerdmans, 1999), Chapter 7 'Bonhoeffer's *Ethics* – A Coda', pp. 301ff.

[22] Green, *Bonhoeffer*, p. 303.

holiness and related terms quite frequently throughout his works,[23] but it is not one of his organising theological ideas. He recognises its importance in the Bible, but he is also acutely aware of the burden of its history. He wants to correct what he sees as massive distortions in its use in Christianity, and his own decision is to communicate it largely through other terms. He therefore raises the question as to whether the word itself is redeemable for current and future usage in our culture. This is a dilemma that frequently faces theologians and others who use Christian language, and indeed any other traditional language. Should they try to rehabilitate terminology that is archaic or has gathered inappropriate associations or that for various other reasons seems to communicate inadequately today? Or should they substitute other words and risk losing touch with the sources and the tradition?

There is, of course, no general answer, but what about the case of holiness? I suspect that it is one of those core terms which has such richness and density of meaning that, on the one hand, it is virtually inevitable that it will be powerfully misused as well as powerfully used, and that, on the other, it is always worth rehabilitating. Such rehabilitation usually requires hard work, and I see Bonhoeffer having done a good deal of that, existentially as well as intellectually. He follows what is often the best strategy. He continues to use the word, and, more broadly, especially insists on the need to re-engage continually with Scripture, which is the only really effective way for its Christian significance to be grasped. At the same time he connects it strongly with other words and ideas, which help to renew its intensity of meaning and reinterpret it with reference to contemporary life. That work began very early, as I have suggested, and one of the main labours was what Benjamin Reist called his 'ethical intensification of all theological concepts'[24] which reached its culmination in his *Ethics*. What Bonhoeffer, according to the new German edition, there took as his starting point underlines its value as a hermeneutic of

---

[23] Cf. the entries under *Heilige, Heiligkeit, Heiligtum, Heiligung* in the *Gesamtregister*, DBW 17, pp. 619–21.

[24] B. A. Reist, *The Promise of Bonhoeffer* (Philadelphia: J. B. Lippincott, 1969), p. 53.

holiness, which is suspicious of many ways of conceiving it, yet does so in the interests of its retrieval.

He begins by radically questioning the classic fundamental ethical questions: How can I be good? and How can I do good? These concerns with the self as moral agent and with the betterment of the world through human agency are replaced by 'the utterly and totally different question "What is the will of God?" '[25] Bonhoeffer's answer is that the will of God is realised in Jesus Christ. This is the central thought of the *Ethics*. A key statement is:

> The place which in all other ethics is occupied by the antithesis of 'should be' and 'is', idea and accomplishment, motive and performance, is occupied in Christian ethics by the relation of reality and realisation [*Wirklichkeit und Wirklichwerden*], past and present, history and event (faith), or, to replace the equivocal concept by the unambiguous name, the relation of Jesus Christ and the Holy Spirit. The question of good becomes the question of participation in the divine reality which is revealed in Christ. Good is now no longer a valuation of what is, a valuation, for example, of my own being, my outlook or my actions, or of some condition or state in the world. It is not the real in the abstract, the real which is detached from the reality of God, but the real which possesses reality only in God. There is no good without the real, for the good is not a general formula, and the real is impossible without the good. The wish to be good consists solely in the longing for what is real in God. A desire to be good for its own sake, as an end in itself, so to speak, or as a vocation in life, falls victim to the irony of unreality. The genuine striving for good now becomes the self-assertiveness of the prig. Good is not in itself an independent theme for life; if it were so it would be the craziest kind of quixotry. Only if we share in reality can we share in good.[26]

This theological account of reality and the good clearly draws ethics into coincidence with holiness. Phrases from that passage might serve as descriptions of essential features of Christian

---

[25] Bonhoeffer, *Ethics*, p. 188; DBW 6 S.32.
[26] *Ethics*, pp. 191f.; DBW 6 S.34–5.

holiness: 'participation in the divine reality which is revealed in Christ' or 'the longing for what is real in God'; and the key underlying question for this ethical holiness is: What is the will of God? The explicit mention of holiness is in that passage's pivotal theological concept: 'the relation of Jesus Christ and the Holy Spirit'. It is therefore appropriate to read the rest of the *Ethics* as unfolding the implications of the reality of Jesus Christ being realised through the Holy Spirit; and that also might serve as an initial definition of Christian holiness. Bonhoeffer is sometimes criticised for saying little about the Holy Spirit, but here he begins his *Ethics* by making the relation of Jesus Christ and the Holy Spirit the theological key to all that follows.

If the central biblical statement on holiness is the injunction of Leviticus to be holy because God is holy, with the New Testament seeing this embodied in Jesus Christ, then Bonhoeffer is defining ethics in line with classic biblical teaching on holiness. Where he springs a surprise, in the interests of both intensifying the meaning of holiness and also correcting misinterpretations of it, is in his linking it so strongly to 'reality'.

Here, negatively, he strikes at the root of many common associations with holiness. It is often seen as rare, as an ideal to be striven for but attained only by a few saints, or by others only ultimately after much purification; and as separated from the sin, ambiguity and impurity of most of life. In other words, it often goes with a sharp separation into two spheres, the holy and the unholy, which can have many variants or analogues, such as sacred and secular, revelation and reason, church and world, and so on. By identifying reality as what is real in God, and further identifying it as the reality of Jesus Christ, Bonhoeffer sets up the basic tasks for his ethics. He must undermine thinking in terms of two spheres by unfolding the meaning of the reality of Jesus Christ as the one encompassing sphere; he needs to unfold the accompanying concept of realisation through the Holy Spirit; thinking in terms of two spheres arises because there are real differentiations to be made between God and the world, so he needs to offer some form of differentiation that can help in doing Christian ethics; and he also needs to give content to the structure and dynamics of the ethical life that results.

That agenda is a description of what he in fact undertook,

and it helps in seeing the coherence of the pieces he wrote between 1940 and 1943. He was following through the requirements of the fundamental thoughts about 'Christ, Reality and Good' put forward in the earliest piece. There are many possible approaches to his carrying out of the agenda. Clifford Green, in his coda on Bonhoeffer's *Ethics* mentioned already,[27] offers an illuminating commentary on the *Ethics* by linking it, point after point, with Bonhoeffer's involvement in the plot against Hitler for which he was eventually executed. It is worth summarising some of the convincing connections made by Green. He shows that Bonhoeffer's description of types, such as 'the tyrannical despiser of humanity', are barely concealed portrayals of Hitler and his followers. Ethical stances based on reason, principle, conscience, duty, absolute freedom and private virtuousness are judged inadequate precisely to those times. They are weapons 'which in the present struggle can no longer be sufficient'.[28] Correspondingly, descriptions of the recommended stance of 'free responsibility' show again and again the marks of being worked out in the midst of the dilemmas posed by resistance to Hitler and by participation in the plot. This is especially so in relation to matters of life and death, conscience, lying, statecraft and readiness to take on guilt.

So realities of concrete history are intrinsic to Bonhoeffer's ethics. As Green also discusses, though more briefly, besides that extreme situation, the *Ethics* also attempts to do justice to the realities of ordinary life.[29] Overall, Green's approach shows both how sensitive to context Bonhoeffer's ethical writings are, and also how he was trying to live out his own ethics.

My approach is different, being aimed at drawing from Bonhoeffer a set of concepts with the assistance of which the meaning of holiness can be developed and intensified for us this century. My thesis is that Bonhoeffer offers at least one key concept in dealing with each item on the agenda just given – the uniting of spheres in the reality of Jesus Christ, the realisation of that reality through the Holy Spirit, appropriate

[27] See above, note 21.
[28] Green, *Bonhoeffer*, p. 306.
[29] *Bonhoeffer*, pp. 321–7.

differentiation between God and the world, and the structure and dynamics of ethical living. Overall, this amounts to a set of concepts which are as helpful in renewing and enriching our theology of holiness as any other I know, and has the added advantage of Bonhoeffer's life and death offering the the sort of illumination Green indicates.

The Reality of Jesus Christ versus Two Spheres

Bonhoeffer's basic conception of reality is that God is 'the ultimate reality without and within everything that is',[30] that in Jesus Christ the reality of God comes together with, enters into, the reality of the world, and that 'all concepts of reality which do not take account of Him are abstractions'.[31] Some implications of this are then given:

> In Christ we are offered the possibility of partaking in the reality of God and in the reality of the world, but not in the one without the other. The reality of God discloses itself only by setting me entirely in the reality of the world, and when I encounter the reality of the world it is always already sustained, accepted and reconciled in the reality of God. This is the inner meaning of the revelation of God in the man Jesus Christ.[32]

My first key concept is that of the world sustained, accepted and reconciled through being united with God in Christ. Bonhoeffer plays many variations on this theme in the rest of the *Ethics*. Perhaps the most important one is through the events of incarnation, crucifixion and resurrection. He emphasises the affirmation of the world in the incarnation, the judgement of the world in the crucifixion and the transformation of the world in the resurrection. They might be correlated with the threefold simultaneity, mentioned above, of a holiness, embodied in Jesus Christ, enacted through living completely in the world, completely abandoning the attempt to make

---

[30] Bonhoeffer, *Ethics*, p. 194; DBW 6 S.39.
[31] *Ethics*, p. 194.
[32] *Ethics*, p. 195; DBW S.40 [sustained, accepted and reconciled = *getragen, angenommen, versöhnt*].

anything of oneself, and relying completely on God. Later, in a key summary statement, Bonhoeffer says:

> In Jesus Christ we have faith in the incarnate, crucified and risen God. In the incarnation we learn of the love of God for his creation; in the crucifixion we learn of the judgement of God upon all flesh; and in the resurrection we learn of God's will for a new world. There could be no greater error than to tear these three elements apart; for each of them comprises the whole ... [33]

This is a rich concept, a condensation of the whole Gospel story, focusing on its climactic events but also embracing creation and eschaton, and theologically developing Nicea's *homoousion*.

With the help of this conception of reality at the opening of his *Ethics* Bonhoeffer first does a critique of thinking in terms of two spheres. He ranges over an array of dichotomies: God/world; holy/profane; supernatural/natural; Christian/ unchristian; *regnum gratiae/regnum naturae*, revelation/reason. His analysis has far-reaching implications not only for ethics and holiness but also for every doctrine, for basic Christian identity, for church practice, and for epistemology:

> Just as in Christ the reality of God entered into the reality of the world, so, too, is that which is Christian to be found only in that which is of the world, the 'supernatural' only in the natural, the holy only in the profane, and the revelational only in the rational.[34]

It may be that every Christian theologian has an implicit or explicit metanarrative of flourishing and corruption in Christian history. With respect to his vital concept of reality as it affects ethics, Bonhoeffer's narrative is of biblical and Reformation (especially Lutheran) flourishing, with signs of corruption beginning soon after the New Testament, and thinking in two spheres becoming dominant twice: 'for the first

---

[33] Bonhoeffer, *Ethics*, pp. 130–1; DBW 6 S.148–9. Cf. Ford, *Self and Salvation*, pp. 247f.

[34] Bonhoeffer, *Ethics*, p. 198; DBW 6 S.44 [the revelational only in the rational = *das Offenbarungsmässige nur im Vernünftigen*].

time in the Middle Ages, and for the second time in the pseudo-Protestant thought in the period after the Reformation'.[35]

He describes two-sphere thinking as so ingrained that it is extremely difficult to abandon. His main therapy is to 'direct our gaze to the picture of the body of Christ Himself, who became man, was crucified and rose again'.[36] This indicates the ecclesial intensification of his ethics, which make them inseparable from Christian community (how he works this out is beyond the scope of this paper) without any ecclesial imperialism in relation to the world. Because he refuses a two-spheres account of church and world there need be no competition between them for space or power. The initial application of this to ethics is in his treatment of the four mandates of labour, marriage, government and church.

Realisation as Transformative Conformation to Christ

Asking how the basic reality (*Wirklichkeit*) of Jesus Christ is realised (*Wirklichwerden*) through the Holy Spirit is very different from asking how a principle applies to a situation:

> The enquiry is directed rather towards the way in which the reality of Jesus Christ, which for a long time already has comprised us and our world within itself, is taking effect as something now present, and towards the way in which life may be conducted in this reality. Its purpose is, therefore, participation in the reality of God and of the world in Jesus Christ today, and this participation must be such that I never experience the reality of God without the reality of the world or the reality of the world without the reality of God.[37]

[35] Bonhoeffer, *Ethics* p. 196; DBW 6 S.41. It would be a worthwhile project to test this historical narrative, and also to compare it (especially as regards the implications for holiness and ethics) with others, such as those which take the period from Augustine to Aquinas as the unsurpassed high point of Christian theology.

[36] *Ethics*, p. 205; DBW 6 S.52–3.

[37] *Ethics*, p. 195; DBW 6 S.40–1.

In line with that early statement Bonhoeffer later tries to conceptualise how the reality continues to be realised with our participation. How does he describe it?

First he uses types, what in ancient ethical discussion were sometimes called 'characters'. There are the types (listed earlier) that have failed to measure up to the times, but there is also a culminating type who combines simplicity and wisdom.[38] The reality of this is seen in Jesus Christ. It is explored further through Jesus Christ incarnate affirming humanity in face of its despisers; Jesus Christ crucified, judging 'the successful man'; and the Risen One, forming a new world that overcomes the idolisation of death.

Then comes the key concept: formation (*Gestaltung*) or conformation (*Gleichgestaltung*) according to the form (*Gestalt*) of Jesus Christ. The culmination of his first paragraph on this is as near as he comes to a definition of Christian holiness:

> ... formation comes only by being drawn in into the form of Jesus Christ. It comes only as formation in His likeness, as *conformation with the unique form of Him who was made man, was crucified, and rose again.*[39]

In the next paragraph the reference to key New Testament texts on being transformed in the image of Christ suggests transformation as a further key word. This is, therefore, about transformative conformation to Jesus Christ. Once again Bonhoeffer develops his thought by reference to the incarnate, to the crucified and to the Risen One, followed immediately by the ecclesial implication: formation 'means in the first place Jesus's taking form in His church'.[40]

Bonhoeffer raises a set of difficult questions about this ecclesial conformation, and his answers give a good deal to discuss, especially when he proceeds to fill out his metanarrative of Western history from the early church to his own time.

---

[38] *Ethics*, p. 68; DBW S.67 [simplicity and wisdom = *Einfalt und Klugheit*].

[39] *Ethics*, p. 80; emphasis follows the German, DBW S.80: *Gestaltung gibt es . . allein als Hineingezogenwerden in die Gestalt Jesu Christi, als Gleichgestaltung mit der einzigen Gestalt des Menschengewordenen, Gekreuzigten und Auferstandenen.*

[40] *Ethics*, p. 83; DBW 6 S.84.

But for present purposes I just want to make a few remarks about his concept of conformation.

First, the language of *Gestalt* is well suited to Bonhoeffer's concern for the whole of life and the whole of Jesus Christ. It even has an aesthetic dimension, which is most marked in his musical imagery of *cantus firmus* and polyphony in the *Letters and Papers from Prison*.[41]

Second, transformative conformation acts as a hermeneutical key not only to Scripture but also to human history, and sets the task of relating the two in a way which, while definitely not fundamentalist, yet gives decisive authority to the scriptural witness, and priority to the will of God and an ethic of holiness.

Third, the concept is well suited to a mediation between Catholic and Protestant traditions of holiness, which is not a compromise but reaches through both in order to conceive holiness in response to the urgencies of the present and the future.

Differentiation: Ultimate and Penultimate

Eberhard Bethge sees the concept in the *Ethics* of 'the ultimate and penultimate' or 'the last things and the things before the last' (*die letzten und die vorletzten Dinge*)[42] as 'the most fruitful of Bonhoeffer's creative formulas' and also as being unconsciously present in his theology for a long time.[43] The last word, the ultimate, is justification, which is by grace alone and faith alone, setting life on a new foundation, that of the life, death and resurrection of Jesus Christ. Bonhoeffer goes on to describe somewhat lyrically how faith is never alone, but, insofar as it is the true presence of Christ, is accompanied by love and hope, giving full life before God.[44] It amounts to a holistic holiness in transformative conformation to the *Gestalt* of Jesus Christ. This event is ultimate, final in two crucial senses.

[41] See Ford, *Self and Salvation*, especially pp. 253–9.

[42] Bonhoeffer, *Ethics*, pp. 120ff.; DBW 6 S.137ff.

[43] Eberhard Bethge, 'The Challenge of Dietrich Bonhoeffer's Life and Theology', in Ronald Gregor Smith, ed., *World Come of Age* (London: Collins, 1967), p. 72.

[44] Bonhoeffer, *Ethics*, p. 121f.; DBW S. 139.

First, it is final qualitatively, 'by the nature of its contents'.[45] It is God's free word, not necessitated by anything in history or to be achieved by following any method. Second, it is final in temporal terms, and so always in fact is preceded by penultimate things; there is a preparation for it. These penultimate things are not such in themselves, but only through being directed towards the ultimate. So the penultimate is an inherently relational concept, and is designed to give priority to the freedom of God while yet affirming the significance of the penultimate and in particular the freedom of humanity before God to be human and to do good.

This is Bonhoeffer's alternative to two-spheres thinking, but it can easily revert to that if the ultimate and penultimate are taken as mutually exclusive spheres. Then the radicality (or, in the terms of this paper, the uncompromising holiness) of the ultimate is set against a penultimate which insists on realistic compromise. In a vivid paragraph he contrasts these:

> Radicalism hates time, and compromise hates eternity. Radicalism hates patience, and compromise hates decision. Radicalism hates wisdom, and compromise hates simplicity. Radicalism hates moderation and measure, and compromise hates the immeasurable. Radicalism hates the real, and compromise hates the word.[46]

The unity of these is, as one might expect, in Jesus Christ incarnate, crucified and risen, the *Gestalt* of a holiness which is utterly involved in the penultimate for the sake of the ultimate. 'Christian life is participation in the encounter of Christ with the world',[47] beyond all radicalism and compromise.

The fruitfulness of this concept is seen in several ways. As Bonhoeffer develops it, the penultimate allows both for a full affirmation of the realm of the natural, of the right to life, and of the importance of doing good (without that being understood as justification by works), as well as for discrimination

---

[45] *Ethics*, p. 123; DBW 6 S.140.
[46] *Ethics*, p. 130; DBW 6 S.148.
[47] *Ethics*, p. 133; DBW 6 S.151 [*Christliches Leben ist Teilnahme an der Christusbegegnung mit der Welt.*]

between the natural (what is directed towards Christ) and the unnatural (such as the Nazis were doing).

The ultimate and penultimate also gives a dynamic, historical structure within which to do ethics in ways that avoid what Bonhoeffer rejects, such as ethical theories or principles or programmes or ideals to be 'applied' to reality. It is structured and normative but affirms both divine and human freedom, and insists on the continual need for ethical and political discernment in one concrete situation after another. The danger of vacuity in a contextual, freedom-centred ethic is met by the reality of God being freely bound to the world in the definite *Gestalt* of Jesus Christ.

This conceptuality is also of great importance for theological epistemology, as Janz shows.[48] He shows how the epistemology and ontology of *Act and Being* are completed by the concept of ultimate and penultimate in the *Ethics*. This is too complex a matter to open up here, but it is extremely important and is an achievement that has not been recognised so far. In his articulation of the ultimate and penultimate, Bonhoeffer's subtle and precise engagement with philosophy and theology culminates in a close relating of ethics and epistemology which simultaneously affirms the integrity of the world, the natural and human freedom, while keeping them radically open to the ultimate. God is both united with the world in Jesus Christ and free, other, transcendent; and this is understood historically and eschatologically. Time is therefore also built into the dynamics of transformative conformation to the living Jesus Christ, whose ultimacy blesses the penultimate which prepares the way for it. The whole structure is Christological, and it is in his Berlin lectures on Christology that we find some of the clues linking the epistemology of *Act and Being* with the *Ethics*.[49]

I think that in the present situation Bonhoeffer's contribution of a theological epistemology inseparable from an ethic of holiness has considerable promise. By affirming the importance of the penultimate he insists on the continuing importance of rationality and philosophical rigour, and avoids

---

[48] Janz, *Redeeming Modernity*.
[49] See Janz, *Redeeming Modernity*, especially Chapter 6 'Penultimacy, Relationality and Ontology'.

the 'radical' temptations of dogmatism, fideism, foundation-
alism, nihilism and positivism. He stands as a warning for
theologians who, in reaction against forms of rationality and
philosophy that dismiss the reality of God, take refuge in
philosophies which renounce rational and ethical norms. But
he also offers a way to question epistemologies and ontologies
that are closed to the ultimate. Janz explores the contemporary significance of Bonhoeffer by showing how the
discussions in *Act and Being* have many parallels with current
debates in Anglo-American philosophy, such as that between
Hilary Putnam (who advocates rational normativity along anti-
realist lines) and Thomas Nagel (who advocates it along realist
lines). It is, Janz suggests, wiser to follow Bonhoeffer's
example of rigorous argument with 'centrist' philosophies,
while also opening up room for genuine transcendence, than
to be seduced by those poststructuralist, postmodern philosophies whose enmity to many of theology's enemies makes
them seem attractive allies, but whose anti-rationalism, anti-
subjectivity and relativism are actually hostile to a treatment of
the penultimate which allows for its orientation to the
ultimate.

The Structure of Responsible Life

The final key concept is the structure of responsible life.
Bonhoeffer sums this up in the beginning of his discussion of
it:

> The structure of responsible life is conditioned by two
> factors; life is bound to man [*Mensch*] and to God and a
> man's own life is free. It is the fact that life is bound to man
> and to God which sets life in the freedom of a man's own
> life. Without this bond and without this freedom there is no
> responsibility. Only when it has become selfless in this
> obligation does a life stand in the freedom of a man's truly
> own life and action. The obligation assumes the form of
> deputyship and of correspondence with reality; freedom
> displays itself in the self-examination of life and of action
> and in the venture of a concrete decision. [*Die* Bindung
> *trägt die Gestalt der* Stellvertretung *und der* Wirklich-
> keitsgemässheit, *die Freiheit erweist sich in der* Selbst-

zurechnung *des Lebens und Handelns und im* Wagnis *der konkreten Entscheidung.*][50]

Freedom is a theme running through Bonhoeffer's whole theology and is a most illuminating hermeneutical key to it, as Ann Nickson has shown.[51] Here at the heart of his *Ethics* Bonhoeffer gives a concentrated set of concepts describing the *Gestalt* of life before God. It is a substitutionary responsibility alert to the reality of world and self, and committed to the risk of free decision in specific circumstances, even if that means accepting guilt. This is the culminating *Gestalt* of the *Ethics*, taking up the other concepts that I have discussed. Representation or substitution (*Stellvertretung*) ties it to the centre of Bonhoeffer's Christology, and deserves to be worked through in relation to Jesus Christ's life and resurrection as well as his death. Correspondence with (or appropriateness to) reality likewise connects to the basic Christological affirmation of the one reality of God coming together with the world. Calling it a form (*Gestalt*) indicates that it is further developing Bonhoeffer's understanding of ethics and holiness as transformative formation or conformation. And the full affirmation of divine and human freedom in all the complexities and ambiguities of history, with their demands for risky decision-taking, is the further ethical determination of the more formal concept of the ultimate and penultimate.

It is tempting to develop this further, but I have done so at length in *Self and Salvation: Being Transformed,* where the concept of substitutionary responsibility is pivotal and is discussed in relation to Bonhoeffer's life as well as his theology. I will just add one comment on that notion of the venture (*Wagnis*) of concrete decision. Here is a hint at that striking feature of holiness at its liveliest: its generativity, its unpredictability, its combination of newness and utter rightness – rightness in relation to God, to other people, to the realities of history and to self. To conform to the one who creates new life is to shape new life, new lives, new communities, a new world,

---

[50] Bonhoeffer, *Ethics*, p. 224; DBW 6 S.256.
[51] Ann Louise Nickson, '*Divine and Human Freedom in the Theology of Dietrich Bonhoeffer*'. Unpublished Cambridge University Ph.D., 1998.

with all the amazing freshness and uncategorisable beauty of holiness.

Conclusion

I have tried to carry out a largely analytic and conceptual task in relation to Bonhoeffer on holiness in his *Ethics*, and have at various points indicated his relevance to theology for the future. There are of course many questions and possible developments and critiques, but the first task is to try to do descriptive justice to his achievement, and that has been more than enough for one short paper. Bonhoeffer's achievement does, I think, even for those who have disagreements with it, set a standard for a Christian theology of holiness which is not easy to meet. But, more importantly, it offers a genuinely habitable form of holiness in which, utterly involved with God and with the world, one can be freed from the concern to 'make something of oneself'. I will end with what I called earlier Bonhoeffer's somewhat lyrical description of this living before God:

> As surely as faith is the true presence of Christ, so surely, too, is it accomplished by love and hope ... When we encounter Christ, everything that Christ is and has is made our property; yet my life is justified solely by that which is the property of Christ and never by that which has become my own property. Thus the heaven opens over our head and the joyful tidings of God's salvation in Jesus Christ come down like a shout of rejoicing from heaven to earth, and we believe, and, in believing, we have already received Christ to ourselves; we possess everything. We live before God.
>
> We never knew before what life is. We did not understand ouselves. Only by our own potentialities or by our own achievement could we try to understand ourselves and to justify our lives. In this way we could justify ourselves to ourselves and to a god of our own imagining, but we could have no means of access to the potentialities and the works of the living God; we could have no conception of a life which should proceed from these potentialities and works of the living God. We could not conceive of a life on a foundation other than ourselves, sustained by a power other than our

own. Yet this is the life that we found when Christ justified us in His way. We lost our own life to Christ, and Christ became our life. 'I live; yet not I, but Christ liveth in me' (Gal. 2.20). Christian life is the life of Christ.[52]

---

[52] Bonhoeffer, *Ethics*, p. 122 (I have changed the translation's masculine third person to first person plural); DBW 6 S.139.

18

Holiness *in extremis*: Jewish Women's Resistance to the Profane in Auschwitz[1]

Melissa Raphael

Although a number of commentators would regard the conjunction of the words 'holy' and 'Auschwitz' as blaspheming against both its victims and their God, this essay will argue that the concept of holiness is indispensable to a post-Holocaust theology of presence. For if it can be shown, as this essay intends to do, that even one Jew resisted Nazi profanisation and re-established, even momentarily, the sphere of the holy, then the covenantal obligations of Israel were being honoured and Auschwitz remained fit for, and indeed invited, God's presence. Two key theological points inform this argument. First, Abraham Joshua Heschel insists that the immanent presence of God is dependent on human partnership with God: 'The presence is not one reality and the sacred deed another; the sacred deed is the divine in disguise.'[2] Second, Emanuel Levinas has argued that God is revealed 'discretely' only as 'Trace' discernible in face-to-face interhuman relations: that confrontation with the other that is a fundamentally ethical moment revealing the holiness of the face as that singularity

---

[1] For a full-length feminist study of the meaning of holiness in Auschwitz see Melissa Raphael, *The Female Face of God in Auschwitz: A Jewish Feminist Theology of the Holocaust* (London and New York: Routledge, 2002). For a synopsis of the arguments developed in the latter study see Melissa Raphael, 'When God Beheld God: Notes Towards a Jewish Feminist Theology of the Holocaust', *Feminist Theology* 21(1999), pp. 53–78.

[2] *God in Search of Man* (New York: Farrar, Straus & Cudahy, 1956), p. 113.

which must not be harmed.[3] Now the face is a traditional metonym for divine presence in Jewish theology and, in its human form, the presentative image of God. So if Levinas and Heschel are right, then it can be argued that the cleansing of the body – especially the face – from the profane is a restoration of the obscured face of God. This is an act for the sake of God as a means by which God can behold God in the world, and for the sake of humanity as a revelation of God as an accompanying God whose nature may not be to alter quasi-magically our conditions, but who does not abandon us.

The intimation of holiness in *any* situation is a signal of the immanence of God. This is where I begin and yet, as a feminist, I must also insist that patriarchal models of God do not define the holy because these sanction injustice against women and Godself, whose image they bear. In which case, for a feminist theologian to seek the holy in Auschwitz is to seek for phenomena other than those shaped by masculinist values through which the divine presence could be phenomenalised. My focus, then, will be women's acts of care for their own and other bodies – washing them, holding them, sewing coverings for them – all of which are traditionally, but not exclusively, part of female gender performance and which correlate with the Jewish account of the work of Shekhinah – the female figure of the indwelling presence of God.[4] These acts also correlate with Judaism's broader account of the mediation of God through the human work of sanctification of the world.

As Arthur Cohen has put it, 'the presentness of God is his holiness'[5] and from a post-Holocaust perspective I will argue that it seems possible to discern a causal relationship between

---

[3] Emanuel Levinas, *Difficile liberté* (Paris: Albin Michel, 1963), pp. 28–9.

[4] The Shekhinah features in biblical and rabbinic literature, but it was during the late twelfth and thirteenth centuries that kabbalism rendered the Shekhinah a separate feminine hypostasis; a manifestation of God in the world. It should be noted that it is only in contemporary feminist writing that she is not subordinated to the masculine being and attributes of God. See further, Ephraim Urbach, *The Sages: Their Concepts and Beliefs* (Jerusalem: Magnes Press, 1979), pp. 37–65.

[5] Arthur Cohen, *The Tremendum: a Theological Interpretation of the Holocaust* (New York: Continuum, 1993), p. 17. See also David Blumenthal, *Facing the Abusing God: A Theology of Protest* (Louisville, Kentucky: Westminster/John Knox Press, 1993), p. 7.

the holiness of women's relational acts and God's self-manifestation or presence. In the attempt to resist the dehumanising encroachment of radical material and spiritual impurity by notional cleansing of the body and face, these women continued the ancient Jewish work of making the world *gottwirklich*, even in Auschwitz. For the face is a reflective surface by which the glorious radiance of the Shekhinah shines back into the world. God would be present and knowable in the reflection of her image in the 'clean(ed)' human face so that the redemptive process of divine/human (re)union could be sustained.[6] This is a redemptive presence whose blessing consists not in miraculous saving interventions but in its own reward of having done that which Jews were covenanted to do, namely to mediate the blessing of God's love, justice and beauty to God's creation and to experience its effect. It is blasphemous to seek God's ineffable presence as instrumental to some human purpose, but it should be asked why humanity should seek the presence of God; a minimal answer is that a world that is fit for God will be abundantly fit for human beings. In other words God's willing for us to sanctify her world is her willing that we should be blessed.

To say that God-She is holy is to say that her moral and rational personality defines love, justice and beauty in such a way that the 'female' face of God is illuminated by the moral, spiritual and material cleanness of peaceful, protective relationships in aesthetic conditions, which point towards and celebrate the creativity of God and which protect the conditions of her presence. In the holocaust situation, whose own moments were aesthetically unredeemed, we can intimate the holy in Auschwitz wherever, and however tenuously, such relational, 'female' Jewish values and practices are enacted for the sake of human dignity and therefore for the sake of God in whose image the dignity of persons is founded.

[6] It must be emphasised that such an argument is necessarily retrospective and does not licence strictly historical judgements on Jewish women's religious experience at the time. I cannot speak on behalf of dead and surviving victims but only from my present vantage point as a Jewish feminist in imaginative sympathy with her European foremothers. Note that my use of the term 'covenant' is in accordance with that of non-Orthodox Jewish feminism in the tradition of Judith Plaskow and Rachel Adler.

This is an essentially ethical approach to the production of holiness. That the separative dimension of *kadosh* has ethical ramifications is indisputable.[7] It is not to reduce Judaism to ethics in a manner typical of the nineteenth-century Reform movement to argue, as Buber does, that Jewish holiness is not subject to any division of holiness by works or by grace; rather holiness consists in 'true community with God and true community with human beings, both in one'.[8] Irving Greenberg's view, that the urgent command rising out of Sinai and Auschwitz is for humanity to be active partners in the covenantal relationship and honour the image of God in the human face,[9] is also both ethical and theological and prompts my suggestion that it is in so far as the relationality of home and family was sustained in Auschwitz (as it was in groups of mutually supportive, quasi-familial camp sisters)[10] that we can call Auschwitz-Birkenau holy without blaspheming against the dead. To care for another with deeds of loving kindness (*chesed*) was to perform what Rabbi Yitzak Nissenbaum called at the time *kiddush hahayim* – the sanctification of God's name in everyday life rather than in death. If the Jew could observe no other commandment they could still honour their foundational covenantal obligation to God to be holy as God is holy; to the God who says to Israel: 'You shall not profane My holy name, that I may be sanctified in the midst of the Israelite people – I the Lord who sanctify you' (Lev. 22.32).[11]

The Profanisation of Women in Auschwitz

It has been instructive for me to read the Levitical text in conjunction with that of the Polish Catholic Pelagia Lewinska's account of her experiences of degradation in Auschwitz. The

[7] Isidore Epstein, *Judaism: A Historical Presentation* (Harmondsworth: Penguin Books, 1959), p. 23.

[8] Buber, *On Judaism* (New York: Schocken Books, 1967), p. 111.

[9] 'Voluntary Covenant', in Steven L. Jacobs, ed., *Contemporary Jewish Religious Responses to the Holocaust* (Langham, MD: University Press of America, 1993), pp. 44, 77–105.

[10] See Judith Tydor Baumel, 'Social Interaction among Jewish Women in Crisis during the Holocaust', *Gender and History* 7 (1995), pp. 64–84.

[11] Cf. Buber, *On Judaism* [Preface to the 1923 edition], p. 9.

(in all senses) repulsive character of these experiences suggested the phrase 'excremental assault' to Terrence Des Pres as a way of summarising the Nazis' attempt to destroy the Jews even before their death, and perhaps more comprehensively than by their death. His phrase encapsulates not only the *modus operandi* of the Final Solution, but also, from a feminist perspective, the means by which unchecked patriarchal power can make all things available (that is, profane) for its own use. Here, the profane is, it seems to me, not merely equivalent to the secular, but both the quality and product of a kind of patriarchal political rule which colonises, breaks, spoils, wastes or uses up what is holy to God and appropriates it for the expansion of its own power and sphere of operation. Nazism represented a demonic, but logical, conclusion of the patriarchal world-view which, where political conditions permit, objectifies all things as disposable means to power, or destroys them in order to destroy God's means to the self-revelation which judges their project. This absolute offence to the divine appointment of the world reached its defining terminus in Auschwitz: the machinery of Nazi/patriarchal *Lebensraum* exposed.

The Nazi crime commonly regarded by Jews as the 'most difficult to forgive or to forget' was their crime against the humanity of the Jews and Jewish self-respect. In the camps and ghettos (and under the conditions of ban preceding these), 'whatever a human being ever cherished was degraded'.[12] In Auschwitz, the absence of sanitary facilities in the women's camp of 14,000 women was, as Pelagia Lewinska has observed, a deliberate way of erasing the humanity of women; condemning them to die in and as excrement. (The one water tap was forbidden to Jewish women.)[13] The surface of the body was broken and covered over by lice and fleas, encrusted with mud and filth, suppurating sores and boils, cracked by sunburn and frostbite. Additional to the physical erasure of her face, the loss of each woman's name and its replacement by a number

---

[12] Eliezer Berkovits, *Faith after the Holocaust*, (New York: Ktav, 1973), pp. 78–9.

[13] Pelagia Lewinska, 'Twenty Months at Auschwitz', in Carol Rittner and John Roth (eds.), *Different Voices: Women and the Holocaust* (New York: Paragon Press, 1993), p. 87.

erased her personhood; her stench and visage further prohibited approach, touch, relationship and knowability.[14] Moreover, Jewishness itself was fouled. Auschwitz not only prohibited the media of the holy, it also desecrated them. Some women, for example, were given pieces of *talles* (prayer shawl) to wear as underpants.[15] Others were given strips of fabric made of torn prayer shawls to hold on their ill-fitting shoes. By this means the symbols and possibilities of (male) prayer were trodden into the mud and, for those many who suffered uncontrollable diarrhoea, literally shat on.

Although Nazism was a secular, racist ideology rather than an intentionally religious one, the Nazis were virtuosi in the production of the numinous spectacle of (quasi) non-natural power and force. In Auschwitz, the over-powering will and force of the Nazi would have compelled in most a terrorised abjection, a feeling akin to what Rudolf Otto describes as 'numinous unworth'; that is, a 'feeling of absolute "profaneness"', a self-abasement or 'submergence into nothingness before an overpowering, absolute might';[16] a consciousness of the sin (or more precisely, racial fault) of being a Jew. The word *Sheiss* or shit was the guards' common mode of address to Jews in Auschwitz. Corpses were referred to as *Scheiss-Stücke* (pieces of excrement).[17] 'Creature feeling' – the sense of being unclean before pure (male) power – was induced by making the Jew repulsive to self and other, allowing the Nazi to justify his 'purification' of that Jew by insecticidal gas and fire. The function of Auschwitz was not only to torment, but to purge

---

[14] See, e.g., Livia Bitton-Jackson, *I Have Lived a Thousand Years: Growing Up in the Holocaust* (London: Simon & Schuster, 1999), pp. 83, 92; Terrence Des Pres, *The Survivor: An Anatomy of Life in the Death Camps* (Oxford: Oxford University Press, 1976), pp. 53, 57, 66; Kitty Hart, *Return to Auschwitz* (London: Granada Publishing, 1983), pp. 107, 135; Olga Lengyel, *Five Chimneys: The Story of Auschwitz* (New York: Howard Fertig, 1995), pp. 22, 44–6; Lewinska, 'Twenty Months at Auschwitz', pp. 85–93.

[15] Lidia Rosenfeld Vago, 'One Year in the Black Hole of Our Planet Earth: A Personal Narrative', in Dalia Ofer and Lenore J. Weitzman, eds., *Women in the Holocaust* (New Haven and London: Yale University Press, 1998), pp. 273–84 [p. 281].

[16] Rudolf Otto, *The Idea of the Holy. An Inquiry into the Non-rational Factor in the Idea of the Divine and its Relation to the Rational* (London: Oxford University Press, 1958), pp. 51, 10.

[17] Lengyel, *Five Chimneys*, p. 83.

Europe of racial 'impurity', swallowing and voiding the Jew (of God) and covering over this digested Jewish waste with ever more Jewish waste – even while it was still alive. Where women were pushed and fell into an abyss of self-and other-loathing, the face of God disappeared from view and the darkness closed over Auschwitz altogether. But that the darkness was also pierced by the light of the divine countenance will be the contention of the rest of this essay.

Now, there is no doubt that the women's camp in Auschwitz-Birkenau was primarily and obviously characterised by chaos and cruelty (and that this was systematically generated between as well as against Jewish women themselves). But there were also women who, not selected for immediate death, sought to preserve some vestiges of their former lives as persons in community. There were, of course, observant women who tried to adapt domestic practices governed by halakhah to the camp situation. But my argument does not depend on these observant women who lit candles on the Sabbath from anything which would burn, or made matzot at Pesach almost from air, literally marvellous as such acts may be. Mine is not an argument exclusive to Orthodox women's practice, but one intended to be inclusive of the considerable religious, social, political and geographical diversity of Jewish women in Auschwitz and other death and concentration camps.

I am more immediately concerned with that inclusive category of women who, as 'camp sisters' could and did reconstitute some of the purificatory and relational functions of the home in the camps through the establishment of familial or quasi-familial groupings as described or assumed in most women victims' memoirs and by feminist historians of the Holocaust like Judith Tydor Baumel, Joan Ringelheim (in her early work) and Myrna Goldenberg. Often women would have been able to help others only because of their slightly more fortunate circumstances or by the earning of hierarchical privileges. Nonetheless, Israel's is a corporeal election, 'because the election of Israel is of the flesh, a Jew remains in the service of God no matter what he believes or does'.[18] Even where Israel is

---

[18] Michael Wyschogrod, *The Body of Faith: Judaism as Corporeal Election* (New York: Seabury Press, 1983), p. xv.

'unclean', the divine presence is among them (*Sifra* on Lev. 16.16). In which case, where women gathered together in the mutually supportive pairs or groups this constituted a form of sacred assembly. Parts of the camp then constituted a morally separate enclosure whose even temporary boundaries marked women's fundamental opposition to the profanity of their situation, surrounded on all sides as they were with moral degeneracy, filth, disease and death.[19]

Women's Sanctification of Auschwitz

It should become clear that this reading of the holocaust literature – and women's memoirs in particular – is not an alien feminist import but a theological possibility inherent in Judaism itself. However, few historical or theological studies invite such a reading. There have, for example, been a number of historical studies which have described how observant Jews (largely and normatively, male) heroically refused to surrender the means by which Israel could remain 'a holy nation' on terms presented and defined by men and largely for men and in honour of essentially masculine modes.[20] The literature, by now an Orthodox metanarrative in itself, is nonetheless a moving testament to male religious resistance to profanisation. In the camps men sometimes found ways to wear *tefillin*, hold services with prayers learnt by heart or written out by hand, study Talmud through the recitation and analysis of passages from memory, establish *yeshivot* using the same means, and engage in Talmudic dispute as they trudged to, from, and sometimes during, slave labour. But it was Torah-educated men, not women, who:

> lived in the nightmare kingdom as if it were just another day, patiently confronting the never-before-imagined questions

[19] It would, of course, be possible to interpret these acts psychologically as expressions of a basic survival instinct. However, while Judaism is a practical religion designed to preserve life, the religious anthropology of the present paper suggests that human acts can also point to values, intentions and meanings that transcend (but do not devalue) bodily survival.

[20] One of the best known of these studies is that of Irving Rosenbaum, *The Holocaust and Halakhah* (New York: Ktav Publishing House, 1976).

and finding answers. May a father purchase his son's escape
from the ovens, knowing that the quotas will be met and
another child will die in his place? May one pronounce the
blessing over martyrdom over a death from which there is no
escape? What blessing does one make before being turned to
ashes?[21]

There is no doubt that observant Jewish men's determination
to maintain the marks and practices of holiness in the face of
torture and death was an affirmation of the transcendental
meaning of Jewish life. But it is unhistorical and theologically
partial to read male (usually Orthodox) holocaustal observance
as if it summarises the essence of Judaism and the experience
of the Jewish people as a whole, with women's pieties being
recounted as a kind of 'special mention'.[22] Secular feminist
historians of the Holocaust have long insisted that the genocide
was not gender-blind and nor should be its historiography. I
would want to add that theologically and phenomenologically,
the subsumption of female into male experience ignores the
role of gender in the production of holiness during the
Holocaust (and at any other times).

The masculine production of holiness consisted in awesome
feats of spirit and memory that were the fruit of dedication to
study over many years. The male 'wandering Jew' (as
Christendom disparagingly referred to him) formulated a
Judaism that was adaptable to migration. Masculine Judaism
was (de)portable because it sanctified the world in ways that
were spoken, textual and theoretical before they were practical,
and sometimes (as in the case of the appointment and
functioning of the Temple) regardless of whether they were
practical. So, for Jewish men a form of sacred space is established wherever ten Jewish men are gathered for prayer. Some

---

[21] Jonathan Sacks, *Faith in the Future* (London: Darton, Longman & Todd,
1995), p. 241.

[22] In his *Hasidic Responses to the Holocaust in the Light of Hasidic Thought* (New
York: Ktav Publishing House, 1990), pp. 99–105, Pesach Schindler gives a six-
page account of Hasidic men's spiritual resistance in the camps and ghettos.
Schindler notes that descriptions of Hasidic women's 'activities' as he puts it,
are rare. He cites only the resistance of one woman, Perele Perlow, wife of the
Koidenever Rebbe, who organised women's prayer and study sessions in the
Vilna ghetto.

Torah-observant men did continue to pray, study, and celebrate the festivals in the camps, despite their prohibition.[23] And for Hasidic men sacred space would have been concentrated simply where the Rebbe was or, in his absence, where his teaching was propounded.[24] Perhaps most significant to the present discussion, rabbinic Judaism has taught that wherever men are studying Torah the presence of the Shekhinah is summoned into their midst.[25] In short, during the Holocaust, while men remained subject to the types of rituals and practices of purity and separation also commanded of women (such as the preparation of kosher food and the maintenance of menstrual purity laws), their sanctification of the world was also (and especially prior to the founding of the State of Israel) far more cerebral, consisting to a far greater degree in words and arguments committed to memory.

In Leviticus 19.1–2 'The Lord spoke to Moses, saying: Speak to the whole Israelite community and say to them: You shall be holy, for I, the Lord your God, am holy.' Yet in this period, women's sphere of the holy was (and in Orthodoxy, remains) the home – and Nazi Germany had taken this from her. The worlds of communal prayer, study and halakhic dispute had never been hers (even if for some Eastern European Jewish women the world of trade was a far from alien one). Bereft of the specifically female media of the Jewish holy, how were women to be holy as God commanded? Where Rabbi Mendele Alter of Pabianice died in Treblinka, reputedly preaching and practising the meaning of Jewish holiness even as he entered the gas chamber, how did or could women reveal and invite the presence of the holy? The rabbis have said that 'over one who uninterruptedly studies God's word ... even the angel of death can win no victory'.[26] But how could women, who did not study God's word, have won any sort of victory over the Nazi angel of death?

[23] See Eliezer Berkovits, *With God in Hell: Judaism in the Ghettos and Deathcamps* (New York and London: Sanhedrin, 1979).

[24] See Seth Kunin, 'Judaism', in Jean Holm, ed., with John Bowker, *Sacred Space* (London: Pinter, 1994), p. 140. Kunin's points are general and not made in the context of the Holocaust.

[25] Urbach, *The Sages*, p. 42.

[26] Cited in Sacks, *Faith*, p. 241.

If Orthodoxy is right that the meaning of Jewish womanhood is to take physical and spiritual care of the family and to pass Jewishness onto her children, and much of this has to do with maintaining the types of halakhically governed purity and separation forbidden, irrelevant or materially impossible in the camps, then how – if at all – might these female practices of Jewish sanctity have transported themselves into Auschwitz where children and their mothers were killed on arrival and husbands and wives separated from one another?[27] Whereas, for men, the 'signs and remembrances' of *tefillin* ('phylacteries') (Exod. 13.9) and *tzitzith* (fringed garments) (Num. 15.39) are laid upon the male body as a reminder to observe God's commandments and 'to be holy to their God', these could not be worn by women as a sign of resistance. The marks of the holy – the beards and head-coverings – that observant men in the ghettos refused on pain of torture and death to remove from their head and face also signify gender differentiation in the production of the holy. The resistant male Jewish face still wore the holy.[28] Circumcision had left a mark of covenantal inclusion that could not be erased. But by what sign would women resist the demonic, and remember and bear in and on their bodies their Levitical priestly vocation to be holy as God is holy?

There are two connected ways of answering this question. One way is to reflect further on the Jewish concept of holiness; the other, and subsequent to that, is to develop a (counter)-reading of the Orthodox ideology of female sanctity which already assumes difference in the fulfilment of women's covenantal obligations. First, with regard to the Jewish concept of holiness, I have already indicated that the relationship between holiness and human will is particularly significant to the theological contemplation of Auschwitz, not despite but

[27] Observant women did of course endeavour to mark the Sabbath and festivals in the death and concentration camps. But the conduct of these is gendered and women's primarily domestic obligations relating to the Sabbath and most festivals could not be undertaken outside the home.

[28] For example, after a beating during which the Germans had sought to remove his hat, the Zabner Rebbe defiantly walked to the train that would take him to his death covering his head with both hands (Schindler, *Hasidic Responses*, p. 99).

because of its prohibition of the ordinary exercise of Jewish will. As Eliezer Berkovits rightly notes, holiness is 'not about Being but Becoming'. That is, 'The sacred *is* not, but has to be brought into being as the result of someone's action or behaviour ... Israel is *made* holy by God and becomes holy by sanctifying itself.' Holiness is a this-worldly 'challenge to Israel, a task, a responsibility'.[29] For a Jew the task of holiness is to come to reflect but not to imitate God; not to be hubristically 'like unto God' (Gen. 3.5), but to model oneself on the divine attributes of compassion and loving kindness: by acts of *avodah halev*, read here as service of the heart, or *avodah begashmiut*, worship of God through the conditions of everyday life. In which case, wherever women maintained relationship, the service of the heart in a place dedicated to its opposite, they sanctified Auschwitz and carried on Israel's covenantal task of making the world fit for the indwelling of God. Indeed, they did not merely *continue* that task, for their acts were powerful in precise proportion to the demonic power those acts resisted. Here the truly numinous spectacle was not the horror of the flaming chimneys but the *mysterium* of human love that is stronger than death, the *tremendum* of its judgement upon demonic hate, and the *fascinans* of its call to God to come into a world which had cast God out. Although not all commandments have a spatial focus, in general, Jewish 'sacred space becomes such through the performance of God's word'.[30] It is through God's word that Jews purify the world; set it apart from evil. Wherever women undertook acts of service or loving kindness in a place that was entirely repellent to both, they purified the world of Auschwitz. They established a separate bounded space that was wholly/holy other to that of the bounded camp of Auschwitz and therefore fit for God.

Because holiness is not a material property of things or persons, the question of women and the mediation of the holy in Auschwitz is not primarily an historical question, but a theological one. God wants Israel to be a holy nation. That the holiness of Israel consists in its being obligated to be 'a nation of priests' is the basis of my argument. Defining priesthood

---

[29] Berkovits, *Faith After the Holocaust*, p. 59.
[30] Kunin, 'Judaism', p. 141.

broadly as the mediation of the holy, the art of consecration, we need to see how women in Auschwitz might have continued to fulfil Israel's covenantal mission to mediate God's presence to the world as a kingdom of priests and a holy nation (Exod. 19.6). I have suggested that women embodied their Jewish vocation when they sought to remove from their faces and bodies the marks of the profane – the filth – that the Nazis commanded them to bear, so as to purify themselves for, and as a revelation of, divine presence. For ultimately God's presence is re-membered not by dressing the body in pieces of fabric or by the fashioning of facial hair, but by will and act. Women's loyalty to this quintessentially Jewish task of making God present to the world would have consisted in a form of religio-ethical action: in effect – if not always intention – their protecting and tending of the holy image of God in those suffering with them.

Not all Jewish theologians could agree with this for, as David Shapiro notes on behalf of Orthodoxy, it is above all the obser-vance of *law* that allows 'man' (as he puts it) to achieve 'the goal for which he was created : the attainment of his Godlikeness – the unfolding within him of his divine image'.[31] But the study and practice of halakhah does not and cannot 'unfold' women's divine image because women are not positioned in relation to that discourse as speaking subjects and agents or decisors. In their status as objects of the law – 'silent recipients, outsiders to the process',[32] they are not normatively human; a screen of patriarchal prohibitions, customs and exemptions has been interposed between women and this mirror onto God.

Yet it is also possible to say that in spite of the Orthodox gendering of halakhic operations, and in some ways because of it, women *do* attain the 'Godlikeness' Shapiro refers to. I come now to my second (non-Orthodox) contention: that Orthodox ideologies of femininity offer us a clue to women's resistance to profanisation in Auschwitz. Granted, on the one

[31] David S. Shapiro, 'The Ideological Foundations of the Halakhah' in Jacob Neusner, ed., *Understanding Jewish Theology: Classical Issues and Modern Perspectives* (New York: Ktav Publishing House/Anti-Defamation League of B'nai Brith, 1973), p. 108.

[32] Rachel Biale, *Women and Jewish Law: An Exploration of Women's Issues in Halakhic Sources* (New York: Schocken Books, 1984), p. 8.

hand, women's traditional vocation has been a practical, domestic path of care, which some would justifiably construe as an alienation of religious labour (and in Eastern Europe especially) marked by their exclusion from the *beit midrash* or house of study and prayer. But on the other hand, and more positively, in its domestic replication of the divine order, the practicalities of Jewish women's religious lives also allowed those lives to finally transcend the practical. In one sense the female sacred sphere is the realm of the everyday – the profane understood as the non-special. But in another sense it is a central – perhaps *the* central – locus of the sacred. For in Jewish sacred geography the home (called by rabbis a *mikdash maat* – a small sanctuary) replaces the destroyed Second Temple. The preparation of kosher food, celebration of the Sabbath and maintenance of family all sanctify Jewish life in the absence of the Temple cult. In Diaspora Judaism the family table – a space at the heart of the female sacral sphere – replaces the Temple's sacrificial altar as a central locus of the holy. Orthodox Judaism has not, therefore, rendered (married) women irrelevant to the consecration of the world. It has taught that the 'female' home, and indeed 'female' virtues, are redemptive and model the proper human posture in relation to God.[33]

The intrinsic religious significance of the Jewish home may explain why nineteenth-century Jewish protofeminists, contemporary Jewish feminists and contemporary Orthodoxy as a whole, have all, if for different reasons and in different ways, affirmed the sanctity of female domestic observance. Of course, there is little doubt that much Orthodox rhetoric on the sanctity of the home is sentimental and performs an ideological function: that of compensating women for their lack of public religious authority. And the conservative ideology of femininity produced by the nineteenth-century Western European embourgeoisement of traditional Jewish sexual politics can hardly be adopted uncritically.

---

[33] See, e.g., Hayyim Schneid, ed., *Family* (Philadelphia: Jewish Publication Society of America, 1973), p. 94; on the 'femaleness' of Jewish religious virtue see Jacob Neusner, *Androgynous Judaism: Masculine and Feminine in the Dual Torah* (Macon, GA: Mercer University Press, 1993), esp. pp. 83–123.

Nonetheless, and in spite of itself, Orthodox rhetoric can suggest a properly feminist construction of female sacral power. Religious feminists who wish to affirm female difference, rather than erasing it in the name of equality with the male norm (as Reform Judaism has done), must be interested by the Orthodox contention that women have, in effect, through their own purificatory and separative practices, the priestly power to transform their space into a shrine; to house the presence of God.[34] As such women's vocation is, arguably, as much a priestly vocation as that of men.

Of particular significance is the female invitation of God as Shekhinah into the Sabbath home through the domestic separation of holy from profane time and space. God blesses and hallows the Sabbath (Exod. 20.11) as the means by which the world is recreated. In mystical understanding, women in their turn realise that recreativity of the Sabbath by the hallowing practices of purification: of the washing and cleaning of bodies and objects in readiness for the holy event that is the arrival of the Shekhinah, the Sabbath Bride.[35] To repeat: there is no doubt that domestic labour *as such* should not be sentimentalised: at the time of the Holocaust, preparations for the Sabbath would often begin almost as soon as the Sabbath was over, and for poor women especially these could be sheer (often unelected) drudgery. But with mystical intentionality or interpretation, domestic preparation for the Sabbath – making the house and its inhabitants gleam and shine – was work of cosmological significance, not only preparing but facilitating and participating in the inner meaning of the Sabbath: a sacred marriage within God, and between God and Israel, that would recreate and restore the tired and damaged world.[36]

[34] Hyman E. Goldin, *The Jewish Woman and Her Home* (New York: Hebrew Publishing Co., 1978), pp. 71–2.

[35] For an account of women's pre-war Sabbath purifications see Yaffa Eliach, *There Once Was a World: A 900 Year Chronicle of the Shtetl of Eishyshok* (Boston, New York & London: Little, Brown & Co., 1998), pp. 408–9.

[36] Cf. Kathryn Allen Rabuzzi's *The Sacred and the Feminine: Toward a Theology of Housework* (New York: Seabury Press, 1982), which argues that all housework re-enacts the primordial creation of order out of chaos.

So it is here, in the traditional domain and values of Jewish female sacrality, that a feminist theologian can ground her search for indicators of human transcendence and divine immanence among women in Auschwitz. If one transposes this domestically centred Jewish theology into Auschwitz, women's experience there takes on a different hue. To take one example (space does not permit more), after being taken from Auschwitz to Belsen, Bertha Ferderber-Salz, her niece, sister-in-law and another young girl were able to maintain what she calls their 'communal household' in Belsen. This Belsen 'household' is what she herself calls 'home'.[37] Here she and the other women supported one another emotionally and helped keep one another clean. They shared food, tried to wash each other's hair with 'coffee', and used needles improvised from splinters of wood to knit and sew one another garments made from the unravelled threads of their blankets.

Ferderber-Salz herself does not theologise her acts. But reading her memoir from a theological perspective, in covering and protecting the Jewish body, the members of her camp 'household' also covered and protected the divine spark. They made a sanctuary for the spark of the divine presence which saved it from being extinguished.

Acts of purification set things and persons apart, whether in the home or other enclosure. Sara Nomberg-Przytyk remembers that 'it was important to wash, even if it meant rubbing your face with a fistful of snow. The effort to wash your face is an expression of life.' The Dutch women on the block of the *zugangen* (new arrivals) lacked the will to do this and many of them died almost immediately.[38] Other women survivors have testified to the need to keep as clean as was possible in the labour and concentration camps, futile and tokenistic as the attempt might have been.[39] As Lewinska expresses it, 'for some

---

[37] Bertha Ferderbar-Salz, *And the Sun Kept Shining* (New York: Holocaust Library, 1980), p. 163. Cf. Frida Michelson's account of how, within the verminous filth of the Riga ghetto, she and her friend Sonia worked for several days to make their tiny apartment into a home. (*I Survived Rumbuli* [New York: Holocaust Library, 1979], pp. 71–2.)

[38] Sara Nomborg-Przytyk, *Auschwitz. True Tales from a Grotesque Land* (Chapel Hill and London: The University of North Carolina Press, 1985), p. 19.

[39] Hart, *Return*, p. 107; Lengyel, *Five Chimneys*, pp. 47, 123.

of us [physical cleanliness] was something more, an act of will
to show ourselves we could defy Auschwitz'.[40] Livia
Bitton-Jackson remembers how, during a brief respite from
Auschwitz, a forced labour factory in Augsberg provided her
with clean white sheets on her bunk, soap, showers whose flow
of water could be controlled, and clean towels. Her response to
these is couched in the language of Jewish mystical theology:
'As we get out of the showers, a secret spark of self-esteem is
nurtured deep within. It's a divine message. A promise of
redemption.'[41]

In these cases, washing should not only be understood as the
physical act of wiping away material dirt in the rare instances
that that was possible. Rather it could be an act of *seeing through*
Nazism and *seeing through* the effects of Nazism to the divine
image reflected in the darkened mirror of the begrimed
human face. The acts of some women in Auschwitz can be read
as attempts to maintain the reflective quality of the material
world (so well-known to the theology of the Sabbath) in the
reflective quality of the face which is, above all, presentative of
personhood, both human and divine.

Alan Unterman has observed that the holy is that which
transcends the natural, 'corrupt' environment,[42] and it seems
clear that in the cases of the women just cited cleanliness
represented something more; it was not just that relative cleanliness was more physically comfortable than dirtiness; it was
also, and perhaps above all, a signifier of the peace and order
that we find figured in the theology of Sabbath and for which
so many longed. The holy is that which God wishes to be set
apart from harm; and theologically, the association of cleanliness with order, peace and safety is explained by the way in
which bodily and other types of material cleanliness are a
precondition and sign of holiness. Cleanliness is a signifier of
the moral and spiritual health or cleanness on which the
blessings of peace and order in the home, the House of Israel,
the world and the cosmos depend. Rabbinical Judaism teaches
that the body is the vessel of the holy spark and so must be

---

[40] Lewinska, 'Twenty Months', p. 97.
[41] Bitton-Jackson, *I Have Lived*, p. 146.
[42] Alan Unterman, *Jews: Their Religious Beliefs and Practices* (London:
Routledge & Kegan Paul, 1981), p. 136.

kept clean and healthy. It must not be neglected and one must wash daily as part of the glorification of its creator (T. Shabbath 50b).

In which case, to say that the holy was present in Auschwitz is to say that it had something crucially to do with women cleaning (however notionally and ineffectually) their own and other bodies – their 'face' – from the afflictions of physical and spiritual defilement. To do so was to declare not only a bounded sacred *space*, but also a bounded sacred *time*: a momentary Sabbath in Auschwitz, which by its nature restored the face of God to a world de-faced by the exercise of patriarchal power.

To those who have internalised the patriarchal denigration of female domestic labour, these acts of purification may seem a rather slender basis for a theology of divine presence in Auschwitz. But valorised as sacral, indeed priestly, these acts can be interpreted without bathos as the exercise of one of the two types of holiness (*kedushah*) known to Judaism. Theirs was not the hierarchical *kedushah* in which the holy can be mapped by a graded series of holy things enjoying varying degrees of purity: places in the holy land, the ranks of priest, sacrifice and so forth (though the circle that was Auschwitz was at the furthest possible distance from the holy centre). Rather, theirs was a non-hierarchical *kedushah* which is established by the intention to consecrate or dedicate an act to God.[43]

The (De)portation of the Holy into Auschwitz

Some elements within rabbinic Judaism assert that the destruction of the Temple was a sign of Shekhinah's desertion of the Jewish people on account of their sins. More representative, though, is Rabbi Akiba's view that because God is compassionate and loving, Shekhinah is always present and shares Israel's suffering in exile.[44] In the absence of the

[43] I am indebted to David Blumenthal here for his distinction between the two types of holiness known to Judaism (*Facing the Abusing God*, p. 24–6).

[44] Michael E. Lodahl, *Shekhinah/Spirit: Divine Presence in Jewish and Christian Religion* (Mahwah NJ: Paulist Press, 1992), p. 53.

Temple, the home is the place of her presence. I have argued that it is in seeing where the symbolics of the (destroyed) home could be transposed into the anti-home of Auschwitz that it becomes possible to argue that the priestly vocation and its redemptive effect could be deported into the women's camp in Auschwitz-Birkenau. But it is also important to say that the symbolics of the home do not exhaust the necessary or sufficient conditions for God's presence in Auschwitz and may also suggest more stable intimacies than Auschwitz could normally sustain. That women who had suffered a series of deportations out of the sphere of the holy could nonetheless fulfil God's command to make God a sanctuary so that God could live among them (Exod. 25.8) is a possibility inherent in Judaism because Jewish sacred space is mobile. In the early biblical period, sacred space is established wherever Jews are encamped in the barren wilderness around them. And from the rabbinic period, to the present 'God's presence is not tied to a specific place. Instead it is tied to the presence of God's people, i.e., Israel, who bring God's presence to wherever they are.'[45]

It is the sheltering of the divine presence (Shekhinah) in whatever wilderness Israel might find itself, that links the redemptive qualities of the home to those of the (assaulted, homeless) body(ies) of Israel in Auschwitz. To clarify: the Priestly documents of the Hebrew Bible describe the *mishkan* or 'Tent of Meeting' – the portable wilderness shrine where for Moses and the people the divine presence resided in its holy of holies (see Exod. 25–27). Within this was the shrouded chest that was the ark of the covenant of which unauthorized approach and touch was forbidden (Exod. 25.10–22; 37.1–9; 1 Sam. 6.19; 2 Sam. 6.6–8).

Now it seems to me that the *mishkan* is also a portable metaphor evoking how women's holding, caring encirclement of bodies created a form of home where that was possible, or if not that, a portable and temporary sanctuary for God; a kind of *mishkan* in the Holocaust wilderness. During the Holocaust, Israel was bereft of the synagogue and home which had replaced the functions of the Temple. Whereas the masculine

[45] Kunin, 'Judaism', pp. 121, 129.

mishkan consisted in the capacity of the memory to be a sacred chest in which to carry and mediate the presence of God in words spoken from inside the head, for women, exempted/prohibited from the sacral performativity of words, the holding body became a mobile sanctuary of the divine spark and God sought to return, here, to this portable tent of meeting – the body/ark which in Auschwitz was carried 'in the midst of their uncleanness' (Lev. 16.16).

While I would insist that the image of the *mishkan* in Auschwitz is no mere linguistic conceit, it must be emphasised that relational acts of service to bodies could not render the women's camp in Auschwitz-Birkenau a sanctuary *qua* place of protection. Such acts may have resacralised the Jewish body, but not Auschwitz itself: there were no places on earth where a Jew was more vulnerable, more absolutely exposed to harm, than a death camp. The victimised female body was under attack; a ruined sanctuary that could offer little refuge to Shekhinah, and often none at all. The body/sanctuary had been entered and defiled. Shekhinah was both exposed to the profane gaze and obscured by the covering marks of its profanation. Whereas the holy desert ark was protected from the contagion of unclean or profane touch by tented layers of animal skin and cloth, the exposing and consuming touch of Auschwitz tore all protection from the holy.

But conversely, the profane can be transformed into the holy by the blessings of sanctifying touch. And in the end, the Nazis' profanatory degradation of women in Auschwitz could not, in fact, desecrate them: for holiness is not a quantity that can be found and destroyed. Holiness is known in a perception of the relation between created things and God. Because it is a category of willed relation, rather than being a material property of objects, it cannot be taken away from those objects by physical force. Just as the Torah scrolls are, in fact, too holy to profane, only God can (dis)appoint the holiness of her own children. It is on the certainty of this that the argument of this essay has rested. Namely, if the Jew, even the dying Jew, remained holy to God, within the precinct of God and therefore fit for God, then God could be a sanctificatory presence in judgement on Auschwitz. For wherever things and persons are sanctified Israel is not cut off from God, her name cannot be blotted out and forgotten by God – a more total and final meaning of Jewish death than any Nazi Germany could conceive.

19

Holiness Ungendered

Susan F. Parsons

One of the critical questions that concerns holiness has to do with the conditions for its possibility in human being. To speak of holiness is not only to ascribe to the divine a peculiar awe-inspiring quality, but also to implicate human beings as ones who may be touched and transformed by holiness in their lives. For the Christian, this mutuality of God and humanity is taken to the limit in the suggestion that we too may become holy, and thus that in our human being, the holiness which is divine, may come to be manifested. Such promise leaves the theologian with a philosophical task of seeking to understand the way in which this holiness might be encountered and enfleshed. For as holiness is understood to be a revealing of God that comes to be known and received by faith, so it is also to be a revealing of the human being as made in God's image, in the fulfilment of which the life of faithfulness is to find its vocation. How this can be so is one of the tasks for a philosophical theology to undertake.

For us to address this question today is to encounter that particularly modern issue of gender, of what it is to be woman and to be man, an issue which has become the locus for so many of the troubled assumptions and projects of Enlightenment humanity. For the issue of gender calls into question the nature of this common humanity by asking about our differences, and at the same time, calls into question the assumptions about our differences that are used to divide us. In drawing attention to gender issues, feminists have argued that claims about what is common to women and men are andro-centric, thus rendering women silent by a false inclusivity, while claims about difference are exposed as self-serving assertions of power over the other, that can no longer pretend disinterest.

This dilemma of difference challenges theological anthropology to the core, and brings us to the question of who is the human being who is to be holy and who is to reveal the holiness of God? It is this matter of who I am that the gender issue poses so starkly in our time.

Ours is a postmodern age, when the inheritance of the Enlightenment is being scrutinised and deconstructed, and thinking with gender plays its part in this. Its challenges to modern humanism are profoundly unsettling, and leave us in a changed situation today. The intensification of the Enlightenment project, in its promotion of the value and the power of the human being, is presented with great moral conviction as the way for the divine image to be seen and realised. Women becoming divine, and women exercising power within the church's life, are invitations for this holiness to be made present among us, manifested in gendered human beings. However, there are also voices that call us into the deeper questioning of this humanism. Some gender theorists are taking up the suggestion that the human being of modernity is misconceived, and that in undermining its image, we may not only free our thinking from the conundrum of gender difference, but also find there is a way open to holiness that is not constructed by human will. It is the purpose of this essay to begin to describe this way, and to do so from the midst of the gender debate, as exemplified in two contemporary writers. Through this consideration, we may glimpse something of the philosophical problematic within which theologians must articulate human formation in holiness.

The Problematic of Holiness

This paper begins with an understanding of holiness as the coming to matter in my life of the grace of God, by which grace I am called to find myself in God, I am to know the end of life in the fullness of divine love, and I am to be as a sign of this transcending, this ever-being-taken-out-of-myself, in the flesh and blood I am given. Holiness is thus a concept in which are gathered up the defining moments of a believer's life, in coming to discern one's human vocation, to trust in God's future, and to be the medium in which these come to matter together. Vocation, expectation and mattering are all to be found within the living of holiness, as I come to be caught up in the difference of God and to be given back to myself in the most tender charity. Holy living takes place in this enactment of love between humanity and God, and is thus entirely and ultimately Christ-centred. Holiness is the coming to matter in my life of the grace of God's coming to matter in Christ.

Discourse concerning holiness has been re-emerging throughout the last decades of the twentieth century, perhaps associated with the thriving trade in spirituality and the outpouring of fascination with the symbols of heaven, represented in the visual and performing arts and exchanged in the common language of the Internet. The commodification of these symbols, whereby they are materialised into purchasable and therefore economically valued objects, and are made visually available as the power of heaven to be yours for a click, is the process that feeds the virtual reality of advertising. So angels on greeting cards and calendars, saintly bliss on the faces of users of aftershave, the Virgin Mary's approving smile on a pair of boots, the footballer – arms outstretched on the hill above Rio – proclaiming the good news of control over private spaces; all of these signify the business that holiness has become. In-your-face transcendence can be had now, and in the holding of it, satisfaction that fantasies will indeed become reality is guaranteed. Such phenomena speak to me of a humanity that has lost its way to that which lies most at its heart, and that is effectively sealing off every exit from this desperate bewilderment in the very production of so many alternatives. Proliferation breeds contempt, and so the manufacture of promises becomes ever more vociferous and demanding of trust. These all-too-sketchy thoughts concern our present situation, the situation of a world that longs for a redeeming even as its own best offers fail and fail again, and thus a situation into which holiness of living comes with a very particular problematic and a very real urgency. In what way is holiness to be found?

These things have come into focus for me in consideration of the problematic of gender and of the urgency of thinking how it is to be human. For the global economy that now shapes our intercultural living has been sustained throughout its development in modernity by an account of our humanity, an account that is no longer naïvely believable in the time of postmodernity. Believing that the self is a centre of decision-making whose choices emerging out of a presumed freedom are effective determinants of its bodied life, believing that the self is a speaker whose use of language expresses the inwardness of its subjectivity, believing that the self is an agent whose exercise of power makes a difference to the world — all of these have become the commonplaces of a modern humanism that is now called into question, not least by gender. For it has been the critical role of feminists to challenge each one of these beliefs as the trace of the man behind the productive machine, as it has been their constructive role to set up alternative representations, empowered and spoken and chosen by women. In postmodernity, the dilemma of difference that haunts all attempts at a universal humanism breaks through the identities of woman and man, which have been made to bear its weight and sustain its interests. Thus the problematic of gender is to be found along the fault lines of the troubled beliefs of modern humanism, marking the precarious way of our being human today.

Commodification, now operating under the logic of its own generation, no longer requires these humanist myths of origin, and with their abandonment, the difference of only two which has been gender dissipates. There is then a kind of strange relief at being presented with the necessity for choosing the self-understanding that we are to live by, according to our own standpoint or situation, so that here too, with regard to our humanity, we can have it any way we like it. In that celebratory choosing of a style, the loss of ourselves to ourselves is masked, and repeated. For the invention of myself is the problem (left in Nietzsche's wake), that with the death of God, the human has come to fill up the universe with its will to power, even as its heart aches in the contradictions of its own self-valuing. The fashioning of myself according to my own image, and the positing of a god in whose eyes I may be recognised, and the disciplining of a life to re-present the value of my self in public – all of these that may at first have appeared to be joyful, become the requirements of the work of self-production into which humanity has fallen, and within which it can only speak of being woman and man as a controlling gesture. Gender has become a sign of our self-limitation, no longer understood as a limit imposed by nature and explained by biology, but as a constructive work of establishing the boundaries within which my life is to be meaningfully lived. With the imposition of chosen gender, human beings resign themselves to their own horizon and are consumed in a striving to live up to its expectations. Discourse concerning holiness is to be heard here too, for in the promises of gender identity, of being woman and man, has been the presentation of a vocation, an expectation, and a mattering. Does the demise of identity signal another way of holiness?

A study of gender and holiness brings me to these prevailing themes of our time, and requires of me as a theologian a thinking with faith into the conditions for their appearance. It is this attention to the conditions of our thinking that has given rise to a reconsideration of modernity as itself a harbour of the nihilism manifested in postmodernity, and that finds openings in the present for new things to be said and to be received. So Foucault's recommendation that we refuse the blackmail of the Enlightenment[1] opens the way for a rethinking of how it is human to be, and in this will take place a certain destruction of the humanism that has been fronted by gender. That what has been called 'anti-humanism' will appear as collaboration with the worst implications of postmodern developments is precisely the prophetic moment into which theology is called to come in faith, and like all such moments, it bears the most intense fragility. For what is to be said of holiness is in the living of it. Its calling is to the birth of God amongst us and its hope is in the birth of the whole creation into God, in both of which is the work of love that becomes my life. So there is a 'logic of self-involvement'[2] that puts the believer at risk in acknowledging as holy the difference of God, and in letting herself become the place of its disclosure. It is to seek and to articulate understanding of this faith in our situation today that theology finds its vocation, and this essay its purpose.

The work of two women has become important in discussions of gender today, each of them trained in and informed by

[1] Michel Foucault, 'What is Enlightenment?' Catherine Porter, in *The Foucault Reader*, ed. Paul Rabinow (London: Penguin, 1987), p. 45.
[2] Donald D. Evans, *The Logic of Self-Involvement* (London: SCM, 1963).

philosophical study, each of them widely published and read in different ways as a voice of wisdom, and each touching upon matters that concern theology in its articulation of faith. My interest here is in drawing out of their work the assumptions that inform their thinking about gender and about being human, and in this analysis, to attend to what it is that is being said here about the form of human being – that form in which holiness is to come to dwell.

A Determined Performance

Martha Nussbaum's is the determined performance. Anyone who has heard her speak or encountered her quite prolific writings will have some indication of the tremendous energy and single-minded commitment that she gives to her thinking. She writes with conviction that a universal language of humanism is available to us, that the framework it provides for ethical and legal judgements is necessary in respect of the pluralism characteristic of our world, and that the deliberate reasoning it requires of individuals is to be the disciplined learning whereby we come to understand and to agree these things together. These three elements bear closer scrutiny, for within them lie the problematic of gender and the urgency of human being which Nussbaum's ethical writings in particular seek to address. She has been formulating the language of humanism throughout her investigations of philosophy, literature and law, and throughout her involvement in multicultural projects concerned with justice around the world. Among the ideas of what is human that are presented in diverse periods and cultures, she finds pattern emerging which she takes to be revealing of what is common to all human beings, and in which she recognises herself and the people of today's world, living and struggling with joys and sorrows that unite us in some sympathy across time and space. This conception of a common humanness appears by a process of inductive reasoning, being posited as the best explanation for the observable overlapping of interests and concerns experienced in a pluralistic world, and indeed claimed by Nussbaum herself to be 'the fruit of many years of collaborative international work'.[3] This becomes for her a concept in which each individual should be able to shelter, from whom protection of our basic humanity is expected, and with whose guidance those things that make and keep us human can be properly noticed and valued.

Variously called Aristotelian essentialism, neo-Stoicism, and Kantian liberalism, this humanism is for Nussbaum the most urgent requirement in the face of the fragmentation of human life into tribal particularities, and of the disrespect for the basic dignity of human beings that threatens the peace of the world. What is needed from this conception of ourselves, in which we recognise one another as human, is that it guide decisions regarding the courses of action by which that recognition can materialise in the circumstances and structures of our lives. This has become important to Nussbaum in the gender debate, for in the conception of common humanity, women and men know one another to be human in the same way, and may be helped to correct all those failures of proper recognition that still torment, devalue and diminish the humanity of women everywhere. The neo-Stoic character of her thinking is evident here in the insistence that gender does not belong with the essentials of our humanness, but is rather a distinction of our actual lives into which we are variously and arbitrarily socially constructed. The Kantian categorical imperative that both presumes and enacts human liberty accompanies this interpretation of gender, making it self-contradictory to use gender as a decisive reason in moral debates about persons, and encouraging that same sense of awe which Kant expressed for 'the starry sky above me, and the moral law within me'.[4] As for essentialism, Nussbaum translates Aristotle's naturalism into a scheme of human capabilities, the enhancement of which is the project of a global politics to secure. As she says, 'We cannot avoid having an account, even if a partial and highly general account, of what functions of the human being are most worth

---

[3] Martha Nussbaum, *Sex and Social Justice* (Oxford: Oxford University Press, 1999), p. 9.

[4] Nussbaum, *Sex*, p. 79. The quote is from the conclusion of Immanuel Kant, *Critique of Practical Reason*, and is attributed by Nussbaum originally to Seneca's *Moral Epistle* 40.

the care and attention of public planning the world over.'[5] This framework is intended therefore to order and prioritise social policies in such a way that human functioning may operate most smoothly within an efficient and just system of world government.

Nussbaum insists that this conception of our humanness and of its implications in understanding and leading our daily lives is the product of rational deliberation, for which each individual has a capability. It is thus the way of thinking that is most needed for a democracy, and the one she is most determined to demonstrate in the performance of her own arguments. There is in her writing an effort to lead us into this right thinking about our humanity, and a conviction that with this right approach to the problems before us, we will be able to resolve the tangled moral and political issues that trouble our times. Thus she writes of human beings as ones who 'participate (or try to) in the planning and managing of their own lives' and who 'wish to enact their thought in their lives – to be able to choose and to evaluate, and to function accordingly'.[6] Such, she explains, is one of the key functional capabilities that are generally derived from her reading of Aristotle. What is interesting about her development of this notion of reasoning is that it has neither the hierarchical nor the teleological ordering that were both necessary in the Aristotelian conception of *phronesis*, precisely the baggage that needs to be discarded if such an understanding of moral reasoning is to be acceptable in liberal discourse today. Whereas for Aristotle, such reasoning is the highest practice of our being human, whereby the other activities of our lives are to be directed towards their very enhancement and completion, for Nussbaum this reasoning appears in a flattened listing of capabilities one after another, taking its place among, and thus sharing the status of, the others, such as bodily health

[5] Nussbaum, *Sex*, p. 34. This chapter of the book incorporates material from her earlier essay 'Human Capabilities, Female Human Beings' in *Women, Culture and Development*, ed. M. Nussbaum and J. Glover (Oxford: Clarendon Press, 1993), which itself incorporates material from a number of earlier essays, including 'Human Functioning and Social justice: In Defense of Aristotelian Essentialism', in *Political Theory* 20 (2) (1992), pp. 202–46.

[6] Nussbaum, 'Human Capabilities', p. 78.

and integrity, emotions, affiliations, play, and control over one's environment. What this masks, however, is the way in which such reasoning is actually the fundamental requirement for the list of capabilities to be drawn up at all, and further, the way in which its appearance in a list of other important things renders its primary necessity for the fulfilment of one's being human, benign.

This has at least two implications which a critical reading of Nussbaum needs to draw out. She explains that practical reason means 'being able to form a conception of the good and to engage in critical reflection about the planning of one's own life'.[7] What her arguments reveal, however, is that a conception of the good is already being offered to us, is already determined, so that we are to understand the good to be that awesome highest value which both forms and guards the boundaries of our human living, and we are to come to be taught that its manifestations among us are here in the constitutive elements of human being that have already come to be figured in the list. The self-involving character of Aristotle's notion of practical reason, whereby I am to deliberate, to interpret, the features and experiences of my life, and in that being interpretative, am to ascend towards a conceiving of the good for which my life is purposed, this risky thinking in which my being human comes to be formed becomes, in Nussbaum's work, the requirement of an obedience to a posited highest value in which the universal human figure looms large. The point here is not that there is no room for individual freedom of judgement and decision, which is the besetting anxiety of liberalism, but rather that the logic of *phronesis* does not proceed from an indicative statement about what is good that is then to be applied as imperatives in particular situations and dilemmas. Moral reasoning for Aristotle is not to proceed by argumentation from principles to conclusions, no matter by what method the principles may be established. Indeed this may be deemed to be the most dangerous kind of thinking so far as formation in the character of human being is concerned, and because the whole of Nussbaum's effort recommends

---

[7] Nussbaum, *Sex*, p. 41.

precisely this kind of lawful functioning of the mind, our being human becomes a determined performance.

The second thing to notice here is how very intolerant, and proudly so, such a scheme becomes. On a number of occasions, Nussbaum refers to discussions in which her vision of essentialism is questioned or challenged by those who seek to affirm the value of difference, and specifically of different conceptions of what that highest value might be and what it might require in practice. Affirming the traditional values of differing cultures and letting 'the radical otherness' of divergent world-views be respected is one of those academically trendy manifestations of postmodern relativism that Nussbaum disdains,[8] and that she seeks to bring to order by her method of reasoning towards the one universal and defensible account of humanness. What she misses, however, in her attacks on these 'antiessentialist conversations' is the very extent to which her own presentation is only rendered possible within postmodernity and thus the way in which the postmodern speaks itself in her words, whatever she says. Such a raising up of the human being to fill the place of God, to generate the values by which its living is to be disciplined, and to regulate its practices so that everything functions efficiently, is precisely a consequence of the erasure of the horizon of transcendence and the appearance of all things human only as will to power. Nussbaum's writing is haunted by the disturbances to the system that might erupt through the failure of humanity to resign itself to its own true reality, and is driven by the urgency of teaching this wisdom to the foolish so that such resignation might be completed. Yet what makes this presentation possible at all is precisely the absence of any such convincing description of our situation, an absence that provides the space for the appearing of the powerful case she presents, but then disobediently lingers behind with disturbing reminders of human frailty.

As a theologian concerned with the enactment of love between humanity and God in which holiness is to matter, how much I am drawn to a careful attention to the problematic and the urgency disclosed in this humanism. It speaks from a desire

[8] Nussbaum, 'Human Functioning', see especially the opening section, pp. 202–5.

to know the truth and to be set free within it, and yet can only construct a scheme into a void, in the context of which its requirements seem, after all, to be good, or better than nothing, we might say. So the human being is to be bodied forth here, clothed with the essential functional capabilities in which it is best represented in the public forum, and is to find its place within the whole body of humanity, with whom it speaks in a common language, and amongst whom it learns to shape its individual expectations and needs so that the quality of life of the common body may be enhanced. In this flourishing of the body of humanity is the end for which we are told we are here, and for the promotion of which our actions are to be directed by reason. With what renewed insight then come the words of St Paul to me, as he enters the public arena in Athens to speak among the philosophers of the time in their seeking of truth.[9] How astonishing, indeed how deeply offensive, is his proclamation that such truth is now revealed in the displacement of a body. That he should draw us to a resurrection from the dead, and thus not to a qualitatively flourishing life; that he should speak of the call of one in whom a new thing is accomplished, and thus not a determined performance; that he should ask our reason to find itself at precisely the moment of its being utterly turned over – all of these speak an understanding of holiness in which the coming to matter of God in human form gives us to ourselves in another way.

'Hip Defeatism'?

Judith Butler's is the 'hip defeatism', or such is the charge of Nussbaum made against the one she calls 'the professor of parody' in a recent issue of *The New Republic*.[10] Butler is a professor in the department of Rhetoric and Comparative Literature at Berkeley, although it is not on this basis alone that Nussbaum would exclude her from the lofty ranks of philosophers, as a mere sophist or rhetorician.[11] Butler's writings in

---

[9] Acts 17.16–34.
[10] Martha C. Nussbaum, 'The Professor of Parody: The Hip Defeatism of Judith Butler', in *The New Republic*, 22 February 1999, pp. 37–45.
[11] Nussbaum, 'Professor', p. 40.

gender theory are marked by a distinctive style, by a startling conjunction of ideas, and by an intellectual courage both to attend to some of the most agonizing contemporary philosophical questions and to risk herself in the asking of them. Her work presents a way into the turn of modern thinking into its postmodern modes and, as such, is excitingly adventurous and unexpectedly disquieting. Widely known as the author of a book most appropriately called *Gender Trouble*,[12] Butler is a disturber of assumptions. Aside from Nussbaum's obvious irritation that Butler is being undeservedly praised as innovative, when in fact 'before Butler', as she repeatedly says, these things have been said and said more clearly, itself evidence of Nussbaum's own commitment to the originating subject – there is the more revealing challenge to Butler's 'quietism' that leaves politics behind, in favour of playful parodies and ironic gestures. It becomes plain in the course of Nussbaum's diatribe against a philosophy that simply cannot be serious unless it engages with law, that she has herself stopped short of the critical self-reflection into which Butler's thinking further takes us. While for Nussbaum, gender constructions are among the many accidents of the human situation that are to be kept in proper perspective by a guiding reason, for Butler, gender is understood to be the prevailing discourse into which the human being as subject is being constituted by modern thinking, and by which the human being has been inscribed into a text of sexual desire that informs the emergent subject in its self-representation. To give this attention to the problematic of gender and of the urgency to interpret the form of the human is for Butler to read the contemporary situation with a difference, a difference that bears on the matter of holiness before us today.

It is the case that one of the so-called unoriginal themes in Butler's writing is her development of the notion of the performative force of language, which she takes as a way of understanding not simply how an individual uses language to perform acts that make a difference in the world – the primary way in which J. L. Austin spoke of how we do things with

[12] Judith Butler, *Gender Trouble: Feminism and the Subversion of Identity* (London: Routledge, 1990).

words[13] – but more especially, how it is that language performs
the individual into the world. Thus Butler considers it
important to ask both what it is that is being performed in
speech-acts, such that the saying of something becomes its
doing, and what it is that that performing itself discloses.
There is for Butler here, following Wittgenstein and others
(like Ryle), no interest in speculation about the internal world
of the speaker to discover either the prior mental acts or that
ever-neurotic jumble of feelings, that might come to be
expressed in words, but rather an attention to the ways in
which language reveals what is commonly thought, and re-
situates or recites the speaker into these prevailing modes of
thinking. Language precedes me, and in this precedence lies
its hold over who it is that I come to understand myself to be,
and its openness to being spoken by me in new and interesting ways. 'Language,' she suggests, 'sustains the body not by
bringing it into being or feeding it in a literal way; rather, it is
by being interpellated within the terms of language that a
certain social existence of the body first becomes possible.'[14]
There is a mutuality in language evident in Butler's writings
that suggests the dependence of language upon my performing of it in various manifestations, and my dependence
upon it for the forms in which I come to know myself. In its
performative nature therefore, language is mutually disclosive
of what is understood it is to be human, and of myself within
this understanding, and it is mutually regulative in providing a
scheme of thinking in the grammar of which I come to be
identified, as I also twist it into the particular shapes of my
embodying of it.

So follows the understanding that there is a textual nature of
the world, of gender identity as it is inscribed into human flesh,
and of sexual desire as it finds expression and seeks satisfaction
in speech-acts. Nussbaum had already written disdainfully of
this 'planet known as Textualité' located 'somewhere in the vast
reaches of literary-theoretical space', and she keeps on trying to

[13] J. L. Austin, *How To Do Things With Words* (Oxford: Clarendon Press,
1962).
[14] Judith Butler, *Excitable Speech: A Politics of the Performative* (London:
Routledge, 1997), p. 5.

bring it back to the real world of materiality on planet Earth, for she says, if we choose 'to follow theory into our lives ... refusing to acknowledge what is common to all ... the texture of the human world will be differently perceived ... Then we will, I think, not *be* human beings any longer.'[15] Yes, quite. For Butler has consistently argued that the real world of materiality so-called is a work of interpretation in which matter comes to be disclosed in the ways of our understanding of it, and thus that what we say is 'real' or foundational in this understanding is performed into this place in our saying of it, and we cannot escape the circularity, the being-dependent-upon, of this thinking. Matter comes to matter, in our sensitivity to it and in its yielding to us, and in the mutuality of this beckoning is again the disclosure and the regulation that language performs in thinking and that I am also to be responsible for. This is what it is human to be, so that one finds Nussbaum's determinate conception of what that being already must be, has the effect of reducing me to a function. For Butler, the notion of what is real is beyond us, a most blunt acknowledgement of our finitude, by which it becomes plain that the positing of the really real is simultaneously a postmodern possibility into which the human will to exceed itself beyond finitude is being said, and a postmodern fiction in which the intensifying of the real in the disneyfication of the world everywhere re-enacts the founda-tional myth of modernity.[16] We can no more conjure up what is real or natural about being woman or man, than we can describe what is real or natural about sexual desire – or rather, in the conjuring up of these things is the very interpretative performance of our human being, that cannot acknowledge its own fragility, for fear, and in this is the profound self-deception of modern humanism.

In one of the passages that Nussbaum takes to be 'a mystifi-cation that eludes criticism because it makes few definite claims',[17] Butler writes of the consequences of this exposure of

---

[15] Nussbaum, 'Human Capabilities', p. 242, her emphasis.

[16] See, e.g., Jean Baudrillard, 'Simulacra and Simulations' tr. Paul Foss, Paul Patton and Philip Beitchman, in *Selected Writings*, ed. Mark Poster (Oxford: Blackwell, 1996), pp. 166–84.

[17] Nussbaum, 'Professor', p. 38.

the will to an identity that characterises humanism. For when we expose the human subject who comes to be represented in modernity, and when we ask what it is that is being disclosed and regulated in the thinking of this human subject, we encounter the workings of power. I understand Butler's to be an exposure of the taking of power by the human subject, who, in order to maintain itself in power, must assert the intrinsic value of its free agency and must demand conformity with this posited identity. In this process, however, is also a subjection, for the subject would not be recognisable at all, that is, represented either to itself or in the *polis*, and would not be capable of any agency at all, were it not to choose to submit to the regime in which its distinctiveness has been cast. Several times in the introduction to a most difficult book, *The Psychic Life of Power*,[18] Butler seeks expression of the problematic of subjection, revealed in the determinations of gender and of sexual desire, and she does so by asking questions that call forth my thinking.[19] She writes:

> What does it mean for the agency of a subject to *presuppose* its own subordination? Is the act of *presupposing* the same as the act of *reinstating*, or is there a discontinuity between the power presupposed and the power reinstated? Consider that in the very act by which the subject reproduces the conditions of its own subordination, the subject exemplifies a temporally based vulnerability that belongs to those conditions, specifically, to the exigencies of their renewal ... How is it that the power upon which the subject depends for existence and which the subject is compelled to reiterate turns against itself in the course of that reiteration? How might we think resistance within the terms of reiteration?[20]

[18] Judith Butler, *The Psychic Life of Power: Theories in Subjection* (California: Stanford University Press, 1997).

[19] Interestingly, it is precisely these questions that stimulate a thinking which Nussbaum finds 'teasing, exasperating', compared to her own didactic style of saying what is so. Indeed she is impatient with having to wait for this mind (Butler's) to 'pronounce', and feels 'bullied' into thinking 'there must be something significant going on'. Who, one wonders, is reinscribing herself as subject in these sayings, and into what? 'Professor', p. 39.

[20] Butler, *Psychic*, p. 12. Cf. similar passages on pp. 9 and 11.

Because such quietist hip defeatism 'offers support to an amoral anarchist politics',[21] Nussbaum is unable to appreciate the difference that lies in this struggle to articulate the place of hope. If I as theologian go on to say that it is precisely this place in which holiness is to begin, it will be of no consolation to Nussbaum's deepest suspicions of religious obfuscations. However, let us see what might begin to be said here.

Is Holiness to be Ungendered?

In Butler's questions, I find so many resonances with the language of St Paul as he seeks also to articulate what is the way of holiness, and as his words come to us through a tradition of interpreting the formation of the believer's life. For St Paul is in many ways appealing to the soul, understood as the exercise of our interpretative being, and stirring this soul awake into a faith in which the soul is to be most fully alive and most fully revealing of the God who gives it life. At times, he calls to the soul in his preaching and letters, and at times he reflects upon the soul as it hears and receives its vocation. In both, it seems to me that his words come close to these questions of Butler which have to do with the struggle of the soul, finding itself to be in the midst of power, or in Butler's terms to be caught up in chains of linguistic signification, which cannot be left behind at the same time as they seem to bind the soul against its own responding to its own most urgent vocation. Every bit of thinking in which it engages seems both to presuppose and to reinstate its being subject to that over which it cannot rise up to dominate, and yet that within which its very life has come to be enfleshed. Its presupposing of subjection is the same as its reinstating itself in subjection. So there appears, as Butler suggests, this 'temporally based vulnerability', or as St Paul says, this body of death,[22] which seems both to be the place of the soul's proper belonging as human, and its most pernicious obstacle to

---

[21] Nussbaum, 'Professor', p. 44.
[22] Romans 7:24 '*tou somatos tou thanatou toutou*'.

completion in the life of God. In what way is the soul to know its calling? In what way am I to find myself in God in these conditions of my living? For St Paul, it is in this place that Christ appears, and thus here that he begins to speak of the dislocation of the subject which takes place as the soul finds its own form to be that of Christ. For Butler to ask whether there is 'a discontinuity between the power presupposed and the power reinstated' is precisely to attend to that moment, that gap, that opening, in which the subject might be dislodged for the birth of a soul into God. For St Paul to say that this is the place in which I am continually to interpret myself as one who lives 'in Christ' is to hold open that gap into which holiness comes to be born in me.

There is too in Butler's work a concern to interpret what is the law that governs humanity in our time, and in this interpretation to seek for the ways of resistance. In particular, she has investigated the workings of the regime of gender and the matrix of heterosexual desire into which the modern human subject has come to be represented, and to which it now finds itself in subjection. There is in the operation of this law a compulsion to repeat it even as there is a dependence upon it for what is deemed to be distinctive human identity, a repetitious circle of thinking. So her question is again poignant – how is it that the power of this law turns against itself in the course of its reiteration? In her words, 'How might we think resistance within the terms of reiteration?' Could this be more plainly the question with which St Paul has to do, as he considers that law which is at work in himself, and asks in what way its hold on his life is to be broken, for its very commandments further consign him to the limits of its terms? Could this be more plainly the question of an expectation that must be thought by a soul, in the thinking of which it begins to find the end of its life in the fullness of divine love? How might we think this resistance which is grace with the terms of our constructed lives? What Butler calls 'politics' takes place here, as we enter into uses of language that subvert this law, into speech-acts that undermine its authority as they parody its requirements, and in this is a refusal of the horizon which this law erects and sustains as necessary by its powerful presence. Our task is, as she says, 'to refigure this necessary "outside" as a future horizon, one in which the violence of exclusion is perpetually in the process of being overcome'.[23] Such a future is what the good news of the coming of God in Christ is to proclaim, and in the saying of it and in the living from it, is to be the holiness that transgresses, that breaks open the hold of law. To perform this holiness is ever to sit uncomfortably with the political demand to reinstate law of some kind, and to enact, again and again, this holding open of the future for the coming of God. This is the delicate and fragile place of a holiness that lives from beyond itself, which is taken out of itself in Christ, and re-sited/recited into God.

Finally it is from Butler that the word mattering has come to be newly significant.[24] Butler's work with the notion of 'bodies that matter' is a demythologising of the ontology that lies within conceptions of what is natural, as these are explained and gain credence in modern biology, and as these come to be fixed in notions of what is woman and what is man, and of what it is that is sexual desire. Such thinking on her part consistently resists the power of this naturalism, which is set up to provide the bearings for our understanding, and in the process confines that understanding to its requirements. In postmodern times, we are already aware however of the void into which such naturalistic thinking is performed and of the effort it requires to insist upon its own necessity. Butler's suggestion is to think of bodies not as some prior existing empirical matter to which our understanding and our freedom is bound, but rather as their effect. Bodies are what come to matter in our interpreting of them. In our thinking and speaking they come to be represented in ways that are disclosive and regulative, and in this is the mutuality that characterises the human way of being as interpretative. Is this too a way into the language of St Paul? For he appears to be speaking of prior existing matter or flesh, and so seems to be requiring of us an ontology before we can understand our faith. Yet is not the flesh, and certainly is not the body, for him too, the effect of an interpretation rather than its cause? Thus is not the challenge

[23] Butler, *Bodies That Matter: On the Discursive Limits of Sex* (London: Routledge, 1993), p. 53.

[24] See also Helen Oppenheimer, 'Mattering', in *Studies in Christian Ethics* 8:1 (1995), pp. 60–76.

of that faith of which he speaks, the challenge of finding the flesh and blood we are given to be taken out of themselves and given back to us again in the purest charity? Our bodies are to be turned into love, and to come to matter as this love, and nothing else. If this might be a recitation of words deep within the Christian tradition, then we are brought in the thinking of holiness to the very matter of our lives. Holy living is the coming to matter in my life of the grace of God's coming to matter in Christ, and in the dislocation of the subject and the transgression of law which this mediates, God comes to be born anew in my flesh.

20

The Communion of Saints and Other
Religions: On Saintly Wives in
Hinduism and Catholicism

Gavin D'Costa

'Saints' and 'Holiness' as Interreligious Concepts?

The Roman Catholic theologian, Elizabeth Stuart, is not alone
in suggesting that canonisation be extended to include Hindus
and Protestants:

> [T]he growth in ecumenical and multi-faith consciousness
> within the Roman Catholic Church does not seem to have
> touched the canonization process. The offence that the
> promotion of [Edith] Stein's canonization causes to many
> Jews is simply ignored, as are arguments which first began to
> be formulated in the 1960s in the wake of Vatican II for the
> opening up of the process to include non-Catholics, like
> Dietrich Bonhoffer and Martin Luther King, and non-
> Christians such as Gandhi. The Church may no longer
> declare that 'outside the Church there is no salvation', but
> this is not borne out in its lists of saints. The canonization
> process is one of the many indications, but perhaps the
> clearest, that at the end of the twentieth century the Vatican
> is little changed except perhaps in a few externals from the
> Vatican of the beginning of the twentieth century.'[1]

---

[1] E. Stuart, *Spitting at Dragons. Towards a Feminist Theology of Sainthood*
(London: Mowbray, 1996), p. 34.

421

I disagree with Stuart on a number of points. While Anglicans have been generous enough to honour the Roman Catholic Archbishop Oscar Romero as a martyr, in the beautiful stone carvings at the entrance to Westminster Abbey in London (even though the Roman Catholic Church has not pronounced him a martyr – thereby making this a dubious ecumenical gesture), I cannot deal with Christian ecumenism and saints in this present essay. I want to stick with Stuart's question about canonising a Hindu. At the level of formal canonisation I do not think Stuart's proposal at all appropriate. This is not because there are any lack of very holy Hindus, or because the Roman Catholic Church has any problems with affirming that holiness, truth and grace exist outside its visible social boundaries. Vatican II made the latter quite clear. My main objection would be on the grounds that canonisation is an *intra-ecclesial act* retrospectively identifying a person whose life conforms to, but more often extends and sometimes problematises, the understanding of the orthodox Christian faith in terms of practice, doctrine and liturgy. Such a person is also the object of the cult of veneration, whereby the faithful grow in the Roman Catholic faith through active communion with that saint. Authentic active veneration has tended to be judged by the number of miracles performed by the saint/candidate. One point of canonisation, at least as argued in the Second Vatican Council, is to link the earthly church with the heavenly church: Roman Catholic saints are embodiments of the presence of the risen Christ within his Church; their holiness is the extension of the story about God's holiness in the ecclesial body of Christ.

Hence, in my view, to canonise Gandhi, or the present Dalai Lama once he has died, as some advocate, would be a gross act of imperialism, if not downright historical falsification. I imagine that the offence caused to some Jews, cited by Stuart, regarding the canonisation of the Jewish-born Roman Catholic convert, Edith Stein, would also be paralleled in some Hindu and Buddhist groups were Gandhi and the Dalai Lama declared saints. No doubt the Chinese government would also protest at the Dalai Lama being canonised, even if their disagreement would be for very different reasons. Admittedly, to some of the BJP party in India, Gandhi's canonisation would simply confirm their suspicions that he had betrayed Hinduism.

Four issues emerge from all this. First, Gandhi and the Dalai

Lama are not Roman Catholics and did not choose to be, and in that sense it would be unacceptable to call them saints in the technical liturgical sense. (Of course, all I am saying about the Dalai Lama is subject to correction, since he is alive at the time of writing this essay.) Secondly, one needs to acknowledge that the list of saints does contain men and women who were not baptised as Christians, such as Mary's mother and father, Anna and Joachim. However, these cases are *sui generis* and relate to the special relation between Christians and Jews. Thirdly, if Roman Catholics deem Gandhi and the Dalai Lama to be holy, it is open to discussion as to how, if at all, such figures might be acknowledged liturgically. Finally, and perhaps more fundamentally, what precisely is involved in deeming such non-Christians 'holy'? I want to address this final question for the rest of this paper, admitting straightaway that I have no clear answer.

Following the growth of the history of religions one finds numerous books and studies that assume saintliness and holiness are 'trans-religious' concepts, or 'cross-religious' concepts.[2] By trans-religious, I mean a concept of holiness that the researcher creates, or at least assumes as universal, and then finds among many different religions, thereby often running against the self-interpretation of the said saint, and their tradition. This is true of Rudolf Otto, and William James, as it is of John Hick, and even postmodernist writers, who should know better, such as Edith Wyschogrod.[3] By 'cross-religious', I mean a tradition-specific notion of holiness, such as found in neo-Hinduism or liberal Roman Catholicism, which then finds parallels, or mirror-reflections, within other traditions. Karl Rahner supported such a theological history of religions. While I am far more sympathetic with the 'cross-religious' approach, it still often faces the problem of running into conflict with the self-description of the valorised saint and his or her community. However, it is sometimes the case that a Catholic saint-*type* might well be found within Hinduism, and that person would

[2] See, for example John Stratton Hawley, ed., *Saints and Virtues* (Berkeley: University of California Press, 1987).

[3] See E. Wyschogrod, *Saints and Postmodernism: Revisioning Moral Philosophy* (Chicago: Chicago University Press, 1990).

also be seen as a saintly example of holiness within their own tradition. Alternatively, that which Hindus might proclaim saintly, may be found to be deeply questionable by some Roman Catholics. It is at this metaphoric conjunction of two different streams of 'holiness' that some of the most interesting flotsam appears.

For the rest of this paper I want to look at the streams and the flotsam, not in any hope of answering the many difficult questions raised, but in the hope that their precise difficulties may become more apparent. I shall look at the life of a Hindu *devi* and Christian saint, Roop Kanwar and Edith Stein respectively, remembering that such designations – 'saint' or *'devi'* – are contested from within and from outside each particular tradition. Roop Kanwar, the Hindu good and holy wife, is according to many a *devi*, a female goddess.[4] I should also add that the government of India and the State of Rajasthan have outlawed veneration to Roop Kanwar, this Hindu *devi*. Our Roman Catholic 'good wife', Edith Stein, is technically a saint. She was beatified on 1 May 1987 in Germany, and canonised by Pope John Paul II in Rome on 11 October 1998; and many Jews and Catholics are outraged by her canonisation. Hence, I proceed with some trepidation, as I fear that some feminists, along with some Hindus, Jews and also Christians may find some of what follows offensive, for differing and sometimes overlapping reasons. However, being 'holy' has always been offensive to some, for it touches our deepest fears, taboos and fantasies.

Roop Kanwar – the Hindu devi?

Roop Kanwar, an eighteen-year-old Rajput woman, is venerated by many Hindus as a saint, as a female goddess (*devi*), capable of showering blessings upon those who visit the site of her 'heroic'

---

[4] *Devi* is the general term for a goddess: the feminine form of *deva*, a god or celestial power. In the earliest texts (*Rg Vedas*) the term is used to refer to the wives of the gods, or to parts of religious worship personified as goddesses (see II, 1; II, 11 for example). Only in the post-Vedic period does the term become used for *the* Goddess and also then becomes used for the many local goddesses of the *Siva* pantheon.

death in Rajasthan in September 1987. At an analogical level of comparison, she fulfils the three general criteria of canonisation within Catholicism (if they were applicable to Hinduism – which they are not, not least because in Hinduism there is no central structural authority that could adopt such a process):

1. doctrinal orthodoxy, even though contested by the local and national government, and by various orthodox and liberal Hindus;
2. heroic virtue, likewise contested;
3. now actively venerated, even while legally banned.

That there should be such controversy over her veneration is hardly surprising. One should recall that Joan of Arc was burnt by one group of church theologians, while another group from the same church would later canonise her. Roop Kanwar, according to Mary Daly, was burnt by patriarchal Hinduism and could only be valorised by a religion which exalted cruelty towards women.[5] Roop Kanwar was, by the majority of eye-witness accounts, and by those who knew her, a woman who *voluntarily* undertook *sati*. Her death, which I regard as tragic and horrific, finds its orthodox defence in the eighteenth-century text, *Stridharmapaddhat. Guide to the Religious Status and Duties of Women*, written by the Hindu orthodox pandit, Tryambakayajvan, who employs Sanskrit religious law to show why *sati* allows a woman to become truly virtuous. Tryambakayajvan's treatise was written for the royal court of Thanjavar (Tanjore), South India.[6] In what follows I present *one* reading of Kanwar's death through the constructs of Tryambakayajvan. There are no first-hand accounts from Kanwar. Her relatives, family and eye-witnesses to her death all testify to Kanwar's voluntary self-immolation. I shall assume this to be so, at least for the purpose of the comparison that I undertake.

Sati is the death of a woman with her (dead) husband on his funeral pyre. ('Widow burning' is an incorrect rendition, as the *sati* chooses other than 'widowhood', for she is not technically

---

[5] M. Daly, *Gyn/Ecology. The Metaethics of Radical Feminism* (London: The Women's Press, 1978), ch. 3.

[6] Throughout, I rely exclusively on Julia Leslie's translation of Tryambakayajvan in *The Perfect Wife: The Orthodox Hindu Woman According to the Stridharmapaddhati of Tryambakavajivan* (Delhi: Oxford University South Asian Series, Oxford University Press, 1989).

a widow until the funeral pyre is lit.) Etymologically, *sati* is the feminisation of the Sanskrit word, *'sat'*, which means 'true, real, good' and even 'virtuous'. It is also connected both etymologically and emblematically with the goddess *Sati*, wife of *Siva*, who kills herself – but in such differing circumstances that David Kinsley rightly says: 'It is not altogether clear, however, that *Sati's* suicide provides the mythological paradigm for suttee.'[7]

Five qualifications are necessary before outlining Tryambakayajvan's arguments. First, the politics of describing this tradition has been rightly criticised: both as potentially defamatory to Hinduism; and in its misogynistic voyeurism. Mary Daly suggests that this type of hagiography is pornography. I cannot claim any detached status in writing this. I have deep respect for aspects of Hinduism, as well as many questions. No Hindu friend of mine seeks to defend this tradition. I find *sati* deeply abhorrent and believe that Daly is partly right in her analysis: it reflects Hindu patriarchy's destruction of women; but is there something more to be explored? I do not believe that the practice can be dismantled until the full power of its ideology is revealed and understood. Secondly, the history of the practice is complex, as is the question of the number of women who have died in this manner. It is a dangerous form of scholarship to pretend that this religious saintly 'ideal' for women can be divorced from forced *sati*, for which there is ample horrific evidence, or that it can be divorced from dowry murders, female infanticide, child brides, and abortions of female foetuses. Neither can it be divorced from the fact that the legal Hindu tradition, like most religions including Christianity, has been constructed by men. Thirdly, *sati* is now illegal in India (since the 1829 Suttee Regulation Act), and was strongly opposed by some orthodox Hindus throughout Hindu history, and also in the present day. Fourthly, in modern India there are many women and men who still regard *sati* as an act of heroic virtue. Julia Leslie writes:

---

[7] D. Kinsley, *Hindu Goddesses. Visions of the Divine Feminine in the Hindu Religious Tradition* (Berkeley: University of California Press, 1986), p. 40. For a fuller account of the variant myths, see Wendy Doniger O'Flaherty, *Siva. The Erotic Ascetic* (Oxford: Oxford University Press, 1973). O'Flaherty properly makes the connection that Kinsley misses: incest.

'*sati* remains as an ideal. While the numbers of women who died in this way have always been statistically small, the ideal of such women and such a death is reverenced throughout traditional India today.'[8]

Roop Kanwar's case is a clear example of such reverence. Many Hindus from all castes proclaimed her a goddess (*devi*). However, soon after her death, 3000 women marched in Jaipur in protest with banners proclaiming: 'A woman's murder is a challenge to the entire sex.' Some weeks later at a pro-*sati* rally in Jaipur, 70,000 men, women and children marched together, proclaiming Kanwar a *devi*, and an estimated $3 million was collected at the meeting for a shrine to venerate Kanwar. *The Times*[9] estimated that over two hundred thousand people all over India defied the government ban to honour her death and deification.

My exploration is into the logic of the *dharma* that is behind such veneration, or to put it differently, an attempt to understand *sati* intra-textually. This is not an attempt to justify it. I have chosen the most difficult example of 'saintliness' within Hinduism that I could think of because it raises such difficult questions, and makes for some painful comparisons.

In as brief and non-technical a manner possible, I now want to outline the basic argument advanced by Tryambakayajvan, who cites numerous older legal Sanskrit texts and scriptures, and whose methodology is not unlike that of the medieval disputation. The work is extremely orthodox both in the authorities cited, and the methodology employed. It is divided into five sections: introduction and parameters to the study; a detailed list of the duties of the Hindu wife (the only path of sanctification for a woman in Tryambakayajvan's view); an outline of the inherent nature of women; the duties of all women (as sisters, friends and the other roles they might play) – where the discussion of *sati* takes place; and finally, stories and quotations about women. The basic position is contextualised in terms of cosmic righteousness, the *dharma*, that if followed by men and women in their different roles, will result

---

[8] J. Leslie, 'Suttee or Sati: Victim or Victor?', in J. Leslie, ed., *Roles and Rituals for Hindu Women* (London: Pinter Publishers, 1991), pp. 175–9 [p. 176].
[9] 17 September 1987.

in social and cosmic harmony. Things were once in such harmony, and the stories of the virtuous wives of gods are set in this golden epic period, before human history began. The proper role of a woman is to be a devoted wife (*pativrata*), and that of the man, a devoted and righteous husband – until his wife dies. He is then able to pursue his dharma as a forest dwelling ascetic (*vanaprasthya*), prior to the final stage of total renunciation (*sannyasi*). *Sati* comes into play if the husband dies first. His life can be defined without his wife, if she dies first. The symmetry is not exact.

Hindu *dharma* entails an extremely complicated set of duties, set out for every caste group and each sex in all stages of development. Tryambakayajvan outlines two possibilities for the woman whose husband dies before her: *sati*, dying with one's husband, which he sees as the preferable route; or widowhood (*vidhavadharma*), which has numerous duties analogous to the celibate ascetic first stage of the man (*brahmacarya*). In his advocacy of *sati* Tryambakayajvan makes some very important points, so that *sati* can be understood appropriately. First, *sati* is to be distinguished from suicide, and therefore does not break the legal prohibition of suicide in Hindu law. It is distinguished along the same lines that the warrior who fights in a righteous battle, and knows that he will be killed, is not thereby guilty of suicide, but is rather virtuously (like the famous Arjuna of the *Bhagavad Gita*) following his proper *dharma*. The warrior, like the widow, must not fear death, for in doing their duty courageously, they will be reborn in a higher form, to be eventually released from the *karmic* cycle. (At the Roop Kanwar rally, a spokesman for the demonstration criticised those who oppose only *sati*, and not other religious forms of 'suicide': 'Jains are known to die by fasting. Buddhists are known to immolate themselves. So why apply this law only to us?'[10] He was referring to a by-law introduced in Rajasthan (in 1987) after the Kanwar case to fine and imprison surviving *satis*, and apply the death penalty to those abetting the practice.)

Secondly, all ritual actions accrue merit, normally for the one undertaking the action. There are three types of ritual action:

---

[10] I. Badhwar, 'Kalyan Sing Kalvi: Beliefs Cannot be Repressed', *India Today*, 31 October 1987, p. 20.

obligatory (*nitya*) ones that are performed daily, e.g., praying; occasional ones that must be performed (*naimittika*) such as on the occasion of marriage; and optional (*kamyaa*) ones that need not be performed, except to gain the merit accorded to that action. For Tryambakayajvan, *sati* is in the latter category. In Tryambakayajvan's eyes, any forced *sati* would not be *sati* at all. While he is pessimistic about the widow's capability of living properly as a widow, due to the supposed nature of women, he is clear that only those who aspire towards the ideal will be capable of *sati*. The alleged voluntarism of the act has been severely criticised: 'If a woman does not have the right to choose whether she wants to marry, and when, and whom, how far she wants to study, whether she wants to take a particular job or not, how is it that she suddenly gets the right to take such a major decision as whether she wants to die?'[11]

This criticism misses one important point – that her choice is not a right, but a matter of following two possible duties. Within the *dharma* there is no place for 'rights' outside of these duties. Similarly, regarding the question of rights, a man has none outside his duties. The important difference between men and women here is that a husband has no such *sati* option. However, one should remember that consistently within the *dharma* there is no attempted 'equality' between caste or genders, for righteousness is served in following the duties prescribed. Equality is an extremely modern ideology. Hence, *intra-systematically*, *sati* is an optional ritual to which is ascribed considerable, if not unique, merit, both for the woman and for her husband, and both their families.

Thirdly, it is this unique transferential merit that gets us to the *dharmic* core of *sati* (at least in its Hindu orthodox intra-systematic sense), and it is an important exception to the Hindu law of *karma*/merit, which normally holds that all actions can reap good or bad merit by one who undertakes the action. Normally, one must undergo the consequences of such action, and only through compensation and reparation for one's wrong actions (through fasting, doing ritually merito-rious acts, etc.), can one eventually attain release (*moksha*). The

---

[11] K. Madhu and V. Ruther, *In Search of Answers: Indian Women's Voices from Manushi* (London: Zed Books, 1987), p. 21.

merit due to the *sati* is threefold. First, the woman's ritualised act of righteous devotion releases her from all bad merit that she has accrued during her life. Clearly, the good wife who is defined by doing her duties, which include obeying her husband, will have less incentive to atone for her own wrong-doings. On the other hand, and secondly, a bad wife has every reason to perform *sati*, for this will be a definitive chance to purify herself. Tryambakayajvan puts it clearly, indicating that intentionality and consequence are not unilaterally identified:

> Women who, due to their wicked minds, have always despised their husbands (while they were alive) and behaved disagreeably towards them, and who none the less perform the ritual act of dying with their husbands when the time comes – whether they do this of their own free will, or out of anger, or even out of fear – all of them are purified of sin.[12]

The latter two causes (anger and fear) can certainly conspire towards forced *sati*, but it is clear that Tryambakayajvan is not intending to support these forms of *sati*, for his argument is precisely to extol the free choice of *sati* because it is *dharmically*, intra-textually, coherent and attractive in securing righteousness in the world. For Tryambakayajvan, *sati* has the quality of 'sufficient atonement' (*prayascitta*) for the deeds of the bad wife. As one of the epic husbands puts it, in a dialogue cited by Tryambakayajvan: 'it is through the merit of being a devoted wife that a woman attains the highest heaven. If she does not do this, even if she has bathed in all the sacred places, she will go to hell.'[13] The ritual efficacy of this atoning act is extremely powerful, for it easily outdoes the ritual efficacy of bathing in sacred places, which is usually enough to cancel out some serious shortcomings.

The third and most significant meritorious aspect is the transferential merit gained for the husband, by the wife's *sati*. This is quite extraordinary, for normally, as we have seen with the first two points above, merit is strictly accrued by the one who undertakes the ritual act. Around 700 CE, this exception is

---

[12] Sdhp. 43r.7–9; Leslie, *Roles*, p. 186.
[13] Sdhp. 44r.3–6; Leslie, *Roles*, p. 186.

introduced into the tradition. The *sati atones* for the sins of her husband and has the power, in her action, to release him from the fires of hell (a provisional, not eternal hell). In earlier texts, it is clear that this atoning power also applies to the wider families in the marriage and to those who visit the shrines of such *devi*. Tryambakayajvan cites many texts. Here is one showing the extent of the *sati*'s atoning power. One begins to understand why the Rajput crowd (who support *sati*) want to venerate Kanwar as a *devi*. Her self-sacrificial love of duty breaks the bounds of hell, as through her free act, she liberates her husband, even if he is a brahmin-killer (clearly a most heinous crime):

> Even in the case of a husband who has entered into hell itself and who, seized by the servants of Death and bound with terrible bonds, has arrived at the very place of torment; even if he is already standing there, helpless and wretched, quivering with fear because of his evil deeds; even if he is a brahmin-killer or the murderer of a friend, or if he is ungrateful for some service done for him – even then a woman who refuses to become a widow can purify him: in dying, she takes him with her.[14]

Or with more dramatic and succinct force, Tryambakayajvan cites another verse: 'Just as the snake-catcher drags the snake from its hole by force, even so the virtuous wife (*sati*) snatches her husband from the demons of hell and takes him up to heaven.'[15] It is this force of virtue which defies the demons of hell that make the *sati* capable of bestowing blessings upon those who visit her shrine. As one Indian woman is reported to have said, when attending the Kanwar pro-*sati* rally: '*sati* is not possible for all women, only those who are very blessed. I have come here for the blessings of this holy place.'[16]

Tryambakayajvan touches on lots of other interrelated matters, which I cannot pursue here. What is so startling about the intra-textual logic of his exposition of the *dharma* is the positioning of *sati* as heroic virtue, whereby the freely

---

[14] Sdhp. 43r.4–5.; Leslie, *Roles*, p. 185.
[15] Sdhp. 43r.4–5.; Leslie, *Roles*, p. 185.
[16] *The New York Times*, 19 September 1987.

undertaken self-sacrifice of a woman is able to atone for her sins, for the sins of her husband and for the sins of others, both her family and relatives who know her and her devotees who never knew her. The good woman has soteriological power. This transferential merit, which seems to break most normal *karmic* rules, is what constructs the ideal holy and good woman. In the midst of an apparently horrific misogyny, women suddenly are able to be saviours, victors, saints, and not victims – even if, tragically, only in their willingness to die. For one single moment, the woman becomes (in Julia Leslie's words) 'victor'; in *sati* 'victims find a path through a maze of oppression, a path that to them spells dignity and power'.[17] Leslie refuses to glorify this dignity, holiness and power; but neither does she simply dismiss it as does Mary Daly.

What is so disturbing, although so very different, is a similar or analogous intra-textual logic of transferential merit displayed in the life of some Christian saints. Here again we see women within a predominantly male-constructed theological tradition, attaining sainthood via death – which is at some level freely chosen, and at some level reflecting the soteriological power of the good woman, the saint, the faithful bride of Christ.

Edith Stein – a Catholic Saint

One of the most controversial elements of the Jewish convert Edith Stein's canonisation, was the transferential merit she accorded to her death. If Kanwar died for her own sins, her husband's, and their families', the Carmelite nun Edith Stein viewed her death, which she did not desire but could not avoid, as an atonement for her own sins, the sins of the church, the German people – and the sins of the Jewish people (of whom she was one). Elizabeth Stuart indicates how her canonisation caused international protest within the Jewish community. Stuart was not the only Roman Catholic or Christian to be outraged by Stein's canonisation either.[18] But first, let me

[17] Leslie, *Roles*, p. 177.
[18] For example, see H. J. Cargas, ed. *The Unnecessary Problem of Edith Stein* (Lanham: University Press of America, 1994).

briefly outline the relevant contours of Edith Stein's life which allow us to see the significant analogies between Stein and Kanwar. She, like Roop Kanwar, was claimed to exemplify orthodox doctrine and practice to an extraordinary degree, was venerated by some groups, and seen as a shining example of a woman mediating soteriological power. On all these three counts, there was, as with Kanwar, intra-tradition dissent as well as extra-tradition dissent.

I shall sketch some biographical moments within her life, using at times some of Stein's own commentary. Edith Stein was born in 1891, the seventh child of a well-to-do practising Jewish family. She was born on Yom Kippur, the Jewish day of atonement, which Stein's mother saw as auspicious, as did Stein. Later, Edith would see her life as an atonement for Jewish disbelief – among other sins of the world. Her father died when she was three. At the age of 15, she declared herself an atheist, without religion. She was intellectually outstanding among her peers. During 1913–15 she studied at the University of Göttingen, under Husserl. Husserl's young colleagues, Adolf Reinach, Roman Ingarden and Max Scheler were Jews who became Roman Catholics. (Pope John Paul II was to discuss Scheler in his doctoral work and was a personal friend of Ingarden.) Stein recalls that what impressed her most about Catholicism was its teachings on marriage. She very much desired to be married, and eventually would be: as a bride of Christ, by taking sacred vows and holy orders in the Carmelite tradition. She, like Roop Kanwar, would find in her husband the image of God, and would seek to follow him everywhere, even through death. Two important events happen in Stein's life during the First World War. The first is her doctoral dissertation under Husserl, written on empathy. Still an atheist, she is able to empathise with the notion of religious sacrifice.[19] The second event was the death of Reinach on the Western front. Anna Reinach's consolation in the cross shook Edith, who had

---

[19] 'I myself may be an infidel and yet understand that someone else may sacrifice all his earthly possessions for his faith. Thus I acquire by empathy the concept of *homo religiosus*, and though it is alien to my thinking, I understand him.' E. Stein, *On the Problem of Empathy*, tr. Waltraut Stein, 3rd edn. (Washington DC: Institute of Carmelite Studies Publications, 1989), p. 114.

gone to sort out Adolf's philosophical papers at the request of his widow. Edith notes this as her turning point: 'This was my first encounter with the Cross and the divine strength it imparts to those who carry it. It was the moment when my unbelief collapsed. Judaism paled and Christ shone forth; Christ in the mystery of the cross.'[20] The transferential merit of the cross, and the participative redemptive suffering undertaken freely by those who follow the groom, would become increasingly central for Stein.

On 1 January 1922, Stein was baptized into the Roman Catholic Church taking on the name of Teresa, after Teresa of Avila, for it was the Carmelite life that attracted her greatly. Her mother was devastated, and Stein was advised not to enter the order in deference to her mother's hurt. She lived with nuns and continued a formal philosophical education, turning to the study of Aquinas, women's education and spirituality. In 1933 the Nazi's enacted anti-Semitic laws and Edith's teaching position at Münster ended. Seeing the course of anti-Semitic currents, she seeks an audience with Pius XII, but fails. Instead she wrote to him; he did not directly reply to her questions but instead sent her his blessings. In 1933, she writes that during the Holy Hour at the Carmel of Cologne-Lindenthal:

> I spoke to our Saviour and told Him that I knew that it was His Cross that was being laid on the Jewish people. Most did not understand it, but those who did understand must accept it willingly in the name of all. I wanted to do that. Let Him only show me how. When the service was over I had an interior conviction that I had been heard. But in what the bearing of the Cross was to consist I did not yet know. I was almost relieved to find myself now involved in the common fate of my people.[21]

Edith always considered herself Jewish, so it is clear that she feels this cross is hers in a double sense: being Jewish, and being Catholic. This is important for a proper sense of her understanding of transferential merit. Eventually, the pull of Carmel was too strong, and she applied for admission, was accepted,

---

[20] *Inside the Vatican*, October 1998, p. iv.
[21] *Inside the Vatican*, p. vii.

and returned to tell her family – and mother. This was to prove as painful, if not more, than sharing the news of her conversion to Catholicism. After going to the synagogue together on 12 October 1933, she agrees with her mother that the sermon was 'beautiful' and that Jews can be pious and devout – if they have not yet learnt about Jesus. Stein writes that her decision to enter Carmel is incomprehensible to her mother and most of the family, but not her sister Rosa, who would eventually be baptised and perish together with Edith. In her clothing ceremony on 15 April 1934, Edith takes on the name Teresa Benedicta of the Cross. Of this name, she writes retrospectively in 1938:

> By the cross I understood the destiny of God's people which, even at that time, began to announce itself. I thought that those who recognized it as the Cross of Christ had to take it upon themselves in the name of all. Certainly, today I know more of what it means to be wedded to the Lord in the sign of the Cross. Of course, one can never comprehend it, for it is a mystery.[22]

The theme of Edith taking on suffering for the atonement of others, especially the Jews, becomes stronger and stronger as Nazi anti-Semitism grows around her. This understanding is also connected with her marriage to Christ, for the cross is the seal of the marriage. She must follow her groom into death if necessary, and her death will then be an atonement for others, especially the Jewish people. In 1938 she uses the image of Queen Esther from the biblical book of Esther to construct her own self-image. She writes of the 'shadow of the Cross which is falling on' her people. She trusts:

> in the Lord's having accepted my life for all of them. I keep having to think of Queen Esther who was taken from her people precisely that she might represent them before the king. I am a very poor and powerless Esther, but the King who chose me is infinitely great and merciful.[23]

Three years before she was murdered in Auschwitz on Thursday 9 August 1942, she wrote on 9 June 1939 a passage

---

[22] *Inside the Vatican*, p. ix.
[23] *Inside the Vatican*, p. ix.

that further elaborates this theme. One should note in this quote three important points: first, that her marriage to Jesus means her joyful acceptance of her own death; second, that her own death will be redemptive to others; third, these others will be Christians and Jews. The bride's death ensures transferential merit.

> Even now I joyfully accept the death which God has destined for me, in total submission to His most holy will. I beg the Lord to accept my life and my death for His honour and glorification, for all desires of the most holy hearts of Jesus and Mary and the Holy Church, and especially for the preservation, sanctification and perfection of our Holy Order, particularly the Carmel in Cologne and in Echt, for *the atonement of the unbelief of the Jewish people and for this: that the Lord may be accepted by his own people* and that His Kingdom may come in glory, for the salvation of Germany and for world peace, and finally for my relatives both living and dead, and all those whom God has given me: that none of them may perish.[24]

While many critics have found in this quote evidence of her alleged anti-Semitic attitude and her replication of the myth of Jewish hard-heartedness, this citation cannot properly be read in this manner. Her incomplete autobiography, *Life in a Jewish Family*, gives an account of her own Jewish family life in an attempt to present the normal human face of ordinary Jews in the light of the 'horrendous caricature' that drives Hitler and the Nazi party.[25] For those who think that Stein was negative about Judaism, her comment on her mother is instructive: 'Her faith and trust in God remained unshaken from her earliest childhood and was her last support in her hard struggle with death. I am confident that she has found a most merciful Judge, and that she is now my most faithful helper on my own journey toward my homeland.'[26] Edith is simply concerned to take upon

---

[24] *Inside the Vatican*, p. x, my emphasis.

[25] E. Stein, *Life in a Jewish Family: Her Unfinished Autobiographical Account*, tr. J. Koppel, (Washington DC: ICS Publications, 1986), p. 23. She neither romanticises nor defames the community she knew through her childhood and her mother's piety is both revered and respected.

[26] *Inside the Vatican*, p. ix.

herself the sins of the world, specified in terms of her own historical context.

By 1936 Stein completed two important works: one on Husserl and Aquinas; and the other, *Life in a Jewish Family.* In 1936, her mother dies, at the very moment when Edith renews her vows in the Cologne Carmel. After her mother dies, Rosa joined her and was baptized. In 1938 Edith takes her final vows, and in December of that year moves to Holland, concerned for the safety of the other nuns because of her Jewish roots. Above, I cited a vital passage from 1939, whereby we see Edith connecting her death and atonement. This theme becomes very central in these last days.

On 26 July 1942, after the Archbishop of Utrecht ordered a denunciation of the Nazi treatment of Jews to be read in all Dutch Roman Catholic churches, the Nazis ordered a round-up of all Jewish converts. Records show that the Nazis promised not to touch converts if bishops, from all denominations, did not interfere with their action towards the Jews. Protestant churches were going to join in the protest; however, only the Catholic bishops went ahead, and only Catholic Jews were rounded up. Rosa and Edith were arrested on the evening of 2 August. Edith's last reported words as she left with her sister, were: 'Come, let us go for our people.'[27] On 9 August, Edith and Rosa were gassed at Auschwitz.

Similarities and Differences – Tentative Conclusions

To recount Edith Stein's life and Roop Kanwar's is gruelling in different ways. We are left with many difficult questions. I only want to outline some similarities by way of a tentative conclusion so as to open up further questions in need of exploration. None of what I say should eclipse the significant historical and theological differences between Kanwar and Stein. A universe exists between them. One woman is a significant Roman Catholic intellectual, the other a simple Hindu wife. Each woman operates and acts in an entirely

---

[27] There is some controversy as to the source and authenticity of this quote. Dutch Carmelites attribute it to Maria Desling, a lay volunteer in the extern quarters of the Carmel in Echt, where Desling worked with Rosa Stein.

different cultural, intellectual, social and religious world, although both women are married to men who die. This is not to confuse the literal and symbolic, but simply to indicate that in the religious world-view that each woman inhabits, the alleged differences between the literal and symbolic might not operate so strictly and clearly. Furthermore, those who proclaim their importance do so in very different terms: a saint is not a *devi*. So amidst asking the question of whether analogically there is holiness and sanctity to be found in the lives of these two women, we should recall that analogy is the process whereby similarities are found within a greater and more fundamental dissimilarity.

First, by marrying men, both women apparently understood that the occasion of the death of their husband had sealed, and would seal, their own lives. Both, in different ways, saw in their husbands the image of God, such that their own death in following him would not now hold any fear. For both, marriage entailed following a path upon which redemption for themselves and others meant voluntarily accepting an early death, due to circumstances entirely beyond their control.

Second, both believed that their deaths would have atoning value, to themselves, and more so to others. Death, and the suffering it entailed, was a means by which transferential merit could be enacted. For Kanwar, being the 'good wife' (*pativrata*), allowed her to atone for her own sins, and quite uniquely within the Hindu tradition, for her husband's sins, and their families, and the devotees who would subsequently flock to the site of her death. Tryambakayajvan calls the *sati* sufficient atonement: *prayascitta*. For Stein, being the good wife, allowed her to atone for her own sins, for her family, both Catholic and Jewish, for the sins of Jewish disbelief, and for the sins of the German people. Clearly, she does not atone for her husband's sins, as does Kanwar. But for both, their families by blood and by marriage are positively affected by the atoning death that both accept.

Third, Kanwar and Stein both had freedom and, equally, both had none. This is a delicate point. At least via Tryambakayajvan, Kanwar *chooses* her death. *Dharmic* law allows one other option – widowhood. This is the extent of her choice. For Stein, her choice is equally limited. First, she renounces her freedom in becoming a religious, and marries her Groom to find a greater freedom. If it is His will that she die, then she develops within herself the willingness to accept this gracefully, even to desire it. Her marriage, after all, is sealed by the cross, and the cross is her name and destiny. Her historical choice is equally limited. The Nazis were closing in, and Edith and her friends were trying to arrange for her safe passage to Switzerland where Jews were still safe. Matthew Monk even suggests that she chose not to hurry these arrangements so that she could face death in solidarity with her people.[28] The fact that she is proclaimed a martyr by the Roman Catholic church implies that she chose this death as testimony to Christ.[29]

Fourth, Stein's understanding of sacrifice and transferential merit is not unique to her gender or her religious order. In the history of Roman Catholic spirituality, it is to be found in many epochs, although there is something particularly interesting in the parallels evoked in the marriage imagery that Stein herself employs, and Kanwar's situation as a bride. Kanwar's sacrificial death and transferential merit are unique to her gender, who in Tryambakayajvan's eyes have no other option than marriage. This is not true for the Hindu tradition as a whole, which sometimes allows for a female renouncer. Furthermore, while *sati* is only open to women, Tryambakayajvan argues against the exclusion of Brahmin wives from such choice. Hence, it is open to all caste groups and all women. Nevertheless, the symbolics of marriage are central for both Stein and Kanwar.

Finally, segments within both communities venerate the soteriological power of these women's lives and deaths, even though both communities pay special attention to their deaths as definitive ways of viewing their lives. Protesters against *sati*, like Daly, argue that on no account can it be seen as anything other than murderous misogyny. Protesters against Stein see this and more. First, there is the murderous anti-Semitism in the church embodied in Stein's comment, made in 1939, when

---

[28] M. Monk, *Edith Stein* (London: Catholic Truth Society, CTS Twentieth Century Martyrs Series, 1997), p. 26. This is difficult to substantiate.

[29] See K. L. Woodward, *Making Saints. How the Catholic Church Determines Who Becomes a Saint. Who Doesn't, and Why* (New York: Simon & Schuster, 1996), pp. 138–42, especially on the fact that her original process did not involve the claim to martyrdom. It took 21 years to change the claims within the process: from confessor to martyr. Exceptionally, she was proclaimed as both.

writing of the shadow of the cross upon the Jewish people: 'If only they would see this! It is the fulfillment of the curse which my people called on its own head.'[30] Second, murderous misogyny is found in the virgin martyr: 'for she rejects marriage to a human husband in order to become the bride of Christ; one form of marriage is exchanged for another. One form of submissiveness to men is exchanged for another which demands renunciation, pain and death. Complete autonomy for women is simply not an option.'[31] The real problem that is never faced by such critics is that neither Stein nor Kanwar apparently sought such autonomy, and the former, as a formidable independent intellectual, thoughtfully sought and practised the opposite.

Both women apparently followed a path, sanctioned by their religious traditions, whereby their own death brings redemption to others. To gloss it: they die selflessly on behalf of others, in a way that scandalises many and causes others to proclaim their special value. If as a Roman Catholic and despite the numerous objections, I affirm Stein to be a saint, which I do, can I really be so horrified, as I am, that Kanwar is a *devi*? I do not yet know how to answer this question, but have tried to make out a case whereby Kanwar's death is seen to have analogical similarities to that of Stein's such that Kanwar is rescued from the claims that her death was futile, tragic and a product of patriarchy. In fact, if we are able to navigate these counter claims, and I am not sure that I am entirely successful, then we might even glimpse in the midst of such deaths, horrific as they are, an insight into holiness. Such holiness is disturbing and troubling – and so it should be.[32]

---

[30] Monk, *Stein*, p. 24.

[31] Stuart, *Dragons*, p. 16.

[32] I am grateful to Stephen Barton, Gerard Loughlin, and to the audiences at the University of Durham and Wesley College, Bristol who responded to versions of this paper.

21

Material Poverty or Poverty of Spirit? Holiness and the Liberation of the Poor

Denys Turner

Though I have no formal definition of holiness to offer, I should begin with two general observations about holiness which, though incomplete, are perhaps, for our purposes, sufficient.

The first is rather personal. As a young boy at a Roman Catholic boarding school in the 1950s, I was fed on a hagiographical diet which successfully conveyed to me an image of sainthood as faultless moral rectitude. I seem to remember, incidentally, that it appeared to be a prerequisite of achieving a flawlessly holy life that you were born of what were described as 'poor but honest parents' (which, my parents being reasonably prosperous, appeared to rule me out on the ancestral financial ground if not on the moral); but I think I was less discouraged by the lack of parental qualifications, or by the obviously daunting moral labours which lay ahead – for I was young, and thought I was capable of anything – as by the unappealing prospect that I might actually achieve it and succeed in becoming what I perceived to be the quite objectionable moral prig some of these saints were praised for having become.

It was somewhat later in life that I discovered how truly flawed many of the saints were, being impressed for example by Jerome's uncontrollably bad temper and by Augustine's only partially redeemed neuroticism. And it was much later that Herbert McCabe told me, in the course of speaking about something quite else, that of course, Christians need a parish community in order to be forgiven on a Sunday for all that they have been up to during the week. And it seemed to me when he said this that in that thought was contained the nub of holiness itself. Holiness starts from a fact: that we are all forgiven. It is necessary that we sin, as Julian of Norwich says, but 'sin is behothely', sin is part of the scheme of things from all eternity, part of that scheme of things whose purpose and meaning is love; and in that eternal love, from all eternity we were forgiven, and so we were forgiven *before* we sinned.

Now a saint is simply a person whose life has been turned inside out by that forgiveness and whose life is refounded upon it as upon a primordial gift, a gift which is primordial because it is given in our very birth, given *before* our birth in our very conception in the eternal word of God. And though this gift is already given to us, we must needs *seek* forgiveness, as Jesus taught us. But we must seek forgiveness not because if we did not we might not find it; nor do we seek it in that anxiety which fears that if we do not seek it in the right spirit, or in the right way, we might not be given it – for that is nothing but the absurd proposition that we be forgiven only if we possess the moral credentials required, which is but to say that we will be forgiven only if we do not need to be. We *seek* forgiveness because it is *in the seeking itself* that we are forgiven, for it is from the divine mercy itself that our seeking arises. Therefore, it is in that seeking that our lives are refounded and reformed not upon our own moral achievements, but upon our inadequacies, not therefore upon our moral rectitude, but upon the failures of pride and egoism which taint even our moral achievements. That recognition, and that seeking, a seeking which is freed, 'liberated' from the self-centred, egoistic, moodily self-obsessed moralistic models of holiness of my youth, is true 'poverty of spirit', a detachment from the self-possessiveness of the righteous prig; it is an abandonment and an ultimate trust. And a holiness born of such parentage will be, I suppose, in some genuine sense, 'poor but honest'.

As a second observation, I note the difficulties with which the cause of the canonisation of Oscar Romero meets in the Vatican. Now I know that some of you might scruple, and on good theological principle, about this practice of canonisation, and I know that, principle apart, it can be and has been abused in all sorts of ways. But I think some such process is justifiable in order that the Church might acknowledge, for itself and for the whole world, the existence of true *miracles* of divine forgiveness, interventions of divine mercy which are visible, palpable in persons and lives, in which whatever else is visible, forgiveness is. And that said, it is truly worth a comment that a pope who has hastened to canonise more saints in 22 years than have been canonised in the whole preceding history of the Catholic church, procrastinates over one of the few twentieth-century martyrs who has evoked a genuinely universal cult.

Why? One speculates, but not with excessive rashness, that the reason is political. I mean, that the Pope has political reasons for his reluctance. I suppose that he would deny this. I suppose that he would put his reluctance down not to his own politics, but to the 'political' nature of Romero's martyrdom, which, on some accounts of holiness, muddies the waters, mixes in with the distilled purity of the spiritual the murky, ambiguous tints of the political – a scruple not unlike that with which I, for one, contemplate the martyrdom of that supremely 'political' Christian saint, Thomas à Becket. For Romero defended the poor against state repression and government-supported paramilitaries; every week he denounced the oppressions of the poor in sermons delivered on the Church's radio broadcast of Sunday mass in the Cathedral of San Salvador; and the day before he was assassinated he had appealed to the army's rank and file to disobey illegal and immoral orders. I *suppose* you can ask whether his martyrdom was truly a *Christian* martyrdom, or only a merely *political* one. But I should say simply that if you ask a bent question you are bound to get a crooked answer and that there is an implied 'politics' – a contentious assumption not merely about the nature of spirituality and holiness, but also about the nature of politics itself – contained in the very formulation of the question. There is, in short, politics enough in the supposition itself that the 'spiritual' and the 'political' are in that way mutually exclusive.

Now I am aware that this sort of observation is a commonplace today and that the appearance of opposition and disjunction between the ideal of 'spiritual' poverty on the one hand, and the inevitably political work of doing justice to the poor on the other, has been subjected to much, and much effective, theological critique.[1] And I do not wish to rehearse

[1] Practically every work of liberation theology offers some form of critique of these dualisms, but see Gustavo Gutierrez, *A Theology of Liberation* (London: SCM Press, 1974), especially chapter 1, for a classic statement.

here the arguments which have been constructed in criticism of the 'dualisms', as they are commonly called, between the personal and spiritual and the collective and political, except at a rather distant remove of conceptual clarification. I ask you to be just a little tolerant of the seeming intellectualism of my approach. I do agree that even good concepts cannot get you all the way to the required actions, whether of personal or of social transformation. But for sure, *bad* concepts can paralyse action as much as thought, and I do think that underlying the sort of theological failures which live on today in our residual dualisms of spirituality and politics, there remains lodged a bedrock of bad thinking about God. Today, I want to do a limited thing, therefore, which is to dig around a little in the area of those foundations and to take a closer look at what we might unearth. I suppose that in the end you might still convict me of intellectualism, but I will risk it, for my purpose is one of liberation of mind, in the obscure academic's belief that doing so might have some role in the liberation of heart and flesh, a belief I know to be scarcely credible in our dismally anti-intellectualist times.

Dualisms and Anti-dualisms

But to our task. Twentieth-century Christian interpretation of biblical texts about poverty are much divided over the question of whether they should be understood in a 'material' or in a 'spiritual' sense. In Matthew's Gospel Jesus is represented as having counted as 'blessed' the 'poor in spirit', but in Luke's account it is 'you poor' who are blessed. And some have seen in this different language at least a difference of emphasis; others – for example, some of the followers of the school of 'Liberation Theology' – have seen in the apparently slight verbal difference between these two texts a very radical shift in theological priorities. For in the Matthean version what is praised, it is said, is a spiritual disposition of detachment from worldly goods, from possessions, wealth, power and secular influence, a disposition which is principally an *individual* ascetical response, a disciplining of human possessive desire so as to liberate the soul for an entirely new relationship with the goods of the world and ultimately for the personal possession of the 'Kingdom of God'. Whereas, according to the Liberation Theologians, the Lucan version seems to praise the actual poor themselves, and therefore praises not merely a disposition of ascetical detachment from goods, which one might nonetheless actually possess in abundance, but the condition of actual deprivation itself. To them, the poor of the world are given not only the preaching of the gospel, but also the 'Kingdom of God' itself, for they are, in their poverty, in some way both a visible *symbol* of the eternal Kingdom of God which transcends all history, and also the historical agency of its coming to be on earth in time. For it is in the poor and by their transforming action for justice that God's work of bringing about the Kingdom is done. Hence, these theologians say, a radical trans-formation of theology and Christian life is called for by Luke's version of Jesus' saying, a transformation which is summarised in the demand that Christian theology and practice should make a 'preferential option for the poor': in the Christian's solidarity with the poor are found at one and the same time both the transcendent symbol and the historical agency of God's justice.

For the purposes of our discussion, let us call this first interpretation the 'spiritual' or 'ascetical' interpretation, which relies upon Matthew's emphasis on 'the poor *in spirit*' to bring out the 'interior', personal and individual significance of poverty, and the second, which emphasises the political and historical dimensions of Jesus' challenge, the 'material' or 'political' interpretation; and let us note further how Western Christian theology has in recent times tended to become polarised around these two interpretations as if they were mutually exclusive. Much recent discussion seems to imply that you will have to make a choice of one or the other, but not both: to the extent that you *affirm* that Jesus was calling for an interior transformation of worldly desire, an inner detachment, then necessarily and to the same extent you must *deny* that he was making a political call on the poor themselves to take up the historical task of transforming society for the reign of justice; but equally, to the extent that you affirm this revol-utionary role of the poor, to that same extent you deny that Jesus demanded a corresponding interior and spiritual trans-formation. Now clearly this polarisation of 'spiritual' and 'material' understandings of the meaning of poverty is theologically unsatisfactory, but it is also paralysingly inhibiting of Christian practice, since it appears to offer equally unacceptable practical choices to the Christians as to way of life: either that of pursuing the ideal of poverty as a purely interior, and therefore as a socially and politically decontextualised individual detachment of spirit, or else that of working in solidarity with the poor for a political transformation of society, as if conditions of personal transformation and detachment were an irrelevant distraction from that fundamentally public and political task.

Of course the existence of this theological and practical predicament is familiar enough to Western Christians, and it has to be said that I have somewhat overstated the absoluteness of the predicament. Most particularly, on the side of the 'Liberation Theologians' of the South, there is little desire to defend such polarisations – in fact they would hold Northern theology as very largely responsible for creating and sustaining the theological and practical foundations from which these polarisations derive. There, in the philosophical divorce of 'theory' from 'practice', in the conceptual oppositions enforced between the 'individual' and the 'social' and between the 'private' and the 'public', are found the theoretical justifications for historical processes of 'modernisation': the separation of Church and state, the 'liberation' of reason from the constraints of faith and the historical momentum of secularisation and of the privatisation of religion. In short, what all this inertia of philosophical and historical tradition imposes upon contemporary Christian theology is a dead weight of 'individualism' which has powerful implications not only for a radical moral relativism, but, in harness with it, also for a 'privatisation' of the spiritual. Hence, an account of 'poverty' which confines it within a region of the private 'inner' world which, in turn, is set in relations of opposition to the social, and of notions of spiritual and personal transformation set in opposition to the revolutionary transformation of relations of exploitation and oppression of the poor by which the wealthy and powerful achieve their wealth and power.

Now it is certainly true that much recent theology emerging from the Southern hemisphere is resistant to these dualisms of theology and practice so endemic to Western thought, which they identify as historically linked with the political and economic hegemony of the capitalist world as its material context: for that capitalist world remorselessly secularises the social as it privatises the religious. It is also true that *in principle* the 'Third World' theologies of Latin America, of parts of Africa and the Far East, offer a much healthier integration of those polarisations which so typically characterise the theologies of the West. The Peruvian Catholic theologian, Gustavo Gutierrez, explicitly rejects the theological strategies which set Matthew and Luke in opposition to one another in the name of an opposition between the material and spiritual meanings of poverty,[2] for he wants to draw upon *both* meanings so as to recreate a synthesis between the two. In fact, what he thinks is 'revolutionary' about his theology is not that he espouses 'political' revolution in the name of the poor of the world as being in any way opposed to a spiritual – and so non-political – transformation of the 'individual', but that he *opposes the opposition* between these two dimensions of poverty, the material and the spiritual. On this matter he is explicit and concrete:

> Only by rejecting poverty and by making itself poor in order to protest against it can the Church preach something that is uniquely its own: 'spiritual poverty', that is, the openness of man and history to the future promised by God. Only in this way will the Church be able to fulfil authentically – and with any possibility of being listened to – its prophetic function of denouncing every injustice to man. And only in this way will it be able to preach the word which liberates, the word of genuine brotherhood.[3]

Yet, merely to propose the transcendence of these false oppositions is not by itself to achieve that transcendence: mere theological formulae have no power in the face of the massive inertia of an hegemonic Western culture, nor even can the concrete mobilisation of revolutionary poor in the name of such formulae – in any case hardly much more than a pious aspiration in view of the overwhelming dominance of the agencies of globalisation and the world markets – by itself offer

---

[2] Gutierrez, *Theology of Liberation*, pp. 287–306.
[3] *Theology of Liberation*, pp. 301–2.

the critique of the *intellectual* foundations of that hegemony. I say this, and offer the thought that this intellectual critique is absolutely necessary even if I make no claims that intellectual critique is by itself sufficient except in alliance with concrete movements of practice, for this would be but to reaffirm the bifurcation of thought and practice which it purported to reject. Still, if not sufficient, I re-emphasise, the systematic critique of Western philosophical, political and religious dualisms is absolutely necessary and I am not convinced that even the theologies of the South, for all the legitimacy of their theological option for the poor and for all their *intended* transcendence of a dualistic theological culture, has yet provided us with the tools for that thoroughgoing critique of the philosophical and theological foundations of those dualisms which we need.

Here I propose to make a bold claim based on a proposition which, in recent times within the academies of the Western world, has become a truism. The truism is that the sum total of philosophical, cultural, religious and political ideas sustaining those fatal theological dualisms collectively form an intellectual complex which we have come to call 'modernity' as a fact and 'modernism' as an ideology. Many Western intellectuals seek the resources for the rejection of this ideology in what they call 'postmodernity' as a counter-ideology, deeming our age to be, correspondingly, '*post*-modern'. And within the contrasts envisaged here, 'modernity' is conceived of as the age of reason, as being the age in which by the methods of a self-contained, self-sufficient, self-developing rationality, human progress triumphs as an inevitable, evolving narrative of the scientific and technological domination of nature, reclaims from the mystifications of faith and superstition its own autonomy, and asserts the hegemony of reason and theory over irrationality and of the dominance of human nature over all else in creation. By contrast, 'postmodernism' as a counter-ideology 'deconstructs' this narrative of an inevitable historical progression, denies the universalist claims of the rationalist, abandons the modernist confidence in the stability of the human mind's relationship with the world, sees nothing to be of universal value, no knowledge to be certain, no fixed relationship between language and world, but that there is only the morally relative, the cognitively fragmentary, the culturally particular – nothing absolutely 'given' to human mind or will objectively, everything subjectively 'constructed' and therefore vulnerable to critical deconstruction.

That, in a word, is the truism: that the intellectual critique of the dualisms of modernity must be accompanied by the despair of any constructive theoretical and moral rival to it, for postmodernity is incapable of sustaining such hope, indeed removes the foundations for it. I call it a 'truism', but not because I believe it to be true – in fact I regard it as false and as being little else than the abject betrayal of intellect yielding feebly to the cultural impact of global capitalism. Rather, I call it a truism because it is widely held, as a matter of highly prescriptive fashion within the Western academies, to be the only intellectual possibility open to us, given the necessary deconstruction of modernity. And so widely held is this ideology of postmodernism that it is almost as generally fashionable within the academic schools of Western theology to seek a parallel *theological* deconstruction, a recasting of Christian thought and belief in postmodernist terms.

Now the bold claim which I want to outline in this paper is that if we are to seek the foundations of an intellectual critique of the dualisms of 'modernity' they will not be found within the deconstructions of the *post*-modern, but rather within certain tendencies of the theologies of the *pre*-modern era; specifically within the traditions of medieval mysticism. I will do no more than outline some reasons why we might want to consider this possibility seriously; otherwise, I will merely add to these rather speculative and general thoughts the proposition that within the doctrines of God and of spiritual poverty found within those medieval traditions it might be possible to identify some of the intellectual and theological resources needed for the *systematic* transcendence of the polarisations and opposi-tions between the spiritual and the material, between the 'inner' individual and the 'outer' social, and so for the transcendence of the dualism between poverty of spirit and the political witness to justice for the poor with which a 'modernist' culture has so beset us.

Spiritual Poverty

The 'spiritual' meaning of poverty has a long and venerable Christian history, but it received its most powerful expression in the late medieval and early modern periods of Western Christian history. In sixteenth-century Spain, one of the great mystics of the Western Christian tradition, St John of the Cross, perfectly expresses this significance in a series of paradoxes embodying the two components of the medieval conception of spiritual poverty, one negative, one positive. The negative component is that of 'abandonment', that to possess God one must abandon the desire for anything worldly, indeed anything creaturely; the positive component is that in thus coming to possess God alone one becomes capable of relating in a new way to that same world, to that same creation, precisely insofar as one can now do so with a desire stripped of all possessiveness, with a desire free of all exploitativeness, with a desire which is a purely contemplative enjoyment of all that God has made. John of the Cross spells out the paradoxes expressive of this double aspect of poverty of spirit:

> To reach satisfaction in all
> desire satisfaction in nothing.
> To come to possess all
> desire the possession of nothing.
> To arrive at being all
> desire to be nothing.
> To come to the knowledge of all
> desire the knowledge of nothing.
>
> To come to enjoy what you have not
> you must go by a way in which you enjoy not.
> To come to the knowledge you have not
> you must go by a way in which you know not.
> To come to the possession you have not
> You must go by the way in which you are not.[4]

Here, within the early modern period, John of the Cross summarises briefly, but very completely, the doctrine of

---

[4] *Ascent of Mount Carmel*, 1.14.11, in *The Collected Works of St John of the Cross*, tr. K. Kavanaugh and O. Rodriguez (Washington: ICS Publications, 1991), p. 150.

spiritual poverty or 'detachment' which he inherited from the late medieval German mystical tradition, particularly, if somewhat indirectly, from the fourteenth-century Dominican friar known as 'Meister Eckhart'. What is common to that tradition and John is the conviction that 'poverty of spirit' is essentially an ascetical discipline of human desire, a purification or purgation of the human desiring power of all its tendencies to possessiveness. For without this purgation of desire's possessiveness, it is impossible, both John and Eckhart say, for a person to love God except as an object of possession, a 'thing', in effect, therefore idolatrously as just another creature. Indeed, so fundamental a condition of love is this 'detachment' and spiritual poverty that Eckhart can even say that he values it above love itself:

> I have read many writings both by the pagan teachers and by the prophets and in the Old and in the New Law, and I have enquired, carefully and most industriously, to find which is the greatest and best virtue with which a man can most completely and closely conform himself to God, with which he can by grace become that which God is by nature and with which he can come most of all to resemble that image which he was in God and between which and God there was no distinction before ever God made created things. And as I scrutinise all these writings, so far as my reason can lead me and instruct me, I find no other virtue better than a pure detachment from all things ... The teachers have great things to say in praise of love, as had St Paul, who says: 'Whatever I may practice, if I do not have love, I am worth nothing at all' (1 Cor. 13, 1–2). And yet I praise detachment above all love.[5]

What, then is this 'detachment' or 'spiritual poverty'? Before we can answer that question with any degree of fullness it is necessary to explain a little about Eckhart's doctrine of God, in particular his doctrine of the supreme *oneness* of God. Here, Eckhart draws upon an important neo-Platonic element of the

---

[5] *On Detachment,* in *Meister Eckhart, Essential sermons, commentaries, treatises and defense,* tr. Edmund Colledge and Bernard McGinn (New York: Paulist Press, 1981), pp. 285–6.

Christian tradition, one which joined hands in the middle ages
of the Christian West with important influences from medieval
Islamic and Jewish thought, particularly that of Ibn Sina and
Moses Maimonides.

The Poverty of God

'Anyone who beholds the number two,' says Eckhart, 'or
beholds distinction does not behold God, for God is one,
outside and beyond number, and is not counted with
anything';[6] and in saying this he embodies a very typical
paradox of Eckhartian theology. Do you mind if here we do
just a little metaphysics? God is one and in him there is no
distinction. That is clear. Yet it cannot be the case that the
oneness of God is of that kind by which we designate the
uniqueness of any creature, for if, say in this room, there are
28 objects of various kinds, and another object which is
unique – something there is and can only be one of, such as
the autograph of a Beethoven sonata – then there are 28 plus
1 objects in the room, that is 29. Now for sure, Eckhart says,
God is one and unique, for 'anyone who beholds the number
two ... does not behold God'. On the other hand, God's
oneness is not just another item in a series, countable as an
additional thing when one has counted everything else, for
God's oneness, unlike the oneness of a creature, puts him
altogether beyond counting in any list of objects of any kind:
he is, Eckhart says, 'outside and beyond number, and is not
counted with anything'.

Conduct, for a moment, an impossible thought-experiment:
suppose you were to count up all the things in the world – an
absurd supposition, of course, for there is any number of
different ways of counting; still, somehow count all the things
that there are, have been or ever will be, and the sum adds up
to the number n. Then I say, 'Just a minute, I am a theist and
there is one being you have not yet counted, and that is the
being who created them all, God'; would I be right to say that

---

[6] *Commentary on Exodus*, 15.58, in *Meister Eckhart, Teacher and Preacher*, ed. and
tr. Bernard McGinn, Frank Tobin and Elvira Borgstadt (New York: Paulist
Press, 1986), p. 63.

now the sum total of things is n + 1? According to Eckhart, emphatically no, for, again, I repeat, God is 'outside and beyond number, and is not counted with anything'. So God is one, but not countable; utterly individual, so not many; utterly individual, and so beyond all possibility of being included with anything else, and yet, because not countable in any series, not distinguishable as one individual is from another; utterly distinct from anything and everything in creation and yet not distinguishable at all in the way in which one thing in the world is distinct from any other thing in the world. Therefore, God's oneness makes him totally and absolutely *other*, from creation; and yet that same oneness sets God's total transcendence not, as one might suppose, in some relation of *opposition* to creatures, but, on the contrary, in a relation of total immanence and 'withinness' to all creatures. For God's transcendence, rooted in his oneness, cannot be of that kind which belongs to creatures, such that being 'this' necessarily entails not being 'that', as being this dog means not being that cat, being this sheep means not being that dog, being this chalk means not being that cheese. This is why Eckhart can summarise all his paradoxes about God in a simple phrase: God's being, he says, is an *unum indistinctum,* a oneness which is not-distinct. For God is supremely distinct from all creatures in this alone, that only he is the being which is not distinct.

It is no wonder that Meister Eckhart finds his most appropriate names for this paradox of the utterly transcendent-immanence in the metaphors of the so-called 'negative theology', for it is a paradox beyond all thought and language. God, Eckhart says, is a 'transcending nothingness', a 'desert', an 'abyss'; he is a Godhead which is completely 'naked', purely simple, and even 'poor', ultimately stripped bare of any properties, attributes and descriptions. Nor is it surprising that in describing how this transcendent God, describable in every way and in none, and present immanently within every soul, he should use exactly the same names to describe that place in the soul where the transcendent oneness of God is to be found: namely in the soul's deepest interiority.

'Sometimes,' he says,

I have spoken of a light that is uncreated and not capable of creation and that is in the soul. I always mention this light in

my sermons; and this same light comprehends God without a
medium, uncovered, naked, as he is in himself ... and that
light has more unity with God than it has with any of the
powers of the soul ...

It is a divine 'spark' in the soul

which has never touched either time or place. This spark
rejects all created things, and wants nothing but this naked
God, as he is in himself. It is not content with the Father or
the Son or the Holy Spirit ... it is not content with the simple
divine essence ... but it wants to know the source of this
essence, it wants to go into the simple ground, into the quiet
desert, into which distinction never gazed ... [and] this
ground is a simple silence.[7]

This nakedness and 'nothingness' of the soul, this 'ground'
and 'desert' in which the divine nakedness and nothingness
meets with ours, is the achievement of, and the deepest meaning
of, 'poverty of spirit' or detachment. In short, it is only in this
poverty that we can meet God in his poverty – nakedness meeting
nakedness, the abyss meeting the abyss. And you might suppose,
from what Eckhart says, that what he offers us is a doctrine of
poverty *so absolutely spiritual* that it stands in correspondingly
absolute opposition to the material world of social relations and
the real world of poverty; *so absolutely interior* as to exclude from
its ambit anything of the exterior world. And yet nothing could
be further from the truth. For it is precisely in and through
Meister Eckhart's resolute insistence upon the utterly spiritual,
utterly interior, utterly transcendent nature of this meeting
place of God and the soul in spiritual poverty, that the fracturing
of spiritual and material, the setting against one another of
interior and exterior, transcendent and immanent is healed.

Poverty and 'Knowing God'

What, then, is the practice of detachment and poverty of
spirit? I think that as we can say that detachment is the

---

[7] All quotations from *Sermon* 48, *Ein Meister Sprichet*, in *Meister Eckhart,
Essential Sermons*, p. 198.

solution, so the problem is not human desire itself, but its possessiveness. Poverty of spirit is the strategy of dispossessing desire of its desire to possess its objects, and so to destroy them. For Eckhart it is not just that, in addition to our other desires, we also desire to possess; as for John of the Cross, possessiveness for Eckhart is pandemic; all our desires are infected by it, all that we desire we desire *qua* object of possession; no matter how unpossessible an object may be in itself, possessiveness will convert it into a possible object of possession, will make a property of it, will 'privatise' it, as it were. We are, in relation to the world, like the tourist who looks at nothing but obsessively photographs everything, destroying the objective beauty of what he sees in a frenzied desire to contain it within the tiny compass of his little black box, to take away and have for himself. In just such a way the undetached person diminishes and denatures his world and cannot even properly enjoy it. He cannot meet with reality on its own terms, but only in terms of his own egoism. Detachment, for Eckhart, is not, therefore, the rejection of worldly desire, but the restoration of desire to a proper relation of objectivity; as we might say, of contemplative reverence for creation. That is why Eckhart says that spiritual poverty is the basis of the true possibility of love, and that is why, for Eckhart, it is more fundamental than love, being the condition of its possibility.

After all, as another fourteenth-century writer, the English author of the *Cloud of Unknowing* puts it, anyone can love God 'for what he can get out of him'. But such a 'God' is not God. Any 'God' we could possibly love without spiritual poverty is not the true God badly loved, but not God at all, the mere godlet of our own invention. What is more, because possessive desire is a form of dependence on its object, the God of our own desire is a form of ego-need, a God on whom we depend not in freedom but in slavery, one for whom, therefore, God would have to be but a tyrannical master whose omnipotent will could only crush the human will into servile submission: not, therefore, the God of love who emancipates and sets the will free, but a godlet who stands to our humanity as an addiction stands to our freedom. For, like all addictions, possessive desires at once destroy what they desire and are enslaved to what they destroy. The gods of the undetached may be poor diminished little things: but they are, for all that, poor diminished little tyrants.

Possessiveness is, therefore, the principle of destruction of nature and creation and this is because first of all it is the denaturing of God: it is, in short, the root of idolatry. But that root of possessiveness at its deepest reaches down into the soil of the ultimately possessive desire *to be a self* my ownership of which must necessarily be set against and exclude God's: for that is the nature of the property-relation, that which is 'mine' is 'not-thine'. That possessiveness is the desire that there should be at my centre not that unnameable abyss into which, as into a vacuum, the nameless Godhead is inevitably drawn, but an identity I can own, an identity which is defined by my ownership of it. That is the ultimately destructive form that attachment can take, for it is an attachment which seeks to infill that nothingness with images of self and with its own private means and 'ways' to God. Such a selfhood must necessarily expel God from the place which it occupies, for it fills the space where God must be with the 'I' which excludes him. This is the 'I' which refuses to be the 'nothing' which can be one with the nothingness of God. Consequently, any God it does affirm it must affirm in exclusion of the I which affirms it. These are the perverse, inverted dialectics of the unpoor in spirit, the dialectics of the 'exterior' person who is trapped in the polarisations of interiority and exteriority so as to seek God 'within' rather than 'without', in the privacy of what I claim as 'mine'. For the truly detached person there can be no such distinction. That is also why Eckhart is so insistent upon the absolute transcendence equally of God and the self, beings beyond every possibility of being appropriated within some intelligible, meaningful, desirable, possessible structure of selfhood. That is why, for Eckhart, 'my' self is not in the last-resort mine at all. To be a self I must become the void, the 'nothingness' and the desert of poverty of spirit. To live in poverty of spirit is to live without an explanation, without personal motive, namelessly one with the nameless God.

Hence, the strategy of detachment is not that of focusing created desires upon God. It is, rather, the critique of desire, the dispossession of its inherent desire to possess, to make 'mine', determinable, countable, possessible, all things, self, neighbour, creation and God; and in being the critique of that instinct for possessiveness it cuts to the root of that corresponding instinct to set one object against another, 'mine' against 'yours', God against creation, 'inner' against 'outer', soul against body, spiritual against material. It is thus that the practice of this spiritual poverty is a strategy of *opposing oppositions* between one desire and another, between the desire for God and the desire for created things, as if the desire for God were just another created desire for another created object. It is only for the spiritually unpoor that that opposition could exist. To be 'poor in spirit' is not therefore to be desireless of creation – still less is it the rejection of creation in order to desire only God, nor is it to desire nothing at all, even God. Rather, it is to desire out of that nothingness of self and God, so that, from the security of this featureless desert of the soul, which nothing created can enter, we can desire all things with a desire truly divine, because it is desire 'without a why', without interest, utterly free of the desire to possess, utterly free to enjoy all.

Knowing God and Doing Justice

Perhaps it is now possible to see how, on this account of it, 'spiritual poverty' cannot be set in any relation of opposition to the fundamental commitment of Jesus' teaching of justice for the poor. For in Eckhart's theology, spiritual poverty is not set in contrast with the concern for justice for the poor as are the 'inner' and the 'outer', the 'spiritual' and the 'material', the 'private' and the 'public', the 'individual' and the 'social', the 'transcendent' and the 'immanent'. Very far from it. It is true that Eckhart attaches primary importance to 'spiritual' poverty – if, after all, it is 'more important than love' then equally it is 'more important' than the commitment to justice for the poor which is but a form of the expression of that love. But the 'greater importance' of detachment and spiritual poverty is not because the pursuit of it is to the *exclusion of* concern for the materially poor, but rather consists in the fact that poverty of spirit is the *necessary condition of the possibility* of love and the concern for justice. Indeed, it is only poverty of spirit which can liberate the person from those dualisms between 'inner' and 'outer', the 'spiritual' and the 'material' which set spiritual and material poverty in opposition to one another in the first place.

For, as I have said, poverty of spirit is that disposition of soul which *opposes those oppositions.* Rather than the 'spiritual' being opposed to the 'material', it is only the truly spiritual person who can transcend the opposition between the spiritual and the material, between the personal and the political: for the spiritual person, these oppositions simply do not and cannot exist: for him or her they are found in perfect, seamless continuity. It is only for those who lack poverty of spirit that those oppositions function so as to trap them into either a private and socially meaningless individuality or else into a spiritually vacuous social activism. Spiritual poverty, therefore, takes an axe to the root of those 'modernist' dualisms of epistemology, psychology and political theory which contrain us to contemplate only mutually exclusive options between a privatised religiosity neglectful of the poor and an unspiritual ultra-leftism which has no place for the transcendent Godhead who calls us into justice for the oppressed. Spiritual poverty as a personal lifestyle sets us apart from the consumerism of a capitalist mentality. Without that poverty of spirit it is impossible for any person, as Eckhart says, to love God, neighbour or creation except in blasphemous idolatry. But even more fundamentally than that, spiritual poverty redeems that whole capitalist culture of possessive individualism, challenges its entrapment in the dualisms and polarisations on which is founded its paralyses of thought and action, its ideological, and *therefore idolatrous,* betrayals of the poor in its midst.

Ultimately, therefore, it is only the poor in spirit who can truly know that naked, poor, God, the knowledge of whom is to know, and to do, the justice he demands of us in respect of the materially poor. As Gustavo Gutierrez famously has said: 'to know God *is* to do justice'. Just so. But it is only the poor in spirit who thus know God. That is why, and it is Eckhart who teaches it, it is only the poor in spirit who can do justice to the poor: and if it is Eckhart who teaches it, it was Oscar Romero who lived it, that 'Saint Oscar' who, in the last interview he gave, three weeks before it happened, predicted his death and forgave his assassins. Romero was far from being a flawless man himself. But the meaning of his life – which deserves the Church's celebration – lay in the fact that he himself, long before his martyrdom, had had to learn, painfully, that he could not seek holiness unpolitically except at a price paid by the poor and that therefore to avoid the politics of holiness was to reproduce but a higher, apparently spiritual, but ultimately self-indulgent, parody of the real thing. After all, he was appointed Archbishop of San Salvador as a 'conservative', one who would resist the 'politicisation', as the Vatican supposed it to be, of the Central American church. It took the shock of another martyrdom, that of his friend Fr Rutilio Grande, to force him to listen to the voice of the actual poor and to hear in that voice the word of God speaking to him of his *failure* as a Christian leader. In short, the theological lesson of Oscar Romero's conversion – of his holiness – was that he learned poverty of spirit from the materially poor.

Flawed man as he was, therefore, Romero was enabled to draw many another flawed person into that gift of human solidarity which is the gift of forgiveness, because first it was given to him by the poor. Thereby he met that fate of which the poor have all too much experience, that fate which Herbert McCabe has described as the whole meaning of Christian living, because it was the whole meaning of Jesus' life: 'If you do not love, you are scarcely alive. But if you do love, you will certainly be killed.'[8]

---

[8] Herbert McCabe often used to say this in lectures and sermons, though I have been unable to find a published source. A 'Liberation Theologian' *avant la lettre,* and one with a better sense than most of the inner-connectedness between the doctrine of God and the practice of justice, Herbert sadly died in June, 2001.

22

Whose Sanctity of Life? Ricoeur, Dworkin and the Human Embryo

Robert Song

Historically, disputes over the doctrine of the sanctity of life have been associated with a variety of moral issues, and three in particular: those of abortion, euthanasia and capital punishment. However, recent developments in artifical reproductive techniques and biotechnology have raised in a new and sharper form the question of the sanctity of life in relation to the embryo. *In vitro* fertilization treatments regularly lead to the creation of more embryos than will be finally implanted in the womb; research into early embryonic development, often for ultimately therapeutic purposes, requires the destruction of embryos; pre-implantation genetic diagnosis allows parents the chance to weed out embryos that are found to be carrying the genes for serious physical disorders; and so-called 'therapeutic' cloning offers the possibility of taking embryonic stem cells and developing organs or other bodily tissues which can then be reimplanted without fear of tissue rejection.

All of these techniques raise the question of the ontological status of the embryo. Much of the debate over this has tended to assume an all-or-nothing quality – that the embryo either is a full human person, deserving of the rights granted to all other human persons, or that it has no such status, and has no claim on us which would finally prevent us from destroying it should the need arise or the benefits be great enough. One of the superficially most attractive responses to this has been to elaborate a developmentalist account of personhood, according to which personhood is better seen in terms of a sliding scale or a spectrum, rather than a discrete *Sic* or *Non*. In this chapter I will mount a critique of two such accounts, by philosophers who are not primarily known as bioethicists, Paul Ricoeur and Ronald Dworkin. Both in different ways attempt to break the deadlock, but neither, I shall argue, is finally decisive. I will also integrate into this discussion an account of the nature and meaning of the sanctity of life that raises the question of whose sanctity of life is finally in question.

Paul Ricoeur and Communal Wisdom

Paul Ricoeur's discussion of the status of the embryo and foetus emerges in the course of an analysis of Kant's categorical imperative.[1] The second version of the categorical imperative, that one should act in such a way that one always treats humanity, whether in one's own person or in that of another, never simply as a means but always at the same time as an end, conceals, Ricoeur argues, a conflict between respect for the law and respect for persons. In the application of the moral law to particular situations, treating persons as ends in themselves may require precisely coming into conflict with the requirements of the law. The resolution of this is, he claims, a matter of practical wisdom and a special form of concern for the other, which he terms 'critical solicitude'.

The question of respect for persons at the beginning of life is presented as a case example of such a conflict. But it is a conflict complicated by the question of the ontological status of the embryo. Traditional accounts of this have tended to be vitiated, he argues, by the acceptance or rejection of a substantialist ontology of the embryo, such that one side asserts the ontological significance of the new genotype that exists from the moment of conception (or, in a more moderate form, suggests that there is sufficient doubt that one should not risk homicide); while the other attaches dignity only to the possession of consciousness or to fully developed personal capacities such as reasoning or whatever. But both have tended

---

[1] Paul Ricoeur, *Oneself as Another*, tr. Kathleen Blamey (Chicago: University of Chicago Press, 1992), pp. 270–3. For an introductory overview of the book as a whole, see Charles E. Reagan, 'Philosophical Essay: Personal Identity', in *Paul Ricoeur: His Life and His Work* (Chicago: University of Chicago Press, 1996), pp. 73–99.

towards a certain Kantianism of outlook, that the entity concerned is either a person or a thing, either entitled to be treated as an end in itself with a complete panoply of rights, or merely inert nature which can be treated as manipulable object.

Ricoeur rejects this dichotomy, and proposes that a narrative account of personal identity, such as the one which he develops earlier in the book, should be used to ground a different understanding of the embryo. Accordingly, he asks whether practical wisdom should not give moral consideration to 'the phenomena of [biological] thresholds and stages that put into question the simple alternative between person and thing'.[2] This would allow qualitatively different rights to be assigned at different stages of foetal development: 'the right not to suffer, the right to protection (this notion itself presenting several degrees of "force" or "emphasis"), the right to respect, once something like an exchange, even assymetrical, of preverbal signs is begun between the fetus and its mother'.[3] This developmental ontology is then set in the context of a further thesis about the inseparability of metaphysics and practice. While unconditional 'right-to-lifers' are correct to recognise the inseparability of the ontological status of the foetus and the manner in which it is treated, they have relied on a substantialist ontology based in large part on old theological considerations about ensoulment. By contrast, proponents of the opposing thesis, while sometimes accepting progressive development in moral respect for the foetus, have often failed to recognise that this also requires a progressive ontology.

Ricoeur's account of the matter undoubtedly has a number of attractions. In particular, his refusal to cast the question in terms of the Kantian divide of person and thing is an important and illuminating insight. It makes clear the dangers of an approach to the embryo which allows it to be the object of morally unconstrained technological manipulation: indeed it might help to clarify the otherwise inexplicable desire on the part of those who deny personhood to embryos in the early stages of development, and therefore defend research on them

---

[2] Ricoeur, *Oneself as Another*, p. 271.
[3] Ricoeur, *Oneself as Another*, p. 272.

to the point of destruction, nevertheless to talk about wishing to treat them 'with respect'. In the broader moral sphere, refusing such a Kantian dichotomy also opens out the possibility of an approach to animal and plant life which regards non-human creatures as bearers of moral worth in their own right. While much philosophical and theological work has been done here in relation to animals, it is striking that relatively little has been done with regard to plants: one of the notable features about theological contributions to the recent debates on genetic modification of crops has been the inability to articulate moral categories that might illuminate our vague unease at the unremitting instrumentalisation of plant life which such intervention constitutes.[4]

Nevertheless it still raises questions. Even if we abstract entirely from the question of a substantialist ontology, there are still grounds for maintaining a significant caution on both the metaphysical and ethical questions. Of course it is appropriate to attach different rights to human beings at different stages of life: there is little point in proposing a putative right not to suffer if an embryo does not yet have the neurological substrate necessary for pain signals to be transmitted; nor is there value in an unborn child having the full range of civil or political rights that it will be unable to exercise meaningfully until it is born, or is a child, or is grown up. Rights are properly specified in relation to the kinds of beings which are to bear them. But all of this is compatible with maintaining that early embryos should be granted the one right which they arguably need, namely the right to life.

To say this is not, of course, an argument for the early embryo's right to life, but merely to assert that a progressivist account of embryonic and foetal rights is quite compatible with such a position. A more important ground for reserve about treatment of the embryo which does not turn on a substantialist ontology is in fact signalled by Ricoeur himself. It concerns the nature of existence in a technologically formed culture. 'The fear of the worst', he recalls from Hans Jonas, 'is a necessary component of all the forms of long-term

---

[4] Whether Ricoeur's dialectical, narrative-based ethics is capable of this task is, however, another matter.

responsibility demanded by the technological age.'[5] This justifies caution in the matter, for example, of the treatment of surplus embryos created by infertility treatments, which he thinks would be part of the practical wisdom required in such morally conflictual situations.

Why does he think such caution is indicated? He gives no reason, and it is left open to the reader to supply the lacuna. One possibility might be an implicit appeal to a causal slippery slope argument, according to which destroying surplus embryos would create a culture in which human life would progressively be devalued: first embryos, then foetuses, then newborns, then those with severe disabilities, those who are old or economically parasitic or delinquent or morally unconforming, would become subject to increasingly oppressive discrimination and worse. Such appeals to slippery slopes have more value than their critics often assert: they are not always a polemical device. Nevertheless a considerably more compelling account than is usually provided is needed of, as it were, the surrounding geography, if something is to be satisfactorily construed as being part of a slippery slope of social causation. A more promising approach is to return to his thesis about the inseparability of metaphysics and practice, when this is set in the context of a technologically-minded society. No doubt it is a general truth that a culture's metaphysical commitments will be shaped by its social practices, but it is one of the features of our technological age that its restless, unceasing instrumentalisation of the material world – and in particular, here, the human body – renders it incapable of recognizing anything outside of that which has been or should be normalised. The gap between representing and intervening has become vanishingly slight in many areas of scientific endeavour, and perhaps nowhere more so than in the new biotechnological sciences.[6] In consequence, the intelligibility of talk of respect for the

---

[5] Ricoeur, *Oneself as Another*, p. 272.

[6] I should make clear that this point is concerned with the cultural rationality of science; it is not as such an epistemological point within the philosophy of science.

given or of the moral claim of the physical body has become increasingly open to question. Our metaphysics has become, or is becoming, corrupted by our practice.

Of course, assertions about the importance of respecting the given could become a guise for a crudely unhermeneutical approach to the body, as if moral norms could be simply read off from biological 'facts'. But such misunderstanding should not be a cause for rejecting some notion of the given. A good hermeneutics of the body will recognise that the body will only be read well by those who are themselves morally well formed. It is only the virtuous community that will see properly. The problem with the readings of the body that are afforded by modern technological medicine – and think here for our purposes of the body of the embryo – is that they are in danger of being corrupted by the dominant technological mentality and the social practices which feed it. The notion of the unmanipulable is foreign to such a mindset, and yet – to return to the topic of this chapter – it is precisely the notion of the unmanipulable, that which may not be tortured to destruction for human gain, which must be at the centre of the notion of the sanctity of life. It is only a sanctified community which will properly discern when one should talk of the sanctity of life. In other words, one answer to the question of whose sanctity is at issue is that it is the community's. Ricoeur is right to say that wisdom in these matters is a matter of communal *phronesis*, but if we are to be cautious about instrumental approaches to the embryo, it is precisely because the mindset of the dominant culture does not easily allow us to think wisely about the issues at stake.

Ronald Dworkin and the Meaning of Sanctity

To explore this notion of the sanctity of life further, I turn now to a second contemporary philosopher, Ronald Dworkin. Dworkin is best known as a philosopher of law, whose arguments for the language of rights against both legal positivism and the dominant moral utilitarianism form the basis of his widely discussed defence of the constitutional role and interpretative methods of the US Supreme Court. In his book *Life's Dominion*, he turns to the politically and constitutionally fraught questions of abortion and euthanasia.[7] His aim in the book is to pour oil on the troubled waters of the debate by arguing for two central points: first, that despite what they each think, both sides to the debate agree on much more than they realise, and second that, again despite what they each think, both sides should regard the issue as fundamentally religious in nature, and therefore something with respect to which the First Amendment prevents Congress from passing laws that restrict individuals' freedom.

I shall concentrate for the present on the first of these arguments, drawing out some implications for the second later on. Dworkin argues that both sides of the debate, in both abortion and euthanasia, in fact agree on a notion of the sanctity of life, and that realising this would take much of the heat and sense of irresolubility from the public controversies. The notion of sanctity of life he proposes is subtle and requires some more detailed elucidation. He starts by distinguishing two different kinds of objections to abortion, which he claims have never been properly analysed (and from now on I will ignore euthanasia and restrict the discussion to abortion alone, noting again that our final object is the considerably more circumscribed question of the status of the early embryo). One kind of objection to abortion claims that the foetus is a creature with interests of its own, including pre-eminently the interest in staying alive; these interests ground rights, including the right not to be killed. The foetus is therefore to be regarded as a full moral person from the moment of conception, to be treated with the same respect and attributed the same rights as a grown adult. This objection to abortion he terms the *derivative* objection, since it is derived from the interests and rights which it assumes all human beings have. The second kind of objection he calls the *detached* objection; this asserts 'that human life has an intrinsic, innate value; that human life begins when its biological life begins, even before the creature whose life it is has movement or sensation or interests or rights of its own'.[8] Abortion on this view is an insult to 'the sacred character of any

---

[7] Ronald Dworkin, *Life's Dominion: An Argument about Abortion and Euthanasia* (London: HarperCollins, 1993).

[8] Dworkin, *Life's Dominion*, p. 9.

stage or form of human life'.[9] He calls this the *detached* objection, since it does not presuppose any particular rights or interests of the foetus, or views about its personhood, but rather that 'it is intrinsically a bad thing, a kind of cosmic shame, when human life at any stage is deliberately extinguished'.[10]

Dworkin argues that the debate over abortion is wrongly understood if it is construed in the first way, as if those on one side think that foetuses are full moral persons, and those on the other that, since foetuses have no interests or rights, they therefore have no intrinsic value at all. He gives a variety of reasons for thinking that the debate should be taken in the second way, that it is in truth a debate about how to interpret the intrinsic value or sanctity of life. On the one hand, with regard to those who assert women's reproductive rights, Dworkin claims that the derivative interpretation of the debate would imply that they believe that the foetus has no intrinsic value, which despite some rhetoric is in general plainly untrue. On the other hand, with regard to the pro-life side, he claims that it is difficult to make sense of the idea of the embryo or early foetus having interests, since to have any interests presupposes at least some elementary level of consciousness, such as that necessary for the capacity to feel pain. Moreover, he argues, a detailed probing of the pro-life position reveals inconsistencies with the claim that the foetus is treated as a moral person with the right to life: for example, even in cases where a mother's life is at stake, one ought never to perform an abortion, since it can never be right directly to kill one person even in order to save the life of another; and yet pro-lifers typically are quite willing to accept this as an exception. Thirdly, Roman Catholic theologians have, over the centuries, espoused a number of different positions about the timing of the ensoulment of the foetus; it was only in the nineteenth century that it was officially pronounced that ensoulment began with conception, and therefore something like the intrinsic sanctity rather than full personhood of the early embryo must have been the dominant idea until then.

---

[9] *Life's Dominion*, p. 9.
[10] *Life's Dominion*, p. 13.

It has to be said that these arguments, at least in relation to the pro-life side, are not deeply compelling. For example, it is surely arguable that one can *have* an interest in continuing to exist without being able to *take* an interest as a subject in one's continued existence. And even if that were not so, it is possible for something to be a bearer of rights without those rights being grounded in that being's subjective or felt interests: a right is quite properly analysable as the correlative of a duty, and it could well be that we have duties to an early embryo which, as a matter of logic, give rise to its having rights over against us, regardless of the presence or absence of states of consciousness. This is the same logic that gives a legitimate sense to talk of animal rights. Again, Dworkin does not address himself at all to the range of different approaches moral theologians have used to address the question of abortion when the mother's life is at stake. And it is also doubtful if anti-abortion activists are likely to be won over to the idea that they have misunderstood all along what they were protesting against. Those at least who have bombed abortion clinics or shot doctors are executing summary justice on those they regard as murderers, not simply crying cosmic shame at the loss of a much prized value. They may be wrong to do so, but they have a better sense of what they are wrong about than Dworkin grants.

However it is his notion of sanctity of life which is of particular concern to us now. Dworkin distinguishes three kinds of value: subjective or personal value, instrumental value and intrinsic value. Something is *instrumentally* valuable to me if it helps me get something else that I want: money or medicine might be two examples. Something is *subjectively* valuable 'only to people who happen to desire it': the greater glory of Derby County Football Club happens to be subjectively valuable to me, but sadly not to many others. By contrast, something is *intrinsically* valuable, 'if its value is *independent* of what people happen to enjoy or want or need or what is good for them'.[11] Within the category of intrinsic value he draws a distinction between things which we value incrementally – 'what we want more of, no matter how much we already have' – and things

[11] *Life's Dominion*, p. 71.

which we value only once they exist. Knowledge might be an example of the former, but the concept of the sacred applies only to the latter: 'It is not important that there be more people. But once a human life has begun, it is very important that it flourish and not be wasted.'[12] The category of the sacred, in this sense of something which we value once it exists rather than incrementally, is not something which is confined to human life. It applies also, for example, to works of art: 'I do not myself wish that there were more paintings by Tintoretto than there are. But I would nevertheless be appalled by the deliberate destruction of even one of those he did paint.'[13]

For Dworkin, then, something is sacred or (to use a secular term) inviolable, if it is intrinsically valuable – that is, valuable regardless of any individual's instrumental or subjective evaluations of it – and if 'its deliberate destruction would dishonor what ought to be honored'.[14] But in virtue of what does it become sacred? How does human life or art – or, he also instances, human cultures or species of animals – come to be intrinsically valuable, something whose destruction would be a shame? Dworkin's answer is that its intrinsic value lies not just in the final product itself, but in the creative *investment* which it represents. Artists invest their creative genius and the resources of their cultural traditions in works of art; nature over evolutionary millennia invests in the various species of animals; generation upon generation have invested themselves in human cultures; and in the case of human beings, both nature and parents (and, for the conventionally religious, God) invest in the creation of a human child. The sacredness of an individual human life reflects therefore

> our wonder at the divine or evolutionary processes that produce new lives from old ones, at the processes of nation and community and language through which a human being will come to absorb and continue hundreds of generations of cultures and forms of life and value, and, finally, when mental life has begun and flourishes, at the process of internal personal creation and judgement by which a person

[12] *Life's Dominion*, p. 74.
[13] *Life's Dominion*, p. 74.
[14] *Life's Dominion*, p. 74.

will make and remake himself ... The horror we feel in the
willful destruction of a human life reflects our shared inartic-
ulate sense of the intrinsic importance of each of these
dimensions of investment.[15]

It is the sanctity of life understood and grounded in this way to
which both conservatives and liberals subscribe. And in relation
to the status of the embryo and foetus, they differ not in this
basic understanding of the sanctity of life, but in their interpretation of this fundamental value. For conservatives it is
principally the natural investment reflected in the biological
dimension of a human life that is important, whereas for
liberals the creative value of the human investment in a life is
overriding. This leads to their different emphases in the
question of abortion: the conservative will see any frustration of
the natural, biological investment as the supreme error, and
hence will defend the continued life of the foetus; while the
liberal will see the potential human waste in sustaining an
unwanted pregnancy as the greater evil. Furthermore, it is easy
to see why those who are religious might be inclined to the
former, since they will see God as the author of everything
natural: it would be quite appropriate for them to insist that
abortion is wrong, not on the derivative grounds that the foetus
is a moral person, but on the detached grounds that 'the deliberate destruction of something created as sacred by God can
never be redeemed by any human benefit'.[16]

Like Ricoeur, Dworkin's account is an attempt to avoid all-or-
nothing approaches to embryonic and early foetal life. He does
this by arguing against such 'derivative' understandings of the
debate and in favour of a 'detached' account of the sanctity of
life. This gives rise to a gradualist spectrum, based not on the
moral significance of progressive biological thresholds, but on
differing people's perspectives on the relative investments by
nature and human beings in a particular life. Whereas
Ricoeur's theory attends solely to the moral and metaphysical
issues, Dworkin's is decisively shaped by the desire to move
forward the political and constitutional debate. Yet, as I argued

---

[15] *Life's Dominion*, p. 84.
[16] *Life's Dominion*, p. 92.

earlier, his arguments against the derivative objections to abortion are unpersuasive. And even if they were effective, in relation to the status of the embryo the points I considered above in comment on Ricoeur – that a technological age is virtually incapable of the necessary vision to address the question – would still give ground for taking a relatively cautious approach.

More striking, however, for a discussion of the sanctity of life is his conception of it as a property of something. To talk of the sanctity of life is to talk of its intrinsic value; and the answer to the question, 'Whose sanctity?' is straightforwardly the embryo's or foetus's – just as it might be the work of art's, or the animal species'. Yet this conceals an ambiguity which finally detracts from his position as a whole. Despite his account (which I quoted above) of the sanctity of a human life which has some overtones of wonder at a *mysterium tremens*, there is nothing in it of a sense of the genuinely transcendent. There is intrinsic value in a human life, but nothing that is finally inviolable. It is a value to be weighed against other values, which might outweigh it. This is true not merely for liberals who might be more inclined to justify abortion or embryo destruction, but also on Dworkin's view for conservatives, since one of the reasons he thinks they should favour his take on the sanctity of life is that it provides them with a rationale for their practice in difficult cases such as abortion when the mother's life is at stake. Yet viewing the sanctity of life in this way does not really capture the idea of unmanipulability that I have earlier suggested is part of the core notion of the sanctity of life.

In this regard it is worth comparing Dworkin's account with that given by Helga Kuhse.[17] Kuhse views the sanctity of life not in terms of a property of a living being, but straightforwardly as a doctrine which can be summed up in a single deontological principle: 'It is absolutely prohibited either intentionally to kill a patient or intentionally to let a patient die, and to base decisions relating to the prolongation or shortening of life on considerations of its quality or kind.'[18] To believe in the sanctity

---

[17] Helga Kuhse, *The Sanctity-of-Life Doctrine in Medicine: A Critique* (Oxford: Clarendon Press, 1987).

[18] Kuhse, *Sanctity-of-Life*, p. 11.

of life is to assent to that principle, not as such to ascribe value to particular beings. Now of course it is arguable that the two are analytically interconvertible: that is, that Kuhse believes that if one is to conceive sanctity of life as a property of something, it should be understood to mean the absolute inviolability of that thing – absolute inviolability being spelled out along the lines of the principle. But for Dworkin the conversion of his account of sanctity into a deontological principle, if it could be done with any degree of exactness, would reveal precisely the vagueness of application that is of concern to the conservatives. The phrase 'sanctity of life' is being used towards ends very different from those traditionally associated with it.

These considerations, and a number of others which I have not detailed,[19] suggest that the political and constitutional problems which Dworkin hopes to ease remain as far from being resolved as ever. He is persuasive neither that conservatives should drop a derivative account of the matter, nor that his interpretation of the sanctity of life will adequately fill the gap. Indeed it is difficult to suppress a creeping sense that Dworkin uses the language of sanctity of life to seduce the conservatives into accepting that abortion is a religious matter and therefore something which it would be unconstitutional for Congress or state legislatures to prohibit, a position that is, of course, finally liberal. Once the smoke clears, what remains unscathed is the fundamental and seemingly intractable logic of the abortion debate: namely that it is not clear why one section of society should tolerate what it regards as the killing of innocents, simply because another section of society does not regard it as such.

Towards a Broader Framework

In criticising Dworkin, I touched on the idea of the relationship of the sanctity of life and the transcendent, as well as on the idea of impersonal values which might be of no subjective or objective value to anyone, but which still should be respected.

---

[19] See, for example, Govert den Hartogh, 'The Values of Life', *Bioethics* 11 (1997), pp. 51–4.

In different ways both of these raise the question of the relation of the sanctity of life to Christian faith, and it is to this that I turn finally.

For Dworkin, the sacredness of life is something which can be affirmed by those with no religious faith; and in this he no doubt draws in part on a long-standing American tradition of the explicit use of the language of the sacred in public alongside the constitutional evacuation of religion from the public square (Jefferson's original draft for the Declaration of Independence, which finally read 'We hold these truths to be self-evident', was 'We hold these truths to be sacred and undeniable'). Kuhse likewise is clear that the sanctity-of-life doctrine in medicine is now fully part of conventional secular morality. But she is also clear that the absolute prohibition of killing is merely a hangover from the West's religious past: it had its source in a theistic framework, and makes little sense outside of it. The rise of Judaism and, particularly, Christianity 'contributed greatly to the general feeling that human life is valuable and worthy of respect': this led to 'a gradual expansion of the circle protecting human life, outlawing not only the killing of slaves or "barbarians", gladiatorial combat, and human sacrifice, but also abortion, infanticide, and euthanasia'.[20] For those who are unpersuaded by such religious beliefs, it would be more compelling to reject the idea of the sanctity of life. This would allow bodily life to be regarded as a mere *bonum utile*, instrumental to higher goods such as desirable states of consciousness; and it would also pave the way for the properly humane quality of life ethic that she proposes.

Kuhse is not the only moral philosopher to believe that a self-consciously post-religious ethic is needed, and that this should be identified with utilitarianism: Derek Parfit and Peter Singer, amongst others, have expressed similar aims.[21] What is interesting for our present purposes is her assertion that belief in the sanctity of life makes sense only within a religious or theistic framework. I will leave aside some of the broader issues this

[20] Kuhse, *Sanctity-of Life*, p. 17.
[21] Derek Parfit, *Reasons and Persons* (Oxford: Clarendon Press, 1984), pp. 453–4; Peter Singer, *Rethinking Life and Death: The Collapse of Our Traditional Ethics* (Oxford: Oxford University Press, 1995), pp. 1–6, 187–222.

raises, and comment only on the questionable adequacy of interpreting the sanctity of life solely in terms of a deontological principle. The sanctity-of-life principle as she states it is severed from any broader framework of meaning which might give it a more general intelligibility. Of course, it is precisely such severing which allows it to be transferred to a secular context and function as 'the theoretical bedrock of medical ethics and the law'.[22] But it is also such severing which makes adherence to the principle doubtfully sustainable over any period of time: it may be broadly accepted for a while, but without the social mediation of some broader conception of the good, such equilibrium as it has is finally liable to be unstable.

Historically, of course, Christian theology provided the intellectual articulation of that broader framework, and the Christian church the immediate social mediation of it. For Christian theology now the first task must be that of recalling the fundamental theological commitments through which the sanctity of life must be interpreted. For example, we could refer to Karl Barth's writing on respect for life. 'Respect,' he writes, 'is man's astonishment, humility and awe at a fact in which he meets something superior – majesty, dignity, holiness, a mystery which compels him to withdraw and keep his distance, to handle it modestly, circumspectly and carefully.'[23] And yet life itself is not the origin of this respect, but rather the command of God. In determining this grounding, Barth rejects the frequent theological resort to 'all kinds of general religious expressions and to the assertions of non-Christian humanism', turning instead to the incarnation:

> We may confidently say that the birth of Jesus Christ as such is the revelation of the command as that of respect for life. This reveals the eternal election and love of God … This gives it even in the most doubtful form the character of something singular, unique, unrepeatable and irreplaceable … This characterizes life as the incomparable and non-

---

[22] Kuhse, *Sanctity-of-Life*, p. 16.
[23] Karl Barth, *Church Dogmatics*, vol. 3, part 4, tr. A. T. Mackay *et al.* (Edinburgh: T&T Clark, 1961), p. 339.

recurrent oppportunity to praise God. And therefore this makes it an object of respect.[24]

Christians reject the notion of intrinsic human dignity or sanctity of life if that means something aboriginal or self-derived, and certainly if it means something finally grounded in human valuing. More apposite than intrinsic dignity is what Helmut Thielicke calls 'alien dignity', the idea that the value of human life is something wholly derived from God, and yet wholly integral to human beings.[25] Because it is bestowed by God, it cannot be earned or lost; it is not dependent on people's investments or subject to technological caprice; it cannot be manipulated or weighed or found wanting. And with this we come to another and final answer to our question: whose sanctity? The answer for Christians can only be: God's sanctity.

Conclusion

I should make clear the very limited number of things for which I have argued here. This paper has not provided any defence of the absolute inviolability of the embryo, nor has it broached the substance of the issue of abortion in any depth; to do these with any seriousness would, aside from anything else, require both a fully contextualised dimension to the argument and a thoroughly theological orientation. I have merely tried to suggest, first, that some of the arguments for rejecting an all-or-nothing approach to the status of the embryo, while they have genuine virtues (not least in rejecting a residual Kantianism), are not finally cogent, or at least would still demand caution in the uses to which embryos are put; and second that *if* sanctity of life is to be understood to imply the deontological principle of absolute inviolability, that will only be a culturally stable conception if it is set within a broader teleological framework.

---

[24] Barth, *Dogmatics*, p. 339.
[25] See Karen Lebacqz, 'Alien Dignity: The Legacy of Helmut Thielicke for Bioethics', in Stephen E. Lammers and Allen Verhey, eds., *On Moral Medicine: Theological Perspectives in Medical Ethics*, 2nd edn. (Grand Rapids, MI: Eerdmans, 1998), pp. 184–92.

For Christians, the sanctity of life is finally constituted by the alien dignity bestowed by a holy God, and truly perceived by a community of believers who are, in Christ, themselves being sanctified.

23

Worship and the Formation of a Holy People[1]

Daniel W. Hardy

Introduction

Western civilisation has been moving progressively to a more and more analytic-descriptive approach to life in the world. That much is to be seen in the attention – bordering on rapture – accorded to scientific discovery and technological innovation. The 'sense of wonder before the intricacy of the universe' that promote and accompanies the sciences, and the uses to which they are put in education and technologically-based industry, always anticipating 'still more startling breakthroughs', is infectious, led by those who appear to be great heroes steadily climbing Everest after Everest to universal admiration. For all its fascination, however, this is all quantitative description, importing us all into a quantitative universe in which we are to be instruments in production and consumption. And it creeps steadily into other subjects, including the range of them normally included in theology – biblical, historical, philosophical and theological – as people become more preoccupied with what is provably the case. Even qualitative issues, the standards and norms by which people live and hope, are made into objects for analytic description, as 'cultures' strangely shorn of their drive toward *goodness* and needing 'historical' research. All this betokens the deepest weakness of

---

[1] A version of this essay appears also in Daniel W. Hardy, *Finding the Church: Shaping Insights and Practices of Anglicanism* (London: SCM, 2001).

modern life and understanding: its self-justifying unwillingness to contemplate the very holiness of God.

Here, however, we shall set our face in the direction of 'prospecting' and ascertaining the qualitative. Not only that, we shall be primarily concerned with the supremely normative, that is holiness – and in particular the holiness of God – in order to try to find how it occurs, how it is generated, how it is transmitted and what are its proper effects. As a topic, it always stretches beyond what human beings – not least this one – are capable of. In fact, it should do that, for of itself it is the peak of reality.

We will pursue the topic into a particular set of important connections: how holiness occurs in sociality, and how the true holiness is achieved in ecclesial form and practice, especially as that is constituted by worship. It is a fascinating but also highly demanding topic, no less than attempting to conceive what is the intensity of the holiness proper to God and how that is made manifest in human sociality; and we here can only aspire to indicate some of what is involved.

While this topic is highly important to the recovery of what the empirical Church should be if it is to be the Church that is of God, it also intersects with a much wider quest that is both religious and worldly: what is the right kind and level of intensity to achieve in the planning of the extensity of life in the world? For the world today, totally preoccupied with increasing complexity, change and the search for pragmatic success – varieties of what I would call extensity – in what does its fullest intensity of well-being consist? And how, both in worship and in the manner in which the Church at worship exemplifies the holiness of God for human society, is this intensity to be mediated in these extensities? Still further, how might this anticipate an 'intensive extensity' of the Kingdom of God, the goal of a transformed life for this world?

Holiness and the quality of sociality that proceeds from it have suffered, separately and in their interconnection, in modern understanding and practice. Why? The causes lie in the constituent elements of modernity and what follows it, but also in the unwillingness of the faithful to identify and redevelop their central concerns in a fashion that is intelligible to modern understanding and life. It seems to me that it is axiomatic that concepts and practices not reworked through the use of current notions will eventually lose their purchase on contemporary life. Nowhere is this more the case than with holiness and sociality – and for that reason I will attend especially to the possibility of using current notions to revivify them. At the same time, we will need to be careful lest we be drawn into using categories that, while attractive and popular, end in domesticating holiness and the quality it bestows on sociality. We need to be attempting the reverse, finding ways of developing these notions and practices that are more, not less, true to them.

True Holiness

At the outset, it needs to be seen that holiness, sociality and worship are, or should be, extremely rich and powerful notions and practices, and therefore capable of orientating vast ranges of life in the world. To put this rather graphically, they have to do with the mountain-tops, valleys and ascents of reality and human life, and as such are extremely exciting, as well as full of implications for human understanding and practice – those very spheres so often detached from them. They are not to be 'flattened' or domesticated as if they were all on the same plane, as they so often are today. That, indeed, is what happens when they are considered as varieties of 'religion', 'experience' and 'culture'.

There is, and ought to be, no more demanding topic than 'the holy', for in it we have a designation of what is fullest and most complete, not only in human awareness and conviction but also in reality, and not only relatively full but completely so. As such, there is no ready way to 'locate' or 'describe' it by means of reality, understanding and practice found in the world.

For those in the Judeo-Christian tradition, ' the holy' and 'God' are mutually defining terms. Before we discuss that, however, there is some value in looking at the holy where the association with God is not developed. In ancient (Greek) times, where there is no developed association for the terms, that is with God, or in (modern) times, where positive associations are suspended for the sake of comparative study, 'the holy' designates the domain proper to the fullest or supreme. It is, as it were, what is proper to the fullest or supreme – its 'propriety' as we might call it, if we free this word from ideas of decorum or manners. Similar to this is its capacity to be fully whatever it is, a 'self-capacity' – as distinct from what I have called the 'capacity for finitude' that marks kinds of creation[2] – and to maintain itself fully 'according to its kind', as distinct from an admixture with what is lesser or different. These are what lie behind the issue of 'purity'. Conventionally, purity is closely associated with separation from the impure; that is, it is conceived in terms of binary oppositions whereby the 'pure' is itself by distinguishing, or separating, itself from the impure. More fundamental, however, is its capacity to maintain its fullness according to its own kind, without reference to, or collapse into, other kinds. Suffice it to say that '*propriety*' and '*purity*' or '*self-capacity*' and '*capacity for self-maintenance*' are primary ways of designating what is 'holy'.

As having its own propriety and purity, the holy resists comprehension in the other terms normally available, even those we normally find to be most fundamental: it is not containable in the ontological (the science of being), the cosmological (the science of the existent) or the historical. We should not slide too easily into suppositions 1) that the holy *is*; 2) has spatio-temporal extension; or 3) has historical duration. Respectively, that would be 1) to 'contain' the holy in an ontological system, to identify it with, or employ it as the sacred epitome of being; 2) to make it 'immanent' in creation as its primary determinant; or 3) to place it within historical process as its overarching principle. There are ways of safeguarding the holy in each of these methods of explaining life in the world: it can be said that the holy – unlike forms of being – has its being in itself; or that the holy – unlike created life – is self-caused; or that the holy – unlike historically contingent events – is without external conditions. But these do not take us far in understanding the holy as such, its '*propriety*' and '*purity*' or '*self-capacity*' and '*capacity for self-maintenance*'.

And we should not easily suppose that the holy can be fully

---

[2] See Daniel W. Hardy, *God's Ways with the World: Thinking and Practising Christian Faith* (Edinburgh: T&T Clark, 1996), p. 158.

grasped by theory, aesthetic contemplation or ethical determination. For it falls beyond the sphere of reference of philosophy, science, morality and aesthetics: it is their 'sting and prod', surpassing them in its own unsurpassability. This was nicely stated recently:

> Philosophy dreams of returning to itself and itself alone, eternally. The history of European philosophical systems, each claiming to be more 'scientific' than the next, provides ample evidence of thought's self-infatuation, whether in the guise of a solitary bravado or speaking with the megaphonic ventriloquy of 'world historical spirit.' But beyond and better than these second thoughts of first highest thoughts, and certainly better than the venom of their only partially repressed frustrations, come other claims, irreducible to empirical science or philosophical totality but more sincere and more elevated – moral claims. Better than science are the demands of morality, of goodness, and above morality itself, absolute but constituting the very sting and prod of morality, are the even higher demands of holiness, the unsurpassable 'you shall be holy because I am holy'.[3]

In other words, we must not suppose that holiness is directly cognisable, can be contemplated aesthetically, or can be morally ascertained as the Good. It is more likely to draw each of these beyond itself to a primary 'fullest' that has its own propriety and purity.

The same applies to linguistic signification. Strictly speaking 'the holy' does not signify by the means we normally suppose, that is by

> Straightforward or oblique correspondence, or through a coherence, whether synchronic or diachronic or both ... It leaves correspondence and coherence behind, or rather *beneath*, drawing them upward in its train, reaching higher, disturbing, giving pause, imposing too much, tracing what is already gone and not yet come, and as responsibility and obligation is both irreducibly present and beyond at once.[4]

[3] Richard A. Cohen, *Elevations: The Height of the Good in Rosenzweig and Levinas* (Chicago: University of Chicago Press, 1994), p. xiii.
[4] Cohen, *Elevations*, p. xv.

That is not, of course, to say that there is no access by such means to holiness, but in order to be even partly adequate, they need to be carried by holiness beyond their usual limitations:

> The holy, which alone is the essential sphere of divinity, which in turn alone affords a dimension for the gods and God, comes to radiate only when Being itself beforehand and after extensive preparation has been illuminated and is experienced in its truth.[5]

How are we carried beyond these limitations to holiness? If we look at human history, the holiness we have identified – '*propriety*' and '*purity*' or '*self-capacity*' and '*capacity for self-maintenance*' – seems to have been uncovered through different kinds of ascesis of understanding and life. In China, for example, the question of human nature – whether 'selfish and asocial … naturally benevolent and therefore socially responsible … or naturally evil and in need of control by rites'[6] – was foremost. In Greece and throughout the Western tradition, such issues came to the fore as the intellectual community (concerned first with cosmology and the constituent elements of the physical universe) 'acquired an internal density and hence a push to higher levels of abstract self-reflection' as to the necessary conditions for human well-being: 'the issue was the purity of the ideal of goodness and how much compromise there should be with worldly and sensual goods'.[7] The fact that 'holiness' was uncovered in such differing, historical, abstractive and reflective ways, does not suggest that it is not 'real', however, but only that differing conceptions of the reality of 'holiness' arise in human beings and their social interaction. Furthermore, in some very fundamental sense, the reality of holiness seems to *attract* attention to itself.

[5] Martin Heidegger, quoted in Jean-Luc Marion, *God Without Being* (Chicago: University of Chicago Press, 1991), p. 40.
[6] Randall Collins, *The Sociology of Philosophies* (Cambridge, MA: Harvard University Press, 1998), p. 146.
[7] Collins, *Sociology*, p. 146f.

Holiness and God

So far, we have struggled to identify the features of the holy, and the ways by which they have been sought out by natural means. These are important, because they are operative in, if not constitutive of, many of the most basic institutions of human life. But it is a matter of question whether they can ever be open to the fuller dimensions of the holy. They smack of formalism and constraint, and in those ways are untrue to holiness itself.

In the Judeo-Christian view of holiness, we meet something much more full, a holiness filled with the perfection of wisdom and goodness and therefore beautiful:

> The law of the LORD is perfect,
>   reviving the soul;
> the decrees of the LORD are sure,
>   making wise the simple;
> the precepts of the LORD are right,
>   rejoicing in the heart
> the commandment of the LORD is clear,
>   enlightening the eyes;
> the fear of the LORD is pure,
>   enduring forever;
> the ordinances of the LORD are true
>   and righteous altogether.
> More to be desired are they than gold,
>   even much fine gold;
> sweeter also than honey,
>   and drippings of the honeycomb.[8]

Within the relationship of Hebrew society with the Holy One comes an immense freedom with God, within which is the possibility of right sociality itself.

Here, holiness and God are mutually defining. God is a holy God (Josh. 24.19); holy is he! (Ps. 99.3, 5); who can stand before this holy God? (1 Sam. 6.20); the Lord our God is holy (Ps. 99.9); holy, holy, holy is the Lord Almighty (Isa. 6.3; Rev. 4.8); the Holy One of Israel (Isa. 37.23); I will show myself holy

---

[8] Psalm 19.7–10 (NRSV).

(Lev. 10.3); he showed himself holy among them (Num. 20.13); the Lord Almighty is the one you are to regard as holy (Isa. 8.13); there is no one holy like the Lord (1 Sam. 2.2); who is like you, majestic in holiness? (Exod. 15.11); you alone are holy (Rev. 15.4).

And holiness is the attraction to God, what *calls* and *moves* people. Divine things are beautiful, and that attracts and motivates people: 'there is a splendor, a beauty, about God and his ways that *lures* human beings to him'.[9] Not only that, but it is – for those who will contemplate it – infinitely satisfying, while also infinitely humbling. Jonathan Edwards expresses this beautifully:

> Holiness ... appeared to me to be of a sweet, pleasant, charming, serene, calm nature; which brought an in-expressible purity, brightness, peaceableness and ravishment to the soul; and that it made the soul like a field or garden of God, with all manner of pleasant flowers; that is all pleasant, delightful, and undisturbed; enjoying a sweet calm, and the gently vivifying beams of the sun. The soul of the Christian ... appeared like such a little white flower ... low and humble on the ground, opening its bosom, to receive the pleasant beams of the sun's glory ...
>
> Once, as I rode out into the wood for my health, in 1737, having alighted from my horse in a retired place, as my manner had commonly been, to walk for divine contem-plation and prayer, I had a view that for me was extraordinary of the glory of the Son of God, as Mediator between God and man, and his wonderful, great, full, pure and sweet grace and love, and meek and gentle condescension. This grace, that appeared to me so calm and sweet, appeared great above the heavens. The person of Christ appeared ineffably excellent, with an excellency great enough to swallow up all thought and conception. Which continued, as near as I can judge, about an hour; which kept me the greater part of the time, in a flood of tears, and weeping aloud. I felt withal, an ardency of soul to be, what I knew not otherwise how to express, than

[9] Gerald R. McDermott, *Seeing God* (Downers Grove, IL: Inter-Varsity Press, 1995), p. 114.

to be emptied and annihilated; to lie in the dust, and to be full of Christ alone, to love him with a holy and pure love; to trust in him ... and to be perfectly sanctified and made pure, with a divine and heavenly purity.[10]

It would be a mistake to suppose that the basis of these views is in some kind of mystical ascent to this pure holiness, as if this were an alternative to the struggles with holiness we discussed before. On the contrary, it lies in the 'discovery' of the nature of the propriety of holiness, that is inherently *relational*. That is the significance of the Psalmist's words praising the *holiness* of laws, decrees, precepts and commandments. This is not, as is so often assumed, to sanctify *human* law; it is to recognise that the holiness of the Lord is in these ways of conferring holiness on the people. The propriety of the Lord, the Lord's holiness, is relational, in establishing a holy relationship with a people called to be holy.

Something similar, but also different, is found in Jonathan Edwards, for whom the holiness of God consists in the one through whom he is mediated for human beings; 'This grace that appeared to me so calm and sweet, appeared great above the heavens. The person of Christ appeared ineffably excellent, with an excellency great enough to swallow up all thought and contemplation.' And, a little later in the same *Personal Narrative*:

God in the communication of his Holy Spirit, has appeared as an infinite fountain of divine glory and sweetness; being full and sufficient to fill and satisfy the soul: pouring forth itself in sweet communications, like the sun in its glory, sweetly and pleasantly diffusing light and life.[11]

As the Jew rejoices in the true righteousness – the holiness – of God as that is conferred through the precepts of God, so Edwards rejoices in the inherently relational holiness of God as conferred through the Word of God that is the Word of life. In both cases holiness is a relational propriety that capacitates or invests human beings with intimations of itself – its propriety –

---

[10] Jonathan Edwards, 'A Personal Narrative' in *A Jonathan Edwards Reader*, ed. J. E. Smith *et al.* (New Haven: Yale University Press, 1995), pp. 287–288, 293.
[11] Edwards, 'Personal Narrative', p. 293.

by which they can identify it, at least in part. But now we are on the verge of a larger issue about how the propriety is self-established and how it invests others with something of itself.

Monistic or Trinitarian Holiness?

What appears in the two places just discussed – the Psalms and Jonathan Edwards – but also much more widely in the Hebrew and Christian Scriptures, is the *relational propriety* of the holiness of God. The issue cannot be left there, however. How is this to be conceived?

At one level, what this suggests is that the holiness of God is not to be seen in monadic terms, as if it were properly itself only when independent from all else. It is possible, of course, to conceive of God in such terms, as an eternally pure self. What is suggested by the God whose holiness is intrinsically relational is different: here is one whose holiness is inherently related to all else, a holiness that is comprehensively relevant – a 'richness' with maximal 'reach'. Although stated in quite different terms this bears some resemblance to what is suggested by Eberhard Bethge's description of Dietrich Bonhoeffer's theology: 'concreteness is the attribute of revelation itself': 'concreteness, being essential to and a genuine attribute of revelation, includes temporality, historicity, involvement, and the realities of the day'.[12] But in the case we have been discussing, such close affinity with the concrete realities of life in the world seems to me to be implicit in the relationality that is proper to holiness as such: the holiness of God is intrinsically related to all else.

There is another important issue here. How does holiness involve itself in the range of life in the world? It is common to distance the two – the holiness of God and the issues of the world – either making them 1) competitive with each other, or 2) co-present. These options are clearly to be seen amongst modern Christians when they argue about the primacy of the revelation of God in Scripture: 1) by some, observance of its

---

[12] Eberhard Bethge, 'Bonhoeffer's Life and Theology' in *World Come of Age*, ed. Ronald Gregor Smith (London: Collins, 1967), pp. 33, 38.

moral pronouncements is made a precondition for engagement with world-issues (homosexuality, for example), and 2) by others Scripture is to be accorded parallel value to (co-present with) worldly practices. In both cases, scriptural holiness and world are held in a dyadic, two-term, relation.

If, however, the propriety of holiness is one of intrinsic relation to all else, we must be very careful to honour it. This means that the relationality that is inherent in the propriety of the holiness of God must be clearly displayed:[13]

1. Holiness is intrinsically complex, *triadic* rather than dyadic: it stands not at a distance from the world, but is inherently related to the other, as one set of relations related to other relations by a stable relation.
2. Holiness, itself a set of relations, is related to other relations by a mediating relation.
3. The relations of holiness to itself and to a relational world are complex.
4. Holiness and the world must not be seen independently of their (mediating) relation: to do so is to ignore their relation.
5. The relation between holiness and the world cannot be constructed from particular features of either: there is no way to construct a triadic relation out of any number of merely dyadic relations (dyadic relations are 'degenerate triads').

Followed through carefully, this would correct the consistent modern tendency to collapse all relations into dyadic pairs, a God conceived on monistic terms versus a world similarly seen, or seen in binitarian terms, or in dualistic terms. As a clarification of the relations inherent in the holiness of God, it illuminates the ways in which this holiness incorporates reference to the complexities of the world, as well as the closest affinity to them.

The argument deserves to be taken one step further still. So far we have seen holiness as intrinsically relational, and

---

[13] See Peter Ochs, *Pierce, Pragmatism and the Logic of Scripture* (Cambridge: Cambridge University Press, 1998), p. 255f. Ochs' use of Charles Peirce is in connection with the reading of Scripture.

relational in a triadic pattern. Properly seen, as it appears in the passages quoted from the Psalms and Jonathan Edwards, the holiness of God is *performative* – performing in triadic patterns – and appreciated by those who perform according to his holiness. 'The ordinances of the Lord are true and righteous altogether ... Moreover by them is your servant warned; in keeping them there is great reward.'[14]

> I felt withal, an ardency of soul to be ... emptied and annihilated; to lie in the dust, and to be full of Christ alone; to love him with a holy and pure love; to trust in him; to live upon him; to serve and follow him, and to be totally wrapped up in the fullness of Christ; and to be perfectly sanctified and made pure, with a divine and heavenly purity.[15]

The holiness of God is not only relational and complex but also inherently dynamic and performative. The performance of holiness in God has a counterpart anticipated within it; the performance of this holiness by human beings in history. The two are related in the same triadic pattern we have discussed.

As I have expressed it elsewhere, albeit in ontological terms I would use more cautiously now:

> God is one whose *being* is *directed*, directed toward human life in the world. His well-being, therefore, is that which occurs in the direction of his being. It is, so to speak, achieved in the direction of his being. Correspondingly, human well-being in the world arises through the direction of his being toward us and our world, and as our lives are conformed to that.[16]

In other words, the holiness of God performs its direction toward human life in the world, and does so through a concentration of holiness in relationship that is inseparable from the extending of the holiness of this relationship with his people in the world.

This gives rise to a renewal of Trinitarian understanding. We see that God is not a kind of inert, Platonic perfection, but 'is himself in maintaining the consistency of his life in an ordered

---

[14] Psalm 19.9b, 11.
[15] Edwards, 'Personal Narrative', p. 293.
[16] Hardy, *God's Ways with the World*, p. 25.

but energetic congruence with his world'. That is, the Trinity immanent in God is his consistent performance of holiness, but this is maintained – as the Trinitarian economy in the world – through God's energetic congruence with the world.[17]

Refining Holiness

As exciting as it is to contemplate God's self-maintaining performance of holiness, we would be failing if we did not also respond to the intensity of what occurs in it. For God is a crucible of holiness, a refining fire in the enacting and extending of it,[18] rightly evoking religious affections such as 'fear, hope, love, hatred, desire, joy, sorrow, gratitude, compassion and zeal'.[19] The 'fullness of all possible good in God, [the] fullness of every perfection, of all excellency and beauty, and of infinite happiness'[20] happens there not simply as a state of affairs, but through a concentration of intense energy within the relationality intrinsic to God.

And 'this infinite fountain of good ... send[s] forth abundant streams, that this infinite fountain of light should, diffusing its excellent fullness, pour forth light all around'.[21] Notwithstanding this – we have called it the intrinsic direction-ality of God – it meets resistance from all that is less, which supplants the relationality 'natural' to God by fragmentation. So merge all the dyadic relations mentioned before, fragmenting the relations inherent in God reducing the 'refining fire' of God's holiness to separate flames, as it were. Thenceforth all that – by virtue of God – is inherently related, is – by virtue of this resistance to God – fragmented.

But that does not stand as the end of the story. In God, that is in the Father's relation to the Son, there is the most direct relation to human beings even if supplanted by the

---

[17] Hardy, *God's Ways with the World,* see pp. 80–2.
[18] Cf. Jer. 6.29–3-; Isa. 1.25; Isa. 48.10; Mal. 3.3.
[19] Jonathan Edwards, *A Treatise concerning Religious Affections,* ed. J. E. Smith (New Haven: Yale University Press, 1959), p. 102.
[20] Jonathan Edwards, *Ethical Writings,* ed. Paul Ramsey (New Haven: Yale University Press, 1989), p. 432f.
[21] Edwards, *Ethical Writings,* p. 433.

fragmentation introduced by human beings. God has placed himself in enduring relation to an unholy humankind yet it continues to be opposed by human beings. In Jesus and his eventual death on the Cross, we find these two meeting in another kind of crucible, the repulsion of humankind and the holiness of God persisting through suffering to death. And the fragmentation between human beings and God is burnt away in this refining fire.

So the holiness of God – the fire in God by which full holiness is generated and sustained in its relation to all else – eventually refines even that which opposes it, thereby healing the fragmentations introduced by those who resist it. It is a highly dynamic and healing 'holiness', well beyond simple conceptions of relationship through effective 'communication'. And by the way, it reveals the deficiencies of forms of theology that bypass the dynamism of God's holiness by employing bland conceptions of 'knowing God' through God's 'self-communication': they avoid the refining fire of the holiness in God and in the Cross of Christ.

Holiness Enacted in the World

The ways by which the holiness of God may be enacted in the world reach far beyond what is conventionally associated with 'religion'. They are as wide-ranging as the dimensions of life in the world, but all of them are seen in their proper interaction. 'Global' names for these dimensions would include the natural, ecological, historical, societal, political, economic and cultural/symbolic. Following the triadic logic of holiness outlined before, they are to be seen as inherently related to each other in the performance of holiness, rather than as functionally isolated in the pursuit of pragmatic success. In the long term, no one or two of these dimensions can flourish by ignoring the consequences of its actions on the others. 'Can any making of our selves and making of our world not also be a response to the world and a respecting of the earth?' is the question rightly posed by the English literary critic Jonathan Bate in a recent book *The Song of the Earth*.[22] The deeper

---

[22] Jonathan Bate, *The Song of the Earth* (London: Picador, 2000), p. 282.

question is whether the holiness of God can be mediated other than through the recognition and refinement of the inherent relations of all people in the world in all the dimensions of life in the world, natural, ecological, historical, societal, political, economic and cultural/symbolic? This is a matter that needs a great deal of serious investigation, but which we cannot pursue now.

The key vehicles for the performance of holiness in the world are not so much the scientific and technologically based economic developments that fascinate us so much, as those capable of *maintaining* and *directing* the inherent relationships of all people in all the dimensions of life in the world, to their fulfilment. Typically, these vehicles for holiness will be the social institutions by which these relations are mediated, such as – in the broadest sense – social polity and law.

First, how do we build the social institutions capable of responding to technological, social, political and cultural globalisation? As one of the advocates of the 'third way' in vogue today stated it,

Civil society is fundamental to constraining the power of markets and government. Neither a market economy nor a democratic state can function effectively without the civilizing influence of civic association.[23]

The more fundamental question, however, is how the holiness of God is performed in civic associations of all kinds. How are the multifold relationships of people in all the dimensions of human life to mediate the 'wonderful, great, full, pure and sweet grace and love' as established through the refining fire of God? What is to be the form of society that will free human beings fully to flourish in the world, and achieve the ends God has placed before them?

Second, how is the law to guide us? That in some measure it can is shown by both the Old Testament and by the respect for the law – even if only a relative respect – seen in the New Testament. In our terms, the law does attempt to arbitrate between people in the many dimensions of their existence.

[23] Anthony Giddens, *The Third Way and its Critics* (Cambridge: Polity Press, 2000), p. 64.

Furthermore, it is itself directional, moving by incremental steps, by a combination of stability and forward movements. The law is not so much a highly coherent set of norms for the whole of social life, or even their interpretation in particular cases, as it is the *development* of the norms needed for the well-being of society,[24] and the punishment of those who offend against society. Although the laws provide stability, they are clearly contingent: as one expert said, 'all laws can be repealed; all are provisional'.[25] They are examples of what has been called 'principled law generation'.[26]

Civil society and the law, conceived in these terms, are not capable of fully achieving holiness in society. This always remains beyond them, as 'source', 'sustenance' and 'end' rather than 'achievement'. Nonetheless, civil society and the law are profoundly important as contingent, provisional historical approximations to the good, both in the freedom that they enable and in the limits to freedom that they prescribe. In that respect, they are like historical forms of what is called 'negative theology'. They approximate the holiness of God in the good of society, while denying that this good – how human beings order themselves – is fully good, or in accordance with the holiness of God. Their value is more proximate: they serve as correctives to presumptuous claims made by those who wish to co-opt society and its people for their system of individual interest. What is especially interesting about them, society and law, is their underlying thrust as derived (so Christians would claim) from God energising them as they reach for the good, even in the inadequacies of their attempts to achieve it. When used of society and law, that is a fascinating thought – that our contingent, provisional, incremental attempt to achieve the good are energised by the very good that they never fully achieve; the 'correction' exercised in legal practice is a necessary anticipation of, but insufficient for, the good. So every attempt to guide, to enact justice, to embody mercy and to punish and forgive, must pass through the refining fire of

[24] Peter Morton, *An Institutional Theory of Law* (Oxford: Clarendon Press, 1998), p. 197.

[25] Morton, *Institutional Theory of Law*, p. 150.

[26] Morton, *Institutional Theory of Law*, p. 176.

God's justice in order to partake of the unnamed qualities of goodness and to be energised by goodness itself. But the occupational hazard of society and law is ignoring both the demands of holiness and the energy of goodness that flows from it in the provenance of God.

Worship as Performative Holiness

Human society and law presume, but do not in practice attend to, the task of mediating holiness in the world. They have their counterparts in the social life and polity of the Church, where – properly speaking – the task of mediating holiness in the world is attended to. The difference, one might say, between human and 'divine' society lies in the fact that the church is – properly speaking – a movement directed by and to the holiness of God. Facing the holiness of God, and performing it within human social life, is the special provenance of worship. There all the interrelated dimensions of life are to be raised to the holiness of God.

The mode is affirmation of praise, as that which 'raises' the holiness of God in human life and society. As George Herbert wrote:

Seven whole days, not one in seven,
I will praise thee;
In my heart, though not in heaven,
I can raise thee.
Small it is, in this poor sort
To enrol thee:
E'en eternity's too short
To extol thee.

Correspondingly, the occupational hazard is to treat it as a routine ritual practice of community-formation unmotivated by – and inert in the presence of – the holiness of God.

Yet if we see worship as the situation in which the relational and directive propriety of the holiness of God is intrinsically present in social enactment, there is a direct connection between the contingent human attempt to 'worship' and the inner dynamic of the holiness of God. So this worship is not primarily human attempts to 'ascend' to God, but the situation in which human beings are held by, and moved forward by the very holiness of God. Whatever movement they make toward the good occurs because of the formative, freeing and energising attraction of the holiness of God.

Yet worship also occurs within human resistance to, and fragmentation from, God. And in it, people must – in order to be held and moved by the holiness of God as they worship – participate in the refining fire, not as it is within God, for that is too intense and great, but as it occurred in the Cross of Christ. As they do so, worship within the intrinsic relationality of God becomes possible again. Then they find themselves 'proved' as people, in all the dimensions of their existence with each other, as they are *lifted*, not into eternity but to a higher historical goodness that, in some measure, exemplifies the holiness of God. Although they may yearn for something much more 'ideal', and for something much more definitive and final, 'a final end to their sin', as it were, worship is actually much more the real anticipation by historical human beings of the eventual holiness of the kingdom of God. The steps by which they move forward to his holiness are concrete embodiments – not complete but nonetheless determinations or anticipations – of the good toward which God's holiness draws all.

Through the refining fire of the Cross of Christ, then, worship is placed within the sphere of the relational and directional propriety of the holiness of God. There are those who see it in timeless terms, as an instant in which, as the Word of God is preached in its fullness to the faithful individual, he or she is transformed. But it seems to me that the logic of God's holiness – with its passage through the refining fire of the Cross of Christ, and the consequent restoration of relationality, directionality and complexity of intersection with the world – suggests the importance of forms of worship that are necessarily more time-laden and social. The pre-eminent form of such worship is the Eucharist, and we must pause to try to understand how it manifests the logic of God's holiness.

Like drama, the Eucharist is a patterning of particulars – particular people in a particular setting in a particular time-scale, in which the various dimensions of their life in the world are infolded, within dramatic actions – in order to signify the reality of their intrinsic connection to the inner dynamic of God's holiness. As such, it is a particular and unrepeatable event of signification that emerges from, and embodies, a complex interaction between circumstances, actors, text and audience, where presence, participation and involvement with a specific set of people at a specific place and time are necessary. It and they are not however separated from 'the world', with all its complex relationships – natural, historical, social, political, economic, cultural – but serve to bring all these into the action in which they are engaged. (For them not to do so is to lapse into lesser kinds of relationality – dyadic ones as distinct from triadic ones – than those found in the holiness of God.) At the same time, the Eucharist enacts the intrinsic connection of all these to the inner dynamic of God's holiness, which depends not on the efficacy of the dramatic action but on the efficacy of God's holiness in it.

Its focus is the enactment of holiness, not as something general and timeless but as what is the 'refining fire' of Christ in this place, in this set of circumstances, for these people, and through them all others, now; and the effects of this holiness are to be seen in the energising of these people for and within the holiness of God as that reaches the whole world in all its complexity. Hence it is an occasion of performing – and thus learning – the quality of God's holiness in action, whose implications are seen as it reconstitutes the life of those involved, forming their multifold interactions with others.

What occurs in this performative event of signification is the refining holiness of God in Christ as performative in *all that we do* in our enactment of goodness with each other and with the world. The Eucharist is our dramatic working out of refining holiness *within* the self-involving, self-enactment of God in human history and life.

Unlike the near-dualism of much theology, separating God from God's action in the world and linking them by notions of correspondence,[27] and unlike attempts to identify God with temporal world-process, the conception of God that is invoked in the Eucharist is one of the 'primal divine drama',[28] in which

[27] This is the effect of modern conceptions of the Trinity, e.g., 'the immanent Trinity is the economic Trinity' (Rahner).

[28] Hans Urs Von Balthasar, *Theo-Drama* (San Francisco: Ignatius Press, 1994), vol. 4, p. 325.

God's inherently self-giving holiness is fully intertwined with God's eschatological self-actualization. Hence the Eucharist is the 'forming of human freedom' in ethical responsibility *within* the refining Cross of Christ as restoring the intrinsic relationality and movement of God's holiness. It is this in which the efficacy of the Eucharist consists.

Worship and the Formation of a Holy People

The ways by which people most commonly suppose that worship affects human life and understanding are much more simple than those we have been considering here. We have seen the relational, directional, purifying characteristics inherent in the holiness of God, and found them to be mediated in the multiple dimensions of human life in the world. But most understanding of worship and its effects is focused on personal transformation, the ethical transformation of one-to-one relationships or on communal *koinonia*. The risk is that, by isolating person from person, or the need and ethical demand of the other from the holiness of God within material relationships, or the community from the needs of social order in the world, the impact of the holiness of God in worship is seen much too narrowly. I do not want to gainsay the value of such explorations – for example, the notion of the radical ethical demand of the other as used by David Ford in *Self and Salvation*[29] is highly instructive – but it seems to me that we need to look to what we might call the 'software platforms' which allow the dynamics of persons, interpersonal relationships and communities to operate most effectively. How does worship affect a holy people through a polity that 'guarantees' right kinds of personal discipline, interpersonal relationships and communities?

Perhaps the central question is how worship enacts *holy trust* as the basis of society. It is widely recognised that the well-being of a society is based on trust: 'Any long-range attempt at constructing a social order and continuity of social frameworks

---

[29] David Ford, *Self and Salvation* (Cambridge: Cambridge University Press, 1999).

of interaction must be predicated on the development of stable relations of mutual trust between social actors.'[30] In ordinary terms, trust involves:

1. endowing others with trust, thereby liberating and mobilising them to act freely without fear; and
2. encouraging sociability and association with others thereby enriching the field and intimacy of their relationships – creating moral density between them.

At least five societal circumstances are necessary for these:

1. Normative coherence, indicating what people can be counted on to do.
2. Stability of social order providing settled and clear 'space' for people to exercise their gifts.
3. Transparency of social organisations, providing assurance of expectations.
4. Familiarity of environment, enabling people to be 'at home'.
5. Regular systems of accountability , to assure the observance of standards.[31]

Taken together, these provide the 'ordinary' social form for human freedom and flourishing.

To speak of 'holy trust', however, is to invoke the active presence of One by whose 'refining fire' life is restored for inherent relationships within the multi-dimensional life of the world. To speak in these terms is to suggest the possibility of relationships between people that embody trust of the highest order, bonds in which human beings may flourish most fully together.

How does this arise from eucharistic worship? It comes from a variety of things enacted in it:

1. Pre-commitment, in which people cede their initiative and security to that which comes preveniently from the holiness of God.

---

[30] Adam Seligman, *The Problem of Trust* (Princeton: Princeton University Press, 1997), p. 14.

[31] Cf. Piotr Sztompka, *Trust: A Sociological Theory* (Cambridge: Cambridge University Press, 1999), pp. 122–5.

2. The coming together in a small situation of expectation, where people are prepared for God to establish a high density and intimacy of relationships.
3. Readiness to undergo refinement – transformation from their fragmentation – by the fire of God's holiness in the Cross of Christ.
4. Openness to a 'moral density' in which together they are infused with a high degree of interdependence, as enacting the relational dynamics of the holiness of God.
5. A symbolic enactment of the refining activity of the holiness of God in the sacrifice of Christ.
6. Active connection with, and embodiment of holiness in, the multiple dimensions and relations of the wider world.

Worship understood in such terms is indeed the means by which a people is formed as a holy society. And it exemplifies the truest possibilities for all society.

Suggestions for Further Reading

Allison, D. C., 'Jesus as Millenarian Ascetic', in *Jesus of Nazareth Millenarian Prophet* (Minneapolis: Fortress, 1998), pp.172–216.

Almond, P. C., *Rudolf Otto: An Introduction to his Philosophical Thought* (Chapel Hill, NC: University of North Carolina Press, 1984).

Anderson, B., 'The Holy One of Israel', in D. A. Knight and P. J. Paris, eds., *Justice and the Holy* (Atlanta: Scholars Press, 1989), pp. 3–19.

Augé, M., *Non-Places. Introduction to an Anthropology of Supermodernity* (London: Verso, 1995).

Barr, J., 'An English Example – "Holy"', in *The Semantics of Biblical Language* (Oxford: Oxford University Press, 1961), pp.111–14.

Barton, S. C., 'Christian Community in the Light of 1 Corinthians', *Studies in Christian Ethics* 10 (1997), pp. 1–15.

Bebbington, D. W., *Evangelicalism in Modern Britain. A History from the 1730s to the 1980s* (London: Unwin Hyman, 1989).

Bebbington, D. W., 'Holiness in Nineteenth-Century British Methodism', in W. M. Jacob and N. Yates., eds., *Crown and Mitre: Religion and Society in Northern Europe since the Reformation* (Woodbridge, Suffolk: Boydell Press, 1993), pp. 161–74.

Bebbington, D. W., *Holiness in Nineteenth-Century England* (Carlisle: Paternoster, 1999).

Bockmuehl, M., 'Jewish and Christian public ethics in the early Roman Empire', in G. N. Stanton and G. G. Stroumsa, eds., *Tolerance and Intolerance in Early Judaism and Christianity* (Cambridge: Cambridge University Press, 1998), pp. 342–55.

Borg, M. J., *Conflict, Holiness and Politics in the Teachings of Jesus* (Lewiston, NY: Edwin Mellen Press, 1998).

Bossy, J., *Christianity in the West 1400–1700* (Oxford: Oxford University Press, 1985).

Bowker, J., *Hallowed Ground. Religions and the Poetry of Place* (London: SPCK, 1993).

Brown, D. and Loades, A., eds., *The Sense of the Sacramental. Movement and Measure in Art and Music, Place and Time* (London: SPCK, 1995).

Brown, P., *Society and the Holy in Late Antiquity* (Berkeley: University of California Press, 1982).

Brown, P., *The Cult of the Saints. Its Rise and Function in Latin Christianity* (London: SCM, 1983).

Brown, P., *Authority and the Sacred* (Cambridge: Cambridge University Press, 1995).

Burton-Christie, D., *The Word in the Desert. Scripture and the Quest for Holiness in Early Christian Monasticism* (New York: Oxford University Press, 1994).

Bynum, C. W., *Holy Feast, Holy Fast: The Religious Significance of Food to Medieval Women* (Berkeley: University of California Press, 1987).

Carver, F. G., 'The Quest for the Holy: The Darkness of God', *Wesleyan Theological Journal* 23 (1988), pp. 7–32.

Chavchavadze, M., *Man's Concern With Holiness Within the Anglican, Catholic, Reformed, Lutheran, Orthodox Traditions* (London: Hodder & Stoughton, n.d.).

Chilton, B., 'Purity and Impurity', in R. P. Martin and P. H. Davids, eds., *Dictionary of the Later New Testament and its Developments* (Downers Grove, IL: InterVarsity Press, 1997), pp. 988–96.

Clements, R. E., 'The Concept of Abomination in the Book of Proverbs', in M. V. Fox, *et al.*, eds., *Texts, Temples, and Traditions* (Eisenbrauns, 1996), pp. 211–25.

Coakley, S., ed., *Religion and the Body* (Cambridge: Cambridge University Press, 1997).

Coats, R. H., 'Holiness: New Testament and Christian', in J. Hastings, ed., *Encyclopaedia of Religion and Ethics* (Edinburgh: T&T Clark, 1913), vol. 6, pp. 743–50.

Cohn, R. L., *The Shape of Sacred Space* (Chico: Scholars Press, 1983).

Coon, L. L., *Sacred Fictions. Holy Women and Hagiography in Late Antiquity* (Philadelphia: University of Pennsylvania Press, 1997).

Countryman, L. W., *Dirt, Greed and Sex. Sexual Ethics in the New Testament and their Implications for Today* (London: SCM, 1989).

Davies, J. G., *Every Day God* (London: SCM, 1973).

Dieter, M. E., *et al.*, *Five Views on Sanctification* (Grand Rapids: Zondervan, 1987).

Douglas, M., *Purity and Danger* (London: Routledge & Kegan Paul, 1966).

Douglas, M., *Natural Symbols. Explorations in Cosmology* (London: Barrie & Jenkins, 1973, 2nd edn.).

Douglas, M., *In the Wilderness: The Doctrine of Defilement in the Book of Numbers* (Sheffield: Sheffield Academic Press, 1993).

Duquoc, C. and Floristan, C., eds., *Models of Holiness* (New York: Seabury Press, 1979).

Eliade, M., *The Sacred and the Profane* (New York: 1959).

Elliott, A. G., *Roads to Paradise. Reading the Lives of the Early Saints* (Hanover: University Press of New England, 1987).

Elliott, C., 'Structures, Sin and Personal Holiness', in H. Willmer, ed., *Christian Faith and Political Hopes* (London: Epworth Press, 1979), pp. 107–22.

Elliott, J. H., *The Elect and the Holy: An Exegetical Examination of 1 Peter 2:4–10* (Leiden: E.J. Brill, 1966).

Elliott, J. H., 'The Epistle of James in Rhetorical and Social-Scientific Perspective: Holiness-Wholeness and Patterns of Replication', *Biblical Theology Bulletin* 23 (1993), pp. 71–81.

Evans, C. F., *Humanity, Holiness – And Humour* (The Michael Ramsey Memorial Lecture, St. Mary's College University of Durham, 1995).

Fenn, R. K., *The End of Time. Religion, Ritual, and the Forging of the Soul* (London: SPCK, 1997).

Flanagan, K., *Sociology and Liturgy: Re-presentations of the Holy* (Basingstoke: Macmillan, 1991).

Ford, D. F., *Self and Salvation. Being Transformed* (Cambridge: Cambridge University Press, 1999).

Frank, Georgia, *The Memory of the Eyes. Pilgrims to Living Saints in Christian Late Antiquity* (Berkeley: University of California Press, 2000).

Gammie, J. G., *Holiness in Israel* (Minneapolis: Fortress, 1989).

Gawronski, R., *Word and Silence: Hans Urs von Balthasar and the Spiritual Encounter between East and West* (Grand Rapids: Eerdmans, 1995).

Geertz, C., 'Centers, Kings, and Charisma: Reflections on the Symbolics of Power', in *Local Knowledge* (London: Fontana Press, 1993), pp. 121–46.

Gillett, D. K., *Trust and Obey. Explorations in Evangelical Spirituality* (London: Darton, Longman & Todd, 1993).

Greer, R. A., *Broken Lights and Mended Lives. Theology and Common Life in the Early Church* (University Park: Pennsylvania State University Press, 1986).

Grossman, A., 'Holiness', in A. A. Cohen and P. Mendes Flohr, eds., *Contemporary Jewish Religious Thought* (New York: Free Press, 1988), pp. 389–98.

Guroian, V., 'The Lost Meaning of Sainthood', in *Faith, Church, Mission. Essays for Renewal in the Armenian Church* (New York: The Armenian Prelacy, 1995), pp. 109–16.

Hauerwas, S., *Sanctify Them in the Truth. Holiness Exemplified* (Edinburgh: T&T Clark, 1998).

Hawley, J. S., ed., *Saints and Virtues* (Berkeley: University of California Press, 1987).

Hawthorne, G. F., 'Holy, Holiness' in R. P. Martin and P. H. Davids, eds., *Dictionary of the Later New Testament and its Developments* (Downers Grove, IL: InterVarsity Press, 1997), pp. 485–9.

Heffernan, T. J., *Sacred Biography. Saints and Their Biographers in the Middle Ages* (New York: Oxford University Press, 1988).

Hinchliff, P., *Holiness and Politics* (London: Darton, Longman & Todd, 1982).

Hodgson, R., 'Holiness Tradition and Social Description: Intertestamental Judaism and Early Christianity', in S. M. Burgess, ed., *Reaching Beyond: Chapters in the History of Perfectionism* (Peabody: Hendrickson, 1986), pp. 65–91.

Hodgson, R., 'Holiness (NT)', in D. N. Freedman, ed., *Anchor Bible Dictionary*, vol. 3, pp. 249–54.

Horbury, W., 'Land, sanctuary and worship', in J. Barclay and J. Sweet, eds., *Early Christian Thought in its Jewish Context* (Cambridge: Cambridge University Press, 1996), pp. 207–24.

Horbury, W., 'The Cult of Christ and the Cult of the Saints', *New Testament Studies* 44 (1998), pp. 444–69.

Houtman, A., et al., eds., *Sanctity of Time and Space in Tradition and Modernity* (Leiden: E.J. Brill, 1998).

Jeffrey, D. L., ed., *English Spirituality in the Age of Wesley* (Grand Rapids: Eerdmans, 1987).

Jenson, P. P., *Graded Holiness. A Key to the Priestly Conception of the World* (Sheffield: Sheffield Academic Press, 1992).

Johnson, E. A., *Friends of God and Prophets. A Feminist Theological Reading of the Communion of Saints* (London: SCM, 1998).

Jones, D. R., 'Sacrifice and Holiness', in S. W. Sykes, ed., *Sacrifice and Redemption* (Cambridge: Cambridge University Press, 1991), pp. 9–21.

Jones, O. R., *The Concept of Holiness* (London: Allen & Unwin, 1961).

Kadushin, M., *Worship and Ethics. A Study in Rabbinic Judaism* (New York: Bloch, 1963).

Knight III, H. H. and Land S. J., 'On Being a Witness: Worship and Holiness in the Wesleyan and Pentecostal Traditions', in E. B. Anderson and B. T. Morrill, eds., *Liturgy and the Moral Self* (Collegeville: Liturgical Press, 1998), pp. 79–93.

Lash, N., 'Hollow centres and holy places', in *The Beginning and the End of 'Religion'* (Cambridge: Cambridge University Press, 1996), pp. 183–98.

Lattke, M., 'Rudolf Bultmann on Rudolf Otto', *Harvard Theological Review* 78 (1985), pp. 353–60.

Loades, A., *Searching for Lost Coins. Explorations in Christianity and Feminism* (London: SPCK, 1987), pp. 39–60.

Lossky, V., *The Mystical Theology of the Eastern Church* (Cambridge: James Clarke, 1957).

Louth, A., *The Wilderness of God* (London: Darton, Longman & Todd, 1991).

Magee, P. M., 'Disputing the Sacred: Some Theoretical Approaches to Gender and Religion', in U. King, ed., *Religion and Gender* (Oxford: Blackwell, 1995), pp. 101–20.

Markus, R. A., *The End of Ancient Christianity* (Cambridge: Cambridge University Press, 1990).

Matthews, M., *Rediscovering Holiness* (London: SPCK, 1996).

Matzko, D. M., 'Postmodernism, Saints and Scoundrels', *Modern Theology* 9 (1993), pp. 19–36.

McGinn, B., *et al.*, eds., *Christian Spirituality. Origins to the Twelfth Century* (London: SCM, 1989).

McLaughlin, E., 'Women, Power and the Pursuit of Holiness in Medieval Christianity', in R. Ruether and E. McLaughlin, eds., *Women of Spirit: Female Leadership in the Jewish and Christian Traditions* (New York: Simon & Schuster, 1979), pp. 99–130.

Meeks, W. A., *The Origins of Christian Morality. The First Two Centuries* (New Haven: Yale University Press, 1993).

Miles, M. M., *The Image and Practice of Holiness. A Critique of the Classic Manuals of Devotion* (London: SCM, 1989).

Minear, P. S., 'The Holy and the Sacred', *Theology Today* 47 (1990–91), pp. 5–12.

Moltmann, J., *The Spirit of Life. A Universal Affirmation* (London: SCM, 1992).

Neusner, J., *The Idea of Purity in Ancient Judaism* (Leiden: E. J. Brill, 1973).

Nicholl, D., *Holiness* (London: Darton, Longman & Todd, 1981).

Nicholl, D., *Triumphs of the Spirit in Russia* (London: Darton, Longman & Todd, 1997).

O'Donovan, O., *Resurrection and Moral Order. An Outline for Evangelical Ethics* (Leicester: Inter-Varsity Press, 1986).

Otto, R., *The Idea of the Holy* (Oxford: Oxford University Press, 1923).

Oxtoby, W., 'Holy, Idea of the', in M. Eliade, ed., *The Encyclopedia of Religion* (New York: Macmillan, 1987), vol. 11, pp. 431–8.

Packer, J. I., 'Richard Baxter on Heaven, Hope and Holiness', in J. I. Packer and L. Wilkinson, eds., *Alive to God. Studies in Spirituality* (Downers Grove, IL: InterVarsity Press, 1992), pp. 161–75.

Pelikan, J., *Human Culture and the Holy* (London: SCM, 1959).

Peterson, D. G., *Hebrews and Perfection. An Examination of the Concept of Perfection in the 'Epistle to the Hebrews'* (Cambridge: Cambridge University Press, 1982).

Peterson, D. G., *Possessed By God. A New Testament Theology of Sanctification and Holiness* (Leicester: Apollos, 1995).

Poland, L., 'The Idea of the Holy and the History of the Sublime', *Journal of Religion* 72 (1992), pp. 175–97.

Porter, S. E., 'Holiness, Sanctification', in G. F. Hawthorne, *et al.*, eds., *Dictionary of Paul and his Letters* (Downers Grove, IL: InterVarsity Press, 1993), pp. 397–402.

Powell, S. M. and Lodahl, M. E., eds., *Embodied Holiness. Toward a Corporate Theology of Spiritual Growth* (Downers Grove, IL: InterVarsity, 1999).

Raphael, M., *Rudolf Otto and the Concept of Holiness* (Oxford: Clarendon Press, 1997).

Rogerson, J. W., 'Holy, The', in R. J. Coggins and J. L. Houlden, eds., *A Dictionary of Biblical Interpretation* (London: SCM, 1990), pp. 295–6.

Rubenson, S., *The Letters of St. Anthony. Monasticism and the Making of a Saint* (Minneapolis: Fortress, 1995).

Ryle, J. C., *Holiness. Its Nature, Hindrances, Difficulties and Roots* (Cambridge: James Clarke, 1952).

Seitz, C. R., 'God as Other, God as Holy', in *Word Without End. The Old Testament as Abiding Theological Witness* (Grand Rapids: Eerdmans 1998), pp. 13–27.

Sheldrake, P., *Images of Holiness. Explorations in Contemporary Spirituality* (London: Darton, Longman & Todd, 1987).

Smith, J. Z., 'Earth and Gods', *Journal of Religion* 49 (1969) pp. 103–27.

Soeding, T., 'Heilig, heilig, heilig. Zur politischen Theologie der Johannes-Apokalypse', *Zeitschrift für Theologie und Kirche* 96 (1999), pp. 49–76.

Squires, A., *Asking the Fathers* (London: SPCK, 1973).

Staniloae, D., *The Experience of God* (Brookline, MA: Holy Cross Orthodox Press, 1994).

Stouck, Mary-Ann, *Medieval Saints. A Reader* (Peterborough, Ontario: Broadview Press, 1999).

Sun, H. C. T., 'Holiness Code', *Anchor Bible Dictionary*, vol. 3, pp. 254–7.

Terrien, S., 'The Numinous, the Sacred and the Holy in Scripture', *Biblical Theology Bulletin* 12 (1982), pp. 99–108.

Theissen, G., *A Theory of Primitive Christian Religion* (London: SCM, 1999).

Thomas, G. J., 'A Holy God Among a Holy People in a Holy Place: The Enduring Eschatological Hope', in K. Brower and M. Elliott, eds., *The Reader Must Understand* (Leicester: Inter-Varsity Press, 1997), pp. 53–69.

Thompson, R., *Holy Ground. The Spirituality of Matter* (London: SPCK, 1990).

Vauchez, A., 'The Saint', in J. Le Goff, ed., *The Medieval World* (London: Collins & Brown, 1990), pp. 313–46.

Von Rad, G., *Holy War in Ancient Israel* (Grand Rapids: Eerdmans, 1991).

Weinstein, D. and Bell, R. M., *Saints and Society. The Two Worlds of Western Christendom 1000–1700* (Chicago: University of Chicago Press, 1982).

Wells, J. B., *God's Holy People. A Theme in Biblical Theology* (Sheffield: Sheffield Academic Press, 2000).

Wilken, R. L., *The Land Called Holy. Palestine in Christian History and Thought* (New Haven: Yale University Press, 1992).

Wilken, R. L., 'The Lives of the Saints and the Pursuit of Virtue' in *Remembering the Christian Past* (Grand Rapids: Eerdmans, 1995), pp. 121–44.

Williams, R., *The Wound of Knowledge. Christian Spirituality from the New Testament to St John of the Cross* (London: Darton, Longman & Todd, 1990, 2nd edn.).

Williams, R., 'Holy Space' and 'Holy Ground', in *Open to Judgment. Sermons and Addresses* (London: Darton, Longman & Todd, 1994), pp. 101–4 and 134–7.

Wimbush, V. L., ed., *Discursive Formations, Ascetic Piety and the Interpretation of Early Christian Literature. SEMEIA* 57 (Atlanta: Scholars Press, 1992).

Wimbush, V. L. and Valantasis, R., eds., *Asceticism* (New York: Oxford University Press, 1995).

Wolterstorff, N., 'Liturgy, Justice, and Holiness', *Reformed Journal* 39 (1989), pp. 12–20.

Woodward, K. L., *Making Saints. How the Catholic Church Determines Who Becomes a Saint, Who Doesn't, and Why* (New York: Simon & Schuster, 1990).

Wright, D. P., 'Holiness (OT)', in D. N. Freedman, ed., *Anchor Bible Dictionary*, vol. 3, pp. 237–49.

Wyschogrod, E., *Saints and Postmodernism. Revisioning Moral Philosophy* (Chicago: Chicago University Press, 1990).

Yoder, J. H., *The Royal Priesthood. Essays Ecclesiological and Ecumenical* (Grand Rapids: Eerdmans, 1994).

Zizioulas, J. D., *Being as Communion. Studies in Personhood and the Church* (Crestwood, NY: St Vladimir's Seminary Press, 1993).

Index of Modern Authors

Abel, F.-M. 166
Alles, G. D. 23–4, 33, 36–7, 40, 42
Almond, P. 24, 27, 33–4, 39, 41
Anderson, A. A. 19
Anderson, B. W. 102
Anderson, G. A. 157
Aumann, J. 333
Austin, J. L. 414

Badhwar, I. 428
Bailey-Wells, J. 104, 197
Balthasar, H. Urs Von 495
Barrett, C. K. 207
Barth, K. 34–5, 474–5
Barton, S. C. 199
Bate, J. 490
Baudrillard, J. 415
Bauman, Z. 3, 49
Baumel, J. T. 384
Baumgartner, W. 155
Baxter, R. 292–4
Bebbington, D. W. 63
Berger, R. 88
Berkovits, E. 385, 390, 392
Bethge, E. 374, 486
Biale, R. 393
Bitton-Jackson, L. 386, 397
Blackwell, A. 86
Blau, E. 70
Bloch, M. 55–6
Blumenthal, D. 382, 398
Bockmuehl, M. 203–4, 208
Bollandus, J. 320
Bonhoeffer, D. 361–80
Borg, M. 177, 190
Borsook, E. 90
Bosker, B. M. 151
Boullec, A. le 165
Brauer, J. C. 295
Brown, P. R. L. 101, 325
Broyles, M. 86
Brueggemann, W. 109, 113–15
Brunner, E. 35
Buber, M. 125, 384

Bulgakov, S. 342
Bultmann, R. 35–6
Butler, J. 413–14, 416, 419

Cameron, E. 332–3
Campbell, C. A. 45
Capps, D. 45
Cargas, H. J. 432
Carrithers, M. 63
Carroll, M. P. 326
Casey, M. 52
Caughey, J. 300
Charles, R. H. 158, 160
Childs, B. S. 123, 125
Chilton, B. D. 135
Clark, E. A. 242, 250
Clément, O. 280
Clements, R. E. 128
Coakley, S. 194
Cohen, A. 382
Cohen, G. M. 157
Cohen, R. A. 481
Colley, L. 76
Collins, R. 482
Conversi, D. 73
Costecalde, C.-B. 95, 99
Cunningham, L. S. 317

Dahl, N. 208
Daly, M. 425
Daunton, M. 83
Davidson, R. F. 24
Davie, J. 69, 71
Davies, D. J. 55, 64
Davies, G. 69
Delehaye, H. 320
Delooz, P. 321, 323, 326
Dembitz, L. N. 162
Des Pres, T. 386
DiVito, R. A. 112
Donne, J. 284
Dorvial, G. 146
Doss, E. 69
Douglas, M. 50, 115–18, 209

Drijvers, H. 248–9
Duffy, E. 78
Dunn, J. D. G. 170, 171, 174, 178–9,
    181, 188–9, 196, 199
Durkheim, E. 49
Dworkin, R. 465–70

Edwards, J. 485, 488–9
Eichrodt, W. 98–9
Eisenstadt, S. 89
Eliach, Y. 395
Eliade, M. 13–14, 37–9, 62
Elliger, K. 110
Endres, J. C. 157, 162
England, E. 313
Epstein, I. 384
Evans, C. A. 133
Evans, D. D. 406
Evans-Pritchard, E. E. 15–16
Evdokimov, P. 342, 348–9, 355
Everard, J. 295–6

Fardon, R. 50
Farmer, D. H. 318, 325
Ferrone, V. 82
Fontaine, J. 247
Ford, C. 324
Ford, D. F. 362, 374, 496
Forster, R. 313
Foucault, M. 406
Fraser, P. M. 147, 153–4
Frederbar-Salz, B. 396
Fries, J. F. 12
Fürer-Haimendorf, C. von 57

Gaborieau, M. 316
Gambero, L. 354
Gammie, J. G. 195
Gartner, B. 175
Gauchet, M. 90
Geertz, C. 55
Gibbons, B. J. 295
Giddens, A. 491
Gilley, S. 87, 329–30
Girouard, M. 69, 88
Godelier, M. 58–9
Goldin, H. E. 395
Gordon, J. M. 299–300, 303, 310
Gougard, D. 247, 251

Green, B. 278
Green, C. J. 365, 369
Greenfield, L. 73, 76
Gutierrez, G. 443, 447

Hall, P. 70
Hanegraaf, W. J. 63
Hardy, D. W. 477, 480, 488–9
Harl, M. 146, 156
Harris, H. A. 156
Hart, K. 386, 396
Hartogh, G. den 472
Hastings, A. 76
Hauerwas, S. 194
Hawley, J. S. 423
Hayward, P. A. 316, 325–6
Hayward, R. 128, 159–60, 197, 211
Heelas, P. 3
Heidegger, M. 237, 482
Hengel, M. 147
Henschenius, G. 320
Herbert, G. 285
Heschel, A. J. 107, 381
Hill, C. 293
Hill, R. 77
Hindmarsh, B. 303
Hodgson, R. 202
Hooker, M. D. 198
Hooker, R. 284
Hopkins, E. 310
Horbury, W. 197, 322–3
Howard-Johnston, J. 316, 325
Hufton, O. 319
Hunter, D. G. 250, 253–5, 257

Idelsohn, A. Z. 151

Jacobs, S. L. 384
Jacobson, H. 152, 154
Janz, P. D. 364, 376
Japhet, S. 145, 150
Jaubert, A. 158
Jenkins, T. E. 65
Jenson, P. P. 105–6, 128, 172, 200
Joosten, J. 102

Kearney, H. 73
Kerlin, M. J. 338
Kinsley, D. 426

Kitchen, J. 317
Knabenbauer, J. 166
Knohl, I. 97, 111
Knowles, D. 278, 320
Kocijančič, G. 220
Koehler, L. 155
Kugler, R. A. 119, 162
Kuhse, H. 471, 473-4
Kunin, S. 390, 392, 399

Landy, F. 119
Lane, W. L. 208
Laporte, J. 144
Lash, N. 31, 193, 212
Latimer, H. 280, 288
Lattke, M. 36
Lead, J. 296
Lebacqz, K. 475
Lengyl, O. 386
Leslie, J. 425, 427, 430-2
Levenson, J. D. 131, 135
Levinas, E. 236, 382
Lewinska, P. 385-6, 396
Lewis, C. S. 103, 337
Lincoln, A. T. 210
Lindbeck, G. A. 104
Lodahl, M. E. 398
Lossky, V. 227-8, 340-1, 343-4, 351
Ludwig, T. M. 24

MacCulloch, D. 82
McDermott, G. R. 484
MacIntyre, A. 194
McKane, W. 20
Macken, T. F. 330
McKenzie, P. 47
McKnight, S. 198
McLean, A. 90
Macquarrie, J. 45
Madhu, K. 429
Malina, B. J. 209
Malinowski, B. 54
Marett, R. R. 41
Martin, D. 69
Martin, M. 73
Mauss, M. 57
Mayr-Harting, H. 278
Meeks, W. A. 202, 209
Meland, B. 24

Meri, J. W. 316
Michelson, F. 396
Milgrom, J. 101, 104, 110-12, 116, 141, 148, 162
Miller, W. T. 154
Minear, P. S. 205
Moberly, R. W. L. 127, 130, 196
Mol, H. 50
Monk, M. 439-40
Moritz, T. 33
Morton, P. 492
Moscovici, S. 61
Motyer, J. A. 130
Müller, H. P. 93, 99, 101
Mumford, L. 69
Munden, A. 314
Munnich, O. 146

Naudé, J. A. 106
Nelson, R. D. 106
Neusner, J. 174-5, 394
Newman, J. H. 330
Newton, M. 176
Nickelsburg, G. W. E. 146, 157, 197
Nickson, A. L. 378
Nomborg-Przytyk, S. 396
Nussbaum, M. 408-12, 415-17

Ochs, P. 487
O'Flaherty, W. D. 426
Oman, J. 45
Oppenheimer, H. 419
Otto, R. 6, 8, 10-13, 22-47, 48, 102, 120, 168, 386
Ouspensky, L. 341
Owen, J. 291, 293-5
Oxtoby, W. G. 29, 32, 95
Oylan, S. M. 104, 112

Pannenberg, W. 15, 17
Parfit, D. 473
Pelikan, J. 87
Perkins, W. 293
Peterson, D. 195
Platzer, M. 70
Poland, L. 43-4
Porter, R. 70
Pratt, J. H. 299-300, 304
Price, R. 326

Proudfoot, W. 43
Puhl, J. 277

Qimron, E. 176
Quinot, M. 341

Rabuzzi, K. A. 395
Rad, G. von 108–9, 125
Radcliffe, T. 206–7
Rainer, M. R. 236
Raïssa, M. 338
Randall, I. M. 310
Raphael, M. 23, 33, 40–2, 52–3, 103,
  381
Rapp, C. 325
Rappaport, R. A. 50
Reagan, C. E. 461
Reist, B. A. 366
Rhodes, J. T. 277
Richard, L. J. 289
Richie, A. 70
Ricoeur, P. 461–4
Ringgren, H. 109
Rivers, I. 289
Robertson, R. G. 152
Robinson, C. 316
Robinson, J. A. T. 361
Rokkan, S. 72
Rosenbaum, I. 388
Rosenbaum, M. 155
Rosenfeld Vago, L. 386
Rosner, B. S. 202
Rousseau, P. 246, 325
Ruther, V. 429
Ryle, J. C. 303–4, 309

Sacks, J. 389–90
Sanders, E. P. 172–5, 179–83,
  188–9
Sandevoir, P. 165
Sarna, N. 142, 154
Sauer, G. 132
Sawyer, J. F. A. 209
Schindler, P. 389
Schleiermacher, F. D. E. 5–6, 31
Schmemann, A. 347
Schneer, J. 83
Schneid, H. 394

Schürer, E. 143, 146, 153, 166
Schweitzer, A. 26
Scott, G. 277
Segal, J. B. 150
Seligman, A. 497
Shapiro, D. S. 393
Sharpe, E. 29
Shutt, R. J. H. 153
Sibbes, R. 295
Silbermann, A. M. 155
Singer, P. 473
Singer, S. 167
Smith, H. P. 19
Smith, J. 288
Smith, W. R. 48
Snaith, N. H. 99, 168
Soboul, A. 316
Söderblom, N. 6–10, 41
Söding, T. 4–5, 14,
Sommerville, C. J. 283
Southall, A. 70
Spiegel, G. M. 327
Spurgeon, C. H. 300
Stăniloae, D. 227
Stancliffe, C. 248–9, 251
Starkey, D. 70
Stein, E. 433–6
Steiner, F. 100
Stibili, E. C. 322
Stone, M. E. 197
Stouck, M. 316
Strugnell, J. 176
Stuart, E. 421, 440
Sztompka, P. 497

Tabory, J. 151
Tambiah, S. J. 55–7
Taylor, J. 285–7
Terrien, S. 119
Thomas, G. J. 198
Thomas, T. 287
Thompson, M. B. 208
Thurston, H. 332
Tillich, P. 36, 105
Tomasi, S. M. 322
Tov, E. 146
Tripp, D. K. 293
Twain, M. 22

Urbach, E. E. 382, 390
Unterman, A. 397

Valin, H. 72
Van der Leeuw, G. 11, 49
VanderKam, J. 146, 157, 162
Vanhoozer, K. 121
Vermes, G. 170

Wach, J. 24, 36
Wakefield, G. 293
Walker, A. 120, 314
Whaling, F. 306-7
Wildberger, H. 123, 128-9, 134
Webb, C. C. J. 223
Weber, B. 155
Weber, M. 53
Weeks, S. 123, 126

Weima, J. A. D. 202-3
Wellhausen, J. 119-20
Wenham, G. 154
Wevers, J. W. 146
Williams, M. H. 143
Williamson, H. G. M. 123, 135
Wilson, E. J. 100, 108
Wilson, L. 301
Wilson, S. 316, 320, 322, 323, 325-6
Woodhead, L. 193
Woodward, K. L. 321, 335, 439
Wright, D. P. 104, 111, 170, 195
Wyschogrod, E. 194, 362, 423
Wyshogrod, M. 387

Zahrnt, H. 22